CULTURE:
The Anthropological Perspective

Marc J. Swartz
David K. Jordan
University of California, San Diego

John Wiley & Sons
New York   Chichester   Brisbane   Toronto

Library of Congress Cataloging in Publication Data

Swartz, Marc J
    Culture: anthropological research.

    Includes index.
    1. Ethnology. 2. Culture. I. Jordan,
David K., joint author. II. Title.

GN316.S98   301.2   79-9211
ISBN 0-471-03333-2

Printed in United States of America

10 9 8 7 6 5 4 3 2 1

PREFACE

This book focuses on the concept "culture." Every chapter is concerned with how culture works as the basis of human life and society. From the role of culture in hominid evolution to its operation in economics, politics, kinship, language, and religion the "prescriptive shared understandings transmitted from generation to generation by social learning" are shown to be the key to understanding humanity.

With all the traditional emphasis here on culture and its all-pervasive role in things human, it needs to be made clear that culture is not viewed as "timeless and changeless." Culture is a vital and dynamic force that is always in the process of development. There is no separate chapter here on "social and cultural change" because it is our view that every chapter concerns social and cultural change. This book takes development or change as a central aspect of culture itself, so that, as Alexander Pope said in the eighteenth century, while "the proper study of mankind is man," the proper study of culture is the study of change.

Forces for cultural continuity are carefully considered and their effects shown in all areas of human life, but so are forces for cultural development, alteration, and change. The book often leaves crucial theoretical issues open and presents several sides to important questions, but it does provide a single guiding framework in its emphasis on culture, cultural continuity, and cultural change.

Culture is incompletely shared in every group, a fact that is explicitly addressed in this book. There is no idea here that culture is a monolithic structure that all group members equally possess. The distribution of interrelated but separate and distinct elements of culture among different individuals, different situations, and different relationships is viewed as the basis of social structure. Our view of social structure, in fact, is an almost completely cultural one. Incomplete sharing is not just a matter of different statuses and roles, however. Individual differences do exist, and our treatment of personality is from the perspective of how quite different sorts of people come to participate in highly similar types of behavior in every society.

As this suggests, this book attempts to increase the student's understanding of other people whether in "exotic" societies or his own. Societies other than the readers' are presented in some detail and diversity. These people are not treated as exhibits in an ethnological museum but as humans to be understood within the same framework as the more familiar humans of everyday experience.

Each of the chapters (except Chapter 11) begins with a case. The case describes real individuals in interaction, responding to motivations, performing roles, and acting according to shared understandings. Following each case (except the first) is an analysis, which abstracts from the interaction the issues that will be dealt with in the chapter and points out that for a real understanding of what is going on in the interaction, the analyst must have some understanding of the kinds of problems the chapter will discuss. After this the chapter itself begins.

Each chapter treats some material that is not necessarily directly relevant to the case—there is no reason to confine the chapter to the case it illuminates—but the discussion is brought directly back to the analysis of the case whenever that is germane. The effort, in each chapter, is to provide a realistic reference point that can give a student a sense of how the material in the chapter can be used in analyzing the events of everyday life as it is lived in a variety of societies and to provide a clear example to make the concepts of the chapter as clear as possible. For the sake of variety, no two cases are taken from the same culture area.

Cases are curiously difficult to find in the anthropological literature. Most ethnographies are much richer in generalizations than in the instances that lead to generalization. The examples that are provided in ethnographic accounts rarely provide enough data about individual actors to allow any very adequate reconstruction of their motives, roles, or understandings. Two cases in this book (those in the chapters on culture and religion) are based on unpublished field materials of our own. One case (Chapter 9, Language) uses material that has not formerly been subjected to anthropological study. A fourth case (Chapter 1, "What is Anthropology?") is abstracted from Herodotus. The remaining four cases are condensed, paraphrased, or occasionally quoted from published ethnographies, ethnographies that can be assigned in full as supplementary reading materials for a course if the instructor so desires.

This book is one of three anthropology textbooks involving the same authors and taking the same general perspective. The other two books are _Origins: Human Evolution and Culture_ (written with Laurie Benz and S. L. Washburn) designed for use in courses in physical anthropology, and _Anthropology: Perspective on Humanity_, intended for a comprehensive introductory anthropology course.

Marc J. Swartz
David K. Jordan

ACKNOWLEDGMENTS

This book would never have been written were it not for Audrey R. Swartz (Mrs. Marc J. Swartz). Her unflagging support and assistance from beginning to end cannot be overstated. Like the others whose names are mentioned here, she is not responsible for any errors we may have committed, but her help has been crucial throughout. The typing of Kae Knight, June Wilkins, and Joyce Krause has brought order where there was chaos and light where there was darkness. Their good-natured and intelligent efforts have vastly benefited this book.

It is difficult to know where to start in citing the colleagues, associates, friends, and willing correspondents who have contributed to our efforts. Our colleagues at the University of California at San Diego have been generous, gentle, and kind in their discussions with us and in their comments on various stages of the manuscript. Outside the Department of Anthropology at UCSD we are especially indebted to Herbert Stern and Chris Wills of the Department of Biology. In our department Roy G. D'Andrade, F. G. Bailey, Joyce Justus, Gananath Obeyesekere, Theodore Schwartz, Melford E. Spiro, Shirley Strum, and Donald F. Tuzin have been particularly helpful.

We are also grateful for the help of John Aguilar, Peter W. Black, Richard Coleman, Harm J. De Blij, C. Paul Dredge, Cecil French, Bernard Gallin, Eleanore R. Gerber, Gerald Hyman, Thomas W. Johnson, Glenn E. King, N. I. Lobachevsky, Thomas Maretzki, Michael Murphy, William O'Barr, James Peacock, David Potter, J. Paul Reid, George Saunders, David Smith, Arthur Soybel, Philip Staniford, Victor Turner, Bonno Thoden Van Velsen, Carlos Velez-I, and Susan S. Wadley.

M.J.S.
D.K.J.

CONTENTS

CULTURE:
The Anthropological Perspective

SECTION ONE

Meeting Ourselves: The Emergence and Development of Anthropology

The term "anthropology" literally means "the study of human beings," but anthropology as an academic discipline and intellectual tradition obviously must be something more specific than that. In a modern university anthropology stands in contrast to such other fields as sociology, psychology, economics, linguistics, history, biology, and so forth, all of which represent, in various senses, studies of human beings.

While it is true that anthropologists have traditionally been the only students of human life to devote attention to the traditions of small-scale societies, they nevertheless also study most of the same groups of people studied by other disciplines. The differences between anthropology and these other fields are often less a matter of subject matter than of emphasis, of method, or of intellectual tradition. These differences give the anthropological study a different flavor. Generalizing broadly, anthropologists are more constantly concerned with comparison between and among different societies than other disciplines are. Whether the problem has to do with religious symbolism, or the relation between biology and intelligence, or the analysis of systems of economic exchange in modern Latin America, an-

thropologists tend to view the problem in what has come to be known as the "cross-cultural perspective."

The cross-cultural perspective has given anthropolgy a unique burden among the social sciences, for it is only anthropology that is directly concerned with exploring "all the possibilities" in human affairs. To the anthropologist, a tribe of 50 souls is as important as a nation of tens or hundreds of millions, for every style of being human contributes to our knowledge of human variation and human potentiality. This has often proved an important perspective—correcting generalizations of other disciplines that were too narrowly based on data from a single society. By introducing material from other societies that may run counter to the generalizations, scholars are forced to try new and better formulations to take account of all the cases.

The traditional method of anthropological data gathering has been intensive fieldwork, often conducted against difficult odds in uncomfortable corners of the globe, devoted to gaining information about human life by direct observation, direct interviews with people living the lifeway being studied, and direct participation in that

1

lifeway insofar as that is possible for an outside observer. Like the historian's text or the psychologist's subject, the anthropologist's informant is the source of the information from which the anthropologist and his colleagues painstakingly build the archive of observations of human custom from which generalization gradually becomes possible.

The central theoretical concept of anthropology is "culture." Although anthropologists disagree somewhat about exactly what this means, and although precise definitions are therefore hard to give, still there is a core of agreement on the general view that culture has something to do with the understandings that human beings have of the world, and that as different human groups share different understandings of the world, so the world has different cultures. The central emphasis in anthropology on discovering how human animals came to be able to understand their world in a way that other animals could not, and on discovering the diversity of human understandings of the world, is a unique anthropological preserve. No other discipline takes culture in general as its central object of analysis. The insights into the life of our species that are gained through a close and comparative examination of this central fact of human existence are important both practically, in our attempts to understand and direct our everyday lives through development programs of various kinds, and also in the attempt of each

of us to grasp more completely what it means to be human in general and what it means to belong to one cultural tradition rather than another. The urbane Roman playwright Terence was the author of one of the most oft-quoted lines of classical antiquity: Homo sum; humani nil a me alienum puto, *"I am a man: and I maintain that nothing human is alien to me" (Heauton Timorumenos, 77). He meant this as a statement of principle. But in the Roman world a full appreciation of what it meant to be human was not possible in the modern sense. To a large extent, because of the findings of anthropology, each of us in the present era may claim the heritage of the entire human race as his own. A knowledge of anthropology makes it possible to live in a cultural world much larger than that inhabited by most people in times past, for the broad understanding of human culture in all its variants and vagaries, promotes a unique breadth of insight into the anthropologist's own society and his place in it.*

In Chapter 1 we trace the history of anthropology. Beginning with the findings of an ancient Greek visiting Egypt, we will see how the problem of human cultural difference has been understood from that time to our own, and we particularly explore the increasingly sophisticated ideas held over the years by professional anthropologists about the nature of human culture and the significance of its countless variations.

1

What Is Anthropology?

How the past perishes is how the future becomes.

ALFRED NORTH WHITEHEAD
ADVENTURES IN IDEAS, 1933

Anthropologist Margaret Mead with informants on Manus Island, Melanesia.

What is anthropology?

How have the various emphases of anthropological research changed over the years?

How is anthropology related to other fields?

What overall ideas or methods hold the different branches of anthropology together?

What studies have anthropologists conducted?

What kinds of issues have they disagreed about?

An Ancient Greek in Egypt: A Case of Early Anthropology

Herodotus was a Greek, born about 484 B.C. in the seacoast town of Halicarnassus (modern Bodrum) in what is today the southwestern corner of Turkey. He was probably a political exile from his home town: after his cousin, a noted poet, was executed by the reigning tyrant of the place, he voyaged extensively through the lands of the eastern Mediterranean and North Africa. His travels supplied material for a monumental *History* of the Greco-Persian wars, which was much appreciated in Herodotus's own time in Athens and other cities of Greece. The *History* devotes a full chapter to the Egyptians, whom he visited about 450 B.C. Here is a short fragment of it:[1]

About Egypt itself I shall have a great deal more to relate because of the number of remarkable things which the country contains, and because of the fact that more monuments which beggar description are to be found there than anywhere else in the world. That is reason enough for my dwelling on it at greater length. Not only is the Egyptian climate peculiar to that country, and the Nile different in its behavior from other rivers elsewhere, but the Egyptians themselves in their manner and customs seem to have reversed the ordinary practices of mankind.

For instance, women attend market and are employed in trade, while men stay at home and do the weaving. In weaving the normal way is to work the threads of the weft upwards, but the Egyptians work them downwards. Men in Egypt carry loads on their heads, women on their shoulders; women pass water standing up, men sitting down. To ease themselves they go indoors, but eat outside in the streets, on the theory that what is unseemly but necessary should be done in private, and what is not unseemly should be done openly. No woman holds priestly office, either in the service of goddess or god; only men are priests in both cases. Sons are under no compulsion to support their parents if they do not wish to do so, but daughters must, whether they wish it or not.

Elsewhere priests grow their hair long; in Egypt they shave their heads. In other nations the relatives of the deceased in time of mourning cut their hair, but the Egyptians, who shave at all other times, mark a death by letting the hair grow both on head and chin. They live with their animals—unlike the rest of the world, who live apart from them. Other men live on wheat and barley, but any Egyptian who does so is blamed for it, their bread being made from spelt, or Zea as some call it [a kind of wheat (*Tricitum spelta*) common in the ancient Mediterranean lands]. Dough they knead with their feet, but clay with their hands—and even handling dung. They practice circumcision, while men of other nations—except those who have learned from Egypt—leave their private parts as nature made them. Men in Egypt have two garments each, women only one. The ordinary practice at sea is to make sheets fast to ring-bolts fitted outboard; the Egyptians fit them inboard.

In writing or calculating, instead of going, like the Greeks, from left to right, the Egyptians go from right to left—and obstinately maintain that theirs is the dexterous method, ours being left handed and awkward. They have two sorts of writing, the sacred and the common.

They are religious to excess, beyond any other nation in the world, and here are some of the customs which illustrate the fact: they drink from brazen cups which they scour every day—everyone, without exception. They wear linen clothes which they make a special point of continually washing. They circumcise themselves for cleanliness' sake, preferring to be clean rather than comely. The priests shave their bodies all

[1] The translation used here is by Aubrey de Selincourt (1954, *Herodotus: The Histories*, Harmondsworth: Penguin Books, pp. 115–123). We have reparagraphed and slightly abbreviated the text. Additions in brackets are also ours.

over every other day to guard against the presence of lice, or anything else equally unpleasant, while they are about their religious duties; the priests, too, wear linen only, and shoes made from the papyrus plant—these materials, for dress and shoes, being the only ones allowed them. They bathe in cold water twice a day and twice every night—and observe innumerable other ceremonies besides. Their life, however, is not by any means all hardship, for they enjoy advantages too; for instance, they are free from all personal expense, having bread made for them out of the sacred grain, and a plentiful daily supply of goose meat and beef, with wine in addition. Fish they are forbidden to touch; and as for beans, they cannot even bear to look at them, because they imagine they are unclean (in point of fact the Egyptians never sow beans, and even if any happen to grow wild, they will not eat them, either raw or boiled).

They do not have a single priest for each god, but a number, of which one is chief priest, and when a chief priest dies his son is appointed to succeed him. Bulls are considered the property of the god Epaphus—or Apis—and are therefore tested in the following way: a priest appointed for the purpose examines the animal, and if he finds even a single black hair upon him, pronounces him unclean; he goes over him with the greatest care, first making him stand up, then lie on his back, after which he pulls out his tongue to see if that, too, is "clean" according to the recognized marks—what those are I will explain later. He also inspects the tail to make sure the hair on it grows properly; then, if the animal passes all these tests successfully, the priest marks him by twisting round his horns a band of papyrus which he seals with wax and stamps with his signet ring. The bull is finally taken away, and the penalty is death for anybody who sacrifices an animal which has not been marked in this manner.

The method of sacrifice is as follows: they take the beast (one of those marked with the seal) to the appropriate altar and light a fire; then, after pouring a libation of wine and invoking the god by name, they slaughter it, cut off its head, and flay the carcase. The head is loaded with curses and taken away—if there happen to be Greek traders in the market, it is sold to them; if not, it is thrown into the river. The curses they pronounce take the form of a prayer that any disaster which threatens either themselves or their country may be diverted and fall upon the severed head of the beast. Both the libation and the practice of cutting off the heads of sacrificial beasts are common to all Egyptians in all their sacrifices, and the latter explains why it is that no Egyptian will use the head of any sort of animal for food.

The methods of disembowelling and burning are various, and I will describe the one which is followed in the worship of the goddess whom they consider the greatest and honour with the most important festival. In this case, when they have flayed the bull, they first pray and then take its paunch out whole, leaving the intestines and fat inside the body; next they cut off the legs, shoulders, neck, and rump, and stuff the carcase with loaves of bread, honey, raisins, figs, frankincense, myrrh, and other aromatic substances; finally, they pour a quantity of oil over the carcase and burn it. They always fast before a sacrifice, and while the fire is consuming it they beat their breasts. That part of the ceremony done, they serve a meal out of the portions left over.

* * *

I was told that Heracles was one of the twelve gods. Of the other Heracles, with whom the Greeks are familiar, I could get no information anywhere in Egypt. Nevertheless it was not the Egyptians who took the name Heracles from the Greeks. The opposite is true: it was the Greeks who took it from the Egyptians—those Greeks, I mean, who gave the name to the son of Amphitryon. There is plenty of evidence to prove the truth of this, in particular the fact that both the parents of Heracles—Amphitryon and Alcmene—were of Egyptian origin. Again, the Egyptians say they do not know the names of Poseidon or the Dioscuri, or receive them as gods amongst the rest. But surely, if they had taken the name of any god from the Greeks, it is precisely these they would have been most likely to notice—unless I am greatly mistaken in my belief that the Egyptians were already at that time a sea-faring nation, and that some of the Greeks, too, used the sea. Being sailors, the Egyptians would have learned the names of Poseidon and the Dioscuri even before that of Heracles.

* * *

[The worship of the god, Dionysus, is performed in Egypt with some of the same rites as in Greece.] I will never admit that the similar ceremonies performed in Greece and Egypt are the result of mere coincidence—had that been so, our rites would have been more Greek in character and less recent in origin. Nor will I allow that the Egyptians ever took over from the Greeks either this custom or any other. Probably Melampus got his knowledge of the worship of Dionysus through Cadmus of Tyre and the people who came with him from Phoenicia to the country now called Boeotia.

The names of nearly all of the gods came to Greece from Egypt. I know from the inquiries I have made that they came from abroad, and it seems most likely that it was from Egypt, for the names of all the gods have been known in Egypt from the beginning of time, with the exception (as I have already said) of Poseidon and the Dioscuri—and also of Hera, Hestia, Themis, the Graces, and the Nereids. I have the authority of the Egyptians themselves for this. I think that the gods of whom they profess no knowledge were named by the Pelasgians—with the exception of Poseidon, of whom they learned from the Libyans; for the Libyans are the only people who have always known Poseidon's name, and always worshipped him. Heroes—men, that is, who have been subsequently deified—have no place in the religion of Egypt.

These practices, then, and others which I will speak of later, were borrowed by the Greeks from Egypt. This is not the case, however, with the Greek custom of making images of Hermes with the phallus erect; it was the Athenians who took this from the Pelasgians, and from the Athenians the custom spread to the rest of Greece. For just at the time when the Athenians were assuming Hellenic nationality, the Pelasgians joined them, and thus first came to be regarded as Greeks. Anyone will know what I mean if he is familiar with the mysteries of the Cabiri—rites which the men of Samothrace learned from the Pelasgians, who lived in that island before they moved to Attica, and communicated the mysteries to the Athenians. This will show that the Athenians were the first Greeks to make statues of Hermes with the erect phallus, and that they learned the practice from the Pelasgians—who explained it by a certain religious doctrine, the nature of which is made clear in the Samothracian mysteries.

The Aims of Anthropology

In this account of Egyptian life and religion, the ancient Greek Herodotus shows himself to be a dedicated student of humanity and its variety. Even though he lived and wrote some 2500 years ago, his work shows most of the characteristics of the discipline of anthropology. In his description, he not only tells his readers what Egyptians of his time did and believed, he also contrasts this with life in other groups including and particularly his own society. He turns the attention of his ancient (or modern) readers to how Greek and Egyptian religious beliefs and practices influenced each other; and in his discussion of what the Greeks borrowed from the Egyptians, he shows a concern with the development of human institutions and practices that has always been a characteristic of anthropology. It is perhaps too much to say that Herodotus was a full-fledged anthropologist, but his claim to being the father of anthropology is as strong as his claim to being the father of history.

Herodotus' monumental work, *The Histories* (De Selincourt 1955), from which the discussion of the Egyptians is taken, includes descriptions of most of the peoples in the world as it was known by the Greeks of his time. Herodotus' basic approach to understanding these people was similar to that used by modern anthropologists, but with this crucial difference: the work was not guided by an explicit concept of "culture." Herodotus tells his readers what peoples in various distant places did, but he treats their activities and beliefs as isolated practices and separate customs not unified by a shared, learned culture.

Anthropology is devoted to the study of humans as cultural beings. Like Herodotus, anthropologists concern themselves with the variety of ways people live, with the development of those ways over time, and also with the development of the human body and the ways people's bodies influenced their lives. Unlike Herodotus, anthropologists look at different human groups from the perspective of the different cultures these groups share. A main objective of anthropology is to go beyond simply understanding the groups themselves and beyond just increasing understanding of our own societies, to an increased understanding of all humanity through achieving a better grasp of how culture works in the lives of all humans regardless of where or when they live. The task of anthropology is to examine the whole array of human societies and lives in order to contribute to the fullest possible understanding of humanity as a whole.

Anthropology is a social science in that it studies the social arrangements found in human groups, how individuals live in these different sorts of groups, and the means by which the different ways of life found in these groups come to be, persist, and change. It is a biological science in that it is concerned with human evolution and with human physical variation as this occurs in different parts of the world at different times. It is also a humanistic discipline that examines the values, art, and philosophy of people—wherever and whenever they live or lived—for the beauty, richness, and meaning they have.

Herodotus. Often thought of as the father of history, Herodotus can also claim to be the first anthropologist.

Culture as the Basis of the Anthropological Approach

Although Herodotus and other early anthropologists (or proto-anthropologists) did not use the concept, all modern anthropologists agree that "culture" refers to shared ways of believing, evaluating, and doing that are passed from generation to generation and from person to person within a group through the process of learning. Each human group has its own distinctive culture, which provides the basis for the way group members make their living, relate to one another and outsiders, deal with the supernatural, and all the other aspects of the group's way of life.

Beyond this agreed-on part of the definition of culture, there are fairly substantial differences among anthropologists as to just what the concept can most usefully refer to. We develop the definition used in this book in the next chapter. That anthropologists disagree about some of the meaning of the central concept of their discipline should be no cause for dismay, however. Anthropology refers, after all, to a body of phenomena of staggering complexity. To understand the field's distinctive approach, it is enough to recognize that its practitioners all agree that culture is learned rather than biologically transmitted, that it is shared by the members of a group, and that it is the foundation of the human way of life.

We speak of "culture" in two different senses. In its broadest use, it refers to the means by which all human groups adapt to the world and to each other. This is the sense intended when we say "Humans are cultural animals." In its narrower use, "culture" refers to what has been learned and is shared by the members of a particular group. Thus we can speak, for example, of Navajo culture, referring to the distinctive Navajo way. Sometimes the word "culture" is used to refer to a social group that shares a culture. In this use, one sometimes hears such statements as "The people in this culture do that."

Another characteristic of culture about which all anthropologists agree is that the learned and shared material which makes up culture is patterned, or organized. This means that the different elements in a particular group's culture influence each other. Thus, anthropologists would agree that the religious beliefs a particular people have are related to at least some other aspects of their culture, perhaps, say, to their family patterns or to the structure of political authority in the group. Some anthropologists go further and believe that every part of culture is related to every other part and that when parts seem unrelated it is simply because investigation has not been carried far enough. Other anthropologists believe that all parts are related to some other parts, but that it is not productive to assume each part is closely connected to every other; this, they maintain, is a matter to be established by investigation, not by assumption.

An important but unsettled issue in the definition of "culture" concerns the phenomena to which the concept refers. Some anthropologists think it is most fruitful to think of culture as constituted of beliefs, ideas, and values. Others think that patterns of behavior, if they are common to the members of a group, should also be included. Still others believe that the tools, dwellings, weapons, and artwork characteristic of particular groups should be included in addition to ideas, beliefs, and values and customary patterns of behavior. Edward Burnett Tylor, one of the most influential of the nineteenth-century anthropologists, used this most inclusive definition in the opening of his 1871 book *Primitive Culture,* where he defines "culture" as "that complex whole which includes knowledge, belief, art, morals, law, custom, and any other capabilities and habits acquired by man as a member of society."

Tylor's view includes things in people's minds (knowledge, belief, and morals), the way people behave (custom and habits), and things that people produce (art and law). Inclusive definitions of culture based on Tylor's view have served anthropology for a long time and still do. However, we offer a narrower definition of culture in the next chapter and try to show the advantages it has.

All anthropologists agree that morality is part of culture, but they differ in their views of how important it is in human life and how pervasive. Many anthropologists see morals as making up one part of culture just as other sorts of ideas make up other parts. Following in the tradition of the French theorist Emile Durkheim, other anthropologists view morality as fundamentally involved in every other part of culture. This last view often includes the idea that human culture is distinctive in having moral force connected to the socially transmitted notions of how to do things. That is, humans learn how things ought to be done, not just how they can be done. Nonhuman primates and other mammals, we now know, depend on what they learn from the previous generation to a considerable extent; thus, their basis for living is similar to, although simpler and less rich than, the human cultural basis. A major difference is the moral force that plays a vital role in human culture, but is absent (or at least much less important) from the socially learned ways of acting that form the foundation for much of primate life.

Anthropologists also have a variety of different views regarding the relation between culture and individual behavior. Many anthropologists emphasize the group nature of culture and its independence from particular individuals. They stress the fact that culture, because it is transmitted from generation to generation, exists before the birth of the particular individuals living at any one time and continues after they die. Some anthropologists think of people as "culture carriers." That is, they view all humans as more or less passive agents who learn culture during their lives and who pass on what they have learned to other individuals before they die. Other anthropologists give more emphasis to individual actors and their behavior, partly because they view them as active parties who may change what they learned and what they transmit to others. These anthropologists stress that individuals may know what their culture calls for in a given situation but not do it anyway. They also call attention to the fact that in no known social group does every member share everything he or she has learned with everyone else. This view, which regards culture as a key determinant of human behavior but not as one that works automatically or without change, is the one we adopt here.

Whatever specific view of culture different anthropologists take, agreement is sufficient to provide the basis for the distinctive anthropological perspective. That perspective has two related parts. One part consists of the way anthropology goes about trying to understand how a particular society works by examining every aspect of the group's life in the context of its own culture. The other part is the use of cross-cultural comparison, which we consider in a later section.

Culture as the Context

A central element in the anthropological perspective is an insistence on looking at specific aspects of a group's way of life in relation to the whole culture shared by the members of the group. This is what would be expected given the view that culture is patterned. Herodotus tell his readers that the Egyptians are "religious to excess, beyond any other nation in the world . . . ," but he does not put his finding in the context of other parts of Egyptian culture. A modern anthropologist would examine how religious beliefs and practices are related to each other and how they fit in with beliefs in other spheres of life. What did the Egyptians think about the relations between humans and gods? Was this similar to how they thought about the relations among humans themselves? What did their religion hold about the fate of the dead and how people could influence this? How did this compare to beliefs about good and evil and to the treatment of criminals on earth? Modern anthropologists would go further afield in trying to understand the religion of the Egyptians and would look at the general meanings of cleanliness in order to understand the cleanliness Herodotus tells us was required of priests and then relate this back to whatever else they had found about religion. They might examine beliefs and values concerning food in general in order to get a better understanding of the foods priests did and did not eat and of the meaning of animal sacrifices and this would be related back to their growing understanding of religion. Anthropologists would not look at each part of religion as an isolated belief or custom as Herodotus did.

In short, the anthropological approach to understanding religion in Egypt would be to investigate all aspects of the Egyptian culture. What was discovered in looking at the similarities and differences between the nature of relations between humans and gods and the nature of relations between humans themselves would lead to investigations of Egyptian politics (since the Egyptian rulers were considered divine) and this could lead to investigations of agriculture since only an economy with a great deal of surplus could support the sorts of political and religious beliefs and practices found in Egypt. The anthropological approach to understanding religion in Egypt, and, in fact, the anthropological approach to understanding any set of ideas and practices found in any group, is to investigate all aspects of the group's culture as each aspect's relation to the problem being studied emerges in the course of the investigation. An anthropological investigation of Egyptian religion would allow us to see it in relation to other beliefs and other practices and to see how the interconnected religious and nonreligious aspects of culture influenced each other. This is what is meant by putting the objects of anthropological interest in their cultural *context*. It is fundamental to the anthropological approach to try to increase understanding of any part of a people's way of life, whether religion or anything else, by putting the behavior, beliefs, and values dealing directly with that way of life in the *context* of the group's whole culture.

Fieldwork and the Anthropological Perspective

Before going on to the second part of the anthropological perspective, the uses of cross-cultural comparison, it is useful to examine briefly the relation between that perspective and the way information is gathered in the field. Since culture is the basis for almost everything the members of a group do, the anthropologist's interest in culture leads to a concern with every aspect of life. The typical procedure for studying a society is to live with the people and to participate in as many of their activities as possible. Through taking part in their work and leisure activities, their ceremonies and rituals, and the daily round of their lives, the anthropologist gets a closer and fuller knowledge of their culture than would otherwise be possible. The fieldworker talks with his hosts about the things that go on in their community and asks them to explain the meanings, values, and beliefs that are associated with the activities he has seen and participated in. This field technique is called "participant observation."

Through this technique the anthropologist comes to understand aspects of culture that never would be discovered by formal interviews or questionnaires. Everyone is blinded to some extent by his own culture and does not look for beliefs or values very different from those in that culture. Participant observation is the technique most likely to minimize the omissions and distortions that come from this partial blinding. In daily activity and conversation, at least some of the parts of the culture of the group being studied that would have been missed because of the influence on the observer of his own culture are presented so strongly and persistently that their presence cannot be ignored.

Participant observation also provides the best means available for discerning the organization of culture. Through daily experience with the members of a group and firsthand experience of the group's way of life the anthropologist comes to see connections among different parts of its culture. If, for example, there is a value on male assertiveness and toughness, as there is in the cultures of a number of groups including some in Latin America, the anthropologist will be exposed to behavior that shows the influence of this value in such diverse aspects of life as child care and politics.

The participant observer will see that fathers do not usually hug or pat their children, and will hear people wonder about the manhood of a father who cuddles his children or frequently speaks fondly to them. In politics the researcher will hear political leaders spoken of approvingly as "bulls" and men who have used violence in the settlement of political disputes praised as being very manly. The opportunity provided by being present to see, to hear, and to ask gives a basis for understanding the behavioral consequences of a value such as male toughness and for discovering the influence of such a value on types of behavior where that influence might not be expected. Participant observation gives fieldworkers the opportunity to see and understand aspects of a group's culture not present in the fieldworker's own culture.

Herodotus traveled a great deal; we saw in his description of Egyptian beliefs and practices that he made inquiries about the objects of his studies in Egypt, but he did not do participant observation. He did not live in any part of Egypt for a long period of time and did not achieve the familiarity with individuals and the extensive opportunities to observe what they do that are required for participant observation.

Culture and Cross-Cultural Comparison

Herodotus was more like modern anthropologists in his use of explicit comparisons. Not only did he compare Egyptian practices to those of Greek society, he also compared them to those of the people of Samothrace (an Aegean island), and throughout his book we find him using such comparisons as a characteristic means of examining the customs or beliefs that interested him. The scope and the detailed nature of modern comparison is, of course, quite different from that practiced by the ancient Greek, but the aims are highly similar.

Anthropologists make a point of comparing cultures of people in different parts of the world and in different periods of human history. They try to find out how the way of life of a particular group is similar to and different from the ways of life of other peoples. Just as anthropologists look at particular parts of a group's culture in the context of the group's whole culture, so also they try to look at the culture of each human group in the context of human culture as it occurs in all societies and time periods. If the members of a particular group do something that is done by no other group, then our understanding of what they do will be different from what it would be if what they do is similar to what is found in other groups. To take a rather lurid example, consider the following royal edict for the punishment of criminals in Burma. This edict was to be inscribed on stone pillars in every village.

A thief is to be punished with one or the other of these punishments. He is impaled. His breast is split open with the axe. He is roasted. His intestines are taken out. His legs and limbs are cut off. His eyes are taken out. Patches of his flesh are taken off. He is skinned and smeared with salt. His skull is split open and boiling oil is poured in. He is buried in the earth up to the neck and a plough driven over him. He is skewered to the ground and trodden over by elephants. He is pinned alive to a tree. He is buried alive. He is beheaded . . . .

The thief shall suffer various torture such as being flogged with a leather strap with iron thorns; being beaten with a cane with thorns; having his ears and nose cut off; having his skull trepanned and molten iron poured in so that the brains boiled like porridge; having his mouth fixed open with a skewer and a lighted lamp put inside; being skinned in strips from the neck to the hips, so that the skin falls in strips round the legs; being skinned alive from the neck downwards and having each strip of skin as soon as removed tied by the hair so that these strips form a veil around him; having bits cut out of the flesh all over the body; being horseshoed and made to walk; having the head nailed to the ground by a spike thru both ear-lobes and then being dragged round and round by the legs; being pounded till the whole body is as soft as a straw mattress; having the body curled into a bundle and chopped to pieces; having cuts made all over the body and salt or alkali rubbed into the gashes; having bits of flesh cut off while alive and given to the dogs; being beheaded and being wrapped with rubbish and baked alive [Than Tun 1973; quoted in Spiro 1973:278-279].[2]

These extraordinary measures intended to deter crime were first decreed by thirteenth-century kings, but some of them were used into the eighteenth and nineteenth centuries. If the early Burmese were the only people whose culture produced such fierce punishments, our understanding of those punishments and of the Burmese would be very different from what it is given that similar punishments were used in Europe (among other places) during the same time period. As the sixteenth-century German woodcut reproduced here shows, splitting open people accused of crimes, gouging out their eyes, and other horrors were by no means limited to Burma. During the same period that Burmese authorities were visiting such punishments on accused criminals, similar treatment was being given in parts of Europe. In fact, extreme measures of this sort were used in Europe at least as recently as the Nazi period and continue in various parts of the world even now.

One point that comes out of this very limited comparison is that great cruelty as an official policy is not limited to a single group, a single part of the world, or a single era in history. Inhumanity is a widespread human trait. But comparison can take us a good deal further than that. We can increase our understanding of both the kindgom of Burma and the social and cultural arrangements that give rise to torture by a more detailed comparative examination of societies where torture is used. Having established that it is used in similar circumstances in the different groups, the examination would begin by trying to find out the similarities among groups that inflict terrible punishments on accused criminals. Do all of them, for example, have a political arrangement centering around an extremely powerful ruler? Do societies where this sort of treatment occurs always have populations composed of ethnically or economically different subgroups or both?

The answer to these questions is yes. Officially decreed torture and mutilation are more likely to be found in societies having both heterogeneous populations and a strong ruler than in societies with only one or neither of these traits. The next step in the comparison is to turn the question around. Instead of asking what traits are common to societies practicing torture, we

[2] @ 1973 by The Regents of the University of California. Reprinted from *Ethos*, Vl. 1, No. 3, Fall 1973, pp. 278-279, by permission of The Regents.

Sixteenth-Century German Punishments. The similarity between the practices shown here and those in Burma described in the text means that such corporal punishments are not distinctive to either group.

now ask whether all societies having the two traits practice torture as an accepted policy. The answer to this is no. There are societies with a strong ruler and a heterogeneous population where accused criminals are not so harshly dealt with. This last result tells us that there is more to the presence of official torture than the kind of government and the composition of the population. A study seeking to discover what else is involved in producing this sort of punishment would compare other aspects of the societies that practice it. Do all societies practicing it have a cultural view of human nature which includes the idea that fear is the most effective means of getting people to do—or refrain from doing—something? What other cultural beliefs and values are found in the severe-punishment societies? If this last question leads to the discovery of further aspects of culture present in all severe-punishment societies, the next step is to ask whether all societies having these cultural aspects practice torture. Following this general procedure, more and more can be learned about what gives rise to the phenomenon and what values, beliefs, and practices are commonly associated with it.[3]

Cross-cultural comparisons are the anthropological equivalent of laboratory experiments. If a chemist wants to know what effect temperature has on the electrical conductivity of a solution, he varies the temperature at which he takes the electrical measurements. Students of humanity cannot, of course, experiment with the ways of life of the people they study. Instead, they use the differences between actual societies and cultures to provide the variation that allows them to examine the effects of particular aspects of life whether these be type of government, composition of population, views of the nature of humans, or anything else.

Studying the widest possible range and variety of societies and cultures makes cross-cultural comparison more fruitful. An example will make this clear. Two psychologists carried out a study of the relationship between age of weaning and emotional disturbance using eighty young children from Kansas City (Sears and Wise 1950). This study found that the later a child was weaned, the more disturbance the child manifested. Obviously this finding would be more important if it applied to children in all societies.

To find out whether early weaning is associated with little disturbance and late weaning with much disturbance, an anthropologist used data on weaning and disturbance from thirty-seven different societies (Whiting 1954; Whiting and Child 1953). The accompanying figure, a summary of Whiting's findings, shows that when the range of weaning times is expanded beyond what was found in Kansas City a completely different result is obtained. In Kansas City only five of the eighty children studied were weaned later than seven months and none was weaned later than a year. In the sample of thirty-seven different societies, in all societies save two, children were weaned between twelve months and six years old. For that sample, as the table shows, the later the weaning, the less the emotional disturbance for the child. This is the opposite of what was found in Kansas City, but it does not prove that the Kansas City study was wrong. What it shows is that by looking at a phenomenon such as weaning over a wider range of variation than occurs in a single society we can

---

[3] The fact that the different parts of a culture are related to each other introduces the need for considerable caution when comparing things from different cultures. The ancient Incas cut out the hearts of victims as part of their religious rites. The practice has a superficial resemblance to the ways accused criminals were treated in Burma and Europe, but a comparison that failed to take account of the Inca practice being part of a religious complex rather than a criminal one would be seriously misleading. Because of the dangers of comparing practices and beliefs that are only superficially similar, some anthropologists are wary of the results of comparing different cultures.

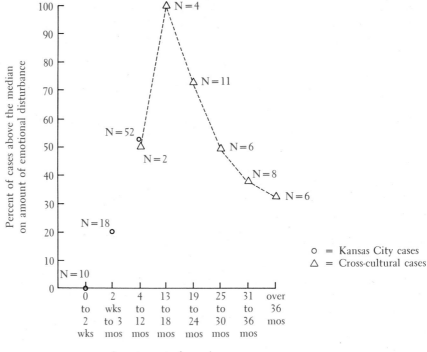

The Relationship of Emotional Disturbance and the Age of a Child at the Onset of Weaning.

(Data from Whiting 1954:525.)

get a fuller understanding of the effects of that phenomenon. The comparative study shows that if the child is weaned after the first year, the later it is, the less emotional disturbance for the child. Data from a single society suggest that the opposite is true if weaning occurs before the end of the first year, but other early-weaning societies would have to be studied to determine whether this was generally true. In any event, the use of thirty-eight different societies showed an aspect of the relationship between age at weaning and emotional disturbance that did not emerge from the study using data from Kansas City only.

Cross-cultural comparison, like the participant observation that provides the basis for most of our knowledge of other societies and thus the material for comparison, is a central part of anthropology's effort to contribute to humanity's understanding of itself. There are branches of anthropology that deal with the biological and prehistoric aspects of human life and with language. These branches have their own specialized methods and techniques. We consider the different branches of anthropology after a brief discussion of the field's history, which will provide a basis for understanding the diverse interests included in it.

The Emergence of Anthropology

We have already seen that Herodotus, the ancient Greek, has a strong claim to being considered the father of anthropology, if not the first true anthropologist.[4] It is unlikely, however, that he is the first person to carry out anthropological inquiries. In fact, it is surely true that long before writing was developed people looked at the practices, beliefs, and values of members of groups other than their own and that they tried to understand these and to compare them with their own much as we have seen Herodotus doing. An interest in human behavior and its variety, a wish to understand one's own group and its similarities to and differences from other groups must be as old as humanity itself. What is distinctive in the emergence of anthropology is not, then, this interest but its increasingly systematic pursuit.

Early European views We have seen that Herodotus was less than a full-fledged anthropologist in that he did not formulate or use the culture concept and any of its related theories. But he did show interest in many of the areas of life that still concern the anthropologist—religion, technology, language, politics, and various aspects of daily life—and he did practice some limited comparisons. We saw Herodotus comparing Egyptian gods' names to those of the Greeks and we noted that his writings were rich in other comparisons. The Egyptians were a people that particularly interested Herodotus, and in a passage of the *History* not included here he notes that some Babylonian burial practices were similar to those of the Egyptians, but that the Babylonians were unique in burying their dead coated with honey. The comparison of burial customs, like his religious comparisons, was mainly aimed at establishing similarities and differences between groups in order to determine what contact the groups had had and how they had influenced each other; a persistent anthropological interest.

Six centuries after Herodotus's time the Roman historian Tacitus wrote a detailed description of the German tribes. Herodotus, for all his intelligence and honesty, could not avoid bringing to his studies of other peoples a viewpoint he shared with his fellow Greeks: that their own culture was vastly worthier and nobler than that found in any other group. This view is part of what is called "ethnocentrism," an important concept that we discuss in the next chapter. Tacitus's descriptions of the German tribes do not suffer so much from obvious ethnocentrism as they do from distortion resulting from something that has long affected attempts to understand foreign groups and continues to do so today—the "myth of the noble savage." This myth can introduce just as much bias into an account of a group's way of life as did the sort of ethnocentrism Herodotus displayed. The noble-savage view holds that all societies which seem simpler and less complicated in social life and technology than the observer's embody all manner of virtues absent in more complex groups. Tacitus believed that the Germans and their way of life had

---

[4]For an excellent discussion of Herodotus, Pliny the Elder, and other ancient, medieval, and Renaissance writers concerned with describing and understanding societies and cultures in addition to their own, see Hodgen (1964). Slotkin (1965) quotes extensively from ancient, medieval, and later writers on anthropological issues and provides useful commentary and historical notes.

everything that was genuinely worthwhile and that was generally absent in his native Rome.

The Dark Ages dimmed interest in factual accounts of societies outside of Europe, although fantastic tales of dog-headed people, of groups of giants and dwarfs, and of people who did not eat but lived off the aroma of apples all received considerable attention. The works of the Greeks and Romans were neglected in the medieval period, and it was not until the sixteenth century that the interest and understanding of human diversity they showed reappeared. The accounts of such explorers as Columbus brought the existence of peoples quite different from those of Europe to attention and raised the problems of how there came to be such different ways of life. In general the Europeans thought of the other peoples of the earth as savage, crude, and hardly human. The seventeenth-century social philosopher Thomas Hobbes expressed a widely held view of life in what he called "a state of nature" in his book *Leviathan*. In societies without the sort of political organization and legal regulation with which he was familiar he said there was "no account of time; no arts; no letters, no society; and which is worst of all, continued fear, and danger of violent death; and the life of man, solitary, poor, nasty, brutish, and short" (1881:94–95).

"The fall" as an explanation of cultural diversity One of the most common Renaissance explanations for the ways of life of non-European peoples was that they had fallen from a higher state of cultural development at an earlier period. According to this explanation, the peoples of the Americas, Africa, and Asia shared common ancestry with Europeans, but over the centuries their isolation from Europe took its toll, and they lost more and more of the practices, beliefs, and values that constituted what the Renaissance writers considered a proper, human way of life—that is, their own. Sometimes this extremely ethnocentric explanation of how non-European culture came about took a theological form, and instead of geographic isolation being the cause of what were viewed as barbaric ways of living, they were attributed to a fall from divine grace.

A somewhat later European explanation of the differences between themselves and the people of the rest of the world was that there were distinct and separate species of humans rather than a single one. In this view the cultural differences between groups were due to their basic biological differences. This early racial determinism began to gather strength in the seventeenth century and was widespread among both scholars and laymen in the eighteenth and nineteenth centuries. It differed from some of its modern counterparts in believing all humans to have a single origin, usually as the offspring of Adam and Eve. Originally, it was believed, all humans were biologically similar, but over the millennia there was degeneration from the original, Adamic condition. The peoples of Europe remained closest to the physical condition as it was at Creation, but in Asia, Africa, and the Americas there had been physical deterioration caused by climate, disease, and breeding. This deterioration was taken to be responsible for the sorts of cultures found in the non-European groups just as Europe's "superior" culture was the result of the physical state of Europeans. The close kinship of the physical-deterioration view and the cultural-deterioration view will be obvious. In some cases, at least, the two views were intellectually and emotionally rooted in the biblical doctrine of the Fall of Man. The idea was that all people were fallen (from Paradise), but non-Europeans more so.

The idea of progress and evolution The attempt to explain the differences between European culture and the cultures of the rest of the world through the process of degeneration from a formerly homogeneous cultural or racial condition continued into the eighteenth century. In that same century, however, an opposing principle began to become prominent in explaining cultural differences. This was the principle of "progress." An early adherent of the view that cultures change by becoming more complex and more refined, Giambattista Vico, held that all cultures developed from a single primordial condition. Although each had its unique history, all went through similar phases of development. Consistently with this view, Vico believed it was possible to learn about the past condition of an advanced culture, namely, Europe, by studying contemporary people elsewhere in the world who were still in an early stage of development and thus lived as the earliest humans did in an earlier period. This idea follows logically from the view that all human groups pass through the same evolutionary stages and is referred to as "unilineal evolution," because it envisions only one line of development for all societies. Vico was not the only eighteenth-century thinker to invoke evolutionary change as the basis for understanding social life. Similar ideas are found, for example, in the works of the philosopher Immanuel Kant and the encyclopedist Denis Diderot.

In the nineteenth century the predominant type of explanation of human history and cultural diversity was an evolutionary one. However, in the first half of that century the most important advances were in prehistory rather than in the development of theory. Drawing on the writings of the Greeks and Romans, some eighteenth-century scholars believed that human tool-making went through three stages: stone, bronze, and iron. Actual evidence that there was a period when Europeans did not know how to work metal was not discovered until the early part of the nineteenth century when the Danish archaeologist R. Nyerup dug up stone implements that were unquestionably earlier than the earliest recorded history. From the accounts of travelers, explorers, and missionaries it was known that there were people living in the world who made their tools from stone, but it had not been proven previously that this was ever so in Europe. In 1836 C. J. Thomsen used the tools Nyerup had found together with other evidence to show that the three stages of technological development proposed by the Greeks and Romans had actually occurred.

At about the time of Thomsen's discoveries, an amateur antiquarian named Jacques Boucher de Perthes was presenting evidence which proved that humanity was much older than contemporary opinion held it to be. He unearthed stone axes that were undoubtedly far older than any man-made objects had previously been thought to be. He argued that the makers of

UNILINEAL EVOLUTIONISM *The view that all societies pass through the same stages of development in the course of their history; also called "parallel evolution."*

C. J. Thomsen. The interpretation of ancient tools by C. J. Thomsen proved that human culture had evolved.

these tools must have had a fully human way of life, including language, in order to have made the tools and, further, that this was far earlier than the Bible indicates as possible. His views were scorned and condemned as heretical for two decades, but when supporting evidence was discovered in England around 1859, they were finally accepted by most of the leading scholars and scientists concerned with human history. For many of these scholars the existence of humans more ancient than had previously been known was also supported by the discovery of the first true human fossil, a specimen of Neanderthal, in Germany in 1856.

The advances in prehistory made by Boucher de Perthes and other nineteenth-century archaeologists contributed to the development of evolutionary thinking. The idea that peoples everywhere passed through similar stages of cultural development was supported by the proof that Europeans had once had a technology based on stone similar in many ways to the technologies being used by some contemporary, non-European peoples. In the middle of the nineteenth century, a number of influential works dealing with the evolution of human society and culture appeared. In 1861 Johann Bachofen published *Das Mutterrecht* [The Mother-right] in which he tried to show that all human societies were originally ruled by women. In the same year Henry Maine's *Ancient Law* appeared. Maine argued that originally all interpersonal relations were based on kinship (what he called "status"), but as society progressed these relations came to depend more on freely undertaken relations with which individuals pursued their own interests. (This basis for these relationships was called "contract.") Charles Darwin's famous book, *The Origin of Species*, was published in 1859, and although it was not primarily concerned with human culture and society, it gave an important impetus to the evolutionary point of view in general.

Bachofen and Maine were attempting in their different ways to find general principles of cultural development and to explain the existence of diverse cultures. Like the thinkers of previous centuries they believed that the way to do this was to discover the processes by which all human cultures changed over time. They (correctly) believed that if universally applicable laws of cultural change could be found, these laws would make it possible to understand how their own culture came to be as it was and how the cultures of groups outside Europe were to be understood. This goal is still central in anthropology, but many contemporary anthropologists do not share a basic assumption of nineteenth-century writers like Maine and Bachofen that every society goes through the same sequence of stages and that most of the differences between societies are due to their being in different stages. For most nineteenth-century anthropologists, the reason all societies developed in the same way, the basis for all going through the same stages, was that all humans have the same mental equipment. Societies developed at different rates, but because of the "psychic unity of mankind," it was assumed they developed in the same way.

The late nineteenth-century evolutionists agreed that the basic stages in evolution were savagery, barbarism, and civilization. This sequence was first

Charles Darwin.
Darwin's hypothesis of evolution opened a new era in the analysis of the development of different kinds of animals.

proposed by the eighteenth-century philosopher Montesquieu, but it was developed into a working tool for the classification of living and historically known groups by later researchers. Lewis Henry Morgan, a practicing attorney but nevertheless the most influential early figure in anthropology in the United States, used the three stages just mentioned. He refined them by dividing each of the first two into an upper, a middle, and a lower part. Lower savagery was the condition of humanity at the time of the transition from an apelike to a human condition. This stage is represented by no living group. Middle savagery was characterized by communal owning of all property and by a technology based on chipped stone tools. Morgan put the Australian aborigines in this category. Village life was a characteristic of lower barbarism, and agriculture and animal husbandry of middle barbarism. Upper barbarism was characterized by the use of iron and the Homeric Greeks are put in this category.

A similar scheme was used by Edward Burnett Tylor, whose definition of "culture" we mentioned earlier. Tylor used archaeological evidence quite as much as descriptions of the ways of life of living peoples in his attempt to establish the uniformity of cultural change, particularly with respect to religion, his central interest. Like Morgan, Tylor believed that all societies developed through highly similar stages and that during each of these stages there was so much resemblance between societies that inferences about the past of a "civilized" society could be made by studying a contemporary "savage" or "barbaric" idea. We have seen that Vico had the same idea in the previous century. This method of reconstructing the past was called "the comparative method." Herbert Spencer, another important figure in evolutionary studies of humanity, compiled an enormous, multivolumed work, *Descriptive Sociology*, which was intended to provide the basis for this reconstruction by making available vast amounts of descriptive material from a variety of societies at different stages.

The comparative method (not to be confused with cross-cultural comparison, which is discussed on pp. 12–16) was a key part of nineteenth-century unilineal evolution, and some of evolutionism's basic difficulties come from the way the method was used. It is entirely legitimate to infer that regularities that are present now were also present in the past. Water surely boiled if heated to 100 degrees centigrade at standard pressure in the Pleistocene just as it does today. *If* communal ownership of goods is associated with a hunting-and-gathering economy as regularly as a temperature of 100 degrees is associated with boiling, we could infer that a Pleistocene group which practiced hunting and gathering (as indicated by their tools) surely had communal ownership of property as well. The difficulty is that the association between cultural beliefs and values on the one hand and tools that survive in the ground on the other is a complex one, and there is considerable cultural variation among different contemporary peoples with similar tools.

The main evidences we have of the culture of prehistoric groups are their tools, bones, and dwelling sites. To infer such things as the nature of property rights, the type of government, or the kinship system from archaeological

Louis Henry Morgan. Morgan was probably the most influential early writer in American anthropology.

Edward B. Tylor. Tylor argued that inferences about the past of European society could be drawn on the basis of evidence from contemporary "savage" or "barbaric" societies.

Franz Boas. Boas rejected
cultural evolutionism and
insisted on painstaking
empirical studies.

ETHNOGRAPHY *The
description of a society's
way of life.*

DIFFUSION *The
transmission of cultural
traits from one society to
another; sometimes called
"cultural borrowing."*

remains, we would have to establish first a close relationship between certain kinds of tools and the aspects of culture governing property, politics, or kinship. The nineteenth-century evolutionists did not succeed in establishing such relations. The associations they used between technology and cultural forms were more the product of their speculations than of empirical findings. The comparative method they used is a perfectly acceptable one. What is not acceptable is using it to reconstruct history when the regularities that are its base have little or no foundation in the real world of social life.

Franz Boas: cautious empiricist Franz Boas, working between the 1890s and 1940, shared some of the evolutionists' interests in studying the historical development of culture, but he vigorously rejected unilineal evolution and the comparative method. He believed that Morgan, Tylor, and the rest were guilty of having invented the sequences of change they presented as explanations of cultural development. For him there was no acceptable proof of the view that all societies went through the same, or even similar, stages of development. He rightly emphasized the poor quality of the descriptions of non-European groups the evolutionists depended on and their willingness to use traits (whether they were kinship terms or pottery designs) outside their cultural context as the basis for establishing their sequences of cultural development. Boas worked for the improvement of the quality of ethnographic information—"ethnography" is the description of a society's way of life—and he insisted that traits could only be useful in reconstructing history when they were examined in their full cultural context. He believed that pottery design, for example, had to be looked at with regard to what it meant to the people who made it and how it served to influence the way pottery was used. The history of a kinship term could be found only when the term was seen as a part of the whole system of terms and relations among kin in each of the societies using the term.

For Boas it was essential to uncover the history of human inventions, customary practices, and other aspects of culture because he believed that cultural phenomena could be understood only through a knowledge of their past. Much of the work Boas did was devoted to investigating diffusion, which is the transmission of cultural traits from one group to another. A number of writers around the end of the nineteenth century believed that all human cultures resulted from diffusion from one or a few centers of cultural development. One of the better known of these views held that almost everything originated in ancient Egypt and diffused from there to the rest of the world at different rates and with different degrees of completeness. Boas rejected these extreme diffusionists as fully as he did the unilinear evolutionists, but the rejection applied only to the attempt to explain the variety of human cultures through unfounded speculations concerning the transmission of traits from one group to another.

Diffusion was a vital source of cultural change for Boas, but it was not the only one, and its occurrence had to be proved in every case. It could not be assumed. Diffusion rather than independent invention was accepted as the basis for the presence of a trait only if the similarities between the trait and associated parts of culture in two or more groups were so great that only transmission could explain them. More than this, either the groups among which there had been diffusion of traits had to be currently in contact or the path of the diffusion through other groups had to be established. Boas believed that every group had a unique history and that its present state was the result both of its cultural borrowings (i.e., diffusion) and of internal development. His rejection of extreme diffusionism did not mean that he rejected the process of diffusion when it could be demonstrated, and his objections to unilinear evolution did not mean he was unwilling to accept culture change from internal sources. He simply insisted that any processes that were presented as explaining the current state of a culture had to be fully proven with reliable evidence.

Boas's concern with careful fact gathering and avoiding unsupported theory led him to oppose even modest and empirically justified generalizations about how culture develops and changes. Boas's reluctance to generalize was so strong and his influence on American anthropology so great that for the early decades of this century the discipline as practiced in the United States was almost without theoretical generalizations. Boas's lasting contributions include an insistence on high standards of research, a concern with each group's culture as an integrated, functioning whole, and a stimulation of interest in linguistics and human biology. Although he believed laws of cultural development would probably never be discovered, he thought psychological laws concerning the acceptance or rejection of new cultural traits might be found some day. Boas's 1911 book, *The Mind of Primitive Man,* effectively demonstrated that there is no scientific basis for using racial differences to explain cultural diversity and that *Homo sapiens* is a single species among whose members there is no significant difference in mental ability. Boas's numerous students, including such anthropologists as A. L. Kroeber, Clarke Wissler, Robert Lowie, Cora Du Bois, Ruth Benedict, and Margaret Mead, diffused his influence throughout the field. No single individual affected the development of American anthropology more than Franz Boas did, both through his own work and through the work of his many distinguished students.

The functionalists Boas reacted to the evolutionists by rejecting their approach, but he retained their interest in discovering how societies, especially non-European societies, came to be the way they are. In England, A. R. Radcliffe-Brown and Bronislaw Malinowski rejected both the evolutionists' approach and their objective of reconstructing the history of social development. They differed from one another in important ways, but they agreed that since documentary evidence of past events was not available for most of the societies that interested anthropologists, it was futile to try to discover what had happened in those societies in the past. For them the task of anthropology was to describe and explain the workings of contemporary, mostly non-European, societies.

One of the most striking ways Radcliffe-Brown differed from Boas was in emphasizing social structure rather than culture. Drawing on the work of the

A. R. Radcliffe-Brown. Radcliffe-Brown held that the principles underlying social order could be derived only from direct observations of actual social relationships.

Bronislaw Malinowski. Malinowski believed social practices could be understood by finding what biological need they served.

French sociologist Émile Durkheim, he taught that close observation of actual relationships among individuals making up a group would provide the basis for understanding the principles underlying their social order. In his scheme the group's social structure was the sum of these relationships. During a career that began in the first decade of this century and continued into the fifth, his writings and lectures examined the contributions religion, law, economics, politics, and the rules of property inheritance and descent made to the maintenance of the social structures of African, Australian, and other societies. He referred to the contribution of a practice or belief as its "function": "The social life of the community is here defined as the *functioning* of the social structure. The *function* of any recurrent activity, such as the punishment of a crime, or a funeral ceremony, is the part it plays in the social life as a whole and therefore the contribution it makes to the maintenance of the structural continuity" (1952:180).

Like Radcliffe-Brown, Malinowski believed that the way to understand a social practice was to determine what contribution it made. Unlike Radcliffe-Brown, Malinowski sought to establish how the practice contributed to the satisfaction of individual biological and psychological needs rather than to the maintenance of the group's social structure. Malinowski also considered himself a "functionalist," but the focus of his type of functional analysis was different from Radcliffe-Brown's. The following passage shows the sort of approach Malinowski favored.

> It is a commonplace to say that humanity advances on its belly, that you can keep the multitude satisfied by bread as well as circuses, and that the materialistic factor of satisfactory food supply is one of the determinants of human history and evolution. The functionalist only adds that the motives which control the parts of this process, and which become broken up into the passion for gardening and hunting, into the interest or greed for suitable exchange and marketing, into impulses of generosity and munificence, must all be analyzed with reference to the main drive, that of hunger. The integral function of all the processes which constitute the cultural commissariat of a community is the satisfaction of a primary biological need of nutrition [Malinowski 1944:155].

Malinowski has been criticized for overemphasizing the uniqueness of various human groups and thereby retarding an increase in the understanding of human culture as a whole. His attempts to explain social practices as means of satisfying biological and social needs has been viewed as circular and unenlightening. To say, for example, that marriage is related to the sexual drive does not help us understand why in some societies one man marries one woman ("monogamy"), in others one man marries two or more women ("polygyny"), and in a few one woman marries two or more men ("polyandry").

Radcliffe-Brown is not susceptible to these criticisms, of course, since his functionalism is different from Malinowski's and focuses on the contribution beliefs, values, and practices make to the maintenance of the social structure.

The main criticism of Radcliffe-Brown is that his approach fails to take account of the dynamic nature of society and culture. What he called "structural-functionalism" (partly to separate his position from Malinowski's, which he rejected) assumes that society is in equilibrium and is changeless in its basic form. Since the enduring social structure is the foundation of all explanations in structural-functionalism, this theoretical position leads unavoidably to looking at whatever society is being studied as a static entity. Many anthropologists believe this to be an unacceptable distortion of the reality of social life, which they understand as constantly changing, though at different rates in different time periods.

Radcliffe-Brown's theoretical position has had more influence in anthropology than Malinowski's has. Malinowski's fieldwork in the Trobriand Islands is his most widely recognized contribution. The quality of his descriptions of Trobriand life surpassed all previous ethnographies, and his work set a standard for research that still prevails. He not only obtained full accounts of culturally prescribed patterns of activity, but he also recorded the actual behavior of individuals in a variety of circumstances. He demonstrated that people in the society he studied followed the dictates of "custom" no more automatically than we do. He showed, for example, that Trobriand men faced painful conflict in the problem of the inheritance of their property. The Trobrianders have a matrilineal society, that is, membership in clans and the inheritance of property pass through women, and a man's heirs are his sister's children, not his own; Trobriand fathers, however, love their children and want them to have their belongings. Malinowski provided for the first time a basis for understanding this and other dilemmas arising from the differences between personal inclination and cultural prescription. Malinowski's functionalism had some influence in bringing out the place of the individual in the operation of culture and in isolating related complexes of cultural practices ("institutions") concerned with the same human needs. His most significant effect on anthropology, however, has been in providing a model for fieldwork.

Radcliffe-Brown reported in detail only his initial fieldwork in the Andaman Islands, which was not particularly distinguished, but his theoretical writings and his teaching make him a central figure in the discipline's development. His students, some of whom also studied with Malinowski, include such important figures as E. E. Evans-Pritchard, Meyer Fortes, Raymond Firth, Max Gluckman, Fred Eggan, S. F. Nadel, and many others. These anthropologists and their students are the core personnel of British social anthropology, and their work has greatly influenced modern anthropology all over the world. However, the American emphasis on history, which centered around Boas and his students, was strong enough to lead a substantial number of American anthropologists to reject functionalism from the beginning. Many others have been leery of its emphasis on stability and changelessness. Nevertheless, its impact has been and continues to be a substantial one.

Contemporary Evolutionary Views

Interest in evolutionary explanations of cultural change did not end with Boas's attack on the nineteenth-century formulations of this viewpoint. Some contemporary evolutionary views do not insist upon a single line of development for all human cultures in the way the views of L. H. Morgan did; however, one of the most influential social and cultural evolutionists of the current period, Leslie White, stresses the similarities between his own and Morgan's views.

Whatever the similarities or differences between White's and Morgan's positions, White has had an important influence on American anthropology. The core of his understanding of cultural evolution is found in what he called "the basic law of cultural evolution." This "law" (many consider it a definition) holds that: "Other factors remaining constant, culture evolves as the amount of energy harnessed per capita per year is increased, or as the efficiency of the instrumental means of putting the energy to work is increased" (1949a:363–393). In White's view every human culture can be divided into three parts: economic and technological; social; and ideological. The economic and technological is fundamental to the other two, and social structure and ideology can be understood, for White, only through reference to that foundation. The basis for relations among people and for their values and world view is, in this scheme, determined by their society's ability to harness and use energy and by the way the products of harnessing are distributed. In this view all groups begin with only the energy that humans can produce with their own muscles, but they all move on to the quantity of energy that can be released by fire, by flowing rivers, and so on, through animal power and up, for the most advanced, to the atom. White argues that peoples with similar sorts of energy production and use have similar sorts of social structures and "ideologies."

White defines "culture" in a way similar to Tylor's omnibus definition. For White, "culture" refers to "traditional customs, institutions, tools, philosophies, languages, etc." (White 1949b:73). Because a group's culture existed before the birth of any particular member of the group and because it will survive beyond any particular member's death, it is, White argues, supra-individual and cannot be explained psychologically. Because culture provides the basis for the relationships found in a group, it cannot be explained by reference to the group's social structure either. In fact, culture can be explained, says White, only by reference to culture. He used the term "culturology" to refer to what he considers the correct focus of anthropology. His explanation of slavery illustrates the way culturology is applied.

> Slavery as an institution will exist and endure only when the master can derive profit and advantage by exploiting the slave. This is only possible when a family group is able to produce considerably more than it requires for its continued existence. The efficiency of production is of course determined by the degree of technological development. Slavery did not exist . . . before the Neolithic [i.e., New Stone Age] times because culture had not developed sufficiently to make it

possible for a producer to be more than self-supporting. . . . Consequently, we have no slavery in early periods of human history, nor, in the modern world, among people of low levels of technological development [1949c:128].

Culturology, then, uses the technological aspect of culture to explain the other aspects of culture and society. White's culturology has not been accepted by many anthropologists. The argument that social structure and psychology are useless as explanations of culture has not convinced even most of those researchers who are interested in the relationship between technology/economics and cultural change. White's students and followers, however, have developed and elaborated his views into a number of related positions, often collectively referred to as "cultural materialism." Cultural materialism is an active and influential school of thought which continues to apply the idea that culture and its changes can be understood best through the study of economics and technology.

An evolutionary position related to White's but different in important respects is often referred to as "cultural ecology." The founder of this extremely influential view, Julian Steward, did not assume that cultures follow a single line of development. He simply set out to discover similarities between cultures or groups of cultures in the ways they develop. He found such similarities to be present among groups living in similar environments and having similar means of dealing with those environments in terms of getting food, shelter, and defense. He summarizes this approach by saying: "I have endeavored in various studies to demonstrate how cultural-ecological adaptations—the adaptive processes through which a historically derived culture is modified in a particular environment—are among the important creative processes in cultural change" (Steward 1953:320).

Julian Steward. Steward founded an approach, often called "cultural ecology," that stresses environmental adaptation.

Steward's cultural ecology is *not* a simple environmental determinism. In every culture he believes there is a "cultural core" made up of those aspects of the culture most closely related to subsistence activities and economic arrangements. His studies show that the interaction between similar cultural cores and similar environments produces similarities in cultural development. He discovered similarities among hunting-and-gathering bands, for example, and among city-states based on irrigation agriculture. Because his theory held both that a single line of evolution was not to be assumed and that there were similarities in cultural development among a number of different types of cultures, he referred to his general theory as "multilinear evolution." His similarity to White and the cultural materialists is found in his emphasis on technology and economics as part of the "cultural core," but he differs from them in believing that these factors do not determine all of a culture's characteristics. Steward also differs from White in specifically maintaining that psychological characteristics can play a part in determining the development of cultures.

Whatever their differences, Steward, White, and other recent evolutionists all attempt to deal with the reality of social and cultural change. American anthropology has stressed change from its earliest period. This is partly due to the fact that until the middle of the present century most American anthropologists did their research in American Indian groups where social and cultural change was rapid and striking. In sharp contrast are the British functionalist anthropologists whose understanding of society as essentially changeless was based on fieldwork in Africa or other areas where the British colonial policy of indirect rule froze or at least seriously retarded social and cultural change. American anthropologists also had an abiding interest in prehistory that their contemporaries in Britain generally did not share. A knowledge of the archaeological record with its endless successions of differences made it very difficult to be satisfied with theories that did not explain change. Thus, American anthropology has always focused on the processes of cultural development over time. This focus can be seen in Boas no less than in White and Steward. It is legitimate to view Boas, White, Steward, and cultural historians like A. L. Kroeber as commonly concerned with looking at cultures as they change over time. This stands in opposition to Malinowski and Radcliffe-Brown whose basic interest was in how society and culture operate when looked at as changeless and outside of history.

Culture and Personality

Although evolutionists gave a central place to the "psychic unity of mankind" as the source of uniformity in cultural development, their interest in the dynamics of mental functioning was extremely limited. Boas believed that psychological laws would eventually be discovered to explain regularities in cultural borrowing and change, but despite the later interests of his students his own work gave virtually no attention to the study of the psychological phenomena that were to provide these laws. The structural-functionalism of Radcliffe-Brown was concerned with how beliefs and practices operated to maintain social structure, but it had little interest in examining questions about what brought individuals to hold these beliefs and what was involved in their carrying out the practices. In fact until the 1920s anthropologists were almost entirely unconcerned with the study of the personalities of the people whose cultures and societies they were trying to describe and explain.

A major change in this situation came through Malinowski's interest in psychology, which was rooted in his theoretical emphasis on the relationship between culture and the satisfaction of biological and psychological needs. While he was working in the Trobriands, a friend sent him some of the writings of Sigmund Freud. Freud's formulations of personality functioning caught his attention, and he began a debate with an English psychoanalyst, Ernest Jones, concerning the usefulness of the Oedipus conflict for understanding personality formation in a society like the Trobriands where descent is through women and authority over the child is vested in the mother's brother rather than in the father. Part of Malinowski's 1927 book, *Sex and Repression in Savage Society*, is concerned with the role of that conflict in Trobriand personality, and he explicitly addresses himself to the "manifestations of the unconscious" in the members of that group.

Ruth Benedict. Benedict held that in every group there is a dominant type of personality configuration and that most group members are influenced by that configuration.

At about the same time Malinowski published his views on some of the relations between personality and culture in the Trobriands, Ruth Benedict, one of Boas's students, began to present hers. In 1934 in *Patterns of Culture,* she set forth a forceful and highly influential statement on the relationship between culture and personality. Her basic position was that in every group there was a dominant type of personality configuration and that in the course of development almost every individual is molded into that configuration. Those members of the group who had the genetically determined temperament most congenial to the group's dominant personality type were most successful and admired, and the dominant type was viewed as the normal type of personality for all the members of the group. Benedict's famous statement "Culture is personality writ large" expresses her belief that the sort of emphasis and style found in a culture is simply a self-perpetuating expression of the shared personality emphases and styles found in the group members. She is interested in looking at groups with respect to such questions as: Is the extreme expression of things valued or is moderation prized; does suspicion and grandiosity find expression in wide areas of life?

Margaret Mead, also a Boas student, concerned herself in the 1920s and 1930s with the relationship between human nature and culture. In her justly famous 1928 book, *Coming of Age in Samoa,* she examines the popular notion that it is part of human nature for adolescence to be a time of emotional tension and conflict. The reasoning behind her study is that if the idea is correct, then tension and conflict will be found in all human adolescents, regardless of the culture of their group. She found, however, that adolescence in Samoa does not entail the upheavals that it does in urban American society and that therefore adolescent stress is a culturally determined phase in individual personality development rather than one rooted in the basic nature of humanity. In a similar vein she studied male and female personality traits in three Melanesian societies to try to find out whether fixed and general differences in behavior between the sexes were present regardless of what culture was being considered. In *Sex and Temperament in Three Primitive Societies* (1935) she showed that some traits thought of as typically male are absent in males in some groups and that some "male" traits are found in females in other groups, and the same is true of females and the presence of allegedly female traits. Mead's contributions, which extended over five decades, are by no means limited to her investigations of human nature or, even, to the field of culture and personality, but she was one of the founders of the subfield, and the issues she raised long ago remain vital.

One of many issues that interested Mead was the effect of child training on the individual's acquisition of culture and on personality development. This topic is a central one because culture is transmitted from generation to generation through the training of children, and, according to psychoanalytic personality theories long influential in anthropology, it is in childhood experience that the most fundamental personality traits are established. In the late 1930s psychoanalysis was becoming quite influential in anthropology, and attempts to understand the relationship between personality and culture centered increasingly on studies of child training. Abram Kardiner, a practicing psychoanalyst, held a series of seminars attended by a number of anthropologists from 1936 to 1940. Among those there were Ralph Linton, Ruth Bunzel, Ruth Benedict, and Cora Du Bois, whose study of the people of Alor plays an important part in the fourth chapter of this book.

Kardiner and his seminar worked out a three-part relationship between culture and personality. In this scheme attention is focused on the institutions that influence child training, such as child-training practices themselves, the economic arrangements that affect the availability of the parents to tend the child, and the housing arrangements that influence the people and situations the child will encounter. These are called "primary institutions," and, because they are uniform for the members of a group, they produce important similarities in their personalities through the common childhood experiences they bring about. Substantial personality differences between group members exist, but the shared characteristics, called "Basic Personality Structure," lead all of them to have similar tendencies and similar conflicts. The conflicts in the Basic Personality Structure find expression and some resolution in such cultural forms as religion and myth, called "secondary institutions."

Attempts to find personality similarities in the sharers of a culture have not been limited to Kardiner and his co-workers. A substantial number of anthropologists and social psychologists have dealt with the problem from a variety of different perspectives. Their basic position has been that because culture provides the ways people do things, including the raising of their children, it would be surprising if individuals raised according to one culture were not more like each other than individuals from different groups with different cultures. Similarly, because cultures are effective foundations for group life only when the ways of behavior they prescribe are followed, it is important to know the role of personality similarities and differences in producing the motives that lead individuals to follow the prescriptions. These motives are generally believed to result, at least in part, from the culturally prescribed child-training practices.

An important type of study relating child training to culture has been carried out by John Whiting and his associates. These studies mainly use the Human Relations Area Files, which were founded and inspired by George Murdock to make ethnological work of all types more efficient and practical. The files provide an indexing system for ethnographic reports (some published nowhere else), making it possible to establish relations between one sort of practice and another sort with relative ease. Whiting and his coworkers found a number of important associations between the ways people raise their children and practices customarily found among adults. One study, for example, of the relation between the severity of aggression training (how much children are punished for showing aggressive behavior) and the type and amount of aggression found in supernatural practices and beliefs (do people believe in witchcraft or sorcery?) found that in societies with severe aggression training a belief in witchcraft was more likely than it was in societies with less severe training.

Many culture and personality studies have been done from a nonhistorical perspective, and from the time of Benedict there has been a tendency to study both personality and culture as though they were changeless. However, one of the most important researchers in this area, A. I. Hallowell, also carried out some of the earliest studies of the relationship between culture change and personality. In two studies of the Ojibwa Indians that appeared in the 1940s he demonstrated that although there were some changes in shared personality traits over time and with different amounts of contact with members of different societies, the most striking thing was the continuity of personality. These studies suggest that common personality characteristics are more resistant to change than culture is. They also suggest that there is considerable flexibility in the relation between culture and personality and that to view culture as "personality writ large" is to over-simplify this relationship.

Like evolutionary studies, functionalist approaches, and studies of culture history, the study of culture and personality remains an important part of anthropology. Culture and personality research reached the height of its popularity in the early 1950s, and a number of anthropologists still devote their main research and teaching efforts to various aspects of this field. However, interest in culture and personality is less widespread than it was earlier, and psychological interest among a large number of anthropologists now is more in the direction of examining cultural influences on how people think (cognition) than it is on how their whole personalities are related to their cultures. This new interest, which we shall examine in the next section, fits well with the older personality interest, and together the two promise to provide a fuller understanding of the issues concerned with the relationship between individuals and their societies and cultures.

A. Irving Hallowell. Hallowell carried out some of the earliest studies on the relationship between culture change and personality showing that under some circumstances personality is more resistant to change than culture is.

Linguistic Models

Linguists have made great progress in developing formal methods for describing languages accurately and comparing them usefully. Many of the logical ideas used in the analysis of language have been adopted into the general vocabulary and approach of descriptive anthropology. The analysis of sound systems in particular has provided a wealth of useful analogies in the analysis of other cultural conventions. Many early anthropologists had noted the usefulness of the logical models that could be borrowed from linguistics. The most famous linguist in the early years of this century was perhaps Edward Sapir, an authority on North American Indian languages.

A more recent example of the influence of linguistic models on other kinds of anthropological problems is found in the work of Claude Lévi-Strauss. Lévi-Strauss has sought to discover the structure of the myths found in groups as diverse as the Homeric Greeks and the Indians of the Amazon Basin in

Brazil. He tries to discover the logic(s) by which the mythological system of one group can be related to the mythological system of another group and by which one myth can be interpreted in light of another. He aims to discover the basic structure of the human mind as it is in humanity everywhere regardless of cultural differences. Although Lévi-Strauss's work is not directly imitative of linguistic studies, it is inspired by some of the same logic that underlies linguistic analysis.

Anthropologists have also been interested in the relationship between the way people think and the way their language works. In the middle years of the present century a great deal of interest focused on the proposition that grammatical categories in different languages code experience differently, which would mean that speakers of different languages perceive and experience the world differently. This hypothesis was associated particularly with the names of Benjamin Lee Whorf and of Edward Sapir. The "Sapir-Whorf hypothesis" (which we discuss in more detail in the chapter on language) did not prove susceptible of simple demonstration, and some anthropological linguists today regard it as a dead issue. Others, however, continue to investigate problems that are derived from it, although with greater focus on vocabulary than on grammar. One study, for example, has demonstrated the influence of the color vocabulary of a language on the tendency of its speakers to remember some colors and forget others (Berlin and Kay 1969).

Much of the most recent work on the relation between language and thinking has focused on two areas, one, childhood acquisition of language and, two, the meanings of sets of words. Studies of childhood acquisition of language have flourished particularly among linguists and psychologists, while studies of meaning have been more prevalent among anthropologists. The terms "ethnosemantics," "ethnoscience," "new ethnography," and "cognitive anthropology" have been used to describe the methods and findings of those who have sought to study the ways that people categorize experience and exhibit their categories in language. Much of this anthropological work—some would say *too* much—has concentrated on understanding the relation between sets of kinship terms and how the terminology relates to the system of kinship statuses in various societies, but other types of words have also been investigated.

The foregoing sketch of the history of anthropology should give some idea of the diversity of approaches that have been and are being used in the field. The sketch has emphasized social and cultural anthropology, but even the brief references that have been made will make it clear that interest in language, human biology, and prehistory have existed and developed along with the concern for describing and explaining contemporary societies and cultures.

Claude Lévi-Strauss.

Lévi-Strauss has produced influential studies examining mythology as a means for discovering the structure of the human mind.

Major Subfields of Anthropology

Anthropology is traditionally divided into four major subfields: social and cultural anthropology; archaeology, or prehistory; anthropological linguistics;

and physical anthropology. Specialties within the subfields will be noted as part of the discussion of each field.

Social and cultural anthropology The majority of anthropologists working in the United States, Britain, Canada, New Zealand, Australia, and other past and present members of the British Commonwealth specialize in social or cultural anthropology. On the European continent this same specialty has fewer practitioners and is often referred to as "sociology," while the term "anthropology" is taken to mean what English-speaking scholars refer to as physical anthropology and, sometimes, prehistory. At one time American anthropologists in this subfield usually referred to themselves as "cultural anthropologists," while people trained in the British tradition called themselves "social anthropologists." In the last few decades, however, the difference between the American sort of work focusing on "culture" and the British sort focusing on "social structure" has diminished, and a number of American anthropologists have begun to use the term "social anthropology" interchangeably with "cultural anthropology." At the present time it is difficult to see any consistent differences among anthropologists who refer to themselves and their work by one term as opposed to the other. Either term can apply to concerns with describing how various groups of people live and explaining both the similarities and differences among the groups and the particular cultural configurations found in each.

The factual basis for all social and cultural anthropology comes from descriptions of the ways of life of human groups. These descriptions are ethnographies, and any anthropologist who writes such a description is an ethnographer. Because the vast majority of professional social and cultural anthropologists do fieldwork involving describing the life (or some part of it) of the group they are studying, they are all ethnographers, whatever other fields may interest them.

Ethnology is the systematic comparison of different societies and cultures. Some anthropologists consider ethnology their main interest, and the Human Relation Area Files, mentioned previously, is one of their important tools. Many anthropologists, however, are involved in ethnology, as they are in ethnography, as part of whatever particular problem they may be pursuing, because cross-cultural comparison is often involved.

Social structure is an area of concentration that often employs ethnological comparisons. Specialists in this subject seek to determine the nature of social arrangements in human societies and the sources and consequences of these arrangements. Because kinship ties provide a fundamental social relationship in all societies and are the main source of these relationships in many societies, specialists in social structure often devote a great deal of their attention to kinship groupings. Political relations are also key elements in the social structures of all societies, and anthropologists who specialize in the study of politics are often interested in social structural questions going beyond politics.

Economic anthropology deals with the ways people in different societies produce food, shelter, tools, weapons, and such and how they are distributed

ETHNOLOGY *The systematic comparison of different societies and cultures.*

once produced. Like political anthropology and all the other specialties in the field, economic anthropology retains an interest in the whole culture of the society being studied and looks at its special subject matter in the context provided by noneconomic areas of life.

Religion is the focus of another specialty. Anthropologists who concentrate on this area do not limit their attention to the major world religions (Christianity, Islam, Judaism, Buddhism), but study the beliefs concerned with supernatural beings and forces as they occur in all human societies. The anthropology of art, another specialty, also casts a wide net and studies art as an integral part of every human culture. The study of folklore and mythology is a separate specialty with connections to the interest in art based in the common concern of the two specialties with symbolism, context, and meaning. Folklore, myth, and art are studied in their own right, and they are also used in studying other aspects of culture and the human mind. Lévi-Strauss and others use the myths and folktales of a group to discover the basic nature ("structure") of human culture. Anthropologists who work in this tradition are called "structuralists," and structuralism is itself a specialty in social and cultural anthropology. (Structuralists should not be confused with social structuralists, who are interested in social arrangements and the principles governing them rather than in the fundamental relations between different aspects of culture.)

Myths and folklore are also used by psychological anthropologists. Those interested in the relationship between how people think and culture sometimes use myths and folktales to help establish the sorts of categories and contrasts characteristic of thought in a particular society; those seeking to discover such common personality characteristics as motives and basic conflicts sometimes use the same material.

"Applied" anthropology is another specialty within social and cultural anthropology. This field attempts to use the understandings achieved through the anthropological study of groups and their cultures to deal with their problems. Medical anthropology is the largest area of applied anthropology, and here anthropologists use their understanding of the organization and culture of hospitals, for example, to help them serve patients more effectively, or they use their knowledge of groups' beliefs about illness, treatment, and health to assist physicians and health workers in providing care.

Archaeology, or prehistory In an important sense archaeology is a branch of social and cultural anthropology rather than a separate field. The main goal of archaeology is the same as that of cultural anthropology: to describe and explain the ways of life of human groups. The difference is that archaeology deals with human groups, sometimes called "extinct societies," known only by their physical remains. Cultural anthropologists observe people's behavior and talk with them about the things they do and believe; they also map their settlements, diagram their houses, study their manufacture of tools, and so on. Archaeologists can only do things involving physical remains since the people they study are long dead. The field is sometimes called "prehistory," and the study of documents as a primary source of information is usually precluded.

(Archaeology of historically known peoples is not normally the province of anthropologists, but of historians and classical archaeologists).

Archaeologists' data are limited to the kinds of evidence that survive hundreds, thousands, tens of thousands, and, even, hundreds of thousands of years. From the remains of settlements and from tools, art objects, and such evidence as the pollen preserved in soil and fossilized animal and human feces ("coprolites"), archaeologists reconstruct as fully as possible the life of the groups they study. The techniques they use include establishing the dates of remains through a variety of methods mostly based on the decay of radioactive elements, magnetic reversals, geological strata, the presence of extinct animals, and counting tree rings. They study the "sites" they dig up in well-established and extremely painstaking ways to preserve all possible evidence. The inferences they are able to make about the culture of the groups that lived in the sites are sometimes astoundingly rich.

Through comparing the findings at different sites dating from the same time period, archaeologists are able to reconstruct the distribution of cultural traits over wide geographic areas. The study of sequences of remains at a single site and the comparison of results from different sites furnish a record of cultural change over much longer periods than would otherwise be possible. Prehistory also provides information about human groups that would otherwise be entirely unknown. Archaeology has had a central role in the development of humanity's understanding of itself since the early nineteenth century and continues to be a vital part of that effort through its increasing ability to reconstruct the past.

Linguistic anthropology   We have already mentioned the concerns of linquistic anthropology with the application of linguistic models and ethnoscience. In addition, linguistic anthropologists have been concerned with historical applications of language study and with recent developments in the field of linguistics proper.

Some of the earliest anthropological interest in language was historical. Linguists in Europe and America made great strides in the nineteenth century in developing ways of interpreting language change through time. Early in the nineteenth century Rasmus Rask demonstrated that languages derived from a single, earlier, "parent" language (as Italian, French, and Romanian are derived from Latin) exhibit regular correspondences in their sound systems. Jacob Grimm (today famous also for the fairytales he compiled with his brother Wilhelm) demonstrated in detail how this worked for major European languages, and the correspondence principle is today known as "Grimm's law." Grimm's law and other findings of historical linguistics were developed through work on European languages, for which earlier historical documents could provide some guidance and a check on the results.

For historical anthropologists, the findings of historical linguistics of European languages also have provided tools for approaching the history of languages in other parts of the world, such as Africa, Siberia, and the Americas. One of the most recent of these attempts was "glottochronology." Glottochronology, associated particularly with the work of Morris Swadesh, is

Jacob Grimm. Grimm demonstrated a system of sound correspondences between European languages.

a technique of dating the time when two sister languages began to grow apart from each other. The technique involves counting the proportions of words that have been replaced in their core vocabularies, on the assumption that the rate of word replacement is relatively constant over the centuries.

Since the late 1950s, the field of linguistics has undergone a substantial change because of the wide acceptance of the approach of Noam Chomsky and his associates, called "transformational grammar." The essential insight of transformational grammar is that the actual words pronounced (the "surface" structure of speech) are to be analyzed as the final reprocessing of various idea categories and structures by successive application of various "rules" (the "deep" structure of speech). The effect of transformational grammar in linguistics has been to reorient linguistics to a new way of looking at the structure of language and to set out for linguistics a rather different set of research problems, focused particularly on the analysis of grammar. In anthropology the effects of the "transformational revolution" in linguistics are only beginning to be felt. The logical models borrowed from linguistics in the past (and variations on them) continue to be useful in the analysis of culture, but the transformational models have yet to be assimilated (*if* indeed they productively can be) into anthropological approaches to culture.

The science of linguistics born out of the philological tradition of Jacob Grimm on the one hand and the anthropological tradition of description on the other, has come to be an independent discipline, and many of its concerns (such as grammatical theory) are today only marginally connected to anthropology. Nevertheless, the continued and unavoidable anthropological concern with language, or at least with selected aspects of language behavior, means that fruitful borrowing of ideas and methods from linguistics may be expected to continue indefinitely.

Physical anthropology   Physical anthropology studies the biological foundations for human life and culture. Its three main subfields are human evolution, or paleoanthropology; human variation, or race; and comparative studies of primate anatomy and behavior. As in the other fields, there have been significant advances during the past decade or so. In physical anthropology these advances are partly because of new discoveries and partly because of the use of newly developed techniques and theories from genetics and other areas of biology as well as from anthropology.

Human evolution, or paleoanthropology, is concerned with the development of *Homo sapiens sapiens* (modern humanity) from its earliest beginnings in ancient and long extinct primates. This subfield combines an interest in physical evolution with an interest in the development of the capacity for culture, and accordingly its main evidence includes the tools and other archaeological evidence of ancient humanity's way of life as well as ancient human and animal bones. In the past few years there have been important discoveries in this subfield, which, together with advances in techniques for establishing the age of the finds, have led to greatly increased knowledge of the earliest periods of human history.

The study of nonhuman primate behavior and anatomy has assumed greater importance for all of anthropology in recent years. Through the investigation of the ways of life of both free-living and confined monkeys and apes, physical anthropologists have made significant contributions to the understanding of the relationship between the physical structures and ways of life of early humans and prehumans. The anatomy of early fossil forms is increasingly looked at in the context of the behavioral abilities of similar forms found in the entire range of living primates, and this perspective is proving highly productive. Similarly, the ecological relations of the earliest humans and their prehuman ancestors are better known now than they ever have been before because of the results of studies of the ecological relations of contemporary nonhuman primates whose environments and abilities are similar to those of the ancient human forebears.

The study of human physical variation is concerned with the physical differences of human groups. Such different groups are sometimes called "races," although this term involves difficulties. Until the past few decades this specialty dealt with differences in such characteristics as skin color, head form, and stature. Now there is at least as much interest in differences in blood types and immunological factors because the genetics of the transmission of these traits is better understood than is that of the transmission of skin color and other such striking characteristics. Advances in genetics, including population genetics, have been vital to the development of this field. The relatively new science of molecular biology is proving useful in studies of racial differences as well as in nonhuman primate work and paleoanthropology.

Anthropology and Related Fields

Anthropology is not the only field concerned with human behavior, society, and history. One thing that distinguishes anthropology from other fields of study is its breadth: unlike many other disciplines concerned with human beings and their behavior, anthropology consistently looks at the problems of human life as they occur in the widest possible range of human societies. It studies familiar societies and exotic ones, societies in which cities, industry, and agriculture are central features of life, societies in which people spend much of their time hunting game and collecting the products of wild plants, societies in which kings and councils or presidents and legislatures rule, societies in which there are no recognizable political offices or formal government, and many others.

Despite its extremely inclusive interests, all the work done in anthropology is related to at least one of the following three major goals:

Describing as fully as possible the ways of life of groups of people from every corner of the earth and every period of human history and the physical characteristics of the people who live in those groups.

Gaining a fuller understanding of the particular groups it describes while increasing understanding of humanity in general.

Attempting, in connection with the last goal, to find general principles governing the ways people live.

Sociology is, in many ways, the field most closely related to anthropology. The main differences between the two are anthropology's more frequent concern with societies that developed outside the European[5] urban-industrial tradition, anthropology's greater interest in using comparisons among different societies as the basis for understanding, and anthropology's concern with the biological aspects of human life. Although sociologists sometimes base their studies on historical materials, they do not usually concern themselves with the understanding of extinct societies without written records as anthropology does. Because of its interest in the past and in development over time, anthropology shares important interests with history. Similarly, archeology's use of the physical remains of extinct societies is similar to anthropology's approach to such societies. However, anthropology's interest in the past differs from both in that it is more concerned with the general principles governing social and cultural processes, and it is usually more interested in societies that do not have written records of their past. Economics, political science, and psychology all address themselves to problems of great interest to anthropology, but they differ from it in dealing with limited areas of human life instead of its whole scope from biology through history, art, technology, religion, and all the rest.

Anthropology, then, is distinguished from other fields concerned with understanding humanity by the scope of its interests, by its attention to non-European societies, and by its attempt to understand humanity in all societies and all periods of time. It is also different in the way it approaches the specific problems it deals with. The basis of this distinctive approach is to be found in the anthropologist's pervasive concern with culture as the foundation of human life. As part of a deep concern with culture, the anthropologist gathers the necessary information through the closest and most prolonged possible association with the people being studied. Similarly, the most important reason for anthropology's insistence on comparing the ways of life of people in different parts of the world and different eras in history is that such comparison helps to illuminate the culture of each group as well as to establish the basis for finding what is common to all humanity and what is distinctive of particular societies or groups of societies.

SUMMARY

Anthropology attempts to describe and explain human ways of life as they occur in all societies and at all periods in history from early prehuman ancestors to the present. Anthropology extends into the social sciences, the biological sciences, and the humanities. Its breadth of interest and its concern

[5]"European" here means found in Europe or in areas occupied mainly by people of European origin.

with peoples from all parts of the world distinguish it from the many applied disciplines. It is also distinguished by its dependency on the concept "culture" as the basis for its approach and by its use of cross-cultural comparison as a routine part of many types of studies.

Historically anthropology can be traced back as far as the ancient Greeks and Romans, whose interest in the variety of peoples they encountered in trade and travel led them to reflect on the nature and source of differences in human culture although they did not make the concept "culture" explicit. The medieval period in Europe contributed little that was useful to the attempt to understand human life in its variety and time depth, but in the Renaissance there was a renewal of interest and thought. By the eighteenth century there was some useful work concerned with human culture and its development. This work begun to consider evolution as the central process in cultural development, and, in the nineteenth century, evolutionary explanations maintaining that all human groups went through the same stages of development were common. Early findings of prehistoric tools and fossil remains bolstered the evolutionary view by providing evidence that Europeans had gone through the stages of development seen in contemporary non-European groups. By the beginning of the nineteenth century the importance of diffusion in the development of culture was receiving more attention, and in the United States evolutionary views came under strong attack as speculative and ill founded. Nevertheless, evolutionary theories of cultural development are still important in modern anthropology, as are those that grew out of the attacks on this view. An interest in personality psychology became important in anthropology after World War II and led to the development of culture and personality studies. Recently there has been considerable work in cognitive anthropology, which looks at the relation between how people think and their cultures. Linguistic anthropology has developed a great deal since the earliest interest in European, and especially non-European, languages, and out of the interest in language and its analysis a number of important approaches to the study of culture and society and the structure of the human mind have emerged.

Anthropology has four main branches: cultural and social anthropology; archeology, or prehistory; lingustics; and physical anthropology. Each branch has subfields, but all are directed at the overriding anthropological goal of attaining the fullest possible understanding of humanity and its ways.

SUGGESTED READINGS

HARRIS, M.   1968   The Rise of Anthropological Theory. New York: Thomas Y. Crowell.

A comprehensive treatment of the history of anthropology from its very earliest beginnings to the present. No other work is so complete in its treatment. The author's views are prominent in his summaries, and it is sometimes difficult to determine what is opinion and interpretation and what various theorists actually said.

HAYS, H. R. 1958 From Ape to Angel: An Informal History of Social Anthropology. New York: Capricorn Books.

An easy-to-read book written in a popular style. For a quick overview of the sorts of ideas and data that have influenced the development of the field, this is excellent.

KARDINER, A., and E. PREBLE 1961 They Studied Man. Cleveland: World Publishing.

Concerns psychological aspects of the study of culture from Darwin and Spencer through Benedict and Freud. A serious and important history written for general readers.

VOGET, F. 1975 A History of Ethnology. New York: Holt, Rinehart and Winston.

A very complete history of anthropology viewed within the framework of the intellectual history of the West.

SECTION TWO

Modern Anthropology: Three Guiding Concepts

The human way of life is based on socially learned understandings that are shared among the members of a group. Many of these understandings are learned as part of the process of growing up. They carry what might be called a "moral charge," and those who share them feel the understandings "ought" to be followed. These socially learned and morally forceful understandings make up what is called "culture," the topic of central concern in this book and the field of anthropology.

The first chapter of this section, Chapter 2, opens with an account of an attempt to settle a dispute between two elderly brothers who belong to the Bena ethnic group in East Africa. The role of culture in the attempted settlement is traced, with attention to how culture changes, works, and fails to work. The general properties of culture, how it is organized, and how it operates in the lives of people in a number of different societies all over the world occupy attention throughout the chapter.

A key aspect of culture is how its component shared understandings are distributed among people and over different situations. People not only share some general notions of what to do and how to act, but they also have specific expectations of how they should behave toward different sorts of individuals in various circumstances;

that is, the relations among people are carried out according to shared understandings about how the participants in those relations should act. The sum of these mutual expectations makes up the social structure of a group. A picture of the social structure of a Spanish village emerges from a description of a conflict over water rights between two men and their allies. The concepts and perspectives that emerge from this case in Chapter 3 are used in considering the way human relations are ordered in a wide array of groups.

The importance of shared understandings and group participation in human life cannot be allowed to obscure the fact that individuals, not institutions, actually carry out activities. We sometimes treat "culture" and "society" as though they had the ability to do things even when we know all behavior comes from individual action. In Chapter 4, the last chapter of this section, we direct our attention to questions about how different people with different interests and different goals somehow come to behave according to the understandings they share. The trials and tribulations of a young man trying to get married on the island of Alor in Indonesia open this chapter. Through examining his life and the events involved in his attempts to marry, some basic ideas for relating personality to culture are presented and applied.

2

Culture

Three things are necessary for the salvation of man: to know what he ought to believe; to know what he ought to desire; and to know what he ought to do.

ST. THOMAS AQUINAS
TWO PRECEPTS OF CHARITY, 1273

Tanzanian teacher instructing village students.

What is distinctive about the human way of life?

How does culture change?

How can we understand behavior quite different from our own?

Death by Witchcraft, Hatred, and Official Misbehavior: A Case of Culture in Action

A large group of villagers in Tanzania, East Africa, are seated on the ground in a semicircle. Two elderly men are standing erect, hands clasped behind their backs, facing some men, including the headman of this ward of the village, seated in chairs. The two men have made statements explaining why they have come before their fellow villagers. The assembly is a *baraza*, which is a dispute-settlement session long used by the Bena, the ethnic group of people in this case. The dispute between the standing men concerns an accusation of witchcraft. The older man, Kaka, is accusing the younger, Mdogo, of having killed a number of the older man's children with "medicine." The younger man, who is the brother of the older, denies that he has harmed any of Kaka's children. He says instead that Kaka has killed his, Mdogo's, children in exactly the way Kaka says he killed Kaka's chil-

dren. The people seated on the ground and in the chairs begin to question the elderly brothers. The first question is directed to Kaka, a man of considerable prestige. He is asked how he knows his chldren did not die "because God willed it" rather than by witchcraft. Kaka is visibly angered by the question and uses his hands and arms to gesture as he heatedly says that God might take one of his children, but since three have died in less than two years, it must be witchcraft.

The headman breaks in on Kaka's rather impassioned answer to warn him that he is not behaving as someone appearing before the *baraza* should. "Stand properly," the headman says, "and do not wave your arms around like that. If you will not behave respectfully, I will fine you." Kaka ignores the headman's warning and continues to wave his arms and shout.

The seated people ask Kaka if he has seen any medicines that his brother might have used to kill his children. Instead of speaking to the whole

Benaland in Tanzania.

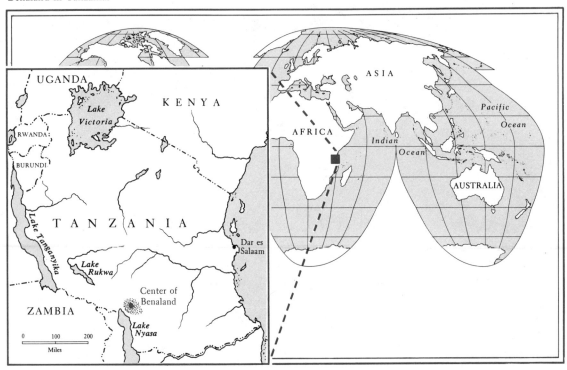

company, Kaka turns to his brother, Mdogo, and shouts: "You know you have medicines. You have destroyed my children with your poison." The headman begins to interrupt the enraged man to warn him again that he must behave with more restraint and speak only to the assembly, not directly to the man he has accused of witchcraft murder.

Kaka's rage overwhelms him at this interruption. His face contorted with emotion, he shakes his fist at the assembled company. "Fools, horses! My younger brother eats my children and your foolishness helps nothing!"

The company is shocked by the display. A man leans over to the headman in charge of the hearing. After a whispered consultation the headman gets up and seizes the elderly man by the arm and begins to lead him away from the area where the questioners are sitting. The old man resists and the headman, young and powerful, drags him down the path screaming and protesting.

Confusion reigns at the court area. There is more disapproving comment about the headman's behavior than about Kaka's. But initially

both are criticized. After some minutes the headman returns and reports quietly to several influential men who had been seated next to him that while he was gone he struck the old man twice on the back with his hand. The men who hear this are visibly agitated and after talking together leave the court area and go to the courtyard of the absent village chief's house. (He is the headman's superior, and had he been present, he would have been in charge of the *baraza*.) There, Kaka is seated on a chair holding a swollen left knee with his hand. The men who had been told about the "beating" by the headman talk to him in a conciliatory way, but he will not be conciliated. The headman is present but silent.

Holding his left hand, parallel with the ground, Kaka strikes it with his right to make clapping sounds. In anger and despair he shouts: "Kaa, kaa [no, no]. He eats my children and they do not help me. They say I myself am a witch. Kaa, kaa! Clap, clap. They have young men beat me, though I am old. Kaa, kaa! [Seeing the anthropologist seated near him with a small tape recorder:] They bring white men with machines

Headman Dragging Kaka Away from the *Baraza* immediately Prior to "Beating" Him. Both the headman and Kaka violated important understandings, but their violations came to be evaluated differently.

to torment me. Kaa, kaa, clap, clap. I come to them with my trouble, my big trouble, and they torment me."

Nothing is said in the courtyard about the old man's behavior. The whole discussion centers on what the headman did, how badly Kaka is hurt, and who will take him to the government dispensary about 15 miles away. The headman is very quiet during all the discussion and speaks only to say that he will push the old man to the dispensary on his bicycle. The headman says nothing to justify his actions although the view that he has seriously erred is made quite explicit, and the government dispensary is chosen to inspect and treat Kaka rather than the closer and more adequately equipped mission hospital because the assembled men agree that "the government must see what has happened here."

The old man, Kaka was taken to the dispensary from which he was sent to the mission hospital by the government medical aide. It was established that his knee was bruised and swollen, but nothing more. However, while the old man was at the hospital, he contracted pneumonia and within two weeks was dead. His death was not directly due to the treatment he received at the *baraza*, and the mission doctor said his knee injury had no part in his fatal illness.

The headman did not come out of the *baraza* well. From the end of the case and for some months afterwards, villagers, including some who were not at the *baraza*, remarked that "he had broken his name"; that is, his reputation was ruined, and he was no longer worthy of respect. His main offense was said to have been violence. Everyone agreed that physical violence in general was a very bad thing and that for a political official to have been involved in it was particularly bad. It was also agreed that the headman did not run *barazas* well and that if he had run this one properly, there need not have been trouble and violence.

Analysis of the Case

What have we seen in this case? We saw two people from the Bena group in East Africa with a serious dispute bringing it before their fellows at a formal and generations-old proceeding called a *baraza*.

The dispute settlement hearing, the *baraza*, was not created for this quarrel; it existed before. A number of ways of behaving are clearly involved in this *baraza*, and in Bena dispute settlement in general. We see:

In the dispute one person has accused the other of wrongdoing before an assembled group although both feel aggrieved.

There is a prescribed way for people to stand and act when they present their cases and are being questioned: hands behind the back; speaking only to questioners and not to the other litigant; not shouting; being respectful.

There is a person, a political official, "in charge," but everyone present questions the two men equally.

The charge in the case is that someone's children have been magically murdered, and the countercharge is that the actual witch is the accuser, not the accused. The questioners do not imply any doubt about the existence of killing by magical means. (Belief in this existed before the case presented here and before the participants were born, so that not only the means for settling the case but also the vehicle of the dispute were available before the events described occurred.) However, they want to find out if these particular deaths were really due to magic or were "natural" ("God wanted them"). The charges are between brothers, and the dead children are very close kin of the accused killers, but no one finds this shocking or difficult to believe.

Kaka, the accuser, stimulates a reaction among the participants in the hearing by raising his hands, shouting, and calling the questioners "fools" and "horses." The reaction to this is shock and disapproval, but when the headman acts physically against Kaka, the old man's behavior is put aside, and the headman becomes the focus of disapproval. There is great interest in seeing that the "government" gets full details about the old man's injuries with the clear implication that action may be taken against the headman for his behavior. No one, including the young headman, suggested that Kaka's behavior (initially shocking and disapproved) had any role in what happened, much less that it justified or even mitigated what the headman did.

How can we understand what happened in this case? Clearly the people involved were acting in accordance with some kind of common understanding of what was happening and of what sort of behavior was acceptable and not acceptable. There they all were: sitting around and asking questions, standing with their hands behind their backs, and answering. How is it possible for them to act together for the common objectives of ending the dispute between the elderly brothers and finding out if there is a witch in their midst? What lies behind their behavior?

To answer these questions, we need to examine some parts of this case more closely and to pull out the elements that will help us understand it. As we do, we will try to develop means of understanding as much of human behavior in general as possible.

Shared Understandings

The first thing that we can see is that the people at the *baraza* have a common, or shared, understanding of at least some of what is happening. All those present know that the two old men standing in the ring of seated people are the ones who have a dispute. They also know how they and the disputants are to act: Their job is to ask questions, and the old men are to answer them. They show that they know what to do by doing it. Their understanding of how disputants should act and how they should not act is shown by their reaction to Kaka's waving his arms and calling the assembled company "fools" and "horses." Their common reaction to the headman's dragging Kaka away and hitting him shows they have definite shared ideas about how the person in charge should and should not act.

By their acceptance of the old men's statements we can see that at least some of the people present feel death can be caused by witchcraft and that it can also be caused by natural means ("God wants them"). The possibility that brothers may well be the killers of each others' children causes no obvious dismay. Although these understandings are shared by those involved in the case, people in other groups elsewhere in the world do not share them or necessarily agree with them.

If most of us were to walk upon the East African scene just described and see people sitting around on the ground and two men standing in the middle of the rough circle formed by the seated ones, we would certainly not know what they were doing. Even if we figured out that they were trying to settle a dispute, we would have no way of knowing what sorts of behavior would be acceptable.

The belief that a person can and will kill others by witchcraft is not found everywhere. Most members of industrial societies do not believe this; some economically and technologically simple societies such as the Ituri pygmies do not believe it, either. On the other hand, there are societies where any cause for death other than magic is discounted, for example, the Jivaro of South America, who believe all men are immortal unless killed by magic.

The transmission of shared understandings For people to share understandings, they must somehow be transmitted from person to person. We have just seen that although the participants in the dispute settlement share important understandings among themselves, members of a variety of other groups do not share these understandings. This means either that the transmission was not biological or that the biological differences among human groups are sufficient to explain differences among the shared beliefs found in different groups.

There are many difficulties in explaining differences in shared beliefs as the consequences of biological differences, but three are particularly important.

1 The biological differences among major human "races" are hardly larger than the differences that are found *within* each of the races.
2 Some groups that are biologically very similar to one another have quite different shared understandings.
3 Some groups that are quite different biologically have quite similar shared understandings.

We conclude from these facts (and others) that shared understandings are transmitted by learning rather than by biological inheritance. Learning is, in fact, the basis for human social life. The dispute case of Kaka and Mdogo could not have taken place if all those present had not learned similar understandings about how people should and should not act in such a situation. Without shared understandings about the way to go about trying to settle a dispute, the people could not have begun as they did. Without clear understandings about shouting and disrespect on the one hand and the use of violence on the other, the affair would not have ended as it did. Generally, social activities can only occur when those involved in them share at least some common understandings of what is going on and how everyone should act. The only way they get these essential understandings is through learning.

The moral element is shared understandings Understanding things in the same ways, however, is not all that is common to the members of a social group. The understandings have moral force. The understandings people share are not just descriptions of the way things are or ideas about ways things can be done. They also contain a "prescriptive"[1] element; that is, the shared understandings tell people what things *should* be like and how things *ought* to be done rather than simply state what they are like and how they can be done.

The response to Kaka's arm waving, shouting, and name-calling shows the moral element in the shared understandings about how people behave at *barazas.* Kaka behaved as he should not have, and the others present reacted with the shock and disapproval that comes from witnessing a moral violation. The complete about-face that occurred when Kaka was subjected to violence does not mean that his behavior before the *baraza* was approved. It was simply that the headman's response to his shouting and abandoned gestures was taken as even more unacceptable. Both men's actions were looked at in the light of shared understandings about how people *ought* to behave and were judged improper and unacceptable but not equally so. The headman's behavior was viewed as worse.

Three types of shared understandings The sorts of shared understandings concerning how things should be done are called "procedural understandings." Understandings about the nature of the world and its contents ("Witchcraft causes death," "The earth is round," "Disputes can be settled") that the members of a group feel ought to be accepted[2] are called "descriptive understandings" or "beliefs." Another type of shared understanding is devoted to what is desirable, beautiful, or good and what is undesirable, ugly, or bad. These shared understandings are called "values." In an important sense they are basic to procedural and descriptive understandings because they are used to evaluate the others and their consequences. All three sorts of shared understandings, however, have moral force even when they seem to be strictly utilitarian guides for how to do things or descriptive accounts of how things are.

If you insist 2 and 2 are 5 and refuse to concede that the correct answer is 4, the response many people will make to you will demonstrate that even the arid statements of arithmetic have moral force among people who share arithmetical understandings.

---

[1] "Prescriptive" (meaning that something positive must be done) as used here includes "proscriptive" (meaning that something must *not* be done), since both refer to what is required.

[2] People in various groups have means for supporting their understandings about the nature of the world and its contents. These means range from appeals to authority ("The ancestors taught us this" or "Science tells us") to empirical demonstration ("Dropping a feather and a nail in a vacuum proves that wind resistance is what makes objects fall at different speeds"). For our purposes, the important point is that people hold the beliefs and think they ought to be accepted. There is no need in this context to try to adopt standards for differentiating among different beliefs or different means for supporting those beliefs, although this can be done.

Imagine coming upon someone pounding in a nail with a monkey wrench while a hammer is right beside him; your understanding of what tools are for and how to pound in a nail will be violated, and the moral force in your understanding—the prescriptive element—will be clear in your response to what you see ("You will ruin the wrench," "It would be faster with the hammer," etc., even if, in fact, you are not sure these statements are really true).

Shared understandings and predictability A crucial element in understanding human life is the recognition that social life is impossible if people cannot predict each other's behavior with a rather high probability of success.

In examining and rejecting the idea that people's understanding of what is happening is due to biological factors, we have eliminated one source of making behavior predictable. Nonhuman animals are biologically far more restricted in what they can learn than man is. For most animals, species membership sufficiently restricts behavior so that a member of a particular species from one area will behave very much like a member of the same species from a different (but environmentally similar) area even though there has been no contact between the animals from the two areas and no chance to learn from one another. It is not that learning is unimportant for these animals; rather it is that the biological restrictions on what the animals can learn keep the range of behavior within rather narrow limits. A dog from California does not act very differently from a dog from Maine, and should they be brought together, the basis for the ways they act toward one another is established by the limited range of responses dogs have.

In contrast, the biological restrictions on what humans can learn to do are very wide and cannot serve to provide the basis for a socially manageable, limited range of behavior. A group cannot continue to exist, or begin to exist in the first place, if its members have no idea what to expect of each other or how to interpret each other's behavior. To live together, people have got to learn common understandings of the sorts of behavior that are and are not acceptable in given situations. They also have to learn how to interpret and evaluate what other people do. This does not mean that there is no room for individual variation, that people are robots acting strictly in accord with detailed computer programs. It does mean that their behavior may not vary across the vast range of human potential. A trivial example will make this clear.

One of the authors was double-parked once, and a woman rather indignantly said, "Do you know that you are illegally parked?" The author replied, "Do you know that Ulan Bator is the capital of Outer Mongolia?" She was completely taken aback and left speechless. The reply had (purposely) gone outside the range of expected variation. Had it been, "I am sorry, I will move" or, even, "You are a nuisance. Go climb a tree," she would have known how to respond.

If people act in ways that are completely outside the limits of what those who deal with them expect, it is impossible to do anything requiring joint action, and relations are too painful and difficult to maintain. If only a few

Human Diversity. The biological restrictions on human diet are very wide, but unlike other animals, exactly what human beings eat and how they eat it is determined primarily by what they learn.

people consistently behaved in ways that defied prediction, they could be ignored, locked up or killed as madmen or criminals, or sent away. If, however, most people were unsuccessful in predicting the behavior of most others most of the time, group life would be impossible. In real social life there are limits on the ranges of things people are likely to do in all common sorts of situations, and these limits give everyone in the situations an idea of what they are supposed to do themselves and what other people are likely to do. The limitations are provided by shared understandings that give all those who have learned them a similar idea of what is happening, what to do when such things are happening, and how to evaluate the whole event. This is just the sort of thing we saw in the dispute-settlement case. The sorts of morally charged shared understandings that were involved in the participants' behaving and evaluating in the ways they did throughout the case are the foundation for human social life wherever it occurs.

Culture: The Basis for Human Life

As we saw in the previous chapter, anthropologists define "culture" in a number of rather different ways. Throughout this book we will use a definition that combines some of the key elements found in all of them in a way intended to promote our ability to describe and explain behavior. In this definition the type of shared and prescriptive understandings seen in the East African dispute settlement are the components of culture. The culture of a group is the sum of the morally forceful understandings acquired through learning and shared by the members of that group. Without culture human groups could not have begun in the first place; nor could they have continued to exist if they somehow had lost it. Because of the results of human biology and evolution, there is no alternative to shared understandings to provide the techniques for dealing with the physical environment and making it yield the means for satisfying needs for food, temperature regulation, and protection from disability and premature death. Culture is both the basic human adaptive device and the foundation for social life.

Culture and human beginnings It is important to understand that humans are not animals that somehow came to have their present physical form (or some earlier but similar form of it) and *then* acquired culture as the basis for their means of getting food and shelter and living with one another. Humans are *cultural animals:* they are not only completely dependent on culture for their adaptation to the environment and to each other, but also their very bodies were—and are still being—shaped by culture even as that culture itself develops.

Human evolution, like the evolution of all other species, is based on "natural selection." This is the name given to the process whereby those members of a species that can best deal with the environment and with their fellow species members produce more surviving offspring, and these offspring, because of their greater numbers, contribute more to the heredity of the evolving group. Since their contribution is greater, and since it includes the traits that made them more fruitful, the whole species comes to resemble them after enough generations have gone by. New traits with adaptive advantage arise through mutation from time to time, and these combine with the earlier ones and gradually produce a species quite different from the original parent species. The new species, of course, does not stop evolving; natural selection continues as long as there are reproducing biological forms. But species can remain relatively unchanged for a long period, especially if their environment does not change significantly,

It is difficult to know in any detail or with much certainty just how natural selection operated in those groups of extinct apes that were our ancient ancestors, but there are two sorts of evidence that indicate that they used tools as part of the adaptation. In the first place, there is evidence that shows that more than 10 million years ago, there were apes whose teeth were importantly different from those of other apes living in the same time. Apes use their teeth for defense and in regulating their social relations through bluffing and fighting as well as the main impliments in obtaining food. The apes with teeth less well suited for those purposes used something else and this must have been tools.

A second sort of evidence comes from studying modern primates. We know that a number of different species of primates use sticks and stones and such as part of their adaptation and that some of them even alter the natural objects they use in what may be thought of as a sort of tool making. Now, if a trait is present in a number of different but related species such as apes, monkeys, and humans, it is quite likely that the trait or some early form of it was present in the earlier species ancestral to the various living species. This, together with the evidence from ancient teeth, strongly indicates that there were tool-using primates many millions of years ago and that humanity is one of the species descended from them.

The other species descended from the common ancestors evolved in different environments, and natural selection in those species produced dependence on such behaviors as arboreal living, but the forerunners of our species continued the tool use of the common ancestors and developed it enormously. This dependence on tools meant that those members of our emerging species who were better able to learn to use sticks and other objects and whose manual skills were greater had an adaptive advantage over their less skilled fellows. These more skilled manipulators and better learners became more and more common as the generations went by, and this led to an even greater dependence on tools, which, in turn, led to more adaptive advantages for individuals with certain physical traits that helped in tool use (a two-legged gait, for example, freed the forelimbs to hold tools, and a thumb which could work in opposition to the fingers allowed finer use of the hands). As learning became more and more important in the species's adaptation, biological mutations that produced individuals better able to learn more and to devise new tools brought an adaptive advantage to those individuals who were born with the mutations, and the traits connected with them eventually became established in the members of the group. The evidence now available shows that our ancestors had bodies quite similar to ours for more than a million years before their brain size (and presumably mental capacity) approached ours; manual and other physical ability came first, with mental ability following after.

There was an interaction, then, between the importance of tools and the learning necessary for tool use and the emergence of a physical form that was compatible with tool use and learning. In the early millions of years of human evolution both the tools and the learned understandings required for their use were very simple, but as time went on and physical traits more suited to tool use became more elaborate so did the understandings. Learning itself also became more elaborate: as the species came to depend more on learning, what was learned had to be *shared* understandings, transmitted from one generation to the next and from one individual to another. In this way culture developed in concert with the development of the increasingly human body. The ability to learn shared responses was the main adaptive strategy of the species, and there was no alternative to using it as the basis for social relations as well as for dealing with the environment.

The earliest dependence on learning was not, in all likelihood, fully cultural; although the understandings that were learned were shared, they were probably not morally forceful. Morality requires symbolic skills that the ancient apes did not have. As with the development of the body, however, both the need for moral force and the ability to have it developed along with the increasing capacity to learn. As we just saw in our discussion of predictability, it is the distinctively human range of learning ability, the variety of things we can learn, that makes it essential there be moral force to restrict the sorts of behavior we are likely to engage in in various situations. Until this range was fairly wide there was little need for moral force, but when the range of possible learning became wider through evolutionary change in the body, the same neural equipment that allowed the wider learning was also available for providing moral force.[3]

The fundamental point is that humanity and culture developed together and that culture is now and always has been the basis for distinctively *human* adaptation and for *human* social relations.

Culture and social relations The fundamental role of culture in physical adaptation and its role in ordering social life are intimately connected and intertwined. Imagine group life breaking up because of too much interpersonal unpredictability. Without group life everyone would be separate from everyone else, and the understandings concerning toolmaking, food getting, shelter construction, and protection from environmental dangers could not be transmitted to the next generation. The new generation would not exist anyway because the parents could not stay together long enough to rear the children even if they managed to conceive them. Obviously, a group that had the prescriptive understandings members needed to get along with each other would have to have the understandings concerning dealing with the environment or it would not survive. In fact, the understandings dealing with how people act around and toward each other and those dealing with how to cope with the physical world are sometimes so closely connected that it is impossible to tell which is which or at least where one ends and the other begins. Thus, how food is shared depends upon understandings concerned with how people treat each other as well as with part of the physical world (food). The same is true of dividing the work in building a shelter.

[3]In Chapter 11 the fact that for chimpanzees and several other nonhuman primates there are no sexual relations between mothers and sons is examined as an indication of possible "protomorality" in our ancient ancestors.

All human groups—now and in the past—have a culture, which includes as an irreducible minimum shared understandings that allow people to live together and provide the basis for satisfying the survival needs of the members of the group. It is not necessary that every member of a group share all the understandings contained within the culture of the group—even in simple societies that is difficult or impossible—but this does not lessen the necessity that some understandings be shared by all and all understandings be shared by some, to a limited extent at least.

Incomplete sharing of culture A group may contain a few blacksmiths, or only one, at a given time, and the understandings needed to work metal may not be shared by other group members. There is a shared understanding, however, between the smith and the others about what he does and about the usefulness of his product, and this links him to the rest of the group in his capacity as smith. The smith transmits his understandings of how to work metal to his successor and does so in a way that makes clear he is not only teaching how you *can* work metal, but also teaching the way you *ought* to work it. The metalworking understandings may be shared by only two members of the group, but they are nevertheless part of the group's culture, and all the members of the group who deal with the smiths share understandings about them and their work.

There are nontechnical areas of social life where not all members share all understandings within the group. It is not unusual, for example, for women to have understandings about how to act toward other women that are not shared by men, and, moreover, the men are not expected to follow them. In fact, they are often obliged *not* to follow them.

Many understandings are not shared by all members of the group; rather, they are distributed among special subgroups. These restricted understandings are the basis of activities that are the subject of other understandings found in the rest of the group. We have already seen this for the blacksmith and the other people in his group: The majority do not have the understandings to work metal (it may even be understood that it is improper for them to do so), but they do know what to expect of the blacksmith with regard to the general outlines of how and when he works, what his products should be like, and so on.

Similarly, in all groups men have a number of understandings that women do not fully share and vice versa, which means that most men do not know how to act as women do in some ways, and most women do not fully know how to act as men do.[4] However, everyone in one subgroup has a clear idea of what is to be expected of the members of the other subgroup. These understandings are shared and morally forceful, and they link the subgroups together in the sense that they make relations possible despite incomplete sharing of understandings.

Thus, saying culture is made up of prescriptive understandings shared by

[4]This sort of distribution of understandings is examined in the next chapter as part of the discussion of statuses.

LINKING
UNDERSTANDINGS
Shared understandings that
make it possible for people
to know what to expect
from members of social
groupings to which they
do not belong.

the members of a group does not mean that all understandings are shared by all members. Subgroup members have understandings they share only among themselves, but this does not disrupt group life so long as there are "linking understandings" that allow others to know what to expect of them. Linking understandings shared between members of subgroups (men and women, specialists and nonspecialists, etc.) that make it possible for people to know what to expect from members of social groupings to which they do not belong.

Even when understandings are shared throughout the group, they are not necessarily followed by everyone all the time or the same way. Behavior must be sufficiently predictable for most people to have some idea of what most of those with whom they associate will do under most circumstances, but it is not necessary for group survival for every individual to do everything exactly as culture prescribes. We need to be able to predict what others will do, but only to the extent that we can understand their behavior in order to adjust our own to it.

Not all shared understandings affect all relationships. Only a few prescribe behavior for everyone under all circumstances. Usually only a limited range of understandings are involved in a particular relation and as long as these are more or less followed, the relation can go on despite considerable differences among the participants regarding other issues. Jones may feel a strong obligation to attend all anthropology lectures while roommate Smith feels this to be a trivial matter. So long as Smith and Jones share enough understandings about using their shared room and each other's possessions, it is likely they can continue to live together. To generalize predictability is essential in the limited setting in which particular people deal with one another, but shared understandings concerning behavior outside those settings are not nearly so important to their relationship.

Violating and maintaining cultural prescriptions In the case at the beginning of this chapter we saw that the old man, Kaka, behaved in a way that shocked and surprised the people at the *baraza*. Shouting, swinging his arms, and hurling insults at the assembled company are behaviors in sharp violation of culturally prescribed behavior at *barazas*. The existence of these shared understandings did not stop Kaka from behaving as he did despite the fact (to be examined later) that he probably shared these same understandings. Still, the understandings served to limit the violation through the agency of the headman. On the basis of the understandings he held, which he correctly believed those present shared, the headman, having failed to stop Kaka's unacceptable actions by attempts to fine him, finally dragged him away.

Despite the fact that Kaka did not live long enough to be at another *baraza* himself and despite the disapproval the headman's behavior stimulated, the understandings concerning proper behavior in a dispute-settlement session were ultimately supported by the events of this case. No one present at the *baraza* could doubt that the sort of behavior Kaka showed brought severe disapproval. Villagers who were not at this particular *baraza* got the same message in the accounts of what happened spread by participants.

Someone, in this instance, Kaka, had behaved contrary to shared understandings concerning proper behavior and was punished for doing so. This punishment, in the form of general disapproval and the headman's physical intervention (itself disapproved, but that is another matter to be considered separately), demonstrated to everyone who saw or heard about it that there really are shared understandings and that behaving contrary to them has serious consequences. Such a demonstration serves to keep people's understandings of what constitutes proper behavior sufficiently alike and sufficiently prescriptive or forceful to prevent the *baraza* from becoming an unworkable bedlam.

Punishment is not the only means by which the force and uniformity of shared understandings are maintained. Rewards are at least as effective in doing this. Very few *barazas* involve the sort of unacceptable behavior seen in Kaka's case. The vast majority of them are highly successful in settling disputes. In general, villagers experience or see (if they are personally involved, or are spectators) that behaving in accordance with shared understandings in the *baraza* brings a solution to difficulties. This sort of reward has the same effect as punishment in keeping shared understandings similar and forceful.

The rewarding and punishing process, of course, is how the understandings were instilled—many of them in children by their parents—in the first place. Learning the understandings this way in the early years gives them moral force, which then originates within the individuals who have learned them. Thus, external rewards and punishments, the social expression of moral force, often work together with internal rewards and punishments. These last come in the form of feeling good about doing things in prescribed ways or feeling bad about not doing them that way (see Chapter 4, "Personality").

There are, then, means to promote and maintain the effectiveness of cultural prescriptions, but this does not mean that those that are shared must be followed at all times for group life to continue or that all of them are shared by everyone. Part of the vitality of human life and part of being able to adapt to new conditions and situations comes from the flexibility that is, in ways we will consider, part of culture.

Basic and entailed understandings The components of culture are unequal in several ways, an important one being that some shared understandings are basic to others. If the more basic understandings are accepted, the other understandings closely attached to them are likely to be followed at least partly as a consequence of that acceptance. Another way of saying this is that some understandings structure or arrange experience in such a way that other understandings are consequences of them. We can call those that structure experience in a fundamental way "basic understandings" and those that flow from them "entailed understandings." An example will clarify this.

Among the people of Truk atoll[5] in the Pacific, powerful moral force is

BASIC
UNDERSTANDINGS
*The parts of culture that
fundamentally structure
the experience of those
who share them.*

ENTAILED
UNDERSTANDINGS
*Understandings that are
held partly as a
consequence of accepting
basic understandings.*

[5] Truk atoll is a huge coral reef enclosing the largest lagoon in the world. There are five major inhabited islands within the reef and a number of smaller ones.

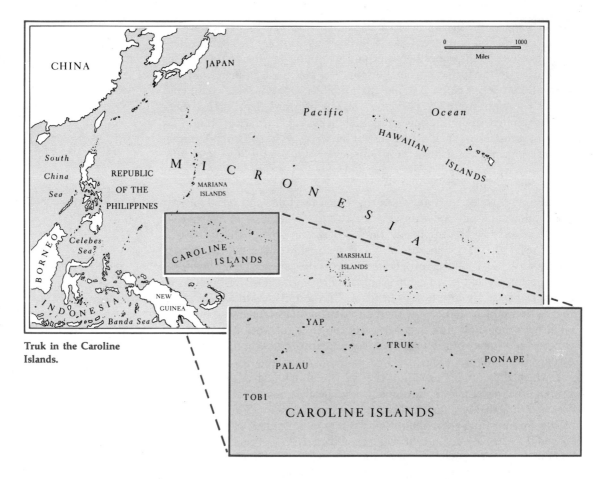

Truk in the Caroline
Islands.

attached to learning and accepting the understanding that when people die,
their ghosts sometimes remain in the area where the poeple lived before
death. Ghosts are also understood to be like living people and physical objects
in general in that they can be seen if there is enough light. It is believed,
however, that ghosts fear and avoid light. Anyone who does not share these
beliefs is viewed as entirely abnormal rather in the way someone in this
society would be if he refused to believe that bricks sink when they are thrown
in the lake.

When the basic understandings concerning the nature of ghosts on Truk
are accepted, the particular understanding that ghosts do not stay around in
the daytime follows easily. It is an entailed understanding; that is, if you
understand the nature of the world as any sane Trukese does, the absence of
ghosts in the daytime is a fact of experience. It does not mean that there are
no ghosts; rather, it means that ghosts avoid light.

Similarly, the Trukese believe that carrying a light at night is an excellent
way to avoid encountering ghosts. As the Trukese understand it, if there is a
ghost that can be vaguely seen where the dark is not too deep at night, he will

Trukese Funeral. Trukese ghosts are the spirits of dead relatives; the spirit leaves the body after three days, and members of the family of the dead stay near the grave until it goes, when they ask it not to harm its living kinsmen.

flee when you shine your light on him. Again, the belief about how to chase away ghosts is entailed in the morally supported understandings concerning the existence of ghosts, their visibility given sufficient light, and their fear of light.

Basic understandings—closed to experience Note that the ghost and visibility understandings are "closed" to experience. Nothing can happen that will put them in doubt. If you do not see ghosts in the daytime, that is as would be expected because ghosts are understood not to be around in the day. If you think you see one at night, but he is not there when you shine your light where you thought he was, that is what the basic understandings about ghosts, visibility, and their abhorrence of light would lead you to expect. Everything that experience tells you supports the shared understanding about ghosts and their qualities.

It is generally true that basic understandings are "closed" to experience in that they provide the framework *for* experience. These understandings are so basic to what people experience that nothing that happens can cast doubt on them. If you share the Trukese understandings about ghosts, the fact that they can never be seen clearly does not mean that they do not exist. It simply confirms the understanding that they hate light.

It is characteristic of basic understandings that anything that happens confirms them, and nothing can occur to prove them wrong. A well-known anthropological example of this concerns the understanding of the cause of misfortunes held by the Azande who live on the border between Zaire and the Sudan in Africa. When people suffer harm, it is thought to be because of witchcraft practiced by an enemy.

The Azande store their grain in special, closed structures raised off the

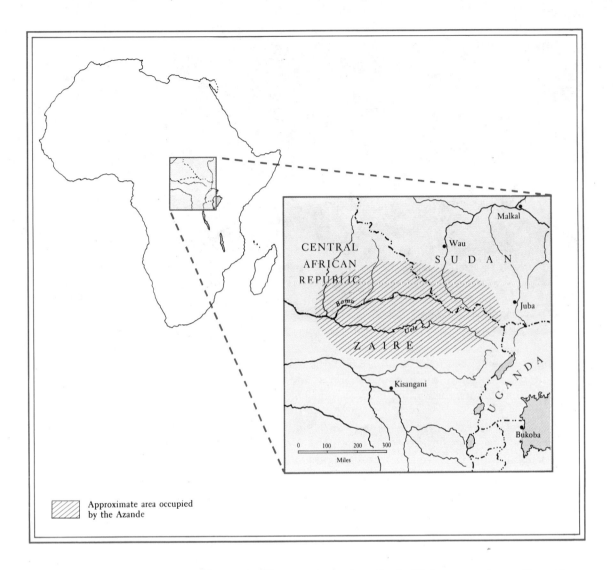

Approximate area occupied
by the Azande

**Azandeland in Central
Africa.**

ground by posts. There are many termites in their area, and sometimes these insects weaken the posts of the granaries so that they collapse. People are sometimes sitting under the granaries to avoid the hot sun when this happens, and the falling structures kill or injure them. One view of such a misfortune is that by tragic chance people happened to be under the granary just as its termite-weakened posts gave way. This is not the Azande view.

> [The Azande knows] that the supports were undermined by termites and that people were sitting under the granary in order to escape the heat and glare of the sun. But he knows besides why these two events occured at a precisely similar moment in time and space. It was due to the action of witchcraft. If there had been no witchcraft people would have been sitting under the granary and it would not have fallen on them, or it would have collapsed but the people would not

have been sheltering under it at the time. Witchcraft explains the coincidence of these two happenings [Evans-Pritchard 1937:70].

For the Azande, the fact that the granary fell on people is proof that witchcraft was behind the misfortune, and no proof could be offered to cast doubt on this. The basic understanding concerning the cause of misfortunes, like all basic understandings, is closed to experience because it provides the basic framework for that experience. Just as a scale cannot be used to find its own weight, a basic understanding cannot be tested against empirical reality. **The units of culture—in the minds of sharers** "Culture" does not refer to behavior or to such products of behavior as tools, art, and other artifacts. Culture is made up of shared, prescriptive understandings that reside in people's minds. When we discuss the organization of these understandings we will see that although the units composing culture are only found in the minds of individuals, the organization of these units often emerges only in the relations between two or more people and is therefore not in the mind of a single person. We will return to this, but basically what it means is that although understandings are in people's minds and nowhere else, assessments such as which understandings are more important and which less sometimes come out of the interaction of several different individuals and are not wholly in any one person's mind. To use one term, the organization of culture is partly "superorganic": It is above or beyond the single individual, but the components of culture never are.

Azande Granary. Granaries such as the one in this picture sometimes collapse on people sitting under them. When this happens, the deaths of the people are attributed to witchcraft. Such tragic occurrences are understood in Azande culture as necessarily resulting from human will, not chance.

Distinguishing Culture and Behavior

An important reason for distinguishing behavior and culture can be seen in the case with which this chapter began. That Kaka shared understandings

about how to behave with all the people who were there was shown by his following those understandings at the beginning of the hearing. However, he behaved contrary to those understandings as the hearing went on, despite his sharing them. Shared understandings are a powerful guide to behavior, but they are not the only force working to influence how a person actually behaves.

Cases of deviance aside (and they are quite important because everyone fairly often fails to follow some understandings that he shares with others), there are other important reasons for distinguishing between culture and behavior. Perhaps the most obvious is the one related to the deviance Kaka showed. He shared the understandings with other people, but he did not allow them to guide his behavior because he was overpowered with anger. It is possible for a whole group to be "overpowered" by external circumstances so that although they share understandings, they do not use them to guide their behavior.

The Plains Indians of the United States are a well-known example of this. They understood that a life based on buffalo hunting was the proper and desirable life, but the buffalo were killed off by outsiders. For a period of time after this they shared prescriptive understandings requiring activity involving buffalo hunting, but they could not follow these prescriptions because the buffalo were gone.

Our understanding of these people would not be advanced by the view that the culture dependent on buffalo hunting vanished as soon as the behavior guided by it became impossible. The fact that the members of this group share prescriptions for behavior they cannot follow is an essential element in determining their behavior and must be taken into account by all those interested in them.

Another important reason to distinguish between culture and behavior is that people sometimes behave in the same way, but do so according to the guidance of different understandings. Only by distinguishing the understandings they share from the common behavior they exhibit can we really understand what we see. We find similar behavior but different understandings fairly often when members of different groups cooperate in some task. During World War II soldiers from different groups fought the Nazis together and did many of the same things (saluting, drilling, fighting the enemy, etc.). Members of some groups shared the understanding that what they were doing was combating a great evil (Nazism), while members of other groups shared the understanding that they were risking their lives for something of no moment to them (e.g., some members of the King's African Rifles).

Finally, it is important to recognize that in most human affairs behavior does not cause behavior. If you push me, it is true that my falling is caused by your behavior. But this is much like the movement of one billiard ball causing the movement of another. People are very different from billiard balls, however, and after I finish falling, my behavior toward you will be partly determined by my understanding of what has happened, what our relationship is, and the understandings I have about how to act in that situation.

Similarly, when one group of people moves into the territory of another group of people, the resulting behavior of both groups (they fight, one moves out, they live together) can only be understood if we examine the understandings shared among the members of the two groups and not just the behavioral fact that they came together.

The understandings people share are inferred from their observable behavior (what they do and what they say), but they must not be confused with that behavior. If we consistently distinguish between culture on the one hand and behavior (and the products of behavior) on the other, we are in a much stronger position to understand both the ways culture works to influence behavior and the influences on culture itself.

So far we have been looking at culture without regard to how it develops over time. The next section is concerned both with how understandings persist and are transmitted from generation to generation and how understandings are modified, added to, and abandoned.

Cultural Continuity and the Transmission of Culture

The prescriptive understandings shared by the members of any group are constantly developing and changing. Archaeology and history show beyond doubt that although cultures change at different rates, they all change throughout their existence. Despite this, at least some of the understandings that constitute every group's culture are older than any of the people who make up the group. This is so because of the nature of the transmission process. Culture is transmitted across time through social learning (i.e., people learn from each other), and each generation must learn from the people they depend on from birth onward (i.e., their parents and their parents' peers) in order to survive. The new generation thus comes to learn some, at least, of the understandings that constituted the culture of the members of their group before they were born.

Because these understandings have moral force for the adult generation (if they did not have such force, they could not serve to make group life possible), they are taught to a new generation in a way likely to bring about their effective learning. These understandings are viewed as morally essential to the most important people in the universe of the young members of the group: the adults on whom the young must depend for life itself. Both the desire and the ability of the established generation to teach these understandings to their successors are very great. Thus, the culture of every group will show at least some continuity with the past; and at least some of the prescriptive understandings held by the preceding generation will also be found in the culture of the new generation.

Since new understandings do emerge and old ones change, it is important to remember that this happens in the minds of people who have already learned many understandings that may not fit well with the new ones. The "old" understandings, like the new ones, have a moral element, so that even when they are discarded or altered in substance, they may still have an influence on behavior. In many groups in the United States children learn from their parents and other adults that it is never proper to be seen publicly without clothes. When they get older, they are in a position to let other understandings (shared with some group members, but not their parents) overpower this one, and some may come to believe public nudity is sometimes acceptable. However, the earlier understanding was learned and may continue to influence them. Although they do not behave in accord with it any longer, it may still be a potent force in how they feel about how people dress or fail to dress. They might, for example, be inordinately annoyed with those who do not practice nudity, or they may take exceptional pride in their own "naturalness." They have abandoned a part of the culture they learned, but they continue to be influenced by it even though the influence is a negative one.

In this connection it is useful to note that there are different denominations of atheists, especially if the atheists come from religious backgrounds. Most Protestant atheists do not disbelieve in the Immaculate Conception in the same way Catholic atheists do, and Jewish atheists do not disbelieve in the divinity of Christ in the same way Christian atheists do.

Another conservative force affecting the transmission of culture comes from the fact that the understandings a child must learn are the ones that his parents and other adults have found perfectly adequate in dealing with each other and the environment. Unless there are major changes in the social or

Cultural Accumulation and Transmission. This old man in Tanzania is passing on some of his understandings of basketry, which will be part of the total of understandings shared by some members of the next generation.

physical world—such as the Indians' buffalo being exterminated or the arrival of a totally different political system—the understandings that worked for the preceding generation will be just as effective for the new generation that learns them.

In addition, because all the members of the new generation will have been trained in similar ways according to cultural prescriptions for child care, they will share the "old" understandings that result from this type of care. New understandings can become shared only after numerous interpersonal efforts, examples, counterexamples, agreements, disagreements, and so on. Those rooted in common training begin that way. Not all understandings need to be shared widely to work, and some are rapidly adopted by many, but understandings rooted in common early training begin, as it were, with the strength that comes from their being shared.

Not all the forces working for cultural continuity are as closely connected to the transmission process as those we have just mentioned; for example, the connection between different parts of a culture. In the discussion of basic and entailed understandings we noted that entailed understandings (ghosts cannot be seen clearly) follow inevitably from basic understandings (ghosts fear light). As long as the basic understanding continues, the entailed understanding will continue, and this is not due to anything other than the relationship between the two kinds of understanding.

Cumulative Quality of Culture

Cultural continuity is only one aspect of what happens in the transmission of shared understandings over time and space. The other is cultural development, alteration, or change.

The simplest way by which culture changes is through the addition of understandings as time goes on. From the point of view of the evolution of humanity the fact that culture is cumulative is a key one. Because there is virtually no limitation on the size of a group's culture, no matter how many prescriptive understandings may exist at a given moment, more can be added.

The archeological record reveals the earliest human ancestors (now generally) accepted as early forms of *Homo erectus*) and creatures (called *Australopithecus*) related to them but probably not direct human ancestors. Paleoanthropologists and archeologists cannot dig up the understandings that these creatures may have had. They can, however, uncover the evidence from which understandings and changes in understandings can be inferred. They find that these prehumans made and used stone tools around 4 million years ago. In the course of time there were some changes in the tools. To the modern observer, these changes do not seem very great, but they do suggest that there may have been other changes too: changes over time in the culture shared among the earliest humanlike beings.

Changes in the tools are evidence of new hunting techniques as well as of new toolworking techniques, clearly indicating new understandings even from the time before our ancient ancestors had become fully human. It is reasonable to infer that culture has always been cumulative. Human culture did not suddenly begin one day. It was built up by the continual addition of new shared understandings to what each generation inherited from the one before it. The very gradual emergence of distinctly human culture is as much a product of our ancestors' ability to add new understandings to those they inherited generation after generation as it is of anything else.

The culture of any group is the sum of the understandings shared by the members of that group. Because these understandings influence each other, additions to the already existing ones will do more than just increase the number of understandings. The new ones will also alter some that existed previously. We can readily see this if we look at understandings current among some groups in the United States concerning the eating of vegetables.

The understanding that organically grown vegetables are required for maximum safety and nutrition has important implications for what is eaten. It does not exist by itself but is part of a whole complex of understandings, which is, in a number of important ways, the same as a complex of understandings held by people who do not believe that organically grown vegetables are significantly different from others. The two complexes have utterly different consequences for behavior (what is bought, eaten, etc.), and it is instructive to compare them to see how adding to old understandings can lead to such differences.

"OLD" UNDERSTANDINGS	"ORGANIC" UNDERSTANDINGS
Vegetables are good to eat and nourishing.	
Some vegetables are spoiled or unripe, but this is the only thing that can be wrong with them, and it can be guarded against by looking, feeling, and smelling.	
If vegetables are not spoiled or unripe, washing is all that is necessary to protect against harm from eating.	Chemicals sometimes used in growing vegetables enter into the vegetables, and these chemicals are harmful.
Poisons are bad for you and should not be eaten.	The presence of chemicals in vegetables cannot be detected by touch, sight, or smell.
At least some chemicals are poisons.	The only way to be protected from harm when eating vegetables is to be sure that they are grown without the use of chemicals.

If we add the two lists of understandings together, we see that some new ones are perfectly consistent with some old ones. None of the "organic" understandings in any way conflicts with the understanding that vegetables are good to eat and nutritious. The "old" understanding that some chemicals are poisonous is in accord with the "organic" understanding about the consequences of chemicals entering into vegetables; what is more, it is even one foundation for the new belief. However, the view that vegetables are all right unless they are spoiled or unripe is not consistent with the new view of the effect of chemicals when used in growing. One of these two understandings must be abandoned, or if the two are both kept, they must somehow be isolated from each other because they cannot easily influence behavior together.

The "old" set of understandings leads to an understanding about buying and preparing vegetables that might be: "If they look, feel, and smell okay, I can safely buy them and eat them provided only that they are washed first."

The "organic" set of understandings, although composed of some of the same elements, leads to a quite different understanding about buying and preparing vegetables that might be: "The only way I can buy vegetables that can be safely eaten is to know that they are grown without the use of chemicals, because if chemicals are used, no preparation will make them safe."

The addition of new understandings brings about a qualitative rather than just a quantitative change in the body of understandings. This sort of change is not limited to understandings about vegetables or to the culture of certain groups in the United States. Although the relations among shared understandings must not be taken for granted, it is practically impossible for any particular understanding to be totally isolated from all others. Thus, when a new understanding is added, it not only expands the total body of shared understandings, but it also modifies at least some already existing understandings. As new understandings come to be shared, they interact with previously existing ones. In the process of getting larger, culture changes in more than size.

It should not be thought that only new generations add to a body of

Health-Food Store. The shared understandings that lead people to believe that only "organic" foods should be eaten differ from earlier understandings both in content and, especially, organization.

existing understandings. As new elements are added and old ones changed or discarded, the body of understandings shared by the members of a group is always in development. Addition and alteration can take place among any or all members of the group whether they be of a generation that is maturing and getting ready to take its place as fully operating adults, among those already in (or past) full adulthood, or both at once.

Relations among Understandings

The prescribed, shared understandings making up a group's culture are not a random assembly, like pebbles tossed up on a beach. The understandings shared by a group's members are connected in that any one involves at least some of the others, as in the organic food example. They are also connected in certain kinds of relationships. These relationships among understandings, which is what the "organization of culture" means, include the facts that some of them are more important than some others; some are more general than some others; some apply under all circumstances while others apply in only a limited range of circumstances; and so on. Attention to the organization of culture is indispensable because the kinds of relations between understandings can have as much influence on behavior as the content of the understandings.

ORGANIZATION OF CULTURE *The relationships among the understandings that make up the culture, such as which understandings are more or less important, which are more or less general, and which go together with which others.*

For social relations to have the necessary predictability, the participants in group life must not only share understandings (that is, share understandings of what is, what should be, and how to do things), but they must also organize them in a similar way. They must agree, at least minimally, about what is more important and what less; about what circumstances invoke what understandings; and about what understandings come before and after what others. Simple examples will makes this clear.

Say, for example, a group shares the understanding that people do not shove other people and the further understanding that reasonable measures should be taken to prevent others from being harmed. Imagine that two individuals sharing these understandings encounter one another in the middle of a street while a car that only one can see is rushing at the other. Imagine· that the person who can see fails to shove the other out of the way, allowing him to be struck by the car. Finally, imagine that he says he acted as he did because he did not want to shove the other person. It hardly needs to be said that invoking the shared, nonshoving understanding would not save him from severe disapproval. He shares the same understandings others do, but seemingly does not share the organizing understanding that preventing harm is more important than not shoving.

What understandings bring into play what others is also a crucial organizing issue. A whole set of understandings is brought into play by the Bena *baraza,* and their significance comes from their all being needed as behavioral guides at the same occasion and over the same time period. For the main participants, Kaka and Mdogo in our case, the prescription that it is required to stand in the center of the seated questioners is essential. This must be accompanied by knowing about holding one's hands behind one's back, speaking only to questioners and not to one's opponent, not shouting and not using abusive language, and so on. All are required as guides for behavior if the main participants are to behave acceptably in a *baraza*, and thus use the group's main means for settling quarrels. However, having the same understandings others have is necessary but not sufficient. The way the shared understandings are related to each other (i.e., organized) must also be shared for the members of a group to have the basis for the predictability essential to group life.

Organizing understandings Just as it was useful earlier on to distinguish between basic understandings and entailed understandings, or to differentiate some understandings as linking ones, so it is useful to recognize that some understandings (whether basic or entailed, or whether linking or not) serve to *organize* other ones. Much of the necessary organization of shared understandings is accomplished by other shared understandings that concern what is more important and what is less so, what goes together with what, and other relationships. As in the case of the onrushing car and the need to choose between not shoving and letting someone be hurt, most people can easily make the choice between understandings on the basis of shared understandings concerning what is more important and what less. There are also parts of culture that concern which understandings go together with which others. Being a participant in a *baraza* requires that behavior be guided by a number of different understandings. In like manner, being a student taking an exam, a couple getting married, or a person buying groceries calls for more than just a general sharing of culture among those involved. In each case all participants must bring together the same group of understandings and guide their behavior by them if the essential predictability is to be present. This requires a commonly held view of the proper relationships among the shared understandings. Shared "organizing understandings," which dictate the relationships among the other parts of culture, involved and which are learned and transmitted just as the rest of culture is, accomplish this in many situations.

Organizing culture in unusual situations As important as organizing understandings are for producing mutually predictable behavior among those who share them, there are situations where they do not serve. These situations have one thing in common: From the point of view of those involved they are unusual. They all confront their participants with a need to make choices they rarely or never had to make before. The requirement for unprecedented choices can arise from new social or physical situations that bring together prescriptive understandings not previously applicable in a single situation. It can also arise from deviant behavior. This is what happened in our *baraza* example, as we will see. In all these situations, existing shared organizing understandings do not provide a common basis for action and evaluation because they do not automatically provide accepted ranking of the two or more parts of culture that apply to the situation.

ORGANIZING
UNDERSTANDINGS
*Shared understandings that
dictate the relationships
among other
understandings.*

In situations where organizing understandings do not provide the needed organization of culture the only available basis for it is one that emerges from the interaction of participants in the situation itself. It cannot be attributed to any single, generally accepted organizing understanding that existed in the minds of those involved prior to the situation; it is a new organization and can only be understood in light of the situation that gave rise to it.

In our *baraza* case we saw a straightforward violation of what everyone present understood to be proper behavior. Kaka waved his arms, shouted, and—really shocking by Bena standards—called the assembled people "fools" and "horses." They reacted to this in accord with the shared understandings concerning behavior at a *baraza;* that is, they were shocked at his behavior and disapproved of it. However, the disapproval of the young headman's dragging Kaka away and hitting him was so great that Kaka's actions were virtually forgotten and all unfavorable attention—a kind of moral pressure—centered on the headman.

As often happens in all societies, no shared organizing understanding was available for guidance in the novel situation resulting from simultaneous violations of several cultural prescriptions. People do not often shout and hurl insults at *barazas* (in observing over 500 *barazas,* the anthropologist observed such a thing only this one time), and when people do, the proper behavior of the headmen or village chiefs in charge is to levy fines against them. Kaka actively rejected the headman's attempt to fine him, and there is no understanding about what constitutes proper behavior for a chief or headman in that extraordinary circumstance. There is an understanding, and it applies to most situations in Bena life, that violence is not appropriate, which made the headman's response to Kaka's behavior culturally suspect. Still, it is understood that proper behavior at a *baraza* is essential, and it is the presiding official's task to ensure that such behavior is maintained.

Creating a new organization of understandings There was, then, a difficult organizational problem. What is more important: to stop unacceptable behavior with actions beyond those understood as appropriate or to allow unacceptable behavior to continue because appropriate actions will not stop it? Which is worse, Kaka's violations or the headman's response to them?

The case involves conflicting organizing understandings: One holds that it is essential (i.e., more important than other things) to maintain order in the *baraza;* the other holds that violence must be avoided in almost all circumstances. The two understandings clash. Usually they coexist because maintaining order in the *baraza* and avoiding violence usually lead to the same behaviors. The clash between them was the product of an unusual combination of events. To deal with the results of this unusual combination, the people present had to arrive at some common (i.e., shared) understanding of what happened and what to do about it.

This new understanding was partly the result of the unique situation itself. However, the role of existing shared understandings in providing the basis for working out the new common view that finally emerged should not be overlooked. It is worth examining. Both Kaka's actions and those of the headman, if they had been separate, would almost surely have led to disapproval directed at each of them. Why not, then, disapprove of both of them or disapprove more of what Kaka did instead of focus most of the disapproval on the headman's actions?

First, the Bena respect old people. They understand that the proper behavior of young people to old ones is deference and respect, which weights the final organization toward disapproval of the headman's behavior far more than of Kaka's, because Kaka is old and the headman is young. Had Kaka been young and the headman old, Kaka's behavior would have been even more offensive than it was, and the headman's reaction to it, contrary to understandings of proper behavior as it was, would have been more acceptable.

The fact that Kaka's knee had been hurt activated understandings about violence and physical damage. What Kaka did was disapproved, but it left no lasting, visible effects. The headman's actions resulted clearly in a swollen knee, and shared understandings of the rights of injured persons clearly affected the final view of Kaka's case. The insistence that Kaka be taken to a government dispensary so that officials from outside the village could be informed of his injury indicates how seriously it was taken.

Moreover, Kaka had once been a political official and was a man of considerable prestige. It is likely that the headman's behavior would not have been as offensive as it was if it had not violated three separate understandings: the one requiring nonviolent behavior; the one requiring respectful and deferential treatment of important men; and the one governing relations between the young and the old. Also, the headman is the lowest political official, and his actions are not interpreted with the leniency the culture accords to really important people such as village chiefs. The headman's position, no doubt, contributed to the extremely unfavorable reaction his response to Kaka's misbehavior evoked.

Also, the headman was a Muslim in a community where less than 10 percent of the people are of that faith, but Kaka was a Christian like the majority. There is no overt discrimination against Muslims, but being separated in religious belief and practice from most of the people at the *baraza* may have contributed to the vigor with which his behavior was disapproved and the way in which Kaka's actions receded into the background.

Finally, the two or three highly respected members of the community at the *baraza* (the ones who were told about Kaka having been hit) all focused their disapproval on the headman. It is quite likely that had these men disapproved equally of both the headman and Kaka or disapproved more vigorously of Kaka, a different ordering of the understandings concerning the events of the case might have been brought about.

The point is that the organization of the relevant understandings did not result from a single organizing understanding in the minds of all present or, in fact, of anyone present. It came out of the interaction of those present as guided by previously existing shared understandings concerning such apparently unrelated matters as relations with important people, limits on what

Man at Bena *Baraza*. Note that this elderly Bena man, although making his point emphatically, follows understandings concerning proper *baraza* behavior by keeping his hands behind his back.

minor officials can do, the weight of the views of leading citizens, the significance of visible physical injury, and so on.

If a case similar to Kaka's had occurred within a fairly short time, quite possibly the memory of Kaka's case would have led to a similar disapproval of the headman, but such a case did not actually arise during the subsequent months an anthropologist observed. Much of what actually happens in all societies is unique, and neither participation in these events nor evaluation of that participation can be fully guided by the mechanical application of already shared understandings. The understandings already shared by the members of a group before they jointly experience a unique event provide common guides for the evaluation that ultimately produces an organization of the understandings concerning the event. However, despite the role of existing culture, organization is a social product of the immediate situation, not a previously learned understanding. This is just what we saw as the conclusion of the dispute-settlement case.

Conflicting understandings It is important to remember that the violation of cultural prescriptions does not necessarily bring about a need for a new organization of understandings. The need arises when understandings applying to the same situation cannot all be followed without conflict. If either Kaka or the headman had been the only one to violate a prescription, there would have been no difficulty in interpreting and evaluating what happened. It was the joint applicability of two understandings that had not previously been ranked according to which was the more important (i.e., "organized") that led to the need to find a new organization which held that it was more important to avoid violence than it was to stop disrespectful behavior.

The need for new organizations of cultural elements can, and often does, arise without anyone's violating a cultural prescription. When, for example, formerly rural groups move to the city, individuals often find themselves faced with a situation that brings together understandings not previously ranked according to importance. In many rural groups there is an understanding that it is essential to extend unlimited hospitality to kin. An understanding that husband, wife, and children should become as prosperous as possible often accompanies this. The two understandings need not come into conflict in a rural setting because visiting relatives can work on the land and produce their own food or, even, contribute to the prosperity of their hosts. In the city, however, the visitors are usually an economic drain. If they cannot get paying jobs—which often happens—the visitors make it impossible for the hosts to follow both the hospitality and the prosperity understandings. An organizing problem occurs even though there have been no violations of prescriptions. The final resolution of the problem can have far-reaching implications. For example, as a result of the greater emphasis on the immediate family and its well-being, the understandings may be ranked so that the strength of other kinship ties is reduced.

Both broad social changes, such as urbanization, and small day-to-day events such as those seen in our dispute-settlement case, can result in new organizations of culture. Even without adding any new understandings, these new organizations are an important source of cultural change. They lead people to behave in ways they would not have before (e.g., not blaming a person who was disrespectful or refusing hospitality to kin), and these new ways can, in turn, lead to further cultural changes. Giving less importance to kin can lead to a need for retirement plans, insurance, and professional baby-sitters and such to take care of needed services once performed by kinsmen. Adding new understandings is an obvious and important source of the constant change that goes on in every group. The emergence of new relationships among existing understandings, however, though not quite so obvious, is no less important.

It is important to emphasize that cultural development and change does not come only from the addition of new understandings. In fact, even adding new elements of culture in the form of beliefs, procedures, and values requires organizational change. The new elements provide no basis for common understandings and actions until they are organized with existing understandings according to whether the new elements are more or less important than old elements of related kinds, whether they apply in the same or different sorts of situations, and so on. Without a grasp of the organization of the elements of culture we cannot really comprehend either the cultural basis for what people do or how culture changes.

The Organization of Culture as a Whole

So far we have considered cultural organization from the point of view of the relations among relatively small numbers of shared understandings, all of which concern similar issues in a single situation. There is, however, more to cultural organization than that. Large areas of culture are related to other large areas, and sometimes we can discern the presence of a similar sort of organization throughout much of an entire culture.

Earlier in our discussion of "culture," we pointed out that some understandings are "basic" and that if they are accepted, other understandings, called "entailed understandings," will also be accepted. This relationship is an organizational one and is especially important because it is a crucial part of the organization of cultures as wholes. Not all understandings are clearly and neatly related to each other, basic and entailed, the way the Trukese belief in ghosts' fear of light is to the belief that flashlights chase them away. Often the basic understanding is not so closely connected to the less basic ones, and the less basic ones do not follow so smoothly.

Understandings can be more basic than others in that they can concern a broader range of issues or they can have greater decisiveness; that is, those who share them believe they apply very widely and that when they do apply, they should be followed rather than any others that might also apply. Thus, the Bena share a basic understanding that harming other people is to be avoided, and they apply this understanding to situations where outsiders might not easily see its applicability. For example, describing someone's physical appearance by saying "he is a tall man," "she is a slender woman," or any other reference to a bodily trait is understood as harmful (i.e., insulting) and to be avoided. The Bena value accurate description as much as anyone else, but this is outweighed in talking about people by the basic understanding about not doing harm, which the Bena apply even when doing so has a considerable cost in time and energy. If the only way to identify someone is by a physical description, the Bena will usually not identify that person rather than insult him (as they understand it) by noting his distinguishing physical traits. Such widely applied and strong understandings provide a kind of overall organization for the culture shared by a group in the sense that they influence many different sorts of activities and provide a kind of "flavor" to much of what occurs in the group sharing the culture.

Even these fundamental understandings, however, cannot be assumed to be involved in all situations. The Bena do harm people, and in such areas as warfare, child training, and wife beating their shared understandings hold that it is perfectly acceptable to do so. Basic understandings are shared by the members of every human group, but just how large a proportion of the culture is closely connected with a particular basic understanding and what influence it has is a matter to be established by actual investigation.

It may be that every understanding in a culture is influenced by a few fundamental understandings that are, in turn, clearly related to one another in relative importance. A culture like this is as a whole highly and thoroughly organized. A culture may also have many understandings not closely related to one another either through some connection between them or through some other understandings that order the ones not directly connected to each other. In this case we would say that the culture as a whole is loosely organized and composed of parts (related groups of understandings) that are not related to each other in a close way. The parts are organized, but the whole much less so.

It is probably true that the smaller and more self-sufficient a group is, the more thoroughly organized as a whole its culture is likely to be. More nearly every member of the group would have to participate with every other in a wider variety of events and would, therefore, have to share understandings encompassing more of life. The kinds of groups anthropologists have usually studied have cultures more organized as wholes than those found in the nations in which most of the readers of this book live. Both sorts of groups, however, have organized cultures. The difference is whether all or most of the understandings that make up the culture are connected through basic understandings or whether there are important parts (such as those concerned with business life and those with family life) that, although internally organized, are not closely connected with each other.

ETHNOCENTRISM
Understanding and evaluating people, the way they act, what they believe, and what they value according to the culture of one's own group.

Ethnocentrism

More universally fundamental than any other aspect of culture is the phenomenon called "ethnocentrism."

"Ethnocentrism" means understanding and evaluating people, the way they act, what they believe, and what they value according to the culture of one's own group. From what we already know about the prescriptive under-standings shared by the members of a group it will be clear that they provide a basis for comprehending and evaluating whatever the sharers encounter. Part of what people encounter is made up of members of other groups. The fact that people use their culture to understand and judge these "outsiders" will not be surprising because the understandings people share with the members of their own group account for most of the understandings available to them.[6] Ethnocentrism, then, is the unavoidable consequence of the fact that individuals must use their culture in dealing with their experience, including the part of their experience made up of encounters with members of different culture groups. Understanding the way ethnocentrism works involves understanding the way culture works because ethnocentrism is simply the application of shared, prescriptive understandings to one part of experi-ence. It is no different in operation from the application of these under-standings to other areas of experience.

People judge or evaluate most of what they experience according to the values of their group. It is perhaps less widely understood that we also comprehend our experience according to shared understandings. Besides involving an important influence on whether we like or dislike what we encounter, ethnocentrism also shapes our conception of *what* we encounter by assigning meaning to it. Consider the following example.

An anthropologist on Truk experimented by translating American jokes into Trukese to see what the people of the atoll thought of them. It must be understood that from the age of puberty until well into middle age Trukese men and women devote a good deal of time to sexual affairs, mostly extra-marital, and this is considered the normal thing to do. It must also be understood that Trukese men believe that the most interesting and attractive aspect of a woman is her genitals. Men can discuss this topic at great length and with a minuteness of detail a person from a different cultural background would think possible only among gynecologists. The joke told a group of Trukese men was:

> A man is leaving a friend's house on a bus after having spent a weekend with the friend. As the bus drives away, he shouts to his friend: "Thanks for the food, it was delicious. My room was really comfortable and your wife was wonderful in bed."
>
> The man sitting next to him on the bus could not contain himself. "I've never heard anything like that. How could you tell that man his wife was wonderful in bed?"
>
> "Just politeness," replied the first man, "she was really lousy."

The Trukese men listened solemnly and with interest to the story. At the end none smiled but one said: "Oh, I see. She had bad genitals." The Trukese men understood the story according to the understandings they share about what is important in the world, which is quite as vital to understanding their

[6]There are, of course, idiosyncratic understandings, but they cannot provide the basis for collective action or evaluation until and unless they become shared.

ethnocentrism as how they judge the things that come to their attention. They interpreted the joke according to what was important as seen through their shared understandings. Ethnocentrism works as it does because of this basis for interpretation. The idea that there might be something unusual or particularly interesting about the extramarital relationship is simply not part of the culture of this group. The interesting and important thing is that the woman presumably was found wanting in the crucial feminine characteristic, which is, to the sharers of their understandings, the obvious point of the story. Earlier in this chapter we saw how Trukese understandings about ghosts structure their world and its contents. Believing there are ghosts and that they are visible but never seen because they fear light is a result of the use of culture in interpreting experience. It differs from ethnocentrism only in that the experience does not concern other groups.

Probably the most widely held view of ethnocentrism is that it leads to the positive evaluation of one's own group and its practices and to less positive evaluations of other groups and their practices when they differ. This often results from ethnocentrism, but to fail to examine why it does makes it impossible to understand how ethnocentrism really works. The application of culture is the basis of ethnocentrism. Culture structures the world by indicating to those who share it what needs to be done and how to do it. It is the source for understanding and evaluating what people are trying to do and how well or badly these things are done. By extension the shared understandings that make up culture provide the basis for evaluating people according to what they are understood to be doing and how they do (or do not do) it. An example will make this clear.

Bantu Agriculturalist and Masai Warrior. Contrary to ethnocentric views, a peaceful agriculturalist is *not* a poor example of a warrior, nor is a warrior necessarily an agriculturalist gone wrong.

Among Plains Indian societies and among the Masai of East Africa, warfare is understood as a continuing and desirable aspect of the relations between different groups. Young men in these societies are understood as being almost entirely occupied with developing military skills and virtues. The members of these groups understand what young men do and how they should be judged quite differently than do members of societies where warfare is thought neither permanent nor virtuous and young men have no desire to be warriors. Looked at with Masai and Plains Indians understandings, the young men from other groups *are* interested in military skills because, according to their understandings, that is the way young men are. However, they do very badly at it and are quite unsatisfactory young men. The members of the other groups understand the young men of the warlike societies as "really" having whatever interests their young men are understood to have. For them the warriors are poor specimens of young men, since they do little or nothing of what the more peaceful groups see as important.

Applying one's own shared understandings to members of other groups where the same understandings are not shared not only leads to a more favorable evaluation of the members of one's own group; but it also leads to a misapprehension about what the members of the other group are doing. A peaceful agriculturalist is *not* a poor example of a Masai warrior and cattle herder. A Shoshonian food gatherer cannot be understood as a failed Plains Indian hunter and raider. These ideas, however, are what would result from the two martial groups' applying their cultures to the farmers and gatherers. Similar evaluations result when the more peaceful apply their understandings to the warriors. Ethnocentrism leads inevitably to these sorts of misunderstandings and the negative evaluations connected with them.

Cultural Relativism

In its simplest form "cultural relativism" is the insistence that the behavior of the members of a group can be understood only according to the culture of that group. Proceeding on the ethnocentric view that the understandings shared in one's own group are also important guides to behavior in other groups ignores the existence of cultural differences between groups, and makes it impossible to take account of the influence of a group's own distinctive culture on its behavior.

Cultural relativism can be looked at as part of the intellectual equipment required for understanding the behavior of people from groups with cultures different from one's own. However, there is also the problem of judging or evaluating the behavior of people whose understandings are different from one's own. Obviously, if you wish to know how their behavior would be evaluated by members of their own group, you would have to know the understandings shared in that group. To evaluate their behavior according to understandings different from those they share would produce an evaluation different from their own.

Whether understandings used in judging human behavior ought ever to be different from those shared by the people judged is a moral and ethical question. Although cultural relativism is sometimes taken to be a moral and ethical position which holds that it is a bad thing to judge people according to understandings they do not have, it need not be. Being able to understand the forces that influence behavior is one thing and evaluating that behavior is quite another. Cultural relativism, seen as an intellectual tool, is very different from cultural relativism as an instrument of moral judgment.

The Dani people of western New Guinea (West Irian), as part of their mortuary rites, cut off a finger from the hand of a female relative of every dead person. To understand this, account must be taken of the parts of Dani culture concerning how the dead should be treated. To see how the Dani evaluate the cutting off of women's fingers (and few adult Dani women have more than one or two left on each hand) requires a knowledge of Dani beliefs and values regarding women, relations among kin, and death, all of which involves cultural relativism as a tool for understanding. It passes no judgment on what the Dani do. Cultural relativism as an ethical doctrine, however, would hold that cutting off fingers is a good thing because that is the Dani judgment resulting from their understandings.

However one may feel about cultural relativism as a moral doctrine, it is independent from cultural relativism as an intellectual tool. Using cultural relativism to help understand behavior need not entail a relativistic moral position any more than it precludes it.

Dani Girls with Amputated Fingers. To understand how the Dani evaluate cutting off women's fingers requires a knowledge of Dani beliefs and values regarding women, relations among kin, and the treatment of the dead. Cultural relativism is essential for attaining an understanding of this and other "exotic" practices.

SUMMARY

Culture is the foundation of human life. Through the operation of their culture the members of a group are able to get along with one another well enough to maintain social relations and to provide for their survival needs. The culture of a group is the sum of the morally forceful understandings acquired by learning and shared by the members of that group. The shared understandings that make up culture have the status of *the best* and, often, *the only* ways of believing, doing, and valuing. This compelling quality comes partly from individuals' feeling good when they perceive themselves as acting according to the understandings they share with the other members of their group and feeling bad when they perceive themselves as doing things contrary to these understandings. The compelling quality is also rooted in social experience where behavior viewed by other group members as in accord with shared understandings is rewarded, while behavior seen as contrary to these understandings is punished. Because of the compelling quality, the components of culture are prescriptive; that is, they are experienced as obligatory.

Culture is cumulative in that as time goes by new understandings are added to those already shared. Adding new understandings may do more than enlarge a culture; it may also change its quality. This is so because individual understandings do not stand in isolation from one another. The understandings that constitute a group's culture influence each other, and adding new understandings can change the relationship among understandings that already exist. In fact, although the content of understandings is, of course, a vital aspect of culture, the organization of these understandings is also crucial. How understandings are ranked (which takes precedence over which in what circumstances and which understandings go together) does as much to determine the overall character of a group's culture as the content of the understanding does. When organization is changed, culture changes just as significantly as when content changes, although usually the two change together.

Culture is not behavior; it is a guide for behavior. It exists in the minds of those who share it and is a powerful determinant of what people do, but it is not the only determinant of behavior. Individuals do behave contrary to the understandings they share with their fellow group members, and sometimes factors other than culture determine their behavior in a given situation or more generally. Individual deviance is not the only source of discrepancy between the behavior prescribed by culture and actual behavior. Sometime physical and social changes are sufficiently great that although everyone may wish to put shared understandings into operation, it is impossible to do so. This might be because the necessary resources (e.g., buffalo for the Plains Indians after the near extinction of the herds) are not available, or it might be because the culture has no clear provision for new or unusual circumstances.

Although culture is not the only determinant of behavior, its importance as an influence in shaping people's judgments and perceptions can hardly be overestimated. Culture plays a key role in what its sharers view as good and bad, desirable and undesirable, and important and unimportant. It also plays a vital part in people's views of what is. Culture's fundamental role in both understanding and evaluating experience of every kind produces ethnocentrism, the practice of understanding and judging what members of other groups are and do by the standards of one's own group. Cultural relativism is the recognition that the members of every group behave according to their own culture and that any attempt to understand them without reference to that culture will fail.

SUGGESTED READINGS
More on the case

SWARTZ, M.   1969   The Cultural Dynamics of Blows and Abuse among the Bena of Southern Tanzania. *In* Forms of Symbolic Action. Proceedings of the 1969 Annual Spring Meeting of the American Ethnological Society. Seattle: University of Washington Press, pp. 126–133.

> *A rare attempt to interpret symbolism in a nonindustrial society where the symbolism is not religious or, even, political. It is concerned with how people achieve shared understandings of situations through the use of shared symbols, an aspect of culture that is slighted in the text and absent in other readings.*

Other readings

BARTH, F.   1966   Anthropological Models and Social Reality. Proceedings of the Royal Anthropological Institute 165:20–35.

> *Gives three ways of looking at social anthropology including classical British structural-functionalism, American cognitive categories, and a view based on shared "expectations" somewhat similar to the one presented in this chapter.*

KROEBER, A. L., AND C. KLUCKHOHN   1963   Culture, A Critical Review of Concepts and Definitions. New York: Vintage Books. (First published in 1952.)

> *An all-inclusive review of the different definitions of culture used by anthropologists throughout the history of the discipline.*

SAHLINS, MARSHAL   1976   Culture and Practical Reason. Chicago: University of Chicago Press.

> *Strongly argues for the cultural constitution of reality and against views holding that culture can be explained by outside forces.*

SPIRO, M. E.   1951   Culture and Personality: The Natural History of a False Dichotomy. Psychiatry 14:20–46.

> *The basic argument in this article that personality and culture are the same thing is not accepted by anyone now, but the systematic review of different definitions of culture and their classifications is useful.*

WHITE, L.   1959   Man and Culture. *In* The Evolution of Culture: The Development of Civilization to the Fall of Rome. New York: McGraw-Hill. chap. 1.

> *A clear statement by the most influential contemporary unilineal evolutionist of how he sees culture developing over time. The second chapter, "Energy and Tools," discusses the dynamics of culture change as seen in this theoretical framework.*

3

Social Structure

It seems clear to me that God designed us to live in society—just as He has given the bees the honey; and as our social system could not subsist without the sense of justice and injustice, He has given us the power to acquire that sense.

VOLTAIRE
LETTER TO FREDERICK THE GREAT, 1752

Interdependent activities in carpet washing, Tehran, Iran.

What is the relationship between culture and social relations?

Is sharing a large number of understandings enough to maintain social life?

How are understandings distributed so that people use the same ones in the same situations?

What part do groups play in the organization of social life?

Water, Old Grievances, and "Fixing" the Inspector in Rural Spain: A Case of the Workings of Social Structure

Alcalá, the village concerned in this case,[1] is a Spanish village in Lower Andalusia. It is surrounded by steep mountains with sparse vegetation. The hillside watercourses are dry except during the few weeks of yearly rain. In the greener valleys are springs, white farmhouses, and the irrigation channels needed for agriculture in this dry and hardly fertile land. Alcalá is more cut off than the other villages in these mountains, and few visitors travel the steep and difficult roads and donkey paths linking it to its neighbors and to the provincial capital, Sevilla. There are 2000 people in the village of Alcalá itself and a further 1700 in the agricultural area associated with it. It has a market, shops, a church, and a municipal administration.

Farming is the main occupation in Alcalá. The national government has laws restricting the sale and processing of the village's crops, but these laws are as often violated as honored, and there is an elaborate informal system for the raising, milling, and selling of "illegal" produce. This informal system plays a crucial part in our case, and we will see that one aspect of it is particularly important. There is only one legal grain mill in Alcalá and it is electrically powered, but there are a number of illegal mills that run on the same water needed to irrigate the fields. There are two olive-pressing mills, also water powered, which

are legal but whose production of oil is officially, but not actually, restricted. The inspectors who are charged with enforcing and administering the agricultural laws are universally viewed as corrupt. Although they are, that is too simple a view as we shall see.

We are going to focus our attention on the activities of Fernando, a prosperous mill owner and former mayor of Alcalá, and his longtime enemy, Curro. Fernando has a mill powered by the waters of a stream called El Juncal. El Juncal runs into a larger stream called the Rio. The Rio irrigates a large field belonging to Fernando as well as the fields of a number of other villagers. One day Fernando sent workmen to repair the Rio's streambed. Doing the repairs involved making a small change in the stream's path. Fernando announced that after his workmen had altered and cleared the streambed, they would pave it with cement and thus increase the flow of water to all those who drew upon it for irrigation. One farmer opposed allowing Fernando to make repairs because he claimed that the change in the river's course would cut off his field from water. Few paid attention to this complaint because the farmer had no real right, in most people's view, to draw water from the Rio anyway.

The next year Fernando's real purpose in repairing the stream became clear. He wanted not only to improve the streambed and thereby increase the water flow, but also to divert the waters of the Rio and join them with the waters of El Juncal at a new place. To do this, he would have to cut off from irrigation a substantial part of a field belonging to Curro, a skilled repairer of mills who, through his craft, was friendly with

[1]This case is taken from J. A. Pitt-Rivers, The People of the Sierra, Chicago: The University of Chicago Press, pp. 145–159. Phoenix edition published 1961. With permission.

83

**Water, Old Grievances, and
"Fixing" the Inspector in
Rural Spain: A Case of
the Workings of Social Structure**

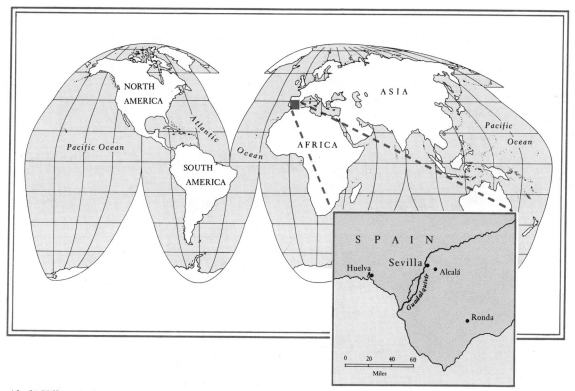

Alcalá Village in Spain.

all the local millers. Unlike the farmer who opposed Fernando the previous year, Curro's claim to water for his field was seen as justified. But there was more to the situation than that.

Curro had been carrying a grudge against Fernando for many years. When Curro's father died, he left his mill to Curro's stepmother, and she sold the mill to Fernando. Curro tried to buy the mill back from Fernando, but he would not sell. The mill is on Curro's land, but is operated by Curro's neighbor and friend, Alonso, on a profit-sharing basis with the owner, Fernando. This mill figures in our case only as the source of the grudge Curro has against Fernando.

The crucial mill is the one Fernando himself operates. His purpose in diverting the waters of the Rio and joining them with El Juncal was to increase the power of his personally operated mill. In the second year of his campaign to do this he actually joined the two streams, so there can be little doubt about his intentions.

The new water arrangement deprived part of

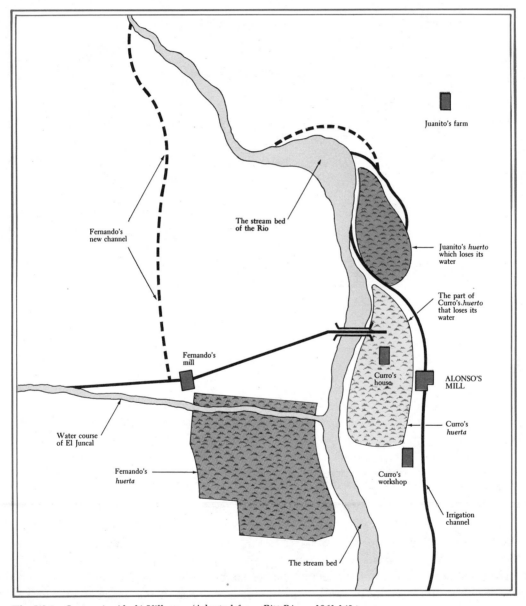

The Water System in Alcalá Village. (Adapted from Pitt-Rivers 1961:143.)

85

Water, Old Grievances, and
"Fixing" the Inspector in
Rural Spain: A Case of
the Workings of Social Structure

Curro's field of the water to which he had a recognized right. The fruit trees Curro had been growing in this area were doomed to die. Several millers downstream from the changed watercourse received less water than they did before. Despite this, only two villagers supported Curro in his opposition to Fernando. One of Curro's supporters was his *compadre*[2] and first cousin, Pepe. Curro was also supported by a man called "El Ranchero" (the cottager), who made his living by producing the plaster needed in building and repairing houses. El Ranchero did not live in Alcalá itself but on a hillside where he mined the raw material for his plaster-producing business. He worked for no one and no one worked for him. His plaster was in steady demand, and he was beholden to no one. He was not an ambitious man and was the local champion of equality and enemy of corruption. He was generally feared because of his outspokenness.

Despite his slender support in the community, Curro pressed his case against his old enemy, Fernando. Curro went to the town hall to complain about Fernando's changing the water supply and was told that he must notify Fernando that his field was being damaged. When Curro sent a message to Fernando telling him this, Fernando offered him money in compensation for the damage.

Curro indignantly refused the compensation. He said he wanted his rights, his field in good condition, not the alms given a beggar.

[2]The person who is god-parent at a child's baptism in Spain and other Spanish-speaking countries enters into a relationship with the child's father or mother in which each calls the other *compadre*. Often *compadres* help each other throughout life and support each other in times of trouble.

Curro told everyone he talked to in the village that Fernando would become all powerful and would crush them all, but no one—including the millers who had to face the competition of Fernando's more powerful mill and the reduction of water power for their own mills—supported him. Of his three previous supporters only his *compadre* and cousin, Pepe, and El Ranchero stayed with him. The one miller who sided with him originally withdrew his support. Alonso, Curro's neighbor and Fernando's profit-sharing mill operator, stayed friendly with Curro but, along with many others, believed he was being too harsh with Fernando. People knew of Curro's grudge against Fernando and believed Curro was being vindictive. Perhaps because of the discouraging lack of support, Curro talked of leaving Alcalá. He said he would sell the field in question cheaply to anyone else, but that Fernando could not buy it for a million *pesetas*.

Alonso told Fernando what Curro was saying about leaving, and Fernando was encouraged by this to believe the dispute would go well for him. Curro found out that Fernando had heard from Alonso of his saying he might leave the village. Curro complained of the falseness and hypocrisy of men, and Alonso stopped coming to Curro's house for his usual friendly chats.

While all this was going on, a prominent and respected local man, Don Antonio, had been watching with interest. His mill had lost business because of the lower rates of Fernando's mill, and he noted the further development of his competitor's mill with something less than glee. Don Antonio had moved against Fernando before. Fernando was very friendly with the government mill inspectors and used his friendship to

Mountain Village in Southern Spain. The village shown here is very similar in appearance to the village referred to by the fictitious name of Alcalá in this case.

make the "arrangements" whereby he and the other millers carried on their milling with only an occasional fine despite its technical illegality. Nevertheless, Fernando's mill was once raided by an inspector, and he was heavily fined for having more olive oil than his quota allowed. Since Don Antonio also had "friends" outside the village, many villagers believed this raid was the result of Don Antonio's using his connections to express his displeasure with Fernando.

While deciding what to do about his dispute, Curro went to Don Antonio's mill to make some repairs. He decided to try to persuade Don Antonio to help him, despite the fact that Don Antonio was an educated man of refinement (as the villagers saw it) and Curro an ordinary man of the village. When Curro told him his story,

Don Antonio was sympathetic. He told Curro to stop trying to overcome Fernando in the village "where everyone listens to him" and instead to go to the Hydrographic Commission in Sevilla. Don Antonio clearly wanted Curro to win the dispute, but he did not want to be directly involved himself.

Curro was impressed with Don Antonio's advice and went to a lawyer in a nearby town to ask how he should proceed. The lawyer told him it was not necessary to go to Sevilla because Fernando had clearly broken the law against diverting streams without prior government permission.

While Curro was getting advice, Fernando was proceeding with the work on the streams. He believed the people of Alcalá and its area were with him in what he was doing. He felt sure

87

Water, Old Grievances, and
"Fixing" the Inspector in
Rural Spain: A Case of
the Workings of Social Structure

he could square the legal problems once the work was done. Fernando told people that the only way things get done is to do them first and get permission later. He said that Curro had a grudge against him because he would not sell him back his father's mill and that Curro was envious of his wealth.

Curro was encouraged by what the lawyer had told him, and he looked forward to defeating and humiliating Fernando. A friend in the village, however, told him that although his legal position appeared to be a strong one, it would be better to use that position to get a big compensation from Fernando than to go to court because you can never tell if you will win in court. The friend stressed the fact that almost all the water rights in the valley were legally quite vague, and to press a court case concerning this might stir up trouble for a lot of people and make Curro very unpopular.

Curro did not like his friend's advice. He said that now Fernando would have to right all the wrongs he had done him in the last ten years. He said that if Fernando backed down, he would sell him the damaged field for 25,000 *pesetas* (three times its real value). This, Curro told his fellow villagers, was a trivial sum compared with what Fernando would make with the added power of his mill. Anyway, he said, such a sum was appropriate for taking somebody else's water. Curro's extravagant talk did not bring Fernando to settle with him, and the case went to court.

The case was tried in Alcalá. Curro lost, and the court ruled that he must pay all the costs including Fernando's. The court decided the case on the "fact" that Curro had given Fernando

permission to change the streambeds. This had happened, the court ruled, at a meeting of the Alcalá water-users' association. Because of this permission, the decision was that Curro had no claim to damages. Curro denied he ever gave permission. He said the topic of water diversion was not even raised while he was at the meeting. However, two leaders of the association testified that Curro did give permission. Curro claimed that one of them was not even at the meeting. Nevertheless, the leaders' version was accepted by the court, and Curro lost. The use of the leaders' testimony was viewed as a *chanchullo* (dirty trick) by the villagers, but most of them approved of Fernando's victory anyway.

Curro was humiliated by the court's ruling and badly hurt financially as well. He said he would have to sell his land and workshop in Alcalá and move to a nearby town where he could get a job in order to get money to pay his debts. However, he sold a house he had been renting out and borrowed the remainder of the needed sum from his unswerving friend and ally, Pepe. After the case was decided, Fernando told other villagers, but not Curro, that he would wait and see what damages Curro's garden actually suffered when the effects of changing the watercourse were seen, and then he would pay him fair compensation.

The people of Alcalá had no sympathy for Curro. They said he pressed his case because of his vindictiveness, and had he accepted compensation from Fernando, he would not have come to grief. Fernando was respected as a generous man. He could afford to be with the advantages he had, but he was respected nonetheless.

Analysis of the Case

Even the most complete familiarity with the culture of the people of Alcalá would leave us somewhat puzzled by a number of the events in the water-rights case. Curro was deprived of the water needed for his field, and the villagers share an understanding that he deserves either the water or compensation for its loss. When he took his demand for compensation to court, he was defeated by a "dirty trick." The use of such tactics is contrary to another shared understanding; nevertheless, Fernando, who wrongly took Curro's water and who used the dirty trick, had the support of almost all the villagers. Among Fernando's supporters were the millers. They supported him despite the fact that he was also violating their water rights and, at the same time, altering the course of the streams so that his mill would get more water power and be potent competition for their mills.

This case could be taken as just another example of the fact that people often behave perversely and do not, by any means, always follow the shared understandings they talk about and sometimes seem to live by. Such cynicism often appears merited by what we see of human behavior in every part of the world or era of history. It does not, however, increase our ability to explain that behavior. It is no more true that people "ignore" their shared understandings than it is that they always follow the ones that might seem to apply.

Part of the difficulty arising from the apparent violation of cultural prescriptions can be resolved when we understand that not all shared understandings apply equally to all situations. This has to be true if culture is to work as a guide for behavior, because included in the large number of understandings that make up every culture are some that are incompatible with others. A culture may have one understanding requiring people to behave in a friendly and easy-going way and another calling for businesslike behavior and strict giving and taking of orders. People share both understandings, but they maintain predictability by also sharing ideas about when one understanding will be the proper guide for behavior and when the other will be. From time to time we hear people reminding each other that particular sorts of behavior are called for in one setting and not another, as when someone says, "Don't be so formal; this is a party and we're your friends."

To get predictable behavior, then, there must be shared agreement about what parts of culture apply to which situations and people. An important source of this comes from a type of shared understanding called "expectations." Expectations are cultural elements that specify what behavior is appropriate in which situation and toward which people and the kind of response that behavior is likely to produce. Through sharing expectations the members of a group are able to carry out extremely complex activities that involve different people's doing different things in a coordinated way. The expectations they share "distribute" their common culture so that everyone has a clear idea of what he is doing and the sort of behavior others are likely to manifest. A simple example will make this clear.

EXPECTATIONS

Elements of culture associated with statuses that specify what behavior is appropriate in which situation and toward which people and the kind of response that behavior is likely to produce.

Football, expectations, and the distribution of culture Knowing all the rules and techniques for carrying out the various behaviors involved in playing football is not enough. All the players also have to share understandings that enable them to agree that a game is actually in progress, what side they are on, and what position each of them is playing. Crucially, each player must have expectations regarding himself and the other players when particular plays are in progress. These expectations distribute the other understandings—how to pass, block, tackle, run with the ball, and so on—both among the players and in different circumstances so that a game can actually take place. Each player knows what he should do and what he should not do in a wide range of circumstances (his team has the ball, their team has the ball, his team passes, their team passes, etc.), and each player has a very clear understanding of the range of behavior within which each of the other players will act.

Because this is all part of culture and, therefore, learned (instead of inherited biologically), there is great flexibility in what players can do and, even, in the game itself. Individual players in particular positions can be replaced with other players in those positions provided only that they all have learned the same understandings including the understandings about what their duties are in various plays and what to expect from the other players in those plays. The whole game can change as well, through the introduction of new understandings. The new understandings may introduce new procedures—for example, the increase in the importance of kicking field goals in the last decade—or may reassign to new positions ways of behaving that already existed, as, for example, when a lineman carries the ball in the "end-around" play.

The game has great flexibility because both the techniques of play and the assignment of particular kinds of behavior to particular positions are learned. At the same time, the learned behavior has significant rewards and punishments in addition to players' own feelings about doing things correctly and well. These come from the referee, the coach, the members of the player's own team, and the opponents. These rewards and punishments help assure at least enough order for the game to go on.

The example of football may seem to be distant from our concern with the analysis of the water-rights case this chapter begins with; however, football (and other sports) involves some of the processes fundamental to that case and has the advantage of being culturally uncomplicated. In much of life there is some doubt about what situation is actually occurring and what people in the situation are expected to do. In football this is remarkably clear, and much of the appeal of the game lies in its being a group activity in which the performance of individuals and collections of individuals (teams) can be measured against clearly applicable understandings about what should be done and who is responsible for doing it.

Outside of games we are often uncertain whether we are in one situation or another. When we take a car back to a mechanic because he has not really fixed it, we sometimes do not know if the situation is one that calls for a straightforward statement of the difficulty still remaining or a more-or-less angry exposure of the dishonesty of charging money to fix something that is still broken. Should we act toward the mechanic as a friendly customer come to chat about a shared difficulty or an outraged victim at the end of his patience? Will he act like a reasonable craftsman willing to consider his customer's complaints, or will he deny any possible responsibility for the continued trouble? In football and other sports, these problems do not occur because if we know the rules of the game, we have a clear understanding of what is happening and what we can expect from all players.

"Status": expectations and categories   A main reason games give those who follow them clear understandings of what is happening and what to expect from all involved in the play is that the "statuses" of those involved are defined very fully and clearly. A status is a social category, a way of grouping people together and all the expectations culturally assigned to the people of the category. When we identify a football player as a quarterback, we are classifying him with all the other quarterbacks we know about, and we expect from him a definite range of behaviors. Quarterbacks are expected to call plays (or, at least, transmit the coach's choice of plays), pass, hand off to other backs, and so on. Other players are expected, according to their statuses, to hand him the ball at the beginning of the play, block members of the other team who are, in *their* statuses, expected to tackle him, and carry out other expected behaviors.[3]

In football games it will be clear that no status exists without other statuses that interlock with it. There can be no ball holder without a kicker and no blockers without tacklers. The same is true in the wider and more "real" areas of life. There are no students without teachers and no husbands without wives. Every status depends upon at least one other for its definition, and the expectations of the mutually dependent statuses dictate complementary behaviors. A salesman groups those he sells to into the culturally provided category customers, and his expectations for relations with them fit together with the expectations they have of him in the status salesman. Because of the interlocking and complementary character of statuses, to understand any particular status, it is essential to examine it together with those regularly connected with it.

No one in any human society has only a single status. Everyone places himself and is placed by others in a number of different categories with

STATUS   *A social category and all the expectations assigned to the people in the category.*

[3]A popular use of the word "status" may cause some confusion here. In this usage "status" refers to the honor or deference someone receives; thus, a quarterback of a championship team has more status than other quarterbacks, and the quarterback on a team has more status than other team members. This usage differs drastically from the one common in the social sciences, which assigns status equally to quarterbacks and water boys. "Prestige" is a useful word for the honor associated with a status. Quarterbacks probably have more prestige than other kinds of players because that position is more honored. Among occupants of the high-prestige status quarterback, the person occupying that position on the championship team probably has more prestige than other occupants of the same status.

The Distribution of Culture. Each player must have expectations regarding what he and other players will do when particular plays are in progress; otherwise, the game cannot be played.

different behavioral expectations under different circumstances. The same person will, according to what is happening and who else is involved, be classified and classify himself as a young person, a man, a son, a student, a husband, a salesman, a customer, a friend, an enemy, a voter, and many others. In any given situation this person will act according to the expectations attached to the status he sees himself occupying, and he will evaluate the actions of others in that situation by the same expectations. He will assign to others statuses that are complementary to the one he has given himself. For example, if he places himself as a student he may assign others to the status fellow student and others still to the status teacher.[4]

A person must understand which of his many statuses he is in at a given time and what statuses the other people involved with him have then. The same is true of every other person in the situation. As we saw in the football example, statuses are always mutually dependent on other statuses. If our person acts as a husband toward another and she acts toward him as a friend, the unmet expectations of both parties may be considerable and might even lead to a severing of relations between the two.

[4]The actual process is a bit more complicated. The assignment of statuses is a back-and-forth exchange and mutual adjustment. One person starts by acting in the status of, say, student and using the expectations of that status. The other person, however, may react as a friend or social partner. This may lead the first person to abandon his original self-assigned status and adopt the friend status and its expectations. Alternatively, the second person may not persevere in applying the expectations of a friend (because, for example, the first person says, "Quit fooling around, we've got to study") and will accept the status of fellow student.

Status, individual differences, and limits Interpersonal relations are always based on statuses. People do not deal with each other on an entirely individualistic and idiosyncratic basis. Culture plays a key role in that people behave toward one another within the limits of the expectations attaching to the categories to which they assign one another and themselves. Both the categories and the expectations are defined by shared understandings, not individual preferences. This does not mean that there is no room for personal choice and individual style in human relations. Which part of the behavior expected of a status an individual emphasizes and how he carries out that behavior is determined individually, but status provides limits or ranges that are ignored only at the price of disapproval in its many forms.

A doctor can joke with a patient or be very serious, he can prescribe one medication or another—or none at all—but whatever he does, he must convince the patient that he is concerned about his health. If he does not do the latter, the patient will say that "the doctor acts funny," "he is not my idea of a doctor," or "he doesn't know what he is doing." The patient may stop going to him, may tell his friends not to go to him, or may even try to get the doctor's license revoked. The patient, in his status, must show the doctor through his behavior that he is willing to help the doctor find out what is wrong with him and that he will cooperate in doing what the doctor tells him to do. If the patient shows himself unwilling to act toward the doctor within these limits, the doctor will say that he is a bad patient, or, perhaps, "he is wasting my time." The doctor may tell the patient not to come to him anymore if the patient will not behave within the limits of the patient's status.

For the statuses of both patient and doctor, there is a clear limit on the amount and degree of individual variation that will be tolerated. Occupants of these statuses will be condemned or excluded from them if they fail to meet their attached expectations at least minimally, and the same is true of all statuses. Almost always room for some individuality exists, but the status sets clear limits and requirements for behavior. Social relations, the way people act toward one another in real situations, are guided for the participants by the statuses they occupy in those relations.

Status and social structure "Social structure" refers to the collections, or sets, of interrelated statuses occupied by the members of a group. We can speak of the social structure of the family referring to the related statuses mother, father, son, and daughter. Similarly, we can speak of the social structure of a village or town when we are concerned with such statuses as neighbor, farmer, mayor, and such, and how they are connected. The social structure of an entire group can also be studied; in larger groups, this means examining mainly political and economic (and sometimes religious) statuses and their connections. The advantage of looking at the relations between people from the standpoint of the statuses they occupy will be clear from what we have said about the ways statuses influence behavior.

Looking at interpersonal relations from the point of view of the statuses

SOCIAL RELATIONS
The way people act toward one another in real situations.

SOCIAL STRUCTURE
The sets of interrelated statuses occupied by the members of a group.

Bengali Mother and Children. In the social structure of this family the mother is expected to provide food, and the children are expected to accept it and to cooperate with her in certain understood ways.

of the participants is also important because the connections between statuses influence behavior almost as much as the expectations in the statuses themselves. This works in a number of different ways. Some statuses require other statuses. For example, in Bena society if a person is to be an influential member of the *baraza* (the dispute-settlement meeting discussed in Chapter 2), it is essential that he be both male and rich. Other statuses are connected and influence their occupants' behavior by presenting them with conflicting guides for their behavior. In many societies women with young children have expectations in their status as worker that are in conflict with the expectations of their status as mother. Still other statuses are connected in more indirect ways as will appear in further analysis of the water dispute in Alcalá.

A complete description of the social structure of a group includes all the expectations in all the social categories of people in that group and the connections between them. This description shows how culture is distributed by telling what sorts of things are to be done by what categories of people. One further refinement is needed, however, and it appears when we look at interpersonal relations as if they were, in effect, between statuses; that is, when we look "under" the actual person-to-person behavior at the culturally provided expectations that guide this behavior.

Roles and the relations between statuses   When we remember that "status" refers to a social category and *all* the expectations associated with it, it is clear that this total collection of expectations is divided according to what the various relationships involving the status call for. Some expectations attached to the social category are appropriate in all relations, while others are appropriate only in relations with occupants of one particular status. It is within the range of expectations associated with the status physician for the occupant of that status to tell the occupant of the status patient to "strip to the waist." Nevertheless, a physician who gave this command to his office nurse when she came to tell him the next patient was ready would not be seen to behave as an occupant of the physician status is expected to behave when classified as a member of that status.

The portion of all expectations associated with a status that is used in relations with occupants of some other status is called a "role." The status physician has roles that provide expectations in the physician's relations with patients, nurses, other physicians, hospital administrators, and a few others. The distribution of shared understandings over the roles that make up a status can be as important to predictable relations as the distribution of shared understandings over different statuses.

The expectations in one role of a status may be very different from the expectations in other roles of the same status, and an occupant's behavior may be quite differently received in these different roles, but all the roles will be associated with the same category. Patients may view a physician very positively as a result of the way he behaves in his patient-care role, while nurses and technicians may view him very negatively as a result of his behavior in his medical-supervisor-and-boss role. Both the patients and the nurses and technicians will have no doubt he is a physician and both groups will understand, if it comes to their attention, that the behavior appropriate in one of his roles is different from the behavior called for in another.

The roles are not completely independent, however; if the physician behaves in a way that his nurses and technicians will not tolerate, his ability to maintain his role toward his patients is jeopardized, and, similarly, if patients will not enter into the physician-patient role connection with him, his ability to continue in the medical-supervisor-and-boss role toward his staff becomes doubtful. The roles of a single status, then, are often quite different in the expectations they entail, but performance in one role of a status can influence performance in others and may even affect occupancy of the status.

Every person in every society has a variety of statuses; and every status, with the possible exception of infant, involves more than one role. The total collection of expectations attached to a status needs to be looked at with respect to which expectations are called for in specific relations the occu-

ROLE   *The portion of all expectations associated with a status that is used in relations with occupants of some other status.*

pants of the status enter into. These "packages" of expectations taken from the total collection belonging to the status are what guide role behavior. The contents of the packages can differ, or a number of expectations may appear in several or all of them. Either way, behavior in one role can affect behavior in other roles, and the ability to occupy a status is affected by performance in all the roles of that status.

Back to water: status, roles, and "favors" We are now in a better position to consider the initially puzzling fact that most of the millers did not oppose Fernando's change in the streambed, despite the reduction in water power it would cause for them. On the basis of the shared understanding that people have a right to compensation if water is taken away from them, we would expect that they would have made claims against Fernando. But water is not the only matter about which there are shared understandings.

There are, of course, a vast number of shared understandings in the culture of the people of Alcalá. It would be next to impossible to go through them all, even if we knew them, to find some that might help us understand the millers' reactions to what Fernando did. Concentrating our attention on the relations between those most directly involved in the case, however, is a likely shortcut for understanding what happened. After all, the statuses and roles that form the basis of social structure distribute most of the other shared understandings over situations and among people through their being assigned—as expectations—to different individuals who belong to the various statuses involved in those situations. Let us begin with the statuses Fernando and the millers occupy relevant to the central events in the case and see whether considering the expectations they involve helps us understand the outcome.

First, what is Fernando's status? He has many, as everyone has, but a critical one for his relations with the millers is the one in which he intercedes for the millers when they are in danger of being fined by the government inspector. The Spanish laws regulating agriculture are complex, but, for the present purposes, the most important one is that all private milling is illegal. To continue in their business, the millers must somehow lessen the effects of this regulation, and it is done through Fernando. When a miller is about to be fined, he goes to Fernando and tells him of his trouble. Fernando, in turn, goes to the inspector and makes an "arrangement" whereby the fine will not be levied. Fernando is able to make the arrangement because he is the inspector's "friend." He is also the miller's friend. Local people often say that nothing gets done in this part of Spain without friendship. "Friendship" clearly involves doing favors and doing them without regard to at least some formal regulations or laws.

Fernando's status with respect to the millers, then, involves two roles: one relating him to the government inspector and another relating him to the millers. A similar expectation, one involving "favors," is found in both roles. Fernando is the dispenser of favors to the millers and the receiver of favors from the inspector. In his role with the millers he is asked for favors;

in his role with the inspector he asks for favors. That Fernando asks for favors on the millers' behalf does not matter to the inspector. To him, it is Fernando who is asking for something, and that is what is crucial for the inspector's relations to Fernando. We know that statuses and the roles that are their constituent parts are categories with expectations attached. Fernando is expected to do favors for the millers, and the inspector is expected to do favors for Fernando, but there are expectations going the other way as well (see accompanying diagram). Since Fernando and the inspector are "friends" and friends do favors for each other according to the culture of this group, we need to know what favors Fernando does for the inspector and what favors the millers do for Fernando.

Time			The "Flow of Favors"	
1	Millers	← Fernando	←	Inspector
2	Millers	→ Fernando	→	Inspector

Exactly what Fernando does for the inspector is not clear from available accounts, but there is some reason to believe that whatever else he may do he gives the inspector money. Fernando may well also help the inspector in the latter's role with his government superiors, but we will examine that later. What is important here is that the expectations attaching to the status friends involve the *exchange* of favors. In the friendship relation between Fernando and the millers, he is expected to do favors for them by preventing excessive fines, and they are expected to do favors for him.

The favors the millers are expected to do are not so specific as the favors Fernando is expected to do for them. However, this makes them no less real and does not diminish the strength of Fernando's expectation that they do them. Generally, they are expected to give him support when he needs it and to apply standards less strictly than they would to people not occupying his status. His change in the streambeds did not cut off their water supply entirely, only diminished it. Moreover, he did say he was going to pave the streambeds with cement, which would ultimately increase everyone's water flow. Supporting him, or at least not siding against him, did require going against the shared understanding that people with rights to water can properly demand compensation when those rights are infringed; but supporting Fernando was a favor, and shared understandings require friends to do favors for each other. The requirements of the favor involved were within the limits of what friends expect of one another, and to maintain the role of friend, the millers have to meet those expectations.

The most essential part of the miller role is concerned with the farmers who pay to have their grain processed. To operate their illegal mills, the millers need Fernando as go-between. They also obviously need the farmers to bring them grain. The farmers, in turn, need the illegal mills because if they take their grain to the village's one legal mill, they will have to sell it at the government price. This price is so low that if it were all farmers could get, they could not even afford life's bare necessities. Thus, the farmers must have the illegal mills operating just as the millers must have the farmers bring them grain. Without Fernando in his go-between status, the millers would have to close down their mills, and the farmers would be in desperate economic trouble. The fact that the farmers of the village also supported Fernando despite his having clearly violated an important shared understanding is probably at least partly due to their knowledge that without his "favors" the illegal mills they depend on would close.

Different roles, different expectations   Despite their support of Fernando, the millers also depend on Curro to remain in business. One of his statuses is mill repairer. Without the understandings in that status their mills cannot be maintained. They also depend upon a status (we will call it "go-between") whose expectations include making arrangements with the government inspector. Thus, because there are no other people active in those statuses in the small village of Alcalá, the millers need to maintain working relations with both Fernando and Curro (see accompanying diagram).

MILLERS' ROLES TOWARD STATUSES OCCUPIED BY DISPUTANTS

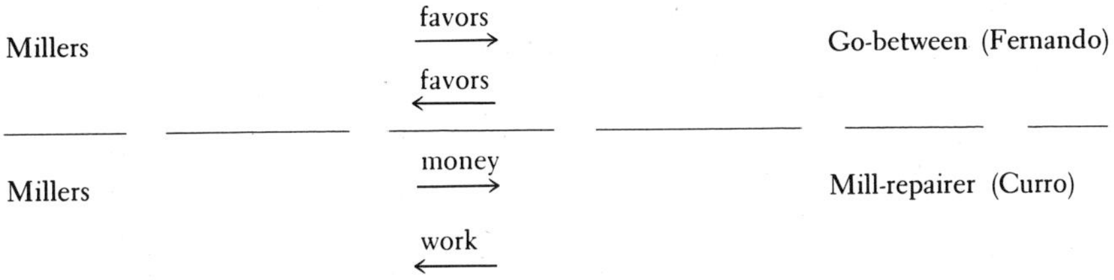

Millers	favors $\longrightarrow$ favors $\longleftarrow$	Go-between (Fernando)
Millers	money $\longrightarrow$ work $\longleftarrow$	Mill-repairer (Curro)

It might appear that efforts to meet the expectations of the statuses involved would lead the millers to side equally with Fernando and Curro. This, however, did not happen, and the reason is to be found in the different roles connecting them to the mill-repairer and go-between statuses. As we saw, it is an expectation of the miller role toward the go-between to return his favors by doing him favors. The role connecting miller to mill-repairer does not involve expectations of mutual favors. Its central expectation is that money be given in return for repair work.

We do not know how Curro reacted to the millers' siding against him. He may have changed his behavior toward them in his status as fellow villager,[5] but he had no basis for feeling his expectations as mill repairer had not been met. Thus, men who occupied the status miller had no basis in any of the roles making up that status to understand that it might be expected of them to support Curro. If the occupants of a miller status had supported

---

[5]People are frequently connected to each other by two or more different roles that are part of two or more different statuses on both sides of the relation.

Curro and not Fernando, and none did in the end, they would have done so outside their relations with Curro *as millers*.

The general point here is that the statuses and roles in a group serve as a guide to the application of particular shared understandings to specific people in various situations. Many kinds of forces affect behavior, but the requirements of maintaining social relations are extremely potent. The millers could have opposed Fernando (one of them did for a time), but their choice of whether they would do so was very much influenced by the different sorts of expectations in the roles that connected them to Fernando and to Curro. If they failed to meet Fernando's expectation that they do favors for him, he might fail to meet their expectation that he do favors for them. The loss of his favors as go-between would seriously endanger their means of earning money as millers.[6] They might feel so friendly toward Curro or so full of hate for Fernando that they would be willing to do this, but the only miller who did soon gave up his support for Curro and joined the others on Fernando's side.

Another aspect of expectations   It will now be clear that the occupants of a status are influenced in their relations with the occupants of another status by the expectations of the roles connecting the two statuses. But expectations in one relation can also affect behavior in a different relation. This can be quite simple, with the mutually influencing expectations in the different relations being obviously complementary to each other. Thus, the shoemaker expects the tanner to supply leather so that the shoemaker can provide shoes to meet the expectations of the customer that he have some for sale. Each relation can proceed only if the expectations in the other relations are met. However, expectations that affect behavior in a number of different relations do not always fit together nicely. Sometimes meeting expectations in one relation makes it very difficult, or even impossible, to meet the expectations in another relation.

We saw that Alonso was Curro's friend and also Fernando's partner in running a mill. Both of his statuses called for Alonso to support the occupants of the connected status, but meeting this expectation in one relation made it impossible for him to meet the same expectation in the other. At first he tried to remain neutral and thus maintain his relations both with his friend and his partner. However, his constant association with both of them and their expectations made it impossible to behave without at least appearing to favor one over the other. Finally he told Fernando that Curro had

[6]This is an interesting example of the interplay of cultural organization and the organization of social relations. Some millers, at least, had to choose between meeting Fernando's expectations as go-between and acting according to the shared understandings that held that Curro had been the victim of a dirty trick and deserved compensation for his lost water. Data are lacking, but it is likely that Curro in his status as villager properly expected these understandings to be followed. By ranking one set of expectations above the other the millers are, of course, organizing the understandings contained in those expectations at the same time they are arranging (as more and less crucial) the social relations. See the discussion of the organization of social relations, pp. 99–104.

said he was going to leave the village. This was probably a response to the role requirement that he help his partner, but it was not necessarily an attack on his friend. Nevertheless, Curro took it to be that and understood Alonso as having irreparably violated the expectations of their friendship relation. The conflicting expectations in Alonso's relations with the principals to the water dispute had become impossible to reconcile, and one of the relations was severed as a consequence of what was interpreted as meeting an expectation in the other. More generally, expectations in one relation can interfere with maintaining another relation.

A final facet of how expectations have influence beyond the particular relations where they guide behavior can be seen by examining El Ranchero's support of Curro in the water dispute. El Ranchero earns a living by making plaster from raw material on his own land. He works for no one and he has no employees. His plaster is in demand for building and repairing, so he is assured of a constant, if modest, income. This occupation removes him, as being a farmer would not, from the complexities of selling crops to illegal millers and the social relations necessary for them to stay in operation. He is, in fact, noted for his independence, and his outspokenness inspires fear among many of his fellow villagers.

In his status as villager (everyone living in Alcalá has that status) El Ranchero is expected to be silent about corruption and to go along with majority views in such things as the water dispute. The return for meeting these expectations is being granted esteem. Losing the esteem of a considerable number of those with whom there is frequent contact is a serious matter for anyone, but El Ranchero is in a better position to bear this than many others are. He is without ambition for more money or for gaining prestige through rising to high positions, and his modest income is secure. His support for Curro, like his criticism of the government, results in nothing more than gossip because most people are afraid to confront him. Not everyone having the same collection of statuses El Ranchero had would act as he did, of course. The point is that expectations in his relations with the other villagers impose a clearly smaller "cost" for opposing the go-between and criticizing the government than would be borne by most other villagers. For El Ranchero, the freedom from restrictive expectations in some important relations makes it easier to behave without too much constraint in other relations. This is an instance of the way the *absence* of certain kinds of expectations in one sort of relation influences behavior that is not a part of those relations.

The Organization of Social Relations

The "organization of social relations" refers to the connections between social relations resulting from the ways the expectations in those relations influence each other. As we saw in the series of relations involving inspector, go-between, millers, and farmers, the expectations in each relation are dependent on each other in vital ways. In fact, the series of interlocked

ORGANIZATION OF
SOCIAL RELATIONS
*The connections between
social relations resulting
from the ways the
expectations in those
relations influence each
other; this can also
be called "social
organization."*

expectations can be traced even further. The inspectors have to meet their supervisor's expectations that they report at least some violations of the milling laws or they will lose their jobs. The farmers and millers, at the other end of the series, have to meet the expectations of their families, who depend on their getting money the only way they can, as farmers and millers.

If expectations in one of these relations change, expectations in connected relations are also likely to change. Were the supervisor's expectations of the inspector to change so that, for example, the inspector was no longer expected to levy *any* fines, it is obvious that not only the particular relation between the inspector and the go-between but also the others we have been considering would change substantially. If we examine a single relation in isolation from all others, our ability to understand that relation is very much reduced because such an examination would provide no basis for seeing the effect of the organization of social relations. Even if we know all the expectations on both sides in the single relation we are considering in isolation, we would not know the influences on those expectations stemming from other relations.

A relatively complete understanding of a relation requires that we know something of what is expected of the participants in *other* relations. The expectations in these other relations can materially affect how the first rela-

Division of Labor in an Early Nineteenth-Century Printing Shop.
The contribution each individual makes to the finished product can only be understood if we consider it in the context of the complete network of social relations.

tion operates (i.e., how the people guide their behavior in that relation) in the ways we considered in the last section. As we saw, expectations in different relations can be mutually dependent, or they can interfere with each other, or the absence of certain expectations in one relation can free behavior in others. This sort of interlocking, or mutual influence, of expectations provides the basis for the organization of social relations whether or not the participants in these relations are aware of it. Participants need not know that their expectations in one relation are influenced by expectations from other relations for that influence to have effects. So long as individuals respond to the expectations of those they interact with, the sources of the expectations make no difference to their effectiveness. Thus, the organization of social relations does not depend upon participants' awareness of the connections which bring about that organization.

In the Alcalá case we saw that the relation between the millers and the go-between is connected to the relation between the go-between and the inspector even though the millers know little about the details of the latter relation. This means that the organization of these relations does not depend upon a shared understanding, found in the minds of participants, about what the organization is or ought to be.

The organization of culture and of social relations Both culture and social relations are organized, but their organizations are different in important ways. The organization of culture is in people's minds. The organization of social relations is by the influence those relations have on each other through conflict, mutual dependence or complementarity, and other sorts of connections we have just seen expectations in different relations to have. The organization of social relations comes from the way people actually act toward one another. These actions are influenced by other relations the people have, and people need not be aware of the source of the influence for it to be effective. Thus, the organization of culture exists in people's minds, but the organization of social relations occurs in their behavior.

The difference between the organization of social relations and the organization of culture points to a vital fact of human life: People participate in relations and contribute through participation in those interconnected relations to the maintenance of statuses that they may not know about. Even if they know about them, they may not approve of them or think them necessary. The series of relations centering around farming and milling in Alcalá provides a good example of this.

Farmers may not know the details of the relation between the supervisor and the inspector, and they may see the connection between that relation and their relation with "illegal" millers or they may not. It does not matter to the farmer-miller relation one way or the other. All that matters is that the farmers participate in relations with the millers. By participating they contribute to the maintenance of the inspector status and the supervisor status. The supervisor could not operate as such if he had no inspector to supervise; the inspector could not operate if he had no go-between to help him levy fines;[7] the go-between has no function without millers; and the millers are subject to fine only if they have farmers who give them something to mill. The farmers need know nothing of much of this. They may know or they may not, but it makes little difference to the operation of the system of relations. Simply by maintaining a relation with the miller the farmers are supporting the existence of the status of supervisor and all the others in the system.

One consequence of this whole system of relations is that the go-between has more power and prestige than most other residents of Alcalá. The people of Alcalá have an egalitarian ethic which holds that men should be equal, and none should have more power and prestige than others. But Fernando does have more power and prestige than others do. The farmers, by maintaining relations with millers, contribute to Fernando's power and prestige, however little they approve of it and whether or not they are aware of it. Similarly, by participating in a relation with millers, the farmers contribute to the continuation of the status of supervisor despite the possibility that they are unaware of such a status and the near certainty that they would disapprove of it if they knew about it.

What we have just seen is an example of people whose behavior contributes to a system of relations they need not be aware of or, if they are, need not think good or necessary. That connections between social relations operate without necessarily being in individuals' minds has many consequences. These can be summarized by saying that the organization of social relations leads to results (e.g., the prestige of the go-between) that would not be comprehensible from a knowledge of culture alone.

The effects of maintaining social relations   More of how social relations, and by extension the organization of social relations, work to influence human behavior can be seen by considering further. In deciding how to act in specific instances people often have to consider more than their own immediate wishes and the shared understandings that apply to the behavior at hand. The choice people face in real life is not just whether or not they want to do something. The issue is not even whether what they are considering is held in a favorable light by the understandings they share with others. Beyond these it is necessary for people to consider what effect their particular actions will have on their existing social relations.

Many of us have experienced situations in which we felt called on to do something we did not wish to do and, sometimes, something shared understandings held to be wrong. Someone, for example, asks if he may copy your exam. You do not really want him to have the benefit of your efforts when he failed to do the work you have done. Moreover, by agreeing to his cheating you are participating in behavior understood as bad by many you share culture with. Yet you do it.

---

[7]The inspector needs to levy fines to meet his supervisor's expectations, but if he puts the millers out of business through his fines he will be in the same hopeless situation as he would be if he levied no fines. He needs to know which millers can absorb fines and not go out of business, and the go-between is his souce of local information.

What is at stake in allowing the copying or not is the whole bundle of understandings attached to the relation with the other person, not just the single issue of copying. Your decision is probably based (in part, at least) on your view of your relation with the would-be copier. Refusing might disrupt or end the relation with that person, which affects your response. On the basis of the shared understandings concerning copying you would have refused; on the basis of your personal views and preferences you would have refused. However, on the basis of your wish to continue your relation with the copier—or your relations with his friends who might think you mistreat him by refusing—you agree to the copying. Among the variety of bases for behavior's being contrary to what is called for by shared understandings is the important one that people often have to choose among alternative actions not only according to their cultural acceptability but also according to their likely effect on relations with others. For people to maintain social relations they value, they sometimes have to do things that they personally do not like and that may even be contrary to some of their shared understandings.

People do not *have* to want to perform certain behavior to perform it. A common basis for this is that they may see a social relation they wish to maintain as dependent on that performance. They may not want to perform an act—whether it be copying, going to work, or giving to charity—but they perform it whether they do or not because they think it vital to some valued social relation.

Social structure, social relations, and the business of living Social relations, and the social structure that makes them possible, may sometimes lead people into circumstances they find disagreeable, but they are indispensable for accomplishing the things group members view as important and desirable. The farmer may not like the existence of the go-between status with its prestige and power. Even so, the farmer's relation with the miller contributes to the continuation of that status and makes it possible for the farmer to earn a living the only way he knows how. Earning a living is crucial to a farmer's occupying two statuses clearly desired by their occupants and understood as basically worthy: family head and adult village male. Thus his participation in the relation with the miller should not be viewed as wholly contrary to his wishes and shared understandings. The social relation with the miller is part of the means provided by the village social structure whereby farmers are able to earn a living.

Some consequences of the social structure and the social relations based on it, then, the farmer views as desirable, but others he dislikes and still others he does not know about. What is important for the understanding of behavior is that the farmer and everyone else in every organization of social relations participates in those relations for the value derived from the participation. People may not know about, or may not like if they do know about, all the aspects of their social relations, but these relations are the only culturally provided means to attain what shared understandings hold as "good" or necessary.

The difficulty in having alternative means to get what is generally desired comes from the fact that social relations are needed to do most things, and these must have a shared basis or they will not work. If a farmer in Alcalá does not want to deal with an illegal miller, he has three choices. He can sell to the legal mill, but if he does so, he will not be able to support himself or his family. He can try to change the laws that make illegal mills necessary, but he cannot do this alone, and in a country without any established means for the formation of popular political groups, what shared understandings will he use for this? Or he can give up farming, but the village has no provision for him to make a living in any other way.

People do not have to accept the social relations provided them by their shared understandings. To get new ones, though, they have to have other people who not only agree existing relations are less than desirable, but also share expectations in the new ones that will take their place. Note especially that a general agreement that something new would be better is not enough. There must be a foundation in the detailed agreement necessary for predictability.

Social structural change goes on constantly in all societies as statuses change their membership categories, their expectations, and the situations in which they are used as guides for action. Given that many relations are connected with many others, the changes in one relation will spread out to others and can alter the whole system of social relations. The need to agree on the expectations in a relation and what people and situations it is appropriate to somewhat checks the rapidity of change, so what is most common is relatively slow change over fairly long periods of time. Participants' dissatisfaction plays a role, but it is not enough by itself.

To sum up thus far, social structure provides people with a limited number of means for achieving culturally valued ends. It often forces them to choose between maintaining the social relations that constitute those means or giving up the ends. To maintain the relations, they may have to behave in ways they do not personally like and that are not understood as proper or good. Taking this with what we saw of the organization of social relations, it will be clear that social structure is an independent influence on human behavior.

Groups and the Distribution of Culture

So far our attention has been centered on how cultural elements are distributed among different statuses through their different expectations. In Alcalá the mill-repairer status includes the expectation that its occupant can keep milling machinery in working order so that the culturally valued task of grinding grain can go on. Other Alcalá residents do not share the understandings needed for maintaining the mills themselves, but they do not have to because they can count on the mill repairer. Whole groups also are understood as responsible for particular kinds of things. In almost all human societies, for example, the nuclear family, which is made up of parents and their offspring, has the main responsibility for caring for infants and young children. This assures that so long as culture actually guides behavior young children will be taken care of, and it frees other groups from direct concern with this activity. Similarly, there are groups that are understood as devoted to food production, others devoted to amusement, still others to religious activities, and so on.

A group is a collection of people, of course, but it is distinguished from other collections by two things. First, its members are aware of their membership and, second, they carry out activities jointly or cooperatively. Examples of groups include a student council, the workers in a factory department or office, and the members of a particular church. The people of Alcalá constitute a group in that they hold joint religious festivals and other village-wide activities not described in the discussion of the water dispute. If they did not have the festivals and other joint activities, they would not be a group. The people who live in white houses, women who have clefts in their chins, and men who have been in wars are not groups. They are categories of people in that they have some characteristic in common, but unless they think of themselves as group members and do something together, they are not groups. If all the people who have been in wars form an association such as the Veterans' League and if the Veterans' League meets or otherwise carries out projects involving the members, it becomes a group. A series of statuses made up of, say, leather producers, shoemakers, and shoe buyers is not a group because those involved do not think of themselves as belonging to a group. If the cobblers and leather makers banded together into a union or craft guild, they would be a group because the one missing quality, awareness of group membership, would then be present.

GROUP   *A collection of people who are aware of their group membership and who carry out activities jointly or cooperatively.*

New Guinea Groups at the Start of a Battle. Sometimes groups can have relations with each other in a way analogous to individuals'. Groups do this when they are acting as unified entities.

Groups and understandings concerning them   Groups must be distinguished from the shared understandings that are their basis just as social relations must be kept separate from the statuses and roles that guide the participants in those relations. People share understandings about what groups ought and ought not do, and these understandings may or may not be followed by the actual members of the groups. The fact that some nuclear families do not care for their infants and young children as culture prescribes does not change the fact that such care is culturally assigned to nuclear families. The families that do not follow the prescription will almost certainly be judged as "bad" families in the same way that individuals would be censured for violating the expectations of their statuses.

People share understandings about groups, which is the basis for their members' and also for nonmembers' knowing what to expect from them. These understandings include criteria for membership as well as prescriptions for what they are to do. Some groups are based on relations of kinship, and membership is only possible for those born to particular parents. In many societies there are groups in which membership is based on descent in the male line or on descent in the female line. A person belongs to one of these kinship groups according to the one his father or his mother belongs to. Other societies have kinship groups made up of the relatives of both parents. The last sort is found in this society as well as among most Eskimo groups, some ethnic groups in Ethiopia, the Gilbert Islanders in the Pacific, and others. In the urban parts of North America and much of Europe, however, the bilateral kin groups (i.e., groups based on both parents' relatives) are sometimes social categories rather than groups since the members never do anything jointly or cooperatively and do not think of themselves as members of such a group. Whether kinship forms the base for groups or for categories, membership is not voluntary, and people have no choice about being considered members. Birth is the sole criterion. (Family and kinship are discussed more completely in Chapter 5.)

Kinship status as determined by who the parents are is a criterion for membership in important groups in every society, but it is often not the sole criterion, even for membership in groups of kin. A group may be composed, to take an example that is important in a number of societies, of the descendants of a particular ancestor (i.e., kinship-status criterion) who live in the same area (residential criterion). Other groups may be based on a combination of residence and interest, as when, for example, the people who live in a neighborhood and want to work for a new park in their area form a neighborhood association. Still other groups can be made up of people who neither live near each other nor share ancestors. The musicians in a band may live anywhere in a city but are united by their common activity and their mutually agreed-on ability to play instruments.

In addition to the cultural elements that set the criteria for group membership and indicate what a group is supposed to do, there are others that prescribe the quality of group relations and how important the group is to

its members and others. Some groups are understood as being supportive, emotionally warm, and tolerant in their evaluation of their members' behavior. Other groups are culturally defined as more businesslike, demanding, and strict in evaluating performance. Groups and membership in them may be understood as more important than what they do. In many societies, for example, people are expected to support their families regardless of how family members may violate shared understandings. In late dynastic China (a period roughly extending from the fifteenth century to the early twentieth century) the importance of family membership was so great that it was not only improper but also illegal for a person to testify in court against a close relative. Membership in other kinds of groups is thought of as contingent upon the proper behavior of the other members. A person might be expected to quit working for a company that cheated its customers.

Groups and statuses   In a number of ways, then, groups are the subject of shared understandings. These understandings are partly separate from those that concern the separate statuses in the group. Because only individuals can act, and only through their actions can groups meet (or fail to meet) their cultural assignments, it is worthwhile to consider for a moment how the culture that is assigned to groups can affect behavior. In part it comes about through the expectations of the groups' constituent statuses. If the occupants of the statuses father, mother, son, and daughter *all* meet the expectations associated with those statuses, most of the shared understandings concerning the nuclear family will be met. A single individual cannot do this alone, however. If a woman met every expectation in her status as

Group of Tongan Chiefs. Chiefly rank establishes membership in this group on the Pacific island of Tonga. Only chiefs are allowed to play the billiardlike game pictured. Group boundaries are so strict that in former times a commoner who tried to assert membership in the chiefly group by playing the game would have been put to death.

mother, this by itself would not make the nuclear family she belonged to culturally conforming. Only if most of the others in the family met the expectations of their family statuses could the family fulfill the shared understandings regarding family behavior and task performance. Most of the cultural prescriptions assigned to groups can be met if all or almost all occupants of the group's statuses meet their expectations.

Whatever cultural elements are not taken care of by assignment to individual statuses are part of another status, that of group member. In addition to being mothers, or sons, or fathers, the family members have a common status, family member, and in it they are expected to behave similarly. Everyone who holds the status family member may be expected to defend other occupants of that status against outsiders. There may be other expectations in the group-member status, so that regardless of whether it is a son dealing with a father, a mother dealing with a daughter, or any other combination, all the family members are expected to be tolerant and kind in dealing with all the others. It is through the combined expectations in the particular statuses that make up a group and those in the status-group member that all the culture associated with a group comes to bear as a guide for behavior.

Group membership and the working of groups   Group membership is sometimes a goal in itself. People, for example, may want to belong to, say, a religious group because of their view of the worth of that group and for no other reason. Group membership may also be a necessary step in reaching some other goal; that is, the culturally provided means for doing something may entail membership in one or more groups. In the Oyo kingdom of the Yoruba people in Nigeria during the nineteenth century, political power was divided between the hereditary king and a secret cult group, the Ogboni Society. The head of this group had the power to have the king killed if he and his group believed the king guilty of misrule. People who belonged to certain kin groups could get political power through joining Ogboni. They might value membership in the group on religious grounds because this group was concerned with relations with the ancestors, or they might want to belong in order to have a part in the politics of the kingdom. In either case the group played a key role in the lives of individuals and in the religion and politics of the kingdom (Morton-Williams 1967:53–60).

Groups, then, like social relations in general, can be seen as providing commonly understood means and ends in specific circumstances and for particular people. Also like social relations in general, maintaining or establishing group membership can have its own influence on behavior. We saw in the water dispute and in considering exam cheating that people, to maintain a relation, carry out particular behaviors whether or not the behaviors are desirable in themselves. The same sort of thing applies to behavior related to group membership with the further fact that whole relations may be maintained not because they are necessarily personally or culturally valued for themselves, but because they are understood as necessary for group membership.

It will be clear that groups are part of the distribution of culture. Their position as ends in themselves and as culturally provided means to other ends influences people to act in ways that contribute to the maintenance of the groups. Naturally, particular groups can break up without having much, or any, widespread effect. The members of the X family may all die or may be unable or unwilling to continue relations with each other. The disappearance of a specific family or other small-scale group has little general significance, although when the specific group is understood as very important, as a royal family often is, or is central to many relations as a factory group in a one-company town is, the consequences can be considerable.

The breakup of a *type* of group is more complex, and considering such phenomena tells us more about how groups work. For nuclear families in general to break up (and the same is true of lesser changes), the people who participate in them must undergo one or several changes. The understandings in which the family is an end as well as those in which it is a means to some other end must be reassigned to other relations not in the family group; or the understandings (of both kinds) must change. For example, if the family vanished, child rearing would have to be assigned to some other group. Were this to happen, the changes in areas of life outside the nuclear family would be considerable as relations in these areas took on the understandings that had been in the family or were affected by the need to readjust behavior and reassign expectations because they were centered on the now-vanished family.

In fact, the nuclear family group has never ceased to exist in a known human group, although substantial differences in its constituent relations and in the understandings associated with it are found in different groups and in the same group over time. Other kinds of groups cease to exist quite regularly. The medieval guilds in Europe are one example, and the Plains Indian soldier societies are another. To understand such phenomena and the less dramatic but more common ones found in the gradual change of groups' relations and associated understandings requires a considerable knowledge of the distribution of culture and of the ways social structure works. So far there has been little discussion of the differences between types of groups and the connections between groups. We turn to those topics now.

Differences between Kinds of Groups

Groups differ in what they are expected to do, the quality of the relations among their members, and in other ways we have just considered. They also differ in a number of ways that are relatively separate from these. For example, without regard to what the groups are expected to do, whether the members support each other, and so on, the members of some groups are in direct, face-to-face contact with each other. Every member of this sort of group has a relation with every other. The nuclear family is always a group of this sort. Other examples of this kind of group are small, isolated villages;

work crews; seminars at universities; and nomadic bands. These are often called "primary groups."

In another kind of group the members are not all in direct relations with each other. Everyone in these groups has direct ties with *some* other members, but everyone does not have a relation with everyone else. The large kinship groups anthropologists have found in some parts of the world include groups spread out over wide areas, and they are usually of this type. Other examples of "secondary groups," as these are called, are big corporations, colleges, and whole societies. A "society" is the most inclusive group to which people think of themselves as belonging, and it is unusual for all the members of any society to have direct relations with all the others. The relations among the members of a society are organized, but members may well not know of the existence of some other member. The same is true of relations in all other groups of this type.

Another sort of group that is important in understanding humanity is called a "corporate group." As with many terms applying to human behavior, this one is given different meanings by different anthropologists. Two characteristics often used in defining this term are group ownership of property and group responsibility for the actions of individual members. Sometimes the two characteristics are used together and sometimes separately. There can be no doubt that groups having joint responsibility affect their members differently from those that do not. In societies where revenge is practiced, for example, it is sometimes considered acceptable to kill one person in retribution for a murder commited by some fellow group member of his. Similarly, property-holding groups are different from groups without property, and this is true whether the property is land, buildings, animals, or religious rites. One important characteristic of such a group is that its members are under special pressure to act as their fellows think they should because otherwise they can be cut off from access to the group's property.

The property-owning and common-responsibility characteristics do not always occur in the same groups, so while we recognize that both influence how groups work, we must choose between them. Here, "corporate group" will be defined as referring only to groups that have common responsibility. Property-owning groups can be designated "property-owning group (corporate)" and "property-owning group (noncorporate)," depending on whether or nor joint responsibility is present.

The Relations between Groups

So far the discussion has dealt only with the internal operation and organization of groups. Now we turn to the ways groups are related to each other and the consequences of these relations.

Groups can make each other's operation difficult. The peer group of adolescents in America, much of Europe, and elsewhere makes demands on

PRIMARY GROUP
A group in which members have direct, face-to-face relations with each other, and every member has a relation with every other.

SECONDARY GROUP
A group in which members have direct relations with some other members, but everyone does not have a relation with everyone else.

SOCIETY *The largest group people think of themselves as belonging to. It is almost always a secondary group.*

CORPORATE GROUP
A group whose members are responsible for each others' actions. There are property-owning corporate groups and others that do not jointly own property.

members' time, and the shared understandings associated with the group call for behavior that brings it into conflict with the nuclear-family groups its members also belong to. Groups can also support each other. The Bena dispute-settlement session described at the beginning of the last chapter supports other groups by providing a means for ending conflicts between their members, as when it mediates family quarrels, for example. At the same time, its requirements do not interfere with the requirements of the other groups its members belong to. The *baraza* meets mainly on Sundays and at other times when the other groups its members belong to do not require their presence. Membership in a *baraza* group does not normally call for money or other resources needed in other groups (save for a member who is fined), and it presents no problems in requiring loyalty that is called for by other groups its members belong to.

Groups need not be either strongly mutually supporting or in serious conflict, but each calls for its members to guide their behavior by the culture associated with it while it is operating. Because, however, everyone in every society belongs to a number of different groups, culturally provided means must be available to allow each group's members to know when that group and its associated understandings rather than another should be the basis for action. Without such provisions groups could not function.

Individuals recognize what group is the appropriate focus of attention in basically the same way that they recognize their own status and the statuses of those they are dealing with. Take, for example, a woman who belongs to a family group where her statuses are wife and mother and an office group where her status is manager. The personnel of the two groups are likely to be different, and the settings are almost certain to be different with one location and type of room for the office group and a quite different location and type of building for the home group. The issues that face her in one group are such things as the family budget, a child's progress in school, and relations with other families, while the office group presents issues having to do with work schedules, payrolls, and so on. When she walks into her office, she knows the understandings associated with the work group and its social relations are the proper guides for her behavior. Her concern with the family will usually be put into the background until she returns home.

People are sometimes forced to decide between participation in one group and in another. Shared organizing understandings often make this choice obvious. The woman in our example would often be acting in accord with a shared ranking of different understandings in putting her family's needs over her office group's needs if such a choice were forced upon her. Should one of her children fall ill and her husband be unavailable, she would be criticized by everyone (probably including her boss) if she did not leave the office to go home and care for him. Sometimes this sort of choice is not so clearly made, and shared organizing understandings do not exist. For example, if everyone in the family wants to go on a trip and she has been asked to do important work at the office, her behavior is likely to be viewed as improper by the members of one of the two groups whichever decision she makes.

When different groups are totally separated in their activities, times of operation, and demands, the relations between the groups pose few problems for their members, and the groups operate without mutual interference. A literary-discussion group that meets only at night and ends early poses no serious problems for a work group that meets only in the daytime. People can belong to both and experience no difficulty. Similarly, quite different groups can exist and even have some of the same people as members if their activities take place over different periods of time. People in military organizations and in residential educational institutions usually still belong to family groups. It is understood that while the person is away from the family, the military or educational group's requirements must direct the person's behavior in most things, and it is also understood that when the person returns home, he will resume family duties. This arrangement may not remove all conflict, but it does allow both groups to exist and to have their culturally assigned tasks carried out.

Indian Aristocrats at a Reception for Queen Elizabeth. Participation in the reception shown here is directly based on membership in an aristocratic caste group; other memberships that the individuals have are not immediately relevant to that participation, nor do they conflict with it.

The Organization of Inclusive Groups

Our main concern has been with relations between small-scale groups. The family, the office group, and the *baraza* generally have only relatively few members. None of these groups is made up of members all of whom belong to some other, smaller-scale group. In the office group some workers may belong to families and some may not. The office is made up without regard to the other groups its members belong to. There are groups, however, whose membership is made up entirely of people who belong to the same sort of smaller-scale groups. The United Nations is an obvious example. All its members belong to national groups, and whatever else the United Nations may be, it is large scale. The organization of such large-scale and inclusive groups can be of two basic kinds, each with different consequences for the group and for the smaller-scale groups whose members compose them.

The inclusive group can be organized through the union of the smaller groups that compose it. This is how the United Nations is organized. Citizens from different countries do not belong directly; their governments represent them. This is a group-of-groups organization.

Alternatively, the inclusive group can be organized directly and without any role being played by the smaller-scale groups its members belong to. The New England town meeting as a form of governmental group is a clear example of this direct organization. Everyone in the town is a member of the meeting and has a right to speak and vote regardless of his standing in such smaller-scale groups as the family, work groups, church groups, or any others.

The different consequences of the two types of organization of inclusive groups can be seen by examining a hypothetical village and the kinds of social relations it would have in each of the two types. In the direct organization all the residents would relate to each other in the village context in the status fellow villager. Individuals would be the unit of organization. Their different statuses in the village's component groups would have no effect, or at least none would be culturally prescribed, on their relations with each other as villagers. Each of them would have his own separate relationship with the village chief, and this relation would be the same for everyone.

Alternatively, the family (or some other small-scale village group) could be the unit of village organization instead of individuals. With this arrangement a person's status in the family group would also be his status in the village group. A man would follow the expectations of his father status, for example, in village affairs as well as in family affairs. In addition to his roles linking him to the other members of the family, however, the father would have a role in this status that concerned relations with occupants of the same status (i.e., other fathers) in other families. Thus, there could be a role in the status father that contained expectations for relations with the fathers in other families. These relations among fathers might form a village council. Every father status in the village could also contain a role connecting the father, and through him his family, to the village chief. The villagers, in

INCLUSIVE GROUP
*A group all of whose
members also belong to
the same sort of
smaller-scale group.*

this group-of-groups organization, relate to each other as family members and through their family statuses. The two ways of organizing inclusive groups are shown in the accompanying diagram.

The consequences of different inclusive-group organizations The two different ways of organizing a village group, or any inclusive group, both work, although we will see that the separate and independent organization of larger groups rarely exists by itself. Each has characteristics not shared with the other, and it is useful to note some of these. The village group that is formed through relations connecting its constituent families uses the strength of the family relations as part of its own cohesiveness. As long as family relations are maintained—particularly, in our example, relations with the father—and the understandings associated with the family group are potent, all that is needed for village-group unity is for relations between the heads of each family and between them and the village head to remain in force. In this sort of village social structure there is usually little serious conflict between an individual's expectations as a member of his family group and as a member of the village group. The strength of the village group, in other words, derives from the strength of the family groups.

It will be apparent, however, that the constituent groups in a larger group with this sort of organization can break away rather easily. If the village chief and some family father cannot maintain their relation, a whole family group may be lost to the village rather than just the individual who is having trouble with the chief. If we think of the village as an organization based not on families but on neighborhood groups held together by a relation

Two Ways of Organizing Groups: group of groups (a) and separately organized inclusive groups (b). One way of organizing an inclusive group is by a union of smaller groups that compose it. A second way of forming inclusive groups is by an entirely new set of relations that supersede those of smaller groupings.

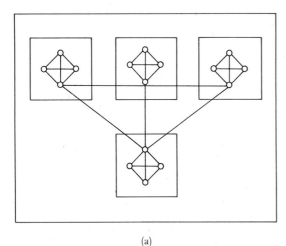

(a)

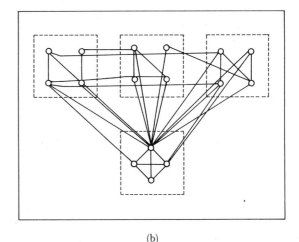

(b)

o = individual

—— = relation based on social structure

▭ = operating group boundary

⌐ ⌐ = group boundary *not* operating in this context

**Village Meeting in
Taiwan.** Families in this
village are united partly
through the family heads'
relations with one another
as participants in village
meetings. This makes a
group-of-groups
organization.

between a few neighborhood-group leaders and a village chief, the danger to
village unity resulting from reliance on a very few relations as the basis of
that unity will be clear. The ability of the village group to do anything
would depend on the near unanimous agreement of the neighborhood-
group leaders. If some of the leaders did not agree, there would be no easy
way for their neighborhood-group members to participate in the village
activities even if they wanted to. Their only role in the village group is the
one in their status in the neighborhood group that ties them to the neighborhood leader. The strength of the neighborhood ties contributes to the
unity of the village, but the possibility of the village breaking up into its
constituents is always present and can result from conflict between only a
few individuals if they are occupants of the crucial statuses of neighborhood
leader and village chief.

The group-of-groups type of organization is found not only in villages but
also in all sorts of inclusive groups including whole societies. Sometimes the
groups that make up the larger society organized in this way are based on
kinship ties, sometimes on regional groupings, and sometimes on class and
caste groupings. The details of the social organization of these sorts of
societies differ, of course, but a central issue for all is what sorts of relations
tie their constituent groups together. Knowing this is indispensable to understanding the organization of these societies.

Inclusive groups organized on the basis of statuses that are not part of
smaller groups lack the potential for splitting (the technical term is "fission")
that the groups made up of groups have. Separately organized groups do not
base their unity on a few key relationships as the ones organized in the other

FISSION *The breaking
up of a group into its
constituent parts; most
often used when an
inclusive group splits
into the smaller groups
that compose it.*

way do. Their unity comes from the strength of all the relations that unite group members as such. This sort of group does not have the limitations that exist when the activities of the group must be restricted to those compatible both with the organization of constituent groups and the interests of the particular individuals who occupy the statuses that join those groups together.

However, relying entirely on statuses that are not rooted in smaller-group membership has problems of its own, particularly when the groups so organized are of the "secondary-group" sort. An obvious problem is that the larger group cannot draw on the strength of the other groups its members belong to. In fact, the strength of these other groups may weaken the unity of the larger group. In a village organized around family or neighborhood groups, people do not have to choose between acting as members of a village group or of the smaller groups. In a village organized without reference to these, they do have to choose. If the family's activities require their services at the same time the village needs them, they may well choose family work. If it happens often, the structure of the village will either change to a group of groups or the village group will cease to exist.

Mixed-group organization Inclusive groups organized completely independently of statuses in some of the constituent groups—families, at least—are very rare. The only example that comes to mind is utopian communities of various kinds. Even in these, where the whole community is supposed to be unitary and undivided, smaller groups develop and a group-of-groups organization emerges after a time.

Statuses in inclusive groups separate from those in the smaller groups do occur, of course. However, they occur *in addition* to the ones members hold in the smaller groups rather than as the sole basis for participation in the inclusive group. A university-faculty group is a good example of this. Instructors are members of departments, of colleges, and of the university faculty as a whole. Each of these groups meets and has its own statuses. A person is a professor of anthropology, one of the faculty members in the liberal arts college, and a member of the university faculty. These statuses have different expectations, but they are overlapping and interlocked. Each group has understandings concerning its activities, importance, and so on, and these too are separate but overlapping. The university can be looked at as organized according to departments, and for some purposes (e.g., the allocation of funds and the employment of professors) the relations between the group's members can be best understood if relations within and between departments are considered. The university can also be looked at as organized according to colleges, and some activities are best understood if relations within and between these groups—as mediated through deans—are the focus of attention. The university is also organized as a whole without reference to departments or colleges. In the academic senate, departmental and college statuses are not supposed to be active, and a shared understanding is that action will be guided by the overall good and interests of the university as a whole, with each member of the senate relating directly to the president. There is both, then, organization involving groups tied together to form a larger group and people independent from the constituent groups directly brought together without reference to those constituent groups.

Many sorts of inclusive groups have both organizations at the same time. Examples are large companies with many departments (manufacturing, transportation, sales), governments with different ministries, whole nations with states, regions, and so on. In all these, both direct membership and membership in constituent groups play parts in the social organization of the inclusive group.

Inclusive groups without leaders In urban, industrial societies and in some others, inclusive groups always have leadership statuses. The smaller-scale groups we have just considered as examples make use of the common practice of having a leader (either an individual or a group such as a council) as the focus of unifying relations. Common as this is, however, it is not universal. Small-scale groups can be knit together without there being a chief or leader of any kind. Until the last few decades a considerable number of societies had no leadership statuses, but despite this they had large-scale inclusive groups. The foundation for this leaderless unity is the fact that different groups have different culturally assigned activities and only through membership in a number of different kinds of groups can individuals do the variety of things their understandings hold to be necessary and desirable. In other words, the distribution of culture itself can be the basis for uniting small-scale groups into an inclusive group.

The Nuer[8] of the southern Sudan in Africa provide a striking example of this. Although they have no formal leadership statuses, groups as large as 60,000 individuals exist and actually carry out joint activities. The Nuer live by herding and by growing millet during part of the year. The nuclear families of brothers live together with the families of other patrilineally (i.e., tracing descent only through males) related men. These small groups of families form hamlets and villages, which are the basic units of Nuer social organization. Because of the extremely harsh environment in which the Nuer live, these hamlets must maintain relations with other hamlets so that if adverse local conditions destroy their food supply, they can borrow from their neighbors. The need to have ties with groups beyond the immediate village is increased by the fact that during the wet season parts of Nuerland are flooded and during the dry season water is found in only a few places. The family groups must move around in the area surrounding their village during the year, which requires that they maintain peaceful relations with the groups that live in the area. The area is populated by the families of men who have a common male ancestor with each other so that the type of kinship ties that form the basis for the village also form the basis for the more inclusive territorial group around the village. The kin ties in the village

[8]This is pronounced "newer," as in "This is new but that is *newer*."

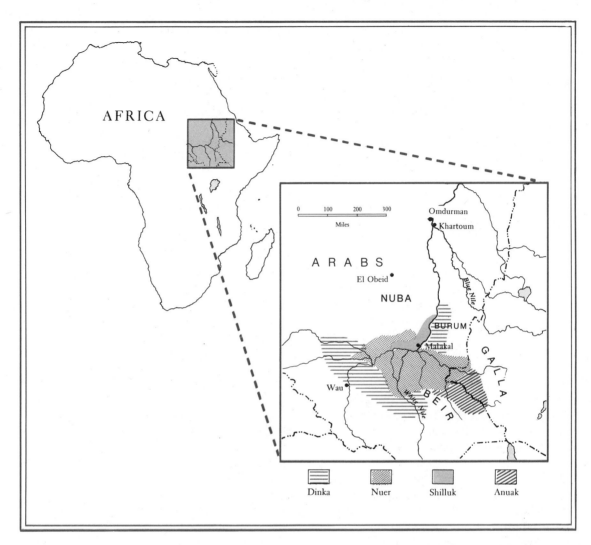

Dinka   Nuer   Shilluk   Anuak

Nuerland in Sudan.
(Data from Evans-
Pritchard 1940:4.)

are closer than those in the broader area, however. In the village the men are the sons of a single father and, perhaps, some of the sons of that father's brothers. In the district around the village all the men are descended from a common ancestor, but the ancestor is two or three generations back. In neighboring districts the men are related through a common ancestor even further back.

The Nuer are extremely independent and warlike people. They raid neighboring groups to steal cattle and this includes other Nuer groups as well as "foreigners." Fighting does not seem to occur within a hamlet or village, but beyond that, raiding and feuding do. The fascinating thing about the relations between Nuer groups is that the same ones that fight each other in some conditions unite against a common enemy in others. If there is a quarrel between two men from different but nearby villages, the men of each village will rally behind their fellow villager in a fight that will be between the two village groups. Should the quarrel involve men from two villages in different districts, each would be supported by the men from all the villages in his district even though there may have been recent fighting between some of those village groups. Should a quarrel involve people from any of the several different Nuer tribes (the largest unit in which they recognize relations of kinship is called a "tribe"), each would be supported not only by all the village groups in his district but also by all the district groups in his tribe. In the accompanying diagram, if a person from village A3 quarrels with a person from village A1, the two village groups will fight each other. If a person from district IA quarrels with someone from district IB, villages A1, A2, A3, and A4 will unite against all the villages in district IB. If a person from tribe I quarrels with someone from tribe II, districts IA and IB will unite against the districts of tribe II.

The Nuer, then, unite into very large groups for martial purposes, and they do this without any reference to leadership statuses. In fact, they have no statuses of this sort that play a part in forming their inclusive groups. The unity comes from the fact that in certain circumstances the only culturally provided means to survive is to become part of an inclusive group, which often involves joining with people who are enemies in other contexts. When there is a quarrel with people from another district, the members of nearby village groups must join together in mutual defense because they will be facing the united forces of the other district. As the British anthropologist Max Gluckman puts this basis for unity, Nuer society is organized "into a series of groups and relationships [in which] people who are friends on one basis are enemies on another. Herein lies social cohesion, rooted in the conflicts between men's different allegiances" (1963a:4).

Forming leaderless inclusive groups need not be based on mutual defense

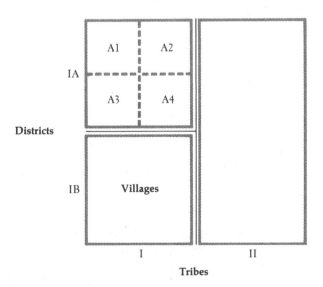

Districts

Tribes

Nuer Sections. If a person from village A3 quarrels with a person from village A1, the two village groups will fight each other. If a person from district IA quarrels with a person from IB, villages A1, A2, A3, and A4 will unite against all the villages in district IB. If someone from tribe I quarrels with someone from tribe II, districts IA and IB will unite against the districts of tribe II. (Based on Evans-Pritchard 1950:144.)

Nuer Dueling. Fission and fusion (separation and combination) are focused on groups uniting with others when quarrels occur.

as it is for the Nuer. Members of different smaller-scale groups may have ties with each other that make them unwilling to have these groups break apart to such an extent that they cannot maintain their relations. The Cheyenne Indians, about whom more will be seen in Chapter 13, "Politics," lived most of the year in separate bands. Their fighting men, however, were organized into Soldier Societies, and all of these save one[9] required that their members be drawn from different bands in the society rather than just one. The members of the Soldier Societies had close ties with each other, which meant that any tendency for the bands to break off relations with each other would be countered by the ties of their member males to men in other bands with whom they shared Soldier Society membership. The military societies drew their members from different bands; that is, the former ties cut across the latter. Gluckman has shown that such "cross-cutting ties" are vital parts of inclusive group organization in many societies where they can form the sole basis for unity and or where they add to the unity derived from common ties to a leader.[10]

[9]One society, the Dog Soldiers, drew its members from a single band, and the Cheyenne always viewed this society as different from and less trustworthy than the other Soldier Societies. It is of some value as a curiosum to note that the term "dogface" used for American soldiers in World War II probably derived from the Cheyenne Dog Society.

[10]Gluckman has discussed his important ideas concerning such ties in a number of places. An easily available and compelling presentation is found in Politics, Law, and Ritual (1965:91–121).

SUMMARY

"Social structure" refers to the relations between people and the organization of those relations. Because of the need for order in social life, people must be able to predict within acceptable limits what other people will do. Culture is the basic solution to this problem for humans, and it forms the basis for social structure. Culture is distributed by social structure so that it is possible to have agreement on which of the understandings shared apply to what sort of people in which circumstances. Statuses are social categories based on shared understandings that specify who belongs in the categories. Other shared understandings, called "expectations," are assigned to these categories, and they concern all the ways the members of the categories should behave under various circumstances and how others should behave toward them. The expectations for a particular relation are called a "role."

Relations are often interlocked with other relations through the effect their expectations have on each other. When the interlocking of expectations in different relations is present, the relations are said to be organized. For this organization to influence behavior, it is only necessary that the participants in the relations in question be influenced by the expectations in their separate relations. It makes no difference whether or not they know that the source of some of these expectations is to be found in another relation, which means that the components of social structure need not all be in a person's mind, as those of culture must, in order to influence his behavior. Social structure provides people with the social relations whereby they may attain goals that shared understandings or personal wishes or both make desirable. There are always a limited number of such means, however, which leads people sometimes to act in ways that may not be culturally or personally desirable. They do so to maintain relations that, whether desirable in themselves or not, are needed to attain desired goals.

Groups are organized series of relations that people recognize as existing and on which they center shared understandings, some of which involve joint or cooperative activities. Group membership may be a culturally desirable end in itself or it may be part of the culturally provided means for attaining some other desired end. Groups are often both. Just as everyone has many statuses, every society has a number of groups. People always have multiple membership and must switch groups from time to time and situation to situation. These groups may be very inclusive, a society being the most inclusive one to which people think of themselves as belonging, or much smaller in scale. Some groups include the members of others, either by uniting the constituent groups while retaining their structure or by uniting the larger group members on a basis independent from the structure of the smaller groups. The last is quite rare as the sole means of uniting large groups, but the two are often combined as different parts of the structure of a single, large group. Different groups are also held together by the fact that their members need the different groups to attain their different ends and strive to avoid their being irrevocably divided.

SUGGESTED READINGS

More on the case

PITT-RIVERS, J. A.   1961   The People of the Sierra. Chicago: University of Chicago Press.

The ethnography from which the case for this chapter is taken.

Other readings

BARTH, F.   1959   Segmentary Opposition and the Theory of Games: A Study of Pathan Organization. Journal of the Royal Anthropological Institute 89:5–20. Reprinted as Bobbs-Merrill Reprint A-370.

An analysis of how political groups recruit members among the Pathan of Pakistan. The groups are based on patrilineal descent, but only the father and his sons form an indissoluble union, and the children of brothers unite and divide according to carefully calculated personal advantage.

GLUCKMAN, M.   1963   Gossip and Scandal. Current Anthropology 4:307–316. Reprinted as Bobbs-Merrill Reprint A-209.

A fascinating discussion of how scandal and gossip serve to unite groups, separate one from another, and help mark the status of "group member."

HOEBEL, E. A.   1954   The Law of Primitive Man. Cambridge, Mass.: Harvard.

This study of Cheyenne law and politics proceeds through the careful analysis of what Hoebel calls "trouble cases" in much the way most of the chapters of this book do. Hoebel uses the concept "postulates" much as "basic understandings" is used here and makes a telling analysis of the relation between politics and culture.

MALINOWSKI, B.   1939   The Group and the Individual in Functional Analysis. American Journal of Sociology 64:938–960. Reprinted as Bobbs-Merrill Reprint S-183.

A classical statement of the effects of multiple-group membership and the relations between groups from the point of view of the individual.

MERTON, R.   1940   Adult Roles and Personality. Social Forces 17:560–568.

This article uses the framework of bureaucracy to consider still-important questions of role performance.

4

Personality

The goal towards which the pleasure-principle impels us—of becoming happy—is not attainable; yet we may not—nay, cannot—give up the effort to come nearer to realization of it by some means or other. Very different paths may be taken towards it: some pursue the positive aspect of the aim, attainment of pleasure; others the negative, avoidance of pain. By none of these ways can we achieve all that we desire.

FREUD
CIVILIZATION AND ITS DISCONTENTS, 1930

The most crucial early experience is social.

What is the relationship between the individual and his group?
How does the individual come to behave as his culture requires him to?
How does he violate its prescriptions?
What is personality, and how is it related to culture?
How is personality related to social structure?

The Puzzle of Individual Behavior: A Case of Wealth, Women, and Trade in Indonesia

Adult men on the island of Alor in Indonesia[1] are preoccupied with an elaborate financial system involving endless debts, loans, profits, and losses. The currency in this system is composed of metal kettledrums (*mokos*) and gongs. Pigs can be traded for these two sorts of valuables, and the men raise pigs mainly to gain control of valuables rather than to add to the regular, daily food supply. Women do not participate directly in the financial system. Their main activity is producing food, and from the point of view of providing the necessities of daily life, their work is more crucial than the men's is. The valuables that concern the men have great social significance, but play little direct part in the business of making a living.

The workings of the financial system center on several kinds of key social events. One is the giving of feasts for the dead to placate the spirits of deceased relatives. Omission of these feasts with their displays of wealth and payment of debts can lead to the spirits' bringing illnesses on their surviving kin. Another focus for financial dealings is marriage. To get a wife, a young man must provide a substantial collection of *mokos* and gongs to the woman's family. He does not have to give his future in-laws all the valuables at once, but he must provide a large down payment before they will allow their sister/daughter to be his wife. The remainder of the marriage wealth is paid over a long period. Frequently, debts still outstanding from the marriage of a couple are assumed by the sons of a marriage after their father's death.

The basic mechanism of the financial system on Alor is lending out valuables with the expectation that the loan will be returned with interest. When a man wants to accumulate marriage wealth for himself or his son, for example, he goes to all those who owe him valuables and tries to get them to return to him gongs and *mokos* of greater value than those he earlier lent them. He also tries to borrow additional valuables from other men. The main goal for all Alorese men is to succeed in this exchange system and to become "rich." It is a deadly insult to refer to a man as "poor," and adult men spend much of their time making "deals" with debtors and creditors. A rich man does not actually have large numbers of valuables in his possessions; rather, he has many people in his debt to call on to provide him with gongs and *mokos*. When a man does manage to get together a large collection of valuables, he almost always passes them on to others either to satisfy old debts or to put others in his debt.

Success in the Alorese financial system comes from a man's ability to get other men to lend him valuables at the same time that he keeps from repaying his debts for as long as possible. The making and repaying of loans is a highly elaborate and time-consuming undertaking, depending on endless dunning of debtors with threats, pleas, and rages (mostly mock) as part of the effort. A man seriously engaged in calling in debts and getting loans will usually make magic to "bring

[1]This case is based on Cora Du Bois, The People of Alor, University of Minnesota Press, Minneapolis. © 1944 by the University of Minnesota. With permission.

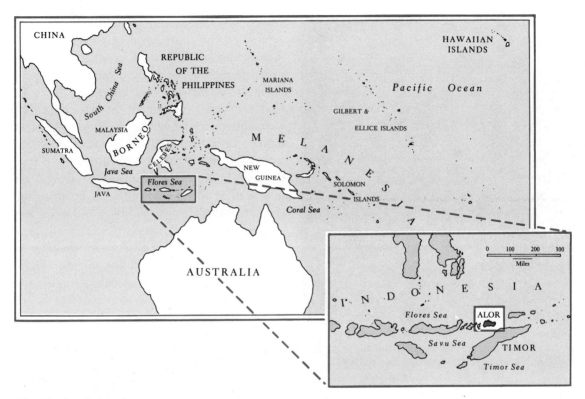

Alor Island in Indonesia.

in the valuables" and will abstain from sexual relations lest his ability to bend debtors and creditors to his will be diminished.

Participation in the financial system is held up to boys as the most important male activity, and even in early adolescence the boys sometimes try to emulate their fathers by accumulating valuables. Active involvement in exchanges, however, most commonly begins with attempts to arrange marriage. A youth's marriage wealth may come mainly from his father, or from some other mature man who has been successful in the sys-

tem, or he may get all the needed valuables by himself. In whatever way the wealth is collected, a man must have it to marry, and he must marry to be thought of as a fully mature and significant member of his group. A few men (but virtually no women) fail to marry; and such hapless males are dismissed as "worthless." Getting the wealth for a down payment to the future in-laws can be, however, full of difficulties for the young man.

The case of Senlaka, a twenty-six-year-old bachelor, shows how trying this can be. Being unmarried at twenty-six is rather shameful in

Alorese Financier. Success in the Alorese financial system is the result of getting others to lend valuables while delaying the repayment of debts as long as possible.

Alor, but Senlaka had a particularly painful introduction to the financial system. When he was in his early teens, his father gave him a piglet, which was to launch him on his financial career and provide the basis for his marriage wealth. Senlaka industriously fattened his pig with the intention of contributing it to someone's death feast or kin-house feast and thus establishing a credit for which he could later demand a gong or *moko*. However, when the pig was ready to be used in an exchange, Senlaka's father unceremoniously took it away from him and, without repayment, used it for a death feast. Senlaka was enraged by his father's actions (even though Alorese parents quite frequently seize their children's property and break promises they have made them), and he resolved to stay out of the financial system. He kept his resolve for more than ten years, but finally he found a girl he wanted to marry, which gave him no choice other than to involve himself in the loans and debts.

His father had died by this time, so he took the single *moko* he had managed to acquire to a successful financier who promised he would invest it to Senlaka's great profit. After some weeks of waiting, his girl's family became impatient and threatened to give their sister/daughter to another man if Senlaka did not produce at least part of the marriage wealth. Senlaka went to the financier and asked for the proceeds from the use of his *moko*, but the older man told him he had to turn the profits from the exchange of Senlaka's *moko* over to another debtor. If Senlaka would give him another *moko*, the financier said, the proceeds from the two could be combined, and Senlaka could satisfy his future in-laws. Another older man told Senlaka that if he could get his valuable back from the first financier, it could be quickly employed in an exchange that would lead to enough wealth to satisfy the girl's increasingly insistent family.

Senlaka demanded his *moko* of the first financier, who said that Senlaka would just have to wait for it. Senlaka then threatened to take the financier before a chief and sue him. He was reluctant to seek government help because doing so would eliminate all chance of getting interest on the loan, but the financier was delaying so

Moko. One of the main objects used in the Alorese
financial system is the *moko,* or kettledrum.

long and the demands for a marriage-wealth
payment were so pressing that he had no choice.
When the financier saw what Senlaka's intention
was, however, he returned the *moko* to avoid the
shame of a court case.

After months of talks with the financier and
others under the constant prodding of his future
in-laws, Senlaka was right back where he started.
His attempts to gain wealth had accomplished
nothing, and the possibility of losing the girl to
a richer man was greater than ever. His only hope
appeared to be the second financier, and he was
not optimistic about what could be expected
from him. He told the anthropologist: "Here
older men try to cheat the young ones. It's a lot
of trouble to get married here. Countries where
there are no gongs (and *mokos*) and where you
don't have to buy a wife are better" (Du Bois
1960:92).

We do not have the details of what happened
to Senlaka, but it appears that he eventually
married the girl. The sort of trouble, even anguish, experienced by Senlaka in getting together
the marriage wealth is not unusual on Alor. The
financial system offers a man a chance to get a
wife and, if he is very successful, to achieve prestige, but, as we see, the costs are often high.

Similarly, marriage once begun has important
rewards, but its course is not often, or even usually, smooth. For a man, marriage is essential to
adult status, to economic security, and to regular
sexual expression. For a woman, marriage is important sexually because wives are rather often
more sexually aggressive than their husbands in
this society. A wife, in fact, has substantial control over her husband in two ways. She can
threaten to withhold food; and she and her
family can cause him extreme financial reverses
by having him fined if he mistreats her. For both
spouses, having children is viewed as a main
benefit of marriage. A divorce can be very costly
for a man, and infidelity, even if it does not lead
to divorce, can lead to the man's being fined.
Despite this, divorce is common and marital
quarrels even more so.

Senlaka wished to marry because without
marriage he could not achieve the status of full
adult and the economic and sexual benefits that
only married men get. Even when he attained
marriage, however, he faced the strong possibility
of divorce and the virtual certainty of many
serious quarrels with his wife. Both the financial
system and marriage on Alor offer individuals a
great deal, but at very real personal costs.

Analysis of the Case

In the case of Senlaka and his attempts to get together marriage wealth we saw individuals doing things: Senlaka tried to use the pig he had been given to start his financial career, but his father took it away from him; the financier used Senlaka's *moko* but did not want to repay it. There can be no question that what was involved were specific people performing particular activities. In fact, of course, this is all there is in human activities. Individuals are the only actors. Cultures cannot perform behavior, and neither can social structures.

At the same time we recognize that only individuals actually do things, we cannot forget that much of human behavior goes beyond the isolated acts of separate individuals. In the last two chapters we saw that people must have some shared understandings in order to live together and that these must be distributed by social structure so that there is at least some agreement about which understandings apply to whom under what circumstances. Individuals are also members of groups and are profoundly affected by their membership. Further, each person must learn some of his parents' (or whoever rears him) understandings. Without them he will not grow up. He may well reject some of the understandings that are presented and taught to him, but he cannot reject them all. The understandings shared with others are the basis for getting along with other people and for dealing with the rest of the world. Culture is man's main means of adaptation, and this is so both for all mankind and for each member of the species.

Our problem is to understand the connection between culture and social structure on the one hand and the behavior of the individual on the other. To do this, we must come to grips with the problems involved in understanding Senlaka's interest in marrying and his return to the financial system despite the very considerable difficulties it presented him from the time he began in it. We know that people need culture and social structure in order to live, but we have not yet looked into the sometimes puzzling relation between individual behavior and shared understandings.

People must have some ability to predict each other's behavior. No individual can work out in the course of his lifetime all the ways of dealing with the world that he needs in order to live and get along with those around him. The two problems are closely connected. Most of the ways people deal with the world, whether they have to do with economics, politics, family, or religion, depend on maintaining relations with other people. These relations, in turn, depend on everybody's having some ability to predict what those around them will do.

Mutual predictability in human behavior can only result from people behaving in accord with shared understandings. In a species that is biologically equipped to carry out as wide a range of behaviors as *Homo sapiens* is, these understandings provide the only possible basis for predictability. To the extent, then, that people share understandings and guide their behavior by them, they can predict each other's behavior and carry on the activities of life. We can call behavior in accord with shared understandings "cultural conformity" and say that it is cultural conformity on the part of individuals that makes group life possible.

A main problem is why people conform to their cultures as much as they do. Some people rarely conform to shared understandings, a larger number do not follow shared understandings much of the time, and everyone fails to conform occasionally. Nevertheless, the continued existence of social groups proves conclusively that most people are culturally conforming much of the time. How are we to understand this conformity? If we succeed in understanding it, we will be in a strong position to understand nonconformity.

Coercion as the Basis of Cultural Conformity

A common and appealing explanation for cultural conformity is that people are *forced* to do the things called for by the understanding they share with others. Senlaka, according to this view, has no choice but to follow the understandings about the necessity for all men to participate in the financial system because of what would happen to him if he did not.

Such an explanation has real appeal. People often do things despite their finding those things unattractive. They may do them because there are direct penalties (e.g., being the object of disapproval, being sent to prison) if they do not. They may also do them because they cannot otherwise get something else they want. It is possible to see Senlaka's behavior in this way. Because he did not want to continue being a bachelor, he was forced back into the financial system despite his personal dislike of it. In this view, it was the coercion based on his desire to marry that led, ultimately, to his conformity.

This as an explanation of the reason for Senlaka's return to finances has the same difficulty that all purely coercive explanations of cultural conformity do. None of them gives sufficient weight to the fact that in even the most coercive situations the individual has some choice. Senlaka could have decided that however undesirable it was to be single, being single was better than returning to the torments of the financial system. The wish to marry clearly played a key role in his decision to start exchanging valuables again, but this decision was the result of a complex mental process. The penalties of being single played a part, but the decision was not wholly determined by the penalties. People often accept penalties rather than do something they think wrong. They also do things they like or think important even if it involves a penalty. No one, in fact, can be coerced into doing anything. Revolutionaries, patriots, criminals, and others have refused to do what was wanted of them all through history despite full knowledge that their refusal would have extreme consequences for them, including torture and death. Less drastically, almost everyone has knowingly behaved in ways other people did not approve of, despite knowing there might be undesirable consequences.

Guardsmen and Rioters. People can be forced to choose between conformity and the consequences of nonconformity, but no more than that.

What coercion can do is force the individual to choose between the consequences of nonconformity, in Senlaka's case, not having a wife, and the nonconformity itself, for Senlaka, staying out of the financial system. A coercion-based explanation of conformity assumes, sometimes incorrectly, that the choice will always be made to avoid the consequences of nonconformity. Such an explanation has the disadvantage of providing only limited help in understanding social and cultural change. It suggests only that people will always accept new things if they are coercively presented to them, when, in fact, the dynamics of change are often far more complex than that.

To understand the ways social groups operate, we must have some idea of how culture actually influences behavior. The coercive effects of knowing other people think things ought to be done in some particular way is not enough to ensure that most people will do them that way. What is needed is a way of looking at individual mental processes that will show the effects of culture together with other influences on behavior, and to this, the concept of personality is basic.

Personality and Its Processes

PERSONALITY *The more or less organized collection of processes that goes on in each human mind.*

The term "personality" refers to the more or less organized collection of processes that goes on in each human's mind. These mental processes cannot be directly observed,[2] but inferences about them can be made from observations of behavior. Personality is *not* behavior, but because its component processes control behavior, it is possible to learn about it from behavior.

[2]An individual can observe some of his own mental processes directly, but as a source of knowledge about personality this cannot defensibly be used in isolation from inferences based on other people's behavior.

Different kinds of processes make up personality. Some processes are compounded of other processes; that is, composed of smaller-scale processes. Among these compound processes, motivation, learning, and cognition have most occupied anthropologists. Each of these compound processes is further complicated by the fact that its operation involves the other two.

Motivation is the compound process that instigates and controls all of an individual's behavior (excepting some reflex actions). Cognition is the compound process by which people know and think about the world, themselves, other people, and everything else. As we will see, motivation draws heavily on what people know and how they think, but at the same time cognition takes place only when it is motivated. Learning refers to gaining new knowledge, and, obviously, there can be no cognition or motivation without learning. Learning, however, does not take place without motivation, which is the source of all complex behavior, and it usually involves some sorts of cognition.

Motivation   A brief examination of how motivation works will show some of the problems involved in understanding how culture affects individual behavior. The compound process motivation is composed of the serial operation of three other processes: drives, means, and goals. A drive is a mental process that begins and maintains action. Some drives (the hunger drive is one) are closely rooted in biology. Other drives such as the self-esteem drive, which is based mainly on social experience, have only distant connections with the inborn constitution of the human organism. Each kind of drive, however, is a whole series of mental events involving sensation, recognition, and the activation of means. Some drives are positive, a seeking for something. Others, in contrast, lead to avoiding or stopping something.

"Means" is a process initiated by a drive. It involves a review of the things the person has learned to find the ones appropriate for the drive he experiences. He must then select (a cognitive process) among these the actions that are congenial to him and, at the same time, likely to reduce the drive and attain the goal he has selected. "Goal" is also a mental process that draws, like means, on what the individual has learned. It, too, involves selections and judgments. Goals, like drives, may be closely linked to biological foundations (e.g., feeling full after eating) or distant from them (e.g., being deferred to or shown respect). Goals can be positive, as in wanting to be rewarded, or negative, as when punishment or pain are to be avoided.

How motivation works   A difficulty in correctly understanding what motivates an individual's behavior is that different motives can be manifested in the same behavior. Imagine a person who is experiencing a sensation of hunger and feeling impelled to do something to reduce this drive. He reviews the knowledge he has about responses to hunger and decides that the means he will adopt is going to a restaurant and buying food. This is likely to accomplish his goal of eating and feeling full. At the same time, a self-esteem drive is operating, and he combines responding to his hunger drive with responding to his self-esteem drive and selects not just any res-

MOTIVATION
A mental process composed of the serial operation of three other processes: drives, means, and goals.

taurant, but an expensive one. The goal of his self-esteem drive is to be treated with deference and to feel he is recognized as an important person. The people who work at the expensive restaurant are likely to do this, he feels, in the course of serving him. In this example, two different motives are involved in a single sequence of behavior, and although they have different goals and different means, the two motives are both directing the person's actions in going to the restaurant.

It is quite common for a person to act according to more than one motive at once. A college education is desirable because of a drive to learn and a goal of attaining greater understanding, but it is also a means to gain prestige, economic security, and a pause before deciding what is to be done with one's life. Similarly, a hunter kills an animal to get food and reduce his hunger drive, but the kill also demonstrates his skill in the hunt and gains him honor and recognition. Killing the animal may also give expression to aggressive, destructive drives. When there is more than one motive for a single sequence of actions, the actions are said to be "overdetermined." Most human behavior is overdetermined whether the individual performing that behavior is Alorese, American, Tahitian, or Spanish.

OVERDETERMINED BEHAVIOR *Behavior that is the result of more than one motive.*

Different individuals can engage in very similar behavior for quite different motives. One person might study because he has a strong drive to acquire knowledge, which is gratified by the means of studying with the goal of knowing more about what is studied. Another person may study because he has a strong success drive, and he uses studying, along with other and different means, to acquire various tangible evidences of success. We can determine which motive is behind an observed behavior only by examining a broad range of the individual's behavior and making inferences from that large sample rather than from a single activity, like studying, examined in isolation.

The Organization of Personality

Everyone has more than one motive for much of what he does, but different motives commonly occur together in different people. Some people, for example, combine prestige motives with other kinds of motives in much of what they do. Others frequently combine aggressive motives with a broad range of different motives. Still others have the search for security as one of the motives for much of their behavior. What motives commonly occur with what others is part of the organization of an individual's personality.

Put generally, the organization of personality has to do with how mental processes are related to each other. One kind of relation, just noted, is that of occurring together. Another kind of relation has to do with relative strength of a motive. For a given person, the prestige motive may be so strong that it is the main guide for behavior even when it occurs with other powerful motives. We might expect an individual whose personality is organized around prestige under some circumstances to go hungry for long

Men Performing *Ketjak,*
or the "Monkey Dance,"
on Bali in Indonesia.
Individuals can carry
out the same behavior for
similar motives and still
have different
personalities.

periods so that he can patronize expensive restaurants when he does eat. His prestige motives would outweigh his hunger motives, perhaps up to the point of starvation.

The organization of personality is entirely within the individual. The organization of a person's personality is not wholly shared with any other individual even if two different people have many of the same, or nearly the same, mental processes. Two people may have the same motives, the same drives, the same goals, and so on; but the personalities of the two may be quite different because the ways in which these processes are related to one another are different. In guiding behavior the organization of mental processes (which process is more powerful than which, which process goes together with which, and so on) is as important as what the processes themselves are.[3]

[3]The organization of mental processes is itself a mental process or, better, a series of mental processes. Organization is fundamental to personality operation and is part of such basic developmental phenomena as those the Freudians refer to as "psychosexual development."

Despite differences in overall personality organization, similarities exist among different people, including similarities in the connections between some mental processes. For example, many people have the same connections between some of their drives and goals. This is especially true for people who belong to the same group. Among Brahmin Hindus the hunger drive is linked only to vegetable-food goals. The linkage between the drive and the goal is so strong for many of these individuals that they will suffer starvation rather than allow their hunger drive to be satisfied with meat. Despite the common organization of a drive and goal, the personality of each Brahmin is unique: The overall organization of personality for each of them is different from the overall organization for every other.

Further, the uniqueness of each personality is not compromised by the fact that there are similarities at levels of organization higher than the simple connections between drives and goals. In a number of different societies, including those in Europe and North America, we find a fair number of people in whose personalities prestige motives are pervasive and powerful. These people are quite different from each other in total personality even though their personality organizations have in common a prominent position for the same motive. Thinking of two different people one knows who both are constantly concerned with prestige will make clear how very different people can be despite sharing an important feature of their personality organizations.

Shared Understandings and Individual Motives

It is axiomatic that human behavior is motivated, and it is a matter of fact that much of human behavior is in accord with understandings shared by the members of the group where the behavior occurs. The sources of the motivation to follow these understandings are sometimes difficult to find. On Alor, for example, the difficulties participants in the finance system experience are clear: Debtors do not readily repay what is owed, and creditors make insistent demands for valuables even if the valuables are not available. Why do people engage in this time-consuming and sometimes unpleasant activity? It is quite possible for the Alorese to maintain their lives without involving themselves in the exchange of gongs and *mokos*, yet almost every man on Alor devotes much of his energy to it.

We can ask the same questions about much culturally conforming behavior in every society. Why do some people in most parts of the United States work hard to get money far beyond what they need to have enough food, shelter, and clothing? Why do people exhaust themselves working on gardens devoted entirely to purely ornamental flowers and nonproductive shrubs? The odd and "optional" areas of life are not the only areas where we see individuals engaged in culturally conforming behavior, behavior in accord with shared understandings. The ways people get food, fight, make love, eat, and relieve themselves are all greatly influenced by the understandings they share with other members of their group. Because coercion alone does not explain culture's ability to guide behavior, we need now to examine the role of learning.

The pervasive influence of shared understandings is partly based in the fact that people have learned these understandings; but learning alone is not enough to explain cultural conformity. People do not always follow modes of behavior they have learned. Senlaka learned about the financial system at an early age, but he refused to participate in it for many years. Everyone in American society has learned about marriage and the circumstances under which it is appropriate; nevertheless, in the last decade or so the number of men and women who live together but do not marry has greatly increased. Surely, none of those involved has failed to learn that marriage is the "proper" state for them, because this is understood by most of the members of the larger group to which they belong. Thus, although it is necessary to know what shared understandings are to be guided by them, knowing is not enough to make them guides. It is a very rare individual who has not said or thought, "I know everyone does that and I'm supposed to, but I'm not going to."

If shared understandings are to serve as effective guides for individual behavior, besides being learned, they must be part of the individual's motives. Some understandings are effective guides for some people because they provide direct gratification for drives those people experience or direct means of accomplishing goals they desire. Many men on Alor are like the first financier in our case. The financier participates in the financial system because it is directly gratifying to him to do so. As we will see, many males on Alor are powerfully motivated to control others. The financial system provides a means for doing just that by providing understandings that enable successful manipulators of valuables to give or withhold wealth from others and thereby control them. The first financier had a powerful influence on Senlaka and, in an important sense, controlled him: He induced Senlaka to hand over his *moko* and then refused to pay it back until he, not Senlaka, decided to do so.

Understandings also find a part in people's motives even when the behavior the understandings call for is not itself gratifying. Senlaka did not enter into the exchange system because he enjoyed it. He did it only when his wish to marry became strong enough to outweigh his wish to avoid the pain he experienced in trading valuables. The financial system was a necessary and unavoidable step in gaining something he wanted, so he guided his behavior by the understandings having to do with trade despite its intrinsic lack of appeal for him.

Shared understandings without intrinsic appeal are also followed by individuals when they feel that not following them will cause more pain than following them. Punishment for not behaving as the culture directs does not automatically prevent such behavior, but it is common enough for people to do things because of the pain they anticipate if they do not do them. Following the rules in taking an exam, for example, may be motivated by a wish to avoid the consequences that the individual believes will follow from cheating. The behavior called for by the rules has no appeal in itself for such people, but it may be preferable to being thrown out of school. The individual, in effect, weighs the benefits of cheating against the punishments for breaking the rules if he is caught and guides his behavior accordingly.

Senlaka finally returned to the finance system in order to get a wife. The rule-following exam taker may be motivated by avoiding expulsion. In both cases cultural conformity is motivated by a wish to attain something for which the behavior required by understandings is an unavoidable step rather than by the desirability of that behavior itself.

Shared understandings can also become an active determinant of individual behavior if the individual is motivated by the wish to follow society's rules. Even when the specific behavior called for by some shared understanding is not gratifying in itself and is not an essential step to something that is desired, the awareness of doing what is required by the culture can be sufficiently gratifying for him to do it on that basis alone. Another form of this process is operating when the individual conforms to shared understandings because not doing so makes him feel bad. In both cases the individual's personal standards of "good" and "bad" lead him to behave in accord with shared understandings and allow him to think of himself as "good," not "bad." This sort of cultural conformity stems from the pressures of what Freudian psychologists call the "superego," and it plays a role in every human society.

For any of these links between shared understandings and motives to work, they must be incorporated in the individual's personality. This takes place through the mechanism of socialization.

Dance Instruction in Bali. Humans are not able to employ their cultures' techniques and procedures until they have had many years of instruction.

Socialization and Shared Understandings on Alor

Mammals have a longer period of childhood dependency than any other animals. Among mammals, the primates have the longest childhoods, and among primates humans are dependent for the longest time (see Chapters 7 and 8). For more than the first ten years of their lives, humans cannot survive without the care of adults, and in some societies this period is much longer. During the dependency period the young acquire their basic personalities. They also learn many of the shared understandings that make up the culture of their groups.

Senlaka found the behavior involved in finance more painful than gratifying, which seems uncommon on Alor. Many Alorese men participate in the exchanges with genuine pleasure despite their universally experienced difficulties. Obviously the men have to learn the procedures for participating in the exchanges, which they do, beginning in adolescence, by observing older men and by limited participation. They learn how to recognize more and less valuable *mokos* and gongs, what to say to debtors and creditors, and so on, in other words, the techniques of the financial system. A great deal of what is done in every society requires the learning of techniques. However, knowledge of techniques alone will not bring anyone to participate in a type of behavior, no matter whether it be Alorese finance or, say, chess in other societies. Individuals must also have drives and goals that make the behavior gratifying. Leaving chess aside, what drives and goals are at the basis of participation in Alorese finance?

As we saw earlier, the Alorese financial system provides its successful practitioners with a fairly considerable ability to control other people. It also provides prestige for those who manage to accumulate large numbers of valuables owed them and are thus thought of as rich men. A close study of the life histories of a number of Alorese men and an analysis of their psychological tests show that these men have a very deep-seated concern with mastering other people and a related wish to be thought important and powerful. The desires for mastery and for prestige have their first and, in many ways, most important roots in early childhood on Alor.

Childhood on Alor When the Alorese infant is born, his mother takes several weeks away from her work in the gardens and devotes herself entirely to caring for it. It is given the breast whenever it cries and is near its mother day and night. Importantly, the father sleeps on a mat separate from the mother's during this time. After a few weeks, however, the mother returns to gardening, and the infant is turned over to an older brother or sister, a grandparent, or some other available relative. The substitute cares for the infant from early in the morning when the mother leaves until late afternoon when she returns. During this period there is no one to suckle the child, and although the caretakers give the baby premasticated food when it cries, it often spits this out and clearly finds it a less than satisfactory substitute for its mother's breast. Little effort is made to toilet train the child during early childhood, and it is not punished for wetting and soiling. Instruction is by example. Children are not directly punished in their early years, but adults tease them a good deal and lie to them (e.g., a crying child will be told its mother is coming even though she is not). Rewards are not an important element in Alorese child training, and children's accomplishments are little noted.

The father is usually a distant figure to children. He is often away on what must seem to children to be mysterious and important business, and his role in caring for the child is much smaller than the mother's and older siblings'. It is not the father who provides for the needs of the child. It is the mother, who not only gives the breast when the child is very small but also provides the food from the gardens. And, as we saw in Senlaka's case, a father has absolute rights over children's possessions and exercises these rights freely. Despite the extreme frustrations the mother causes the child by her absences early in its life, she is the source of almost everything the young child needs and wants. The father, however, provides little or nothing, yet he has great ability to demand and take. There is no basis for a very positive image of him or his relations with others, but because of the presumed importance of his activities and his sexual control of the mother, the father plays an important role in forming the developing child's personality.

The young child on Alor has little ability to bring about the things he wants. He cannot be sure that anything he does is likely to have the results he desires. He will be fed not when he feels hungry but when his mother and, later, other people older than himself are available and interested. He will receive attention and whatever else he wants only at the whim of those around him. On the other hand, the child is allowed free emotional expression, and at quite an early age virtually all Alorese children begin having temper tantrums in which they throw themselves about, cry, and scream. These displays do not regularly result in such things as bringing back an absent mother or getting an older child or adult to do what the child wants, but they are continued for some years in most cases. In later childhood these tantrums disappear, and the child begins to acquire means for caring for himself.

Alorese Child Having a Temper Tantrum. Alorese children throw themselves about, cry, and scream, but they are almost always ignored when they do this.

Girls are trained in food production and begin accompanying their mothers to the gardens at a fairly early age. Girls' lives have significant continuity as a result of their smooth and rapid introduction into adult activities and adult companions. Boys, on the other hand, are left to each other's company from an early age to adulthood. They have to shift for themselves during the day and are given no particular training. They often form small bands and wander about their village areas hunting rats and stealing food from gardens. When either boys or girls reach the later years of childhood, they respond to what they regard as parental mistreatment by running away to the houses of relatives in other villages. Generally the mother goes looking for her runaway after some time and convinces the child to come home.

In adolescence boys begin to try to act like grown men, but their efforts are not particularly encouraged. Alorese have a special expression for the sort of hooting laughter women direct at adolescent males when they first try out the finery men wear and when they do other things grown men do. At about the age of sixteen boys let their hair begin to grow long in the adult-male fashion. As this period goes on, the boys and young men imitate the behavior of successful older men more and more. For example, they begin to eat a midday meal, a symbol of adult status, even if they have to cook it for themselves. They also assume the swaggering gait and vanity about appearance that adult men display.

Girls' adolescence is more structured than boys'. Their work in the gardens and with their younger siblings occupies them a great deal, and they spend more time with adults of their own sex. Girls marry earlier than boys and are launched into an adult career with less aimless waiting and uncertainty.

Helplessness, control, and the Alorese financial system This brief sketch of child training on Alor gives us some basis for examining how the motives necessary for performing the behavior called for by culture become part of the personalities of the members of the culture group. The financial system on Alor involves a number of different sorts of behavior (e.g., lending, borrowing, dunning, and haggling), and these have several different conse-quences for the individuals who participate. One is that opportunities are provided to control other men as the financier controlled Senlaka and an-other is the likelihood of gaining prestige and importance with success. From the beginning of his life the powerlessness of the Alorese child is constantly demonstrated to him. He cannot depend upon his food supply, although in the earliest days of life he could. He cannot stop his mother from aban-doning him. His mother and the others around him lie to him and tease him. There is no dependable way for him to get from them what he wants, yet they are his only source of food, protection, and attention. In addition, from the beginning almost all the relations between people in which the child participates are marked by superficiality and lack of warmth. The rela-tion between mother and child sets the stage for this, but all early experience contributes to it. Du Bois makes this point clearly in her summary of child training in the first stages of childhood: "Children must be left with a sense of bewilderment in placing their loyalties and with an essential ignorance of warm and trustful relationships. The lack of training and praise, as well as the presence of teasing, ridicule, and fear, combined with lack of privileges and esteem, must create in the child an essential distrust of itself" (Du Bois 1960:79).

Given the sort of relationships with which the child is surrounded, it is clear that control of others is an important goal for him. The Alorese child cannot trust others to do things for him, no matter how strong their ties to him may be. Even his mother will leave him and let him suffer. The only way the young child can hope to get things from others is through controlling them, which he tries to do with temper tantrums. However, these only emphasize his helplessness. The appeal of the financial system as a means of gaining control should be obvious. The extreme helplessness of the young Alorese child is not the only basis for participating in the exchanges, but it is an important one. It offers a way of controlling others that is approved by shared understandings as well as effective. Only through its operation can one actually bring others to do the things one wants.

Another key motive in the financial system centers on the prestige goal. We saw in Du Bois's summary of early child training that the child has no trust in himself. If he has no trust in himself, the evaluation he gives himself cannot but be greatly influenced by the opinions of others. An analysis of the psychological tests given to people on Alor shows that they have very low self-esteem. They are not consciously aware of it,[4] but it is a key fact in their personalities, and the drive for self-esteem based on it is a highly potent

[4]In addition to the abundant clinical evidence demonstrating the existence of unconscious mental processes, a number of experimental studies also shows their existence. Stanley Clemes, for example, did a study in which subjects were hypnotized and then given nine words about which they had emotional conflicts and nine neutral words. It was found that although the words were learned equally well, subjects recalled conflict words after hypnosis about half as well as neutral words. The experimenter argues that the selective "forgetting" is due to an unconscious process by which the individual protects himself from conflict (Clemes 1964:62–69).

one. Other means of gaining recognition could be satisfactory sources of gratifying the self-esteem drive, but men on Alor have few means other than the financial system. It is worth noting in this respect that Cora Du Bois, the anthropologist who studied Alor, hired Senlaka as a helper. His willingness to work for her may indicate his search for prestige and control through channels other than the traditional Alorese ones. Perhaps through earning the sort of currency we deal with in this society, he hoped to gain the goals that had eluded him when he sought them through the Alorese financial system. Whether this is so or not, the evidence strongly indicates that people on Alor have a powerful and unconscious self-esteem drive and that it is gratified through the financial system.

Closely related to the low self-esteem characteristic of many Alorese and stemming from the same childhood experiences is a strong aggressive drive. Aggression was originally engendered by and directed against the mother and then against the substitute caretakers. The young child's rage at being abandoned and at not getting food and other desired things cannot be expressed in a way that produces what the child wants. After playing a role in producing the temper tantrums of the first few years, the rage mostly disappears from direct expression and consciousness. The rage drive does not go away because interpersonal relations that produced it are not limited to those between parents and young children, but are found throughout Alorese society, as we saw, for example, in the relations between adolescent boys and women. Overt expressions of aggression are relatively uncommon among the Alorese, however, and only the insane commonly freely vent their anger by assaulting others. Fights, especially between men, are rare. Instead, the drive is expressed in indirect ways, notably in the financial system. Participation in this system is highly overdetermined with the unconscious operation of aggression adding yet another vital element in producing such behavior as running up debts, dunning, and trying to gain control of others.

The finance system, then, serves the motives of the Alorese men in a multitude of ways and, crucially for the continuation of the group, these are ways that make following the culture's prescriptions relatively attractive. Societies only survive if their members use whatever understandings they share at a particular time as actual guides for at least some of their behavior. For such guidance to occur, those understandings must provide a means for gratifying individuals' drives and attaining their goals in approved ways. This gratification is as important for unconscious drives and goals as it is for conscious ones, and the financial system provides gratification for both sorts.

This is not to say that the financial system provides the basis for complete and constant gratification of its participants' self-esteem, aggressive, and control drives, or that it leads all, or even most, of those who engage in it to achieve the prestige they desire. Complete satisfaction for a single individual, let alone a sizable segment of the population, has probably never occurred in any society. What participation in the financial system on Alor does contribute is enough gratification of personality needs to keep most individuals from spending great amounts of their time and energy in trying to get gratification through other means that undermine group existence.

If a large proportion of Alorese, or members of any other society, have to seek individual means of gratifying drives and attaining goals, the mutual predictability essential to social life is lessened or destroyed. Further, the individual means may interfere with such group activities as cooperative work or economic exchange.

Personality and Cultural Change

Personality needs do not prevent cultures and the social relations based on them from changing. On the contrary, new understandings are adopted by individuals because of the new or fuller gratifications they offer. However, massive and sudden change accompanied by absence of approved and shared means for achieving gratification of drives and attainment of goals can lead to social breakdown. Changes imposed on groups by environmental disasters and by outside groups often have this effect.

A brief examination of another society, the Sioux, will show this clearly. Erik Erikson (1945, 1939) demonstrates that child training in Sioux society engenders in the individual strong but unconscious hostility against other group members. The hostility is particularly strong in males who found accepted expression for it in warfare, where its object was the "enemy" instead of fellow group members. When warfare was stopped, the culturally constituted means to gratify the unconscious hostility drive disappeared, and the result was a large number of people engaging in ingroup fighting, crime, and drunkenness.

What this tells us is that a knowledge of the motives involved in following shared understandings is essential to those who would understand social and cultural change. If the behavior (like Sioux warfare and Alorese financial dealings) that gratifies important conscious and unconscious motives is somehow eliminated, it must be replaced with other culturally constituted behavior that gratifies those motives or the consequences for the individual and the group may be drastic.

Without knowing about the unconscious drives and goals involved in Sioux warfare and in Alorese finance it would be impossible to understand the consequences if these patterns of behavior are eliminated. Warfare and the soldier groups that do the fighting could be considered wholly harmful except for the solidarity that results from belonging to the fighting groups. It might be thought that if the fighting groups were disbanded and replaced by peaceful groups which also promoted social ties among their members, there would be no social or individual loss. However, eliminating warfare and not replacing it with other socially acceptable means of gratifying hostility drives is likely to lead to all sorts of personally and socially maladaptive behavior. The difficulties are exacerbated, of course, by the impossibility of gratifying the even further intensified hostility that comes

Sioux Indian Village.
The motives involved in
Plains Indian warfare did
not stop operating when
the warfare itself came
to an end.

from the ex-warriors' being controlled by whoever it was that stopped their valued fighting. Similarly, if the financial system on Alor were suddenly eliminated and marriage made possible without exchanges of valuables, we would expect personal suffering and social disintegration to follow unless means were provided for gratifying aggressive and self-esteem drives.

Senlaka's use of the financial system as a way to achieve marriage suggests another aspect of the relation between social and cultural change and personality. The financial system itself had no net gratification for Senlaka, although the evidence we have from Du Bois suggests that it was intrinsically gratifying for many or most Alorese men. What would happen to the financial system if the majority of participants had the sort of motivation Senlaka had? Little work has been done on the distribution of motives for participation in particular sorts of behavior, but it seems likely that behavior which is not intrinsically rewarding most of the time for most participants will change at a different rate under different circumstances than will behavior that is usually rewarding in itself for most who engage in it.

The general point we have been making is this: To understand social and cultural change, we have to know what personality needs are served by the behavior various kinds of shared understandings call for. Once we know, we can compare the ability of individuals to get gratifications, including unconscious ones, from cultural conformity[5] before and after the changes, and our ability to understand the acceptance of change and its consequences is much increased.

So far we have been considering cultural conformity and change from the point of view of motives stemming from the intrinsic rewards of following shared understandings or from the fact that conformity leads to some other desirable goal. A third type of motive, and one that almost always works toward cultural continuity and against change, is the feeling individuals have that shared understandings "ought" to be followed.

Moral Force

We noted in Chapter 2 that the components of culture all have "moral force." In terms of personality, this means that behavior in accord with shared understandings is partly motivated by the individual's feeling that it is "bad" to do things understood as prohibited and "good" to do things the culture requires. The individual often experiences the workings of these motives by "feeling good" about doing something or trying to avoid "feeling bad" for what he does or does not do. These motives are based in the individual's conscience, or more accurately in the psychoanalytic sense, "superego," and their general effect is to influence the individual toward continuing to do what he learned from his parents early in life.

Some behavior called for by shared understandings entails very limited motivation of this sort; its performance, as we have discussed, is largely brought about by its intrinsic appeal or its part in bringing about something else desirable. Other behavior has much stronger moral motivation and will be continued by many individuals without much regard to whether it contributes to the satisfaction of other motives. A person's refusing to cheat on an exam, even when he knows he will not be caught and will fail without it, is a good example of how powerful these motives can be and how they can override others. Everyone is not equally moved by such motives, but virtually everyone is affected by them. Part of the resistance to change found in every society stems from members' feelings that they *ought* to behave in accord with the understandings they learned before they encountered the "new" ones.

The basis of "ought" in childhood is generally agreed to be the young child's experience with reward and punishment coming from those who care for him. If they believe something is "bad," that thing actually *is* bad for the child in that he will be punished for it and therefore experience it as bad. Similarly, when those who take care of the child believe that something is good, it *is* good for the child in that he will be rewarded for doing it. As the child experiences these rewards and punishments over time, he

American Toilet Training. Children learn to *experience* as good what their parents tell them is good.

[5]"Cultural conformity" means behaving in accord with shared understandings. As they change, so does conformity.

comes to anticipate them and to need the caretakers' intervention less and less in order for him to perform the "good" behavior and avoid the "bad."

Guilt   All this is true for human beings in all societies, but there are important variations within the pattern. First of all, the young child's only important caretakers may be his parents (as in many families in the United States), or they may include relatives and others in addition to the parents (as in Alor). A study of seventy-six different societies (Whiting and Child 1953) reveals that in societies where the parents play a much larger role in child training than anyone else, feelings of personal responsibility for misconduct are very high.[6] Personal responsibility is even more clearly present when the techniques used in teaching the child center around love and its withdrawal. In societies like Alor where people other than parents play an important part in caring for the young child and where training techniques not mainly oriented around love and its withdrawal are used (ridicule is a good example of a nonlove-oriented technique), outside agencies (e.g., spirits, sorcery) rather than personal misconduct will be seen as primarily responsible for misfortune.

The popular name for personal responsibility for misconduct is "guilt." The individual who suffers from guilt is, in an important sense, punishing himself for things he thinks are bad in his behavior. In his earliest years the individual is trained by loving parents, and he has learned what behavior they think is good and what bad; he has also so identified with them that when he commits an act they think is bad, he wants to punish himself as they punished him. Every individual will have a unique set of things that he has been taught are bad and good, but a "core" of shared good things and bad things will be present in sets of members of the same society. These shared things are, of course, elements of culture, and in a society whose members have guilt-oriented superegos or consciences people's anticipation of punishment from within ("pangs of conscience") will incline them to conform to these elements of culture.

Shame   In societies where there are important agents of socialization in addition to the parents and, especially, where nonlove-oriented training techniques are used, people will still anticipate punishment for the things their parents and other caretakers took to be bad. Here, however, identification will not be as complete as in the guilt-oriented societies, and although the individual will have learned what his parents and the others think is good and what bad, he will expect others instead of himself to punish him for "bad" behavior. This expectation of external punishment will incline the individual to conform to shared understandings just as the internally based punishment in individuals with guilt-oriented superegos will. The

[6]In the study "personal responsibility" referred to the belief that acts committed by the individual led to his becoming sick. The absence of personal responsibility refers to believing disease is caused by the acts of persons or agencies other than the one who is sick. It seems highly likely that the belief in disease causes is part of a larger view of responsibility in which the individual does or does not blame himself.

externally based source of punishment is found in individuals with a "shame-oriented superego." Both types of superegos provide the moral force that plays a pervasive role in motivating cultural conformity in all societies.[7]

Individual Differences and Similarities

It is sometimes tempting to think of the personalities of members of groups as "all the same," particularly when the members of that group are physically or socially at a considerable distance from us. Living with people and participating in their daily activities, however, allows us to note the same sort of individual differences we find between the members of our own groups.

Theoretically it is also rather appealing to view all members of a group as having the same personalities, because then it is easier to make formulations about the motivation for the various shared understandings we are interested in. However, in every society where psychological information is gathered, whether in the form of psychological tests, life histories, dreams, or depth interviews, the evidence of substantial individual differences is overwhelming.

At the same time, there are similarities among the personalities of different individuals. An important issue here, one we shall deal with shortly, is that we might think people have similar personalities because they share understandings rather than because they "really" have personality characteristics in common. For the moment, let us say simply that some of what we see as similarity in personality is just that. In fact, there are all sorts of personality similarities among different people, ranging from very broad and general ones to quite specific ones. As a classic in the study of the relation between personality and culture puts it: "Every man is in certain aspects: (a) like all other men, (b) like some other men, (c) like no other men" (Kluckhohn, Murray, and Schneider 1953:53).

Every person has a personality similar to every other person's by virtue of common human biology and psychology, what is called "the biopsychic unity of mankind." The facts that all humans are dependent upon adults for a long period; have to adapt to the culture of some group; learn to live with other humans; have to learn how to gratify drives and attach them to some goals rather than others—all contribute to important similarities in the personalities of human beings regardless of their society or, even, historical period. These broad similarities are further based in such universal human traits as erect posture, opposable thumbs, stereoscopic color vision, and an extremely complex nervous system. The species-wide personality traits produced by these biological characteristics are collectively referred to as "human nature."

[7]Much of the discussion of the motivation for culturally conforming behavior draws heavily on Spiro (1961a, 1961b, 1958:406–422).

For a discussion of shame-oriented and guilt-oriented superegos and differences in their operation and personal consequences, also see Spiro (1961a, especially 120–121).

At the other extreme, in many crucial ways no individual is similar to any other. Earlier we emphasized the uniqueness of every personality, pointing out the distinction between the processes that compose it and the organization of those processes. Individuals can have similar mental processes and still be quite different from one another because the processes are organized differently. Imagine, for example, two people both of whom have strong self-esteem drives and strong hostility drives.

In the first person, the self-esteem drive combines with a wide range of other drives, but his hostility drive mixes with only a limited range of others. When this person eats, he tries to do it in ways that will also contribute to his being able to see himself positively. He eats expensive food and goes to "first-class" restaurants. When he buys things he needs, he tries to get things that will not only do what he wants them to but also bring other pople to admire him for the fine things he owns. In his relations with women, whatever else is involved, he looks for companions who will bring him admiration because of their appearance, wealth, family background, or personal accomplishments. His hostility drive, however, is much less pervasive than his self-esteem drive and occurs only with the other motives that bring him to participate in activities such as sports and war.

The other person mixes his self-esteem drive only with the motives involved in working, but it is powerful there. His hostility drive, on the other hand, is highly pervasive, and most of his dealings with other people involve a drive to cause them psychological or physical pain, regardless of what other processes are involved. Clearly, the personalities of these two men are very different, even with reference to two drives that are important to both of them.

Some pioneering workers in culture and personality studies have been accused by their numerous critics (e.g., Wallace 1961, 1970:22–24, 123–129) of giving too little weight to personality differences among individuals who belong to the same society and share many understandings, and sometimes the accusations are justified. Some students of culture and personality have rendered the two concepts "culture" and "personality" indistinguishable. Ruth Benedict's dictum "Culture is personality writ large" is an excellent example of this view (Benedict 1932:22), and Margaret Mead's important work has been along a similar line for much of her career (e.g., 1953). Overlooking individual differences in the study of the relation between personality and culture can, however, be a serious source of misunderstanding. The psychoanalyst Kardiner, who analyzed the psychological data Du Bois brought back from Alor, says of the individuals for whom there were full psychological records, "Each has some features of the basic personality structure, but each is in turn molded by the specific factors in his individual fate" (Kardiner in Du Bois 1961:548).

Once we acknowledge the uniqueness of each individual, we must also recognize that there are personality similarities among people sharing a common culture. An obvious source of these similarities is having grown up under the influence of the same shared understandings. This happens to all people raised in a group with a common culture.

Another source of similarities in personality works even in different groups with somewhat different cultures. When groups face the same environmental problems, they often evolve rather similar solutions to those problems, which can produce individuals with common personality features even though they belong to different societies. All societies, for example, must deal with some of the same recurrent problems. The herds must be protected; rights to grazing land must be retained although use of the land may be only seasonal; and relations with settled, nonherding peoples must be maintained (Edgerton 1971). Similarities in the shared understandings that form the basis for solutions to these common problems can lead to similarities in the personalities of members of different herding societies even if they are far apart or in different historical periods.

In the same way, common problems and similar solutions to them lead to similarities between the personalities of members of other sorts of groups, such as peasants, poor people in industrial societies, or hunters and gatherers. Similar shared understandings have arisen for dealing with similar problems in each of these kinds of societies, too. These similar understandings affect child training and the experiences individuals have after childhood, which, in turn, produce similarities in personality among members of the different societies. Herders from Africa will be similar in some respects to herders from Asia, and poor people in Rio de Janeiro will have some personality characteristics in common with poor people in New York.

To assess these similarities, no matter what their source, we must draw a clear distinction between what is meant by "personality" and what is meant by "culture."

Differences between Culture and Personality

People from another society often seem to be very much alike, especially if we do not know them very well. Englishmen may, for example, strike us as reserved and Japanese as polite. Even if these are partially valid inferences from observation rather than prejudices, we must still ask to what extent the similarities are due to common personality traits and to what extent they are due to shared understandings held by people with totally dissimilar personalities. The basic issue here is how culture differs from personality, especially as each affects behavior.

One main difference between culture and personality is an organizational difference. Culture is organized by what have been called "organizing understandings" (see Chapter 2). These understandings establish which elements are more important than which others, which ones are basic to which others, and all the other relations among the parts of culture. For these organizing understandings to serve as useful guides for action, they must be shared. They cannot exist *only* in a single individual's mind.

Culture and Personality. These Zulu dancers are all engaging in behavior that is in accord with shared understandings, but individual motives for participating and how these fit together with other personality processes are different for each dancer.

Personality organization, however, is not shared. Which drives are more potent than which, which means are connected to which drives, and the other sorts of relations among the processes that make up personality can only exist in the individual's mind. Personality organization does not depend upon sharing to work. People do resemble each other in some organizational features. Different individuals often have some of the same drive-goal connections or, even, similar ranking of the importance or power of their different drives. This is particularly likely if they belong to the same society or similar ones. Nevertheless, the overall organization—the sum of all the relations among the component processes—of each personality is different from that of every other. There are as many personality organizations in any group as there are individuals; there is, however, only one organization of culture in every group.[8]

Since understanding is a mental process and personality is the sum of an individual's mental processes, it is a simple but important definitional issue to note that all the parts of culture, including organizing understandings, are parts of individuals' personalities. No one's personality, however, is made up entirely of understandings that are shared with others. Everyone has understandings he shares with no one else.

[8]In fact, things are rarely or ever that simple, and there are probably always subgroups with differing organizing understandings. One subgroup, for example, believes the understanding that getting a lot accomplished is the most important work understanding, and another believes that doing quality work is more important. Even with subgroup differences in organization, there can be only a limited number of cultural organizations, and this number cannot be as large as the number of people in the total group.

In addition, some mental processes are not understandings: drives, emotions, motives, basic approaches to learning and cognition, and modes of perception. Many of these processes are molded by shared understandings, but they are not themselves understandings, much less shared ones. Anthropologists and others have done a good deal of work on how personality processes are affected by culture, but however much they are affected, they are not themselves part of culture.

Individuals' personalities, then, are not composed entirely of shared understandings. Culture, however, *is* composed entirely of personality processes. Thus, in addition to the differences between the two arising from the shared organization of culture as opposed to the unique organization of personality, they also differ in that culture is entirely made up of components of personality, while personality is not wholly composed of cultural elements. Table 1 summarizes the important similarities and differences in culture and personality.

Different Personality Roles for the Same Cultural Elements

Because every individual's personality is organized differently from every other's, differences in the relations between the processes that make up the personalities are to be expected. What is a means for one individual may be a goal for another. The drive connected to a particular means in one person's personality may be quite different from that in another. These differences in relations apply to all mental processes involved, including shared understandings. Thus, a shared understanding may be connected to one goal for a particular individual and to a quite different goal for another. In the Alorese case we saw that for Senlaka the understandings concerning participation in the financial system were primarily means for getting

Table 1 Some Important Similarities and Differences in Culture and Personality

	A CHARACTERISTIC OF	
	CULTURE	PERSONALITY
Concept refers only to mental processes	Yes	Yes
Is acquired through social learning	Yes	Yes
Is composed only of shared understandings	Yes	No
Is organized with a ranking of parts according to importance and connection with each other	Yes	Yes
Organization is effective as influence on behavior only if shared by two or more individuals	Yes	No
Organization is effective as influence on behavior whether shared or not	No	Yes

a wife. For other Alorese men, these same understandings were more important as means to get power over other men, gain prestige, and harm others.
On Alor, as elsewhere, people can have quite different motives for following
the same shared understandings.

Part I of Table 2 ("Motives and Behavior in Accord with Shared Understandings") shows how different drives and different goals can be involved
in the motivation to carry out the same culturally patterned behavior. Senlaka and the financier who took his *moko* were following the same set of
understandings, those of the financial system, but with different motives.
Diverse motivations for following a single set of shared understandings are
not, of course, limited to the people of Alor.

In the United States individuals behave in accord with shared understandings on the basis of motives that are at least as diverse as those on Alor.
Some individuals, for example, follow the understandings concerned with
the complex set of behaviors called "going to the university" (involving
such things as registering, paying fees, attending lectures, studying, spending
time on campus, and taking examinations) largely in response to their independence drive. Going to the university is a way for them to get out of the
parents' house or away from their supervision or both. Others are mainly
motivated to follow the same set of understandings by intellectual drives
and goals, and still others by a wish to enhance their standing in the community. The relationship between the understandings concerned with
university attendance and the individual's other mental processes are of a
number of different kinds, but all lead to behavior in conformity with a
shared set of understandings.

Conversely, as part II of Table 2 indicates, a single drive and goal can be
involved in motivating behavior in accord with a number of different sets
of shared understandings. Thus, the self-esteem drive with a prestige goal
is involved with shared understandings having to do with male vanity (dressing and coiffure) and marriage on Alor as well as the financial system. It is
probably not the whole motivation for anyone's participation in any of these
three things, but it is involved in all three for many people. In the same way,
self-esteem is an important drive for many people in most or all societies,
including the one in the United States. This drive and its prestige goal are
part of the motivation for many North Americans' following of shared
understandings in such things as going to the university, buying new cars
frequently or otherwise engaging in what Thorstein Veblen called "conspicuous consumption," and adhering to fashions in dress. Although all these
activities have a number of motives in addition to self-esteem/prestige
attached to them, it is clear that for many people self-esteem/prestige is
one of the elements in their motivation to follow the culture in these areas
of life.

To restate, then, shared understandings provide the basis for behavior
that can serve to satisfy a variety of different individual motives. Equally

Table 2   Motives and Behavior in Accord with Shared Understandings

Drives	I DIFFERENT DRIVES AND GOALS FOR A SINGLE MEANS Culturally Conforming Behavior		Goals
Alor			
Sex, prestige, security, nurturance	——————→		——————→ Marriage
Self-esteem	——————→	Participate in financial system	——————→ Wealth (prestige)
Mastery	——————→		——————→ Control debtors and creditors
Aggression	——————→		——————→ Humble and interfere with others
United States			
Independence	——————→		——————→ Away from home
Intellectual interest	——————→		——————→ Learning
Economic Security	——————→	Attend university	——————→ Increased employment opportunities
Dependency	——————→		——————→ Retain parental support and delay adult responsibility
Self-esteem	——————→		——————→ High educational status

Drives	II DIFFERENT MEANS AND SAME DRIVE OR GOAL Culturally Conforming Behavior		Goals
Alor			
Self-esteem	→ Participate in finance		——————→ Prestige (wealth)
	→ Marriage		——————→ Prestige (adult status)
	→ Male Vanity		——————→ Prestige (admiration)
United States			
Self-esteem	→ Attend university		——————→ Prestige (knowledge)
	→ Buy cars, etc.,		——————→ Prestige (wealth)
	→ Dress as companions do		——————→ Prestige (group identity)

importantly, a single motive can lead people to follow a variety of different shared understandings. Because of these two facts, there is considerable latitude in the way shared understandings fit into different people's personalities.

Limitations on Human Flexibility

The latitude in the way personal motives and the behavior called for by shared understandings fit together is one expression of the great flexibility that is inherent in human biology. People can gratify their drives in a very wide variety of ways, and broad ranges of goals can come to be attached to these drives. Such flexibility makes it possible for individuals with substantial personality differences to be motivated to carry out the behavior called for by their common culture. This flexibility is not without limits, however, and in every human society the available means of gratifying drives do not include all those of which *Homo sapiens* is capable. What behavior is omitted and what is insisted on differs from society to society, but in all societies the range of behavior that occurs is smaller than the humanly possible range. One of the sources of limitations on human behavior is moral motivation.

Moral motives arise from the individual's childhood experience with reward and punishment. Some of the things he does as a child are considered "good" by those who care for him, and he is rewarded for doing them. Other things he does are considered "bad," and he is punished for doing them. Depending on who cares for him, how many caretakers there are, and the kinds of rewards and punishments they use, the individual will grow up either punishing himself with guilty feelings or expecting others to punish him for what his caretakers thought bad. In either case, "good" behavior has appeal for the individual because he has learned it is good, and "bad" behavior produces anxiety because he has learned it is bad.

This is so despite any intrinsic rewards behavior may have. For many North Americans, for example, constantly asking other people to give them things is simply unacceptable. A person *could* gratify his dependency drive and achieve the goal of having others take care of him by endlessly "borrowing" money, food, clothing, and anything else that is needed. Such behavior could certainly be rewarding for many people, but only a rather small number of those who might find it rewarding actually engage in it. They refrain from doing it because they have been taught it is bad, and the rewards they would get from doing it—or think they might get if they were to do it—are more than outweighed by the punishment they would get from themselves because they have learned to view such behavior as bad. Such dependent behavior is acceptable to people in Alor, especially men, and they constantly beg for gifts. The same sort of behavior, although it is humanly possible and would reduce a drive found in North Americans, is rare among them, including at least some whose dependency drive is powerful. In general, even behaviors that could provide drive reduction and goal attainment may be rejected because they cause "pangs of conscience" from within or the anticipation of punishment from without.

For the same reasons, individuals sometimes insist on performing behaviors even when the external gratifications for those behaviors are distant or wholly absent. Not very long ago in the United States, many people felt that they had to care for their aged parents. Doing so was a duty and, for

Eskimo Child Training. Children can be taught that independence of others is a good thing. Notice the way this child is concentrating on how shoes are tied.

many, a burden. Those who did not care for their parents were socially stigmatized, and during that period the motives for caring for an aged father or mother included maintaining a good reputation. Later, although little stigma attached to putting a parent in an old people's home, some individuals still insisted upon keeping him or her at home despite the personal disadvantages. Often, the individual felt he had to do it and that failure to do it would be bad and worthy of punishment. In short, it is now sometimes done because of the promptings of conscience, despite its being the opposite of gratifying to any motives other than moral ones.

Moral motivation, then, can cause people to reject otherwise gratifying behavior and to insist on behavior that is painful in some ways. When a large number of people in a group have the same sorts of moral motivation, it leads to a limitation on the acceptance of new shared understandings and on the abandoning of old ones. The very substantial flexibility inherent in human biology is considerably reduced as far as the members of that group are concerned. Understandings that could lead to gratification do not become part of their culture, and understandings that lead to little gratification are retained because of moral motives.

All we have said about the reduction of flexibility in people depends upon the members of a group having some personality traits in common. To understand how this comes about given the uniqueness of every human personality, we must consider an important aspect of human childhood.

Uniformity in Childhood Experience

Every culture provides its members with solutions to all the ordinary problems of life, including raising children. Because parents have a common culture and, thus, shared ideas about how to treat their offspring, all the members of a fairly stable group (i.e., not changing too quickly) will have had similar experiences in childhood. Parents with a common culture teach their children much the same things. This is how culture is transmitted, and this transmission is part of every individual's childhood.

Another source of common experience stems from the demands the culture makes on parents and how these affect child care. The influence of demands on parental time causes children to have similar experiences despite the individuality of their parents. Kardiner makes this point very effectively for the people of Alor:

> Maternal neglect is caused in this culture by two circumstances—the economic duties of the mother and the attitude of the mother toward the child predicated by her own experience with her own mother. Suppose we assume that occasionally a mother will be kind; how much will this kindness register on the child as long as the mother must take care of the fields? The child does not know the urgency of her tasks. Therefore, the impression of a frustrating mother is created irrespective of her emotional attitude toward the child. Moreover, even when maternal care is in itself good, so many other aspects of ego development are stifled in childhood by other affiliated institutions. Rilpada [one of the men for whom Du Bois collected a full array of psychological data] is a case in point; in spite of good maternal care he nevertheless developed severe inhibitions toward women [in Du Bois 1960:548].

It is particularly noteworthy that in Alor the culturally provided economic arrangements that call for women to do most of the food producing play a role in Alorese childhood experience independent of the personality of any particular mother. The understandings on which these economic arrangements are based do not directly concern how children should be raised, but they nevertheless contribute vitally to the child's being abandoned by its mother and turned over to siblings and others for a large part of every day. Being treated in this way has an undeniable role in the formation of the personalities of those who experience it, and all Alorese experience it without regard to their mothers' particular personalities. This is not, of course, the only sort of influence on the personalities of individuals in Alor. Each person in that society, as is true of each person in every other society, has his own unique set of experiences. Still, the culture of the people of Alor provides everyone with some similar experiences that lead to some similarities in their personalities, and the same is true of every other culture and its effects on the members of the group sharing it.

Modal Personality Structures

On Alor the experiences of women are in some ways different from those of men. Like the men, the women of Alor are also abandoned in early childhood when their mothers return to work, but their ability to identify with adults of their own sex and to move smoothly into adult responsibilities is considerably greater than men's as a result of the key role of females in the economy and their induction into this role at an early stage in their lives. For people of both sexes, though, some similar personality characteristics result from the common experience with their mothers. Kardiner emphasizes the effects of the common childhood situation of hunger and abandonment: "The intermittent appearance of the mother in the morning and at night cannot relieve the situation. In fact, it must in the long run act as an additional irritant, because the only image of the mother that can emerge as a consequence of her intermittent attention is the emphasis on her tantalizing and frustrating aspects to the disparagement of the kindlier side" (Kardiner 1945:148).

He maintains that this common experience leads to common effects in the personalities of the people of Alor: [They are] "anxious, suspicious, mistrustful, lacking in confidence, with no interest in the outer world. There is no capacity to idealize parental image or deity. The personality is devoid of enterprise, is filled with repressed hatred and free floating aggression over which constant vigilance must be exercised" (1945:170).

Kardiner is talking about similarities in personality organization. Anxiety, suspicion, lack of confidence, and the rest are complex mental processes that are highly pervasive in Alorese personalities; that is, they combine with many other processes and can be seen as recurring parts of the motives for a variety of Alorese behavior. The members of every culture-sharing group have some pervasive aspects of their personality structures in common. These common organizational features are referred to as "modal personality structure."

If the self-esteem drive of most members of a group is more powerful than many other drives, this organization of drives would be part of a modal personality structure for that group. Similarly, if most of this group's members have a highly pervasive aggressive motive, this would be another part of the modal personality structure. We get a complete list of the components of a group's modal personality structure through psychological studies of the group's members. Not every member of the group need share all the modal personality structures. On Alor we know that self-esteem is a highly powerful drive and that aggression is a highly pervasive motive, but a given individual

MODAL PERSONALITY STRUCTURE *Common organizational features in the personalities of the members of a group. These features concern which drives are more powerful than which others, which motives are most pervasive, and other relations among personality components.*

Yanomamö Aggression. A pervasive aggressive motive is characteristic of individuals in this South American society and is, therefore, part of the modal personality structure of this group.

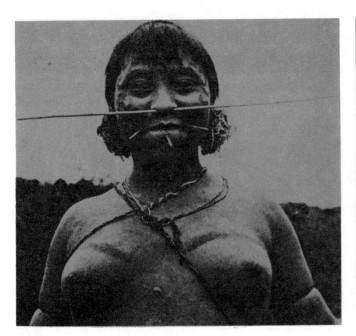

may have a weaker than usual self-esteem drive, and another individual may have a relatively limited aggressive motive.

Modal personality structures are not descriptions of individuals; they are descriptions of *shared* organizations. They are the result of the understandings shared by the previous generation, and they will produce the understandings of the next generation, but they are not themselves culture. No Alorese understanding, for example, holds that aggression should be pervasive in an individual, but this organization of motives is produced by Alorese understandings (most especially those that affect child training), and it will, through its influence on maternal behavior, affect the understandings learned by the next generation.[9] Thus, personality is a vital force in the maintenance and change of culture just as culture is a vital force in the shaping and operation of personality.

[9]Understandings make up part of the contents of personality and those that are shared are, of course, components of culture. This means that part of what is organized in personality is culture, but the organization itself is not culture, and modal personality structures are not culture. It is, however, possible that there be shared understandings that are reflected in modal personality structures. Thus, an understanding may hold something like "It is important to be suspicious in everything you do," which might be reflected in a high pervasiveness of the mental process suspicion in the personalities of a large number of group members. This would be an example of a modal personality structure that reflected a shared understanding. We could only determine this fact, however, through psychological studies because establishing that the understanding about the importance of suspicion was in fact shared would not also establish that it was a common organizational feature of individuals' personalities. The consequences of the understanding about suspicion would also be quite different from the consequences of the organizational feature.

SUMMARY

Human social life depends on individual conformity to the shared understandings that make up culture. The basis for conformity is to be found in the mental processes and the organization of these processes that make up "personality." Anthropologists give most of their attention to three mental processes: learning, cognition, and motivation. Motivation is compounded of three other processes: drives, means, and goals. All behavior is motivated, often by more than one motive for a particular sequence of behavior. Different people may do the same thing for different motives.

Shared understandings influence behavior through being parts of the motivation process. They are connected to motives in three basic ways. The understanding may call for behavior that directly reduces drives and attains goals; the called-for behavior is not intrinsically rewarding, but it leads to gratification or the avoidance of punishment; or the individual is gratified or protected from self-punishment by following the understanding simply because he has learned that doing so is "good" or not doing so is "bad." All three sorts of connections between the elements of culture and individual motives produce culturally conforming behavior; but we need to know which connections are found in various parts of a population being studied to understand both change and continuity. A very general resistance to change in human groups, to take an important example, comes from people's reluctance to abandon behavior when that behavior is the result of "moral motivation." Moral motivation is a vital force in all societies and is the basis for the prescriptive aspect of culture.

The vital role of personality in the operation of culture and social structure leads to the question: How similar and how different may the personalities of group members be if that group is to survive? In fact, there are some similarities among all *Homo sapiens* as a consequence of the biopsychic unity of mankind, and there are further similarities among those who have had more common experiences and face the same sorts of problems. Determining the extent of similarity in personality among the members of the same group requires a careful distinction between personality and culture. The elements of culture, shared understandings, exist as parts of the personalities of the individuals who share the culture. The elements of personality are not, however, limited to shared understandings. Some understandings are not shared, and many components of personality are not understandings but other sorts of processes. Thus, one difference between culture and personality is that although all the elements of culture are personality components, not all personality components are elements of culture. Another difference is that although the organization of culture is shared, the total organization of each personality is found *only* in the individual's mind.

An important consequence of the differing personality organizations of those who share a culture is that components of culture can play different roles in the personalities of different members of the group. Particular people carry out the same culturally conforming behavior for a variety of motives, and the same drives and goals are often involved in motivating different sorts of behavior. This flexibility of fit between culture and personality allows for considerable personality variation among the members of a culture-sharing group at the same time that it provides a basis for cultural conformity sufficient to allow social life to continue. The flexibility is not unlimited, however, and all societies have less variation than humanity's extremely plastic biology requires. The most important source of limitation on variation is the fact that members of the same society have similar childhood training both because of shared understandings about how children should be raised and shared understandings not directly affecting child training, but influencing the behavior and availability of those who care for children. Having many similar experiences in childhood leads to common moral motivation, which is a powerful restraint on individuals' ability to adopt behaviors other than those called for by their culture. The same similarities of experience also produce common elements in personality organization, which exist despite individual differences.

The similarities in personality organization are called "modal personality structures." They result from the understandings shared by the previous generation, and they will produce the culture of the succeeding generation, but they are not themselves culture.

SUGGESTED READINGS
More on the Case

Du Bois, Cora   1960   The People of Alor. 2 vols. New York: Torchbooks. (First published in 1944.)

The source of the case used at the beginning of the chapter. Although it was originally published over twenty-five years ago, it remains one of the most important and useful studies of basic personality structure written. Kardiner's interpretation (chap. 18, vol. II) of Du Bois's material is worthy of close attention for its views on the relation between individual differences and shared personality traits.

Other readings

Singer, Milton   1961   A Review of Studies in Culture and Personality. *In* Studying Personality Cross Culturally. B. Kaplan, Ed. Evanston: Row, Peterson.

A discussion of the interests in the anthropological study of personality as they have developed over the years.

Spiro, M. E.   1961   An Overview and Suggested Re-orientation. *In* Psychological Anthropology. F. Hsu, Ed. Homewood, Ill.: Dorsey.

Argues strongly for the need to consider personality dynamics as part of social and cultural explanations. Looks at Radcliffe-Brown's explanation of joking relations (culturally prescribed joking between people related in particular ways) from point of view of what a psychological perspective would add to it and how inadequate it is without it.

Swartz, M. 1958 Sexuality and Aggression on Romonum, Truk. American Anthropologist 60:467–486.

Adultery and the florid sexual practices associated with it are looked upon as what Spiro called "culturally constituted mechanisms of defense," although the concept had not been developed at the time this piece was written. The article shows how the practice of sadomasochistic sex allows Trukese to express strong hostility without disrupting the even tenor of social life.

SECTION THREE

An Anthropological View of Human Life: The Guiding Concepts Applied

Section Two introduced the concepts of culture, social structure, and personality—three capacities that are the mainsprings of human interaction. In the study of living and historical peoples, anthropologists have considered the characteristics of human behavior using more specialized concepts derived from the basic three capacities. These more specialized concepts have permitted the development of theory and observations focused on particular segments of human activity. In the present section we shall examine five of these specialized areas: economics, politics, kinship and the family, language, and religion. Each of these areas of human behavior involves shared understandings, status relationships, and motivation, but each has also proved to be a convenient unit of analysis in itself, and each has required and inspired specialized development of larger conceptions to deal with the phenomena that anthropologists have found in their examination of a wide range of societies.

The chapter on kinship and the family, Chapter 5, is first. In all societies interaction with kinsmen and the family members is important, especially in the early years of a person's life, but often later on as well. In small-scale societies, nearly everyone may be a kinsman to nearly

everybody else. Accordingly, the study of kinship and family life has been central to much anthropological work from the beginning. The chapter begins with the problems of a middle-aged central African who finds that he is barred from becoming a village headman because he has the wrong kinship status. To make matters worse, his family does not meet village expectations about families. The chapter describes the variety of family structures and of kinship statuses that anthropologists have found around the world and also describes some of the problems that have arisen in trying to understand what is distinctive about them.

The next topic is economics. Chapter 6 begins with the case of a poor Mexican family and the difficulties of its members in getting access to resources to keep them alive from day to day. The problems of this family lead to a discussion of the understandings, motivations, and statuses that are involved in the distribution of resources generally in human societies. Examples from a number of strikingly different societies show how thoroughly the problems of making a living are entwined with noneconomic aspects of life.

The chapter on politics, Chapter 7, begins with the instance of a Cheyenne hunting party.

When two members of the party are caught trying to kill a buffalo on their own instead of cooperating with the party as a whole, everybody loses interest in the hunt and concentrates on punishing the two independents. Why? It is easy to see that the penalties will bring the independents into line, but it is much harder to see what makes the rest of the hunting party cooperate and follow the leaders. Inasmuch as most obedience is not induced by penalties, how, the chapter asks, are people made obedient? The answer to this lies in the concepts of legitimacy, an elaboration of the understandings relating to social statuses presented earlier.

If the chapters on economics, politics, and family and kinship are primarily concerned with social statuses and the understandings that relate directly to them, Chapters 8 and 9, on language and religion, are concerned more with the understandings themselves. Chapter 9, "Language," builds from the description, in his own words, of one man's attempts in Poland in the nineteenth century to create a new, neutral, "universal" language that could be used to alleviate the intergroup frictions that he believed to be caused by the language barrier. He found that it was not easy to create a language, but the language that he created, Esperanto, gained adherents and is still spoken today. The case of Esperanto provides a number of interesting lessons in how cultural understandings are encoded in language, how language comes to be a symbol of social statuses, and how the analysis of language can provide a model for the analysis of culture in general.

Building from an instance of a Chinese farmer suddenly possessed by a god and forced to become a spirit medium, Chapter 8, "Religion," explores what anthropologists have discovered in their investigations of understandings about the world of the unseen. Chinese spirit mediums stand in contrast to almost all the religious concepts of the Western world. The problem that the chapter raises is how it is that the concepts that people hold about the supernatural are credible: how they are motivated to believe and how the form that religion assumes is related to the form of other understandings about the world. Discussions of myth, ritual, and witchcraft are also included here, for the same question is central to these: Why does belief take the form that it does?

Chapter 10, "Applied Anthropology, shows how anthropological knowledge can be applied to the problem of bringing about change in contemporary communities. The case focuses on the inhabitants of a village in Peru, where public health authorities tried to introduce the practice of boiling drinking water in order to reduce the incidence of water-borne diseases in the area. From the experience of this program, the chapter discusses the range of anthropological questions that are raised when any outside agency tries to bring change to the established routines of a community. Getting people to boil their drinking water turns out to be much harder than one might suppose, and the reasons for this lie broadcast across the range of traditional anthropological interests even while applied anthropology itself is one of those interests.

The chapters of Section Three correspond, more or less, to a number of traditional anthropological concerns. Each of these concerns has distinctive terms for the phenomena involved, distinctive methods of investigation, and distinctive questions about human behavior.

5

Family and Kinship

Heaven is ruled by the Lord of Heaven;
Earth is ruled by Lord Mother's-Brother.

CHINESE PROVERB

Family in Sri Lanka preparing meal.

What is a family?

What kinds of families are there?

In polygynous family systems, where do extra wives come from?

What is a kinsman?

What does marriage refer to?

Why is there a taboo on incest?

What happens when a society prohibits marriage with some categories of people or requires marriage with others?

What is a lineage?

How can lineages serve as the basis of social organization?

Why are some kinship terms used for more than one kind of kinsman?

What happens in societies where people marry their cousins?

Sandombu, a Ndembu: A Case of Not Being Chief

The Ndembu are an African tribe living in the far northwestern corner of Zambia, bordered by Zaire to the north and by Angola to the west. Our case concerns Sandombu, a man living in a village called Mukanza, where his mother's brother Kahali Chandenda was headman.[1] Sandombu had for some years been hoping to succeed his mother's brother as headman. As an industrious farmer, he had produced enough surplus wealth to be able to offer free beer to visitors and otherwise entertain them in style, hoping to put them in debt to him so that they would support him at a later time. Relations between Chandenda and his nephew were by no means warm and friendly. This was partly due to Chandenda's poverty and physical condition and partly to his reputation as a dangerous sorcerer.

Kahali Chandenda, even by Ndembu standards, was a very poor man. Part of his leg had been amputated, and when he travelled he had to enlist the help of a younger man to push him on a bicycle. On the credit side of the balance, he had been a famous *chiyang'a*, a hunter with a gun, and was in addition a great "law-man" (*ihaku*), judging and advocating cases with forensic skill and knowledge of custom. But he was old-fashioned and could not cope with the modern duties of a headman. He was also feared as a sorcerer. Hunters are thought to possess exceptionally powerful

[1]The Ndembu were studied by Victor Turner between 1950 and 1954. The following case material comes from V. W. Turner, Schism and Continuity in an African Society: A Study of Ndembu Village Life, Manchester, England: University of Manchester Press, pp. 95–115. Published on behalf of the Institute for African Studies, University of Zambia, by Manchester University Press; First published 1957, Reprinted 1964, 1968, 1972. With permission.

familiars; their strength and skill in killing animals is acquired initially from killing their junior relatives by medicine [i.e., sorcery]. Thus Kahali's accomplishments belonged to a rapidly passing social order, and physically he was a burden to the village and a reproach to Sandombu. His reputation as a man with bad medicine was all that restrained the hostility, felt by several persons against him, from breaking out [Turner 1957:111].

The hostility between Sandombu and his uncle came to a head one day in 1947. Sandombu trapped a small antelope, and, like a good Ndembu hunter, he divided the meat with his village kinsmen. As his mother's brother, Chandenda ought to have received a back leg or the breast of the animal, both very desirable parts. Sandombu, however, sent him less meat and less prestigious meat: part of one of the front legs. When Chandenda saw the little piece of the

Sandombu Making an Initiation Shrine for One of His Wives. Sandombu aspired to the village headmanship occupied by his uncle, Kahali Chandenda.

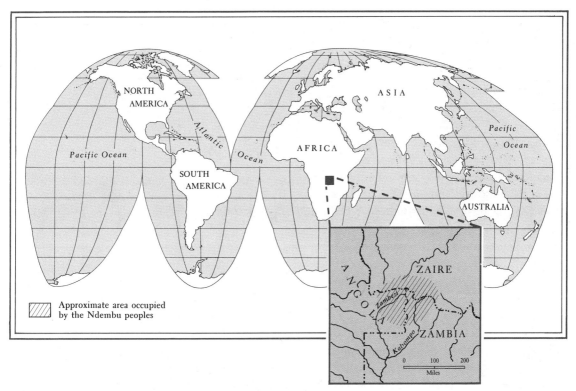

Ndembuland in Central Africa.

antelope that was sent to him, he became angry and refused to receive it. Sandombu, he said, showed that he despised his uncle.

A few days later Chandenda himself went to another village and on his travel killed a bushbuck. He sent his daughter to Mukanza village with the meat. Sandombu took the meat his uncle sent back and divided it, keeping the breast, the liver, one of the front legs, and the head for himself and his wives. This was more and better meat than custom entitled him to. "By giving Kahali [Chandenda] an inferior share of his own meat and by eating a major share of Kahali's meat, Sandombu made it clear that he no longer respected Kahali as an uncle and a headman, and would be glad to see the last of him" (Turner 1957:112).

When Chandenda returned the next day, his nephew Sandombu was away, and Kahali asked Sandombu's wife Malona for some food, for Chandenda was a widower and had no wife of his own at that time. Malona was insultingly slow in preparing anything for the old man, and Chandenda finally went to visit a cousin, who fed him. That evening Sandombu's sister came to Chandenda with Chandenda's niece and told him about the division of the meat and how Sandombu had taken the best parts of the bushbuck for himself.

Sandombu came home late that night, and early the next morning he departed for a week of work as a road-maintenance foreman about 25 miles away from Mukanza village. While he was gone Kahali complained about his behavior in the village forum. Sandombu's wife apparently attended this session, and she wept bitterly and publicly at this shaming of her husband. When Sandombu returned to Mukanza, his wife told him what had happened. A fierce dispute arose between Sandombu and his uncle Kahali Chandenda. Each of them threatened to use sorcery against the other. In the end Sandombu shouted: "I am going to Sailunga Area. The people of this village are worthless. Some people must look out." By this, people thought he meant that he was going to consult with a famous sorcerer who lived in Sailunga Area and to have the sorcerer kill Kahali Chandenda. Turner writes:

Mukanza Village. Residence and political position in Mukanza village are heavily dependent on kinship ties, and the ability to rise to political office comes from having many kinsmen to give support.

It was believed by Mukanza people that Kahali [Chandenda] kept his familiar, an *ilomba*, or water-snake which possesses the face of its owner, in a stream in Sailunga Area; and that Sandombu had gone to pay Sakasumpa [the sorcerer] a fee to shoot the *ilomba* with his *wuta wawufuku* or "night-gun," a piece of human tibia carved in the form of a muzzle-loader and primed with graveyard earth and decomposing pieces of human bodies. When an *ilomba* has been killed its owner also dies.

After a few days Kahali fell ill, and died shortly afterwards. A rumour came to Mukanza village that Sandombu had boasted in Shika that he would kill his uncle by sorcery [1957:95, 98].

Traditionally, divination would have been performed to discover whether the death had been by sorcery and whether Sandombu was the sorcerer. But no divination was performed in this case because the national government had a law forbidding such accusations under penalty of punishment, and people "feared prosecution by the Government for making accusations of witchcraft." When Sandombu returned to Mukanza village, he found that he was not allowed to succeed Kahali to the headmanship "for he had shown himself to be a man with a 'black liver' (*muchima bwi*), a selfish person and a sorcerer. The question of succession was left over for a time. Sandombu was not expelled from the village because there was no positive proof of his guilt, such as might be obtained from the diviner's basket. He had only spoken in heat as had Kahali himself, although good men did not speak in this way" (Turner 1957:98).

The successor to the headmanship was a man named Mukanza Kabinda, who was approved by all and confirmed by the government subchief.

Analysis of the Case

Turner's discussion does not leave Sandombu here. This is indeed only the first of a series of case histories in which Sandombu is an important figure. But we can leave the story at this point (as Turner himself interrupts it) to consider some of the problems that it raises for the anthropologist trying to understand what is happening.

Clearly an important issue is Sandombu's desire to become headman and his resentfulness of his mother's brother who occupies the post. Sandombu, however, lost the succession. Turner is not convinced that this is entirely because he sorcerized Kahali Chandenda (an act, incidentally, which Sandombu told Turner he had not performed, even though other people in Mukanza village were unanimous in their opinion that Sandombu was a sorcerer).

> It is impossible to get any closer to the actual facts of the case for the events are no longer susceptible to enquiry and the account has acquired a mystical character. Why has it by the consensus of all save one acquired this character? . . . The myth of the bewitching of Kahali Chandenda had already in a short period of time become the social justification for the exclusion of Sandombu from the succession. Why had he been so excluded? Was it simply because he was regarded as a selfish and a quarrelsome fellow and a sorcerer to boot? I do not think that this explanation altogether fits the facts. Sandombu was a most generous host to me as well as to others. He was a diligent agriculturalist, who grew much finger-millet and gave away beer brewed from it free of charge. . . . Although he might easily have followed the growing practice of selling beer, he preferred to give it to all and sundry. But there is no doubt that within the limits of his little world he was a highly ambitious man, eager for headmanship and the prestige that even today attaches to that office in the more conservative areas.
>
> That is why he gave away beer and also food, for he wanted to put many people under an obligation to him, and in time to build up a following who would come and live under his leadership in his village. This ambition was a little too obtrusive for his relatives to stomach, since he would boast, even when I knew him, that one day he would become headman of Mukanza Village. This meant only one thing to Ndembu, that he was impatient for office and would stop at nothing, not even sorcery, to obtain his ends. But his hospitality, his obtrusive ambition, and even his wild boasting in his cups, suicidal though it was at the time to his hopes, all stemmed from his position in the social structure [Turner 1957:98–99].

Sandombu, in other words, wanted the headmanship very badly, but even in trying to attain it, he found himself acting in ways that disqualified him for it. Such issues as Ndembu understandings about sorcery, deviance, ambition, political power, generosity, and cruelty are obviously relevant and important in our attempts to understand this case. However, for present purposes, we propose to concentrate on the issue that Turner felt was central to the affair: Sandombu's "position in the social structure." What sort of social structure does a Ndembu village have? And how can a man's posi-

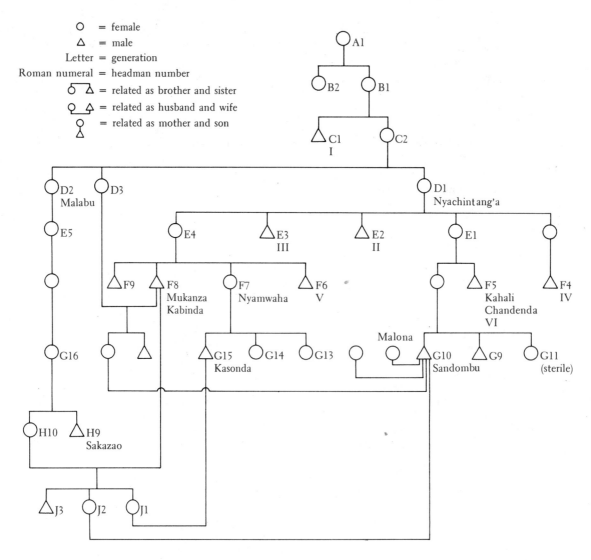

Abridged Genealogy of Mukanza Village.
(Adapted from Turner 1957:96, Appendix I.)

tion in it affect his chances for attaining headmanship or drive him to try to attain it by resorting to techniques that undercut his own chances?

Ndembu villages are typically composed of a few families related to each other through marriage and through descent from a common ancestress through her daughters and their daughters and daughters' daughters. Not all of the women remain in the village; some join their husbands in the villages of their husbands' maternal groups. Accordingly, the men in any village will sometimes be the husbands of the women who live there and sometimes their sons and brothers. The political leadership of a village is vested in senior men who are descendants through female links from the ancestress. One of them is the headman. These men have no legally explicit authority to order people about, but exercise instead a kind of moral leadership, a legitimacy deriving from general agreement that they are appropriate leaders and that the village will be best served by taking their direction seriously. Although the headman is always a descendant of the founding ancestress, there is no clear rule of descent by which the succession to office is established. Instead, when a headman dies, different men in the village press claims for the position. Ndembu try to balance two principles against each other when selecting a headman. One is that the headmanship should not be the monopoly of any single line among the lines of descendants of the ancestress. The other is that candidates of a higher generation should generally be preferred over candidates of a younger generation. The rotation of the headmanship among the lines of descendants is important, in Turner's view, because it provides a motivation for people to remain in the village. The Ndembu consider keeping the village together to be vitally important to their welfare and to the prestige of the people in the village. One way in which people can be induced to stay with a village is the possibility that an individual can become headman at some point. The rotating succession provides a link among the village lineages[2] as equal participants in village life.

> If the leading men in each [lineage] consider that they stand a reasonable chance of succeeding to office they may well hesitate before seceding from the village. The basic membership of long-established Ndembu villages consists of a rather loose association of free and independent elders who are not really constrained by economic exigency or political directive from above to remain together. Nevertheless, if the village is relatively ancient, powerful ties of historical pride may buttress those of kinship to retain the elders' joint allegiance. Perhaps their unity tends to be further stiffened by the possibility of succeeding to the headmanship. The prestige attached to living in a long-established village puts them under a certain amount of moral pressure not to secede from it and "kill the village," as Ndembu put it. Since the headman, among the watchfully egalitarian Ndembu, is hardly more than a *primus inter pares* [first among equals], he cannot coerce village members to remain in the village. The unity and cohesion of villages depends on the fraternal association of generation mates, not on the dominance of a single lineage segment [Turner 1957:104].

In addition to the importance attributed to rotating the headmanship among lines of descendants and to having senior men in the post, it is of course important that a man be responsible enough for people to be eager to follow him. To press one's claim for the headmanship, one must exercise moral leadership. A man must be able to generate a following of village people who want him to be the headman. That is why Sandombu gave away beer.

A leader, in short, should have a following, should be of a line that did not hold the previous headmanship, and should be of the oldest generation

[2]For present purposes we shall use the word "lineage" (as Turner does) to mean a line of descendants from a common ancestor or ancestress. Later we shall redefine the word in a narrower, technical sense.

with eligible men. Not surprisingly, these principles sometimes do not all suggest the same candidate, and different candidates arrange their arguments on the basis of these principles to show why they rather than others should be preferred.

In order to understand Sandombu's situation, we must look at the makeup of Mukanza village and the descendants of the original ancestress. The genealogical chart of Mukanza village (p. 168) is adapted from Turner's own. The individuals are identified by a letter indicating their generation (beginning with the founding ancestress as generation A) followed by a number to distinguish individuals in the same generation.[3]

The inhabitants of Mukanza village were descendants of A1, through her daughter B1, and B1's daughter C2. C2's brother C1 was the first headman of Mukanza. C2 has two daughters, Nyachintang'a (D1) and Malabu (D2). Malabu's line had no further connections genealogically with the descendants of D1 until the marriage of H10 to F8, and it was a more or less independent unit. Members of the Malabu lineage, as Turner calls it, had apparently a clear sense of their separateness and must at times have thought about splitting away from Mukanza village. Turner writes:

> The lineages of which Nyachintang'a (D1) and Malabu (D2) were the respective ancestresses were structurally ready to divide from one another. A few years previously (1928) another [lineage] had split off after actual fighting in the village between the senior men of Mukanza; and it was touch and go, so to speak, whether the lineage (*ivumu*) of Malabu the senior man of which was Sakazao (H9), would not follow suit [1957:100; notation modified slightly].

As we see from the genealogical chart, the headmanship of Mukanza descended from C1 to his sister's daughter's son E2, and from the latter to his brother E3. Presumably it would have been preferable for it to have moved to the Malabu lineage so as to avoid having the Nyachintang'a lineage take the headmanship twice in succession, but the smaller Malabu lineage apparently had no male in that generation who could serve. The same fact appears to have resulted in F4 succeeding his uncle E3 as the fourth headman of Mukanza. The F generation, like the E generation, produced no males in the Malabu lineage. When F4 died, the headmanship passed to the most distant available F-generation male in the village, F6. The Nyachintang'a lineage was itself now developing branches, and it was important for the headmanship not to be monopolized by any one of them, so it is not surprising that F6's successor was F5, Kahali Chandenda.

From the genealogy and from Turner's explanation of Ndembu thinking on how succession ought to run, it seems obvious that F9 and F8 would be prime candidates for the next headmanship. Of the two, Kabinda (F8) had the edge because of his marriage to H10. This was an important link with the Malabu lineage, whose enthusiasm for participation in Mukanza village

[3]The numbers used are the same as those used by Turner. Some individuals are here omitted, and accordingly there are gaps in the numbering system.

might otherwise have been somewhat in doubt. It was, fortunately, a fruitful marriage and one that was often held up by village people as being an ideal and entirely happy arrangement. Sandombu, perhaps with political intent, had married two of Kabinda's daughters. One of these was J2, Zulyana, a member of Malabu lineage. Thus he too forged a link with the Malabu lineage, and if he had had children by this wife, the children would have been Malabu like their mother. In spite of this link, Sandombu was both too closely related to Chandenda and in too low a generation to compete with Kabinda on these grounds. Perhaps part of his annoyance with Chandenda was due to the fact that Chandenda's being his uncle actually made it harder for Sandombu to succeed him, though he apparently did not say so. For several years he had not taken care of the old man as a sister's son ought to do, and Chandenda had in fact been supported by F7 and her children G15 and G13.

If Sandombu wanted to compete with F8, it would have to be done by his showing superior leadership ability, by his having a larger number of village people more eager to follow his leadership than that of F8. Knowing this, Sandombu's exaggerated hospitality and his diligence in raising an agricultural surplus so as to be able to give it away becomes more than just a feature of his personality; it clearly emerges as a strategy, apparently a conscious following of shared understandings, by which an ambitious man might hope to overcome his genealogical position to compete for the headmanship.

Sandombu also had a rival in his own generation, however: a certain Kasonda (G15), who, like Sandombu, had married one of Kabinda's Malabu daughters J1. (The generations in the Malabu lineage seem to have been slightly shorter than those of the Nyachintang'a lineage, so that J1 and J2 were in fact not much younger than Kasonda or Sandombu.) Kasonda also had hopes of attaining the headmanship.

But one factor in particular at that time militated against Kasonda's claim to succeed—his relative youth. Although he had lived for more than ten years in urban areas, five of them in Bulawayo, and although he had acquired a little education in Mission schools, traditional Ndembu notions rated him too young, at the age of thirty-five, to become a headman. In frank conversations I have had with Kasonda about the question of succession, he has told me that he saw his best hope in exerting his influence over his powerful sisters to support the claim to succession of his own uterine uncle, Mukanza Kabinda [F8]. The latter was by that time an old man of about sixty-six and could not be expected to live very long. If he died in a short time, Kasonda would support Sakazao (. . . H9), also in his sixties, for the headmanship. If Mukanza Kabinda's life lasted a further ten years, Kasonda would press his own claims after his uncle's death. Kasonda, although he was careful to maintain the outward show of friendliness towards Sandombu, was privately jealous of him, hated him as a bar to his own advancement, and feared him on account of his widespread notoriety as a sorcerer and friend of sorcerers. If Sandombu were to succeed at the age of about fifty, it might be many years before Kasonda would get the chance to follow him into office, and therefore Kasonda was determined to keep Sandombu out of the running at all costs, by the secret and devious ways of whispered slander. He, more than anyone else, was responsible for the story that Sandombu had bewitched Kahali Chandenda, and he never allowed the episode of the quarrel to become forgotten. For various reasons it suited him well that Mukanza Kabinda, and not Sandombu, should succeed [Turner 1957:102–103].

Turner continues with Kasonda's assessment of the situation. Mukanza Kabinda (F8) is described by Kasonda as having less skill than himself in the eloquence and deliberation that Ndembu value in headmen. Presumably he would call upon his sister's son for assistance, and Kasonda would become the "grey eminence" behind Kabinda's power and the effective headman, obviously an even more likely candidate for eventual succession.

In Sandombu's kinship position we can see reasons for his behavior. Kasonda's kinship position, as probable advisor to his uncle in the event of the latter's succession, as of the proper generation to succeed F5, as a man whose wife and children were of the Malabu lineage and thus who formed one of the few precious links between the two lineages, also helps us to understand his special suspicion and dislike of Sandombu, and we can see why he was unlikely to allow charges of sorcery against Sandombu to die away in Mukanza village.

Sandombu lacked the support he might need for a claim to the headmanship among the descendants of E4 or among those sympathetic to Kahali Chandenda; but could he not have turned to others in the village (people not even shown on the genealogy) for support? Probably not.

Sandombu's mother had only one sister, whose descendants did not live in the village. He therefore did not have a body of mother's kinsmen who might support him. His one sister was barren, and he had therefore no sister's children of whom he might demand allegiance in the name of loyalty to the descent line of their mother (as F8 could demand the allegiance of G15 and G13, for example). Although he had four wives, Sandombu had only one child, a daughter who was widely believed not to be his own. Furthermore, one of his wives had died, and he had divorced another. Lacking children of his own, children of his sister, or even other kinsmen through a mother's sister, he lacked the natural constituency of the Ndembu local politician. Kinship had once again made him the "odd man out," as Turner describes him. Unfortunately for him, odd men out are not well treated by the understandings of Ndembu culture. Sterility is a characteristic of sorcerers. So is excessive zeal and success in gardening. Suspicion of sorcery was unavoidable, and Sandombu apparently even used it on occasion to make people do as he wished, or when he lost his temper, as he appears to have done when he left the village after threatening Kahali Chandenda.

As Turner points out, even his efforts to win support through well-chosen marriages backfired. He was twice the daughter's husband of Mukanza Kabinda, and the daughter's husband of H10 of the Malabu lineage, but these were marriage links that were difficult to exploit, for Ndembu understandings discourage intimacy between members of adjacent generations.

When one's in-laws are in an adjacent generation, one avoids any contact with female in-laws and associates only very unwillingly with male in-laws. Mukanza Kabinda benefited from his link with the Malabu lineage partly because his wife's parents were dead. Sandombu, on the other hand, married into the Malabu lineage in such a way that he could not actually use the link very well. An important man like H9, whose support would have been very useful to him, was rendered permanently distant from him by the marriage. If H9 had not been in an adjacent generation, he might have become an important political ally of Sandombu. As it was, the marriage link was politically useless.

For a man who sought to become headman, Sandombu's kinship position was wrong in almost every feature. To compensate, he had to work to win followers by a reputation for generosity. But that very diligence combined with his sterility to create the impression that he was a sorcerer. His public statements, which were intemperate because of his very desperation, suggested to an already suspicious village that he wanted rather too badly to be headman; a man so eager for the job, it was reasoned, would very likely be willing to use sorcery to get it. And a man willing to use sorcery to become headman was not a very promising candidate for the post. If his kinship position had been more favorable we do not know what he might have been like, but it is tempting to speculate that he might have felt less desperation and much of his behavior might have been quite different. The key issue seems to have been kinship.

Kinship Statuses

When we began our analysis of Sandombu's situation, we noted that Turner sought to explain Sandombu's dilemma by reference to his "position in the social structure." Earlier we defined the social structure of a group as the sum of the social statuses in it and of the relationships among them. Interestingly, all of the statuses that Turner is concerned with in Mukanza village, except the status of headman itself, are kinship statuses. A "kinship status" is one whose occupancy is established by relations of descent from particular individuals or relations of marriage to a particular individual.[4] Thus, Sandombu is a member of the Nyachintang'a lineage; he is in the G generation; and he is married to a member of the Malabu lineage. He is Kahali Chandenda's sister's son, and Kahali Chandenda is his mother's brother. Some of these statuses unite Sandombu with others in a self-conscious group (such as his membership in Nyachintang'a lineage), while some do not (such as his

[4]When two individuals are kinsmen to each other by virtue of descent from a common ancestor, they are said to be "consanguineally" related, or to be "consanguines." When two individuals are kinsmen to each other by virtue of a marriage between themselves or between two of their consanguineal kinsmen, they are said to be "affinally" related, or to be "affines." The terms "consanguinity" and "affinity" are common in the anthropological literature on kinship.

being a sister's son of Kahali Chandenda). All of them define what behavior is acceptable, desirable, or prohibited towards other statuses. A man ought to give a back leg or breast of an animal he has killed to his mother's brother, for example, and failure to do so is failure to satisfy the requirements of the status of sister's son. In most societies in which anthropologists have worked, kinship statuses (such as mother's brother), kinship groups (such as lineages), and other kinship-based relationships (such as being in somebody's G generation) are extremely important, ordinarily far more important than they are in our own society. The Ndembu are in no way unusual in their stress on the importance of kinship. It is a key basis for determining statuses, succession, and inheritance in every human society. Accordingly, the study of kinship has been one of the most conspicuous concerns of anthropological study.

Kinship statuses, of course, are related to the biological facts of reproduction. That is the reason why all societies have statuses that we can reasonably describe as kinship statuses. At the same time, however, kinship statuses are culturally defined and involve expectations about behavior on the part of the people who use them. From the biological point of view, the woman who bears me is my mother, and every person has exactly one mother. From the social point of view, a person's "mother" may be the woman who bears him, or the woman who raises him, or the woman who arranges his marriage, or even any member of a class of women who are, say, wives of his father (whatever those who share his culture may mean by "father"). For years anthropologists have struggled with the relationship between biology, which seems to underlie kinship, and the numerous sets of shared understandings that underlie the social categories of kinship. The social categories often do

Bushman Mother and Children in Botswana. From the biological standpoint, "mother" is the person who bears a child, but shared understandings may include other people in the category "mother." Among the Bushmen, only a child's biological mother can be his social mother.

not correspond perfectly to any simple biological reality, and they are important (as we have seen with Sandombu) for quite unbiological reasons.

Biologically, a child is the product of a mating between a man and a woman, his biological father and mother. The child's biological father is today technically called his "genitor," and his biological mother is called his "genetrix." In theory, neither one of these people is necessary to the child once it is born, so long as *somebody* looks after it. The genitor need not even stay around through his mate's pregnancy and his offspring's birth; biologically his job is finished with conception. In virtually all societies of which we have record, however, a child has both a social father and a social mother. His social father may or may not be the same as his genitor, though he most often is. In our own society, when the social father is not the genitor, he may be a foster father or some other man who is currently married to the social mother. In some other societies he may be long dead when the child is conceived. When anthropologists speak of a child's mother or father, they normally mean his social mother or father. The technical terms, when special clarity is desired, are "mater" and "pater," respectively. A vivid instance of the difference between a genitor and a pater occurs among the Nuer of Sudan, who were studied by E. E. Evans-Pritchard in the 1930s.

GENITOR
A biological father.

GENETRIX
A biological mother.

MATER *A social mother (as opposed to a biological mother).*

PATER *A social father (as opposed to a biological father).*

> A very common feature of Nuer social life is a union I have called ghost-marriage. If a man dies without legal male heirs, a kinsman of his or the succeeding generation . . . ought to take a wife to his name. . . . This is a vicarious marriage, the vicarious husband acting as though he were the true husband in the marriage ceremonies and afterwards in cohabitation and domestic life. . . . Nevertheless, the legal partners to the union are not the man and woman living together. The legal husband is the ghost in whose name the bridewealth was paid and the ritual of matrimony was performed. The woman is *ciekjooka*, the wife of a ghost, and her children are *gaatjooka*, children of a ghost. The family that develops out of a ghost-marriage may be called a ghost-family in acknowledgement of the ghostly status of the pater of the children. It consists of a ghost, his wife, his children born in the union of marriage, and the kinsman who begat these children and acts as father to them. . . . These ghost-marriages must be almost as numerous as simple legal marriages [Evans-Pritchard 1951:109–110].

"Genitor" and "genetrix" are biological terms. They imply only a very restricted social status whose only role behaviors are those involved in the activity of mating and (for the genetrix only) bringing the child to term and bearing it. Strictly speaking, there is no cultural variation at all around the world in the biological statuses genitor and genetrix, even though there is tremendous variation in the behavior of such culturally defined statuses as husband, wife, or lover. Pater and mater, on the other hand, are statuses with more and broader effect based upon shared understandings about behavior and attitudes. The behaviors of a pater towards his child may be expected to vary a good deal from culture to culture inasmuch as the shared understandings that make up different cultures are different. Biology is only the beginning of the family, and although family and kinship systems are related to the biological facts of human existence, the anthropological study of human kinship necessarily is concerned far more with shared understandings about social statuses than it is with biology, more with pater and mater than with genitor and genetrix.

It is perfectly possible for a status such as pater or mater to be shared by more than one person. We can readily imagine a system in which the genitor of the child is its pater, but so is the genitor's brother if he happens to have one. The Todas of southern India used to follow just such a system. The Todas, studied in the early years of this century by W. H. R. Rivers, were polyandrous; that is, a Toda woman had several husbands simultaneously. Rivers wrote of them:

> The Todas have a completely organized and definite system of polyandry. When a woman marries a man, it is understood that she becomes the wife of his brothers at the same time. When a boy is married to a girl, not only are his brothers usually regarded as also the husbands of the girl, but any brother born later will similarly be regarded as sharing his older brothers' rights.
>
> In the vast majority of polyandrous marriages at the present time, the husbands are own brothers [i.e., sons of the same mother]. . . .
>
> When the wife becomes pregnant, . . . the brothers are all equally regarded as the fathers of the child. . . . If a man is asked the name of his father, he usually gives the name of one man only, even when he is the offspring of a polyandrous marriage. I endeavoured to ascertain why the name of one father only should so often be given, and it seemed to me that there is no one reason for the preference. Often one of the fathers is more prominent and influential than the others, and it is natural in such cases that the son should speak of himself as the son of the more important member of the community. Again, if only one of the fathers of a man is alive, the man will always speak of the living person as his father; . . .
>
> When the husbands are not own brothers, the arrangements become more complicated. . . .
>
> It is in respect of the "fatherhood" of the children in these cases of non-fraternal polyandry that we meet with the most interesting feature of Toda social regulations. When the wife of two or more husbands (not own brothers) becomes pregnant, it is arranged that one of the husbands shall perform the ceremony of giving the bow and arrow. The husband who carries out this ceremony is the father of the child for all social purposes; the child belongs to the clan of this husband if the clans of the husbands differ and to the family of this husband if the families only differ. When the wife becomes pregnant, another husband may perform the *pursütpimi* ceremony, and if so, this husband becomes the father of the child; but more commonly the *pursütpimi* ceremony is not performed at all during the second pregnancy, and in this case the second child belongs to the first husband, *i.e.*, to the husband who has already given the bow and arrow. Usually it is arranged that the first two or three children shall belong to the first husband, and that at a succeeding pregnancy (third or fourth), another husband shall give the bow and arrow, and, in consequence, become the father not only of that child, but of all succeeding children till some one else gives the bow and arrow [1906:515–517].

Todas. The Todas are one of the relatively few societies on earth where one woman has several husbands simultaneously.

We can see that biology lurks in the background; a social father or a social mother is obviously a cultural category inspired by biology. Most commonly (and most conveniently) a child's genitor and genetrix are also his pater and mater. Biology is not the whole story, however. This is demonstrated by the sharing of social categories by several people even when the sharing of similar biological categories is impossible.

The Family

Every known human society has some type of co-resident kinship unit that includes children and their mater and makes some provision for the rearing of the children. A majority of the members of every society spend at least their childhood years attached to such units.

That is about all we can say of families if we do not wish to have occasional exceptions appear in the ethnographic record. If we are willing to tolerate less than complete universality in our characterization, however, we can add some nearly universal statements. Normally a family is a unit of economic production (although M. Spiro [1954] has found an exception to this in his study of an Israeli collective farm). Normally a family includes adults of both sexes, at least two of whom maintain a socially approved sexual relationship (Murdock 1949:1) (although K. Gough [1961a, 1961b] has described the instance of the Nayar of southern India, where the husband leaves forever immediately after the wedding and lives with his mother and/or sisters).

Kinds of families   Beyond these few generalizations, anthropologists have found it necessary to distinguish several kinds of "families." One of these is the "nuclear family," sometimes also called the elementary family. This consists of a husband and wife and their children. As it actually occurs around the world as a residential unit, the nuclear family often includes

FAMILY   *A co-resident kinship unit that includes children and their mater and makes some provision for the rearing of the children. In almost* all *known instances, a family is a unit of economic production and includes adults of both sexes, at least two of whom maintain a socially approved sexual relationship.*

NUCLEAR FAMILY *A family consisting of a husband and wife and their children.*

Nuclear Family in New Guinea.   A nuclear family consists of a husband and wife and their children.

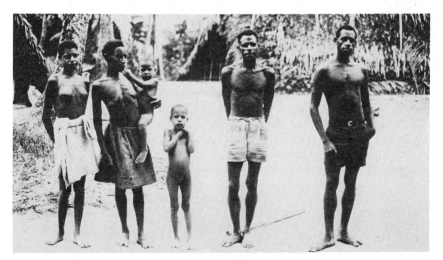

POLYGAMY *A family system in which a family is composed of one man, two or more wives, and the children of these women; or of one woman, two or more husbands, and the children of the woman. Polygyny and polyandry are types of polygamy.*

POLYGYNY *A family system in which a family is composed of one man, two or more wives, and the children of these women.*

POLYANDRY *A family system in which a family is composed of one woman, two or more husbands, and the children of the woman.*

MONOGAMY *A family system in which a given individual has only one spouse at any given time.*

other people (such as a parent or sibling of one of the adult members or the spouse of one of the children), but in societies where nuclear families are recognized as the normal social units, these other people are considered exceptions (even if most families are exceptional) rather than the rule. The family system of the United States is based on nuclear families.[5]

Very often, however, nuclear families are combined, as it were, to form larger familial units, which are the actual or preferred residential units in a society. This combination may proceed in either of two ways. One of these produces the "polygamous" family, which may consist of one man, two or more wives, and the children of these women, or may consist of one woman, two or more husbands, and the children of the woman. A system in which a man may take several wives simultaneously is called "polygyny." One in which one woman may take several husbands simultaneously is called, as we noted earlier, "polyandry." Either system may also be called polygamy. Such systems contrast with "monogamy," where only one spouse is permitted at a time. A polygamous family can be thought of as two or more nuclear families sharing one adult member in common.

Ndembu families are polygynous, and Sandombu, like many other Ndembu, had more than one wife. Some of his wives were clearly selected in order to gain political advantages, just as spouses among ourselves are sometimes selected for purposes of political or economic advantage. Among the Ndembu, as among most polygynous societies, a man considering taking on an additional wife must weigh the advantages in extra labor, new affinal connections, prestige, and, perhaps, pure fun against the disadvantages of another mouth to feed and possible squabbling among wives (and their children) for his favors or resources.

Nuclear families may also be combined to produce a larger family unit when one or more of the children marries and has children, but does not leave the nuclear family. The "children" of one nuclear family are identical with the "parents" of another. Such an arrangement is usually called an "extended family," though some anthropologists break this type into several subtypes, reserving the term "extended family" as a label for only one of them. G. P. Murdock (1949:2), in a survey of 192 societies, found that 47 (24 percent) of them had only nuclear families, 53 (28 percent) had polygamous, but not extended families, and 92 (49 percent) had extended families, some of which were also polygamous. Probably because larger and more complex social groups are in general more difficult to establish and maintain than smaller and simpler ones, societies in which families are preferentially polygamous or extended or both almost always include many nuclear families as well, nuclear families that lack the additional personnel to fit the preferred mode.

[5]The word "family" in American English has wider application than in the technical parlance of anthropology. Anthropologists do not apply the word to a married couple without children, for example, or to the set of all of a person's kinsmen, whom an American might loosely refer to as "my family."

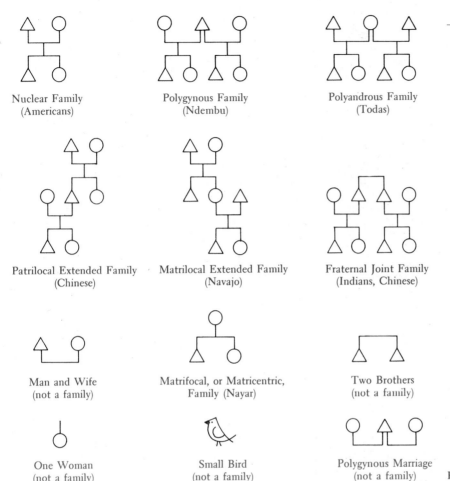

Family Types.

Life in an extended family: the Chinese An extended family system excludes the possibility that people can found a new family when they get married and have children. If extended families are to be formed, either the son's wife or the daughter's husband must be required to move into an already established, and possibly unfamiliar, family. This incorporation of a new adult into a functioning family is not always easy, as we can see by a brief look at the classical Chinese family system.

In classical China it was normal for a bride to move into her husband's household. There she was, like her husband, under the authority of her husband's father, and for most domestic purposes she was also under the authority of her husband's mother. Unaccustomed to the routines of the household, and the object of curiosity of its members (who were concerned at how well she would fit in and inclined to be resentful if she got in the way of their customary procedures), the young bride was frequently isolated and unhappy. In her special relation to her husband, she also posed a threat

EXTENDED FAMILY

A family composed of a husband and wife (or a husband with more than one wife or a wife with more than one husband), plus at least one parent of one of them, plus at least one of their children. A typical extended family might consist of a man and his wife, his mother and father, and his children.

Chinese Bride and Groom, Late Ch'ing Dynasty. In classical China it was normal for a bride to move into her husband's household.

to her husband's parents, for she was in a position to tempt him to evade their authority. The groom's mother frequently felt isolated from her son after his marriage and resentful of the woman that had come between her and her son. This, in turn, made her less sympathetic to her daughter-in-law and more inclined than ever to ignore the girl's unhappy suffering in the strangeness of the new household. The birth of a baby, especially a baby boy, confirmed the importance of the bride to the household and made her burden easier both in increasing her prestige and in providing her with a child on whom she could focus her affections. Perhaps the very desperation with which the Chinese bride loved her child was to make it that much harder for her years later to share him with his wife when he finally got married.

For the young husband, on the other hand, nothing was changed except that he shared his bed with a new member of the household, normally one whom he did not pick and whom he married in response to public expectations or parental order rather than because of any affection he bore her. Authority patterns remained in their usual lines, and the son continued to execute his father's directives (and sometimes to resent it) as he had since boyhood.[6]

[6]This grim picture, particularly of the lot of the young bride, is confirmed by suicide statistics for Hong Kong and Taiwan in the early years of this century, which show the highest rate of female suicide in the years just after marriage and a generally higher rate of suicide among women than among men. Pressures of this kind on young brides are common in societies with family systems that install the bride in a large family unit to which her husband belongs. In India some brides become "possessed" when the pressures of their new circumstances become overwhelming (S. Wadley 1973: personal communication).

Some Chinese families were huge, but anthropologists concerned with China have long stressed that the enormous extended family with dozens of members popularly thought of as the "Chinese family system" was extremely rare even when it was at its most common. The unit into which the average bride married was more likely to contain her husband and his parents and, perhaps, one or two younger siblings of her husband or his parents and a married older brother and his wife and perhaps a child. The unit might contain about four or five people, seldom more than six. What put stress on the young bride was not the size of the group, but the relations of love, authority, and jealousy within the group and her own isolation from the family where she herself grew up and where she was loved.

Incorporating a young bride into her husband's family was of course not the only problem the Chinese family system entailed, but it was probably the most troublesome (see M. Wolf 1972). Life in a Chinese extended family had its positive side too, however. As a social unit it provided for Chinese men from cradle to grave and for Chinese women either from the time they were born until they married out of it or from the time they married into it until they died (and even after, for as an ancestor of the family's male descendants, the woman was honored with sacrifices alongside her husband long after her death). All members worked as they were able for the welfare of the entire family, and all had the assurance of the support of the others in times of illness or misfortune. Unlike some other extended family systems, the Chinese family accorded honor and authority to the eldest members of the family, who became more venerable with each passing year. Where the "youth culture" of the American family system condemns most Americans to deteriorating honor and prestige from their middle thirties (thus, for most of their lives, they are sliding gently downhill), the "age culture" of classical China accorded to every Chinese a gradual increment in his social standing as the years passed. As one observer put it, China turned its old people into community elders; America turns them into dilapidated youth.

Life in a polygamous family: the Ganda   Polygamous systems also have characteristics that make life in them different from life in nuclear families. We have already briefly examined marriage among the polyandrous Todas. Let us consider the polygynous family of the Ganda, an important agriculturalist and herding group in Uganda.[7]

Until the end of the nineteenth century, war, a very difficult life, and ruthless royal government produced a high fatality rate in Ganda society, particularly among men, and women are said to have exceeded men in the population by about three to one. A Ganda family apparently usually consisted of one man and his several wives and their children, occasionally supplemented by the man's widowed or unmarried sisters, sisters of the wife, an

[7]This discussion of the Ganda family of the late nineteenth century is based on Queen and Habenstein (1967:66–87). Some anthropologists refer to these people as the Baganda, of which the singular is Muganda, who speak a language called Luganda, live in Uganda, and so on. It seems to make more comfortable English in most cases to leave off the Bantu prefixes and use the root alone: "Ganda." We have done that here.

English Explorers John Speke and James Grant before the Ganda King in 1862. By the beginning of the 1800s the Ganda lived in a highly organized, martial state headed by the *kabaka*, who was simultaneously the civil and religious leader.

aged parent, or other kinsmen. Each wife had a garden plot of her own, cleared by her husband, but cultivated by her. The men were in charge of herding, although much of this work could be assigned to children, and it is probably accurate to say that women did more of the productive labor among the Ganda than men did and that the bulk of the food supply was in fact supplied by women and children.

Because of their important contribution to family economics, women and children in Ganda society had definite economic value in the eyes of men. At marriage a new husband had to make gifts to his wife's family to complete the marriage and win her economic productivity. Even then her children were not automatically his; they had to be paid for, as it were, by compensation to her family, or else legal control of the children reverted back to the wife's original family.[8] For the child's mother's brother, as for its father, the child represented a source of labor and (if a girl) a source of potential wealth when she was married. Furthermore, the child belonged to its father's lineage (we shall discuss lineages in more detail later) rather than to its mother's, and the mother's brother felt that in exploiting his sister's child he was not injuring a lineage mate. In contrast with fathers, mothers'

[8]The attempt of one of the authors to convince his sister's husband and sister's son of the virtues of this arrangement has so far been unsuccessful. If one is an American, there is no particular advantage to being a mother's brother.

brothers among the Ganda were typically seen as rather frightening figures. Thus, the obvious economic value of wives and children was counterbalanced to some extent by the cost of acquiring and maintaining them.

Despite their expense, the economic importance of women and of their children was surely an important motivation for Ganda men to feel the need to collect wives. Wives were a kind of wealth, but the system was circular in this respect. It took wealth to get wives, but it took wives to produce wealth. Rich men had many wives and much land; poor men had few wives and little land and struggled to get together the price of a new wife who might increase the economic base slightly.

Wealth, work, and wives were importantly related also to the availability of land and to patterns of inheritance. Land was important because a new wife could be of economic use only if there were land for her to work. Land was assigned to a Ganda male by a chief to whom he might attach himself. Land was apparently fairly abundant, and the land to which a man might have access was limited only by his ability to use it, that is, by his ability to marry women who would farm it, an ability that was partly dependent on his ability to accumulate money for the substantial gifts that had to be made to a woman's family at her wedding. Corresponding with the holding of land at the pleasure of one's chief, the Ganda had an inheritance pattern that did not transmit much to a man's children. The oldest son inherited nothing from his father, and other sons could only press their claims with the father's lineage mates. Most of a man's inheritance, including his younger wives, reverted to his lineage group and was assigned to an heir designated by that group. At marriage, a son normally set up a new household, sometimes near his father's compound, sometimes not. Here he began making provision for accumulating wives, with relatively little benefit from his father's earlier successes.

A major point of stress in a family system of this kind comes in the relations between the wives of the polygynous husband. In most polygynous

Ganda Beer Sellers. Men were unable to transmit the proceeds of their economic activity to their sons because of the Ganda inheritance rules.

societies relations between wives are a subject of some difficulty for the men. On the one hand, a man's first wife may beg him to take another wife so that there will be someone to share the work. On the other hand, once he does so, there is often conflict between these women. They are, after all, competitors for the favor of their joint husband, who provides an important enough structural focus for the family that being in his highest favor surely makes life easier than it might otherwise be. It is a commonplace among polygynous African men that one of the greatest problems of domesticity is quarreling wives.

In many polygynous African societies, a prime motivation for a wife to quarrel with another wife is to win a larger share of the common resources for her own children. Details vary from society to society and household to household, but it is clear that polygyny as a family system makes such situations very likely. (In traditional Uganda, this may have been mitigated to some extent by the peculiarities of Ganda inheritance. Inheritance, at least, was not a realistic object of concern because the husband did not control it; that could not solve the problem entirely, however.) The Chinese bride entered the household of her husband as a structurally weak individual at the beck and call of an often hostile mother-in-law. In contrast, the Ganda wife apparently entered the household as a not-quite-equal competitor (and cooperator) with the husband's earlier wives, all under the central authority of a husband who had made some sacrifice (the payment to their original families) to acquire each of them and to whom each of them represented a source of wealth and productivity.

A student once objected to anthropologists' study of polygynous societies because such societies were "unfair to women."[9] It is true that regarding women as an economic and social resource is typical in polygynous societies (as in many other societies) and is an important motivation leading a man to acquire wives. But women in such societies are not by any means always opposed to sharing their husband. For the most part, they fully appreciate the advantages of participating in the household of a successful man, where there are many wives to share the work, even though they also appreciate the fact that there can be friction between the cowives. It appears that once a polygynous family system is established, there is motivation for women to want to marry into multiwife families just as there is motivation for men to want to establish and enlarge them. Whether or not such societies are, in the long pull, "unfair to women," it would be a mistake to imagine that they reduce women to mere pawns in a game of economic one-upmanship. Women and their desires are very much part of the picture.

Polygyny and the sex ratio: where all those women come from One of the questions that most frequently arises about polygamous families is where

---

[9]It could also be maintained that a system which faces men with the problem of looking after a houseful of wrangling, scheming, maneuvering women is unfair to men. Men who live in such societies do, after all, say just that.

one gets the extra men or women that will allow some women to have many husbands or some men to have many wives without depriving many others of even one. In the Ganda case it seems that many men were killed in one way or another. This automatically meant more women in the population than men, and if everyone was to be married, a man would necessarily have to take several wives.

In fact, however, imbalances in the sex ratio can be created (or removed) by means other than extermination of large numbers of members of one sex or the other. Indeed, in most societies there are cultural understandings that interact with death rates and natural inequalities in the sex ratio to maintain a family system that accommodates most members of the society and produces enough new individuals to prevent the population from dramatically declining and eventually becoming extinct. These factors include differences in the preferred age of marriage for men and women, number of spouses preferred, differences in the efficiency of prenatal and childhood care by parents of different ages and for children of different sexes, and the like. We can take preferred age of marriage as an example. If men marry later than women do, then more years of marriage are being accomplished per woman than per man. Measured in years instead of in individuals, there are more female marriage years available to the society than male marriage years.

This fact was perhaps most extravagently exploited by the Tiwi of northern Australia in traditional times. The Tiwi, apparently, were unaware of the relation between sexual intercourse and conception, believing that a woman was likely to become pregnant as a result of contact with certain spirits. C. W. M. Hart and Arnold R. Pilling, who studied the Tiwi in the late 1920s and early 1950s respectively, write of the situation:

> Since any female was liable to be impregnated by a spirit at any time, the sensible step was to insist that every female have a husband *all the time* so that if she did become pregnant the child would always have a father. As a result of this logical thinking, all [female] Tiwi babies were betrothed before or as soon as they were born; females were thus the "wives" of their betrothed husbands from the moment of birth onward. For similar reasons, widows were required to remarry at the gravesides of their late husbands, and this rule applied even to ancient hags who had already buried half a dozen previous husbands in the course of a long life [1963:14].

Older men with power and prestige married quite young girls, and parents were also anxious to betroth their newborn female children to such important figures. When the men died, their widows, now but girls, married again, also to older men. After these men died, their widows, now older and less desirable, married somewhat younger, less powerful and prestigeful men, who were, however, still older than their new wives. When a woman's third or fourth husband died, she was fairly old herself and less desirable as the wife of a powerful or wealthy man. Accordingly, she tended to become the wife of a younger man, perhaps his first wife. Because of the prestige attached to wives, particularly to young ones, it was difficult for a young man to get a wife; usually his first old woman would come to him when he was in his thirties. Even if women did not live longer than men, such a system would still provide more than one wife for older men, because younger men are not married, but all women are. A system of widow inheritance, because it "recycles" older women to younger husbands, has a similar effect. In ancient Israel a widow would often live with an adult son if she had one. If not, she often married her deceased husband's brother, who might sire children for his deceased brother. This custom, called the "levirate," has been found by anthropologists in many societies.[10]

Family and personality Whether a family is nuclear or extended, polygamous or monogamous, has an important effect on the lives of the family members and on the kinds of relationships that can exist between families. The structure of a family, like any other social structure, is a product of understandings about statuses and role behaviors that help people predict each other's behavior and cooperate in the business of life.

A family, because it provides the social framework within which children are raised, also has important effects upon personalities of members of a society, including inculcating in them values and expectations. As we saw in the chapter on personality, the personality of any individual is very importantly influenced by the expectations that are established in him as a child: expectations about whether the world gives or withholds, about how the world may be made to do as one wants, about whether people are to be trusted or not, about whether the world is hostile or harmless, and so on. The structural form of a family probably is not directly related to the expectations that infants come to have, with one possible exception: In family systems that include large numbers of people in the same family unit, there is a higher probability that someone will be around to look after a child's needs as they arise and that a greater pool of wisdom and experience will be available for dealing with unique situations that arise as the child develops. The child will also have an opportunity to observe more ways of being human and will have a greater variety of models for his behavior; the child will also have less privacy in which to deviate from expectations directed toward him. Correlations between particular personality characteristics and particular family constellations are difficult to make with any degree of cross-cultural consistency, however, and with the exception of generalizations about the differences between large and small groups as contexts for child development, little can be said about the effects of family form on personality or vice versa[11]

LEVIRATE *The custom of a man marrying his brother's widow, usually to sire children for his deceased brother.*

MARRIAGE *An institutionalized way of providing that the offspring of a particular woman or of a particular woman by a particular man will be legitimate (i.e., will be the social kinsmen of some people rather than others and the social descendants of one set of ancestors rather than another).*

[10]The complementary custom, whereby a man marries the sister of his deceased wife, is called the "sororate."

[11]For an interesting attempt to do so, see Hsu (1961).

Marriage

The statuses of husband and wife One of the undefined ideas we have been using so far is "marriage." There is a difference between a biological mate and a social spouse, just as there is a difference between a genitor or genetrix and a pater or mater. Different societies have different ideas about how much correspondence there must be between biological and social realities. Some insist that sexual liaisons must be limited to socially defined spouses. Others do not seem particularly concerned about the matter. Anthropologists reserve the terms "husband" and "wife" for the social categories. We also noted earlier that the understandings attached to the statuses of mother or father differed from society to society. It was always possible to identify something that we could conveniently call the mother or father status, we noted, but the greatest possible variation was to be found in the details of the roles involved. Similarly, it is possible in every society to identify statuses that we can call husband and wife, but it is difficult to generalize the definitions in a way that leaves no exceptions. We mentioned the ghost marriage of the Nuer earlier on. The Nuer also exhibit a form of marriage between two women in which one of them, usually a woman who is unable to bear children, assumes the status of husband. Children are sired by a male friend or kinsman, but the woman who is the husband is their pater, and the family unit functions very much as any other family unit would function in Nuer society (Evans-Pritchard 1951:108–109). Another extreme example occurs among the Chinese, where everyone's being married is so important to the ideology of family structure, individual social placement, and ancestor worship that some anthropologists have reported marriages being performed between brides and grooms who were already dead and were represented in the ceremony only by paper images and ancestor tablets (Topley 1956, 1955; Li 1972:179n.).

But such examples are the exceptions, not the rule. They strain the boundaries of any definition we might make, but they do not affect the central themes. Despite these exceptional cases (and others), it is safe to generalize that for most people in any society, whatever else "marriage" does, it provides that under certain circumstances the offspring of a particular woman or of a particular woman by a particular man will be legitimate, that is, social kinsmen of some people rather than others, social descendants of one set of ancestors rather than another.

Marriage prohibitions Not everyone a person meets is an allowable spouse. Quite aside from personal tastes, there are a number of understandings about whom one ought or ought not to marry that restrict the range of choice very considerably. Let us consider the case of an American woman. An American woman may not marry her brother, her father, her grandfather, her uncles, or (in most states) her first cousins. She also may not marry another woman or a child. Her family and community will critize her for marrying someone substantially older or younger than herself. They will object to her marrying

Tutsi Husband and Wife, East Africa. In many societies the statuses of husband and wife involve a lasting relationship with carefully defined expectations. This is by no means universal, however, and particular societies have their own understandings about the permanence of these relations and the clarity with which they are defined.

someone much poorer than she is and will probably feel uncomfortable about her marrying someone much richer than she is. Among most Americans she will be discouraged from marrying someone of a different ethnic group, of a different church, of a different political party, of a different nationality, or of a different language group. She may be discouraged from marrying someone who is a "stranger" from another location. If she lives in the countryside, she may be expected to avoid a city dweller, or if she is an urbanite, a rural man. The family or the community will normally discourage her from marrying someone with substantially more or (worse yet) substantially less education than she has. It may condemn certain occupations for her potential spouse and object to her marrying an undertaker because that seems morbid, an aviator because that seems dangerous, or a junk man because that seems lowbrow.

These constraints can all be stated positively, of course. Rather than saying that the girl must not marry a "stranger," we can say that she must marry a "local." The point is the same. In any society people have understandings about what categories of people are and are not desirable mates. In some cases these understandings are clearly stated and strong, and violations are punished. An American girl who tries to marry her brother will be barred by everyone, using force if necessary, from doing so. Indeed, the question barely arises, for she would not be able to have a legal marriage performed. Nor could she have a legal marriage performed with another woman (though that may change). Previously in some states a legal marriage could not be performed between two individuals of different "races," and some churches still will not perform a religious marriage for individuals who are not both members of the same church.

In other cases the constraints violate less deeply held understandings or understandings that can be overridden in the service of "higher" values, such as the importance of love. Our hypothetical American girl may find family resistance to her falling in love with an Arabian university student, but Americans put such a high value on the importance of love in marriage that she may be able to convince her family that the match should be made even if it in many respects is not an optimal one. Similarly, family members may stop trying to arrange a match with the eminently eligible local banker's son if she makes it clear that she finds him disgusting.

The cultural understandings about desirable, allowable, and prohibited spouses are an important object of anthropological inquiry. The fairly consistent application of an understanding that pretty girls marry only handsome men is unlikely to have important structural effects over a long period of time. On the other hand, the fairly consistent application of an understanding that blacks and whites do not marry each other can have important structural effects upon society, as Americans are increasingly aware. So can the fairly consistent application of an understanding that if your family is named Adams, you should marry into a family named Rockefeller, Ford, or

Chinese Bride Mannikin. The "bride" for this marriage in Taiwan is made of paper and cloth and represents a deceased girl who is to be married to a living husband. Some of the living husband's children by his living wife will honor the "bride's" memory.

Kennedy. Kinship relations are an important source of cultural understandings that have long-term structural effects upon social organization.

Incest Our hypothetical American girl was prohibited from marrying certain kinsmen. All societies prohibit marriage with some close kinsmen, "incest," though the particular categories that are prohibited vary a great deal. Marriage between parent and child and marriage between brother and sister seem to be prohibited in all known societies.[12] Sexual relations between these people occur and may or may not be severely punished, but marriages are impossible. Anthropologists have not yet been successful at explaining why such marriages should be universally prohibited.

One explanation that has been proposed is that the probability of genetic mutation is high enough in such a close marriage to convince members of any society that it is not a good thing to do. However, this explanation is inadequate for several reasons. It assumes that if such marriages were permitted, they would occur with high enough frequency for such observations to be made across several such marriages. It assumes that a high enough rate of serious genetic mutation among marriages would occur to make its observation unavoidable. It further assumes that the persons marrying would be biologically related, not adopted, socially related persons, a situation more common in some societies than in others and rare in a few societies. It also assumes that whatever mutations occurred would be detectable, that is, would be visible in small children. Given the high rates of child mortality in most human societies, any defect that would kill the child without making it look monstrous would go undetected; and attributing mutations that appeared in late childhood or adulthood to birth defects would be unlikely. It confuses biological process with social marriage, ignoring such possibilities as impregnation of the woman by a man who is not her incestuous husband. Finally, it cannot explain why in many societies marriages with some kinsmen are prohibited while marriages with other, equally closely biologically related, kinsmen are allowed or encouraged.

A variant on the same genetic-mutation argument maintains that because of genetic mutation, a society allowing incestuous marriage would die out completely; therefore, there are none left. In addition to the objections already indicated, this argument suffers from an additional problem: That some societies have died out does not explain what motivates people in existing societies to maintain the rule. When the extinct incestuous societies died out (and we have no evidence of any such societies ever having existed), the message that "incest kills" presumably would have died out with them. The hypothetical extinction of these hypothetical societies is therefore not very enlightening.

INCEST TABOO *The prohibition of marriage with particular categories of kinsmen.*

[12]In ancient Egypt, in ancient Hawaii, and among the ancient Incas incest was practiced within the royal family to avoid contamination of the royal line by the blood of commoners. In all three of these societies, similar marriages were prohibited to other people, however.

Other anthropologists have proposed that there is a lack of interest in marriage and mating between people who grow up together. This position assumes (a) that there is, in fact, lack of sexual interest among long-time childhood associates; (b) that marriages are arranged at least partly by the bride and groom themselves and at least in part on the basis of sexual attraction; (c) that brothers and sisters grow up together, or in greater proximity than they do with others, and that both grow up in proximity to their parents; and (d) that when people feel a lack of inclination to do something, they will enact a rule prohibiting others from doing it. The first of these assumptions is supported ethnographically to some extent (see, e.g., Spiro 1958, especially Part VI; A. Wolf 1970), but clinical evidence is not strong. The other assumptions do not hold true universally, even though the incestuous marriage prohibition is universal.

A third argument that is sometimes made is that marriages with other families, other lineages, other tribes, or whatever provide valuable social contacts for people. Whether or not the people in question are conscious of the importance of maintaining such contacts (and they usually are), any society in which family groups failed to maintain outside contacts would lack the necessary ties to get help in emergencies and would die out. Once again, there is an assumption that by permitting parent-child or brother-sister marriages, *all* marriages would be made that way, and the group would not have outside ties. That seems unlikely.

Yet another explanation maintains that mother-son marriages would interfere with the functioning of the family. Such marriages, it has been maintained, would disrupt the socialization of the son by allowing him to indulge the pleasure principle, thereby failing to develop in him an internalization of the reality principle. It would also disrupt the mating of the parents because the son would be taking the mother away from the father. Finally, it would confound authority relations within the nuclear family. (Reasons for the prohibition of father-daughter marriages would presumably be parallel.) The assumptions involved in this are (a) that denial of sexual access to the mother is the only or primary device for instilling a sense of reality in a young man; (b) that the attention of the son to his mother would take precedence over and perhaps preclude his father's sexual access to this woman; (c) that authority is related to marriage but not to parenthood or to marriage order; and (d) that the father would typically still be alive by the time such a marriage might occur. None of these assumptions, however, is true universally (some of them may never be true), and the explanation in any event does not suggest extensions to cover brother-sister marriages in any simple way.

Any of these arguments might explain why there is an incest taboo in some society, but none of them is able to explain why we should find the taboo universally. The picture is made even more confusing by the fact that in nearly all societies other categories of marriage are also prohibited, often just as emphatically as the brother-sister or parent-child matches. Some anthropologists have tried to relate explanations for the brother-sister and parent-child marriage prohibitions to other marriage prohibitions. The universality of the former and the idiosyncracy of the latter have conspired to undercut these attempts.

Such is the state of our knowledge that there is no reason at the moment, beyond probability, why the next society we study should necessarily turn out to have a prohibition on incestuous marriage. Perhaps fresh insights about the nature of marriage or of universality will produce a breakthrough in the years ahead that will allow us to understand the problem of prohibition of incestuous marriages.

Preference and prescription   Just as all societies have cultural understandings prohibiting marriage with some social categories, including kinship categories, so also many societies *require* marriage with some categories of kinsmen. Somewhat confusingly, anthropologists speak of the prohibition as a *pro*scription, and they speak of the requirement as a *pre*scription. Finally, in some societies people believe that it is a good thing, but not a necessary one, to marry a kinsman of a certain category whenever that can conveniently be arranged. Anthropologists speak of this as a "preference."

If proscription is familiar enough to the Western reader, prescription or preference on the basis of kinship statuses may seem a bit strange. An example is provided by the Tungus, a nomadic tribe of reindeer herders of northeastern Siberia. When they were first studied by anthropologists in late Czarist and early Soviet years, the Tungus marriage system involved a preference for two families to exchange brides. Thus, the son of one of the families would marry a daughter of the second, and the son of the second would marry a daughter of the first. This system is often called "sister exchange" in the anthropological literature. When possible, it was preferred that this exchange take place between families already so linked, which could be accomplished by the marriage of cousins.[13] Nature, of course, did not always place marriageable mates in the right structural positions.

When a sister exchange could not be arranged, the inequity was compensated by gifts of reindeer from the groom's family to the bride's and a heavy dowry (equal to about half the value of the reindeer) from the bride's family to the groom's. Such gifts were unnecessary for sister exchanges between cousins. Simple economics therefore dictated that if a man *had* a marriageable cousin, he would marry her. The understandings that the Tungus had about marriages were involved with their understandings about reciprocity and interfamilial contacts in such a way that the set of obligations involved in a marriage contract biased the choice in favor of cousins when available. They can be said to have practiced preferential cousin marriage.

Anthropologists also use the terms "exogamy" and "endogamy." Exogamy, from "ex-" (out) plus "-gamy" (marriage), means "marrying out" and

EXOGAMY *Marriage outside one's own group.*

[13]Specifically, the preference was for male Ego to marry his "cross-cousin," that is, either his father's sister's daughter or (better yet) his mother's brother's daughter. We shall discuss cross-cousins and parallel cousins below.

is applied to the marriage system of a group whose members find spouses outside the group. Endogamy (from "endo-" [within] plus "-gamy") refers to a system where group members find spouses from within the membership of the group. In America we can say that church and ethnic groups are generally endogamous, kinship groups are generally exogamous, and occupational groups are not clearly one or the other, though there may be a slight tendency toward endogamy as a result of the social networks in which spouses are found. A group that proscribes marriage between its own members is always exogamous. One that prescribes marriage between its own members is always endogamous. Exogamy or endogamy are historical facts, merely labels for the marriages that are actually made. Prescription, proscription, and preference are cultural understandings, normally very conscious ones.

ENDOGAMY *Marriage within one's own group.*

Descent and Descent Groups

One of the problems Sandombu had to overcome in his claim for the headmanship was that he was Kahali Chandenda's sister's son, for Ndembu believe that the headmanship should circulate through different lineages. If we follow out the logic of Ndembu succession and look again at the genealogy of Mukanza village (see p. 168), we can on the same grounds

Sakazao. If we follow the logic of Ndembu succession and give attention to the genealogy of Mukanza village, we can almost guarantee that although Sandombu might struggle but ultimately fail to gain the headmanship, Sakazao would gain it effortlessly because of his genealogical position.

almost guarantee that H9, Sakazao, will sooner or later become a Mukanza headman. This is not because of any particular skills he may have, but because the same principle that says Sandombu is too close to the sixth headman to become the seventh also says that Nyachintang'a lineage has held the headmanship too long and that it ought to circulate to the Malabu lineage at first opportunity. Sakazao will become headman because of his descent.

What is "descent"? A person's descent is his claim to membership in a social category or group consisting of his ancestors and persons descended from them, his codescendants. (The biological model underlying the idea of descent is, of course, the birth of a child to its genetrix as a result of her cohabitation with its genitor.) Once again, however, we are concerned with a social category, which does not necessarily involve any direct relationship to biology. For purposes of his social placement, a person is descended from his mater and pater, not from his genetrix and genitor. In all societies there are some expectations about privileges and responsibilities that accrue to a person because of his descent from some ancestors rather than others. The most conspicuous examples are such things as thrones, large estates, and chairmanships-of-the-board. Queen Elizabeth is queen because she is descended from the right ancestors, not because she scored highest on a civil service examination, conducted a revolution, or won an election. Members of the Ford family have been involved with the family motor company for generations, and one suspects that being named Ford gets one certain advantages that being named Smith does not.

Most of us receive at least a few family heirlooms and some amount of money from ancestors by virtue of our descent from them. Some of us succeed to positions (such as head of a family business) for the same reason. Whether we choose to speak of privileges, goods, obligations, or statuses descending to a person or to speak of a person succeeding to privileges, goods, obligations, or statuses, the point is that descent from some ancestors rather than from others can make a difference in a person's position in the world and the understandings that govern his behavior and the behavior of others toward him.

Unilineal descent groups In the United States people recognize descent from both male and female ancestors. The ancestors of an American consist of mother and father, mother's mother and father and father's mother and father, mother's mother's mother and father, mother's father's mother and father, and so on, the number of ancestors doubling with each generation. All of these people are equally ancestors. Americans are said to have "bilateral descent" (two-sided descent) because they trace it through both sides (mother and father) at each generation. Not everything that is inherited is inherited bilaterally in the American system, however. Thus, surnames are handed down from father to children. A daughter receives her father's surname, but she is unable to hand it down to her children. A son is able to transmit the name to his children if he has any. The inheritance of surnames

DESCENT *A person's claim to membership in a social category or group consisting of his ancestors and persons descended from them.*

BILATERAL DESCENT *Descent that is traced through parents of both sexes at each generation.*

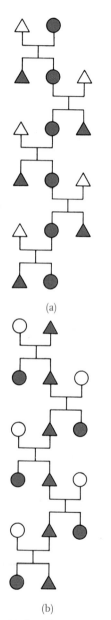

(a)

(b)

Unilineal Descent
Groups: through females
(a); through males (b).

in America is through the father's line. On the other hand, certain things pass only through women. In some American families wedding dresses, wedding rings, and, sometimes, other jewelry and dishes are handed down from mother to daughter. They are inherited through the mother's line.

Because Americans trace descent bilaterally for most purposes, they are members of a large number of potential descent groups at the same time. A family reunion of descendants of my father's mother's mother includes me just as much as a family reunion of descendants of my mother's father's father does, yet the two reunions mostly include different people. They are two different descent groups. If all family reunions were held on the same day, a person would not be able to attend all the ones he was expected to attend: He would be at once a member of several reunion groups because of being descended from so many recognized ancestors. Similarly, if each family-reunion group were to decide to live and work together, any one person would have difficulty deciding where he should be. If all of the groups *insisted* that he work with them, the arrangement would be physically impossible.

This sort of problem in making descent groups work as important social units does not occur if there is a way to avoid having people maintain membership in several groups simultaneously. One common and logically simple way to do this is to give priority to descent through one sex over descent through another. Among the Ndembu descent through women is what determines one's right to live in a village, hold a headmanship, and so on. Unlike American family reunions, where a person has no conventional way to choose which group is prior to which other, a Ndembu knows that the relevant group is on his mother's rather than his father's side, and this goes back as far as ancestors are traced, so there is more concern with his mother's mother's group than with his mother's father's group, and so forth. Putting the stress entirely on male rather than female links is another simple way to limit the number of relevant kinsmen. An organized descent group that establishes its membership by means of a single line, through women alone or through men alone, is called a "unilineal descent group" ("one-line" descent group).

Close to 60 percent of the societies anthropologists have studied include unilineal descent groups as important social groups. These societies range from some of the smallest known—Tobi atoll in the South Pacific had a population of fifty-eight at last count and seven matrilineages—to the largest, that of China, at least up to the beginning of the communist period. The advantages of such an arrangement are clear: Everyone is placed in a discrete social group from birth, a group that looks after his welfare and provides him with a social identity and, typically, with the economic base of his life regardless of his achievements in the world. The unilineal principle prevents confusion about who is in which group.

Lineages   An important aspect of unilineal descent groups is the proportion and kind of everyday activities that the members carry out in common. In some societies unilineal descent groups have little relevance to daily life, and their activities are limited to, say, gathering once a year for collective worship of their ancestors. In other societies unilineal descent groups are the basic landholding groups, the religious organizations, the basis for recruitment to war parties, and determinants of marriage alliances. To occupy itself with the economic or social details of daily life, a unilineal descent group (like any other group) has to be composed of members living close enough to each other to cooperate in their work; that is to say, they must be *localized* in one or a few places. They must also maintain relations (good or bad) with other, similar, localized descent groups. Anthropologists have discovered that it is extremely common for a society to have unilineal descent groups as important social units; it is also extremely common for these groups to be localized and for each of them to be exogamous, so that the relations between the groups include the exchange of spouses among them.

A localized, exogamous, unilineal descent group is called a "lineage." If descent is figured through a line of women, it is called a "matrilineage." If descent is figured through a line of men, it is called a "patrilineage." Mukanza village included at least three matrilineages (Nyachintang'a, Malabu, and D3), each organized of the descendants (through women) of a particular woman and the members of each marrying spouses from outside their own lineage.

Because lineages occur in so many societies and because of their central importance to the social structure of most of the societies in which they are found, the study of lineages has been a major concern of anthropologists studying kinship.[14] There have been three general concerns. One has been the understandings about descent that members of a society use to determine who is in which lineage. A second has been the shared understandings by which a lineage is localized in space, generally called "rules of residence." A third concern has been the relations between lineages, particularly the effects of marriages between their members, which involves many of the issues we touched on earlier in our discussion of preferential and prescriptive marriage. We shall now briefly direct our attention to these three topics in turn.

Segmentation, apical ancestors, and who is in which lineage Earlier we spoke of a lineage "founder," and in Mukanza village Turner speaks especially of two lineages, those founded by Malabu (D2) and by Nyachintang'a (D1). If C2, say, had been construed as the founder of the lineage, then all the members of Malabu's, Nyachintang'a's, and D3's descent lines would have been members of the same lineage. Indeed, for some purposes they are; that is why they all live in the same village. Which people are in

UNILINEAL DESCENT GROUP *An organized social group, membership in which is based on descent traced through a line of ancestors all of the same sex.*

LINEAGE *A localized, exogamous, unilineal descent group.*

MATRILINEAGE *A lineage in which descent is figured through a line of women.*

PATRILINEAGE *A lineage in which descent is figured through a line of men.*

---

[14]Earlier anthropologists sometimes used the words "clan" and "sib" for matrilineage and patrilineage respectively. The word "clan" has more recently been reserved for lineagelike unilineal descent groups (patri- or matri-) in which kinship links with the founding ancestor are asserted but cannot be traced by the members. The word "sib" is today occasionally used for a union of two or more lineages related by a common mythical ancestor.

Sandombu's matrilineage obviously depends upon which of his ancestors is taken as the starting point in the calculations. When lineages own property or titles, when some are wealthy and others poor, it obviously is important to have agreement about who is within and who is not within the lineage. One can think of a lineage as the descendants of one person who is recognized as the founding, or "apical," ancestor ("apical" because he is at the apex, or top, of the genealogy showing members of the lineage). Among peoples who keep written genealogies, the apical ancestor is usually considered to be the first generation of the lineage, and no one before him need be kept track of.

Obviously the apical ancestor himself had ancestors. Choosing one rather than another ancestor as the apical ancestor results in different social groups. In classical China, where the maintenance of written genealogies allowed both ethnographers and participants themselves to keep track of genealogies and lineages going back hundreds (and occasionally thousands) of years, a lineage would occasionally agree to split into two by selecting a more recent ancestor as apical. This was a useful expedient when, for example, one branch of the lineage had become much wealthier than another or when different segments refused to cooperate in lineage activities and interests. Similarly, different lineages would occasionally merge by discovering (or occasionally inventing) a common ancestor.[15]

Some lineage systems do not use the same apical ancestor for all purposes. Instead, a different ancestor is picked depending on the size of group that is required for a given activity or the capacity of the resources available for distribution to more or fewer people. A system that selects different apical ancestors for different purposes is called a "segmentary lineage system." One of the activities to which such systems are particularly well suited is dispute settlement. Consider the accompanying chart showing the segmentary lineage system. The men labeled 1 and 2 have a common ancestor in generation E and are segment mates. Men 3 and 4 also have a common ancestor at E and are segment mates. Men 1 and 2 are not in the same segment with 3 and 4, however, unless we look back for an earlier ancestor, which we find in generation D. If 1 and 2 get into a dispute, it is none of 3's or 4's business. If 2 and 3 get into a dispute, then 1, being a segment mate of 2, comes to his aid, and 4, being a segment mate of 3, comes to 3's aid. Segment mates 1 and 2 are now the antagonists of 3 and 4, and a fight may ensue. In his relations with 3, however, 2 knows that he has the assistance of 1 and can negotiate from a position of greater strength than if he were alone. Of course 1, 2, 3, and 4 could find themselves all on the same side if one of them had need to negotiate with 5, and men 1–6 could all find themselves working together in negotiations with 7. Men 1–6 would in that case work as a unit

[15]Genealogical inventions and omissions are extremely common (though often undetected) and are an impressive device for justifying landownership, political power and position, and so on.

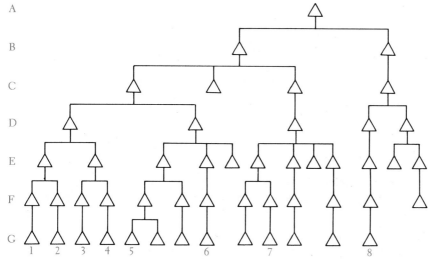

by invoking their common membership in a segment based upon an apical ancestor in generation C. Indeed, they might try to convince 7 to cooperate better with them by making appeal to the fact that he is, if one looks to generation B, a fellow lineage member with them.

Assuming that leadership roles are clear for each possible segment, a segmentary lineage system can be used to mobilize tremendous numbers of people for a specialized, short-term activity such as warfare. When an outside enemy is faced, a tremendous and temporarily united military force can be mustered to meet the threat. Indeed, if profit is to be had, it can be mustered to pose a threat. (On the other hand, the obligation of members to support segment mates at any level of segmentation results in an almost continual state of intersegmental squabbling.) Marshall Sahlans, in a provocative paper (1961), speaks of the segmentary lineage as an "organization of predatory expansion" at the expense of neighboring peoples who are not organized in a similar way. It is particularly characteristic of pastoral, nomadic peoples such as those of northern Africa whose populations are normally sparsely spread over the land, but who, on occasion, unite for a time for group activities. The Mongols were such a pastoralist group, organized in segmentary lineages. This principle of organization was powerful enough that, when other circumstances were favorable and sufficient leadership appeared in the person of Genghis Khan, the Mongols were able to establish an empire stretching from Poland to Persia to Korea, though their ability to maintain it was less impressive.

Residence rules: who moves where at marriage to keep the lineage together If lineages are exogamous, their members must choose spouses from other lineages. And if they are also localized, the members must live to-

UXORILOCAL
RESIDENCE *The*
custom whereby a bride
and groom take up
residence with (or very
near) the bride's parents.

VIRILOCAL
RESIDENCE *The*
custom whereby a bride
and groom take up
residence with the
groom's parents.

NEOLOCAL
RESIDENCE *The*
custom whereby a bride
and groom take up
residence independently
of either set of parents
or other kinsmen.

BILOCAL RESIDENCE
The custom whereby a
bride and groom take up
residence either with the
bride's parents or with
the groom's parents.

gether. How then are spouses to live with each other? This problem is solved in various ways, which are collectively called residence rules.

It is a normal thing among human beings for a child to live with or near its mater until it is married. It is also normal for the pater to live with them, though this has more exceptions. Once a child has been married, complications arise. Unless their original families (families of orientation[16]) are located very near to each other, it is not possible for both the bride and the groom to continue living near their parents and also to live together. They can go to live with (or very near) the bride's parents (an arrangement called "uxorilocal," from Latin *uxor*, meaning wife). The Navajo do this. Or they can go to live with the groom's parents (called "virilocal," from Latin *vir*, husband).[17] The Chinese do this. Or the couple can go somewhere else (called "neolocal"). Americans are neolocal. The Ndembu apparently take their choice, for Turner tells us that some men remain in Mukanza village and their wives come to live virilocally with them, while others go to live uxorilocally in their wives' villages. A system that allows a choice is called "bilocal."

Residence rules are not usually laws or regulations enforced upon members of a society, despite their name. The anthropologist induces the residence rules from his study of actual residence patterns. In most cases, the "rules" he induces correspond to very general expectations that members of the society have about the proper way to behave at marriage. In some societies these expectations allow of few exceptions and have a good deal of moral force. In other societies exceptions are many, and people do not seem particularly disturbed about them.

In classical China a man was expected to bring his wife and live with his father, preferably in the same house. A man who, for financial or other reasons, moved in with his wife's parents instead was always stigmatized as a "supernumerary husband." On the other hand, among Americans, who share a general understanding that the bride and groom should establish their own home, there is a very high tolerance (if little enthusiasm) for virilocal and uxorilocal arrangements and (to the best of our knowledge) no standard derogatory terms for people who engage in these minority residential arrangements.

This technical vocabulary of residence rules is very vague. If a society is "virilocal," that word does not specify whether *all* brides and grooms live with the groom's parents, or only the largest number of them. It does not

[16]Anthropologists distinguish between a person's "family of orientation," where he is born and raised and has the status of child, and his "family of procreation," which includes (in the case of a man) his wife and children and in which he has the statuses of husband and father.

[17]Some anthropologists, especially in the past, have used the words "matrilocal" and "patrilocal" for uxorilocal and virilocal, respectively. The "matri-" and "patri-" terms are easier to remember, but are misleading because they suggest mother and father rather than wife and husband. We have preferred the more precise and more current usage with "uxori-" and "viri-."

say whether they move there immediately upon marriage or ultimately. Some anthropologists have coined terms like "uxorivirilocal" to mean living first with the wife's, then with the husband's, parents. It does not say whether living "with" someone (say, the wife's parents) means living in the same house, the same village, or the same region.

Using a small set of technical terms to describe the great diversity of human institutions and behavior patterns is a perpetual problem. In the discussion of any particular group of people, it tells us very little to say of them only that they are uxorilocal. On the other hand, in a comparative perspective one can contrast, say, bilocal with neolocal groups and consider some of the problems that are likely to arise in one but not in the other. It is important to realize how vague our technical terms really are, but that is not a reason to consider them useless. (Similarly, calling a group "patrilineal" tells us little about what membership in a lineage entails for a person; but certain features characteristic of most patrilineal societies are different from those of most matrilineal or nonlineal societies.)

The operation of different residence rules results in different sets of people living with each other. In a virilocal society the local group consists of men all of whom have been born and raised in the same place (a village, say). The women, on the other hand, except for unmarried girls, may or may not have come from that same area. (This will depend partly upon typical marriage patterns, which we shall discuss shortly.) Virilocal residence is therefore an ideal pattern in a society that has kinship groups which depend on the cooperation of adult men all born and raised in the same place with rights by birth in its products. A patrilineage is just such a group. Not surprisingly, it develops that virtually all of the patrilineal societies we know about are also virilocal, though some other societies are also virilocal.

Table 14 shows the distribution of residence and descent rules in a sample of 428 of the societies that anthropologists have studied. From it we see that patrilineal descent is the most common descent rule in human societies and that virilocal residence is also the most common residence rule. The fit between virilocal residence and patrilineal descent is so good, furthermore, that all but 4 of the 181 patrilineal societies in the sample live virilocally as well.

Table 14   Distribution of Residence and Descent Rules in 428 Societies

RESIDENCE RULE	DESCENT RULE				
	None	Matrilineal	Patrilineal	Double	Total
Neolocal	26	1	1	0	28 = 6%
Bilocal	33	1	3	1	38 = 9%
Virilocal	78	9	177	17	281 = 65%
Uxorilocal	30	32	0	2	64 = 15%
Avunculocal[a]	1	15	0	1	17 = 4%
Total	168 = 39%	58 = 14%	181 = 42%	21 = 5%	428 = 100%

[a]Avunculocal residence is discussed on pp. 588–589.

SOURCE: After D'Andrade 1966:182.

From the table we may also notice that far fewer of the world's societies are matrilineal (14 percent) or uxorilocal (15 percent) than patrilineal or virilocal. The reason for this seems to lie in a very important but not well understood characteristic of social organization, that regardless of whether descent is through men or through women, it is men who actually exercise the most authority in all known human societies. The legendary Amazons, a society ruled entirely by women often represented in ancient Greek art and literature is in fact only that: a legend, without verifiable historical foundation. Even societies in which political power is centered in a queen turn out to have men in positions of power in families and kinship units. Explanations for this phenomenon vary from the greater size and strength of men to the exigencies of bearing and tending children.

Whatever the reason, the fact that authority resides in males means that matrilineal systems have operating problems not present in patrilineal systems. The patrilineage, if it is to be a major organization in society, needs to keep the men of the patrilineage in one place where they can effectively cooperate in the supervision of lineage activities. The matrilineage, if it is to do the same job, needs to organize men, too. That means that it must either keep the men of the matrilineage in one place or allocate authority to the husbands of the women of the matrilineage. If most marriages take place within a fairly small geographical area, this is, of course, not much of a problem. If, on the other hand, people move quite a distance at marriage, it means that if a man goes to live uxorilocally with his wife, he is not around to look after the lineage properties and interests of his home matrilineage. He must leave these to the care of his sister and her husband. In matrilineal, uxorilocal societies, we may expect to find that husbands become more involved with their wives' lineages and their affairs than they are with the lineage affairs of the lineages in which they grew up.

Types of Residence.

Neolocal residence

Bilocal residence

Virilocal residence

Uxorilocal residence

Avunculocal residence

AVUNCULOCAL
RESIDENCE *The
custom whereby a bride
and groom take up
residence with the groom's
mother's brother.*

Another arrangement is possible, and it has been a subject of great fascination for anthropologists. That is "avunculocal residence." All societies in which avunculocal residence is found are matrilineal, and we may see it as a solution to the problem of keeping the men of the lineage located spatially with their lineage mates. In an avunculocal system the groom takes his young bride to live with the groom's mother's brother. *Avunculus* is Latin for mother's brother. When they have children, and raise them to marriageable age, the children take the lineage membership of their mother, of course, and as such they have no claims on the lineage properties of their father or their father's matrilineage. At marriage a girl joins her husband. Neither before marriage nor after is she living where her own lineage has property and rights. Before marriage she is living with her father's matrilineage. After marriage she is living with her husband's matrilineage. The young groom moves away from his father and mother and his father's matrilineage and goes to live with his own mother's brother, presumably in the region where his and his mother's matrilineage have their property. Before marriage he is not living with the men of his matrilineage (with the exception of his unmarried brothers), and after marriage he joins them.

An avunculocal system is in a sense a special kind of neolocal system in that the married couple live with or near neither set of parents and nobody ends his life in the household where he began it. But it is different from other neolocal residence patterns in that the adult men who live together are all from the same matrilineage and are in a position to enjoy and protect the benefits of lineage membership. At first it may strike us as odd that a

Avunculocal Marriage.

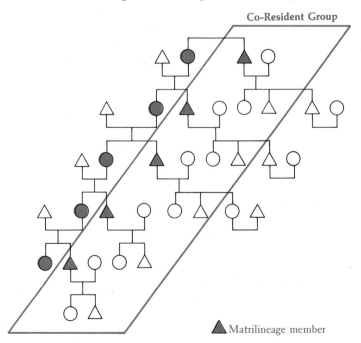

Co-Resident Group

▲ Matrilineage member

bride and groom would go to live with the groom's mother's brother in a place where neither of them had lived previously. But advantages of the arrangement become clear once we recognize that even in a matrilineal system it is the men who manage the resources of the lineage, so that the couple is in fact moving to the groom's economic base.

Our discussion of residence involves us in an important qualification of our original definition of lineage. We originally defined a "lineage" as a localized, exogamous, unilineal descent group, and we said that "localized" meant that the members lived in one or a few places. It is now clear that unless the intermarrying lineages are located right beside one another, only some of the lineage members will live at the "locale" around which the lineage is "localized." As we have seen in the avunculocal situation (which admittedly is rather rare), the minority of the lineage members live at the lineage locale, and most of the people living at the lineage locale are not lineage members. What we mean by "localized" is that the members of the lineage responsible for decision making must be localized in the same locale as the resources belonging to the lineage.[18]

Marriages between lineages: preference and prescription revisited As noted, lineages are exogamous, and the exchange of personnel between them through marriage constitutes an important element of their relationships to each other. Many marriages are deliberately planned with an eye to the forging of links between one lineage and another or between an individual and a lineage other than his own. Sandombu's marriage to J2 was made, insofar as it is possible to determine, not so much because Sandombu felt any attraction to J2 herself, and not because he particularly needed a wife—he already had more than most people—but because he felt that he might increase his chances of political support from the Malabu lineage if he had a marriage link with them. It is possible that his marriage to the (later deceased) D3-lineage daughter of Mukanza Kabinda was arranged with the same type of reasoning in mind.

In many societies there is not only a prohibition on marriage within one's own lineage, and a corresponding prescription that one marry into some other lineage, but there is also a feeling that it is preferable to arrange a marriage with a kinsman. There are several advantages to this. For one thing, kinsmen (both one's future spouse and one's prospective in-laws) may be more trustworthy than other people. For another, a marriage to one of a group of kinsmen in another lineage to whom one is already related in some way strengthens a relationship that already exists and makes it more dependable and hence more usable. If Jones is Smith's father's father's father's wife's brother's son's son's son, Jones and Smith are not very closely related. If Jones is *also* Smith's brother-in-law, the relationship between the Smiths and the Joneses has been made closer.

[18]In the patrilineal society of classical China a woman changed lineage membership at marriage and became a member of her husband's lineage. This appears to be one of the relatively few societies in which a localized lineage could really be literally localized.

COUSIN-MARRIAGE
RULE *A rule to the
effect that marriages
should preferentially or
prescriptively be made
with a person in the
status of cousin; typically,
this status refers to any
same-generation kinsman
of another lineage.*

The preference (or even prescription) for a *kinsman* of another lineage rather than merely a *member* of another lineage as a marital partner is widespread in human societies. For brevity anthropologists speak of such a preference as a "cousin-marriage rule," and the effects of such marriages are discussed as though first cousins were the ones being wed. The target kinsman is not necessarily literally a cousin, but rather a kinsman of the same generation in another lineage. Such a category includes some first cousins, however, and anthropological tradition is not so misleading as it might seem when it sets forth its discussions of preferential marriage with kinsmen of other lineages as though cousins were the heart of the issue. (Besides, things get complicated enough just thinking about marriage to literal cousins, as we shall see.)

Kinship notation Before we proceed with our discussion of marriage to "cousins" in other lineages, it is useful to look at a notational system that anthropologists use in kinship studies. First of all, it should be noted that everyone occupies several kinship statuses simultaneously. Thus, I am a son with respect to my father, a brother with respect to my sister, a father with respect to my children, and so forth. Anthropologists usually describe systems of kinship statuses by reference to a fixed, fictitious participant in the kinship arrangements they are discussing. This "person" is called Ego. Ego's kinsmen are identified in the anthropologist's notes by a series of conventional abbreviations taken from the English words "mother," "father," "daughter," "son," "sister," "brother," "wife," and "husband." Ego's mother is Mo; his daughter's husband is DaHu; his wife's brother's wife's father is WiBrWiFa; and so on. Using these abbreviations, the anthropologist can identify many kinship statuses and relationships that he would not be able to name precisely (or at all) in English (such as Ego's WiBrWiFa, whom we just mentioned).[19] An abbreviation such as "Br" or "DaHu" or "WiBrWiFa" is called a "kintype." By the use of such abbreviations, the anthropologist is in a position to make statements such as: "Mukanza Kabinda was Sandombu's MoMoSiSo."

Cousin marriage Returning to cousin marriage, it is first essential to determine which of Ego's cousins will be available as marriage mates and which will be in his own lineage, hence, ineligible. Let us start with Ego's "patrilateral" cousins, those on his father's side. Ego's Fa and his FaBr are in the same lineage. If it is a patrilineage, it also includes Ego and his FaBrDa. On the other hand, if FaBr can transmit lineage membership to his daughter,

---

[19]Some anthropologists prefer to use single-letter abbreviations: M, F, D, S, H, W, and so on. The only confusion arises between son and sister. By an internationally agreed-upon convention, "S" stands for son and "Z" stands for sister. Beyond this, different anthropologists extend the system as may be necessary to their own work. Thus, some may find a need for terms that do not distinguish sex, and for parent, child, spouse, and sibling use Pa(P), Ch(C), Sp(E), and Ge(G). Some may use "E" and "Y" as prefixes to distinguish elder and younger siblings (ESi, YSi), or what have you. None of these extensions has come into widely standardized use, however.

FaSi cannot, and FaSiDa is therefore sure to be outside the lineage. Ego can marry her. (See part [a] of the accompanying diagram "Lineages and Cousins.") If it is a matrilineage, Ego will be in a different lineage from his Fa and FaBr, but FaBr may have married a woman of Ego's lineage, so Ego's FaBrDa may or may not be outside his lineage. His FaSiDa, however, is sure to be of his father's same matrilineage, and because Ego is not of that matrilineage, FaSiDa is marriageable (part [b] of "Lineages and Cousins"). Therefore, whether the exogamous system is patrilineal or matrilineal, FaSiDa is always of another lineage from Ego and can be exogamously married.

What about Ego's "matrilateral" cousins, those on his mother's side? In a patrilineal system Ego's mother and his MoSi and MoBr are all of a different lineage from Ego. His MoBr can transmit that lineage membership, so that man's daughter, Ego's MoBrDa, is sure to be of another lineage, specifically, Ego's mother's lineage. On the other hand, if the system is matrilineal, Ego is in the same lineage with his Mo, MoSi, and MoBr. In a matrilineal system the MoBr will not be able to transmit his lineage membership to his daughter, who is therefore a possible spouse for Ego. But Ego's MoSi does transmit that membership. Accordingly, once again, MoSiDa is not marriageable, but MoBrDa is. Whether the exogamous system is patrilineal or matrilineal, MoBrDa is always of another lineage from Ego and can be married without violating lineage exogamy rules.

The MoBr's children and FaSi's children are referred to by anthropologists as "cross-cousins" because the siblings in Ego's parents' generation are of the opposite (cross) sex. Given lineage exogamy, cross-cousins are always of a different lineage from Ego.

Notice, however, that the structural effects of Ego's marrying his patrilateral cross-cousin (FaSiDa) are not quite the same as the effects of his marrying his matrilateral cross-cousin (MoBrDa). His MoBrDa is of the same lineage as Ego's mother. A marriage with her represents the same kind of tie between lineages that Ego's father's marriage with Ego's mother represents. If Ego and his father are of the Eagle lineage and Ego's mother and MoBrDa are of the Lion lineage, both marriages represent a union between

CROSS-COUSINS *The children of Ego's father's sisters and of Ego's mother's brothers.*

Lineages and Cousins.

Patrilineage Members

Matrilineage Members

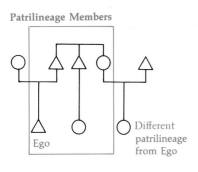

(a)

(b)

the Eagles and the Lions. On the other hand, a marriage with his FaSiDa does not represent the same kind of union Ego's father made (except in the special case where the society is divided into only two lineages).[20] Although Ego's FaSiDa is not of Ego's own lineage, she is not necessarily of his mother's lineage. If, however, Ego's son marries *his* FaSiDa (that is, Ego's sister's daughter), this lady will turn out to be of the same lineage as Ego's mother. The accompanying chart ("Cross-Cousin Marriage") shows diagrams of both patrilateral cross-cousin marriage and matrilateral cross-cousin marriage, with both matrilineages and patrilineages superimposed.[21] Selecting any Ego and tracing his cousins and his marriage on the diagram is easier than describing how the systems work.

The effect of having Ego's marriage be to a woman of his mother's lineage (his MoBrDa) is potentially quite different from the effect of his wife being in a different lineage from his mother. The matrilateral form provides a structure that is compatible, for example, with understandings that some lineages are superior to others. Anthropologists have found many systems of ranked lineages. In some it is understood that women from lower lineages marry into higher lineages (technically called "hypergamy"), and in some it is understood that women from higher lineages marry downwards ("hypogamy").[22] Whether or not there is an understanding that a woman's lineage is superior or inferior to her husband's—and there usually is—matrilateral cross-cousin marriage means that male members of a lineage always get their wives from the same other lineage and always marry their daughters to a different other lineage. In the diagram of cross-cousin marriage, model III, for example, indicates that men of lineage K marry women of lineage L and women of lineage K marry men of lineage J. With respect to lineage K, lineage-L men are wife givers, and lineage-J men are wife takers. If important dowry goods are paid, they will generally travel from L to K to J. If goods or services are owed to one's wife's father, such goods will travel from J to K to L, and services will be performed by J for K and by K for L. Shared understandings about duties owed "by whole lineages" to other lineages or about superiority and inferiority of lineages fit particularly well with such a marriage rule.

The patrilateral form of cross-cousin marriage has the opposite effect. If Ego is in lineage C and takes his wife from D, it cannot be said that C are the wife takers of D, for in the next generation Ego's son will take his

---

[20]As a pencil and paper will eventually show, in a system composed of only two lineages Ego's MoBrDa and his FaSiDa turn out to be the same "person" on the diagram, the same "category" in practice. In such a system, it is impossible to distinguish patrilateral from matrilateral cross-cousin marriage because both principles dictate the same choice of spouse. Some anthropologists worry about that.

[21]When a male Ego is marrying his MoBrDa in good matrilateral fashion, she is of course marrying her FaSiSo, which logically is a patrilateral marriage. To avoid confusion, it is conventional *always* to describe marriage systems from the point of view of a male Ego.

[22]Hypergamy and hypogamy also occur in systems without cousin marriage.

Patrilateral (FaSiDa) Form

I

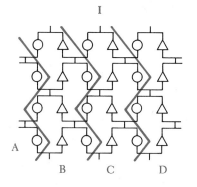

Patrilineages

II

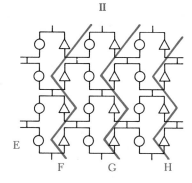

Matrilineages

Matrilateral (MoBrDa) Form

III

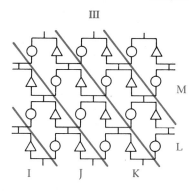

Patrilineages

IV

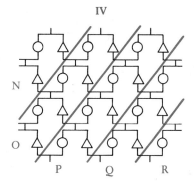

Matrilineages

Cross-cousin Marriage.

wife from B, and his daughter will marry into the lineage her mother came from. In a system of patrilateral cross-cousin marriage, a woman is always marrying her MoBrSo, and therefore she is always back into her mother's patrilineage or her mother's father's matrilineage. This system fits well with understandings that if a lineage such as F on our diagram receives a woman from lineage G in one generation, F will "pay them back" with a woman in the next generation.

Much has been made, particularly by Lévi-Strauss and his followers, of the "exchange" and "circulation" of women that is logically implied by these different forms of preferential and prescriptive cross-cousin marriage rules. One could equally logically think of the women as remaining stationary and speak of the "exchange" and "circulation" of men, of course, though in societies that follow such understandings it is much more common for the men to be thought of as the fixed parts of the system.

The point, in any case, is that the existence of understandings that pre-

PARALLEL COUSINS
*The children of Ego's
father's brothers and of
Ego's mother's sisters.*

scribe marriage with a particular cousin sets the stage for quite different sorts of relationships between lineages (and vice versa).[23]

Cousin marriage for other reasons So far we have considered cousin marriage as though it occurred only in societies with lineages and was related exclusively to trying to maintain ties with people in other lineages. There can be other reasons for the development of a system of cross-cousin marriage; and there are also systems of parallel-cousin marriage in societies that lack exogamous lineages. (Parallel cousins are Ego's MoSiDa, his FaBrDa, his MoSiSo, and his FaBrSo.) Let us begin by considering briefly a case in which cross-cousin marriage does not seem to be motivated primarily by a desire for ties between lineages.

When Malinowski studied the Trobriand Islands during World War I, the Trobrianders (who had matrilineages) explained that the best person to marry was one's patrilateral cross-cousin. As Malinowski explored this, he discovered that this was not a random choice, nor did it have to do primarily with maintaining ties to other lineages. It seemed to derive instead from psychological stresses and political strategies of everyday life. Trobriand fathers, he found, often wished to transmit their property to their children, but this was impossible because of the rule of matrilineal descent and inheritance by which a man's property goes to his sister's son. By insisting upon a system of patrilateral cross-cousin marriage (model II on p. 207), a Trobriand Ego could assure himself that his son would be married to a woman who was under Ego's guardianship and control (for he was her MoBr), and that his son's children would enjoy full inheritance of Ego's property, inasmuch as his son would be married to a woman of Ego's same matrilineage who could transmit that membership. The Trobrianders seemed to be using a "rule" of preferential patrilateral cross-cousin marriage to lessen the potential psychological conflict between a matrilineal system of descent and inheritance and the affection of fathers for their sons.

We noted earlier that parallel cousins will be in Ego's own lineage, hence, not marriageable because of the rule of lineage exogamy. However, not all societies that have unilineal descent groups have exogamous lineages. In some areas (most notably the Near East) endogamous unilineal descent groups exist, often accompanied by understandings about the purity of women and about the danger of their being polluted by men of other descent groups. The advantage of endogamy is that it excludes "outsiders"

[23]Logical elaborations on cross-cousin marriage go beyond those we have been able to discuss here. For example, if in a matrilineal society Ego is allowed to marry neither into his own lineage nor into his father's matrilineage—that is the rule among the matrilineal Navajo, for example—then model II of the diagram becomes impossible, because in that model Ego's wife is always in his father's matrilineage. The system necessarily reverts to the model IV, with its bias toward ranking. In a patrilineal society, the model shown in III provides that Ego's wife is always in his mother's patrilineage, and, accordingly, a double-exogamy rule pushes the system to model I, with its bias toward interlineage relations of reciprocity. There are enough chicken-and-egg problems implicit in all this to keep kinship theorists going for years.

entirely from access to the resources of the descent group and relieves the descent group of any obligations to support or assist outsiders. The endogamous group itself is simultaneously a localized community and a kinship community, with strong loyalties of its membership to itself. The same sense of independence that precludes marriage outside of the endogamous unilineal descent group—one writer calls it a "deme" (Murdock 1949)—may lead to preference for marriage to a close kinsman (or as close as understandings about incest allow) rather than to a more distant one. A parallel cousin is such a person. In an endogamous system, a MoSiDa or FaBrDa is normally about the closest marriageable kinsman available to Ego as a marriage mate.

The ultimate marriage prescription: the Australians Our discussion of "cousin" marriage has been a special case of understandings about who is and who is not a potential spouse for a given Ego. Every society has *some* understandings about which marriages are to be encouraged and which discouraged, which insisted upon and which prohibited altogether. The ones we have been discussing have lineage membership and kinship status central among the understandings that lead to the "rules" of the system. In some societies more elaborate systems of rules for the selection of a mate among kinsmen exist, however, systems that reach a degree of baroque extravagance among such Australian groups as the Arunta and the Murngin, creators of the "eight-section" systems of marriage regulation celebrated in anthropological song and story.

In Australia an entire society is typically divided into two exogamous

Australian Men. The most elaborate systems regulating marriage preference are found among the native peoples of the island continent of Australia.

patrilineal descent groups called moieties.[24] The society is then further divided into two endogamous "generation" groups, membership in which may not be inherited; thus, a child is always in the opposite generation group from his parents but in the same one as his grandparents. (Because different people have children at different ages, these generation groups are, of course, composed of people of all ages.) There are therefore four "sections" of society or kinds of people, differentiated by moiety membership (say, A or B) and generation membership (say, 1 or 2): A1, A2, B1, and B2. If Ego is an A2, he can marry only a B2. His son will be an A1 and will be able to marry only a B1. This is called a "four-section" system.

If each moiety is divided into two exogamous submoieties, there are eight possible kinds of people. This provides the basis of the "eight-section" system. In an eight-section system, in keeping with his membership in the same "generation" category (say, 1) as his FaFa, Ego marries a woman of the same submoiety as his FaFa did; that is, he marries a woman of the same submoiety as his FaMo. He is, in addition, prohibited from marrying a woman of the same submoiety as his Mo, his MoMo, or, of course, himself. If Ego's FaFa is of submoiety A and his FaMo is of submoiety B, Ego will

[24]The word "moiety," related through Old French *moité* to Latin *medius*, meaning middle, is used as a specialized designation for a descent group when the entire society is divided into only two such groups.

Australian Eight-Section System.

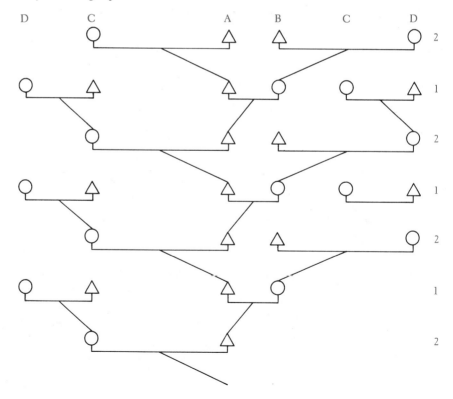

marry into submoiety B. If Ego's WiMo is, say, from submoiety D, his son will have to avoid A, B, and D, and marry a girl from C. Ego's grandson will duplicate Ego's choice and marry a B girl, his great-grandson will marry a C girl, and so on.[25] (See the diagram entitled "Australian Eight-Section System.")

The effect of this is an exchange of women between submoieties A and B and between C and D in generations numbered 1, but between A and C and between B and D in generations numbered 2. (A never exchanges with D, and B never exchanges with C.) The political implications alone of such a system are awesome to contemplate, and it is not surprising that Australian kinship has kept anthropologists fascinated for decades. Sandombu's problem would have been quite different if the Ndembu had been a central-Australian society.

Kinship Terminology

The set of names that participants assign to kinship statuses (words like "uncle," "cousin," and "grandfather" in English or like *hermano, primo,* and *abuela* in Spanish) are called "kinship terms," or "kinterms." Their study is important because a working assumption made by most anthropologists (although sometimes proved wrong in particular cases) is that each kinterm labels a social status with particular expectations associated with all occupants of that status that are different from the expectations associated with occupants of other statuses.[26] An "uncle," in other words, is expected to behave toward his nephew or niece in certain ways and not in others, and the range of expected behavior from him is different from the range of behavior expected from an "aunt" or a "cousin" or a "mother."

KINTERMS (KINSHIP TERMS) *The names that label kinship statuses in a society.*

What has been discovered by the comparative study of systems of kinterms is, briefly stated, that certain patterns of status names (and presumably therefore of statuses) come up in society after society and that there are correlations between systems of kinship statuses on the one hand and such other aspects of kinship behavior as rules of incest, restrictions on marriage, or lineage organization.

Classification and description The cousin (MoSiDa) who fed Kahali Chandenda when Sandombu's wife was too slow was a woman named Nyamwaha (F7), whom Kahali referred to by an Ndembu word that he also used in reference to his sisters. Turner refers to her as a "classificatory sister," that is, a woman classified into the same status category as a sister.[27] Turner

[25]No rule of cousin marriage of the kind we have discussed with other systems will distinguish Ego's potential spouses in an eight-section system, which is really a system of second-cousin marriage: Ego can marry his MoMoBrDaDa, who, it develops, is the same as his FaFaSiSoDa.

[26]Some anthropologists use the phrase "kinship system" to mean system of kinship terms. Such a usage is misleading, but it is indicative of how important they consider the terms to be in the study of kinship.

[27]Turner does not say whether a MoSiDa and a Si have *identical* role relationships with their classificatory brother (Kahali Chandenda in this case) or not. Presumably their roles toward him are at any rate very similar.

does not say what the Ndembu word is that names this status, but presumably it includes *at least* Si and MoSiDa, and it is because Nyamwaha was in this relation to Kahali that he was able to go to her for food when he was spurned by Sandombu's wife. Nyamwaha was apparently so touched by Kahali's plight that she even threw in beer, which Turner makes clear was above and beyond the call of duty. Kahali's "real" sister (his Si) told him "in anger and shame" how Sandombu had divided the meat in Kahali's absence and how he had shorted the old man of his due. Both Kahali's Si and his MoSiDa, both of his classificatory sisters, in other words, were worried on his behalf and were determined to help him. Both felt and acted toward him in the way that was appropriate to the status of a (classificatory) sister, named by a particular Ndembu word.

A kinterm that includes several kintypes is said to "classify" these kintypes together, and a system of terms that contains such classificatory terms is said to be a "classificatory system." A system of terms that does not include classificatory terms is called a "descriptive system." Nearly all kinterm systems classify at least to some extent and at least for kinsmen remote from Ego, but it is still a convenient shorthand to speak of the extent to which one system is more classificatory or more descriptive than another. It is a reasonable working assumption (though it does not always hold) that highly descriptive systems of kinterms are accompanied by kinship statuses that are different and involve different role expectations for nearly every one of Ego's kinsmen; while highly classificatory systems are likely to be accompanied by statuses with more general role obligations that are the same for large classes of Ego's kinsmen.

Some common kinterm systems Some of the most frequently found terminological systems are shown in the accompanying diagram of cousin-term systems. The diagram includes terms for members of the zero and plus-one generations.[28] For some reason, the names of these systems of terms are descriptive adjectives ("generational," "lineal," "bifurcate") for the plus-one generation terms but names of groups of people ("Iroquois," "Sudanese," "Eskimo," "Hawaiian") for the zero-generation terms. These names are too hallowed by use and time to warrant our proposing new names here.

The generational-Hawaiian system is the most classificatory of the lot, using only two terms (one for each sex) for all members of the plus-one generation and only two terms (one for each sex) for the zero generation. It is as though we were to refer to our mothers and our aunts by one word meaning mother/aunt ("maunt"?) and to our fathers and our uncles by one word meaning father/uncle ("funcle"?).[29]

CLASSIFICATORY SYSTEM *A system of kinterms that includes at least one term that refers to kinsmen in more than one genealogical relationship to Ego.*

DESCRIPTIVE SYSTEM *A system of kinterms that includes no term that refers to kinsmen in more than one genealogical relationship to Ego.*

[28]Anthropologists refer to Ego's generation as zero, to his Fa's generation as plus-one, to his FaFa's generation as plus-two, to his son's generation as minus-one, and so on.

[29]The system used in English is approximately the lineal-Eskimo one, except that in English we do not distinguish sex in cousin terms: We are apparently a bit more classificatory than the Eskimo.

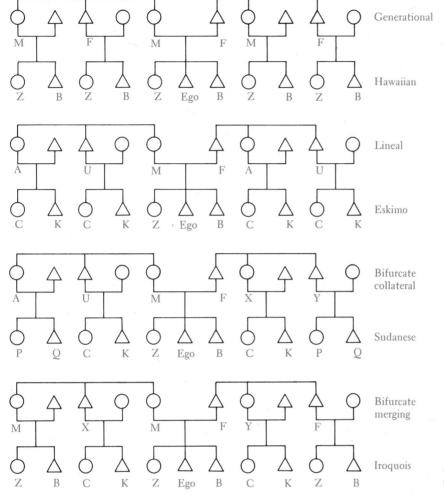

Generational

Hawaiian

Lineal

Eskimo

Bifurcate
collateral

Sudanese

Bifurcate
merging

Iroquois

Common Kinterm
Systems.

The most descriptive among these sets of terms is the bifurcate-collateral-Sudanese, which distinguishes paternal from maternal aunts and uncles and both sets from parents, and which distinguishes parallel cousins from cross-cousins and both from siblings. (It has *not* distinguished patrilateral from matrilateral cousins, so it is still not a completely descriptive system.) Note that in a lineage system (or some comparable system) practicing cousin marriage and using Sudanese cousin terms, marriageable cousins (C and K) are terminologically distinguished from unmarriageable ones (P and Q). The system of kinterms is therefore suitable to a system in which these two statuses are importantly different.

The bifurcate-merging terms differ from bifurcate-collateral terms in that they use the same term for Fa and for FaBr (and the same term for Mo and MoSi). Such a set of terms would also make sense in a system of unilineal descent groups, in which these people are fellow members. The Iroquois terms often associated with bifurcate-merging systems distinguish cross-cousins from parallel cousins (as do the Sudanese terms), but use the same terms for parallel cousins as for siblings. (We think of the Ndembu, where Si and MoSiDa are in the same category.) This would make sense, too, in a strongly lineage-oriented society or similar situation where parallel cousins may be "like siblings" as far as Ego is concerned.

Crow and Omaha kinship terms The matrilineal Crow Indians of the North American Great Plains area used a system of kinship terms that has become (in)famous in anthropological studies because it used the same words for kinsmen of more than one generation. Thus a Crow used one kin-term for his FaSi, FaSiDa, FaSiDaDa, FaSiDaDaDa, and so forth. Another term labeled a status that included his MoBrSo, So, BrSo, FaBrSoSo, and FaSiSoSoSo. Bizarre as such statuses seem to be, the system turns out to be a fairly common one that, together with the very similar Omaha system, is found in more than 100 societies.

In the diagram of the Crow system of terms, the actual words are represented by single letters. Ego's grandparents (A and B) and most of the minus-two generation are not particularly odd. The key to the rest seems to lie in the fact that the Crow were a matrilineal society. Within his own matrilineage, Ego used one male and one female term for each generation (C and D in the plus-one generation, I and J in the zero generation, M and N in the minus-one generation).

The Crow System of Kinterms.

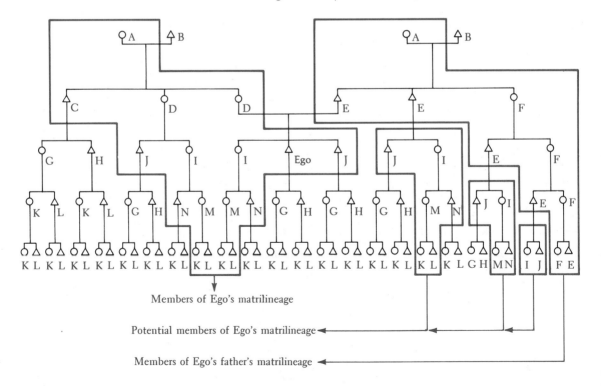

Members of Ego's matrilineage

Potential members of Ego's matrilineage

Members of Ego's father's matrilineage

But Ego's father's matrilineage was also a unit of concern to him, if for no other reason than because it was of concern to his father. The special terms E and F were used for members of it, regardless of generation. What mattered to Ego was not their generation, apparently, but their status as members of his father's lineage. Men of Ego's father's lineage were possible husbands for women of Ego's own matrilineage (even as Ego's father had married Ego's mother), and the terminology that Ego used for their offspring is the same terminology that Ego might have used had they, like Fa, married Ego's Mo. Thus, the son and daughter of any man of Ego's father's lineage is called J or I (classificatory brother or sister), and the daughter and son of a woman called I are called M and N, just as Ego's SiDa and SiSo are called M and N. If we assume that the terminological system represents in some measure the reality of actual social statuses, we must assume that the issue of lineage membership and potential marriage matches was far more important in Crow society than generation was, for that is what would explain why the terminology is as it is.

Men of Ego's matrilineage, of course, could not pass on their lineage membership. Neither could they marry lineage members. Special terms were used to designate their sons and daughters (H and G). Some H's and G's are children of lineage mates of Ego's generation, some of other generations. Some, by American thinking, are close to him (like his own children), while others are distant from him (like the son and daughter of his FaSiSoSo). All alike, however, are children of men of his matrilineage, and that puts them in the same status as far as the terminological system is concerned. Their children are K and L, or "grandchildren," which presumably carried an implication of great genealogical distance.

The Crow system of kinship terms (and the Omaha system, which is virtually identical, except that it is patrilineal rather than matrilineal) probably inspired interest originally because of the difficulty encountered in trying to imagine how the same term could be used for kinsmen of different generations. It continues to inspire interest because it is a vivid example of the fact that kinship terms and the statuses they label are the products of shared understandings of the participants about how to behave toward other people and about how to expect other people will behave toward them. What participants experience as important is what will be recognized by the system of terms. Understandings about kinship statuses and the words that name them are part of the same system of understandings as understandings about descent, residence at marriage, duties in the family, and who can and cannot be married: the kinship system.

SUMMARY

Kinship statuses are social categories. They are related to biology, but are different from it. A child's social mother (mater) is not necessarily the same person as the child's biological mother (genetrix).

A family is a co-resident kinship unit that includes children and their mother and makes some provision for the rearing of children. Nearly always it is also a unit of economic production and consumption and includes both a husband and a wife. A family composed only of a husband and wife and their children is called a nuclear family. Because larger family units are often more difficult to maintain than smaller ones, even societies in which the nuclear family is not the ideal family form usually have some nuclear families. A family in which a man has several wives is called polygynous. The Ganda provide an example of life in a polygynous family. A family in which a woman has several husbands (a much rarer form) is called polyandrous. Either form may also be called polygamous. When a family includes not only a husband and wife and their children but also the wife or husband of one of the children and the children of this pair as well, it is called an extended family. The Chinese provide an example of life in an extended family.

Life in a larger family unit is different from life in a smaller one, partly because the larger number of adults allows the children more constant adult attention and because privacy is much reduced. In polygynous families jealousy between different wives, often because of differences in privileges enjoyed by their children, is a frequent source of discord.

The statuses of husband and wife, like other kinship statuses, are social categories and do not correspond perfectly with biological mates. Every society has rules about who may marry whom, including an incest taboo, or prohibition on marriages between certain kinsmen. The reason for this is still not clear. A prohibition on marriage with some category of individual such as occurs in the incest taboo is called a proscription. Some societies also have preferences and prescriptions, that is, rules about whom one ought to or must marry. A group that allows its members to marry only outsiders is said to be exogamous. One that allows its members to marry only other group members is called endogamous.

Descent is a person's claim to membership in a social group or category consisting of his ancestors and persons descended from them. When descent is traced through links of one sex only, a unilinear descent group may result. Unilineal descent groups that are localized and exogamous are called lineages, and many societies have lineages, which function as major organizing groups in society. In a segmentary lineage system, different apical ancestors are chosen to establish different-sized groups for different purposes. Such systems are capable of generating lineage groups as small as a couple of families and as large as the entire society and may be mobilized, for example, in the resolution of disputes, war, and economic activity.

Residence rules are understandings about who moves where at marriage, and they are related to lineages because different residence rules unite or separate the individuals with an interest in lineage resources. The terms "uxorilocal," "virilocal," "neolocal," and "bilocal" refer to residence rules. Most societies in a world sample are virilocal, which seems to have to do with the fact that men have authority over resources regardless of the descent system. The combination of patrilineal descent and virilocality seems to be particularly stable. Matrilineal systems, in order to keep the men of the lineage spatially near to each other, pose peculiar problems of residence. Avunculocal residence is an example of an arrangement designed to solve some of these problems.

In some societies preferential marriage is practiced toward kinsmen in other lineages, a situation known as cousin marriage, although cousin marriage may also be practiced in nonlineage systems. Cousin marriage has different effects depending upon the kind of marriage link that is prescribed or preferred. The matrilateral form is congruous with systems of socially ranked lineages, while the patrilateral form is congruous with systems of socially equal lineages. A particularly extreme system of prescriptive marriage is found in the eight-section systems of some Australian groups.

Kinterms are names that are assigned to particular kinship statuses. A working assumption is that named statuses are socially different from each other. Several systems of relationships among kinship terms have been discovered to be very widespread over the world as a whole, and, as a result, anthropologists have developed a set of names for these systems. Terms such as "bifurcate collateral" and "Crow" refer to paradigms for the organization of kinsmen into named statuses. Different systems of terms are congruent with different social structures.

SUGGESTED READINGS

More on the case

TURNER, V. W. 1957 Schism and Continuity in an African Society: A Study of Ndembu Village Life. Manchester, England: Manchester University Press.

This ethnography, an important work of political anthropology, contains important data on kinship and how it is used among the Ndembu.

Other readings

DAVENPORT, WILLIAM 1959 Nonunilinear Descent and Descent Groups. American Anthropologist 61:557–569.

A general discussion, with numerous ethnographic examples, of descent groups other than lineages. In combination with Fortes (1953) it covers the idea of descent (as opposed to kinship).

FORTES, MEYER 1953 The Structure of Unilineal Descent Groups. American Anthropologist 55:25–39.

This paper is a classic discussion of lineages and their general definition.

FOX, ROBIN 1967 Kinship and Marriage: An Anthropological Perspective. Baltimore: Penguin.

A readable introduction to anthropological theory in the field of kinship and marriage that has become a handbook in many anthropology courses.

GOUGH, E. KATHLEEN 1959 The Nayars and the Definition of Marriage. Journal of the Royal Anthropological Institute 89:23–34.

This paper is included not only because the subject is raised in the kinship chapter of this book, but also because it is an extremely memorable ethnographic case that vividly brings home the point that marriage is far from self-evidently universal. In combination with Spiro (1954) it provides an entire education in cultural relativity. It also focuses on an important problem in the relevance and nature of universal institutions and definitions.

SAHLINS, MARSHALL D. 1961 The Segmentary Lineage: An Organization of Predatory Expansion. American Anthropologist 63:322–343.

This famous article describes the way in which segmentary lineages allow the integration of the activities of large numbers of people for temporary projects such as defense or aggression and therefore provide a means for the subjugation of adjacent peoples with less-efficient means of organization. It also shows the significance of kinds of kinship links in social organization.

SLATER, MARIAM KREISELMAN 1959 Ecological Factors in the Origin of Incest. American Anthropologist 61:1042–1058.

Most anthropological papers on incest are pretty silly; basically, we do not know why there is an incest taboo. This paper is a little more interesting and provocative than most, and relates human behavior with respect to incest to the behavior of other hominids.

SPIRO, MELFORD E. 1954 Is the Family Universal? American Anthropologist 56:839–846.

This paper criticizes a traditional definition of the family. It also provides data about the Israeli kibbutz family that expands our view of what "family" life might be like. (There is a follow-up note in A Modern Introduction to the Family, 1958. Norman W. Bell and Ezra F. Vogel, Eds. New York: Free Press.)

6

Economics

For no man giveth, but with intention of Good to himselfe; because Gift is voluntary; and of all Voluntary Acts, the Object is to every man his own Good.

HOBBES
LEVIATHAN, 1651

Bushman mother pounding bark.

How are resources distributed in primitive societies?

How are resources distributed in large-scale societies?

What are the symbolic aspects of resource distribution?

How does the distribution of resources relate to social statuses and expectations?

What is money?

How does money relate to the distribution of resources?

What kinds of resource-distribution systems have anthropologists found?

How useful is the idea of reciprocity in studying economic life?

Are there universals in the division of labor in society?

How does the division of labor relate to resource distribution?

The Martínez of Azteca: A Case of Subsistence Economics

Pedro Martínez was fifty-nine years old and lived with his wife Esperanza and six children (ages seven to twenty-three) in a Mexican highland village about 60 miles south of Mexico City when he and his family were studied by Oscar Lewis in 1940.[1] Lewis calls the village Azteca, recognizing the bicultural character of it: The Martínez spoke both Nahuatl, the language of the ancient Aztecs, and Spanish. Like many other "Indians" of the area, they lived economically on the very fringes of Spanish-speaking Mexican society. The Martínez family was desperately poor and always had been. Its members were often forced to borrow money or buy provisions on credit because they were unable to pay for them. As a result they were (like peasants in most parts of the world) normally in debt.

> Pedro couldn't remember a time when he hadn't been in debt. Early this past year, after he had come out of the hospital where he had had surgery, he had borrowed 300 pesos from the widow Isabel to pay medical bills. Then, finding his indebtedness to her irksome because she expected free "legal" advice from him, he had borrowed 150 pesos from a wealthy politico to help pay her

back, and 300 pesos from Asunción to pay other bills. And all this time he was paying back, at eight per cent monthly interest, a loan of 200 pesos from the previous year. At times it seemed as if he were walking forever in a treadmill of old obligations. "The debt remains; only the creditors change" [1959:40].

Pedro's subsistence came in part from crops he grew in communal land in the hills around Azteca. This land was the property of a municipality of seven villages of which Azteca was one, and it was available to any of their inhabitants who wished to work it. Heavy rains washed the topsoil from cleared areas, however, and it was necessary every two or three years to clear more fields.

> Pedro and his sons burned the brush and weeds, cut down young trees, and built new stone fences. . . . But the crops could supply enough corn and beans for only three or four months. So Pedro had to try other means of earning a living as well— making rope from maguey fiber, selling plums, hiring out his sons as farmhands [Lewis 1959:39].

Money that was earned by the two sons who worked as hired hands in the field of a wealthy neighbor, Don Porfirio, was contributed to the common family resources and provided a source of cash for the supplies that the family had to buy, and, of course, for paying off debts from cash borrowings earlier.

The day before the one that Lewis singles out for discussion Pedro had sold one of his two mules in order to pay off his debt to a certain Doña Conde.

> It infuriated him to think that he had to sell it for only 300 pesos when it was easily worth 450. And now he had only one mule left. This meant that the boys could bring only half the usual

[1]Excerpts and material in the description of Pedro Martínez and his family from "The Martínez Family," in FIVE FAMILIES: The Anthropology of Poverty: A Revealing Portrait of Lives, Customs, and Emotions in Mexico, by Oscar Lewis, with a foreword by Oliver La Farge, © 1959 by Basic Books, Inc., Publishers, New York. With permission. Indicated pagination, however, is from the New American Library Mentor edition. Lewis has expanded on the story of this family in Pedro Martínez: A Mexican Peasant and His Family (1964).

amount of wood down the mountains and that there would be little left to sell after Esperanza took what she needed. Besides, during the plum season the boys could earn only half of what they had the year before hauling crates of fruit to the railway station [Lewis 1959:40].

Pedro and his sons were the breadwinners of the Martínez family. They rose before dawn to leave for their work in the fields, either their own fields or those of their employer, and did not return until seven o'clock in the evening. Esperanza and her daughter Machrina, however, spent their day cooking, grinding corn, sewing, buying food in the market, sweeping out the house and the little courtyard, and tending the two youngest boys. Lewis paints a vivid picture of Esperanza's life as head of the domestic sphere of the family's life:

When the men had gone [to the fields to work in the morning] Esperanza took stock of the day's food supply. There was only a little corn dough left, barely enough for the two boys still asleep, and some chile, and cinnamon, sugar, and salt. There was no money because Pedro had used the mule money to buy huaraches [shoes] for Felipe, a sombrero for himself, and a machete for Ricardo

Azteca Village in Mexico.

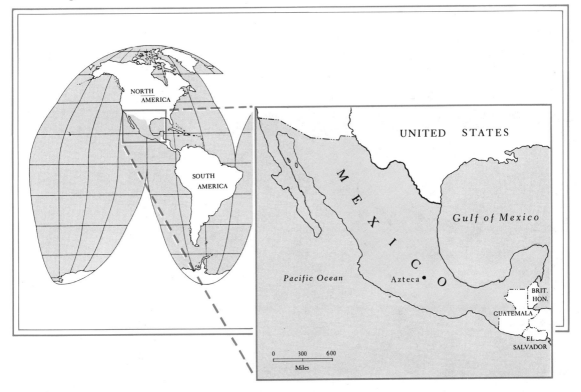

—all badly needed for work in the fields. The rest of the money had gone to the hateful Doña Conde. Where could she borrow now? What small thing could she sell? . . . Even when Pedro gave her larger sums it would usually be spent quickly, either to repay debts or to buy something they urgently needed. . . .

Esperanza wondered from whom she could borrow. She could not ask her cousin Maria for a loan, for she had not paid back the ten pesos borrowed a few days ago. Nor could she approach her Aunt Gloria; she had herself stopped by yesterday to ask for a small loan. . . . No one else nearby ever had enough money to lend, and Esperanza did not want to borrow a small sum at interest from those who had plenty. It was better to sell the turkey even though it would be a long time before she would be able to buy another baby turkey to raise. Esperanza drank her cinnamon tea and went to look for the bird [leaving her daughter Machrina, seventeen, in charge of the house] [1959:43].

She did not sell the turkey in the end, for she was offered only 2½ *pesos*, which was too low a price. Instead she went to call on her sons' employer and got an advance on their wages of 4 *pesos* and 4 liters of corn.

In the afternoon Esperanza visited her married daughter Conchita, who lived with her husband, apparently in the same village:

Esperanza wiped the back of her hand with her shawl and, still standing, said, "Just imagine, I could not sell the turkey today. They offered only two and a half pesos for it." Conchita went into the house and came out a moment later with a sardine tin full of beans. Esperanza dropped the beans into her shawl and returned the measuring tin. They exchanged a few words, Esperanza said, "Thanks, little daughter," and quickly left.

It was five o'clock, not much time to prepare the beans for the men [Lewis 1959:59].

Mexican Village Scene. The pseudonymous village of Azteca may have resembled this back street in Taxco.

Analysis of the Case

This is an undramatic case, although in Lewis's description there are a number of flashbacks to dramatic incidents in the course of the family's history. But the flow of everyday life in the Martínez family immediately raises a number of points that are important in the anthropological study of economic organization.

One thing that immediately stands out is how different Pedro's activities were from Esperanza's. Pedro is represented as a hard worker and as a man very concerned about the welfare of his family and (in other passages) about the welfare and progress of his community. Nevertheless, he did not spend much of his time in his little house, which seems to have been primarily a place for sleeping. Most of his day (or anyway most of this particular day) he spent tending his crops on the common lands outside Azteca. His older sons (ages twenty-three, twenty-two, and eighteen) were also engaged with the crops, either working jointly with Pedro in his fields or working as peons in the field of the wealthy landowner. Pedro's farming efforts did not yield enough food to feed the entire family all year around, and he supplemented with food supplies (and other supplies) bought with cash earned through the production and sale of rope, the transportation of plums in season, and the like. We are told elsewhere that he was also "half a lawyer" and brought in a little cash this way. Esperanza, on the other hand, seems not to have participated in production for the family beyond her sewing (for domestic use only) and keeping the turkey. Her energies, and those of her daughter Machrina, were devoted to maintaining the household and feeding the family with the resources that Pedro and his sons provided. Much of the difficulty of Esperanza's position was that these resources were meager, and her work could be accomplished only with a certain amount of trading and borrowing. Her husband and sons were not always aware of this. Pedro was never told that the beans were a gift of his married daughter, for example, for Pedro and his son-in-law were on very bad terms, and Pedro had forbidden members of his family to have any contact with Conchita and her household.

The Martínez family constituted a single economic unit, with the economic relation of each member to the whole being determined by the member's sex and age. Pedro's work and his wife's work were quite different. Furthermore, they were training their sons to do the sort of work Pedro did and their daughter to do the sort of work Esperanza did. The fact of being male or female in Mexican rural society (as in all societies) involved expectations about what activities one would engage in, expectations that Pedro and Esperanza followed automatically as part of the natural course of things and that they taught their children to follow equally automatically. Occupying the status of man or woman in Azteca required performance of "men's work" or "women's work." In rural Mexico, as in most peasant societies, the type of labor attached to the status of man or woman is so integral a part of status expectations that the failure to conform to the expectations

Mexican Farm Laborers
Line Up for Pay.
By hiring out as peons
Pedro's sons helped add
to the family's shared
cash resources.

about labor endangers one's occupancy of the status. Far more than in urban American society, peasant society tends to make division of labor by sex a defining characteristic of male and female statuses.

In this chapter we shall consider some features of the sexual division of labor as anthropologists have found it in the societies they have studied, and we shall examine some of the reasons that seem to underlie the similarities that have been discovered about what is "women's work" and what is "men's work" in various societies.

Pedro made part of his money by making rope from the fibers of the maguey (agave) plant, a tough, cactuslike succulent that is native to Mexico. Pedro did not make this rope for his own use, but to sell. Presumably the people who bought the rope did not make rope themselves, but earned money in some other way. Pedro was not an independent economic entity. This situation raises the problem of the distribution of products from the producers to the people who ultimately make use of them, the problem of economic distribution, which will occupy the bulk of our chapter.

There are several ways that distribution may occur, and our case illustrates at least two. The more important one for the Martínez family involved the use of money as a medium of exchange, and the Martínez and their neighbors were very concerned with money. Both Pedro and Esperanza were engaged in much borrowing, selling, and earning. Although apparently the bulk of the produce that Pedro raised was for his own family's consumption, he also earned a certain amount of cash. This money, like the wages earned by his sons as peons or in selling firewood or transporting plums, was the family's mode of access to the products that they did not provide for themselves in Pedro's fields. Esperanza needed cash (or credit, with the promise of cash in the future) to buy provisions. Her neighbors presumably understood her desperation when she had no money—they were often reduced to the same state themselves—but without money to lend her they were not in a position to help her. An intricate web of debts is characteristic of most peasant societies.

On the other hand, not all distribution of economic resources involved cash. One person provided Esperanza with food without asking for payment, and that was her married daughter Conchita, who apparently simply gave her mother the tin of beans, in spite of the formal hostility between the households. As far as we can tell from Lewis's account, Conchita did not expect her mother to pay her for the beans. However, their relationship was such that presumably if Conchita had come to her mother in the same circumstances, Esperanza would also have given her whatever she could have spared. Esperanza and Conchita seem to have engaged in occasional exchanges of food (and presumably of other things) on the basis of not very

Mexican Woman and Children Removing Corn from Cobs. In Mexican villages preparation of food is women's work. This rural woman is assisted by the family's children.

Mexican Market. Rural Mexicans grow crops for their own use. They also depend on local markets to sell their produce and as a source for things they do not grow or manufacture for themselves.

closely calculated reciprocity rather than on the basis of cash payments. In this case this kind of distribution of economic resources seems related to prescriptive understandings about how mothers act toward daughters and how daughters act toward mothers in Azteca. Economics here is closely tied to kinship statuses, so much so that kinship and economics cannot even be separated for analysis very easily. Although Lewis does not say so, one suspects that both Esperanza and Conchita would have been horrified at the prospect of Conchita selling her mother the beans for cash or on credit; that was not how moral daughters acted.

In the course of this chapter we shall be much concerned with systems of distribution and exchange, based on money or gifts or accomplished in other ways, and we shall try to see how systems of exchange are related to expectations associated with role relations. We shall also be concerned to see how money relates to other media of exchange and to distinguish between true money, or "general-purpose money," which may be used for a wide variety of exchanges, and media of exchange with more limited use, usually called "special-purpose money," which can be used only in some spheres of exchange and not in others.

Distribution and the Division of Labor

There is no human society in which each person is entirely self-sufficient, performing all the jobs necessary to his own subsistence, depending upon no one, supporting no one. Such people exist, of course—the Robinsons

Crusoe of their societies—but in no society are they a significant proportion of the population. Most people live in constant economic interaction with other people, sometimes providing for the needs of others, sometimes being provided for by others. If this were not done, at least in a minimal way, preganancy would be far more dangerous than it is, sickness would claim more fatalities, and the aged would expire as soon as they could not fend for themselves. Because all children would die within a few hours of birth, the society would not long continue. Hobbes's vision of the "war of all against all" is pure fiction: Such a society has never existed and could not exist. As we saw earlier in the chapter on human beginnings (Chapter 8), social living is part of the primate heritage but a key aspect of this is mutual support and protection. In humans (and only in humans), regular food sharing is universal.

An important problem in the study of human behavior, then, is how people share their means of subsistence. What makes someone share what he has with others? The answer to this question seems to lie in the association of economic production with the culture of the group, as parceled out in the system of social statuses. Each status (as we noted in Chapter 3, "Social Structure") involves a number of roles that relate it to other statuses, roles that are made up of expectations about behavior on each side. Economic activities are virtually always a part of the role behavior appropriate to various social statuses. Sharing the results of productive activity following specific prescriptive understandings about the exact form that sharing will take is also attached to social statuses.

As we noted when we discussed statuses, to occupy a status, one must be able to perform even those role behaviors one does not particularly like. The teacher who is willing to grade papers but not to conduct classes (or vice versa) will not long keep the post, and the husband who eats his wife's cooking but will not take a job is in for marital difficulties. When economic sharing and distribution are associated with status expectations, they too become imperative.

It is useful to view economic activity in the total context of a society's culturally defined statuses and the expectations that make up the roles of those statuses in order to understand how people's motivations are channeled into the productive activities and sharing necessary to the continued existence and well-being of the entire society. This focus on statuses and expectations as a way of distributing tasks and resources involves us with what is usually called the division of labor in society. The phrase "division of labor" refers to the basic (if not particularly profound) insight of economic anthropology that different tasks are distributed by culture among several people, each of whom depends on the others, such that between them they accomplish what must be done. In a rural group such as is presented in our Mexican case, the division of labor may involve the women in cooking, making clothing, cleaning the dwelling, caring for the children, and, in many societies, keeping gardens, while the men are engaged in raising crops, building houses, conducting religious rituals, and, in many societies, herding, hunting, trading with neighboring groups, or conducting war.

Children may be understood as properly occupied with keeping track of the chickens, gathering firewood, tending smaller children, running errands, and the like. The tasks appropriate to each status depend on the expectations making up the roles of that status, which are part of the culture of the society. The anthropologist must therefore approach each society's division of labor anew, expecting it to be different from the division of labor in other societies with which he is familiar. It is conventional to distinguish division of labor by sex or age from other kinds of division of labor, partly because there is somewhat greater uniformity from culture to culture in division of labor by sex and age than in other kinds of division of labor.

Division of Labor by Sex

All cultures include understandings which distinguish between work that is appropriate for women and work that is appropriate for men, and occupancy of the status of man or woman involves expectations that the individual ought to perform the kind of work associated with his status as man or woman. (There are, of course, many kinds of work in any society that may be performed by either sex. The point is that such kinds of work are never the only kind that a society has.)[2] In rural Mexico, Pedro Martínez and his sons raised corn and beans, but Esperanza and Machrina cooked and swept and bought kitchen supplies. Pedro presumably *could* have cooked (and was fond of reminding his wife that it was he who taught her to sweep), and Esperanza *could* presumably have raised corn as women do in many other parts of the world. But expectations in Azteca associated cooking with women and corn growing with men, and both would have felt uncomfortable doing the "wrong" tasks, and would have been the target of ridicule. In fact, the activities that each of them engaged in are for the most part activities associated with male and female statuses over a large number of societies. Although there is tremendous cultural variation in understandings about sexual division of labor,[3] some intriguing similarities have also emerged that anthropologists have been interested in trying to explain.

A study by Murdock and Provost (1973) considered 50 technological activities in a sample of 185 societies, rating each activity in each society as M (performed only by men), N (performed mostly by men), E (performed equally by men and women), G (performed mostly by women), and F (performed only by women). For each activity they then calculated an index of masculine participation based on the proportion of cases and the extent to which men participated. Table 13 shows their results, with the tasks arranged and numbered by the amount of masculine participation.

In this sample there are only two activities in which women are never involved: hunting large aquatic animals (deep-sea fishing) and smelting ores.

[2]The *idea* that men behave differently from women, as opposed to the particular behaviors that are considered appropriate for the two sexes, is probably introduced in earliest infancy as the parent with the milk is distinguished from the one without.

[3]See M. Mead (1949, 1935).

Table 13 Sex Allocation of 50 Technological Activities in 185 Societies

	TASK	M	N	E	G	F	INDEX
1.	Hunting large aquatic fauna	48	0	0	0	0	100.0
2.	Smelting of ores	37	0	0	0	0	100.0
3.	Metalworking	85	1	0	0	0	99.8
4.	Lumbering	135	4	0	0	0	99.4
5.	Hunting large land fauna	139	5	0	0	0	99.3
6.	Work in wood	159	3	1	1	0	98.8
7.	Fowling	132	4	3	0	0	98.3
8.	Manufacture of musical instruments	83	3	1	0	1	97.6
9.	Trapping of small land fauna	136	12	1	1	0	97.5
10.	Boatbuilding	84	3	3	0	1	96.6
11.	Stoneworking	67	0	6	0	0	95.9
12.	Work in bone, horn, and shell	71	7	2	0	2	94.6
13.	Mining and quarrying	31	1	2	0	1	93.7
14.	Bonesetting and other surgery	34	6	4	0	0	92.7
15.	Butchering	122	9	4	4	4	92.3
16.	Collection of wild honey	39	5	2	0	2	91.7
17.	Land clearance	95	34	6	3	1	90.5
18.	Fishing	83	45	8	5	2	86.7
19.	Tending large animals	54	24	14	3	3	82.4
20.	Housebuilding	105	30	14	9	20	77.4
21.	Soil preparation	66	27	14	17	10	73.1
22.	Netmaking	42	2	5	1	15	71.2
23.	Making of rope or cordage	62	7	18	5	19	69.9
24.	Generation of fire	40	6	16	4	20	62.3
25.	Bodily mutilation	36	4	48	6	12	60.8
26.	Preparation of skins	39	4	2	5	31	54.6
27.	Gathering of small land fauna	27	3	9	13	15	54.5
28.	Crop planting	27	35	33	26	20	54.4
29.	Manufacture of leather products	35	3	2	5	29	53.2
30.	Harvesting	10	37	34	34	26	45.0
31.	Crop tending	22	23	24	30	32	44.6
32.	Milking	15	2	8	2	21	43.8
33.	Basketmaking	37	9	15	18	51	42.5
34.	Burden carrying	18	12	46	34	36	39.3
35.	Matmaking	30	4	9	5	55	37.6
36.	Care of small animals	19	8	14	12	44	35.9
37.	Preservation of meat and fish	18	2	3	3	40	32.9
38.	Loom weaving	24	0	6	8	50	32.5
39.	Gathering small aquatic fauna	11	4	1	12	27	31.1
40.	Fuel gathering	25	12	12	23	94	27.2
41.	Manufacture of clothing	16	4	11	13	78	22.4
42.	Preparation of drinks	15	3	4	4	65	22.2
43.	Potterymaking	14	5	6	6	74	21.1
44.	Gathering wild vegetal foods	6	4	18	42	65	19.7
45.	Dairy production	4	0	0	0	24	14.3
46.	Spinning	7	3	4	5	72	13.6
47.	Laundering	3	0	4	8	49	13.0
48.	Water fetching	4	4	8	13	131	8.6
49.	Cooking	0	2	2	63	117	8.3
50.	Preparation of vegetal foods	3	1	4	21	145	5.7

SOURCE: G. P. Murdock and Caterina Provost, 1973, Factors in the Division of Labor by Sex: A Cross-Cultural Analysis, Ethnology 12(2), p. 207. With permission.

And there are no technological activities in the sample in which men are never involved. Nevertheless, it is clear that across the world as a whole there are some subsistence activities that are very largely the domain of men and others that are very largely the domain of women. Murdock and Provost break the table into sections; the first (items 1–14), they call the domain of "strictly masculine activities"; the second (15–23), "quasi-masculine activities"; the third (24–39, 41, and 43), "swing activities"; and the fourth (40, 42, and 44–50), "quasi-feminine activities."[4] The division of labor by sex in the accomplishment of subsistence activities is obviously not random. The shared understandings that are involved in the statuses of male and female members of different societies seem to be influenced by practical considerations of some kind. Murdock and Provost try to explain what some of these might be and identify several factors that might help to explain them.[5]

Factor A: masculine advantage For some activities, the greater physical strength of men is of importance. The comparative advantage of men is made yet greater by the comparative physical incapacity of women while they are pregnant and their relatively smaller mobility when they have to tend small children, a task that is inevitably assigned to women, presumably because of their capacity for nursing and the attachments that develop between mother and child in their first weeks of contact. The relative masculine advantage due to greater strength and mobility is clearly relevant in most of the activities (though not all) in the "strictly masculine" group.

Factor B: feminine advantage Women are in a better position than men to engage in some subsistence activities largely because the advantages that men have in other spheres keep them away from home a part of the time. The advantage that women enjoy *in subsistence activities* is therefore that they are likely to be in the place where certain work must be done while the men are not. Murdock and Provost point out that the activities in the "quasi-feminine" group are ones that "require practically daily attention and are thus relatively incompatible with such masculine tasks as warfare, hunting, fishing, and herding which commonly require periods of absence from the household" (1973:211).

There are some other strictures on what a woman can do, however, even when she enjoys the advantage of being near to the task: Women's work often involves tasks that can be combined with child care and are therefore "relatively monotonous and do not require rapt concentration; and the work is not dangerous, can be performed in spite of interruptions, and is easily

Equadorian Woman Hoeing. Women engage in some subsistence activities largely because men's work in other spheres keeps them away from home much of the time.

[4]The numbers in two of these are discontinuous because the groupings are also influenced by regional distributions that need not concern us here.

[5]We are here interested only in the most important of these, and our factor labels therefore do not correspond with those in the original study.

resumed once interrupted" (J. Brown 1970:1074; quoted by Murdock and Provost 1973:211).

Factor C: degree of occupational specialization   Possibly as a result of the fact that in most societies most women are subject part of the time to child-care distractions from which men are free, the data suggest that as a society comes to involve a complex division of labor by occupation (so that not all families are engaged in the same types of technological activities), men seem to perform the more fully specialized activities. Even cooking becomes men's work when it becomes an "occupation" entered into for money instead of an activity performed in each household for the benefit of the household members only.

Certain activities that are performed by women in hunting-and-herding societies where the men tend to be away from home are performed by men in societies where the men are available to do them. The preparation of meat and skins, leather working, and the construction of shelters are among these.[6] Exceptions occur to most of these generalizations, but it is important to note that the understandings in any society about the division of labor between male and female statuses are not entirely arbitrary, but bear a readily explicable relationship to the facts of life and the biological and psychological necessity of women bearing and caring for children.

True Division of Labor

Division of labor by sex and age is found in all societies, and results from the constraints that biology imposes upon human life. In some societies this is virtually the only division of labor. In such societies all adult men, for example, perform about the same tasks as all other adult men, and they neither cooperate in performing tasks that require different skills or different activities on the part of different members nor distribute the results of specialized labor so that different people become specialists at different activities.

In most societies, however, at least some division of labor is based on criteria other than sex and age. As we noted, Pedro made rope that he himself did not use. He and his sons gathered more firewood than they used (or did before he sold the mule), and they transported plums that were not destined for their own table. In these activities they were engaged in the subsistence concerns of the larger society around them, filling the needs of others in return for money, with which they could, in turn, induce others to fill their needs. Such arrangements are very much the most usual thing in the societies with which we are familiar. Some people are specialists at making pottery, performing religious rituals, constructing houses, healing the sick, or adjudi-

---

[6]In the case of constructing shelters, the fact that the shelters are rather simpler among nomadic herders and hunters may mean that they do not require as much strength to put up, and what is responsible may be factor A again.

TRUE DIVISION OF
LABOR *Division of
labor following criteria
other than sex or age.*

cating disputes. Division of labor following criteria other than sex or age is sometimes called "true division of labor." It is found especially in contexts in which individuals have differences of skill or training that make an important difference to the outcome of the activity or where the task to be undertaken requires the coordinated efforts of a group of people. Pottery making, for example, requires a degree of skill that is acquired over time and with experience. Some people become better potters than others. Certain kinds of hunting, such as the "surround," where the game is chased into a narrow enclosure by people on all sides of it making noise and then is dispatched with comparative ease when it has nowhere to run, require the coordinated efforts of a large group of people, including temporary direction by some.

In general, the more complex the technology of a people, the greater the division of labor, and the more the specialization into occupations. It is no surprise that in complex modern industrial society there are some exceedingly specialized occupations.[7] The greater the specialization that is found in a society, the greater the dependence of its members on one another. The Eskimo hunter travels in a tiny family group composed of himself, his wife (or wives), and his children. This unit is not entirely isolated from other similar units (the hunter's children will marry the children of other hunters, for example), but the hunting family is not dependent on other families in any way for its sustenance. However, the man who spends his time making pottery (or being a personnel manager) is dependent on someone else to produce his food, and society must be organized in such a way that the necessary distribution of resources can occur.

Three Modes of Distribution

The occupant of a social status interacts with the occupant of another social status according to expectations that we have called collectively a role. Many, possibly most, of these relations have at least some cultural expectations about the exchange of physical goods, of labor, or of information that may be used in the manipulation of goods or labor. Most typically, the occupant of one status is expected to give some particular class of resource to the occupant of some other status. His failure to do so subjects him to criticism or worse. Thus if a man is in the status of salesman, he must give his product to someone who is in the status of customer when the understandings about the sale have been met. The salesman cannot refuse to surrender the product without people (such as his boss) criticizing his ability to be a salesman, and certainly he cannot do so and maintain the expected relationship with his customer. He is likely to be fired, sued, shot, or whatever. Pedro's son Felipe

---

[7]Such as manager in charge of hiring workers for a personnel office that hires investigators who establish security clearances for clerks who carry papers and reports between offices charged with coordinating the activities of people and machines engaged in the production of specialized equipment used to produce submarines to facilitate naval espionage on the submarines produced for the same purpose in other parts of the world.

worked on the estate of the landowner Don Porfirio for money. If Felipe had refused to work, he would not have received the money, however ardently he desired it, and if Don Porfirio had not paid him, Felipe would not have worked for him, however much the work needed to be done. The statuses of boss and peon require that both parts of the bargain be fulfilled for the parties to maintain the status relationship.

Economic exchanges, then, are behaviors that take place in the context of people performing roles and fulfilling expectations, just as are all other activities that people engage in with each other. To understand the activity of economic exchange, it is necessary to discover the statuses and the role expectations that are involved in the interchanges.

Economic historian Karl Polanyi has distinguished three general modes by which the distribution of a society's material resources can be carried out, depending upon the expectations that participants have about the statuses of giver and receiver of a given resource.[8] He calls the three modes reciprocity, redistribution, and (market) exchange. The distinction has been widely adopted by economic anthropologists.

"Reciprocity," or reciprocal exchange, sometimes called gift exchange, occurs when resources are presented by one person to another with the expectation on both sides that sooner or later the second will return something of about the same value. When the carpenter gives the blacksmith a chair with the expectation that the blacksmith will shoe his horse some day, that is reciprocity. Bartering is also a form of reciprocity.

"Redistribution" occurs when material resources (and sometimes labor) are consolidated by one authority and then reallocated to the members of the society such that what each member receives is not identical with what he contributed. When the carpenter gives his chair to the king, who gives it to the baker and also makes sure that the carpenter's horse will be shod when that is necessary and that the blacksmith and the carpenter will have bread, that is redistribution.

"Market exchange," or marketing, is a system of exchange that involves buying and selling. Prices are set by supply and demand and are expressed in generalized units of value, typically money.[9] When the carpenter offers the blacksmith a chair in exchange for six gold coins, one of which he plans to use to have his horse shod by another, cheaper blacksmith, that is marketing.

Reciprocal Exchange

As used by anthropologists, the word "reciprocity" refers to more than merely equal exchange between two individuals or groups. It refers as well to the circulation of goods or services because of expectations about statuses

RECIPROCITY *A mode of economic distribution in which resources are presented by one person or group to another with the expectation on both sides that sooner or later the second will return something of about the same value to the first.*

REDISTRIBUTION
A mode of economic distribution in which resources are presented to a central authority, which then allocates them for use to the members of the group.

MARKET EXCHANGE
A mode of economic distribution in which resources are exchanged on the basis of prices established by supply and demand and expressed in generalized units of value.

[8]Although Polanyi published his scheme in 1944, the classic statement of it is Polanyi (1957).

[9]The cross-cultural definition of money has posed some problems that we shall discuss below.

Three Modes of Distribution: reciprocity (a); redistribution (b); and market exchange (c).

(a)

(b)   (c)

that are not exclusively (and usually not primarily) economic. M. Sahlins has made the point clear in a discussion of tribal economics:

> Exchange does not exist apart from "noneconomic" relations. Better said, there is an economic aspect to every social relationship. Father-son, maternal uncle-nephew, chief-follower: each implies a mode of exchange of one kind or another, consistent in its material terms with its social terms. Thus from a relative "you can get it wholesale," and, from a close relative, perhaps for free.
>
> On a more abstract level: the tribal exchange scheme is constructed from the scheme of social segmentation. Each group in the segmentary hierarchy is in the perspective of its participants a sector of social relationships, more or less solidary and sociable . . . ; each sector implies appropriate norms of reciprocity. Differences thus appear in the way people deal with each other, according to the way they are socially divided from each other. The tribal scheme of segmentation sets up a sectoral scheme of reciprocities [1968:81].

In an effort to clarify the idea of reciprocity as an economic system, E. Service (1966:14–15) has suggested a continuum that ranges from "generalized reciprocity," where individuals contribute the fruits of their labors as a matter of course without conscious calculation of return, through "balanced reciprocity," where values are calculated and equivalent items are exchanged, preferably simultaneously, to "negative reciprocity," where efforts are made to exploit the other party as in bargaining or haggling.

The kind of reciprocity that should prevail in a given situation is one of the expectations attached to the statuses of the people involved. The reciprocity that is represented by the gift of beans to Esperanza by her married daughter Conchita is generalized reciprocity; that is, no conscious calculation was being made (at least so far as we can tell) of a particular return. Conchita was not concerned with what she would get back on her "investment" of the sardine tin of beans; rather, she acted as she did because she had beans, her mother needed beans, and daughters ought to help their mothers. It is safe to say that reciprocity tends to be of the generalized kind when the roles involved are roles that involve many interactions of a wide variety. Balanced reciprocity tends to occur when the roles involve less frequent or less diverse interactions. Negative reciprocity seems to prevail when there are few specific status relationships, as between strangers.

Reciprocity as a society-wide economic system occurs particularly in small-scale societies in which small groups of people maintain a wide variety of relationships with each other. It is therefore generalized reciprocity that we are particularly concerned with when we study, for example, societies organized in small tribes or bands.[10]

The transfer of goods, labor, prestige, or what have you from one person or group to another is, of course, at the base of all reciprocity, just as it is at the base of all other economic distribution. A great deal of anthropological attention has been focused over the years on the nature of such transfers in contexts falling in the range between generalized and balanced reciprocity, where the goods transferred are called "gifts," or "prestations."[11] If the gift giving is done in the context of only two statuses, it may approximate a condition of balanced reciprocity, with the expectation of more or less exact and more or less immediate return. If the gift giving is in the context of a large number of closely related statuses, the expectations of return may be less and less direct, until the condition of generalized reciprocity is approximated. In either case, return is expected, whether directly or by the recipient's continued contribution to the system as a whole. Roles are two-way expectations, and just as there are expectations about the donor, so also there are expectations about the recipient of a gift. There is always "repayment" in the sense that unless the recipient wishes to discontinue his relationship with the donor or with the group, he is obliged to conform to the expectations of how a person in his status must act. One cannot accept the advantages of a status without discharging its responsibilities, or anyway not forever and not without criticism. This is true whether the reciprocity is balanced or generalized. (The allowable or preferred time lag before repayment differs from case to case and is not built into the definitions.)

Economic and social advantages of general reciprocity For a small group of people, reciprocity, particularly its generalized form, has considerable advantages as a general mode of economic distribution. There is no society in which some families or individuals do not have hard times, and there are few families or individuals in any society who do not find themselves in difficult straits sooner or later. When generalized reciprocity is the principal means of distributing a group's resources, repayment that is immediate, exactly equal in amount, or in the same commodity is not required. It is a system that looks after the needs of people at times when they are not in a position to "pay" for what they use, as Esperanza well understood when she went to visit her daughter. The distribution of food following kinship or residence patterns in a hunting society or the sharing of labor in an agricultural society means that the hunter who fails to catch anything does not

[10]Balanced and negative reciprocity occur in such societies largely in the relations that members of one group have with another.

[11]The terminology derives from a famous essay by French sociologist M. Mauss (1925), who enunciated the principle that every prestation entailed a counterprestation.

Cambodian Village Family at Dinner. Generalized reciprocity is characteristic of economic exchange within small groups, including the resident family group in most societies. Exact repayment is not expected.

starve and the farmer who has not the labor force in his own family to harvest all his crop at the right time will get it harvested anyway. This is true because economic resources are passed from one person to another regardless of the recipient's ability to "pay" for them. Among the Bena, whom we discussed briefly in the chapter on culture, it is bad manners to visit when people have just slaughtered an animal. The reason is that the visit, whether or not so intended, is necessarily a request for some of the meat, for the Bena host has an obligation to provide some of the slaughtered animal to his guest; he would not be a good host if he did not. In primitive societies, existing on a material base that would not long support a person on the resources he has stored away, the sharing of available resources may make the difference between life and death for some members. In many societies the awareness of this is so great that even relations between parents and children, involving economic exchanges of generalized reciprocity, are phrased in terms of balanced reciprocity: The parents care for the children when the children are young and helpless, and the children are *therefore* expected to look after the parents when the parents are elderly and in their turn helpless.

Balanced reciprocity between antagonists: silent trade When a market economy is not in operation, and when a system of redistribution does not integrate all members of a society, reciprocity is about the only distributive form available, even between potential antagonists. These people often engage in balanced reciprocity. In such a situation the goods exchanged are

Pygmy Women and Children. Pygmies of the Ituri Forest area carry on a trade with agriculturists of the neighboring societies in which industrial trade products are left at pickup spots to which the Pygmies come to replace them with forest products. The Pygmies in this photo wear cloth and smoke tobacco procured through trade.

normally subsistence goods essential to the well-being of at least one of the partners. Confrontation between the partners to the exchange can be avoided by an arrangement anthropologists have often encountered and have come to call "silent trade." Such an arrangement occurs in trading between the hunting-and-gathering Pygmies of the Ituri Forest area of northeastern Zaire and neighboring agricultural societies. Agricultural and industrial trade products are left at established pickup spots around the agricultural villages, and the Pygmies come and replace them with forest products that they have gathered. Particular villages have relations with specific bands of Pygmies with whom this kind of exchange is regularly carried on. If either partner believes he is being shorted, he simply terminates the exchange for a time and then sets it up again with another group in the future. Neither group likes the other: The Pygmies regard the agricultural villagers as plodding bumpkins, and the agriculturalists consider the Pygmies to be midway between humans and animals. But in spite of these feelings, the trade continues in a way that is at least minimally satisfactory to both sides.

Silent trade, though it is a form of balanced reciprocity, can involve quite a high element of anonymity, even more than that which normally prevails in market exchange. This is presumably one of the reasons for the use of silent trade by kidnappers and blackmailers in our own society. It also depends little upon moral force, and very much upon highly specific expectations, which is one of the reasons it is particularly well suited to accomplishing exchange between real or potential antagonists.[12]

Reciprocal exchange, then, normally occurs in the context of other role behaviors, and it is economically significant (and inevitable) primarily in small-scale societies in which members for the most part have a variety of other role expectations besides those relating to economic exchange. In such societies it has the advantage that it provides for some members (such as luckless hunters) who would be deprived of normal means of subsistence without help for which they cannot immediately pay. Reciprocity in other societies takes on a largely symbolic importance that is based on these same characteristics.

Reciprocity as symbolism An important and distinctive aspect of reciprocity as a mode of exchange when an immediate return is not required is that it implies a long-term relationship. The expectation of eventual but not immediate return means that partners to a relation of reciprocal exchange embark upon a relationship that is understood by both to be permanent. Often a series of exchanges may be undertaken less because of the partners' need for the products than because of the implications of good faith and longstandingness that are implied by reciprocity. When this happens, the purely economic aspect of the exchange can be trivial compared with the symbolic aspect.

In our own society reciprocal exchanges are frequently more important symbolically than economically. Consider a dinner invitation: Smith invites Jones to dinner, and Jones accepts. Jones does not actually "need" the dinner that Smith gives him. Accepting the dinner, however, activates a system of reciprocal exchanges that ideally never come out exactly even, which implies that Jones and Smith treat each other in good faith and expect their relationship to continue indefinitely.[13] Because reciprocity without immediate return as an economic form implies (and requires) good faith and a continuing relationship, it provides an excellent symbolism of friendship. If Jones got up from the dinner table and took out his wallet to pay Smith for the dinner, he would be acting according to the wrong set of expectations about the nature of the exchange, would not be symbolizing friendship, and would insult (or dumbfound) Smith. In North America, the person who too quickly or exactly pays his social debts signals a disengagement from the

---

[12]Cultural devices to avoid confrontations between real or potential antagonists are a study in themselves. Besides silent trade, perhaps the most common device is the use of a mediator, or middle man, who negotiates with each side on behalf of the other. Marriage matchmakers are an example of a particularly widespread type of mediator.

[13]The example assumes that Smith and Jones are related to each other as friends. If, say, Smith is a student and Jones is a professor, the symbolism of the thing changes somewhat: Jones "repays" Smith by giving Smith the honor of his company and undivided attention for the evening. Professor Jones probably will not reciprocate by inviting young Smith to dinner. He may or may not repay him by raising his grade at the end of the course or by treating him in a way that raises his prestige or self-esteem.

system of statuses that these social debts imply and makes people suspicious of his motives and of his sincerity.

The ultimate reciprocal system: the potlatch The gift that differs too far from the standard that is expected for a given role relationship implies that the role relationship has been changed and that the statuses of the partners to the exchange are different. When the boss gives his attractive female secretary a box of candy on Valentine's Day, his wife has no reason to complain, for the secretary is being treated like a secretary. On the other hand, if he gives her a diamond bracelet, he is suggesting that the relationship is something quite different from merely boss-secretary, and both the secretary and the boss's wife can reasonably be concerned about his possible intentions.

The giving of inappropriately large or small gifts, because of the symbolic associations implied or denied in this way, can be calculated to embarrass the recipient and show the dominance, superiority, and power of the donor and the dependency of the recipient. Particularly large gifts can embarrass the recipient in another way as well: It is much harder to repay the oversize gift sometime in the future with equal or even greater "generosity." The manipulation of other people by excessive gifts can become an important part of role behavior. The most extravagant example of a system of resource allocation involving this kind of aggressive reciprocity is reported from several peoples (the Haida, Tlingit, Tsimshian, Salish, and Kwakiutl, for example) of the northwest coast of North America. When these people were first studied in the late nineteenth century they still practiced a form of exchange called the "potlatch."[14] A man would sponsor a huge feast, with guests from

Potlatch among the Coast Salish of British Columbia. The Northwest Coast potlatch was a system of delayed gift exchange that lent prestige to those who could give most generously.

[14]The word "potlatch" comes into English from Chinook Jargon, a trade language widely used by nineteenth-century traders along the northwest coast of North America. It has nothing to do either with pots or with latches, but seems to have come from the Nootka "potlatsh," meaning gift or to give.

many distant villages. He would provide them with all the food they could eat and then with food and other goods to take with them when they returned home. Sometimes he would give away or destroy large quantities of other goods, most notably blankets, sea-otter skins, shield-shaped copper plates, canoes, and fish oil; occasionally also slaves. The ability of the host to dispose of vast resources suggested (quite accurately) his ability to organize his kinsmen and followers to provide for his economic needs and contributed to his prestige and the prestige of his group.[15] Forde writes of the situation:

> The chiefs or heads of noble families each had a following of relatives and commoners, on the size and solidarity of which their wealth and authority depended. This gave them influence and a power to command, but no general authority beyond their personal prestige. A chief was in the first place master of his own considerable household, that is the relatives, close and remote, who lived with him and the dependent families of commoners and slaves. . . . If he raised his rank in relation to neighbouring rivals by giving great feasts and presents his group as a whole, be it household, lineage or village, or all three, gained in respect. If, however, he were insulted or degraded the group was correspondingly put to shame. Since the chief symbolized the prestige of those he represented, he could depend on the industry and self-sacrifice of his followers in supplying labour and materials for the preparation of the ceremonial feasts [Forde 1963:89].

Many a man impoverished himself for years by sponsoring one potlatch. During the succeeding years his guests were making efforts to invite him to their own potlatches and pay him back, preferably even more grandly. Forde continues:

> Although the glory of munificence was everywhere paramount, the obligations of repayment played a prominent part, especially among Kwakiutl. The acceptance of gifts at a feast . . . involved an obligation to repay them with considerable interest when the guest in turn gave a feast. A Kwakiutl would sometimes borrow material beforehand, again at high interest, in order to in-

[15]There is variation among the groups who practiced the potlatch. Among the Kwakiutl, for example, who are generally regarded as the classic example, the prestige gained by a successful potlatch devolved on the sponsoring group, while among the Tsimshian it devolved on the individual who sponsored it, and among the Haida on the children of the person who sponsored it. Also it should be noted that originally and usually potlatches were held in celebration of events in family life, such as house building, child naming, death, or totem-pole raising, much as a cotillion, bar mitzvah, or wake is related to family events in American society. Naturally, being able to provide a better potlatch rather than a poorer one would have reflected favorably upon the sponsor, but the frequency and intensity of the use of the potlatch distribution to shame and embarrass guests (either all guests or selected guests) represents in a sense a redirection of its use in response to postcontact changes (changes after contact between Indians and whites became common) in the procedures for winning the right to hold certain prestigious statuses. The present discussion, like most anthropological discussion of the potlatch, focuses on the custom as it was practiced particularly among the Kwakiutl and particularly in postcontact times.

crease the lavishness of his gifts at the feast. Careful record was kept by official tally-keepers of all these gifts which were practically forced loans, and the extent of all obligations was publicly known [Forde 1963:90].

The anthropological understanding of this institution has been affected by the fact that it was on the decline when it was first studied. Further, the destruction of large quantities of supplies has always disturbed the imaginations of white settlers, which has made some informants reluctant to talk about it. In recent years attempts have been made to identify the possible ecological or economic advantages of such a system of aggressive reciprocity. For one thing, that guests came from long distances to a potlatch served to spread the economic produce of one region to other areas. Local shortages could have been relieved to some extent in this way. Furthermore, these societies lacked a state apparatus that could require people to produce food beyond their own use. The use of potlatches to bring prestige to the successful host and shame upon the guest may well have stimulated increased productive efforts. As in some modern societies, prestige and productivity were closely linked. A third possible advantage might have been the fact that because the residents of some area had in the past given a great potlatch and distributed much, they were entitled (and required) to receive from others, and the credit won in an earlier time of prosperity could have tided them over bad times. In a sense the prestige earned by giving a great potlatch was a contributing factor to being invited to be a guest at other potlatches. Unlike many kinds of prestige, it could be eaten (see Suttles 1960; Piddock 1965).

Another possible advantage of the system is that unproductive areas or social arrangements that were not economically efficient did not allow many potlatches. Dwellers in such areas or members of such social units presumably suffered the sting of low prestige with respect to the inhabitants of other settlements. They may have tended to drift away from unproductive regions or inefficient leaders and attach themselves to more successful units, thus adjusting the population to the available resources (after Hazard; quoted by Harris 1971:250).

We have discussed the potlatch as a system of reciprocal distribution of resources, but it must be remembered that the participants were acting on the basis of prescriptive understandings—about prestige, about family events, about morality, about wealth, about enemies—and not on the basis of regional economic or ecological effects or of input-output analysis. The reason for our stress on the effects of the potlatch on the distribution of goods in Northwest Coast society rather than on people's motivations is that the relationship of the potlatch as a system of reciprocal exchange to other systems of reciprocal exchange helps us to understand the nature of reciprocity in general.

Reciprocity and power: the big-man   Although the prestige of the successful potlatch accrued to some extent to all members of the group that sponsored it, at least among the Kwakiutl, there is no question that the greatest prestige went to the man who organized it. This man was also the leader and economically central figure of the group during the long months and years of preparation for the potlatch. Such a central figure is known in anthropology as a "big-man," a term derived from New Guinea pidgin English. M. Sahlins has given a general description of how a person manipulates relations of reciprocity to move into the big-man status.

> Any ambitious man who can gather a following can inaugurate a societal career. The up-and-coming Melanesian big-man depends initially on a small core of followers, mainly his own household and nearest relatives. Upon these people he can prevail economically: he capitalizes in the beginning on kinship dues and by finessing the relations of generalized reciprocity appropriate among close kinsmen. At an early phase, a big-man will seek to enlarge his own household, especially by getting more wives. The more wives he has, the more pigs. . . . [Pigs are important in Melanesia because they are used in feasting and as gifts, and pigs are raised by wives.] Each new marriage also creates another set of affinal relatives from whom he can exact support [and to whom he owes support]. But the leader's career goes into "take-off" when he is able to bring other men and their households into his faction, harnessing their production to his ambition. Usually this is done by helping them in some big way, as to put them forever in his debt [1968:89].

The potential big-man, the manipulator of the system, takes advantage of a position of economic strength (perhaps temporary, and perhaps created mostly by luck) to put others in his debt, a debt they can satisfy partly by supporting him in expanding his power yet further. The big-man in effect makes the system of reciprocity snowball to his favor. The status he creates

New Guinea Highland Big-Men: Huli (a) (b); Kunice (c). The big-man in (a) is leading a ritual; in (b) he is distributing pork in a ritual; the big-man shown in (c) is addressing his followers. Big-men take advantage of positions of economic strength to put others in their debt, which allows them to expand their power yet further.

(a)

(b)

(c)

for himself is potentially a very powerful one, though it has its dangers. The big-man's power base can be undermined by a miscalculation that causes him to assume support from people with different and lesser understandings about their obligations to him. It can be destroyed by the machinations of other big-men who are in opposition to him. It can be weakened or destroyed by his failing to treat his followers in a way that gives them any motivation to continue their relationship with him. It can be weakened by the failure of his crops or his hunting or by illness that takes him away from the constant manipulation of reciprocity and indebtedness that is the basis of his power. Nevertheless, in many parts of the world local-level leadership is built on the reciprocity based power of big-men.

In the chapter on politics and law (Chapter 7) the importance of different sorts of expectations will be emphasized in the discussion of legitimacy and coercion. The big-man is obviously and importantly a political figure. Some of the expectations about him, however, are economic ones. To some extent a big-man is followed in the vague expectation that one is better off following him, perhaps because he may make one wealthy some day. In the terminology of political analysis, he is being followed on the basis of the legitimacy of his leadership. Sometimes, on the other hand, he is followed because of much more limited and specific expectations, for example, because he is very likely to give each of his followers a pig at the next feast. In this case, his leadership is said to be based on "coercion," in the technical sense in which we shall define coercion in Chapter 7. The big-man's following provides a clear example of the way in which political expectations can be involved with the distribution of economic resources.

Reciprocities and more reciprocities: the *kula*   The same peoples who make use of generalized reciprocity as an important system of allocation of resources internally often make use of balanced reciprocity in exchanges with other groups (in exchanges on the occasion of a wedding, for example, or in trading coastal products for inland ones), and they make use of negative reciprocity as well by preying on the occasional stranger or enemy whose goods they seek at as little cost as possible to themselves. The same group can use more than one system of reciprocal exchange, depending on the roles involved, and in some cases (perhaps even most cases) economic interaction in a given role may be one of several kinds depending upon circumstances. An American may *give* his sister a dinner or a room in his house in a system of generalized exchange, but he may *lend* her the money to buy a new car, sometimes at interest.[16]

In some relationships transactions of a generalized and of a more commer-

---

[16]Our research has been rather casual, but we find some American informants who maintain that within the family economic exchanges should all be generalized reciprocity. Money-lending smacks of balanced to negative reciprocity to these people, and charging interest seems like exploitation. Other Americans have no such qualms. Kinship feelings among the latter group are not absent, however: One has the impression that most Americans who will lend money to their relatives at interest lend it at better rates than most banks.

cial nature go on simultaneously. The most impressive ethnographic example of this is the now classic *kula* system of the Trobriand Islands (located off the east coast of New Guinea), studied by Malinowski during World War I. Trobriand men had trading partners in adjacent island groups. To their partners in Dobu, to the south, they gave shell arm bands, and from them they received shell necklaces. These items were highly prized and considered extremely valuable. The necklaces they passed on to other partners to the east, from whom they received in return a supply of arm bands. The entire system, which ultimately involved thousands of people on dozens of islands, can be thought of as circulating necklaces clockwise and bracelets counterclockwise around a wide circle in the southwestern Pacific, with many of these goods going around and around the circle.

It was not expected that the exchange of these valuables would come out exactly even between any two partners on any given occasion, but there was a general expectation that over the long pull one's partner would give about as much as he took. The distribution of *kula* treasures was clearly a case of exchange that falls somewhere between our models of generalized and balanced reciprocity.

If the *kula* had circulated only bracelets and necklaces, however highly treasured, it would have had little effect on the distribution of subsistence

The *Kula* Ring. *Kula* goods circulated over a vast area involving thousands of people on dozens of islands. (Adapted from Malinowski 1922:82.)

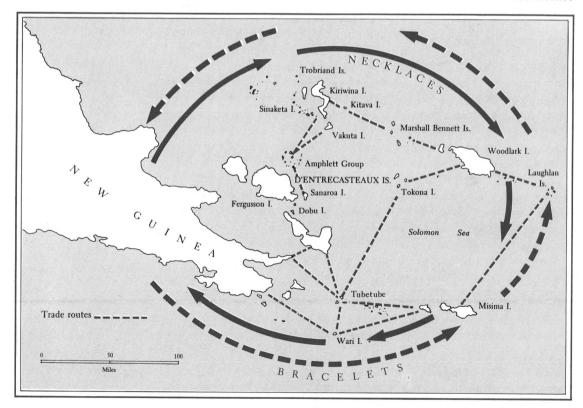

goods. In fact, the trading expeditions provided the occasion for a great deal of balanced-to-negative reciprocity as well, in which individual members of each expedition haggled over other products more directly related to subsistence concerns: fish, coconuts, flour, baskets, mats, vines that could be used for rope, shells that could be made into knives, and the like. The status of trading partner involved mutual expectations about delayed reciprocity and uneven exchange. The fact that such friendly and explicitly noneconomic exchanges occurred was apparently part of what made the *kula* jewelry valuable and the expeditions occasions of social solidarity and rejoicing. On the other hand, an important economic aspect of these exchanges was related to the far less gentlemanly exchanges of subsistence items, which were conducted following commercial expectations of buyer-seller statuses that were of such low prestige among the Trobrianders that expedition leaders insisted that the activity barely occurred or was of little significance.[17] The relationship between trading partners involved differing expectations about the mode of resource distribution depending on the nature of the resources involved. The person who would have haggled for a *kula* bracelet or would have tried to exchange one for baskets and mats would clearly have been a person with the wrong expectations.

Redistributive Exchange

Redistribution has been well characterized by Nash: "A redistributive system of exchange is a form of reciprocity with political or economic centricity. Some central agency collects goods or commands services and then distributes them among the social units and persons who have proferred them" (1966:32).

In a redistributive system, Nash points out, there is still a sense of obligation or the necessity of meeting the expectations associated with various roles, but the society is now differentiated into the "center" and the "noncenter": "Political or economic centers are provided by simple social mechanisms of stratification, chieftainship, temple economies, and other means of providing prestige and power differentials in a society. . . . Redistributive exchange rests on social differentiation along some axis of prestige and power inequality" (1966:32). Thus we find redistribution as a major means of allocating a society's resources in situations where power and prestige are

---

[17]The *kula* situation is similar to some aspects of American economic relations (and Western business practice generally) in which the economic exchange is treated as though it were a very minor part of the relationship. For example, car dealers, stockbrokers, real-estate agents, and others often call customers by their first names, buy them coffee, meals, or drinks, and talk about the weather, golf, or baseball as though the relationship were one between friends The status of friend involves some understandings—trust, mutual assistance, for example—quite different from those of a strictly business relationship. To the extent that the ploy is successful, it means that effective salesmen are the ones who can get customers to give more attention to meeting the salesman's "friendly" expectations of them than to maximizing their own economic advantage.

particularly concentrated in the person of a king, the institution of a temple, or where there is some other government apparatus with power greater than other people or groups in society. In our own society, the collection of taxes to support works in the national interest is an example of a redistributive transaction. Similarly, when a local chief of an African tribe collects tribute and distributes it through the membership on the basis of kinship, support, or whatever, that is also an example of redistribution in operation.

The term is not as useful at the domestic level, but if we choose to apply it, we might say that many households are operated on redistributive principles, for different members turn their earnings over to a common budget, from which they then receive their sustenance. The Martínez household was operated in this way. The reason Esperanza was able to borrow against her sons' wages was that their employer understood perfectly well, just as did the sons, that the money they earned was earned for the family as a whole, and was not their own. All of the resources of the Martínez family were pooled in a common budget, and the distribution of them to accommodate the family's needs was in Pedro's hands. Esperanza had no money for food because Pedro had ruled that the sombrero, the machete, and the huaraches, and paying off Doña Conde, all were more pressing than the immediate household budget. Lewis also suggests that Pedro's sons saw him as a redistributive agent:

> The land was easier to work than the mountain clearing [where Pedro had his fields] and Don Porfirio [the landowner] was less of a taskmaster than Pedro. So the boys were glad of a chance to work for Don Porfirio and to earn some

Redistribution. The concentration of wealth and its reassignment to people on the basis of something other than who brought it is the essence of redistribution. This feast in Tonga involves the redistribution of food.

cash for the family. Pedro could be expected to give them something later on—a new shirt or a sombrero or some pocket money [1959:39].

The interest of redistribution as a system of economic exchange is greater, however, when it is operating at a societywide level rather than in a household only. For example, when it is a major source of economic distribution in a society, redistribution reinforces important political processes, for it involves tremendous power in the hands of the redistributor, be it person or institution. We are all familiar with the disputes that arise around priorities for spending (redistributing) the money collected from us in taxes, and everyone has heard the old proverb, "The power to tax is the power to destroy."

Systems of redistribution can be responsible for the creation or maintenance of differences in wealth in a society. The chief or headman is in a position to siphon off a portion of the resources he collects for the use of his own household or for the use of his friends or relatives. Royal houses are virtually always financed from public funds in this way, as are members of the nobility in most instances. On the other hand, redistribution, as Nash points out, can *also* be a means for reducing differences between the wealth of different segments of society. In the United States graduated income tax is an instance of the use of redistribution intended to take from the rich and give to the poor (or anyway to the commonweal), and for years it was opposed by political conservatives as "creeping socialism" for this reason.

Redistribution was a prominent feature of most preindustrial states and empires, even as it is a feature of most modern nations, particularly socialist ones. Levy describes the government's attention to economic distirbution in ancient Egypt:

> But the state did not only intervene in production. It directed distribution and consumption. It appropriated a fraction (usually large) of the harvest and hoarded it in warehouses, granaries, and depots situated even in the smallest villages or in "supply towns." The stores consisted of food, animals, cloth, metals, even furniture. These resources not only served to defray state expenses but also formed provisions for years of scarcity. The provident state laid up goods for its subjects. The king, it was said, is "he who presides over the food supplies of all," which is also shown by the Bible story of the seven lean kine [cows]. The distributions were made in a twofold spirit—desire for gain, and foresight or paternalism. The king sold dear what he had stored, but he and his administrators felt themselves duty bound to ensure the subsistence of everyone [1964:8].

Like a system of reciprocal exchange, a system of redistributive exchange involves the sorting of members of the society into different statuses, and their performance of roles consisting of sets of expectations between those statuses about what each side may expect of the other. The chief who fails to redistribute what he has collected wins the resentment and enmity of those under him, who may leave or may seek to replace him. The underling who fails to render unto Caesar is liable to find himself in Caesar's jail. The difference between redistributive exchange and reciprocal exchange lies not in the fact that there are expectations, but in what it is that is expected, and in the overall, societywide system of distribution of resources that results from the particular understandings that people follow.

Marketing

Market exchange, or marketing, involves exchange of resources on the basis of prices established by supply and demand and expressed in generalized units of value. Marketing, in other words, involves money and prices. In its ideal form, marketing is characterized by freedom of participants to buy and sell at whatever price suits them in free competition with other buyers and sellers of the same items, and the prices of items are established by supply and demand.

Characteristic of some markets is "haggling," the negotiation between buyers and sellers over the prices of the wares to be exchanged.[18] In theory, if both buyer and seller had perfect knowledge of the supply of the product and the need for it, they could agree immediately on what the "fair" price would be. In much marketing, however, not only is such perfect knowledge lacking, but there is also an element of negative reciprocity involved: Both the buyer and the seller seek to get the best possible bargain for themselves and leave it to the other side to look out for its own interests. If they do not both feel they have an advantageous or at least adequate exchange arranged, they do not make it. When Esperanza Martínez went to sell the turkey, she was not bringing the turkey man her turkey because he needed it, but because she wished to have money (or, more exactly, corn or beans or some other commodity). When he would not offer her what she considered to be an adequate price, she refused to sell. Haggling is one mechanism for establishing what both the buyer and seller consider to be an adequate price. Fuller market knowledge is another way, and the two are not incompatible. But in a market-exchange system, if buyer and seller cannot agree on the price, the Esperanzas of the world do not sell their turkeys, and goods are not distributed.

In market exchange the parties to the transaction are related primarily in the statuses of buyer and seller. In this respect, market exchange differs from most reciprocal exchange, in which the participants occupy statuses such as father-in-law or comrade that involve a large number of things be-

---

[18]In our own society haggling has been made somewhat less obtrusive by establishing fixed prices on some items in some stores, which the potential buyer can take or leave. Haggling still occurs for high-priced items such as houses and cars and in huge orders (as in government and industry) where bids are taken. In a sense the functional equivalent of haggling occurs even at the retail level in that the buyer normally can choose another store or another brand or can wait for a sale, all of which is monitored by experts in marketing research who advise the seller.

Butcher Shop in Rural Taiwan. The characteristic feature of market exchange is that prices are set by a market mechanism (supply and demand), sometimes mediated by haggling, and usually expressed in a uniform standard of value: money.

sides mere exchange of commodities. Marketing also differs from redistribution, which involves general expectations about power and political control in addition to economic expectations. In a sense, people who have a non-economic relationship with each other are not in a position to buy and sell efficiently to each other; their prior status relationship usually involves a concern for one another's welfare that precludes each trying to get the fair market price or the best bargain for himself. On the other hand, people who are not already involved in any status relationship other than buyer and seller are more likely to feel free to be as cold-blooded as they can manage about it.

Market exchange, therefore, is excellently suited to a situation in which the parties to the exchange are unacquainted with each other. Neither knows how much he can trust the other or whether he will ever see the other again. Because the transaction is more or less complete in itself,[19] each side is free to consider the advantages and disadvantages of the transaction, is at liberty to enter the transaction only if it is advantageous (compared with known

[19]The completeness varies. In many societies public opinion, custom, or law allow one to reopen the case if bad faith is later discovered, as in deceptive labeling or packaging. Some merchants, seeking to establish continuing series of purchases from steady customers, extend this possibility to any cases of customer dissatisfaction. Interestingly, attention to consumer complaints is also related to supply and demand.

alternatives), and is protected to some extent against bad faith on the part of the other participant by the fact that no long-term relationship need be maintained.

Market exchange is characteristic of large-scale societies. This is probably partly because people tend not to know each other in such societies, and a system that is to some extent proof against bad faith is appropriate. The status expectations associated with the statuses of buyer and seller are comparatively simple and do not require long knowledge of the other party. They allow even a huge society like those in many modern states to integrate its economic life in spite of the anonymity of its participants.

Even if people did all know each other, the social structure of a large-scale society (not just social class, but membership in such entities as families, neighborhoods, churches, occupational categories, and so on) separates the interests of different people, so that to meet the expectations in some relations (such as the family), they must have different and more restricted expectations in other spheres. Market exchange is a way of keeping some of one's social relationships very severely restricted without disrupting the distribution of economic resources. This, too, makes it congruent with the needs of large-scale societies.

On the other hand, many a society is small enough that participants for the most part already have long-standing status relationships to each other (such as kinship relationships) and do have long-term knowledge of each other. Market exchange, with its implications that every person must look out for himself, may then strike the participants not only as unnecessary, but also as cold, distant, or downright unfriendly. Even in our own society, the proprietor of a small business often feels uncomfortable about having normal business dealings with kinsmen or friends and seeks to transform such interactions by devices like offering them a discount on what he sells. In India and some other new nations where people are more used to systems of reciprocity as total economic-exchange systems, a problem for commercial development has been that the would-be proprietor of a new shop finds his relatives lined up outside the door on the first day and feels obliged to give them what they want for free, often as not leaving him with nothing to sell. Similarly, a person who earns a wage is often importuned by rural kinsmen for financial help or for free room and board to an extent that almost removes the economic (although perhaps not the social) advantages of getting wages.

Money and Monetization

Market exchange, as we noted earlier, involves prices set, however imperfectly, by supply and demand. This is not easily accomplished without the use of money inasmuch as the direct exchange of items has inherent inefficiencies both in supplying all potential customers with items that can be exchanged for a commodity and in establishing a standard price when different transactions involve the exchange of different things. How many pots should one pay for a camel? How many chickens should one pay for a camel? How many folding tents? How many chickens are equal to how many pots? How many chickens or pots are equal to how many folding tents? If the number of pots (or chickens or tents) is high, what is the camel seller to do with them all? One way such problems are efficiently solved is through the use of "money." Money is a unit of value by which different items may be compared and in terms of which they may be exchanged. It is also a physical token of value that provides the means for making an exchange. If the transaction makes use of money, the camel seller no longer has to worry about all those pots.

Of the two functions of money, the first, providing a standard of value, is in many ways the more important. Our own society, by means of checks, credit cards, promissory notes, charge accounts, and the like, has very much lessened the direct use of money as a token of exchange, particularly in large transactions involving hundreds, thousands, or millions of dollars. Modern China has gone even further in eliminating money. There, all transactions between organizations must by law be accomplished by cross entries from accounts in the same state bank. Neither society has done away with money as a measure for calculating the comparative value of different items in common units (dollars, pounds, *yuan*, or whatever), however. Even in Azteca, for all the concern about money, there seems to have been a good deal of credit buying and payments in produce. We remember that Don Porfirio paid Esperanza the advance partly in cash and partly in corn. But as far as can be told from Lewis's account, the values were calculated and the records were kept in a common currency: *pesos*.

The tokens exchanged as money against goods vary a good deal from society to society. In most modern states slips of paper (bills) and metal disks (coins) are used. However, over the world a wide variety of objects have filled this purpose, ranging from cowrie shells in Melanesia to cattle in Africa and from stones in Yap and shells in the Russell Islands to feathers among the Santa Cruz Indians.

Among the Baruya of the eastern New Guinea highlands, bars of salt were used in exchanges with neighboring groups.[20] The salt, which was produced from ashes with great difficulty and labor, was an expensive luxury commodity that was used in certain religious rites. But beyond this use it served as an intertribal currency in the area, and prices of certain items in intertribal trade were given in large, medium, and small bars of salt. A round, pierced stone for use as a stone club was worth one medium bar. Twenty to thirty barbed arrows were worth half a large bar. Five bark capes could be bought with one large bar of salt. The services of a friend traveling to conduct trade could also be bought with one large bar. The services of a sorcerer cost one

MONEY *A unit of value by which different items may be compared and in terms of which they may be exchanged; also a physical token of value that provides the means for making an exchange.*

---

[20]The Baruya are a group of about 1500 people belonging to the group of tribes administratively referred to as the Kukukuku. See Godelier (1971) for a description of Baruya salt currency.

or two large bars. A male dog cost one medium bar, and so forth (Godelier 1971:60f.). What made the salt bars money was not merely the fact that they were traded back and forth, but the fact that they could be exchanged for different kinds of commodities and were used as a unit of value for calculating the worth of different types of commodities. Godelier writes about this problem this way:

> Salt is a luxury commodity, but is it a "money"? In order for a commodity to function as money, it must be possible to exchange it for the totality of the other commodities, it must work as their *general* equivalent. . . . let us take the example of the circulating of a crossbelt of pig's teeth. It cannot be exchanged for a stone axe or for a pig, either dead or alive. It could perhaps be exchanged for feathers but the possibilities of converting it into another product end there. Its circulation is ascribable to the most current barter and if it is a commodity, it is certainly not a money. Stone axes and pigs could conceivably be converted into any other sort of commodity but this is, in fact, not possible because they are too scarce. On the other hand, salt alone can undergo (enter into) all the possible conversions. It therefore functions as money [1971:66].

For the Baruya, salt can be exchanged for more other commodities than anything else, and it is the most general equivalent to other commodities. However, there are surely some things that salt cannot buy, just as there are some things that dollars cannot buy. Money, the folk wisdom tells us, cannot

Money. The tokens used as money vary tremendously from society to society. Shown here are: Yapese stone wheel (a); Maya copper bell (b); African iron hoe (c); Chinese metal coin (d); Aztec gold eagle (e); and North American wampum (f).

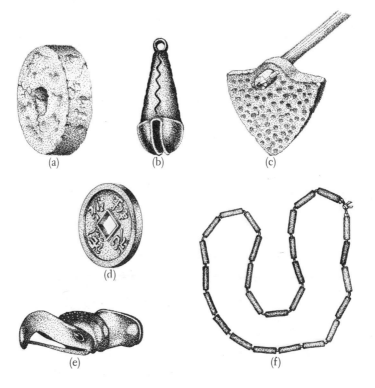

buy happiness. Nor can it buy love, good looks, health, wisdom, time, or so on. When we speak of things that have "sentimental value," we are saying that they have value that cannot conveniently be expressed in money. Depending on how many of a society's exchanges can be expressed in the same currency, anthropologists speak of a society as being more or less "monetized." No society is completely monetized. So far as we know, there is no society, for example, in which for a certain fee each week someone will love you. This does not mean that love is not "exchanged" or that "sentimental value" is not "value," but only that love and sentimental value are not in the same system of exchange as the parts of our existence that are monetized.[21] One of the clearest examples of separate spheres of exchange (clear partly because of its contrast to our own society) comes from the Tiv of northern Nigeria, who were studied by P. Bohannan between 1949 and 1953. At that time Bohannan was able to distinguish three different spheres of exchange, each of which functioned differently. One sphere included food, chickens, goats, household utensils, and some tools and raw materials. These things were exchanged against each other without mediation of currency. A second sphere of exchange included slaves, cattle, a kind of highly valued white cloth, and brass rods. Bohannan notes: "This second category is associated with prestige (shagba) in the same way that the first category is associated with subsistence. Although slaves and brass rods, at least, had some economic value beyond their value as prestige-conferring property, this latter was their main use" (1955:62).

The third category contained only one item: rights in human beings other than slaves, especially rights in dependent women and children, expressed in terms of kinship and marriage. The three categories were ranked such that items in the prestige category were considered more important than items in the subsistence category and items in the dependents category were considered more important than items in the prestige category.

The Tiv distinguished between exchanges of goods between categories and exchanges of goods in the same category. There were firm expectations among the Tiv that any rational man would make efforts to convert his wealth to higher and higher categories as the opportunity presented itself, and the man who did not do so was scorned as inadequate.

Exchanges within a category—particularly that of subsistence, the only one intact today—excite no moral judgments beyond comments regarding the

[21]Some social critics suggest that our society is becoming ever more monetized, and that, in fact, such things as love are becoming part of the general exchange system; more and more, they maintain, our collective understandings allow us to treat love, family welfare, and other parts of our existence as "commodities" to be bargained for or with in the general marketplace. There is also a general impression that modernization and monetization go together. Modernization, of course, even as it encourages monetization in some spheres (such as paying compensation for "mental anguish" or paying fines instead of taking revenge), discourages monetization in other areas (such as selling people into slavery, paying for brides, and buying one's way out of the draft).

"market" luck of one or both of the parties to the exchange. Exchanges between categories, however, excite a completely different sort of moral reaction.

The drive towards success leads most Tiv, to the greatest possible extent, to convert food into prestige items; to convert prestige items into dependents—wives and children. Tiv say it is good (*do kwagh*) to trade food for brass rods, but that it is bad (*vihi kwagh*) to trade brass rods for food; that it is good to trade your cows or brass rods for a wife, but very bad to trade your marriage ward for cows or brass rods [Bohannan 1955:64; quoted out of sequence].

The closest thing to money in this system was brass rods, which were used more than other things in trading between categories. They did not provide a standard measure of value, however.

The Tiv case is particularly interesting because it also provides an example of what happens to prescriptive understandings about exchange when these separate spheres of exchange are united by the introduction of a medium of common exchange between them, that is to say, when all three are monetized by the same currency. With the advent of the colonial administration, true money became available, which was convertible into goods in all three categories as well as into newly imported goods, and the traditional system of separate spheres of exchange began to break down. The monetization of the Tiv economy was imposed upon traditional Tiv values and understandings about how good people behaved and how the system was to be manipulated to the advantage of all. Bohannan writes of this breakdown:

In response to what appeared superficially to be popular demand, the Administration . . . abolished exchange marriage and substituted for it a form of marriage by bride wealth [i.e., a transfer of money from the groom to the bride's family on occasion of the marriage]. . . . Today every woman's guardian, in accepting money as bride wealth, feels that he is converting down. Although attempts are made to spend money which is received in bride wealth to acquire brides for one's self and one's sons, it is in the nature of money, Tiv insist, that this is most difficult to accomplish. The good man still spends his bride wealth receipts for brides—but good men are not so numerous as would be desirable [1955:69].

In other words, there is an ill-fated attempt to preserve the traditional separateness of these exchange spheres by differentiating money received for brides from other money and making it bride money only so as to avoid the implication that brides have entered into the general system of exchange and can be "bought." The situation grows worse.

Today it is easy to sell subsistence goods for money to buy prestige articles and women, thereby aggrandizing oneself at a rapid rate. The food so sold is exported, decreasing the amount of subsistence goods available for consumption. On the other hand the number of women is limited. The result is that bride wealth gets higher—the price of women becomes inflated. Under these conditions, as Tiv attempt to become more and more wealthy in people, they are merely selling more and more of their foodstuffs and subsistence goods, leaving less and less for their own consumption [Bohannan 1955:69].

Hausa Cassava Seller in Niger. Although many peoples have engaged in market exchanges for centuries, integration into a world economy has involved monetization of new spheres, demonetization of previously monetized spheres, and the convertibility of many monetized spheres by means of general-purpose money. All three of these processes have the potential to bring about dislocations in traditional societies.

The monetization of Tiv economy has led to a rush on what were once the most desirable goods, inflating them, causing guilt among those "selling" them, and in general disappointing the expectations of participants without their being able to do anything about it.[22]

It is important to note that it was not monetization of these spheres of exchange per se that caused the dislocations in the Tiv economy, but the monetization of all three spheres with the same currency. In theory, if different currency had been introduced into each sphere, the spheres would have remained more or less separate—they were never entirely separate after all—and the dislocations would not have occurred. Anthropologists sometimes speak of "special-purpose money," that is, money that is restricted to one of two or more spheres of economic exchange in a society, as opposed to "general-purpose money," which serves as a general medium of exchange for all monetized spheres of economic exchange in a society.

Money, and the shared prescriptive understandings about the spheres in which its use is and is not appropriate, provides an instrument to facilitate the market exchange that is very efficient as a means of distribution of resources in large-scale societies. No society is ever completely monetized, and no society ever uses market exchange for all its distribution of resources, but it is apparently impossible for any but a very small society to function without marketing, and monetization of at least some spheres greatly facilitates the marketing process.

[22]Perhaps we should be glad that money *cannot* buy love—yet.

SPECIAL-PURPOSE MONEY *Money that is restricted to one of two or more spheres of economic exchange in a society.*

GENERAL-PURPOSE MONEY *Money that serves as a general medium of exchange for all monetized spheres of economic exchange in a society.*

SUMMARY

In no society are individuals entirely self-sufficient. They depend on each other, at least during a portion of every life. The differences in their activities and the contribution that each makes to the welfare of the others is comprehended by the term "division of labor." All societies have division of labor by sex and by age. There are some cross-cultural regularities in division of labor by sex that seem to be relatable to the biological facts that men are for the most part larger and stronger than women and that women bear and tend children. Variation is tremendous from society to society, however.

Economic anthropologists distinguish "true" division of labor from division of labor by sex or age. In general, the more complex the technology of a people becomes, the greater the division of labor there is and the more specialization occurs, with the result that there is a more acute problem of distribution of resources among members of the society. Anthropologists, following economist Karl Polanyi, commonly distinguish three modes of distribution: reciprocity, redistribution, and market exchange. Reciprocity involves the direct exchange of items with an expectation of eventual return of comparably valuable items. There are several different kinds of reciprocity, depending on the extent to which repayment must be exact or immediate rather than inexact and delayed and on the extent to which participants try to drive bargains. Redistribution involves the collection of resources into a center and their return to the body of individuals who contributed them. Market exchange involves the sale of resources in trade for money at prices fixed by supply and demand. No economy makes use of only one of these modes of distribution, even though one may be predominant and it may be convenient to speak of market economies, redistributive economies, or reciprocal economies.

Reciprocity as a predominant mode of exchange is typical of small band or tribal societies and is particularly suitable to situations in which individuals have little control of their productive capacity. Reciprocity, in most instances, is also the mechanism involved with silent trade. Reciprocal exchanges, because they imply good faith and long-term association, are also often endowed with a symbolic function, and some reciprocal exchanges are largely or primarily of a symbolic rather than strictly distributional nature. Perhaps the ultimate reciprocal system is the potlatch of the northwest coast of North America, which involved individuals and groups in a web of obligations and counterobligations of great economic importance. Power relations with a political big-man are normally also entwined with economic exchange with him, typically on the basis of reciprocal obligations and expectations. *Kula* exchange in the Trobriands also involves long-term relations of reciprocal exchange, though exchange that is economically unimportant.

Redistributive distribution is common in many societies, though it is not the exclusive mode of exchange in any society. Redistribution of all or part of a society's resources by a central authority can be used to maintain differences in wealth or to diminish differences in wealth. The American graduated income tax is an example of a redistributive distribution designed with the latter end in mind.

Market exchange is the basic distributional mechanism in most large-scale societies. It is peculiarly well suited to this because it does not require long-term association between buyer and seller and requires little trust between them. With this system, the anonymity that is inevitable in large-scale societies is no barrier to distribution of resources. Market exchange depends on money, which is both a unit of value for evaluating resources against each other and a physical token that may be used in exchange. Anthropologists speak of the use of money in a sphere of exchange as the monetization of that sphere of exchange. Social and cultural changes that appear with modernization often involve monetization of spheres that were previously unmonetized; they sometimes also involve the opposite as well.

In economic analysis it is important to distinguish between the effects of a custom upon the distribution of resources, on the one hand, and the motivations of the participants, on the other. Participants engage in exchange for a variety of reasons, including understandings about the social statuses they occupy, and the analysis of the distributional effects alone does not provide adequate understanding of the cultural aspects of the distributional system.

SUGGESTED READINGS

More on the case

LEWIS, OSCAR 1959 Five Families: Mexican Case Studies in the Culture of Poverty. New York: New American Library.

This book includes the description of the Martínez family from which this chapter's case is taken.

Other readings

DALTON, GEORGE 1961 Economic Theory and Primitive Society. American Anthropologist 63:1–25.

This paper presents reasons why traditional economic theory cannot easily be applied to primitive economics, which are neither industrialized nor market centered.

MALINOWSKI, B. 1921 The Primitive Economics of the Trobriand Islanders. The Economic Journal 31:1–16.

This article presents a better-rounded picture of Trobriand Islands economics than does Chapter 6 which discusses their economics only from the perspective of kula *exchange.*

MEAD, MARGARET 1935 Sex and Temperament in Three Primitive Societies. New York: Morrow.

This book discusses three New Guinea societies in which the cultural under-standings about how women and men behave take three dramatically different forms, illustrating something of the variation that is possible in the definition of sex roles.

NASH, MANNING 1964 The Organization of Economic Life. *In* Horizons in Anthropology. Sol Tax, Ed. Chicago: University of Chicago Press. pp. 171–180.

This article is a general survey of the kinds of problems faced by anthropologists in examining economic systems.

SAHLINS, MARSHALL D. 1968 Tribesmen. Englewood Cliffs, N.J.: Prentice-Hall.

A discussion of both social and economic aspects of a tribal type of social orga-nization and economic adaptation. Much of the book focuses on the problems of economic allocation.

SERVICE, ELMAN R. 1966 The Hunters. Englewood Cliffs, N.J.: Prentice Hall.

Describes the kinds of cultural understandings and social organization associated with hunting-and-gathering bands, whose economies typically are based on reciprocal exchange.

7

Politics

The use of force alone is but temporary. It may subdue for a moment; but it does not remove the necessity of subduing again; and a nation is not governed which is perpetually to be conquered.

EDMUND BURKE
ON CONCILIATION WITH THE AMERICAN COLONIES, 1775

The vast Zulu empire in southern Africa was carved out by Zulu soldiers like these.

Why do people often accept the decisions of their groups and follow their groups' rules for behavior?

What is the difference between legitimacy and coercion, and what role does each play in politics?

Do politics occur in groups without politicians?

What effect does conflict have on groups?

What special groups are found in the rapidly changing politics seen in much of the contemporary world?

Buffalo, Soldiers, and a Council: A Case of Politics among the Cheyenne

The tribe was moving in a body up the Rosebud River toward the Big Horn Mountain country in search of buffalo.[1] The Shield Soldiers, who were in charge on that occasion, had their scouts out looking for the herds, and when the scouts came in with their report, the order was given that no one should leave the camp or attack the buffalo. Nobody was supposed to shoot a buffalo until the signal was given.

All the hunters went out in a line with the Shield Soldiers in front to hold them back. Just as they were coming up over a long ridge down wind from where the scouts had reported the herd they saw two men down in the valley riding in among the buffalo. A Shield Soldier chief gave the signal to his men. They paid no attention to the buffalo, but charged in a long line on the two violators of the rules. Little Old Man shouted out for everyone to whip them: "Those who fail or hesitate shall get a good beating themselves."

The first men to reach the spot shot and killed the horses from under the hunters. As each soldier reached the miscreants he slashed them with his riding whip. Then some seized the guns of the two and smashed them.

When the punishment was done, the father of these two boys rode up. It was Two Forks, a mem-

ber of the Dakota tribe, who had been living with the Cheyennes for some time. He looked at his sons before talking. "Now you have done wrong. You failed to obey the law of this tribe. You went alone and you did not give the other people a chance. This is what has happened to you."

The Shield Soldier chiefs took up the talk. "Now you know what we do when anyone disobeys our orders," they declared. "Now you know we mean what we say." The boys did not say anything.

After that the chiefs relented. This was not alone because of the fact that the culprits were Dakotas. They called their men to gather around. "Look how these two boys are here in our midst. Now they have no horses and no weapons. What do you men want to do about it?"

One of the soldiers spoke up, "Well, I have some extra horses. I will give one of them to them." Then another soldier did the same thing.

Bear Standing On A Ridge was the third to speak out, "Well," he announced, "we broke those guns they had. I have two guns. I will give them one."

All the others said, "*I pewa*, good."

Meanwhile, someone had been counting up the men. There were forty-nine in the troop at that time, and now it was noticed that five or six were not at hand. When they began looking around, they saw these men way down the creek chasing bison. "Now we will give them a good whipping," shouted one of the chiefs. "Charge on them and whip them, but don't kill their horses."

They all leaped to their mounts to see who could get there first. When the slackers saw them coming, Big Footed Bull, who was among them, took off the blanket he was wearing and spread it on the ground. It was one of those fine Hudson's Bay blankets which the government used to issue to the Indians. He stood behind it with his friends, because he meant it as an offering to the troop. Last Bull, who was one of the Shield Soldier chiefs at that time, called to his men to halt. They stopped, and then they split into two columns

[1]All the material in this case concerns the Cheyenne as they were during the nineteenth century when the vigorous, horse-based life of the North American Plains Indians was at its height. The case is written in the ethnographic present for simplicity of presentation. The buffalo-hunt description that opens the case is taken from a verbatim account by the Cheyenne Stump Horn. From *The Cheyenne Way: Conflict and Case Law in Primitive Jurisprudence*, by Karl N. Llewellyn and E. Adamson Hoebel, pp. 112–113. Copyright 1941 by the University of Oklahoma Press. With permission. The descriptions of the Council of Forty-Four and the priest-chiefs and of the military societies are based on Hoebel (1960) and Grinnel (1923).

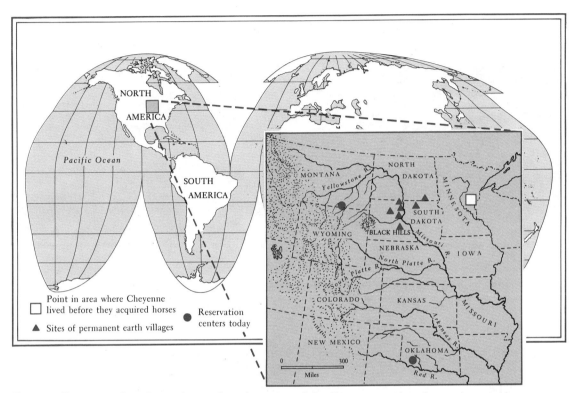

Cheyenne Country: Taking the northern and southern parts of the Cheyenne together, the members of this group hunted over a vast section of the western plains. The people discussed here are northern Cheyenne, whose territory included parts of Montana, Wyoming, Nebraska, and South Dakota. (Adapted from Grinnell 1923:358.)

which rode slowly around the men by the blanket and circled around to the front again. The soldiers dismounted and divided the blanket among themselves, tearing it into long narrow strips of cloth to wear as tail pieces when they were having a dance. They finished by cutting an ear off each of the horses of the culprits. That was how they punished them [Hoebel 1941:112–113].

Large buffalo hunts such as this one occur only when the whole Cheyenne tribe is gathered together. During most of the year the Cheyenne live in ten main bands, each hunting over its own area of the northwestern plains, but in the late spring and summer when hunting is best and grazing for the horses most plentiful, the whole tribe camps in one place. During this time the great religious festivals are held, major military actions are undertaken, and the Council of Forty-Four meets to make the decisions that are fundamental to all important group activities. To understand the organization and operation of such things as the buffalo hunt, or any large-scale

Cheyenne Soldiers. Discipline and tribal unity were achieved among the Cheyenne through the existence of soldier societies, to one or another of which every adult man belonged.

Cheyenne activity, we must examine the council and how it works.

The Council of Forty-Four is the supreme authority in Cheyenne affairs. The military societies, of which the Shield Society is one,[2] have their leaders, but these "war chiefs" are subordinate to the "peace chiefs," the common name for council members. These are men who have proven themselves in battle and are established warriors. If, however, a chief of a military society is appointed to the council, he must abandon his leadership position in the war group, although he remains a member of that group. Both the separation of military and civil leadership and the

supremacy of the civil are clearly recognized and valued by the Cheyenne. The council's supremacy over the chiefs of the military societies is unquestioned. The council decides when and where such group activities as buffalo hunting and tribewide moves shall take place, and the council determines tribal war policy and judges major cases involving criminal acts. As they did in the hunt just described, the war societies act as an enforcement arm for the council's broad policies and specific decisions. In matters of war, however, these societies and their chiefs influence council decisions in an important way.

The Cheyenne have a myth that gives the council a supernatural origin and establishes it as the ultimate authority in the tribe. This myth dramatically portrays the anarchy resulting from

[2] Another Cheyenne military society, the Dog Society, probably provided the nickname used for United States soldiers in World War II, "dogface."

the absence of such authority and how having the council prevents this anarchy and brings order and justice to daily life. The military societies are explicitly seen in the myth as subordinate to the council.[3] The council has five leaders, one of whom is its presiding officer. He is called the Sweet Medicine Chief after the culture hero Sweet Medicine, whom he represents, and who is the founder of the council in Cheyenne myth. Because this leader has important religious as well as political duties as part of his office in the council, he is referred to as a "priest-chief," and the same is true of his four fellow council leaders. Each of these other four priest-chiefs represents a supernatural being, and the ritual activities of the five council leaders are connected with their mystical ties to these beings.

The members of the council, including the five priest-chiefs, choose their own successors when they finish their terms in office. The mem-

[3]For the text of the myth and its analysis, see Hoebel (1960: 39–45).

bers of the council serve ten-year terms. Roughly four council members come from each of the ten main bands that make up the Cheyenne tribe, and when a member finishes his term, he always appoints his replacement from his own band. This makes for a close representation of the ordinary people in the tribe, with roughly one council member for every 100 people (there are about 4000 Cheyenne). Each tenth year a great ritual is held when the new council members assume their duties and the council is supernaturally renewed. The four days and nights of this ritual are presided over by the five priest-chiefs, each of whom has specific ritual duties to perform. These duties are passed along to each priest-chief by his predecessor. The Sweet Medicine Chief is in overall charge of the renewal ritual as he is of council meetings. At the end of the renewal rituals, there is great gift giving, and the poor members of the tribe are especially singled out in receiving horses, robes, and other things of value from the council members.

A Cheyenne Camp, about 1870. Group order depends on a combination of legitimacy and coercion.

Cheyenne outside Medicine Lodge. The supernatural basis for the power of the Cheyenne chiefs and council was crucial to its flexibility and effectiveness.

Each of the members of the council is a dominant figure in his kin group and band, but above all, he is viewed as a "protector of the people" and a "father" to every member of the tribe regardless of family or band. The Cheyenne frequently mention a number of personal characteristics essential to membership on the council and found in all peace chiefs: The members must have an even-tempered good nature, energy, wisdom, kindliness, concern for the well-being of others, courage, and generosity. All the members of the council have a close connection with the supernatural, so, as Hoebel puts it, "The council is not just a body of their wisest men, but a council of men in empathy with the spiritual forces that dominate all life—beneficient forces from which come all good things the Cheyenne heart desires, forces that respond to their hopes and needs so long as the [required] ritual acts are faithfully repeated" (1960:45).

The council is itself the supreme authority. The Sweet Medicine Chief is its presiding officer and has vital religious duties as the representative of the culture hero, but he has no power to decide things by himself. There are other offices within the council for the other four priest-chiefs, but they have the same voice in determining tribal business as do any of the thirty-nine other council members. The council meets in a great tepee, which usually has its sides rolled up. A large audience sits outside the tepee listening to the discussions in which all council members are free to participate and to speak their views fully. When a decision is reached, a crier rides through the camp and announces it to all.

Analysis of the Case

If a collective buffalo hunt is to have a chance of success, most of those who participate in it must act in such a way that they contribute to the joint effort or, at least, do not interfere with it. To achieve this, there must be a decision that the hunt be held, this decision must be accepted by a large enough number of people to provide needed manpower, and there must be some sort of common regulation of behavior during the hunt. The most striking part of the hunt description concerns this regulation and consists of the announcing of the hunt rules and the enforcement of these rules by the Shield Soldiers. In fact, however, the rules and their enforcement are no more crucial than the decision that the hunt be held and the acceptance of that decision. The two kinds of processes, rule enforcement and decision making, are not as separate as they may seem to be.

The Shield Soldiers and their whips It is tempting to think of force as "automatically" effective, but, in fact, it only works when people allow it to. As we saw in Chapter 4, "Personality," when coercion is part of a situation, it is only one element in the complex of factors that determine behavior. When the type of coercion being used is force, and there are other types to be discussed later, people must weigh a number of considerations in deciding what to do. These include how likely it is they will actually have the force worked upon them; how much they wish to avoid the force; and how strongly they want to do (or not do) whatever it is those who threaten to apply the force are trying to stop them from doing (or not doing). Another important consideration is whether or not those who might receive the force agree that what they did was wrong; that is, do those who expose themselves to the possibility of punishment feel that they deserve it?

The Shield Soldiers are an obvious agency of coercion through force. The two boys at the beginning of the hunt description and the five or six men at the end probably hoped they would not be caught in their premature attacks on the buffalo. They could hardly have hoped successfully to resist the soldiers once they were caught. The punishment they actually received was very severe in the case of the two boys, but, as it turned out, less so in the case of the five or six men. What is particularly interesting in both cases is that there was no attempt to escape the punishment. In fact, the group of men made it as easy as possible for the soldiers to get them and put out a valuable blanket for the soldiers to take. Hoebel says of this:

> This laying of the blanket was not bribery or buying off. It was open recognition of error, submission, and a good-will offering. It stayed the beating in good part, as we see it, because it removed the flavor of defiance about the insubordination; but it did not stay all the penalty. The duty of all the members of a society to participate in the administration of punishment and the liability of all members to discipline in case of neglect were stated by all informants as generalized rules and are borne out in several cases [1960:113].

There can be no doubt that force is an important element in the coordination of activity needed for the hunt, but it is important to recognize that it is not the only element. If we consider another bit of the hunt description, it will begin to become clear that force, or any other form of coercion, cannot by itself bring about conformity to rules or support for decisions from a large proportion of a group's members.

Coercion—not enough   We saw that a Soldier Society chief, Little Old Man, shouted to the soldiers that if any of them failed to beat the two erring boys they would "get a good beating themselves." The question as to how this beating might be administered if a large number of the soldiers did not want to follow the chief's orders is one that points to a basic fact of politics: Coercion, whether through beating and property destruction or of some other kind, cannot *by itself* bring about conformity to rules or support for decisions from more than a small part of a group's members.

The beatings and property destruction meted out by the soldiers can obviously keep a few deviants in line, but these beatings are only possible if most of the members of the Shield Society think they ought to be given. Little Old Man could not have beaten his whole group of soldiers by himself if they had chosen to let the boys go unpunished. If most of them actively opposed punishing the two boys, the punishment could not be administered, and the chief's threat to his soldiers would be an empty one. The support for the hunt's rules may have been partly based on fear of the soldiers, but the soldiers' own support for the rules cannot easily be based on fear alone.

There is a basic need for support not based on coercion among at least some group members. The question of the Latin poet Juvenal, *Quis custodiet ipsos custodes?* (Who shall keep watch over the watchers?), is a recognition of the impossibility of an exclusive reliance on force. None of this

Cheyenne Warriors. Little Old Man could not have beaten his whole group of soldiers by himself. Ultimately his authority over them required the agreement of those controlled.

should be seen as a detraction from the real role of force and other kinds of coercion in getting people to behave in accord with rules or in getting their support for decisions. Simply, there are limits to what coercion can do. It is never enough by itself to win support throughout a group.

In fact, there are some other forces supporting the rules of the Cheyenne hunt in addition to the whips of the Soldier Society. The earlier discussion of the Council of Forty-Four and its priest-chief leaders provides a basis for seeing where these forces come from.

Legitimacy and the Council

The Council of Forty-Four and its leaders are closely associated with the supernatural forces that Cheyenne culture identifies as the source of all that is good and necessary in the world. According to the myth of its founding, the council itself is a gift from a supernatural being who specifically intended it as a means of promoting the internal peace and order valued by the Cheyenne. The religious rites required for prosperity and well-being are possible only through the activities of the council and its members. So long as the understandings concerning the nature of the world, the supernatural, and the council's connection with the supernatural continued to be shared, the council had a broad and vital basis for support. This was strengthened by the shared understandings concerning the character of the men on the council; their social ties with other members of the society; and the way the council operated.

A particular action of the council's may not have been agreeable to some or even most of the members of this society, but it still had a considerable basis for support in the understandings that surrounded the council. Everything the council and its agencies did was not dutifully followed by everyone. The rules of the hunt came indirectly from the council, but they were nevertheless broken. Still, the actions and decisions of the council and its representatives enjoyed a basis of support that was independent from the support that those actions and decisions might receive on their merits as these were assessed by the people.

The acceptance of punishment by those who broke the hunt rules can be partly understood as a consequence of the fact that the rules of the hunt and their enforcers are associated with the council and share in its support. For some hunters, this support was not enough to bring them actually to follow the rules when they saw an opportunity to achieve personal advantage, but it was enough to keep even these individuals from attempting to avoid the punishment the soldiers administered to them. The support for the council and for the Shield Society as a representative of the council had an effect on all the hunters including even those who disobeyed. The shared understandings that the council and its agencies are closely connected to all that is good provide those who share them with a general inclination to follow the council's decisions. This inclination could be outweighed by other forces in particular cases for particular individuals, but it was always present and always affected those who had it, even if only to make them willing to accept punishment for behavior contrary to the council's wishes.

This effect results from people's general expectations that the council will provide them with benefits. The myth establishes the council's role as the source of peace and order, and the shared understanding that all its members are men of great virtue devoted to the general welfare helps assure that people will have broad and relatively undefined expectations of benefit from it. Support based on such expectations is called "legitimacy."

LEGITIMACY *Support based on broad and general expectations.*

This kind of political support attaches to anything about which people have these sorts of expectations. What is legitimate may be a special sort of group (the Cheyenne council or a United Nations organization), a particular office (Sweet Medicine Chief or Secretary General), a specific person (the man who is Sweet Medicine Chief), or it may be specific sorts of procedures such as reaching decisions by public discussion, by divination, or by secret vote. We find out what is supported by legitimacy by examining the actual expectations of the people involved. Is it the specific individual who is expected to provide vaguely defined but important benefits such as happiness or prosperity or, rather, that any occupant of a particular status is expected to do this? The answer may be that there are general expectations attached to the office and a further set of expectations attached to the particular individuals who occupy the office at various times. It may also be that people have broad expectations regarding, say, the procedures for decision making (e.g., "The council's open discussions ensure the people's interests will be considered") and also have such expectations for the statuses whose occupants are involved in these decisions (e.g., "Any council member will try to promote the people's welfare").

Cheyenne with Peace Pipe. The *calumet,* or peace pipe, was smoked by most North American Indian groups as a symbol of the legitimacy of political agreements.

Legitimacy is not the only kind of political support; it is not even the only kind that results from expectations. It is distinctive in being composed of *general* expectations. People cannot always tell whether a specific action or decision contributes to the "good life" or "peace," but it is the very vagueness of the expectations that make up legitimacy which gives this form of support its strength and flexibility. So long as Cheyenne were convinced that the council was the source (or one of them) of peace and the good life, they had an important basis for supporting its decisions and the actions of its agencies even in circumstances where the particular decision or the particular action was not itself desirable. Presumably the five or six men who were caught by the soldiers did not really want to give up their blanket, much less suffer the more severe punishment they could well have received. Nevertheless, their understanding that the agency of the council, the Shield Society, was acting as part of what they understood as a general tendency of the council to achieve "good" played a role in their acceptance of the punishment. As we will see in the discussion of coercion, this is not all there was in the hunters' acceptance of punishment, but it was a key element.

It is important to note that liking and legitimacy are not the same. An official may be well liked but not be supported by the sorts of expectations we are calling legitimacy. Similarly, an official who is disliked can be legitimate in that people expect general sorts of benefits from him. "Legitimate" is also different from "legal." A legal official is one who holds office according to an established set of rules, and a legal decision is one made according to these particular rules. Being in accord with rules, however, is not necessarily the same as being the object of general expectations. Rules themselves require support to be effective. This support *may* be through legitimacy if people have general expectations of benefit from the rules themselves. When this happens, actions taken in accord with these rules will be legitimate (with the special meaning that has) as well as legal.

In the United States the Constitution is legitimate for many citizens in that they expect general benefits to come from its use. This is true for at least some people who have never read the whole document and may not even be quite sure about some of its contents. For these people, individuals who are understood to be defenders or upholders of the Constitution thereby gain support, and the same is true of laws that the people themselves (not necessarily the Supreme Court, which they may or may not view as legitimate) see as being in accord with the Constitution.

Coercion As important as legitimacy is in affecting behavior, those who grant it may still not act as the object of the legitimacy requires them to. Some people have general expectations of benefit coming from the Constitution, agree a law is constitutional, and violate it anyway. This is probably what happened with at least some of the rule breakers in the hunt. Some of the violators of the hunt, however, probably did not have general expectations of benefit from representatives of the council, and there are surely Americans who have no such expectations of the Constitution. To gain desired sorts of behavior from all or most of the members of a group, legitimacy must be supplemented by other more immediate and direct supports. Not only can the failure of a few individuals to give support ruin an activity as it did in the hunt, but it can also serve as an example that might lead other group members to allow their general expectations to be overcome by immediate personal desires.

The administration of punishment is a way of countering these examples by showing that what the violators did leads to highly specific (and, in the case discussed here, undesirable) consequences.[4] The members of the hunting party, and all the other members of the Cheyenne group, knew that the Shield Soldiers would punish those who broke the rules of the hunt. They even knew what forms the punishment was likely to take. They had highly specific expectations of what would happen to rule breakers.

"Coercion" refers to the highly specific expectations people have regard-

COERCION *Support based on very definite and narrow expectations.*

[4]A famous story illustrating this concerns Napoleon's treatment of a soldier he saw straggling behind his unit during the retreat from Moscow. Napoleon seized an aide's pistol and shot the man dead. When his staff asked why he had killed the man, Napoleon said: "To encourage the others."

ing the behavior of other people, statuses, groups, procedures, or organizations. Coercion is like legitimacy in that both are forms of political support. It is also like legitimacy in that it is a sort of expectation of others' behavior. Coercion differs from legitimacy, however, in that coercion refers to very definite and narrow expectations. The Shield Soldiers controlled the hunt through coercion. Everyone knew just what would happen if they attacked the buffalo before the group was ready or broke in front of the line of soldiers: They would be beaten or lose valuable property or both. They also believed that the representatives of the council were working to help them and to bring them benefits. The general expectations of the council and the specific expectations of the Shield Society, the council's agent, both worked to mold behavior.

Coercion differs from legitimacy only in that its expectations are highly specific. In the example of the Cheyenne hunt the coercive expectations were negative while the legitimate expectations were positive. Coercion need not be negative, however, and legitimate expectations can sometimes be negative. This will become clearer in examining the way the two kinds of support work.

Types of legitimacy and coercion   If you are told to vote for Jones or your arm will be broken, your support for Jones is being sought on a coercive basis. Whoever threatens you in this way is trying to instill in you a clear expectation of precisely what will happen if you fail to do something he wants you to do. He may fail to instill that expectation (because, for example, you do not believe he can or will harm you or because you feel he can successfully be fooled) or you may not do as he says, even though he has instilled the expectation that your arm will be broken, because you believe that it is better to suffer injury than accept this sort of domination. Whether it works or not, the coercive nature of the bid for support is clear. It is equally coercive, however, if the same man comes to you, and instead of holding out the prospect of bodily damage, says he will give you $10 if you vote for Jones. The expectation of getting a particular and specific reward is just as specific as the expectation of punishment, and, as we will see, some of the same problems and advantages derive from positively based coercion as from negatively based coercion.

The broad and general expectations that make up legitimacy are often of the positive sort associated with the Cheyenne council, but broad negative expectations will also work. The great conqueror Shaka Zulu, who built an empire covering most of southern Africa, had the reputation of being an extremely fierce man. He would point his finger at a retainer or bystander who had offended him (in one recorded case by smiling), and the king's servants and guards would kill the offender immediately. This was a common occurrence at Shaka's court as can be seen in the following quotation from an early European visitor:

> On the first day of our visit we had seen no less than ten men carried out to death. On a mere sign by Shaka, viz.: the pointing of his finger, the victim would

be seized by his nearest neighbors; his neck would be twisted, and his head and body beaten with sticks, the nobs of some of these being as large as a man's fist. On each succeeding day, too, numbers of others were killed; their bodies would then be carried on an adjoining hill and there impaled. We visited this spot on the fourth day. It was truly a Golgotha, swarming with hundreds of vultures [Stuart and Malcolm 1950:78].[5]

What is particularly noteworthy about the sudden violence to which those around the king were subjected is that it served as a basis for political support that was not wholly coercive. It is reported that victims of the royal wrath often made no attempt to escape and that it was not unusual for them to use their last breath to praise the ruler who ordered their death. Whether this can be seen as a legitimacy based partly on broad and general negative expectations—quite possibly mixed with positive ones—is not entirely clear, but it is suggestive. The important point is that if people expect dreadful and unspecified things to be done to them at any time and for any reason, the results in gaining their support are quite possibly the same as those obtained when people expect indefinite benefits. General expectations, whether of benefit or harm, are much broader in their influence than specific expectations. If a person is bribed or forced to vote for a candidate, once the voting is over, the influence of the bribe or force is exhausted. If, however, a person has the *general* idea that he will be benefited or harmed by an official or a policy, this idea will continue to influence his behavior as long as it is held.

Zulu Soldiers. These contemporary Zulus are dressed in the garb worn by Shaka Zulu's troops.

How Legitimacy and Coercion Work

A key difference in the operation of legitimacy and coercion is that coercion requires constant "payoff," and legitimacy does not. The support the Cheyenne council had did not depend upon its successfully providing all members of the group with the particular things they wanted all the time. The council did not lose its ability to have its decisions carried out because a particular hunt was unsuccessful or, even, because a particular military action turned out to be a disaster. People expected the council to provide benefits and they interpreted what the council did in that light. If a hunt failed, it was because the buffalo were scarce or the hunters unlucky. If a battle was lost, it was because of the enemy's strength. It was not because the council had done something wrong. As long as the council was understood to be devoted to the welfare of the people and as long as it was believed to have the means for promoting that welfare through its supernatural connections and the abilities of its members, it won support with little regard to particular occurrences.

[5]This passage from Fynn's diary, quoted in Stuart and Malcolm, as well as many similar accounts from early travelers among the Zulu, are to be found in Walter (1969:109–219). Walter's views of "terror" are closely related to the concept of "legitimacy" as presented here, especially, of course, negatively based legitimacy.

The sort of support that derives from coercion is closely tied to events. A vote buyer cannot successfully get votes over time if he does not pay off, that is, meet the highly specific expectation of those who vote as he tells them to. A hunt policeman must actually do something undesirable to those who break the hunt rules or his effectiveness in keeping order in the hunt, his support in the status of policeman, will vanish. Because it is specific, coercion requires constant payoff. Because it is general and indefinite, legitimacy does not.

Coercion is clearly an "expensive" way to get political support, in that the specific expectations people have must be met with considerable regularity. Moreover, the support that comes from coercion does not spread beyond its original object. If the only reason you support a political candidate in an election is because he buys your vote, the money (or threat) that brought you to vote for him is unlikely to bring you to help him once he gets into office unless he pays (threatens) you again for each specific instance of required support. Similarly, having given your vote by coercion, you are unlikely to vote for other candidates associated with him unless you are coerced into doing this, too.

This is very different from support based on legitimacy. Voting for a candidate of whom you expect broad and general things is not the end of your support for him. If your help is required once he gets into office, the likelihood you will give it is rather great, and, crucially, you give it without any particular payoff from him. The same expectations that led you to vote for him lead you to continue to support him. Moreover, his support for

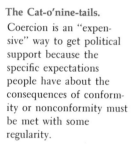

The Cat-o'nine-tails.
Coercion is an "expensive" way to get political support because the specific expectations people have about the consequences of conformity or nonconformity must be met with some regularity.

Politician and Adoring Crowd. Voting for a candidate of whom you expect broad and general things does not end your support for him, and you are likely to consider his wishes and recommendations in a positive light after the election.

another candidate or for some particular action is rather likely to influence you to give the same support. In all this, your support is not tied to any specific actions on the part of your candidate, but only to the maintenance of your expectations of him.

From this it will be clear that legitimacy is not only a more flexible and spreadable form of support, but also a cheaper one to operate. The difficulty with legitimacy comes in establishing it. As the Cheyenne case shows, legitimacy grows easily out of shared understandings about the nature of the world and of the supernatural. It can be established through shared understandings regarding what constitutes the "good man" and the "desirable leader," as in the list of qualities attributed to Cheyenne council members. Without the sort of broad-scale and widely shared culture we see in the nineteenth-century Cheyenne, however, legitimacy is not so easily won from a wide segment of the population of a political group. If the activities carried out by the members of a political group require the participation of a considerable number of people, there must be at least some support based on legitimacy as well as on coercion. This legitimacy may be granted to individual leaders, to offices, to procedures, or to any other part of the political process, but it must be present. In large and culturally diverse groups, however, legitimacy can be expected to play a smaller role than it does in the politics of groups having a more broadly shared body of understandings. Political groups with diverse populations regularly carry out such activities as publicly making claims and charges (propaganda) intended to create or maintain the legitimacy essential to their continued operation.

Politics and Public Goals

The ordinary, conversational, use of the term "politics" provides valuable guides for defining the term. Often when the word "politics" is used, it refers in some way to governments and the statuses and activities associated with the forming and operation of governments. At the same time, "politics" is also used to refer to activities and statuses having nothing directly to do with government. We talk about "office politics," "university politics," "church politics," and so on, and we sometimes characterize people and actions as "political" even when they have no connection with government. This suggests that in ordinary use we think of a rather wide sphere of activity not connected with the business of formal government as having something in common with what is involved in winning elections and passing legislation.

One of the common elements in all these everyday uses of the term "politics" is a concern with goals. A person running for office and his supporters are seeking the goal of being elected, as is the person running against him. A legislative committee considering a law is concerned with the goal of making legislation for the group. It may also be concerned with such other goals as helping constituents, winning future elections, and, perhaps, promoting the common good. Similarly, "office politics" has to do with such goals as winning the boss's favor, getting a raise, attaining a desirable position, or seeing rivals and enemies fail. People we speak of as "political" are usually interested in winning and keeping the favor of their associates—a goal in itself—and in gaining support for whatever specific ends they may be seeking, usually including increasing their own control of the people and resources around them.

Goals, then, play an important part in a good deal of what we speak of as "political." Some goals are strictly private as, for example, the goal of getting a good grade in a course or getting someone to like you. Other goals are public in the sense of their involving a group of people. Wanting a whole group of people to do something, such as hold a buffalo hunt, is a public goal as is seeking something that only a whole group can give, such as a position of leadership or an honor of some kind.

What is "public" and what is "private" is relative to the particular problem being studied. Thus, if we examine the politics of neighborhoods, the families that make up the neighborhood are private spheres, and the family goals are private goals. If we study family politics, however, the families are the group we call "public," and the private sphere is made up of the individual family members. "Politics" refers to activities concerned with establishing and achieving public goals, with what is "public" depending on what sort of group is being studied.

It is important to note that establishing and achieving public goals very often involves opposition. Because the goals we are concerned with are public, a number of different individuals are always involved, which makes disagreement and even conflict very likely. Accordingly, the study of politics is often basically concerned with examining conflict, rivalry, and competition. Power plays a key part in this when we understand "power" to refer to control over other individuals and over resources. Through the use of power, opponents in conflicts concerning public goals try to outdo each

POLITICS *Activities concerned with establishing and achieving public goals, with what is "public" relative to the sort of group being studied.*

POWER *Control over other individuals and over resources.*

other, and each tries to achieve his own goal (having the group carry out one project rather than another or give *him* the office or honor rather than the others who want it are good examples of this). Power is itself a public goal and is, at the same time, an important support in striving for other goals.

When we examined legitimacy and coercion, we saw two important sources of political support; that is, legitimacy and coercion are two ways of gaining power that can be used in achieving goals. One of the main issues in the study of politics concerns how the various parties to political activity are able to get the power they need to attain their goal. Understanding this requires that we find out what basis their power has. In the Cheyenne hunt we saw the basis of power for the Shield Soldiers and the rather different basis for the council's power. Discovering these bases helped explain how the hunt police were able to work toward the goal of maintaining order and how the council was able to operate as the goal-choosing agency for the whole Cheyenne group. Understanding the sources of power within groups and for groups in their competitions with other groups is a key step in political analysis. By examining groups with different cultures, different sorts of resources, and different goals, we increase the variety of kinds of political activities and supports for power considered and thereby increase the generality of our political understanding. These groups can be whole societies, or they can be subgroups as small as the family or as large as the populations of a whole region, and we are not limited in any of them to studying political processes only in formal and recognized governments even if they have such organizations.

Rules: normative and pragmatic   Another aspect of political activity is that it is carried out according to certain rules. F. G. Bailey (1969) has analyzed politics in a variety of groups from the point of view of what rules are followed in the competitions for goals. He views politics as a game in which there must be at least some conformity to the rules or it ceases to be that game and becomes another one. When football players bribe the officials to favor them in decisions, it is still football although the bribers might be censured if caught. Football players who refuse to limit their team to eleven players and insist on having fifteen on the field are simply not playing football as that is understood although they may be founding a new game. Similarly, a candidate for an elective office who pays voters to cast their votes for him may be cheating and might be punished if caught, but he is still within the framework of the election and its rules in that he is trying to win with votes. A candidate who kills his opponent may achieve his goal of getting office and may be starting a "game" of assassination politics, but he is not engaging in *election* politics.

Bailey distinguishes between "normative rules" and "pragmatic rules." "Normative rules" are broad guides for behavior deriving from understandings about what is good and ethical. A shared belief that an official, a group, or a procedure follows normative rules can be an element in its gaining and keeping legitimacy because such a belief can be the foundation for general

NORMATIVE RULES
Understandings about what ought and ought not be done; based on cultural conceptions of what is good and ethical.

expectations of benefit. Normative rules concern what ought to be done and what ought not to be done. "Pragmatic rules" concern what will work whether it is good or bad. They are simply understandings about how to do things effectively without regard for good or evil. There are pragmatic rules for expressing important values, and there are also pragmatic rules for violating values without getting caught.

PRAGMATIC RULES
Understandings concerning how to do things effectively without regard to whether the things are in accord with values or not.

When the Shield Soldiers finished destroying the guns and horses of the violators of the hunt rules, they gave the violators new horses and guns. This action is very much in accord with the Cheyenne value on generosity and the maintenance of group peace and solidarity. It is also an effective means for bringing the violators, and all those who witnessed the violation, to accept their punishment and stay in the group instead of running away. Destroying goods and then replacing them is a pragmatically effective way of demonstrating forgiveness and the benefits of group membership as well as punishment for breaking the group's rules. Pragmatic rules can also be concerned with violating values in profitable ways. How to bribe legislators, coerce officials, and cheat in applying laws are all pragmatic rules because they concern what is politically effective.

The pragmatic and normative rules used in a group's politics are closely related to the group's culture. If the members of a group share the understanding that no decent person does anything for his own interest when that is in opposition to the group's interest, a normative rule in politics holding that all the goals proposed for the group should benefit all the group's members would be expected. Similarly, a shared understanding that holds that people who shake hands and smile are friendly and dependable will probably lead to a pragmatic rule in elective politics holding that those who want to be elected will make gains if they shake hands and smile. There might well also be a pragmatic rule that goals be made *to appear* beneficial to all whatever their real effects might be.

Technical facts and jural rules Pragmatic and normative rules guide people in using resources to attain their goals, but this guidance also depends on the social and physical resources that are available. A pragmatic rule in an agricultural society with a limited supply of land might be to offer people fields in exchange for their support. To do this, however, there must be fields available to give away. A politician may have the undisputed right to expect his brother's support, but this will not help him if he is an only child. Ralph Nicholas (1968:304) calls such factors "technical facts." He defined them as "what members of a society regard as 'necessary.'" As an example he says: "I may have an airtight case proving that land being cultivated by someone else is mine, but if there is a year's backlog of cases in the court, then I will not get a crop from that land this season." Technical facts are unavoidable aspects of social and physical reality that are directly involved in shaping political activity by providing or denying opportunities to participants. Technical facts, of course, do not work by themselves. A crowded court calendar by itself has no effect on the activities of competing political groups. It is through the use of technical facts according to some applicable rule that

TECHNICAL FACTS
Unavoidable aspects of social and physical reality that are directly involved in shaping political activity by providing or excluding opportunities for particular sorts of actions.

these facts influence political activity. The crowded court calendar can be the basis for deriving advantage from an illegal act through the application of the pragmatic rule that this is a way to gain an end. If there is a normative rule that holds people with large families to be the best officials, a candidate's constant mention in speeches of the technical fact he has a large number of relatives is the pragmatic use of a technical fact to win support based on a normative rule.

The expectations that are part of statuses provide an important basis for the mobilizing of resources for gaining public goals. In Chapter 3, "Social Structure," we discussed the formation of feuding groups among the Nuer of East Africa. We noted that these groups are brought together by the expectation of mutual defense that is part of the status of "patrilineal kinsman" (i.e., person sharing a common male ancestor as traced through males). This expectation makes it possible for large groups of soldiers to form and pursue common military goals without formal leadership statuses of any kind, and the effectiveness with which these groups form and operate demonstrates how powerful status expectations can be in political processes.

Expectations (like that of mutual defense for patrilineal kinsmen among the Nuer) that the culture holds to be indispensable parts of a status are called "jural rules." When these expectations are violated, the violator is treated as a "bad" member of the status category or, sometimes, as having lost the right to be considered an occupant of the status. Nicholas (1968) tells us that jural rules are a main means of mobilizing human resources, because it is often through the expectations in statuses that people are brought to support some other individual or group. As among the Nuer, kinship statuses are often used as the foundation for goal-seeking groups, and anthropologists have long been concerned with tracing out the political consequences of the jural rules that unite the members of social groupings. These expectations are not always so simple and straightforward as the mutual-defense expectation that unites Nuer feud groups.

Status expectations and political processes The government of villages in the Trobriand Islands in Melanesia, for example, is based on the expectations in the status clan leader, or headman, of the leading clan in each village. This clan is understood to own the land the village stands on and the surrounding fields. The clan leader is expected to govern wisely, and he has the jural right to the obedience of all those who live in the village his clan owns. If a village-owning clan is considered the senior one in its region, the headman of that village is also considered the leader of the other villages in the area and their chiefs are subordinate to him (Malinowski 1935).

Attaining the headman position by becoming recognized as the leader of the senior clan is an intricate process, and as soon as a new leader has been chosen, the competition[6] to succeed him begins. A main device for attaining the position as successor to the current headman is called *pokala*. It is es-

JURAL RULES
Expectations that are culturally viewed as indispensable parts of a status. Violation of these expectations leads to the violator's being treated as a "bad" member of the status category or as having lost the right to be considered an occupant of the status.

---

[6]Competition is not always part of the process. Sometimes only one young clan member wants the office, and sometimes none wants it.

Trobiand Village Scene.
A claim on the head-manship of a Trobiand village depends on establishing and activating expectations of mutual help between higher- and lower-ranking village men.

sentially a means of establishing and activating expectations of mutual help between higher- and lower-ranking men. A young man who wants such things as additional land and who may want to become the next headman gives gifts such as firewood and fish to a senior man and helps him garden or cares for him when he is sick. When the young man has done what he considers to be enough for the senior man, he publicly requests the land or whatever it is he wants. If it is granted to him, which happens only if he is considered to have done enough to warrant it, his prestige rises. This leads younger men to *pokala* him in turn, which increases his prestige even more in the eyes of the seniors, and with it the likelihood he will be chosen as the next headman (Powell 1960). The ambitious young man uses a culturally provided device for establishing expectations that lead senior men to give him land and accord him prestige, and, if he succeeds in doing this, he has the stature to become headman. In that office his status will include the expectation that the people of the village will follow him. What happens is that ambitious young men use technical facts such as what they are able to give as gifts and services. They do this according to pragmatic rules about what is effective to achieve prestige as defined in normative rules regarding what it is that makes a man important and trustworthy. This establishes relations that lead to selection as headman, which, in turn, establishes relations with expectations that make it possible for the headman actually to lead.

Although the expectations in statuses seem to work well as a basis for politics in Nuer society and, in a different way, in Trobriand Islands society, it is important to remember that in the pursuit of goals there are always a variety of forces at work. Pragmatic rules are always available to participants in political processes, and these may lead to jural rules being ignored or altered by some. Normative rules are vital parts of political activity, but it hardly needs to be said that people sometimes fail to follow even the most cherished ones. Even technical facts can be overcome. For example, a person may not have many "real" relatives, but he may somehow convince people that he does have them or he may adopt them. Because of the variety of available guides for behavior in political activity, we have to examine the complex interactions among norms, jural rules, pragmatic rules, and the environment and remember that each of these elements is almost endlessly changeable. This is true even in rather simple political processes.

In the Cheyenne case we saw that in the implementation of the goal of having an orderly hunt the Shield Soldiers guided their conduct by a number of rules. There was the jural rule that made it their duty to police the hunt and gave them the responsibility for punishing the offenders and the normative rule that held that detractors from the general good must be punished. This last rule provided the immediate basis for the beatings and property damage the soldiers administered. The technical fact that there were only a small number of offenders and a large number of Shield Soldiers was surely important and may have prevented the normative and jural rules from facing a stiff test. The normative rule that offenders must be reintegrated into society played a key part in the replacement of the horses and rifles. The second set of offenders showed an effective use of a pragmatic rule. By getting off their horses and putting out a valuable blanket, they probably saved themselves a beating and the destruction of more of their property.

The course of political processes is clearly a complex one with many alternatives available to participants. F. Barth (1959) emphasizes the importance of individuals making strategic choices in their interaction with other people where these choices are aimed at gaining the goals of the chooser. This approach allows him to examine how individuals attempt to manipulate political systems for their own benefit and to the detriment of their opponents (see, for example, Barth 1963).

Politics with and without Politicians

Political activity is not limited to such groupings as nations, states, villages, tribes, or any such. All social groups can be looked at with respect to their groupwide (i.e., public) goals and the activities associated with choosing and implementing those goals. Some groups have statuses that are wholly or largely devoted to activities having to do with public goals, and others do not.

As recently as the earlier part of this century, anthropologists believed that there were groups without politics. What they meant was that there were groups without leadership statuses or, at least, permanent and full-time ones. Inasmuch as the processes involved in goal seeking in societies without "presidents," "chiefs," or "kings" are similar in important ways to those in societies having such officials, however, it is not useful to view any society as being without politics. We have already considered the Nuer, a group that pursues goals involving large numbers of people without any officials to direct activities. Other societies decide upon and pursue public goals in an open and informal way. A number of hunting-and-gathering societies are of this sort. In these societies there are inequalities in the distribution of power, as there are in all human societies, but those who have

The Ituri Forest in Zaire.

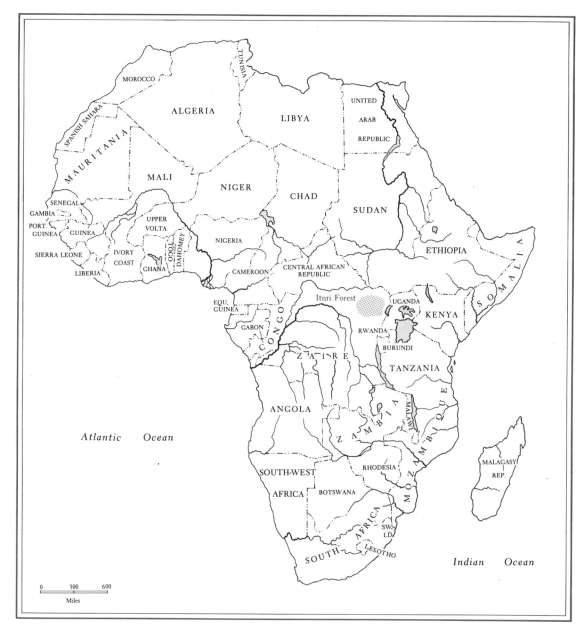

greater control over the actions of their fellows have this control because of their personal qualities or because of temporary conditions rather than because of statuses they occupy.

Among the Mbuti Pygmy bands of the Ituri Forest in Central Africa, most public goals concern the movement of the band, where it should hunt, and what relations should be carried on with the agricultural villages on the edges of the hunting territory. Colin Turnbull describes the politics (in our sense) of this quite clearly.

> All major decisions are taken by common consent, as in other realms of Mbuti life. Men and women have equal say, hunting and gathering being equally important to the economy. Young married couples and youths have the most to say, being the most active hunters and gatherers, but while ability as a hunter carries some weight, too much ability may lead to ridicule. That is, a man who displays himself as a great hunter, and boasts of his achievements too loudly, is somewhat distrusted, and any attempt on his part to use his reputation to gain more say than others will lead immediately to ridicule.
>
> One other consideration determines the extent of influence of a man or woman in economic matters, and that is their knowledge of the territory. Thus, no matter how deserving of respect as hunters, a visiting Mbuti family who do not know the territory well will have little to say regardless of their kinship, age, or other considerations. They will nevertheless be expected to take part in discussions [Turnbull 1965:178–179].

Even this brief quote from Turnbull's fascinating account of the Mbuti shows that the politics of this group can be usefully studied in the same

Mbuti Pygmies.
Although all major decisions result from the equal participation of all those involved, young people are particularly influential because they are the most active hunters and gatherers.

way Cheyenne or Trobriand or American politics can. The absence of leadership statuses is one element in the processes whereby public goals are decided upon and pursued in this hunting society, but it is nothing more than that. Naturally, our examination of the politics of the Mbuti would take into careful account the statuses of those who participate in making a decision about, say, where to hunt. We would note who is young and who old; who a skilled hunter or gatherer and who less skilled; who argued on one side and who on the other; what values were invoked; and so on. We would determine what expectations attach to such qualities as youth (e.g., "If young people are not consulted, they will not join the proposed hunt") and individual skill to identify what the basis is for accepting group decisions.

This is not different in any fundamental way from our study of a group more traditionally examined from the point of view of its politics. In studying a city council, for example, we would note who the chairman was and who simply a council member; who was elected with a large majority and who with a small; and so on. In fact, the basic approach to the study of politics is not determined by the sort of group we are studying. We can usefully examine all political activity to find the sorts of rules and facts involved, and we can do this regardless of the sort of group in which the political activity occurs. The approach applies equally to a Mbuti hunting band and the United Nations. In all cases we are examining the unfolding of human behavior over time from the point of view of the goals the actors are pursuing, the rules and resources they employ in seeking these goals, and the expectations that lie behind their relations with each other. Political anthropologists seek generalizations about the activities associated with choosing and implementing public goals, and they do this through studying politics in a wide variety of groups and cultures. One set of generalizations that has emerged in this field concerns the role of conflict in group activity.

Conflict and unity   Conflict is an inherent part of political processes. These processes (being public) always involve a number of different people, and no two people have exactly the same interests or the same social ties. Conflict obviously divides individuals and drives them apart. Everyone can think of examples of social groups splitting apart on the basis of differences over what the group as a whole should do or how it should do it, and this is true whether the groups are nations, societies, neighborhoods, or families. The British anthropologist Max Gluckman, however, has discovered something about conflict that is a good deal less obvious. Members of a group, paradoxically, may be united by the very conflict that divides them.

Perhaps Gluckman's best-known illustration of this finding is his examination of the effect of rebellion on the maintenance of kingship. He has shown (1963c:110–163) that rebellion, whether in the form of an actual armed attempt to unseat one particular king and install another or in the form of a ritual, serves to make the *status* of the king more secure; that is, the hostility and hatred that are engendered by the operation of a status having great power are directed at the particular individual who occupies that status at

REBELLION *Conflict over which individuals should hold offices or play particular roles in political processes rather than over the effectiveness or virtue of those offices or processes themselves.*

a given time rather than against the status itself. The point of a rebellion is to achieve a state of affairs in which people can say, "The king is dead, long live the king!" This sort of conflict, rebellion, is not over the continuation of the kingship, but over the particular individual who is currently the king. By fighting over which individual should occupy the kingship, its importance is emphasized, and the unity of the group, which stems from shared understandings concerning a status affecting all the members, is made greater even though a particular occupant of the status may be done away with. This sort of political conflict is called "rebellion." It concerns which individuals should hold offices or play particular roles in political processes rather than the virtue or effectiveness of the offices or processes themselves. A rebellion may result in a kingdom's having a new king, but it will not result in a presidential form of government replacing the monarchy.

Gluckman does not maintain that all conflict leads to enhanced unity for the whole society or that there is no such thing as "revolution." A "revolution" is a conflict over the existing statuses and rules of politics and an attempt to substitute new and different offices and rules for the ones that existed previously. Removing King X and replacing him with King Y is a rebellion even if the replacement is by force. Abolishing the kingship and replacing it with, say, a parliamentary government is a revolution even if it is a peaceful change.

REVOLUTION *Conflict
over the virtue and
effectiveness of existing
political processes
and offices.*

Gluckman is fully aware that revolutions do occur and that they sometimes lead to social divisions that may not be healed for a very long time. His emphasis, however, is on the unifying force inherent in rebellion because he believes it to be often overlooked. He believes that the unity which can arise from full-scale political rebellion can also come from the ordinary difficulties and quarrels that arise out of interpersonal relations. These difficulties and quarrels, like the rest of social behavior, are shaped by the understandings shared by the members of a group. The understandings often work in such a way that the quarrels people have do not make it impossible for them to go on living together. Sometimes that drastic result occurs and brings such things as families breaking up, neighbors moving apart, or countries dividing. More commonly, however, there are provisions in the common culture of those who quarrel to use the very quarrels to strengthen the group's unity. Rebellion serves to strengthen the kingship by demonstrating the worth of its status through conflict over it and by draining away dissatisfaction with the system by focusing it on particular officials. In a similar way, other sorts of quarrels unite people despite the presence of differences that have the potential to divide them.

Divide and cohere Gluckman believes that the fact that people are divided in some situations and united in others results in their having an overall unity they would not otherwise have. He calls this "divide and cohere," and it is a social force that results from what Gluckman calls "cross-cutting ties" (see, for example, Gluckman 1965:91–97). It works as follows: In some contexts, individuals are united with members of their families in opposition to members of other families who have different demands and interests; in other contexts, the family is divided within itself by competition for the resources (material, social, and emotional) available within the family, and family members are united with others from different families who are in the same position (for example, sons with sons united against fathers). In some settings, the people of a village are united with one another in opposition to their chief, and in others they unite with their chief in pursuit of common goals in competition with other villagers and *their* chiefs.

No group is so totally united across all sorts of social stituations and contexts that its members can completely give up their ties with members of all other kinds of groups. Members of a particular family, for example, may quarrel among themselves, but they understand that they need each other's support in conflicts with other families, and this helps unify the family. Further, members of different families need each other, as fellow villagers, for conflicts with other villages or with their chief, and this helps unify the village. The existence of these shifting unities, which change as the membership of the groups in conflict changes, is a force for unity that is often strong enough to hold the members of a society together even when they have rather serious quarrels with one another. Conflicts in one context are balanced by unity in other contexts, and the overall result is a continuing force for unity. Sometimes, of course, the balance breaks down and families, villages, or whole societies break apart. This, however, is *despite* the unifying force in the social divisions. One source of conflict may be so strong it leads people to give up the assistance of their opponents in other conflicts, but the need for this assistance is still a force at work for unity even when it is not strong enough to prevail.

Political Change

Much of the earlier work in political anthropology was devoted to showing how various aspects of culture and social structure contributed to the maintenance of a group's existing political system and, more generally, their traditional way of life. This work has made important contributions in showing the sources of social and cultural continuity. Gluckman's contribution in demonstrating the role of conflict in the maintenance of social groups and the continuation of their culture is an extremely important one. However, the point has never been that the politics and culture of the groups that exist at any particular time go on forever without change.

Archaeologists and historians have shown us beyond any doubt that the most constant thing in human life is change. This has been so since humanity emerged and will probably continue to be so for as long as humanity endures. What differs among various sorts of social groups is the rate at which their politics, and other aspects of their life, change and the way in which they change. Sometimes change is so slow as to be almost undetectable, and sometimes it is so fast that we delude ourselves into believing there is no continuity with the past. This is as true in politics as in any other area of life, and an adequate study of politics must take account of this fact.

A major development in political anthropology is the continuing search for approaches to the study of politics that encourage an understanding of how change takes place. In fact, the use of the term "change" is itself somewhat suspect because it implies that political arrangements, or more general social and cultural arrangements, are in one enduring state until something happens to them causing them to "change" into another. Inasmuch as an endless development and alteration of the rules and expectations that underlie politics and social life in general is the constant of human life, it is probably more accurate to talk not about "change," but about "development" or "alteration." The objective in deemphasizing the term "change" is to underline the constancy of alteration and to help prevent looking on political "change" as an unusual or abnormal state of affairs.

Looking at politics from the point of view of the participants' expectations and the rules and technical facts that lie behind their attempts to choose and implement public goals is intended to focus attention on both persistence and alteration and on both development and continuity. It is extremely useful to be able to analyze something like the events of the Cheyenne buffalo hunt and the Cheyenne Council of Forty-Four, even though such an analysis does not allow for developments over time. It is also necessary, however, to be able to examine what forces finally broke down the council and removed from it the ability to formulate public goals for the members of the society. How the changes in technical facts affected the normative rules that made, for example, the council a source of benefit to the entire group could be examined from the historical records, which

Cheyenne and Arapaho Chiefs. The study of political change involves analyzing changes in the participants' expectations and the rules and technical facts that lie behind their attempts to choose and implement public goals. A study of political change among the Cheyenne would have to include an analysis of what legitimacy the Council of Forty-Four had after the United States government took away its official power.

would contribute to our understanding of how political processes operate under extreme stress and over many decades of time. This study would seek to show what legitimacy there may have been after the council's power was largely taken away by the United States government and what sorts of coercion were effective within the group. It would try to describe the alterations in public goals and in the means for achieving these goals as they unfolded over the period from the independent existence of the Cheyenne to today and to explain how this came about.

In political development, new technical facts, new jural rules, new normative rules, and new pragmatic rules all must be integrated into the existing organizations of political understandings that guide goal seeking. These new facts and rules together with the new organizations of understandings that result from integrating them with old ones produce political processes that are quite different from what existed before. In many parts of the world politics as it is today is unmistakably different from the politics that had existed before. Political development and alteration has existed as long as *Homo sapiens* has, but it may be that in the modern era change is faster than it ever was before.

Local Politics in the Modern World
One of the central facts of modern politics in many parts of the world is that events and decisions at the national level affect goal seeking in distant and formerly isolated social groupings. With the end of the colonial administration of huge areas in Africa, Asia, and the Pacific, the newly arisen governments of recently independent nations have passed new laws and taken a new kind of interest in the people who make up the majority in their states. This interest and these laws have had a profound effect on local politics, and political anthropologists have found themselves studying rapidly changing situations requiring them to deal with political processes and groups that earlier anthropologists as recently as the 1940s and 1950s only occasionally encountered.

Factions   One sort of group frequently encountered in modern, local politics is called the "faction." R. Nicholas says of this type of group as opposed to such permanent political groupings as the Nuer kin groups or the Cheyenne council and Soldier Societies: "In situations of rapid social change, factions frequently arise—or become more clearly defined—because factional organization is better adapted to competition in changing situations than are the political groups that are characteristic of stable societies" (Nicholas 1966:55). He defines "faction" as having five characteristics: It is a political group; a conflict group; it is not a corporate group; it is recruited by a leader; and members are recruited on the basis of diverse interests and desires (Nicholas 1965:27–28).

FACTION   *A political conflict group that is not corporate; it is recruited by a leader, and its members belong on the basis of different interests and desires.*

As political conflict groups, factions are not only concerned with establishing and implementing public goals but they are also involved in doing this against opposition. Normally, there are two factions in a political process involving this type of group, but there may be only a single faction if it is in competition with a nonfactional group such as a corporate kin group. Factions are not corporate, and they own no property jointly and the members are not responsible for one another (see Chapter 3 for a discussion of corporate groups). The relatively weak ties among fellow faction members are partly due to the group's not being corporate, but they also result from the fact that people may be in the faction for different reasons. Recruited "on the basis of diverse interests," they need have little in common beyond a wish to work together for each individual's own ends. One thing they always share beyond this is a willingness to work with the individual who recruited all of them. Because faction groups do not have means of recruiting members such as the common descent that brings people into kin groups or the common residence that is the basis for territorial groups, the role of the leader is obviously a crucial one in forming them. Having formed them, faction leaders ordinarily exercise a great deal of power in directing the group's activities. The leader is free to use a wide range of maneuvers in pursuing his group's ends, and this, together with the manner in which factions are recruited, is why factions are so well suited to politics in rapidly changing social situations.

Factions in a Mexican village Factions are found in a great number of societies including those of the urban-industrial world, where they can be seen operating inside political parties, in municipal governments, on school boards, in university student and faculty organizations, and elsewhere. In the Mexican village of Durazno in the state of Michoacán, politics is factionally organized and focused on the office of the *cacique*, or local political boss (Friedrich 1968, 1970). Here, the faction of the current *cacique* is made up of most of his relatives, *some* of the village people who view themselves as "true revolutionaries," and other villagers who want either more land or the help of the *cacique* in matters that concern the state or national government, in which he has a good deal of influence. The opposing faction is composed of the fairly numerous personal enemies of the *cacique*, people who object to his opposition to religion and those who emphasize the fact that although he dresses and lives modestly and espouses egalitarian and revolutionary views, he has enriched himself during his period as *cacique*.

The factions in Durazno are unusual in that they have lasted for a long time, half a century, although factions are usually temporary groupings. They are also unusual in that both the faction of the *cacique* and that of his main opponent have clear-cut—and opposing—ideologies concerning religious, social, and legal matters. Most often, factions have no real ideological commitment, although they may present one in their conflicts with other groups as a pragmatic attempt to gain whatever specific goal they are seeking. In Durazno both of the main factions have actually tried to implement some of the social, religious, and legal principles they espouse in addition to their efforts to gain such other ends as wealth, power, and favorable decisions from higher authority.

Mexican Village Headman. Because of his office, a Mexican *cacique* receives some of the general expectations that are the basis of legitimacy. A *cacique* is expected to have broad abilities to help his people.

Because of his office, the *cacique* in Durazno receives some of the general expectations that are the basis of legitimacy. Any *cacique* is expected to help the people of his village and to have at least some ability to do so. More than this, however, the particular *cacique* of this village is supported by legitimacy deriving from his family background and unusual personality. He is the descendant of a line of no less than six remembered leaders in the village, and a number of villagers believe that only men in this line are "fit to rule in Durazno." His connections with state and federal officials and his forceful manner are further sources of general expectations in those whom he rules. Faction leaders can, and often do, work with support that comes mainly through the positive sort of coercion (for example, "Support me and you will win your court case"), but as the Durazno situation shows, this need not be the case.

Factions in an Indian village A political contest in the agricultural village of Govindapur, Mindapore District, West Bengal, India, provides an opportunity to examine some aspects of factionalism difficult to see in the Mexican example. Nicholas reports (1965:30–46) that in 1959 the Indian government required all villages to elect a four-member representative council (*panchayat*) and a delegate to the regional council. The events in this election in Govindapur show how factions work in a modern rural setting. In this instance, the factions formed because of the intervention of the national government. The election did not bring about totally new political groupings, but it produced some new alignments and brought into public view other coalitions and divisions that had existed for a long time. The leaders of the various factions in the village were mostly the sons of fathers who had been active in village affairs at the beginning of this century. The leaders of the two major factions, one the headman, the other a teacher, were divided by events and conflicting interests that began in 1913 with a quarrel between their fathers over temple land.

Through their kinsmen and clients and with the help of each other's enemies both men built fairly large followings. The two groups had been forming and changing over the whole period since the original quarrel forty-five years before, and each court decision or public dispute brought changes in their memberships. The headman in Govindapur, like the *cacique* in Durazno, had influence with officials in the state and national governments. Through placing one of his allies as local representative for the agency that distributed food and money to the destitute in the Govindapur area, he was able to gain considerable power and many followers. Another faction, less powerful but still important, was jointly led by a man and his maternal cousin; another was made of a number of neighboring families and their followers; and there were two more for a total of six in the village whose population was 677.

The first event directly concerning the election was a visit from an official of the national agency responsible for the village's affairs. In consultation with the headman this official divided the village into two wards, each of which was to elect two representatives. In the time-honored procedure called gerrymandering,[7] the ward lines were drawn so that almost all of the headman's supporters were in one ward and the opposing factions were in another. This ensured election in one ward for the representatives chosen by the headman and his group; in the other ward, the headman hoped the conflict between the various opposition factions would lead them to eliminate each other's candidates.

Since there were six factions in Govindapur, it is obvious that if each one put up its own candidates, there would be so much competition no group could count on winning. Because of this, the various factions temporarily combined with one another into two coalitions for the purpose of the election. The village elections were run as part of national elections, which meant that the national political parties were involved. The headman, like most headmen in West Bengal state at that time, was a member of the nationally ruling Congress party. His faction and those aligned with it used that party's name and were helped by outside election workers sent in by the party. The other alignment of factions associated itself with the Congress party's main national opponent, the Communist party. Some of the members of the factions opposed to the headman were relatively rich landlords, and they had no liking for the Communists as they understood them. For them, however, the real issue was their opposition to the headman and the wish to win in the coming election, so—in a way often seen in factions—ideology was put aside, and the Communist party's help was accepted.

In the election the Congress-party coalition of factions elected both representatives from its ward, and the Communist coalition elected both from the ward where the headman had hoped, vainly it proved, that the different opposing groups would eliminate each other's candidates. The headman's group succeeded in electing the delegate to the regional council. The results, in other words, were fairly close, with each grouping of factions doing about as well as the other. Nevertheless, there are several interesting things to be seen in the events of the election.

Five characteristics of Govindapur factions First, it should be noted that although each of the factions was recruited by a leader, sometimes the "leader" was not a single individual. One faction was led by a man and his cousin, and another was led by a group of neighboring families. This type of joint, or collective, leadership is sometimes called "clique leadership," and it is frequently important in factional politics in all parts of the world.

Second, each faction brought its supporters into action for this particular election; many of the supporters had no lasting commitment to the partic-

[7]This practice takes its name from Governor Elbridge Gerry of Massachusetts whose party divided the state for electoral purposes in 1812 in a way giving itself great advantage by combining its supporters' districts and dividing those of its opponents. The division led to districts of unusual shape, and Essex County, Massachusetts, was divided so that some thought it looked like a salamander. The last part of the reptile's name and that of the governor make up the word for this sort of political division of territory.

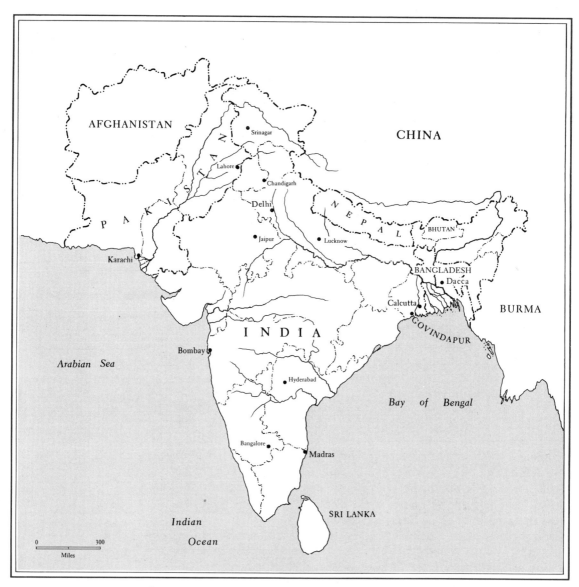

Govindapur Village in Eastern India.

lar faction they voted with. The leaders used all their ties with other people to get the maximum number of supporters for this event. Kinsmen and employees were reminded of their relationship, debtors were told about the conditional generosity of creditors, and tenants were reminded that they lived and farmed at their landlords' pleasure. This is very different from the situation of the Nuer kin groups discussed earlier in which the expectation of mutual defense is enough to rally kinsmen into a fighting group with no leader present at all, and it underlines the importance of leaders in forming factions.

Third, we see in Govindapur that factions combine with each other in much the same way individuals come together temporarily to form a faction. The coalitions of factions formed and acted together because the specific interests each of them represented were momentarily served by joint, instead of conflicting, activity. They stayed together for the common goal of winning the election, but after the election ended, they had no reason to work together and opposed each other as circumstances warranted. This sort of temporary formation of coalitions is found wherever factions are part of the political process.

Fourth, each individual faction in the village election was made up of different people often seeking quite different things. Nicholas (1965:42–46) questioned the members of the six factions about why they were supporting and voting with the faction they were and he found that:

29 percent were related to the faction leader

27 percent depended on the faction leader for their livelihood

19 percent were backing their neighborhood leader

15 percent were giving their support on the basis of caste[8]

10 percent were hoping to defeat an enemy

Each faction, then, had members who were there for different reasons. Not every single member had a reason for membership different from every other because whole families and even caste groups belonged to the same faction, but within each faction there were always a variety of reasons for belonging. This sort of diverse basis for faction membership is found in every part of the world where there is factionalism.

The leaders of the Govindapur factions were supported by the general expectations of some of their members so that, for example, a particular leader's relatives had the broad idea that he would help them or be generally available whenever they needed him. Many other members of factions supported their leaders on the basis of highly specific expectations such as not being pressed for the payment of debts, being allowed to continue working for the leader, or getting a government job. Most individuals, however, supported the leaders of their factions because of highly specific expectations of the sort called coercive. This last fact helps explain the shifting membership of factions: Once a specific expectation is met, there is no further basis for staying in the faction. A person who belongs to a faction because the leader is expected to help him with a court case may well leave the faction once the case is over unless he develops a further expectation of the leader. Because of this, faction leaders must continually instill expectations and

[8]A "caste" is an hereditary social group whose members do not marry outsiders; all members of the same caste have the same general social standing and, sometimes, occupation. In India castes are a central aspect of the organization of social relations.

produce benefits for their members as, for example, the headman did by providing food and money on a recurring basis through his ally who was the local representative of the national aid agency.

As we have seen, much of what happened in the Govindapur election is characteristic of factions everywhere whether it be in Mexican villages, Republican-party conventions, or student organizations. Factions are particularly well suited to new and rapidly developing situations because they are so flexible both in membership and in their ability to work for different goals as these become available. Factions are common sorts of groupings in local politics in much of the world, especially where new problems and opportunities constantly arise as they do in what we call "modern" and "modernizing" societies.

Similarities in Modern and Traditional Politics

Although factions are well suited to many of the kinds of political contests found in rapidly developing situations, they are by no means the only groups involved in such politics. Sometimes they play no part at all. In Govindapur we saw that families which are corporate groups were involved in the election. Caste groups, also corporate, participated as active units. It is true that both sorts of permanent groups joined factions in order to be effective, but it is important to note that they nevertheless stayed together as political groups. In fact, a number of studies of Indian villages show that the local members of caste groups sometimes work together to gain a common goal, usually that of raising their standing in the social hierarchy, and they do so in conflict with the members of higher caste groups, which want to block them.[9] These groups have none of the characteristics of factions and are, in fact, corporate groups, but they nonetheless seize upon the new opportunities afforded by such things as modern legislation, which removes the legal basis for their domination by other castes. The castes are unquestionably involved in modern political activity in India even though they are traditional groups that have existed for centuries and their means of recruitment is, as it always was, by birth. Similarly, in Northern Ireland there has been a bloody struggle for many decades between two traditional groups, the Protestants and the Catholics. That struggle appears likely to go on. It is, however, a struggle between groups that are not factional, although it is a modern struggle in the sense of facing new problems and making use of new opportunities. *Within* each religious group there are factions—usually centering around "moderate" and "extreme" views—but the major conflict groups themselves are recruited by birth as they always have been. Factions play an important role in modern politics, but they are not the only sorts of groups involved, and they may even be entirely absent in particular cases.

[9]See, for example, Cohen (1955) and Beteille (1965).

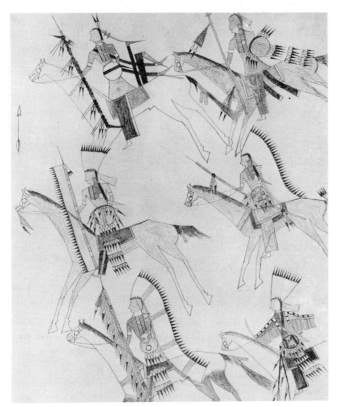

On the Warpath, **Drawn
by Making Medicine.**
Whether it is the
Cheyenne Shield Society
or the Govindapur
election, the specificity of
expectations (legitimacy
and coercion) is crucial
to the study of politics.

What is involved in both traditional and modern politics, no matter what sorts of political groups are operating, is the seeking of public goals with various types of support according to whatever rules and technical facts are at work. Whether leaders or offices are supported by general or specific expectations is as important to understanding the election in Govindapur as it is to understanding the Cheyenne Shield Society and how it dealt with misbehavior. The sorts of rules and the technical facts that apply are crucial in choosing the headman in a Trobriand Islands village and also for the way the *cacique* operates in Durazno. Modern politics are most distinctive in the rapidity with which new goals, rules, resources, and expectations emerge, but they are not qualitatively different from the most traditional sorts of politics. As F. G. Bailey says:

> People have systems of rules which regulate their interactions with one another and the ways in which they make use of resources in their environment. Innovations occur when they come to realize that they are no longer or may soon not be getting what will satisfy them out of the environment: they are then ready to experiment with new rules for their mutual interaction or for coping with the environment, or both [1973:313].

SUMMARY

For people to be able to carry out joint activities, decisions must be made about what goals are to be pursued. There must also be rules for how to behave in this pursuit. It is sometimes argued that people accept decisions and follow rules because "they have to." In fact, people are rarely without alternatives, but they often reject them, accepting instead the group's decision. This acceptance is based on two types of expectations: coercion and legitimacy. Coercion is highly effective in specific instances but is expensive to use and can never be the sole basis for the politics of a group. Legitimacy is easily expanded to provide support for new decisions, new rules, and new officials, and it is very inexpensive because it does not call for those who grant it receiving anything specific in particular situations. Legitimacy, however, is difficult to establish outside groups whose members share many understandings about what public goals should be and what qualities officials should have. All politics concern public goals, and legitimacy and coercion are the main ways that a person gets power in order that his goals and way of doing things rather than someone else's are adopted. Politics is not just the use of power, but power is both a public goal itself and an important means for gaining other public goals.

Politics can be looked at as a game with rules: normative rules about how things ought to be and pragmatic rules about how things can be done effectively whether they ought to be done that way or not. Jural rules, the special expectations attached to statuses that are more compelling than others, are also important in politics. In some social groups most political activity has no basis other than the jural rules that require the occupants of some statuses to give support and assistance to occupants of other statuses. In these groups, and they are usually based on kinship relations, political activity is largely a matter of establishing and using the expectations associated with particular kinds of relationships.

Politics is not limited to groups with politicians, but occurs in all social groupings with goals. Political struggles can divide any of these groups, but, paradoxically, this conflict can have a unifying effect in two ways. One is through the conflict over who should occupy an office, a kingship, for example, which emphasizes the importance of that office and the basic unity of those who grant its importance, however divided they may temporarily be over which individual should have the office. The second is through people who are opposed to one another in one context being united in another so that they cannot break with their momentary "enemies" because they are tomorrow's allies.

That there can be unity in conflict does not mean politics and political groups do not change. In fact, change—or better, development—is the most constant thing in human activity, including politics. A particular sort of political group, a faction, is particularly effective in rapidly changing political situations. It is suited to those situations because its members belong to advance their own particular interests and not because of lasting ties or commitments to the group, its ideology, or its other members. These groups are recruited by leaders, and they are devoted to conflict with other groups over gaining various goals.

Politics, whether "traditional" or the rapidly changing sort now commonly seen, concerns how groups and their members go after what they want. The study of politics is, then, in a sense, the study of groups in action.

SUGGESTED READINGS

More on the case

HOEBEL, E. A. 1960 The Cheyennes, Indians of the Great Plains. New York: Holt.

This is a short, general ethnography of the Cheyennes.

Other readings

BEIDELMAN, THOMAS O. 1961 Beer Drinking and Cattle Theft in Ukaguru: Intertribal Relations in a Tanganyika Chiefdom. American Anthropologist 63:534ff.

Relations between different political units with attention to the minimization of hostility between groups despite serious tensions. Both ethnography and analysis are compelling.

EISENSTADT, S. 1959 Primitive Political Systems: A Preliminary Comparative Analysis. American Anthropologist 61:200–222.

This article classifies political systems according to what they do: perform executive functions, ritual activity, or other coordinated activities.

FRIEDRICH, P. 1970 Agrarian Revolt in a Mexican Village. Englewood Cliffs, N.J.: Prentice-Hall.

A history and political analysis of revolt in the Michoacán village briefly discussed in this chapter. There is a psychological and political examination of the cacique (village boss) that takes account of his motives as well as his ideology. An unusual and rewarding book.

GLUCKMAN, M. 1956 The Frailty in Authority. In Custom and Conflict in Africa. M. Gluckman, Ed. Oxford, England: Blackwell. pp. 1–26.

A classic statement of the idea that society is held together by conflicts that cut across potentially fragmentary groupings. Here Gluckman's general view concerning the social usefulness of conflict is used to examine the basis for political authority.

SAHLINS, M. 1963 Poor Man, Rich Man, Big-man, Chief: Political Types in Melanesia and Polynesia. In Comparative Studies in Society and History 5:285–303. Reprinted as Bobbs-Merrill Reprint A-339.

A modern evolutionary view of politics that compares Melanesia and Polynesia on the basis of economic and interpersonal determinants of political development. Well-written and persuasive.

SCHEFFLER, H. 1964 The Social Consequences of Peace on Choiseul Island. Ethnology 3:398–403.

Scheffler disagrees with Gluckman that conflict is the basis of political unity, and after explicitly rejecting Gluckman's view, Scheffler shows that unity on Choiseul continues despite the absence of conflict. Unity, he argues, comes from ecological and economic forces.

SWARTZ, M. 1968 Bases for Compliance in Bena Villages. *In* Local-level Politics. M. Swartz, Ed. Chicago: Aldine. pp. 227–242.

A discussion of what makes people do what political officials tell them to do. Examines social, cultural, and psychological sources of compliance.

8

Religion

The moment the priest appears from the sanctuary wearing these vestments, everyone bows down to the ground in reverence, and there is deep silence throughout the building. The effect is so awe-inspiring that one almost seems to feel a divine presence.

THOMAS MORE
UTOPIA, 1516

Pakistanis praying at a mosque.

What makes a religious system believable?

How do people communicate with the supernaturals they believe in?

What kinds of religious practitioners are there?

How is sorcery related to religion?

How does divination work?

Religion in Bao-An: A Case of Godly Possession

The Chinese village of Bao-an is located on a broad plain just north of Tainan City, in the southwest of the island of Taiwan, sometimes called Formosa.[1] The people of Bao-an believe that after death some people who have been especially virtuous and important in life can become gods and that most of the gods they worship were once living people like themselves. These gods do not have unlimited power, but their power is very much greater than the power that ordinary human beings have, and they can do a great deal of good for the worshipper who persuades them to use their power on his behalf. The gods do not always act in concert. For the most part, each god is conceived to act in his own sphere, and each intercedes in human affairs following his own agreements and contacts with the human world. The gods are thought to be organized into a celestial hierarchy, similar in broad outline to the hierarchies of human governments, and the gods have official-sounding titles, often with military overtones (for example, kings, generals, and field marshals). They are believed to command large retinues of retainers and troops, and they work through these subordinates, just as an earthly general requires his troops to fight his battles.

Communication with these beings is conducted through prayer and divination or fortune-telling. Chinese folk religion is rich in means of divination. One very authoritative means of communication with gods in southwestern Taiwan is through people who are spirit mediums. Typically, a spirit medium goes into trance and behaves as though he were speaking and acting the words and deeds of a certain god. Village people can then converse with the god, tell him their problems, and receive his advice. The god can write charms against diseases or other misfortunes or can participate in the performance of village rituals. When the need for the divine presence is past, the spirit medium collapses in a chair and revives as though he were coming to after a faint. Most spirit mediums claim to remember nothing of what they said or did while they were in trance, but even those who do remember the activities of the séance insist that they themselves had no control over them, but were merely onlookers. People are hesitant to talk very much about spirit mediums because many of their urban and educated compatriots condemn the séances as superstition and condemn spending money on offerings of incense, food, or flowers to the gods as wasteful.

Until early in 1967, Guo Ching-shoei was an ordinary Taiwanese farmer, not different in any particular way from most of the other men of Bao-an village. He was married and had children and lived with his parents in traditional Chinese fashion. His house was modest, but comfortable

[1]Formosa was ceded to Japan by the Chinese government in 1895 and ruled by the Japanese until the end of World War II. In 1949 the Nationalist government of China moved to Taiwan, where it has remained ever since. The population of the island has been virtually entirely Chinese for several centuries, and although Taiwan has been politically separate from mainland China for all but four years of this century, it has proved an invaluable laboratory for anthropologists interested in traditional Chinese life. The present discussion is based on the research of David K. Jordan (1972 and unpublished) in the late 1960s.

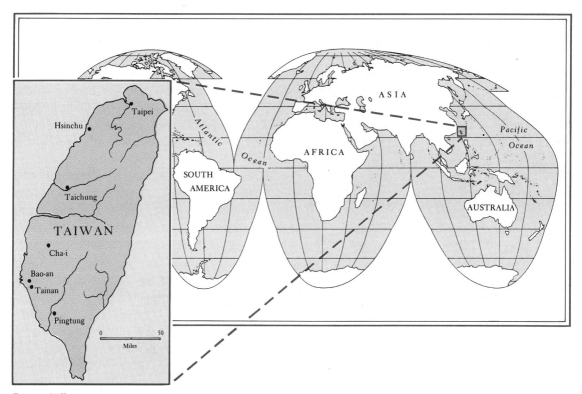

Bao-an Village in Taiwan.

and adequate by local standards. Like his neighbors he liked to stop by the tiny supply shop not far from his house of an evening for a drink of rice wine and light refreshment and talk over the events of the day. Sometimes he had a little too much to drink. On one of these occasions he got into a heated argument with one of his friends, and some other friends persuaded him to go home before a fight broke out. When he got home the other members of his family were in bed. Guo Ching-shoei set about the usual tasks of shutting up the house. Before he closed the door to the central room where the family altar was located, he lit some sticks of incense as he did every night. The routine required that he hold the incense and bow before the pictures of gods over his family altar, before his ancestral tablets at the left end of the same altar, and out into the night, through the door of the house. As he was holding the sticks and standing before the altar he suddenly gave a shout and began jumping around the room, shrieking and leaping like a mad man. His family members stumbled into the central hall to see what was the matter.

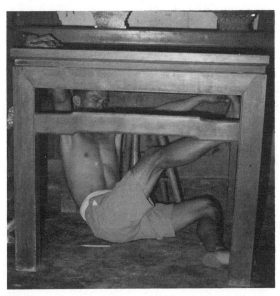

Guo Ching-shoei in Trance. Guo Ching-shoei was possessed very unexpectedly. After great initial agitation, during which he smashed the top of the lower table of his family altar, he remained under the altar all night in the position shown.

Guo Ching-shoei continued to scream unintelligibly and to jump and flail his arms.

A Chinese family altar consists of two tables. One is a high, narrow table, which holds the incense pots, the ancestral tablets, some vases of flowers, candles (usually electric in modern Taiwan), and other equipment used in worship. The lower table is sometimes used to hold sacrificial food or flowers, but especially in poorer houses it is often also used for a dining table, as a place for the children to do homework, and as a general-purpose table in the central hall. Guo Ching-shoei jumped onto this lower altar table and leaped up and down on it. Though sturdy, the table at length gave way. By the time he

settled down, he had broken all the boards out of the top of the table, leaving the four legs and the outline of the top. He sank down into this frame exhausted. As he hung in the frame, bracing his foot against one side and holding to the side supports with his arms, his body became rigid. He hung in this position until morning. As well as it was possible for the ethnographer to establish, Guo Ching-shoei was in trance for about eighteen hours, through most of the next morning. As the story of his possession spread through the village, the people of Bao-an began to assemble before the house to watch what was happening. Guo Ching-shoei's mouth announced that he was possessed by the Great Saint Equal to Heaven,[2] a popular south Chinese deity who often possesses mediums. No one doubted that he was possessed. But everyone knew that people could sometimes be possessed by spirits who were not gods. These spirits might be ghosts of people who had not achieved divine status and who merely wished to receive worship for reasons of vanity or sought to do harm. Some people accepted Guo Ching-shoei's revelation as divine and were prepared to welcome the Great Saint and hope for his alliance and assistance in the future. Others were suspicious and preferred to wait and see.

While Guo Ching-shoei was still in trance, an old man arrived who was also in trance. His name was Guo Tian-huah, and he had been a medium in Bao-an for over thirty years. Indeed, Tian-huah

[2]Great Saint Equal to Heaven is the title assumed by the monkey hero of the popular novel Journey to the West (by Wu Ch'eng-en, ca. 1506–1582), readily accessible to the Western reader in a delightful abridgment by Arthur Waley, entitled Monkey.

was considered to be one of the most competent mediums in the area, and his possessing god, the Third Prince,[3] was a constant ally and friend of the people of Bao-an. Tian-huah was getting old, and many people of the village, especially Tian-huah himself, hoped that the gods would find a new medium of equal skill so that Tian-huah either would not have to continue the physically demanding séances or could at least reduce the number of his séances. The Third Prince (speaking through Tian-huah) declared the possession of Ching-shoei to be genuine and asserted that indeed the Great Saint was coming to help him (the Third Prince) to govern Bao-an's affairs and was possessing Ching-shoei for that reason.

Still, some people were rather dubious. It was better to wait and see, they urged, than to take the chance of mistaking a ghost or demon for a god. The Third Prince (speaking through Tian-huah) announced that the Great Saint (possessing Ching-shoei) would go away, but would return on a certain date to reassert his claim.

Late the morning after he had been possessed, Guo Ching-shoei recovered and was himself again. He was bruised and cut from his adventure and utterly exhausted. And he was the talk of Bao-an village. His neighbor Wang Fuh-ming revealed that a few nights before Ching-shoei had been possessed, he had seen shadowy shapes

Altar Statue of the Great Saint. The Third Prince declared the possession of Ching-shoei to be genuine and declared that the Great Saint was possessing Ching-shoei in order to help govern Bao-an's affairs.

moving about before Ching-shoei's house. Now he understood that they must have been the soldiers of the Great Saint, come to seek a medium. Many people said Fuh-ming was overly imaginative, but some people thought his vision was more evidence that the gods were at work and that Bao-an had received a new medium.

Spirit mediums, when they are not in trance, are just like everyone else. They plow fields, eat with their families, and drink with their friends.

[3]The Third Prince is the title of Prince Lii Ne-jah, an important character in The Investiture of the Gods, a Ming-dynasty historical fantasy by Lu Hsi-hsing contemporary with Journey to the West, mentioned earlier. Unfortunately, no English translation has been published. Some of the material has been included in Werner (1932: 59–65, 247–249, 1922: 305–324). The Third Prince is believed to possess spirit mediums more often than any other Chinese god.

But when they are possessed, they speak with the voice of godly authority, and, not surprisingly, godly authority is very influential in village opinion. When the gods can be made to recommend public policy, they do so with great effect. The political implications of a new spirit medium were by no means lost on village people.

Bao-an village did not have important, long-lasting bitterly opposed factions. When public issues were discussed, it was usually easy enough to work out a common goal and policy. When divisions did occur, they were not always along the same lines. However, at least two elderly and influential village men normally found themselves on opposite sides. Guo Ching-shoei was a friend, though not a close one, of one of these men. The other man, Guo Fang, may have feared Guo Ching-shoei's possession because he thought it would result in divine advantages for the other side. He sought his friend Ming-feng, and together they held a séance of their own, using another means of divination, and announced that they had discovered Ching-shoei's possession to be demonic rather than divine. Few village people paid much attention to them. But Ching-shoei's father was alarmed. He did not like spirit mediums and thought people should avoid becoming involved in the affairs of the world of the dead and the spirits. It bothered him that his son was apparently going to become a medium. He encouraged Guo Fang and his friend Ming-feng in their work and attended at least one additional divination session with them.

The divination instrument they used was a small, wooden armchair about 20 centimeters on a side and 25 to 30 centimeters from the bottom of the rear legs to the top of the back. It might be imagined to resemble a kind of throne in which a godly presence might be believed to seat himself, except that built into the front of the chair and into the open spaces of its arms were wooden pickets that made a sort of fence around it. The chair was held over a table by two illiterate old men, friends of Ming-feng, each of them holding a leg in each hand. As the old men held it, the chair moved over the table, and one of its arms traced lines that Ming-feng interpreted as Chinese characters. He then interpreted the characters as answers to questions being asked. Each time Ming-feng decided that the lines traced represented a certain character or that the character related to their question in a certain way, the chair would bounce down into the table to indicate that the interpretation was correct (one rap on the table) or wrong (two raps). By this means Guo Fang established to his satisfaction that Guo Ching-shoei was not possessed by the Great Saint, as he claimed, but by a demonic presence that was merely pretending to be the Great Saint. Rather than being accepted as a new medium in Bao-an, poor Ching-shoei ought to be subjected to an exorcism to drive out the evil presence that had taken control of his body.

In spite of continued denial of Ching-shoei's authenticity by Guo Fang and his friend Ming-feng, village opinion began to swing more and more in favor of accepting Ching-shoei's possession as legitimate. People became more and more excited at the prospect of a new medium in the village and an alliance with the Great Saint. One village man took the ethnographer aside and told him: "In the festival next year our village will contend with another village for the best place in the procession; if we had another spirit medium, we would have a much better chance of winning the better place; I think that must be why the god has possessed Ching-shoei."

Ching-shoei was possessed again on the predicted day. So was Tian-huah, and once again the Third Prince, speaking to his village friends of long years through the tired body of Tian-huah, told the villagers how fortunate they were to have the cooperation of the Great Saint, manifest among them in the curious speech and movements of their friend Guo Ching-shoei. With widespread approval, a date was set for Ching-shoei's initiation as a spirit medium.

The initiation was held on a festival day, and many of its activities were combined or interposed with festival activities. Basically it included two vital activities. One was an exorcism of possible demons from Ching-shoei's body—just in case. When the exorcism was over, Ching-shoei was still in trance. That was the final evidence that he was possessed by a god, capable of withstanding the exorcism, and not by a demon, who would have been banished by it. The second

important part of the initiation consisted of providing Ching-shoei (still in trance) with a sword and a ball of nails. Both of these are used by spirit mediums to mortify their flesh, causing blood to flow. Mortification of the flesh is common among spirit mediums in China, and it is considered to be a sign of divine presence that the mediums do not show any sign of feeling pain when they cut and puncture themselves. A medium does not mortify his flesh until the community initiates him. When the community accepts him and holds the initiation, he is provided with these tools of his trade. After that, in theory, he can be called upon to go into trance when the gods are needed for advice or to participate in rituals. Guo Ching-shoei was destined no longer to be just an ordinary Taiwanese farmer. Once provided with the tools of his godly trade, he was also a spirit medium, and his life was changed forever. Guo Fang and his friend Ming-feng said nothing more about their private investigations, but accepted their new medium as everyone else did.

Holding Divination Chairs, Awaiting the Descent of Gods. One means of receiving supernatural communication is through the movements of divination chairs, which write characters on a table. Ming-feng used this type of divination in the case to try to disconfirm Guo Ching-shoei's claim of divine possession.

The Anthropological Perspective

In our encounters with peoples of different cultures, it is often in the area of religion that they seem most alien to us. Even when we are able to understand that strange food tastes good to people raised on it or that some new agricultural operation is made necessary by soil conditions we have not known before, it is more difficult for us to imagine why people like Ching-shoei and his fellows believe some of the things they believe. Many people encountering the people of Bao-an and their ideas about divination, alliances with gods, and mortification of the flesh would simply say Chinese are superstitious. If they were missionaries, they might feel it their duty to combat the superstition they saw and introduce the people of Bao-an to a different religious system. Other people might not see the village people as superstitious, but would seek for some higher wisdom in what they were doing, for some metaphysical truths that could be taken from the example for the edification of the observer.

Neither condemnation of Taiwanese religion as superstitious nor the search in it for philosophical verities tells us very much about how it works or about how Taiwanese beliefs about the supernatural fit with their understandings about other things or with their social patterns or personality traits. As a private individual, the anthropologist may be interested in philosophical truths. He may also be motivated to bring about a change in what he sees. As an anthropologist, however, his concern is not with whether what people believe is or is not philosophically valid or whether their beliefs should or should not be exchanged for the beliefs he holds. As an anthropologist, he wants to know how shared understandings about religion are related to other shared understandings and how religious statuses are related to other understandings and statuses. He is interested in the interplay between religious beliefs and personality variables. None of these questions depends on any particular view of the validity of one or another religious system. For the anthropologist, it is immaterial whether or not the Great Saint "really exists" and whether or not he was possessing Guo Ching-shoei. What is of interest is what people believe about the Great Saint and how Ching-shoei and his fellows reacted to Ching-shoei's behavior. In looking for the fit between religious beliefs and behavior and other beliefs and behavior, the anthropologist is not being very helpful if he merely says the beliefs are superstitious or contradictory, or if he decides that a ritual is childish, or if he thinks that a myth embodies a lesson for all humanity, or if he finds that the local view of the nature of prayer is the same as his. None of these findings increases his understanding of the society he is studying. He must view religious understandings in the same way he would view other kinds of understandings, and religious statuses must be considered in the same way other statuses are considered. Religion is part of human culture, and the anthropologist's contribution to religious studies lies in the extent to which he is able to "explain" particular religious understandings or behavior in the context of theories about culture in general or in the context of nonreligious culture or behavior.

Analysis of the Case

Guo Ching-shoei's possession was not the spontaneous creation of a dis-
ordered mind. We do not know what psychological factors motivated Guo
Ching-shoei to behave as he did. We do know, however, that from the
moment he first went into trance until the ethnographer left Bao-an, whenever he acted as a spirit medium, even though he seemed to be in a dissocia-
tive state, he followed a wide range of understandings that were shared with
other people in Bao-an. The possession was a cultural performance, not
merely an inscrutable psychological outburst by one man. The trance, Ching-
shoei's behavior while he was in the trance, and people's reaction to the
trance were all dependent on a series of understandings relating to the supernatural. Because people in Bao-an shared the understanding that there are
supernatural beings, they were able to attribute Ching-shoei's behavior to
divine (or demonic) intervention, rather than merely being puzzled. Because they shared the understanding that gods sometimes communicate
with human beings through other human beings, they were able to develop
an interpretation of his behavior as communication from a god and to discuss
and agree with each other both about what the behavior meant in itself
and about what the implications might be for village life. Because they
understood that supernaturals may be good or bad, there was even a culturally understood channel for counterinterpretations (namely, that the
possessing presence was not a god). These counterinterpretations, however,
were related primarily to the way in which Ching-shoei's behavior should
be permitted to influence group life. Guo Fang did not deny that Ching-
shoei was possessed; he denied only that the village should be guided by his
possession and allow him a position of occasional leadership.

The spectacular performance by Guo Ching-shoei was culturally patterned behavior. Indeed, it is because it was culturally patterned that other
participants understood it as they did and reacted as they did. They too
acted in accordance with religious understandings prevalent in Bao-an. Guo
Tian-huah, for example, attempted to integrate the new medium into the
system of religious statuses in Bao-an by developing an explanation that
the Great Saint was coming to assist the Third Prince. This explanation
was both understood and found credible by other people in the village.
Wang Fuh-ming mentioned the shadowy forms of spirit soldiers that had
been the advance guard. Even though some discounted his view as extreme,
they did not do so on the grounds that the god would not have sent an
advance guard or because supernatural soldiers did not guard Bao-an. They
did so because no one else had seen the sight and because Fuh-ming was
always thought rather imaginative anyway. Importantly, Fuh-ming's vision,
although not disallowed by shared understandings of the village, was not
necessary to the event. If it had been widely believed that no one could
be possessed unless his neighbor first saw supernatural soldiers, perhaps
Fuh-ming's evidence might have received greater attention. The man who
proposed that Bao-an would gain a political advantage in a coming festival
by having one more spirit medium suggested this in order to explain the

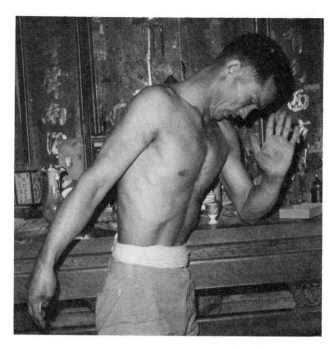

Guo Ching-shoei in Trance before His Family Altar. The Great Saint was made manifest among the people of Bao-an through the curious speech and movements of their friend Guo Ching-shoei.

motivation of the gods in taking a new medium. He too was acting culturally, for he too was integrating a new religious (and political) event into the total pattern of shared understandings of the village and attempting to make Guo Ching-shoei's unusual behavior credible to himself and others around him.

Guo Ching-shoei's performance was dramatic in another important way. For those who believed that the possession was in fact godly (ultimately, therefore, almost everyone in Bao-an), Ching-shoei's words and views while in trance were the words and views of the Great Saint himself. People had contact directly with one of the supernatural beings of their pantheon and could experience for themselves what gods were interested in and how gods wanted people to behave toward them. His possession also provided an example of the absolute power that gods have over the minds and bodies of human beings because Ching-shoei was believed to have no control of the situation himself. Not only did he have no power to speak his own words, but also he could not prevent the possession, and his body was thrown about by the gods without concern to his own comfort. After his initiation, Ching-shoei was to injure himself with the instruments for the mortification of the flesh (balls of nails, sawfish saws, swords, clubs with nails mounted in them) on many occasions when he went into trance. One effect of this mortification upon the people who watched it (whether they watched Guo Ching-shoei or another medium) was to illustrate the ability of the gods to force people to conform to their bidding and to cause such "unnatural" phenomena as the absence of pain. Both of these themes were mentioned frequently to the ethnographer when people in Bao-an talked about spirit mediums. Ching-shoei's possession provided a new channel for communication with the supernatural, in this case, in the person of the Great Saint. It also provided a new, dramatic instance illustrating the influence of the gods upon human life.

The initiation of Ching-shoei was part of this drama and involved the participation (or at least presence) of very large numbers of village people, all of whom shared a general conception of what they were doing and seeing and some general agreement to include Ching-shoei's newfound status in the social structure of the village and to consider his revelations in the formation of individual and village policy. The participation of virtually all of the people of Bao-an in this sacred drama may be hypothesized to have reinforced their shared understandings about the nature of the supernatural and of their relation with it; that is, we may suppose that the event increased (or helped to maintain) both the degree of similarity of understandings from person to person and their conviction of the validity of these understandings (because they were the understandings that it appeared to each that everyone else had and that were defended by all as the most rational or only appropriate understandings).

Ching-shoei presumably had about the same religious understandings that his fellows had in Bao-an. He apparently never received any special religious training, and he was able to manipulate the symbols of the religious system as easily as they were and in a way that both he and they apparently found credible. But he differed from them. In being the man who actually went into trance, he assumed a new social status and appropriate role behavior toward village people, toward his possessing god, and toward the earthly manifestation of the Third Prince, Guo Tian-huah. There was therefore not only a cultural component in the event of his possession, but also a social-structural one. That is what alarmed his father (who did not want his son to occupy that status), and that is what alarmed Guo Fang (who was afraid of the consequences of having a spirit medium in the village who was on such good terms with his rival). Guo Fang's opposition was designed not to change people's understandings about gods, but to change their understandings about how to act toward Guo Ching-shoei and the behavior to expect from him. Guo Ching-shoei was claiming occupancy of a particular status. His father was alarmed but helpless. Guo Fang undertook to dispute the claim and demonstrate instead that Ching-shoei was in another status, that of a man possessed by an evil presence, which required different behavior toward him. Instead of being initiated, he should have been "cured" if Guo Fang's interpretation of the situation had been followed; and instead of being obeyed, he should have been defied. The consequences of having a new man in such a status or of having this particular man in such a status seem to have been what interested people in Bao-an most about the event.

Religious studies in anthropology necessarily proceed from an analysis of culture, the understandings that people have about religion. The distribution of these understandings or the distribution of social relationships as a result of these understandings will concern us somewhat less in this chapter, but these, too, are important to the analysis of any particular religious system. The social structure of a group of people represents the distribution of their understandings and of their expectations about behavior. Although Taiwanese ideas about gods and their relations with human beings are crucial to Taiwanese religious behavior, any given event (such as the initiation of Guo Ching-shoei or Guo Fang's private séances) is also the result of the distribution of understandings and statuses among the participants. In addition, anthropologists have been concerned with the relationship between personality and religion, particularly with what gives religious ideas the credibility and force that they have for those who hold them and with the way in which an individual makes use of the religious understandings of his culture in the formulation and satisfaction of his particular drives, means, and goals. We shall begin by examining the supernatural itself and widespread understandings about how people relate to it and communicate with it.

Communicating with the Gods

RELIGION   *The belief in spiritual beings or forces.*

For years anthropologists have defined "religion" as belief in spiritual beings or forces and have maintained that some such belief is universal. This did not mean that all human beings believed in spiritual beings or forces, but that all known cultures involved shared understandings about them, even if these understandings were denied by some of their members. The case was overstated. It is not true, for example, that such a culture as that of the U.S.S.R. (to the extent that Soviet culture may be considered unitary) includes a widely shared belief in spiritual beings. Very probably such beliefs were universal at one time, but this was not because human culture was impossible without them; instead, it was probably because human culture is especially congenial to the development of such beliefs. Universal or not, the belief in spiritual or supernatural beings or forces is one of the most common human understandings.

Supernatural beings   The postulation of supernatural beings normally implies some relation between these supernaturals and human beings. The quality of this relationship varies from culture to culture, from supernatural being to supernatural being within the same culture, and from person to person with respect to the same supernatural being. The notion that supernatural beings exist and can affect the careers of human beings entails a host of additional questions: What is their influence like? How can humans recognize it? Can it be manipulated to the advantage of particular people? What are the gods themselves like? What are their expectations about human beings? Some peoples discuss questions like these openly and clearly. Others seldom think about them and rarely discuss the relation of one belief to another. They still share understandings about supernatural beings, even if they do not have elaborate theological discussions and even if the understandings seem to be rather disparate and not integrated very logically.

In the culture of Bao-an village several categories of supernatural beings are recognized. One includes gods. The gods are believed to be interested in the affairs of the human world, but some are more interested than others in the activities of any particular human being or of any particular group of human beings. Chinese religion maintains that gods and humans can work in alliances, normally with particular gods coming to the aid of particular people, sometimes in conflict with other gods who are allied with the enemies of these people. In Taiwan a person establishes and maintains an alliance with the gods by offering food, incense, and temple money to particular gods and asking for their assistance in solving his problems. Although some of these relationships are short term and end when the worshipper's problem is solved (or when he decides that the god is not effectively helping him solve it), many such relationships continue for years and generations. Thus, many families in Bao-an village have tried to maintain a lasting special relationship with the Third Prince. When Guo Ching-shoei was possessed by the Great Saint, one man's theory was that the additional alliance with a god not currently worshipped in the village (but assumed to have been recruited by the Third Prince to help him in tending to village problems) would strengthen the position of Bao-an in conflict with other villages in the area. Gods and humans on one side were being ranged in this man's mind against alliances in other, competing villages.[4]

We are immediately struck by the differences between this view of the supernatural and the conceptualizations of such religions as Islam or Judaism. In Islam or Judaism only one supernatural body is postulated, who is always associated with a system of absolute morals, and whose alliance with human beings (if one can use the word "alliance" at all in this context) can never erupt into conflict with other supernaturals allied with other human beings. The Chinese, in common with many other polytheistic peoples, understand gods as limited in power, struggling for different ends, and differentially interested in people depending on how people have behaved toward them. Although Chinese gods are generally moral (having attained their positions as gods because of their virtue as humans), they are willing to return attentions paid to them. Their influence in human affairs is normally a function of their social relations with human beings, and not primarily a function of the virtue or error of the course that their human allies may be following. The ancient Greeks, whose concern with the humanlike private lives of their divinities engaged the imagination of the European nations into our own century, went even further in this direction and understood

---

[4]In earlier times this competition took the form of local wars. In this century the conflicts are largely over prestigeful positions in intervillage ceremonial activities and, to some extent, over political advantage. They rarely emerge into physical violence any more.

godly assistance and opposition as a function of flattery, insult, and pique. A recent encyclopedia of Greek topics provides the following description of the goddess Hera:

> In Homer and in later texts and inscriptions on buildings she was considered primarily as the patron goddess of marriage and the guardian of marital fidelity. Her own union with Zeus, however, had its stormy passages and she found it difficult to tolerate the innumerable escapades of her husband; she pursued with tenacious hatred all the women whom Zeus chose for his mistresses (Io, Leto, and many others) and she vented her spite too on the children of his illicit amours; her persecution of Heracles was notable. . . . One of the most important episodes in Hera's life happened in the Troad. There, [a Trojan named] Paris was asked to judge who was the most beautiful of three goddesses. Furious at her rejection, Hera unleashed her anger on the Trojans and took sides with the Greeks in the Trojan war [Devambez 1967:230].

There is a considerable difference between Chinese or Greek ideas of a multitude of gods with supernatural but limited powers (different as these are from each other) and the view of a unitary, omnipotent supernatural reflected in, say, the Koran of Mohammad. Consider the picture presented by Mohammad:

> Praise be to Allah, lord of the universe, the bounteous, the merciful, master of the Day of Judgement. We worship Thee alone and from Thee alone seek assistance. Guide us onto the right path, onto the path of those upon whom Thou hast bestowed Thy grace, of those who merit not Thine anger, of those who err not [Surah 1:2–7][5].

> Among men are those who say "We believe in Allah and in the Day of Judgement" but who nevertheless are not believers. They would deceive Allah and the believers, but they are able to deceive none but themselves, though they do not know that. In their hearts there is sickness, and Allah has increased that sickness, and for them there will be grievous punishment, for they have lied [Surah 2:9–11].

> It is Allah who created the heavens and the earth and sent water from the clouds; He thereby made fruits for your sustenance and placed ships at your disposal which plough the sea at His order and put the rivers at your disposal, and He set the sun and the moon revolving without end to your service, and the night and the day, and He gave you everything which you desired to receive from Him, and if you would number the favors of Allah you could not calculate them all. Truly man is sinful and unthankful [Surah 14:33–35].

Mohammad's view of Allah, who punishes all liars and to whom human debt is too great for possible repayment, is utterly unlike the Chinese or Greek

[5]Numbering of verses in each Surah follows the edition of Italo Chiussi (1969), from which these passages are retranslated.

The Judgment of Paris
by Lucas Cranach the
Elder.   When Paris did
not select Hera as the
most beautiful of the
three goddesses, she flew
into a rage and sided
against Paris and the
Trojans in the war with
the Greeks.

views of gods.[6] The difference is not just that Allah is a unitary figure, while Greek and Chinese religions include an endless number of gods. It is also a difference in the views of how humans and the supernatural act toward each other. Allah would presumably not concern himself with petty one-upmanship between Taiwanese villages or with winning a beauty contest judged by a human being. Taiwanese gods presumably would be unconcerned about people who chose not to set up alliances with them, and Greek gods never seemed moved to inflict punishment against mere liars. For the believer in Islam, a person's debt to Allah is too vast for repayment. For the Taiwanese farmer, one can bargain with individual gods and pay one's debt in sacrifices.

[6]We are concerned here with strictly orthodox, Koranic Islam. Popular Islam includes the worship of saints (*awliyā*), whose tombs are visited by pilgrims seeking particular blessings. Orthodox Islam has nearly always disapproved of saint worship.

Divination   A person's relation to his gods in most parts of the world involves some kind of communication with them. Most peoples have conventionalized ways to tell the gods about human needs, to ask questions that they want answered, to strike bargains with the gods, or to offer praise.[7] This communication tells both the anthropologist and the participants in the culture themselves much about the understandings they share with regard to the nature of the supernatural and the supernatural's relationship to human beings. When human beings address words to supernatural beings we call it "prayer." When the communication moves in the other direction, when the supernaturals address messages to human beings, we normally use the word "divination" as a label for the activity of human beings in deciphering what is being said to them. The word "revelation" is sometimes applied to the messages themselves, though the word is rarely used by anthropologists. These two halves of human conversation with the supernatural are rather different from each other. Most prayer is speech, often the same sort of speech that would be offered to an important human being. Even when the speech is sung, whispered, or only thought, the communication is much like ordinary mortal communication in that thoughts are formulated by a speaker (or thinker) with the intent that they will be received and understood by another intelligence using essentially the same formulations that are appropriate among humans.

Divination is rather more complicated. Just as people disagree on the nature of supernatural beings, so also they disagree on how supernatural beings communicate with humans. In Bao-an we saw the use of spirit mediums and of a divination chair that worked a little like a Western Ouija board. In ancient Judaism God spoke to his people through the prophets and through events in history. Learning the will of God through historical events is a continuing theme in Western religion. Natural disasters (still called "acts of God"), military triumphs and defeats, astrological events, and untimely deaths are all taken to contain messages. The island of Taiwan was partially occupied militarily by the Dutch at the beginning of the seventeenth century and was ceded to them in 1623 by the Chinese emperor, who hoped thereby to keep them from establishing a colony on the Chinese mainland. Political events and a changing military balance led to Dutch expulsion from Taiwan by local Chinese forces in 1662. The present-day Chinese population of Taiwan consider this campaign to be the moment from which Taiwanese history really begins. To the Dutch who lived through the expulsion (or who died in it), the event was fraught with supernatural significance as well as military and political importance. An extract of a letter by a certain Joannes Kruyf, a Dutch missionary, describes the events of 1662:

PRAYER   *A process in which human beings address words to supernatural beings; the words so addressed.*

DIVINATION   *The activity of human beings in deciphering what are believed to be communications from supernatural beings or forces.*

[7]Not all supernaturals in whom people believe have relations with them. A belief common among many African peoples is that the world was created by gods who subsequently had nothing further to do with it. Africanists refer to these creators as "otiose" (lazy) gods in contrast to gods understood to have a continuing interest in earthly affairs.

Meanwhile there being great want of necessaries in Castle Zeelandia, the soldiers died daily of bloody flux, scurvy, and dropsy; so that in nine months' time, having lost about 1600 men, both by famine and sword, we were forced (for the preservation of our lives) to capitulate.

One cannot without tears think of the unexpected destruction and ruin of so many families, and of nearly thirty ministers, partly in their lives, partly in their fortunes (among whom I had my share, having lost all I had gathered in fifteen years' time), the loss and dishonour of the Company, with other unspeakable miseries—my own being none of the least as it includes the loss of three parts of my library. All of which we ought to look upon as the effects of God's just indignation, on account of our manifold sins [Quoted in Campbell 1903:328].

To Kruyf the Dutch military collapse was an expression of God's dissatisfaction and at the same time a punishment of the Dutch for their sins. There was a message to be read in it.

The devices used to discover the will of the supernatural or to gain information from supernatural beings are many, ranging from observing the direction of flights of birds in the northern Philippines to using tarot cards (ancestors of modern playing cards) in Europe to poisoning chickens to see

Chinese Forces Expelling the Dutch from Formosa, 1662. For Kruyf and his compatriots, a military defeat was also a message from God.

whether they survive or die among the Azande of Sudan. But all these devices are subject to an important constraint: What the supernaturals are interpreted to be saying must be something that people think is believable for them to say. Understandings about supernatural beings and the part they play in mortal affairs are part of culture, and these understandings must not be contradicted by the words that are understood to be spoken by them. Joannes Kruyf sees in his troubles an expression of God's just indignation resulting from the many sins of the Dutch in Taiwan. If Kruyf had read in this event that God was soon to be married and was asking the Dutch to provide a veil for the bride, he would have been thought mad or accused of heresy or both. Kruyf and his compatriots in the seventeenth century, believed that God would be displeased by sins, that people were sinful, and that any disaster communicated divine annoyance. They did not believe, for example, that God might get married, or that God would work disaster on innocent (or even sinful) human beings merely to communicate that he needed a wedding veil. Among the Chinese of Taiwan today, as in Kruyf's time, divine communication is also possible, but no almighty god rules every detail of the universe, and military reverses are not readily interpretable in the fashion in which Kruyf interpreted the Dutch reverses. Indeed, history is not an important source of divine communication. In Bao-an it is believable that gods are concerned with a village or an individual family that worships them and that, among other things, they use the bodies of individual human beings to communicate.

An important practical consequence has to do with what kind of device is used for divination. It must be appropriate to the understandings about what the gods might want to say in their half of the conversation. If the gods are being asked where good hunting may be found, the divination device must not suggest marrying such and such a woman. If the gods are being asked who is responsible for the death of a certain person, the divination device must not respond by telling where there is good hunting. If gods are understood to be protectors of human beings, the divination device must not instruct the inquirer to do something obviously destructive to his interests. One way to provide for a relevant and believable (that is, godlike) response from the supernatural is to use a divination device that can generate only a small number of answers and then ask the question in such a way that all of the answers are relevant. This is akin to flipping a coin. When I decide to flip a coin and that heads means I will eat pork and tails means I will eat fish, then a flip of the coin must tell me to eat pork or fish. It can tell me nothing else. Its answer is necessarily relevant to that question.

Another way to provide for a relevant response from the supernatural is to use a divination device that generates an ambiguous response, subject to many different (and often conflicting) interpretations. From what is known of them, it appears that the ancient Greek oracles worked this way. This is also the way in which several divination systems work that are popular in our own day. Divination by means of tarot cards, for example, may bring up the following oracle if one draws a six of swords (equivalent to a six of spades in modern decks);

Passage away from difficulties; journey by water; success after anxiety; sending someone to represent you in an undertaking [Gray 1960:48].

When this card is drawn for representation of a past or future activity, it can apply to a large range of situations. It is difficult to imagine that such a prediction will not come to pass or that an event has not happened to all of us in the recent past to which the passage *could* with imagination be applicable. Horoscopes work the same way, often adding some very general advice as well that could be followed by anyone anytime with few ill effects. A Chinese divination manual now popular in the United States, the *I Ching*, or *Book of Changes*, also provides ambiguous responses, for example (Wilhelm 1950:201):

Keeping still. Keeping his back still
So that he no longer feels his body
He goes into his courtyard
And does not see his people.
No blame.

Here the message of the supernatural is so unclear that it is difficult to be entirely certain what it applies to. Inasmuch as it is normally offered in response to a particular question, the applicability of the text to the problem at hand requires interpretation.

The act of interpretation by a member of the culture ensures that the shared understandings of members of the culture will be duly taken into account and that the message and its implications for action will be credible to participants. In Chinese temples when passages from the *I Ching* (or other similar texts) are used, each passage is often printed on a slip of paper together with putative implications for some fifteen or so commonly asked questions. In many societies some people are considered experts at reading supernatural messages. When Guo Fang and Ming-feng conducted their séance to find out whether Guo Ching-shoei was truly possessed by the Great Saint, they used a wooden chair held by two illiterate, old men, which was moved over a table to trace various shapes. Ming-feng's job was to interpret these shapes as Chinese characters and then apply the characters to the issue at hand in such a way as to make them relevant. Part of Ming-feng's skill as an interpreter of this means of divination (called a *kiō-á* in Taiwanese) is that he shows great imagination in bringing essentially random lines into correspondence with a village problem so that people feel that they are being divinely and unambiguously guided. The biblical tale of Joseph interpreting Pharaoh's dream shows the same skill:

Joseph said to Pharaoh, "Pharaoh's dreams are one dream. God has told Pharaoh what he is going to do. The seven good cows are seven years, and the seven good ears of corn are seven years. It is all one dream. The seven lean and gaunt cows that came up after them are seven years, and the empty ears of corn blighted by the east wind will be seven years of famine. It is as I have said to Pharaoh: God has let Pharaoh see what he is going to do. There are to be seven years of great plenty throughout the land. And after them will come seven years of famine; all the years of plenty in Egypt will be forgotten, and the famine will ruin the country. [Gen. 41:25–30, New English Bible]

To the outsider who does not share Taiwanese understandings about gods or about the ability of gods to inspire the men who hold the chair, Ming-feng's performance looks like pure fraud; to the outsider who does not believe that supernatural forces could, would, or did inspire Joseph in his interpretation of Pharaoh's dream, Joseph seems a clever cozener. But Ming-feng and Joseph themselves (apparently) believed in the validity of their respective findings, and at least some of the village people accepted Ming-feng's findings on this occasion just as Pharaoh and his court accepted Joseph's. In Bao-an virtually all of the village people frequently resort to this means of divination, guided by Ming-feng or by someone else. And in the Near East in biblical times dreams were an extremely important source for the discovery of unknown things.

In brief, belief in gods normally also involves belief in ways of communicating with them, either through prayer or divination. A major issue in the analysis of divination is how the device used for divination and the interpretations made from the device are kept in accord with shared understandings about what the supernatural would be likely to say. Different divinatory traditions approach this problem differently.

Shamanism The Taiwanese mediums Guo Tian-huah and Guo Ching-shoei can be thought of as another kind of divination instrument. Because they speak in natural language (or in a close approximation to it), their words can be understood by everyone, and they do not require expert interpretation (although some mediums in China do). However, when supernatural forces are believed to possess the bodies and tongues of ordinary mortals, divine behavior other than communication can be enacted. The phenomenon of possession is common throughout most of the world, and anthropologists have been able to make some broad generalizations about it. The word anthropologists usually apply to a person routinely possessed by a supernatural being for purposes of divination or healing is "shaman."[8] The classical

Masked Shaman and His Patient. The classical Siberian shaman is primarily concerned with healing.

[8]The word is taken from Tungusian, the language of a Siberian tribe, the Tungus, famous for its shamans. Some scholars have insisted that the word "shaman" ought not to be used except to describe Siberian shamans. Others have sought to limit its meaning as a technical term: Eliade, for example (1964:5), uses the word to refer to a man whose soul journeys to other spheres and contrasts it with "medicine man," which he uses as a technical term to refer to a man possessed by a supernatural and speaking his words. E. M. Loeb distinguishes between a shaman, who is possessed by spirits, and a seer, who has visions of spirits, but is not actually possessed by them. The term "spirit medium" is used by authors writing about China to refer to Chinese shamans (which is why we have used it here). In America the term "spirit medium" is popularly limited to shamans who are believed to be possessed by the souls of the dead.

location of shamanism is Siberia, though it is found in some form in most parts of the world. The typical Siberian shaman, unlike the Chinese shaman, often inherits his office from his father. Normally he is subjected to a period of intensive training (as are shamans among the Ojibwa of North America, for example, or in some cases among the Chinese. Guo Ching-shoei's case is atypical in the suddenness with which his career began). On initiation the Siberian shaman acquires special costuming and paraphernalia, notably including a drum with which he calls the spirits over which he has control (unlike the Chinese shaman who is controlled by the spirits he serves). Normally the Siberian shaman is primarily concerned with curing disease, which is often interpreted as loss of the patient's soul. In his trance the shaman is believed to seek the missing soul, to find and overpower it, and bring it back to the patient's body, thereby restoring his health. In the realms where he travels, the Siberian shaman may meet good and bad spirits and may experience many things, often describing them to onlookers who are watching the performance.

The central and in many ways most important feature of the typical shaman's performance, however, is that he attempts to cure a patient of illness, in contrast to the Taiwanese shamans of our example. The shaman, in trance, performs a series of gestures, even a dance, around and over the body of the patient. Often he dramatically bends over the patient and seems to be sucking vigorously. After a time he stands up and draws from his mouth the object said to be causing the disease: a stone, a wad of cloth (perhaps bloody), a fragment of wood, or whatever. Some shamans have been found by ethnographers to conceal these things in their mouths before they begin. Before we conclude that they are charlatans, however, we must note that the shamans who have been caught in the act of preparing sleight-of-hand "miracles" have usually been believers in their own magic, just as Ming-feng, in our case, believed in the validity of his divination findings in spite of what looked to the outsider like conscious manipulation. Some shamans have explained that their cure is real, but that the people they are curing require a tangible sign of the removal of the illness. Although they may concede that the objects produced in the sucking cure are produced by sleight-of-hand, they also maintain that the sucking cure itself is effective. Psychologically, they may be quite right. Much illness is psychosomatic. Furthermore, our attitude toward illness and our tolerance for short-term, trivial disorders is very much influenced by whether we think we are sick or not. The patient who can be convinced he has been cured is liable to feel better than the patient who doubts it. If we do not accept supernatural explanations, a shaman's ability to cure people is based entirely upon his ability to convince them through a dramatic performance that they feel better. The difference between the shaman's view of his performance and the anthropologist's view is that although the shaman believes that supernatural power is at work and need only be dramatized, the anthropologist usually believes that the drama stands alone. Both are aware that many patients recover naturally,

SHAMAN *A person routinely possessed by a supernatural being or beings for purposes of divination or healing.*

SUCKING CURE
A typical element in a shamanistic performance wherein the shaman appears to suck a solid object from the body of a patient, to which the patient's illness or other disorder is attributed.

that some patients get worse, and that at least a few patients recover spectacularly after the shaman's performance and apparently as a result of it.

The Chinese shamans in our case had a much wider role in community affairs than curing. When they did do curing, they did not use the sucking cure; rather, they wrote charms on little pieces of paper that were carried on the patient's body or burned over a cup of water, which was then drunk. Giving advice on community and personal troubles rather than primarily directly curing the sick seems especially Chinese and is not shared by shamans in most other cultures. Fascinating as shamanism is to both anthropologists and others, it has proved remarkably hard to characterize with generalizations that do not find exceptions, even if one limits oneself to the Siberian cases. Gustav Ränk, in introducing a series of research papers on shamanism, comments on this aspect of it:

> North-Eurasian shamanism, as is known, does not comprise a completely unified phenomenon, but exists in different gradated forms that not seldom take on a strong local colouring. Not only does the personality make-up of shamans vary, but so do their authority, their pattern of behaviour, and professional equipment, and all this provides a fertile soil for different theoretical reconstructions and generalizations. For every theory advanced there are ample opportunities to find proof for a contrary theory. Research so far is rich in such contradictions [1967:16].

Priests   The shaman is, of course, not the only kind of religious practitioner known to anthropologists. The variety of specialists in supernaturalism is as wide as the ethnographic record itself. One of the most common of supernatural practitioners is the priest. Like the word "shaman," the word "priest" is used to designate a wide class of religious specialists, and the details vary from one culture to another. Typically, the priest stands in contrast to the shaman in that the priest is not possessed by the supernatural and does not directly speak for it. He is knowledgeable in religious rituals and is trained to perform them. As the shaman represents the supernatural made temporarily manifest in the world of mortals, so the priest performs rituals on behalf of the community or of individuals in it and to some extent represents the human world temporarily approaching the supernatural. At least some of his rituals are not concerned with producing specific results, but are simply concerned with, for example, praise or thanksgiving. Often, the association of priests with the world of the gods, especially the fact that the community desires to approach the gods with all appropriate propriety so that the gods will not be angered, requires the priest to observe special restrictions on his private life. A Chinese Taoist priest must normally abstain from eating meat or having sex before and during a religious festival. In the past some Taoist priests also abstained from cereal, which was also considered to pollute the body. Chinese Buddhists take vows of chastity and vegetarianism for life. Roman Catholic priests take vows of chastity and obedience and in some orders take vows of poverty. As a representative of the community and

PRIEST *A religious practitioner able to perform on behalf of the community or of individuals culturally santioned rituals that are directed toward supernatural beings, not all of which are concerned with producing specific results.*

its leader in many of its approaches to the supernatural, a priest must represent the community as the gods are assumed to want it to be: humble, pure, glorious, or whatever.

The basis of a priest or shaman's effective authority is legitimacy. A shaman's legitimacy derives from his trance and from the community acceptance of that trance as a genuine manifestation of divine presence. A priest's legitimacy derives from his special training in the performance of rituals and from his membership in an order of priests in which the community has vested its trust for relations with the supernatural. Priests are rarely self-appointed (though shamans often are). Any anthropology student, for example, could easily learn to read the Roman Catholic mass. It is not secret, and anyone who wishes to do so can acquire not only the texts of the mass, but also detailed instructions for the performance of the mass and detailed explanation of what each step of the mass means. But if the student has not been ordained as a Catholic priest, his mass would not be considered a valid or proper one. Indeed, it would offend most Catholics. The reason is not that the student's mass would look or sound any different from the priest's mass, but that the student has no right to perform it because he is not ordained, and a rule of mass giving is that the giver be ordained. As long as the student is not a member of the priesthood, the mass that he performs is invalid and offensive. There are normally no such rules for shamans. If a person acts as people do when possessed by a god (in China, say), the community must immediately entertain the possibility that he is what he says he is. Only a few followers need accept him before he is established. Community acceptance is not dependent on his mastery of arcane ritual or on his ordination by any authority, but only on general agreement that his

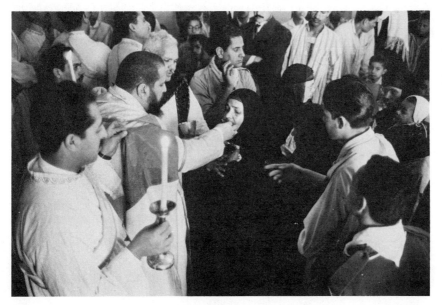

Coptic Mass. A priest's effectiveness, unlike that of a shaman, depends on his having been ordained rather than simply on his doing the right things.

performance is a credible one and a general conviction that there is no reason to believe that he is not possessed by a god as he says he is. The initiation in our case did not make Guo Ching-shoei a shaman, but expressed community acceptance of his claim to that status. The weapons he was provided were not consciously intended as symbols of office (although they served that function), but as inevitable tools of his calling that the community was "teaching" him to use. The attempts made to discredit Guo Ching-shoei involved counterdivination and an attempt to undercut community opinion. The way in which a student would be discredited if he performed a mass without ordination would consist simply of an announcement that he had not been authorized to perform it.

It is difficult to generalize about the statuses of shaman and priest in human society, for each society that has such religious practitioners integrates them differently into the prevailing system of statuses. Among the Jivaro of the Amazon Basin in South America, as in many other tribal societies, shamans are feared. Although they are able to effect cures, their traffic with spirits also enables them to inflict illness, and Jivaro shamans are both respected and despised members of their communities. In classical China priests were also viewed with deep suspicion and tended to be tolerated only as a necessary evil (necessary because only they could perform certain rituals, particularly funerals). They occupied social positions neither of power, wealth, nor prestige, often living in monasteries at the very fringes of society. Like Jivaro shamans, they were feared. One proverb begins: "Do not go singly into a temple [lest you be harmed by priests]." Another traditional saying describes a person whom one fears to approach too closely as being like "the old priest with three catties of charms on his back," which he can use to work harm to those he dislikes. There were, of course, important priests in Chinese history, Taoist and, especially, Buddhist. The point is that most priests were socially marginal men, the objects of fear at some moments and of scorn at others.

In some societies, by contrast, the priestly role is an honored one, and society can even be said to be governed by priests, whose access to the supernatural provides a good rationale for their leadership. In classical India the priests were the highest caste, higher than kings, and even royal houses acted only with full consultation with the priesthood. Contact between priests and others was considered polluting for the priests. Similarly, in ancient Egypt a rich and powerful priesthood exercised tremendous power over society, both as the holder of vast estates and as a major influence in the formulation of national policy. Individual priests in Egypt appear to have been nearly sacrosanct persons.

Just as Ching-shoei was also a farmer, in many societies priests and shamans occupy these statuses only when they are not engaged in economically productive activities. Because the status of priest or shaman is not an economically productive one, societies without very much economic surplus cannot afford to maintain shamans or priests full-time, and priests and shamans normally ply their religious trades only on a part-time basis.

Sometimes priestly activity is part of the set of expectations attached to a status with far wider ramifications. In most societies at least some religious rituals are performed by the head of a household, for example. Thus, Ching-shoei lit his own incense before his altar every night before retiring, the ancient Roman father offered sacrifices and prayers to the spirits of the cupboard and the ghostly guardians of home and crossroads (the *penates* and *lares,* respectively), and many an American household head says a prayer on the family's behalf at sitting down to dinner (or delegates the authority to do so). In many societies the headman, king, or chief has priestly functions as a regular part of his status behavior. Among the Nootka of the Canadian west coast, the chief traditionally acted as a priest in performing the rituals associated with the beginning of the salmon run, and in many agricultural societies the king used to perform religious rites at the beginning of the harvest. It is sometimes difficult to decide whether someone who is both king or priest should be classified primarily as king or primarily as priest.

To summarize, shamans and priests are two kinds of specialists concerned with human relationships to supernatural beings. The shaman (speaking very generally) represents the activities of the gods with respect to human beings, the priest (speaking equally broadly) represents the activities and desires of people with respect to the gods. (If we wish to associate them with the "conversation" of prayer and divination mentioned earlier, shamans represent the gods' side, while priests represent the human side.) The statuses of shaman and, especially, of priest fit into different social structures differently.

Supernaturalism without Supernaturals: Mana Beliefs

Both the shaman and the priest are concerned with supernatural beings, but the supernatural is not always thought of as a "being." People often think of the supernatural as consisting (at least partly) of a force or forces that although not concrete, individual entities like gods are beyond the natural, familiar world. The conceptualization of the supernatural as an undifferentiated, impersonal force is widespread. Anthropologists usually call supernatural force understood in this way "mana."

The word "mana" is taken from the Tahitian, where it is the name given to impersonal, extranatural force pervading all things.[9] Typically mana is conceived of as a force that inheres in all things. For the believer in mana, everything is supernatural to a degree, and everything is more than it ap-

MANA *Undifferentiated,
impersonal, supernatural
force.*

---

[9]The word "mana" is not related to the biblical word "manna," the divine nourishment that was supplied to the Israelites during their wanderings in the wilderness. The word "manna" used in the Bible is believed to derive from the Aramaic *man hu,* What is it?, a term used because the Israelites did not know what the substance was.

ANIMATISM *Belief in mana.*

ANIMISM *The belief that all living beings and natural phenomena that appear to move or have life (sun, moon, rivers, etc.) have individual spirits* (animae), *some or all of which are appropriate objects of worship.*

pears to be. Belief in mana is called "animatism," for it is the belief that all things are imbued with soullike or mindlike supernatural force.[10] This all-permeating force is not evenly distributed, according to the beliefs of most of the animatists that anthropologists have studied; it is concentrated more in some areas and some objects than in others. An object with a very great amount of mana in it can come to have special significance. Charms and amulets are believed effective because of the "lucky" forces that are thought concentrated in them. Sometimes a natural object such as a stone or a stick will be revered because of the amount of mana believed to be concentrated in it.

Our own culture is not without a belief in impersonal force associated with physical objects. Most Americans would be more disturbed by a rape committed on an altar than by a rape committed on a park bench. Both may be made of wood, but the special associations of the altar with religious purposes imbue it with qualities beyond the qualities it has as an object of wood. Most Americans would also be disturbed by a coffee table made of wood from old coffins. Coffin wood is not just wood. Its intimate association with the dead has made it rather special. The feeling about coffin wood is not merely a "natural" revulsion at being reminded of death. In fact, it is not shared by the Taiwanese village people in our case, who reinter the bones of the dead in ceramic vessels and then use the boards from the old coffins (if they are still sound) to make footbridges over irrigation canals. There is no evidence that Taiwanese think there is anything macabre about such practical recycling of the wood.

The fact that physical objects are believed powerful does not imply mana beliefs, however, unless the power is thought to be an integral part of that object. Among peoples who believe in supernatural beings there is often a belief that a particular supernatural being can possess a physical object even as it can possess a shaman. The divination chair in the Taiwanese case is not itself endowed with mana. In ordinary times, when it is not being used in a séance, it is just a wooden object. When it is used to write characters, it is not a power associated with the chair that is writing the characters, but a specific god who is using the chair as his instrument. The little chair is still a chair, and no mana is involved. When Taiwanese farm people offer sacrifice to a god, they often use a statue to represent him. The importance of the statue is not that it is powerful in itself, but that it provides a "seat" for the god, a physical form for him to reside in when he receives the offerings. The divination chair and the god's statue differ from amulets because amulets have power of their own; they are filled with concentrations of

---

[10]Belief in mana is called "animatism," referring to the notion that all things are animate. Somewhat confusingly, this is contrasted to "animism," the belief that all living beings and natural phenomena that appear to move or have life (sun, moon, rivers, etc.) have individual spirits (*animae*), some or all of which are appropriate objects of worship. Probably because of the similarity of sound of these two technical terms the trend in recent years has been to avoid using "animatism" and to substitute a term such as "mana belief" instead.

mana; and they will serve their bearers for good or for ill if correctly manipulated. But the divination chair or the god's statue are merely blocks of wood, tools that may be temporarily used by supernaturals, but that bear no power of their own that people can use for their own ends without regard to the divinities controlling them.

Witches and sorcerers Even as there are specialists who concern themselves with supernatural beings, so there are specialists who make use of undefined supernatural powers. Anthropologists writing in English usually distinguish between witches and sorcerers.[11] Sorcerers make use of a series of procedures to bring about changes in the world through the mediation of impersonal, supernatural power. Usually such procedures are traditional, and often they are secret property, handed down over generations. Although sorcery may be used for socially desirable ends, most cases of sorcery that come to the attention of anthropologists involve harming people over long distances. Many times the sorcerer does not act on his own behalf, but offers his services (for a fee) to a client, who is seeking to right a wrong he believes was done to him by the person who is to be the victim of the sorcery. Although sorcery may be performed secretly, news that he is being victimized usually (and often by design) reaches the target individual. In many cases, this information has dramatic effects upon him, effects that are attributed to the mana manipulation of the sorcerer. Evidence suggests that people can be killed by sorcery. When a person believes in sorcery and also believes that someone is working sorcery against him, he may go into shock. If no evidence turns up to convince him that he is not the victim of sorcery, the continued state of shock can cause serious disruption of his vital body functions and ultimately death (see Canon 1942). One author (Seabrook 1940) has proposed the term "induced autosuggestion" for this process. In one case on the island of Truk that came to our attention, the victim did not go into shock, but simply lost his will to live. He thought himself the victim of sorcery because he heard stones hitting his house at night. Sorcerers are believed to rock houses when working sorcery against the inhabitants, and he associated the stones with this activity. He took to his bed and refused both solace and food. When the ethnographer asked him why he would not eat, he said he was dying anyway, so eating was useless. A few days later he died. Because the power of sorcery to harm is great when the victim believes in it, it is not surprising that some modern governments maintain longstanding laws against it.

"Witchcraft," as the word is used by anthropologists, differs from sorcery in that a witch's power is innate. It requires no ritual activity to bring it into play. Sorcerers actually perform activities with the intent of manipulating mana, but witches manipulate it effortlessly, sometimes even unconsciously. Beliefs about the "evil eye," widespread in Europe and elsewhere, are fre-

SORCERER *A person who makes use of a series of procedures to bring about changes in the world on behalf of the community or individuals through the mediation of impersonal, supernatural power.*

WITCH *A person believed to bring about evil effects upon others through innate powers, and not through the use of ritual. (European "witches" are technically sorcerers, not witches.)*

Nigerian Sorcerer.
A sorcerer's power comes from knowing procedures; that of a witch is innate.

[11]In its modern formulation, the distinction is traced to E. E. Evans-Pritchard's Witchcraft, Oracles and Magic Among the Azande (1937).

quently cited as a classic instance of witchcraft. In most of Europe it was believed that certain people were born with the evil eye and could cause harm to come to others merely by looking at them and wishing them ill or sometimes even without wishing them ill.[12] Because no actual ritual is involved, witches, unlike sorcerers, may be as astonished as the rest of the community to learn of their undesirable effects.

The distinction can be a useful one, for socially and psychologically there is a great difference between a situation in which people try to manipulate the cosmos in such a way as to harm others and a situation in which people fear harm from others and accuse them even when no deliberate mana manipulation has been going on. There is also a difference between a system of mana manipulation such as sorcery that is available to everyone, at least by purchase, and one that is inherited by only a few members of society. The usefulness of the distinction can be overemphasized, however. In societies that believe in sorcery, people may be falsely accused or even falsely convicted of sorcery. In theory this is not a case of witchcraft, for witchcraft involves the belief on the part of all concerned that ritual is not necessary, but it is like witchcraft in its social effects, for people are accused of doing mischief (whether or not they intend to) without evidence of their actually performing any specific acts of hostility.

Among many peoples, the Jivaro of the Amazon Basin, for example, all deaths are attributed to sorcery. The Jivaro believe that a person is by nature immortal, but that he is also by nature so hateful that all historical human beings are sooner or later killed, and at each death divination is used to discover the person responsible so that he may be killed in turn. M. J. Harner, who studied the Jivaro in the middle 1950s writes: "[There is] tremendous emphasis among the Jívaro on ascribing almost all non-epidemic illnesses and deaths, and non-violent deaths, to witchcraft and poisoning. The fundamental assumption . . . is that bewitching shamans are continually attacking one's person and family. This leads, in the cases of assumed witchcraft death, to punitive retaliatory sanctions, in the form of homicide, against the presumed bewitchers" (1972:170–171).

What matters in understanding the effects of these behavior patterns on Jivaro society is not whether sorcery is actually performed, but the process of accusation and revenge against the alleged sorcerer-witch. Harner continues: "With the guilt determined through divination with the aid of a hallucinogenic drug, and the subsequent vengeance probably wreaked on the wrong person (even if one believes in witchcraft deaths), it is clear that the . . . beliefs and practices have repercussions which heighten the sense of outrage and injustice that permeates the society and sets household against household. Under these circumstances, Jívaro witchcraft clearly promotes . . . physical violence" (1972:171).

[12]The famous European and early American "witches" were, in anthropological jargon, sorcerers, not witches. Evil-eye beliefs are widespread, particularly in Christian, Jewish, and Islamic folk societies. Two recent articles discuss the evil eye among Ethiopians (Reminick 1974) and among Slovak-Americans (Stein 1974).

Jivaro Funeral. Jivaro believe that deaths are caused by sorcery, and at each death divination is used to discover the person responsible so that he can be killed in turn.

Briefly, witches and sorcerers are quite different from shamans and priests. For the most part, the former deal with impersonal mana, magically manipulated, while the latter deal with specific supernatural beings.

Religion, Magic, and Science

We saw earlier that it is possible to view human relations with the supernatural as a kind of communication or interaction that is grossly comparable to the kind of interaction that can take place among human beings. Mana, because it is an impersonal force rather than a "being" or a "personality," is related to human beings in different ways from supernatural beings. Mana is manipulated more the way other forces in the universe are manipulated. Some anthropologists, most notably Bronislaw Malinowski, have sought to see beliefs concerning mana and the manipulation of mana as qualitatively different from beliefs concerning supernatural beings and human relations with them. The former they call magic and the latter religion.[13] Sorcery is

MAGIC *The belief in supernatural forces other than supernatural beings and procedures for the manipulation of those forces; the result of applying such procedures.*

[13]In this chapter we have used "religion" as a cover term that refers to belief either in spiritual beings or in spiritual forces. Malinowski's usage limits "religion" to belief in spiritual beings.

magical. Prayer is religious. Religion implies the postulation of supernatural beings and understandings about their nature and the nature of our relationships with them. Religion (usually) implies communication with the supernatural beings, usually through prayer. Magic, on the other hand, is merely a set of techniques, lacking explanations in terms of gods. Although gods may be concerned with the ends a person is trying to achieve when he approaches them, a magical technique works regardless of who uses it. In a sense, magic techniques are just like techniques for doing other things: A technique works or it fails without regard to the moral consequences of its application. Magic is also different from other techniques (which Malinowski broadly calls science) in that magical techniques are not based on careful observation of the laws of cause and effect or on the rational evaluation of actual experiment, but rather on principles that are not in fact valid. Malinowski writes:

> Science is founded on a conviction that experience, effort, and reason are valid; magic on the belief that hope cannot fail nor desire deceive. The theories of knowledge are dictated by logic, those of magic by association of ideas under the influence of desire. As a matter of empirical fact, the body of rational knowledge and the body of magical lore are incorporated each in a different tradition, in a different social setting and in a different type of activity, and all these differences are clearly recognized by savages. The one constitutes the domain of the profane; the other, hedged round by observances, mysteries, and taboos, makes up half of the domain of the sacred [Malinowski 1925:87].

Some theorists have found it useful to distinguish two major principles on which magic performances are often based: homeopathy and contagion. "Homeopathic magic," sometimes called "imitative magic," is based on the proposition that two things that resemble each other in one way will also resemble each other in other ways. Thus, if I perform an operation on one thing, the results of my activity will turn up on the second. If a sorcerer makes a wax figure of someone (the ethnographer, for example) and then pounds nails into it, the rule of homeopathic magic says that because the wax figure looks like the ethnographer, the nails will injure not only the wax figure, but also the ethnographer. Of course, we know that the world does not work this way, but the principle seems psychologically satisfying on occasion. Schoolboys poking pencils through a picture of the teacher or college students burning the dean in effigy know that they are not really hurting him, but they get pleasure from the symbolism of hurting him. They differ from a Haitian voodoo specialist in having different understandings of what they are doing. Both may get psychological satisfaction out of the affair, but the voodoo specialist believes he is also affecting the victim. The schoolboys presumably are aware that they are not doing so. It is when one believes that one is actully harming the person represented by the wax figure or the teacher represented in the picture that the exercise becomes homeopathic magic.

The second kind of magic, "contagious magic," is based on the idea that

HOMEOPATHIC (IMITATIVE) MAGIC
Magical procedures based on the proposition that things which resemble each other are mystically linked, so that what is done to one is also done to the other.

CONTAGIOUS MAGIC
Magical procedures based on the proposition that things once associated with each other continue to be mystically linked, so that what is done to one is also done to the other.

things once associated with each other continue to bear a special relationship. Thus, the sorcerer can perform operations on a piece of his victim's cast-off clothing, or on his victim's hair clippings, nail parings, or feces, and the effect will be worked on the victim. Once again, we know that in fact the world does not work this way, but, once again, the psychological validity of the exercise is very real. Not long ago it was fashionable for a girl to give her beau a lock of her hair when they were to be parted for a long time. He would treasure and admire it and would sometimes even kiss it. Presumably, this was done to the lock of hair as a symbol of the girl friend. Only when the boy begins to believe that his girl friend actively feels the kisses administered to the token can he be said to be engaging in contagious magic.

In fact, of course, magic, science, and religion are not so easily differentiated in practice as they are when one is writing definitions and imagining ideal types. These terms and the concepts they isolate are part of the anthropologist's vocabulary for describing what he finds. In some instances, he may find that it is convenient to change the boundaries of the definitions slightly: The shared understandings of the people he is studying will not necessarily produce magical techniques without theological justification, or relationships with supernaturals that are devoid of magical means of manipulating them, or a system of "scientific" practical knowledge of the real world that is distinct from a system of "magical" ways of dealing with the world.

The Taiwanese spirit mediums in our case sometimes cure the sick by writing charms that bring about the cure magically. These charms are believed to be written by the gods who possess the mediums and, if one strictly follows anthropological vocabulary, would have to be interpreted as a case of gods performing magic: Surely this does not represent a very strict separation of religion and magic in the minds of Taiwanese farmers. Some religious systems include theories about ways in which the gods can be magically coerced. For example, one church in Chicago used to have a sign in front of it advertising a distinctive "system of prayer" that "guarantees" the worshipper will receive anything he asks for, including new cars, money, better jobs, children, cures of illness, television sets, and a host of other items. Presumably such an infallible system of prayer is able to manipulate the power of a supernatural being in the same way in which magic manipulates impersonal power. Magic, furthermore, can involve religious elements. Traditional European sorcerers (or, more often, sorceresses) were believed to control both impersonal magic power and specific supernatural beings (such as familiars) and to command the presence of other supernatural beings at will by means of secret rituals.

The Functions of Religion
All such terms as "sorcerer," "shaman," "magic," "priest," "spirit medium," and "divination" provide a vocabulary with which we can describe the activity related to people's beliefs in supernatural beings or supernatural

Pilgrims at the Vatican.
Theological systems can
provide comforting ideas
when the world does not
seem to be a worthwhile
place and when the
individual does not feel
he can cope with his
problems.

power. None of the terms, however, contributes to solving the problem of why people believe what they believe, or why people find some religious understandings so much more compelling than others.

Religion as explanation   One function that religion serves in society is as a source of explanation. Religion, particularly myth and understandings about how the supernatural behaves, can answer questions that are not readily answerable in nonreligious terms (or to which most secular answers are unacceptable). When we think of religious explanation, we tend to think of explanation of the origin of humanity or of divine intervention in human affairs to produce a certain outcome. In fact, religious systems can provide "information" and "explanation" regarding a vast range of subjects, not just to satisfy intellectual curiosity, but to relieve anxiety or to resolve disagreements. This is the direction of much of the work of Taiwanese spirit mediums. Among the farmers of Bao-an, affairs do not always go well. When a family has a spate of bad luck, when family members are sick one after another, when crops fail, when there are financial reverses, when people quarrel, Taiwanese religion can often find a supernatural explanation. Most frequently the family is haunted by a ghost, often the ghost of one of the family members whose needs after death the family has neglected (Jordan 1971). Where secular understandings can only explain *that* the family has had hard times, religious understandings can explain *why* the family has had hard times. They can also provide ritual means of solving the problem (by pacifying the ghost or exorcising it). The religious explanation here requires not only shared understandings about the continued existence of the soul after death and about the willingness and the ability of the dead under certain circumstances to harm living people; but it also that the family be convinced that its behavior toward the dead relative can be found wanting and that its misfortune is somehow commensurate with the gravity of its failure and the ghost's need. The theology of ghosts provides the intellectual explanation, and such devices as divination or a spirit medium apply the explanation to the situation of a given family. The family's motivation to accept the explanation depends on psychological as well as cultural supports that we can only hint at here. At least part of its acceptance of the supernatural explanation, however, is that there is no competing secular explanation and no secular means of "breaking the streak of bad luck." Religion can provide at least the illusion of information and practical means of coping.

Religion as a source of comfort   Theological systems can also provide comforting ideas in time of crisis, when the world does not seem to be a worthwhile place and when the individual's normal ability to cope is drastically reduced. Religious ideas normally include a conception of an afterlife, for example, which eases the terror of the dying by explaining the experience of death as part of a chain of events that is neither unknown nor unacceptable. Religion provides an explanation when battles are lost or natural events bring disaster upon mortals and their works. Recall that Joannes Kruyf explained the collapse of Dutch imperialism in Taiwan in this way.

Religion as a charter   Religion can also be used to explain a person's situation in relation to other people. French kings ruled by "divine right" because Providence had seen fit to entrust the kingdom to their care. In local wars some 150 or more years ago, the people of Bao-an and their allies were able to hold their own against an alliance of other villages, they say, because they had divine aid; and it is because of the continuation of that same divine aid that they are able to occupy a place of importance out of proportion to their numbers in the area today. Sometimes the subordinate position of a person in human society is explained by religious means. Thus, in Buddhist countries (including Taiwan) one's place in society is believed to be a reward or punishment for behavior in a previous life. In Taiwan (though not in Bao-an) divination is sometimes carried out to reveal the past two lives of a person and explain why his present lot is the logical result of his behavior in past lives.

Often a religious explanation will be invoked to explain the subordination of a whole group of people. After Eve accepts the apple from the serpent and persuades Adam to share it with her, Hebrew tradition tells us that God punished Adam and Eve for violating his prohibition on eating the apple: "To the woman he said: 'I will increase your labour and your groaning and in labour you shall bear children. You shall be eager for your husband, and he shall be your master'" (Gen. 3:16). Thus, the pain of childbirth is explained as well as the subordination of women to their husbands. (The passage has sometimes been quoted by opponents of the women's liberation movement.)

Religious explanation for contemporary practice, like the quote from Genesis about women, often takes the form of myth. A myth is a story which embodies the values that are important to a culture and which has an aura of sanctity about it. When appeal is made to the myth as the justification of contemporary practice, the myth is said to be the "charter" of that practice. Thus, the creation myth in Genesis is potentially a charter for the subordination of women to men.[14] The use of religious myth to increase the legitimacy of contemporary social institutions is found in most societies.

MYTH   *A story that embodies values of a culture and that has an aura of sanctity.*

Later Christian theologians, possibly building on Jewish themes,[15] made use of the biblical history of Adam and Eve in the development of the doctrine of the "Sin of Adam," which is the basis of human wickedness and condemns all people from birth unless they are saved through participation in the sacrifice of Jesus. This participation is ritually expressed through baptism. The necessity of being saved through baptism and the acceptance of Christian life is the backbone of Christian mission activity. The very ancient

[14]Note that nothing in the definition of myth specifies whether the story is true or false. History may come to be myth just as readily as fantasy may. Calling the creation story in Genesis a myth is a statement about how this story functions in Euroamerican society. It says nothing about whether the story is historical or imaginary.

[15]At least one Jewish source (dating from A.D. 70 or later) suggests the infection of mankind with the Sin of Adam. It occurs in the Apocrypha, 2 Esdras 3:21, and, less directly, 7:47–48.

Adam and Eve by
Albrecht Dürer.
Religious explanations
are often given for the
situation of whole groups
of people; thus, Eve's
violation of God's
command is said to have
led to the painfulness
of childbirth and the
subservience of women
to their husbands.

story of Adam and Eve is thus made a justification (though not the only one) of later activity involved with the expansion of Christendom.

Anthropologists have often found religious explanation, usually in the form of myth, used as a justification of practices in which a society engages. It appears that an institution is more strongly supported by people involved with it if it is directly relatable to understandings about the supernatural and the relations between humans and higher forces in the cosmos.

The idea that religious explanations can provide a "charter" for human institutions is a powerful one. The presentation of human institutions as an integral part of the plan of the universe and as having the endorsement of supernaturals naturally provides the institutions with a respectability and an inevitability that is much greater than they would otherwise have.

Religion as a force for social solidarity Besides explanation, another function of religion in human society is to stress to its members their common dependence on and participation in the cultural heritage that they share. When we see religion explaining why the human condition (or the condition of a particular person or group of people) is as it is, religion is not only explaining but also, in a sense, supporting that arrangement by making it fit into a larger picture. But religion can support people's sense of participation in a community in other ways as well. One of the most important ways is through religious rituals. For some anthropologists, ritual is the most important aspect of religion. The French sociologist Durkheim pointed out (1912) that participation in group religious activities has a very stimulating effect on the participant, which encourages him to accept the values of the group and to feel the moral imperatives that are implicit in group membership.

For example, Jones attends a Presbyterian church service, where he prays, sings hymns, and listens to a sermon together with many other people. Jones's sense of the correctness of the values and beliefs of Presbyterian Christianity is increased by his experience of apparently sharing these values and beliefs with other people also participating in the church ritual. At the same time, by publicly attending the Presbyterian church he is making a visible demonstration that he accepts the system of Presbyterian Christianity. Evidence suggests (Festinger 1956) that a visible, public commitment to a system of beliefs (particularly one that is not shared by the rest of the community) makes it much more difficult for an individual to withdraw his support from that system even in his own mind. (We recognize this when we say that someone has a "real investment" in an idea.) Jones's attendance at the Presbyterian service reinforces his Presbyterianism in two ways: First, it gives him the experience of acting out the rituals associated with his beliefs in the company of other people, showing him that he is not alone; and second, it makes a public statement of his support for the church from which he cannot withdraw inconspicuously (and which he is therefore led to support more vigorously).

Jones's neighbor, Smith, attends a Baptist church, which holds services at the same time the Presbyterians do. Another neighbor, Sandor, has just moved in. By attending the Presbyterian church Sandor is placing himself in the same community of believers as Jones. By attending the Baptist church he is placing himself in the same community of believers as Smith. By attending another church, he is separating himself (at least so far as membership in a religious community is concerned) from both of them. Because the services are held at the same time, there is no way he can attend both regularly. He has to choose. Once his choice is made, he is unavoidably more closely united with Jones (or Smith) than he was before, and his difference with his other neighbor is made much clearer because it is now a religious separation. In this way religion both symbolizes social bonds and boundaries and creates and maintains them.

The example of church membership is worth pursuing further. It develops that choice of a church expresses more than just the details of a member's theology. Thus, Sandor may pick the Presbyterian church rather than the Baptist church because (as in many American towns) Jones and other Presbyterians are wealthier or more educated than the Baptists, and Sandor wants to associate himself with that social class. (On the other hand he may prefer the Baptists because he feels "out of his element" among the Presbyterians.) A work by Wilson (1969) has shown that across the United States as a whole there is a fairly consistent relationship between church membership and social class. Presumably social class is not an integral part of religious belief in the minds of most Americans, but it is clear that participation in religious rituals with others "of the same kind" involves for Americans a reinforcement of values and understandings in many areas other than religious belief.

Something similar happens in Taiwan. The people of Bao-an engage collectively in a great many rituals that are related to their religious beliefs. There is one Christian family in Bao-an, theoretically excluded from traditional Chinese rituals because the local Christian church to which they belong formally opposes the rituals. The effect is to take the family out of the community in many other respects, and the family finds it difficult to maintain normal relations with its neighbors, even in activities that have no religious significance. Similarly, Bao-an people who move to other areas find that their religious practices must change to suit their new associates. Many villages in Taiwan send some of their young men (and occasionally a young woman) to universities. Taiwanese student culture is unreligious, occasionally antireligious, following a general desire on the part of students to be "progressive," "Western," or "modern." Many students discover that they are obliged to avoid traditional religious activities when they are at college because participation is regarded as a sign that they do not accept the "progressive" values of their peers and full membership in the community of college students. On the other hand, when they return to their villages, they find that they must participate in religious rituals because nonparticipation is regarded as a sign that they do not accept the values of their families and membership in them. Both memberships are important to them, and they usually find it necessary to demonstrate their loyalty to them symbolically by participation in rituals at home and nonparticipation at college.

Whether it is Sandor's decision to join Jones and the Presbyterians rather than Smith and the Baptists, or whether it is a Chinese college student's decision to be a religionist at home and an agnostic at school, the point is the same: Participation in religious ritual has a social aspect. It unites one with the others who also participate, and religious behavior is often influenced by the desire to symbolize a union with people with whom one feels united on nonreligious grounds, even as it may make people who have little else in common feel that a union exists among them.

Fruitful as it is to consider the effects of collective worship in achieving a sense of group solidarity, some theorists have objected that much religion is not social; that is to say, the ritual is not carried out in large groups, and there is neither the experience of group participation in ritual nor the public demonstration of participation in a shared ritual or in one sect rather than another. However, much private worship (or private divination or whatever) can imply a larger religious community, even if that community is not present at the time. The Haggadah service read in Jewish homes at Passover does not involve the physical presence of all Jews or even of a large number of Jews in the house. It is a household ritual, performed in a small group of family and friends, yet it implies the existence of all Jews as a special and relevant group in which the Haggadah participants are members (or at least sympathizers). Consider the following prayer, spoken toward the end of the service:

> Praised art Thou, Lord God, King of the Universe, for the vine and the fruit of the vine, [and for the produce of the field,] and for the pleasant, goodly, and ample land which Thou didst please to give us as inheritance to our Fathers, to eat of its fruit and to be satisfied with its goodness. Have mercy, Lord God, on Israel Thy People and Jerusalem Thy city and Zion the abode of Thy glory and on Thy altar and Thy shrine. Again build Thou Jerusalem the Holy City, speedily in our days [Roth 1965:109].

Note that each participant in this small-scale home ritual is reminded of his membership in "Israel Thy People." He is also reminded of the "ample land" inherited from his ancestors, where is located the semimystical city of "Jerusalem," in the reconstruction of which he has a special interest. Although the Hebrew nation is not physically present, the ritual implies its existence and the participation of the ritual participants in it. The effect is even amplified by the knowledge that all over the world other Jews are performing the same rites on the same day.

How Religion Is Believable

When the anthropologist is interested in how religion provides explanation, his focus is largely on myth and shared understandings about the supernatural and our relation to it. When he is especially interested in the social effects of religious activity, his attention will be attracted by ritual. Obviously, however, ritual and the understandings of religious culture are closely related. The understandings that people have about the nature of the supernatural and about the relation of human beings to supernatural forces often imply (or at least do not disallow) the rituals that they use to maintain their relations with the supernatural. This is clear in the Taiwanese case with which we began. Taiwanese understandings about the existence and importance of gods are entirely congruent with Taiwanese understandings about ways of communicating with the gods and of getting the gods to do what human beings need to have done. This is not to say that in theory a different system of rituals could not be associated with Taiwanese beliefs about gods; but given the Taiwanese beliefs, some sorts of rituals are required to maintain communication with them, and given the rituals (such as are used to initiate the new spirit medium, or such as include the spirit medium as the spokesman for a particular god), some sorts of beliefs are implied that include such understandings as: There are many gods, they are interested in the affairs of humans, they speak the same language as humans, there are demonic forces that must be guarded against, gods are powerful enough to be of assistance to human beings, disease can be divinely cured, and so forth. The Taiwanese rituals we have seen would make no sense at all in a Christian Science testimonial meeting. And the Taiwanese understandings about gods would not fit at all with Islamic calls to prayer at the mosque.

The relation between natural experience and the superhuman Many anthropologists have been interested in the system of understandings that holds religious belief and ritual together and makes both an integral part of a cultural system. Why is it, they ask, that a given religious system is found credible to people of a given culture? How do religious understandings fit with other understandings about the world? In religion more than in almost any other area of cultural studies anthropologists have tended to ask, "Why these understandings instead of other ones?" The answer has been sought in the proposition that religious understandings are structured in a way that is related to other understandings. People seem to "project" their experience of the natural and human world onto their conceptualization of the supernatural and superhuman world. Thus, we should find in religious beliefs and rituals, it is maintained, reflections of concerns and understandings about everyday affairs of human experience. Ideas are not very compelling if they are utterly unrelated to our experience of the world, and for beliefs about the supernatural to be believable, they must be beliefs that make sense in terms of what we know about the parts of the world that are available to direct experience.

The possible usefulness of this approach has been evident in a number of fascinating findings that have emerged from it. For example, several investigators have discovered what seems to be a relationship between the characteristics attributed to deities and the characteristics children attribute to their parents. In societies in which parents are rough or punitive with children, gods are believed to be inclined to punish people. But in societies in which parents are (comparatively more) gentle and supporting, gods are more often seen as helpful and inclined to alleviate human distress. This finding (which we have rather grotesquely oversimplified here)[16] does not mean that understandings about gods are invented by children or that any individual invents his gods when he grows up on the basis of his experience as a child. What it suggests is that over a long period of time the type of supernatural being that strikes people as most convincing, most to be attended to, and most to be taken seriously as an important element in life is one that accords with their experience of what it means to have ultimate power. And the clearest case of human experience with ultimate power and ultimate

Virgin Mother Carried in Procession in Bolivia. In Catholic countries in which mothers are far more nurturant and supportive than fathers, particular emphasis is placed on Mary, the Virgin Mother, whose qualities are an idealization of those associated with actual mothers.

[16]See Whiting and Child (1953), Young (1965), Swanson (1968), and Spiro and D'Andrade (1958) for more sophisticated statements.

helplessness is the helplessness of the human infant and the comparative omnipotence of its mother or father. When we conceive of beings with power vastly greater (and less understandable) than our own, it is apparently this model that we are best able to understand and relate to. With our memories of our helplessness and our relationship with omnipotent parents come memories of how that power was administered and how it was to be manipulated.

Apparently religious ideas that reflect these impressions are the ones a person is liable to find most readily acceptable and convincing. Each individual learns his religious understandings in the same way he comes to learn other understandings that make up his culture. But the credibility and force of these understandings come not just from the fact that other people hold them or that they "are his culture," but from the fact that they fit into a pattern of his experience and make sense in terms of what he has been through. The despair of many a missionary is not that the people among whom he works do not understand his message, but that they are not very interested in it. What he seldom realizes is that the view of the supernatural that he presents may be at variance with the understandings about what omnipotence or supernatural power and understanding can be like.

Cultural understandings such as those about how power is used are not limited to relations between parents and children or between humans and gods. Such understandings often emerge over and over again in the everyday organization of a people's activities. There are power differences between social classes too, for example. Not surprisingly, there is some correlation between the presence of clearly differentiated social classes in a society and the view that supernatural beings are inclined to punish humans. Table 16 shows the distribution of beliefs about supernatural punishment and of distinct social classes in forty-seven societies.

It appears that differences in power (and apparently disadvantages to those in positions of less power) can be very pervasive themes in a culture. Experience of this situation is not limited to infancy (although it is universal in infancy), but continues through life in many societies. It is a tempting hypothesis that such an experience in the sphere of everyday life makes it especially credible that the postulated gods, who hold much greater super-

Table 16 Beliefs about Supernatural Punishment[a]

		SUPERNATURAL PENALTIES	
		Present	Absent
Social Classes	Present	25	2
	Absent	8	12
			Total = 47 societies

[a]Probability of getting this table if the relationship is random: 5 chances in 10,000 ($p = .0005$).

SOURCE: Adapted from Swanson 1960:166.

natural power, should also have some definite advantages and require close submission on the part of human beings.[17] When supernatural beings use their power in a way that resembles the use of power by human beings who have it, the situation is familiar and makes sense to the religious participant. When supernatural beings use their power in other ways, the situation is less familiar and less believable. Supernaturals who resemble human beings in this respect can be expected to show much greater viability over long periods of time than those who do not.

The proposition that religious understandings are related to (or are an extension of) secular understandings enables us to develop a large number of more specific propositions about particular religious beliefs and behavior and gives us a way of accounting for understandings that do not make very much sense otherwise. Most of the gods the people of Bao-an believe in are, as noted, deified human beings. The Third Prince, for example, has a human biography known to many from a popular classical novel. (The fact that many gods have no historically verifiable existence as human beings is irrelevant to the belief that almost all gods were once human beings even if we have no records of their life on earth.) It follows that human beings now on earth have the possibility before them of becoming gods when they die, and, indeed, one man in Bao-an during my stay was thought by some to have done so.

If we are to see in understandings about gods a reflection of understandings about human life, we are led to ask how it is that people can be promoted to godhood, and it becomes interesting to explore the possibility that mobility through a hierarchy of ranked positions may be a very important part of the Chinese view of the world. Suddenly we can see a relationship between the tradition of social mobility represented by the classical Chinese civil service system (China was the first nation in the world to have a civil service system designed to promote people to the highest positions of the land on the basis of merit) and the possibility of mobility from human to godly status. We also see a special importance in the tight hierarchy of positions in the patriarchal Chinese family and the fact that a person's position in his family advances through a series of discrete stages, each with greater and greater prestige and greater and greater authority. It is not clear how far we want to push an analysis of Chinese understandings about hierarchy and mobility, but at least tentatively the Chinese belief that gods are deified human beings seems to fit with Chinese beliefs about officialdom and about family organization in a way that suggests broader organizing understandings among these things than we would have suspected before.

The issue is not always so straightforward, however. Supernatural beings are often of several different kinds, and people's views of them by no means

---

[17]Swanson (1968) also finds correlations between supernatural punishment and the presence of considerable debt in the society and between supernatural punishment and systems of inheritance in which the first son receives everything and subsequent siblings receive nothing. Obviously, our hypothesis about power is strengthened by these correlations, which, though significant, are not as strong as the correlation with social classes.

always depend on anything so simple as power differences in society. Most cultures include understandings about negative, evil, or demonic forces that frustrate our efforts to accomplish our earthly goals. Demons are often made responsible for disease or death. Often demons seem to have the features of human life that human beings fear the most, including especially the character traits, secret desires, and destructive urges that we most fear in our own psychic makeup. Melford Spiro's work on the Pacific atoll of Ifaluk can provide an example. The total land area of Ifaluk is only $^6/_{10}$ of a mile square. On this tiny fragment of land there were, when Spiro visited it in 1947, some 250 inhabitants. For this many people to live together on so little land, Spiro argues, it is essential that conflict and uncooperativeness be avoided as far as possible. In fact, people get along very well together, and open aggression is virtually nonexistent. Even sorcery seems extremely rare, though it is not unknown. Aggression and hostility seem to have been effectively suppressed in Ifaluk until we look into Ifaluk understandings about supernatural beings. Spiro tells us that the supernatural in Ifaluk is unrelentingly hostile. The hostility that people in Ifaluk apparently do not express but often do feel (at least subconsciously) has been attributed to demonic ghosts. A tremendous amount of psychic energy must be devoted to repressing hostility and aggressiveness in each person, and a great deal of concern is expressed about ghosts. The ghosts can be defended against publicly, however. Spiro would see Ifaluk concern with keeping the aggressive ghosts at bay as a cultural enactment of what is in fact a very private, unconscious worry about keeping the aggression and hostility of each individual under control. The supernatural here is not a reflection of actually existing human behavior; instead, it is a reflection of human experience that is being deliberately and vigorously repressed. The belief in the ghosts and the activities engaged in to prevent the ghosts from harming human beings constitute what Spiro calls a "culturally constituted defense mechanism." This mechanism aids individuals in keeping their own hostility under control because they project their hostile feelings onto the ghosts and practice hostility against them (which is culturally approved). Not all religious understandings can be interpreted as culturally constituted defense mechanisms, but the concept of the culturally constituted defense mechanism is extremely useful in our attempts to understand the psychological importance of many of the understandings people have about the supernatural and how to deal with it.

Spiro makes the case particularly convincing in his examination of Ifaluk ethnography. The pattern of attributing aggression and hostility to supernaturals rather than to humans is in fact fairly widespread in the Pacific. Inez de Beauclair, writing of the Yami, inhabitants of the island of Botel Tobago off the southeastern coast of Taiwan, writes as follows:

> The history of the Pacific proves that the inhabitants of isolated islands do not welcome strangers to their shores. Fearing an attack and greedy for foreign goods, they kill the intruders.
>
> The Yami's oral traditions are strangely silent about such events, though their occurrence is proved by documentation. . . .

It is of interest . . . that historically documented events though dramatic and of importance often fail to enter into the folkloristic repertoire of archaic peoples. These happenings more often than not concern acts of brutality, murder and killings. Lessa [a noted authority on the Pacific] himself notes the instance of the murder of a Spanish missionary, Father Cantova, and his group on Ulithi atoll in the western Carolines in 1719. The memory of this incident, as Lessa convinces himself during his stay on the atoll, had completely vanished. It had not become the object of a narrative that, told and retold, continues to live. It had died with the slayer and the witnesses of the scene.

The phenomenon of omittance puzzles the folklorist and has not yet been explained. However, referring to the Yami, they, as most archaic peoples, live in fear of the spirits of the dead, the *anito* [Beauclair 1969:123–124].

The pattern described by Beauclair, generalizing for the Pacific as a whole, but concentrating upon the Yami, fits very closely with the finding of Spiro in Ifaluk: Hostility and aggression in actual human activities are denied and repressed as much as possible, but these unsavory emotions are attributed to supernatural beings who must be defended against and who are objects of great cultural concern largely because of their symbolic attributes. It is about the ghosts that folklore is generated, not about acts of human aggression, which is better forgotten.

The project of seeking patterning common to religious understandings and to other understandings is by no means always so straightforward as finding that gods are in general parentlike or that a society in which aggression is not allowed expression in interpersonal relations may express its anxieties about aggression in a fear of aggressive ghosts. The work of Lévi-Strauss and his followers on myth has suggested that religious and mythological motifs may focus on general problems of human existence that cannot be resolved. Indeed, Lévi-Strauss suggests that it is problems that cannot be resolved that form the basis for most mythic formulation. In an important paper published in 1955 Lévi-Strauss provides an analysis of the Greek myth of Oedipus in which he tries to show that the story of Oedipus is built up of a series of irresolvable contrasts, each of which represents a contradiction in the human analysis of things. The details of the argument are too elaborate for discussion here, but what is of interest is that the *kinds* of problems to which Lévi-Strauss finds myths address themselves are such questions as (in the case of the Oedipus myth): the undervaluing as opposed to the overvaluing of kinship relations (What are the ties of kinship really about?) or self-made as opposed to descended creatures (How much am I a product of my ancestry or my tradition and how much am I unique?). It is because of the importance of these problems in human experience that their symbolization in myth and ritual renders the myth or ritual interesting to its listeners, and it is because these problems cannot ever be entirely resolved that a myth can continue to be interesting and that the problems can generate large numbers of myths. (In his monumental series of volumes called collectively *Mythologiques* Lévi-Strauss traces the same theme through hundreds of myths in South America.)

Of course, for a myth or ritual to be compelling, one must be able (at least at an unconscious level) to understand the symbolism that is involved in it. People are not motivated by ideas they do not have, and they do not respond to stimuli that they do not (at least unconsciously) detect. Lévi-Strauss has been criticized for apparently assuming that where he can find patterning, the same patterning is of importance to the people he is describing. A thorough study of a religious system with emphasis on the understandings that people have about it and the symbols in it that evoke responses of recognition, however vague, in its participants requires a very long exposure to the culture studied. It also requires a careful analysis of the understandings that are symbolized and how they are organized by participants' shared understandings in such a way that participants have any probability at all of sensing a relationship between a given myth (say) and the world of everyday experience. The significance of placing a red scarf on an altar, for example, cannot readily be interpreted by the ethnographer seeking its relation to other understandings until he knows what understandings people in the culture have about altars, about scarves, and about the color red.[18]

The key problem in the anthropological analysis of religion today is credibility: How is it that people find a given set of ideas about the supernatural compelling and believable? The answer seems to lie in the discovery that patterns of understandings about the supernatural are related to patterns of understandings about other things. The understandings of the supernatural and the understandings of the secular, workaday world reinforce each other at numerous crucial points, and each gives an increased sense of inevitability to the other. This realization is summed up in Clifford Geertz's already classic contemporary characterization of religion as a cultural system: "A religion is a system of symbols which acts to establish powerful, pervasive, and long-lasting moods and motivations in men by formulating conceptions of a general order of existence and clothing these conceptions with such an aura of factuality that the moods and motivations seem uniquely realistic" (1966:4).

Religious understandings and their associated behaviors are to be interpreted symbolically, Geertz is telling us, and when so interpreted, they can be shown to reflect human experience in culturally relevant ways. The effect of the religious expression of patterns of understandings is to increase the credibility of these patterns as an inevitable way of viewing the world. Basic understandings and their entailed subordinate understandings attain an "aura of factuality" that makes that particular organization of the world, those particular understandings, "unique" in that they are seen to be more realistic than other understandings, whether nonshared personal understandings or the shared understandings of another group of people. In this way

[18]A particularly outstanding example of the close analysis of possible symbolic content of ritual activity is Victor Turner's The Forest of Symbols (1967), which describes ritualism among the Ndembu of Zambia.

the religious system is able to maintain the morale and the motivation of people involved in it. For this reason, too, an attack (as by missionaries) on the religious understandings of a people weakens the coherence and perceived validity of larger organizations of understandings in the culture and has an effect that goes beyond change in the religious sphere alone. Similarly, a change in other areas of a culture, to the extent that it involves new organizations of understandings (as about ties of kinship, the expression of aggression, or how children should be cared for), may be expected to cause changes in the emphasis and total organization of religious belief.

SUMMARY

Religious understandings are part of culture, just as other understandings are, and the anthropologist's task is to understand them, not to judge them. For purposes of cross-cultural analysis, religion is defined as belief in spiritual beings and forces. The postulation of such beings or forces is nearly universal in human society, but there is little necessary similarity between the supernatural beings postulated in one society and those postulated in another. Chinese and ancient Greek religion are different from each other and from Islam in their view of the nature of the supernatural. The postulation of supernatural beings normally involves understandings about how human beings communicate with supernatural ones, typically through prayer and divination. Although there is almost no limit to the number of potential channels of communication in divination, a problem for anthropological attention is the way in which the means of divination is suited to the conceptualization of the supernatural.

Shamanism refers to routine spirit possession of a person for the purposes of divination or healing. In his trance the shaman can represent the presence of supernatural beings among mortals. He contrasts with the priest, who is a religious practitioner qualified to perform rituals on behalf of the community that are directed to supernatural beings. The status expectations and social prestige of shamans and priests vary tremendously from society to society.

Belief in nonindividualized supernatural force (mana) is widespread. The practitioners who use ritual to make use of mana to affect the world (as to cure or cause illness) are sorcerers. Sorcerers are distinguished by anthropologists from witches, who also bring about changes through the operation of mana, but do so without conscious manipulation of mana through ritual. Rituals for the manipulation of mana are referred to as magic.

Religion functions in society to provide explanations for the human situation, often through myth. One typical situation is the justification of a contemporary institution by reference to a myth, such as the justification of missionary activity by reference to the Sin of Adam. Another function of religion is promoting social solidarity within or among some groups or statuses rather than others. On the one hand, religious belief is justified in the mind of the participant by his seeing that it is shared, and, on the other, it provides a context for the participant's public demonstration of his belief and cooperation in the community of participants and their shared religious understandings.

Religion appears to be believable when it invokes the same kinds of understandings as other areas of experience. Recent research suggests a relationship between key religious themes of a culture and experience of members of society in a wide variety of other status relationships and spheres of cultural understanding.

SUGGESTED READINGS

More on the case

DIAMOND, NORMA 1969 K'un Shen: A Taiwan Village. New York: Holt.

A general ethnography of a Taiwanese village located not far from the one mentioned in the text.

JORDAN, DAVID K. 1972 Gods, Ghosts, and Ancestors: The Folk Religion of a Taiwanese Village. Berkeley: University of California Press.

A further discussion of the religious system of the village mentioned in the text, including further information on the Chinese spirit mediums that are the core of our case.

Other readings

CANNON, WALTER B. 1942 Voodoo Death. American Anthropologist 44:169–181.

This is a rather gory explanation of the psychology and physiology of death by autosuggestion, complete with descriptions of the pathico-adrenal and sympatico-adrenal systems of vivisected cats and the like. This paper is relevant to the understanding of religions by being a particularly vivid instance of the power of belief and the importance of cultural systems in the individual's construction of reality. This article is cited in the text in connection with witchcraft, but the general issue of culturally mediated constructions of reality is a theme throughout this book.

DOBZHANSKY, T. 1965 Religion, Death, and Evolutionary Adaptation. *In* Context and Meaning in Cultural Anthropology. Melford E. Spiro, Ed. New York: Free Press. pp. 61–73.

This brief article speculates on the importance of "death awareness," presumably a religious feeling, in human evolution.

EPSTEIN, SCARLETT 1959 A Sociological Analysis of Witch Beliefs in a Mysore Village. The Eastern Anthropologist 12:234–251.

A study of witchcraft from the perspective of the analysis of social structure.

GEERTZ, CLIFFORD   1966   Religion as a Cultural System. *In* Anthropological Approaches to the Study of Religion. Michael Banton, Ed. London: Tavistock. ASA #3. pp. 1–46.

This essay presents the "definition" of religion that is quoted in the chapter on religion. It is probably one of the most enlightening and useful works available on the function of religion in helping people to construe reality by means of cultural symbols. Geertz's view of culture is very similar to the view taken in the text.

HOMANS, GEORGE C.   1941   Anxiety and Ritual: The Theories of Malinowski and Radcliffe-Brown. American Anthropologist 43:164–172.

This famous article provides a summary and attempted resolution of one of the most controversial problems in anthropology: the relation of magical practices to the resolution of anxiety.

MANDELBAUM, DAVID C.   1941   Social Trends and Personal Pressures. *In* Language, Culture, and Personality: Essays in Memory of Edward Sapir. Leslie Spier et al., Eds. Menasha, Wis.: Sapir Memorial Publication Fund.

This paper, on the personalities of religious personnel in India, discusses who does and who does not become a religious specialist and how the religious specialist fits into the community.

SCHWARTZ, THEODORE   1973   Cult and Context: The Paranoid Ethos in Melanesia. Ethos 1:153–174.

An interpretation of New Guinea cargo cults as a religious reaction to changing circumstances, which seeks to make the changes in people's situation intelligible in terms of familiar categories of experience. Schwartz seeks to relate the particular form this type of religious interpretation takes to wider themes in New Guinea cultural and psychological life.

9

Language

If I do not know the meaning of the sound the speaker makes, his words will be gibberish to me, and mine to him.

1 CORINTHIANS 14:11

French-Flemish language riot in Brussels.

How do anthropologists analyze language?

How does language reflect cultural understandings about the world?

What models does the study of language provide for the study of other aspects of culture?

How is language related to social structure?

Zamenhof and Esperanto: A Case of Creating a Language

L. L. Zamenhof (1859–1917) was a Warsaw oculist, remembered as the author of Esperanto, an artificially created language designed to serve for all humanity as a second language that would be easy to learn and politically neutral. Zamenhof's objectives and some of his problems in creating Esperanto are set out in the following letter, which he wrote in Russian to a certain N. Borovko.[1]

I was born Byelostok [Polish: Bialystok] (15 December 1859, the 3rd of December in the Russian calendar), in the province of Grodno, in Poland. This place of my birth and of my childhood years gave direction to all my future endeavors. The inhabitants of Byelostok consisted of four diverse elements: Russians, Poles, Germans, and Jews. Each of these elements spoke a separate language and had hostile relations with the other elements. In that town more than anywhere an impressionable soul might feel the heavy sadness of language diversity and become convinced at every step that the diversity of languages was the single, or at least the primary, force which divided the human family into unfriendly parts. I was educated as an idealist; I was taught that all men were brothers, while at the same time in the street and in the court at every step everything made me feel that men as such did not exist: only Russians, Poles, Germans, Jews, and the like existed.

Little by little I discovered, of course, that everything is not so easy as it seems to a child. One after

another I cast aside my various childish utopianisms, and the dream of a single human language was the only one I kept with me. I was somehow pulled toward it, though of course without any clearly defined plans. I don't remember just when, but certainly very early, I developed the awareness that the single language could only be a neutral one, belonging to none of the existing nations. When I went on from the "Byelostok Real School" (then already called the gymnasium) to the second-class gymnasium in Warsaw, I was attracted for a time to the ancient languages, and dreamed that I would some time travel through the whole world and give inflammatory speeches to convince people to revive one of these languages for common use. Later—I don't remember how anymore—I came to the firm conclusion that that would be impossible, and I began to dream, however unclearly, of a *new*, artificial language.

I often began new attempts, in those days, and thought out hugely rich artificial declensions and conjugations and so on.

I had learned German and French in childhood, when one cannot yet make comparisons and draw conclusions, but when I began learning English in the 5th class, the simplicity of English grammar leaped before my eyes, especially thanks to the abrupt transition from Latin and Greek grammars. I noted that a richness of grammatical forms is merely a blind historical accident, not a necessity for a language. Under this influence I began looking through my language and throwing out unnecessary forms, and I found that the grammar began to thaw in my hands. Soon I came to the most minimal grammar, which occupied no more than a few pages, without detriment to the language. And I began to give myself over more seriously to my dream.

Once, when I was in the 7th class of the gymnasium, I noticed the formation of the [Russian] word *shveytsarskaya* (porter's lodge) which I had seen many times, and of the word *kondityerskaya*

---

[1]An Esperanto translation of this letter appeared in *Lingvo Internacia*, 1896, Numbers 6-7. The present text is abridged and retranslated from the Esperanto as quoted in Edmond Privat, 1912, Historio de la Lingvo Esperanto: Deveno Kaj Komenco 1887-1900, The Hague: Internacia Esperanto-Instituto, pp. 22-31.

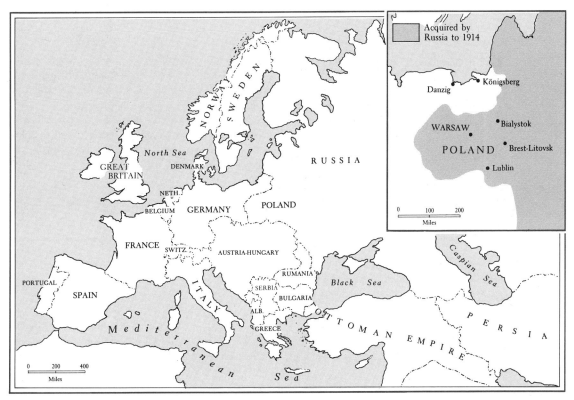

Europe at the End of the Nineteenth Century.

(confectioner's shop). This *-skaya* interested me, and showed me that suffixes provide the possibility of making from one word a number of others which don't have to be separately learned. This idea took complete possession of me.

"The problem [of vocabulary] is solved!" I said to myself. I took the idea of suffixes and began to work enthusiastically in that direction. I began comparing words and looking for constant, definite relations among them, and every day I threw large series of words out of my dictionary, and substituted for them a single suffix defining a certain relationship. I found that a huge number of words

expressed by a base form (e.g., mother, narrow, knife) could be easily transformed into common words [plus suffixes][2] and thus vanish from the vocabulary. The mechanics of the language were now before me, as though in the palm of my hand, and I began to work regularly on it, with love and hope. Soon after that I had written the entire grammar and a small vocabulary.

I should say a few words about the material for

[2]In modern Esperanto: *patr-in-o* (= parent + feminine + noun), *mal-larĝ-a* (= opposite + wide + adjective), *tranĉ-il-o* (= cut + instrument + noun).

L. L. Zamenhof. Zamenhof, an oculist in Warsaw at the turn of this century, believed that the creation of an easily learned, politically neutral language would promote better relations between nations.

convinced me that made-up words were very difficult to learn, and even harder to remember. I became convinced that the material for the vocabulary would have to be Romance and Germanic, changed only as much as was required by regularity and other important conditions of the language. I observed that modern languages already possessed a large stock of available words that were already international, were known to all peoples, and would provide a supply for the future international language. And of course I used that supply.

In the year 1878 the language was already more or less ready, although there was still a great difference between my "lingwe uniwersala" of that time and Esperanto as it is spoken today. I told my friends about the project—I was then in the 8th class of the gymnasium. Most of them were attracted to the idea and struck by the extraordinary easiness of the language and they began to learn it. The 5th of December 1878 we solemnly celebrated the birth of the language. During this celebration there were speeches in the new language, and we enthusiastically sang our anthem, which began as follows:

Malamikete de la nacjes
Kadó, kadó, jam temp' está!
La tot' homoze in familje
Konunigare so debá.

In modern Esperanto this would be:

Malamikeco de la nacioj
falu, falu jam tempo estas!
La tuta homaro en familion
unuîĝi devas.

(Hatreds between nations
Fall away, the time is here!
All humanity into a family
must unite.)

the vocabulary. Much earlier, when I was going through the grammar and throwing out everything unnecessary, I wanted to use principles of economy for words also; and, convinced that it made no difference what form a word had if we simply "agreed" that it expressed a given idea, I simply thought up words, trying to make them short and to avoid having too many letters in them. I said to myself that instead of the 8-letter word "converse," we could equally well express the same notion by, for example, the 2-letter word "pa." Therefore I simply wrote a mathematical series of the shortest easily pronounced combinations of letters, and to each of them I gave the significance of a defined word (thus a, ab, ac, ad, . . . ba, ca, da, . . . e, eb, ec, . . . be, ce, . . . aba, aca, . . . etc.). But I discarded this thought immediately, for the experiments which I did myself

On the table, besides the grammar and vocabulary, lay a few translations into the new language.

Thus ended the first period of the language. I was still too young to come out with my work publicly, and I decided to wait another five or six years and during that time to try out the language carefully and work it out practically. Half a year after the celebration of the 5th of December we finished at the gymnasium and went our several ways. The future apostles of the language tried to talk a little bit about a "new language," and meeting the ridicule of grown-ups, they immediately gave it up; I remained entirely alone. Foreseeing only ridicule and persecution, I decided to hide my work from everyone.

For six years I worked perfecting and trying the language, and I put in a good deal of work, even though the language had seemed all ready in 1878. I translated a good deal into my language, and wrote original works in it, and these further efforts showed me that what had seemed all ready to me theoretically was not yet ready practically. I had to chop out, substitute, correct, and radically transform a lot of things. Words and forms, principles and postulates pushed and obstructed each other, when in theory, entirely apart and in short experiments, they had seemed entirely satisfactory.

But practice convinced me more and more that the language still needed a certain uncapturable "something," the uniting element that gives a language life and defines a completely formed "spirit."

I began to avoid literal translation from one to another language and tried to think directly in the neutral language. Later I found that the language in my hands had already ceased to become a pale shadow of some other language with which I was concerned at any given moment, and had received its own spirit, its own life, a uniquely defined and clearly expressed physiognomy, no longer dependent upon any sort of outside influence. The words flowed of themselves, flexibly, gracefully, and entirely freely, just like a living, mother tongue.

I finished the university and began my medical practice. And now I had begun to think about the publication of my work. I prepared the manuscript of my first *booklet* (*An International Language*: *Preface and First Textbook*, by Dr. Esperanto [one who hopes] and set out to find a publisher. At last, after long efforts, I was able to publish the *booklet* myself in July of 1887. I was very excited before it came out. I felt that I stood at a Rubicon and that the day when my *booklet* would appear I should no longer be able to turn back. But I could not give up the idea that had entered my body and blood; I crossed the Rubicon.

Zamenhof Arriving at Conference Hall in Antwerp for Seventh Universal Congress of Esperanto in 1911. The language Zamenhof invented attracted enough interest so that an international congress was held in France in 1905 and has been held yearly since except in time of war.

Analysis of the Case

Zamenhof's struggle with the language problem in nineteenth-century War-saw and ultimately his creation of a new language (which came to be called Esperanto) provide us with a view of a large number of problems in social, cultural, and psychological life that are all related to language. Language is so much a part of human life that anthropologists have long had a special concern with it, and the analysis of language, to which anthropological studies have importantly contributed, has in recent decades emerged as the separate discipline of linguistics.

Zamenhof, even as a child, was impressed with the fact that particular languages were associated with particular groups and were an important part of the self-image of each of those groups when they were in contact with other groups. Thus, the Russian officials who ran Warsaw (which at that time was, like most of the rest of Poland, a part of the Russian Empire) were distinguished from the Poles both in their own minds and in the minds of the Poles themselves by the fact that they spoke Russian rather than Polish. Indeed, it was a point of official Russian policy in the late 1800s to try to integrate Poland into Russia by restricting the use of the Polish lan-guage and encouraging the teaching of Russian in hopes that Poles would come to think of themselves as Russians.

The Russian policy reflected more than just a realization of the tendency of people to identify themselves with the language group to which they belong. It seemed to reflect also a notion that Russian was "better" than Polish, and a language that was somehow more "moral" or more "proper" to speak. We noted earlier that cultural understandings have a moral com-ponent, that is, that they are perceived as natural and inevitable conse-quences of reality and, therefore, as being the best view of things. A language, too, can have a moral quality, for it is often perceived by its speakers as the "best" or "natural" way to speak. The attitude of the Russian administrators in Poland was that people "ought" to speak Russian, and if they did not, it was their error.

Within Polish society itself, Jews were often thought of, both by them-selves and by their fellow Poles, as being a distinct nationality, not "real" Poles. Zamenhof attributed much of the distinctiveness of Jews in Poland to the fact that they spoke Yiddish, a language derived from German but written in Hebrew script. To the Poles (and to the Russians) the Yiddish-speaking Jews were "foreigners," association with them was avoided, and their activities were restricted because they were thought to be dangerous to Christian Polish society. To the Jews, however, the same language was a treasured mark of their particular heritage and identified them as a distinc-tive and, in many ways, superior group. The importance of language as a symbol of group identity both to the speakers of that language and to out-siders who do not speak it and the feeling that one's own language is superior to other languages are two of the most important and widespread phe-nomena that anthropologists have encountered in intergroup relations.

Whether Zamenhof was right in attributing intolerance and conflict exclusively to language is doubtful. But he correctly noted that at least in Warsaw there were few intergroup antagonisms that did not involve the language problem in some way sooner or later.

Zamenhof's work on Esperanto encountered a great many difficulties, not just in gaining acceptance—the movement to promote it remains small to this day[3]—but in creating the language itself. In thinking about the problems involved in creating a language, Zamenhof necessarily reflected on the different ways in which the languages he knew seemed to arrange the world and to present it in speech. Latin and Greek, he remarks, seemed to put great stress on changes in the terminations of words (called inflections) to indicate relationships between the words of a sentence. Mastering these inflections (and irregularities in them) was one of the major obstacles to learning those classical languages. Polish and Russian are also characterized by forms of this kind. English, by contrast, made much greater use of word order to accomplish what Latin and Greek accomplished with endings, namely, showing how words are related to each other to build larger units of meaning in sentences. It was the observation of this variation between the languages he had studied earlier and English that led Zamenhof to

[3]The number of Esperanto speakers in the world in the 1970s has been variously estimated to be from a few hundred thousand to several million. Many of their activities are coordinated through the Universal Esperanto Association, founded in 1908 and located in Rotterdam, the Netherlands, since 1946.

Esperanto Congress in Varna, Bulgaria, 1978. Zamenhof's language has not been widely accepted, but it is Zamenhof's logic in creating it and decisions he had to make about its structure that provide the jumping-off place for our concerns in this chapter.

consider alternatives for the language he was creating. In the end he elected a grammatical system for Esperanto that was more inflected than English but less inflected than the other languages he knew. He defended this on the grounds that the endings in Esperanto permitted freedom of word order, but he also defended having only a few of them on the grounds that the language was easier to learn that way.

Zamenhof also had to face the problem of what information a language needed to encode about the world. For example, was it important to classify all statements according to the time by having a present tense, future tense, and past tense as in many European languages, or could the time of an action be left out of most sentences unless it was an important point in the discussion as in many Asian and Austronesian languages? Western languages generally require that verbs show the time of the action. Esperanto verbs all show tense. If Zamenhof had known Vietnamese, say, or Malay, he might perhaps have decided that time was not something one needed to know in every sentence and might have constructed verbs without tense. Polish and Russian verbs also always indicate whether an action is completed or continuing. Zamenhof chose not to include this distinction in his verbs. Such decisions could not have been easy for him, at least in cases where the languages with which he was familiar were different from each other. When a language requires that some information be coded into a sentence, the speaker is obliged to observe the world in such a way as to be able to provide the necessary information. If the Russian speaker must decide whether an action is continuing or completed in order to select the right verb (or form of a verb) to describe it, surely he must come to pay attention to continuation and completion in actions he perceives. Does this affect the way he thinks about the world? Does it affect the features of a situation that he perceives or fails to perceive? These questions have not yet been satisfactorily answered, and whatever Zamenhof's conclusions, his decision to include or exclude any given feature as a necessary part of his language must surely have raised doubts in his mind about the philosophical implications that he was going to build into his grammar.

This problem was not limited to tenses of verbs and whether or not verbs should show actions as continuing or completed. Indeed, the problem was not confined to grammar. There is a structure, too, to the vocabulary. We saw in the chapter on family and kinship that various societies recognize different kinship statuses. Esperanto would have to have terms to be used in naming kinship statuses. But which ones? If it were to be an international language, what decision could be made that would in fact be satisfactory to all of its potential speakers? What about other statuses in society or other cultural categories?

Culture involves shared understandings, and many of these understandings are concerned with categories in which a given object, person, relationship, or event may be placed. Consider some cultural categories reflected in English nouns: Jones is a "Methodist"; Smith is a "ratfink"; that is a "salad fork"; she is my "maiden aunt"; his crime was a "felony"; they are "newly-weds." Such categories as these are by no means universal. A felony is a particular type of offense in English common law. The status newlywed is not distinctive to American culture, but the implications of overtures from eager silverware merchants are perhaps different in America from other places. A maiden aunt is a feature of English society whose position is quite unlike that of unwed women in most other societies. The category ratfink is peculiarly American; even though similar categories are named in many other languages, the exact connotations of the word and the particular behaviors that cause one to be classified as a ratfink in America are a product of American shared understandings, not of the natural world. Cultural categories may or may not line up very well from one culture to another, and the words that label them are often not easily translatable from one language to another. In a sense, in creating his language, either Zamenhof had to assume a culture to which the language would be appropriate (and thereby face the possibility that it would not be a truly neutral medium) or he had to create a culture to go with it. (Perhaps one secret of such success as Esperanto has enjoyed is that its use is restricted almost entirely to participants in European culture and almost entirely to international contexts in which other languages also have difficulty because of not being able to handle several different sets of shared understandings.)

Although he does not mention it in the passage that opened the chapter, Zamenhof also had to decide what sounds were to be used in his language. In his instructions on how it should be spoken, he indicated that the pronunciation of all but a few letters should follow Italian or Spanish. Unfortunately for the phonetically precise, Italian and Spanish are not in full agreement about the pronunciations of many of the sounds they have in

Kindergarten for Native-Speaking Esperantists. The children in this photo are sons and daughters of Esperantists from various countries who have had only Esperanto as a common home language. Like other Esperantists, the children speak the language with slightly different accents; but variation in pronunciation of a sound does not interfere with conversation as long as each sound is clearly different from each other sound.

common. However, Zamenhof himself realized (and many Esperantists later came to discover) that there was in fact room for a good deal of variation in the pronunciation of any given sound so long as none of the variants became too similar to variants of any other sound recognized in the language. The issue of what sounds are recognized and how much variation is allowable (or required) has been one of great importance for our understanding of how language works and has provided an important model for much cultural analysis. And the principle that variation is tolerable (and, under certain circumstances, desirable) only so long as it does not cause confusion seems to be applicable to much of culture. For this reason, we shall discuss the sounds of language and discuss them first of all. Then we shall look at some other structural problems and the ways in which different languages classify experience into categories. Next we shall consider the use of language as a sign or symbol that the speaker occupies a certain social status, and finally we shall consider problems of language variants.

The Sounds of Language: Phonemes

The human body is capable of producing an extraordinary variety of sounds, from whispers to shrieks to clapping of hands and growling of stomachs. Any sound that can be voluntarily controlled can be used in culturally patterned ways for communication. Thus, it is a European tradition that an audience expresses approval of a dramatic performance by clapping the hands. Even more enthusiastic approval may be shown by standing up while applauding. In French theatre disapproval is shown by whistling.

Most communication by voluntary noisemaking occurs as speech, of course, and involves the sounds that can be made with the mouth, throat, and nasal cavity. The variety of sounds that can be voluntarily produced with these organs and distinguished by the ear of a listener when they are produced is almost infinite. Raising or lowering the tongue, even very slightly, rounding or flattening the lips, allowing more or less air to pass into the nasal cavity while one speaks—all of these have a detectable effect upon the sound that is produced. Accordingly, all of them may be used to generate the sounds of language.

As Zamenhof noted, language is a set of cultural conventions or shared understandings. Bread is not called bread because there is any association between its ingredients and the combination of muscle movements needed to pronounce the English word "bread," but because English speakers share an understanding that the sounds "bread" will arbitrarily be allowed to represent that object. Naturally, different languages make use of the total, infinite set of possibilities differently.

Significant sounds   Every language that has ever been investigated identifies a relatively small number (between about 10 and about 150) of sounds that are culturally understood to be different from each other and that are then combined to form the words and phrases of the language. These significant sounds are called "phonemes." As we shall see below, one of the most important features of a phoneme is that it is regarded by native speakers as clearly a different sound from any other phoneme. The *f* sound represented in the English words "off," "enough," and "phantom" is a phoneme of English.[4] Similarly, the *t* sound of "Tabby," "scat," and "Tuscaloosa" is a phoneme of English. Linguists describe phonemes (and nonphonemic speech sounds) by the positions of the speech organs involved and by the manner of articulation, refinements that need not detain us unduly here. For the linguist, the *t* sound, which is made by stopping the air briefly by pressing the tip of the tongue against the "alveolar ridge" (the ridge behind the upper teeth), is an "alveolar stop." (Or, since it is the apex, or tip, of the tongue that is pressed against the alveolar ridge, it may be called an "apico-alveolar stop.") Inasmuch as the vocal cords are not used in pronouncing a *t* sound (unlike the similarly located *d* sound), the linguist can more precisely describe it by saying it is a "voiceless alveolar stop." The accompanying illustration shows the major parts of the speech apparatus and the terms by which linguists describe speech sounds.

Because of the inefficiency of our traditional spelling system, linguists

PHONEME *The range of sounds recognized by native speakers of a given language as one sound, such that the difference between one phoneme and another in a given utterance can potentially change or destroy the identity of the utterance. An English example is /t/.*

[4]Note that the spelling of English does not always represent the same phoneme by the same letter. In this example the *f* sound is *spelled ff, gh,* and *ph* in the three words. We are concerned in the present discussion entirely with spoken sounds, not with spelling.

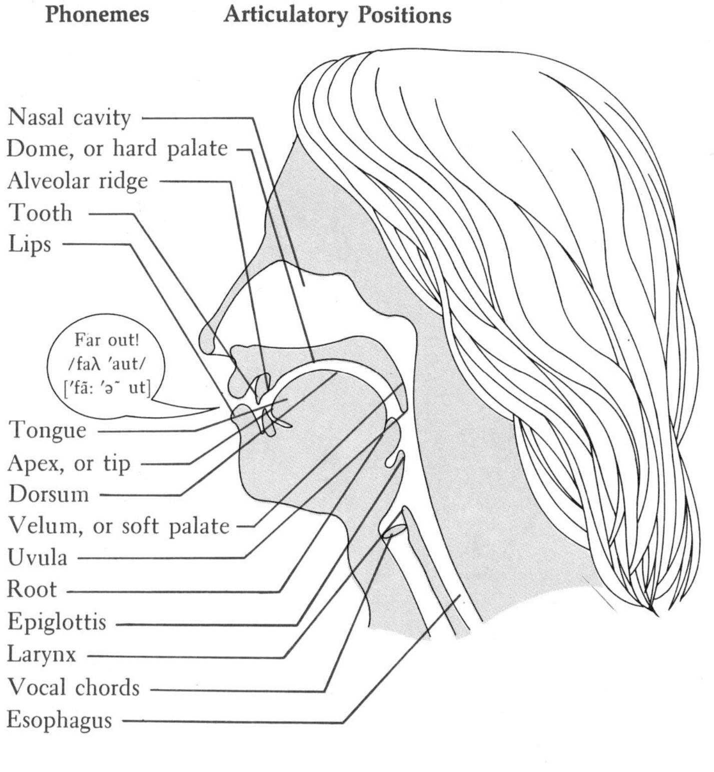

Phonemes   Articulatory Positions

Nasal cavity
Dome, or hard palate
Alveolar ridge
Tooth
Lips

Far out!
/faʌ ˈaut/
[ˈfãː ˈə̃ˉ ut]

Tongue
Apex, or tip
Dorsum
Velum, or soft palate
Uvula
Root
Epiglottis
Larynx
Vocal chords
Esophagus

Cross Section of Student Rapping. The concept of one student rapping is, of course, like the concept of one hand clapping; the diagram is intended to be only a partial representation of the process. Note also that rapping (normally) presupposes the presence of an ear. (Diagram designed by Eleanor R. Gerber.)

have also established special symbols for some of these sounds, symbols that differ from standard spelling. Table 15 lists the phonemes of English as spoken in Chicago with the symbols used by many American linguists and some words (in their traditional spellings) to illustrate the symbols. Phonemic spellings are traditionally indicated by being placed between slanted lines: *cat* becomes /kæt/ in phonemic notation.

Variation: Russian and English A given phoneme is not always pronounced exactly the same way by every speaker, or even by the same speaker in different moods, speaking at different speeds, or when it is followed or preceded by different other phonemes. Returning to the *t* sound of "Tabby," "scat," and "Tuscaloosa," we might note if we listened carefully that some speakers make the sound (at least some of the time) with the tip of the tongue against the upper teeth instead of against the alveolar ridge. And some may place the tongue slightly farther back along the roof of the mouth. Some speakers may use more than just the tip of the tongue and may place a greater surface of the tongue against the roof of the mouth (called the "palate," or "dome," by linguists). All of these are clearly English /t/, and the word "cat" pronounced with any of these variants of the /t/ is still "cat," but they nevertheless sound slightly different.

In Russian, on the other hand, these are variants of two different phonemes. The *t* sound with the tongue on the teeth is different from the *t* sound with the tongue pressed against the palate. We can represent the dental version as /t^d/ and the palatal sound as /t^p/:

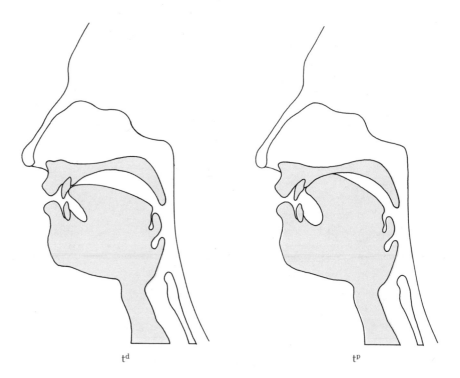

t^d   t^p

Table 15 Phonemes of Standard (Chicago) English

SYMBOL	EXAMPLE INITIAL POSITION	EXAMPLE FINAL POSITION	SYMBOL	EXAMPLE
/p/	pat	cop	/i/	eek
/b/	bat	cob	/ɪ/	bit
/t/	till	greet	/ɛ/	bet
/d/	dill	greed	/æ/	bat
/k/	Kate	sack	/a/	bot
/g/	gate	say	/u/	boo!
/f/	fat	sniff	/U/	book
/v/	vat	sieve	/ŋ/	bought
/θ/	thigh	path	/ə/	but
/ð/	thy	scythe	/ɨ/	children, "get"
/s/	Sal	brass	/o/	—
/š/	shall	brash		
/z/	zoo	grows	/iy/	beat
/ž/	—	rouge	/ey/	bait
/h/	hat	—	/ay/	bite
/m/	me	Tim	/æy/	maid
/n/	knee	tin		
/ŋ/	—	sing	/aw/	bout
/r/	rate	steer	/ow/	boat
/l/	late	steal	/uw/	boot
/w/	watt	—		
/y/	yacht	—		

SOURCE: After Salus 1969:6–8.

Thus, the word "floormat" in Russian is /mat^d/, but the word "mother" is /mat^p/. The two words differ only in the type of *t* sound they have; yet they are understood by Russians to be utterly different words, just as "mat" and "mad" are different to speakers of English. For English speakers the variation between /t^d/ and /t^p/ is trivial and unimportant, and some English speakers studying Russian claim that they are even "unable to hear" the difference. For Russians, the difference is clear and distinct and important as well. Different languages involve different understandings about how the spectrum of possible sounds may be broken up into sounds that make words. No two sounds are ever quite identical, but what is random variation in one language may be the difference between two phonemes in another.

Such a set of words as the Russian /mat^d/ and /mat^p/ are referred to as a "minimal pair," because they are distinguished by only one phoneme being in contrast. Linguists use minimal pairs as evidence that a given language recognizes the distinction between the two sounds as a phonemic distinction. One minimal pair in English is "beet" and "bit." Both vowels are made by placing the tongue high in the front of the mouth and allowing the air to pass over it while vibrating the vocal cords. The difference is that the tongue is slightly higher in "beet" than in "bit." (For most speakers, the lips also pull slightly farther sideways into a smile in "beet" than in "bit.") In Russian

MINIMAL PAIR
A pair of words or phrases in a given language that differ from each other in meaning and in only one phoneme. A minimal pair is evidence that the two phonemes by which the two elements of the pair differ are separate phonemes. For example, "bit" and "pit" distinguish English /b/ from /p/.

(and most other languages) there is no such distinction, and these two vowels of English are understood to be two different variants of the same basic *i* sound. It is clear that the distinction between these two similar sounds is understood to represent two phonemes in English, however, because in English there are numerous minimal pairs based on them (e.g., "seat" and "sit"; "lead" and "lid"; "seen" and "sin"; "feel" and "fill").

Subphonemic variation: etics and emics   As we noted, no two pronunciations are ever exactly identical. The fact that English /i^{beet}/ and /i^{bit}/ are different vowels or that Russian /t^d/ and /t^p/ are different consonants does not mean that there is no variation in the pronunciation of any one of them. Any English speaker can readily produce a whole range of pronunciations of "beet" all of which are recognized by other speakers as the same word, but which are also understood to sound different from each other. Such variation is said to be "subphonemic"; it is not used to distinguish one phoneme from another.

A "phonetic" analysis of a language attends to all of the sounds that the trained analyst is able to hear, whether or not they are phonemic. A "phonemic" analysis of a language is concerned with the sounds that are "recognized" by the language to be significantly different. When a field linguist begins his analysis of a language, he does not know what variation will be phonemic and what variation will be subphonemic. He strains to record every slight distinction that he is able to hear, *just in case* it should turn out to be phonemic. Once he has established what distinctions are phonemic (perhaps by the discovery of a large number of minimal pairs), he may choose to disregard variation that is subphonemic. His notes become much "cleaner," for he can omit the signs for higher and lower tongue positions, for more or less rounding of the lips, for higher or lower pitch, or whatever, except when they are important to phonemic distinctions, that is, to differences between words. A phonetic analysis is concerned with the sound waves in the air and the muscles in the speakers' heads. A phonemic analysis is concerned with shared understandings of those speakers about speech. A phonetic analysis makes use of all the distinctions that a linguist can be trained to hear, because he does not know what may turn out to be important and he does not want to miss anything. A phonemic analysis is in a sense the view from the inside, for it is concerned with the categories that are recognized by the speakers themselves.

The model of phonetic and phonemic analysis in language can be extended to other parts of culture as well. Anthropologists speak of an "etic approach" and an "emic approach" to the study of human behavior in general. In an etic approach the anthropologist is concerned with human behavior as the set of movements that humans make, interpreted without regard to the understandings that these same humans have about what they are doing. This approach makes use of preestablished categories for organizing and interpreting data. An anthropologist who seeks an emic analysis, on the other hand, is concerned to identify the categories into which the

ETIC APPROACH
An approach to the analysis of a society or its culture that makes use of preestablished categories for organizing and interpreting data.

EMIC APPROACH
An approach to the analysis of a society or its culture that makes use of the categories of the people studied for organizing and interpreting data or that takes the discovery of these categories as an explicit research objective or both.

people he is studying classify their experience and the understandings that they have about their behavior and their world.[5]

The concept of the phoneme had not yet been developed when Zamenhof published his language in 1887, and he necessarily spoke in terms of sounds and letters. Yet he clearly understood that a certain amount of variation was to be tolerated in the pronunciation of the new language, so long as one "sound" (phoneme) was not confused with another. His instruction that the new language should be pronounced as Spanish or Italian is not very strange if Zamenhof was in fact indicating the variation to be expected in the pronunciation of phonemes.

Subphonemic variation: levels of patterning Subphonemic variation is not necessarily random. For example, consider pitch. Pitch of a word is phonemic in Hausa, Chinese, and Swedish, but not in English, Arabic, or Yiddish; that is, there are minimal pairs that differ only in pitch in Hausa, but there are no such minimal pairs in English. Nevertheless, English words are always pronounced with some pitch, and differences in pitch are not randomly distributed. When they are angry, most speakers raise the pitch of their voices slightly. This does not change the words into different words, but it nevertheless communicates something: their anger. An even greater increase in pitch is often used in English to indicate surprise. Consider the sentence, "George ate twelve eggs." If we are astonished that anyone could possibly consume so many eggs, our pitch is higher than if we are angry because there are no more eggs for anyone else, and if we are angry, our pitch is higher than if we are merely reporting the fact that George came in eighth in an egg-eating contest.[6]

Similarly, the word "water" pronounced by someone from Delaware is the "same" word as the word "water" pronounced by a Chicagoan. On the other hand, there is a slight and detectable difference, a difference that is related to their respective dialect areas (which we shall discuss shortly). One Chicagoan's pronunciation of "water" may be the same as another's (compared with the man from Delaware), and yet there may be differences between the two Chicagoans that are related to (say) social class or sex. Even

[5]In recent years some anthropologists have used the word "etic" to refer to any approach that ignores the categories and understandings of participants, even if it is not concerned with detailed description. Under this usage, the comparative study of plow agriculture, for example, is regarded as an etic study. The usual argument in favor of emic studies is that human behavior is subject to serious misunderstandings if one does not pay attention to the understandings in the minds of the participants. The usual argument in favor of etic studies is that because different cultures by definition involve different shared understandings, behavior even partly defined by shared understandings is not strictly comparable from one culture to another, and emic comparison between cultures becomes very difficult. Unfortunately for the more extreme parties to this debate, both of these statements are entirely true.

[6]For most American speakers, the change in pitch is not the only difference between these utterances. In this particular example loudness is also an important difference, for many speakers probably the most important one, particularly in distinguishing the angry intonation from the other two.

the same person's pronunciation of the same word may vary from occasion to occasion depending upon whether he is angry or sad or sleepy, and someone who knows him and shares his understandings about how moods are coded in speech can detect his mood by listening to him talk.

Complete understanding of a given language requires that a person understand how the sounds of the language are organized into distinct phonemes. But it also requires that the analyst understand the basis by which a given speaker in a given situation selects one or another acceptable variant of a given phoneme; that is, it requires that the analyst understand subphonemic variation. It is a working rule for linguists and anthropologists that what appears random at one level of analysis (such as the selection of one or another variant pronunciation within the range of variation of a phoneme) is often (some would say always) patterned at another level of analysis. The selection of a higher rather than a lower pitch in the sentence "George ate twelve eggs" makes no difference to the identifiability of the words or to the grammar of the sentence (except as raising the voice at the end may turn it into a question). With respect to these concerns, pitch differences may be random. But in the sphere of showing how the speaker feels about the event, raising or lowering the pitch (as well as varying the loudness, changing the speed, raising the eyebrows, hunching the shoulders, and so on) is part of a set of patterned understandings about how emotions are expressed. At this level, the pitch difference is not random, but must be carefully adjusted to the speaker's meaning. It is necessary for the anthropologist to try to discover not only what phonemic distinctions are being made, but also what shared understandings are involved in making decisions between alternatives at other levels as well.

The application of the proposition that what is random variation at one level is patternable (and usually patterned) at another is not limited to language. It applies equally well to many of the phenomena that anthropologists study. For example, in American clothing a number of kinds of gowns are distinguished: nightgowns, hospital gowns, dressing gowns, academic gowns, and so on. Each of these has distinctive features of styling and is made of characteristic kinds of cloth, which enables an American to tell at a glance what sort of gown he is looking at. Academic gowns (which are further subdivided according to the degree received) are usually worn at graduation ceremonies and are typically rented. Some people buy them, however, especially when they receive a doctor's degree. The cut and styling of such a robe identify it as an academic gown for the doctor's degree. A doctoral robe always has, among other features, a number of pleats running down the front, but the exact number of them varies and is irrelevant to the identification of the garment as a doctoral gown.

At least one prominent American university sells doctoral gowns with different numbers of pleats at different prices. The candidate who buys the more heavily pleated gown shows that he has spent more money. His fellow graduates may interpret this to signify that he is richer than the others, that he loves his alma mater more than they, that his degree means more to him than to them, or whatever. Although the variation in the number of pleats is insignificant at the level of distinguishing a doctoral gown from (say) a hospital gown, the number of pleats is an obvious and significant marker of the purchaser's financial condition and attitude toward his graduation and his university. Pleats, which are insignificant at one level, turn out to be communicating something at a different level of analysis.[7]

We shall come back to these concerns later, when we discuss relations between language and social structure.

The Classification of Experience: Meanings and Morphemes

By itself a single phoneme, such as /t^d/ has no meaning. It is merely a building block that can be combined with other similar building blocks to make a meaningful unit, called a "morpheme." In English, "cat," "-ing," and "Oshkosh" are morphemes. Since "cat" and "Oshkosh" can function in a sentence as words, they are called "free morphemes." However, "-ing" can function in a sentence only when it is combined with one or several other morphemes (in a form such as "cheat-ing"); it is therefore called a "bound morpheme." Another English bound morpheme is the "-er" that occurs in "consumer" or "executioner." The word "undoing" is combined from one free morpheme ("do") and two bound ones ("un-" and "-ing").[8]

When Zamenhof noticed that the Russian suffix -skaya referred to a place, he rejoiced because he had found a way to reduce the size of the vocabulary of free morphemes in his language without reducing the number of potential words. Esperanto accordingly is rich in words compounded of bound morphemes. Indeed, the Russian -skaya that originally gave him the idea turns up as Esperanto -ejo. Thus, the two original Russian words he cites are compound forms in Esperanto, too. If anything, Zamenhof carried the principle further in Esperanto than it is carried in Russian:

shveytsar-skaya (porter's-lodge) = pord-ist-ejo (door-person's-place)

kondityer-skaya (confectioner's-shop) = suker-aĵ-ist-ejo (sugar-thing-person's-place)

Similarly, the Esperanto word for "hospital" is mal-san-ul-ejo or un-healthy-

MORPHEME

A phoneme or fixed combination of phonemes having a meaning and not subdivisible into meaningful constituent parts.

[7]We have been using the phrase "level of analysis" in a way that is common, but rather loose. Some anthropologists would prefer to say that the different levels we have been speaking of are different communication channels.

[8]Sometimes a morpheme can be composed of a single phoneme, such as the English article "a" or the Russian prepositions "k" (toward) and "v" (in). It is convenient to assume that this is a special case of a morpheme being composed of a single phoneme rather than of a phoneme having a meaning; the English /a/, for example, is just as meaningless in the word "arithmetic" as is the /i/, and the Russian "v" is just as meaningless in the word "vodka" as is the /d/.

person's-place (compared with Russian *bol'-nitsa*, sick-place, or *gospital'*, hospital). This kind of compounding is so integral to Esperanto vocabulary that attempts to introduce the "international" word *hospitalo* have been only very partially successful, and in actual conversations the longer, compound word *malsanulejo* seems to be preferred.

Context and classification The same morpheme or word (in the sense of the same combination of sounds) can often have more than one meaning. The English word "cat" may refer to an animal or to a human being. As an animal, a cat may be a zoo animal (such as a cheetah) or a house pet (as in "alley cat" or "damned cat"). As a human being, a cat may be a prostitute, a kind of burglar, or an unsympathetic, selfish woman. In the slang of a few years back any person could be called a cat (though the better sort of person to be was a "real cool cat"). A "father" may be a parent or a priest. "Grades" are found on roads, at meat counters, and after examinations. This situation is called "polysemy" (many meanings), and it is common to all languages. It is of interest to the anthropologist to the extent that one word brings to mind the others. Thus, if a priest is called father, it is important to realize that the word "father" is also (and primarily) a kinship status and that the two meanings are connected. A priest's behavior is expected to be supportive, sympathetic, and authoritative, on the model of the kinship status.

POLYSEMY *The quality of having more than one meaning.*

In addition, the meaning of a word or even a whole phrase can vary according to the broader context in which it is used. The word "cat," as we saw, is already ambiguous, though presumably it normally relates to the house pet. The sentence "It's the cat's miaow" can refer to any one of the meanings of cat that we have discussed (in such a context as the question "What in the world is that noise?") or it can have little to do with a cat as such; but, instead, it can both introduce a positive evaluation of some object and suggest lightheartedness (because it is obsolescent slang). In a yet broader context, other considerations arise, such as the appropriateness of this jocular style. The sentence "Her new coat is the cat's miaow" is quite different in its general impact from "The kaiser's moustache is the cat's miaow" (which smacks of lack of respect) or "My mother's coffin is the cat's miaow" (which implies grossly inappropriate sentiments about the death of the speaker's mother).

Meaning depends upon the shared understandings of the speakers of a language (just as the sounds that humans can voluntarily produce are patterned in different ways depending upon different shared understandings of the speakers of various languages). Problems of context and polysemy have been studied by anthropologists particularly in connection with religious ritual and with personality organization.[9] Anthropologists primarily concerned with language normally attempt to set these problems aside, at least temporarily, and work with the primary meaning of each morpheme or word

[9]Concern with polysemy is central to much personality psychology and psychotherapy. Polysemy is the basis of psychoanalytic dream analysis, for example.

(to the extent that they are able to identify a single, primary meaning). Even the primary meaning of a given word seldom corresponds perfectly with any word in English. People vary from culture to culture in the way in which they understand the world and in the way in which they therefore label and describe it.

One of the most vivid and famous instances of this is in the system of words that are used to name colors in different languages. Color terms have been a particularly profitable area of investigation because scientific measurements exist that can provide a continuous index of shade, hue, and intensity of colors. This means that the vocabulary of one language can be compared with that of another language by reference to absolute measures of light frequency. Perhaps the most famous instance in anthropology comes from the work of H. Conklin among the Hanunóo of the northern Philippines. "Color distinctions in Hanunóo are made at two levels of contrast. The first, higher, more general level consists of an all-inclusive, coördinate, four-way classification which lies at the core of the color system. . . . The second level, including several sublevels, consists of hundreds of specific color categories, many of which overlap and interdigitate. Terminologically, there is 'unanimous agreement' . . . on the designations for the four Level I categories, but considerable lack of unanimity . . . in the use of terms at Level II" (1955:341).

The terms at Level I could be very roughly translated as "black," "white," "red," and "green." However, they did not correspond very exactly with these English words: "In general terms, ["black"] includes the range usually covered in English by black, violet, indigo, blue, dark green, dark gray, and deep shades of other colors and mixtures; ["white"], white and very light tints of other colors and mixtures; ["red"], maroon, red, orange, yellow, and mixtures in which these qualities are seen to predominate; ["green"], light green and mixtures of green, yellow, and light brown" (1955:341–342).

Conklin points out that there are two distinctions in this, one between light and dark, the other between dryness and desiccation (red) and wetness or freshness (green), a division that makes particular sense in terms of plant life. "Green" is not a highly valued color, but "Clothing and ornament are valued in proportion to the sharpness of contrast between, and the intensity (lack of mixture, deep quality), of 'black,' 'red,' and 'white.'" (Level II terms are used only when greater clarity about color is specifically required.)

Conklin's point in his article was to stress that even systems of color that were very different from those with which the analyst was familiar could be reduced to understandable propositions, and that, further, the ability or inability of people to perceive a color was independent of their tendency to name it. What his study shows also is the extent to which words for colors can vary between languages. It provides us with an excellent example of a color-term system based on entirely different principles from our own, one that reflects a very different way of understanding and labeling color.[10]

[10]The definitive anthropological work on color terms so far is Berlin and Kay (1969).

Food? Whether tadpoles, frogs, and freshwater crabs are classified as vermin, pets, forbidden objects, sacred creatures, or (as here) food depends on the shared understandings of the speakers of the language involved.

A common experience of anthropologists is that people generally have a well-developed terminology for describing what is important to them and a less well-developed terminology for describing what they are little concerned with. English speakers eat rice occasionally. Southern Chinese, however, eat rice much more often and are far more concerned with rice and its cultivation and preparation. An English speaker learning a southern Chinese dialect finds himself suddenly forced to select from a variety of different words every time he wants to say "rice" depending on the state of growth or preparation the rice that he is talking about is in. The accompanying dia-

Choosing the Right Word for "Rice" in Taiwan.

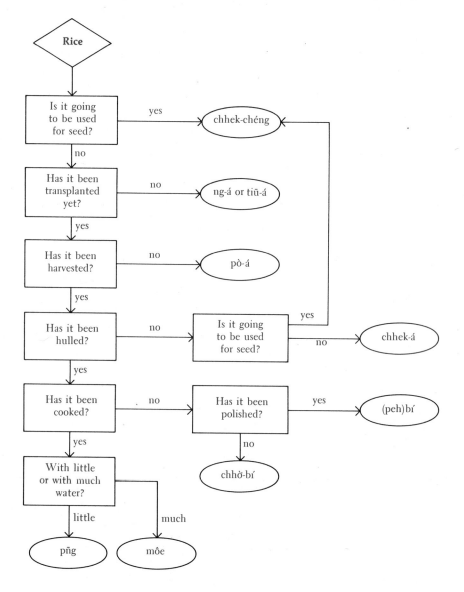

gram that we developed shows a method for selecting the correct word for "rice" from among nine different words used in southern Taiwan.

Componential analysis Much anthropological investigation has focused on sets of words that name related but different concepts, such as kinship terms, names of different kinds of trees, color names, names of diseases, and the like. The effort in "componential analysis" has been to identify the "components" of meaning that distinguish one word in the set from another. By way of example, let us consider the four words *ē*, *ū*, *bē*, and *bô*, in the following Taiwanese sentences:

COMPONENTIAL ANALYSIS *A mode of analysis of sets of words or phrases that seeks to establish the minimum features that distinguish any one item in a set from any other.*

i ū súi	She is pretty.
i bô súi	She is not pretty.
i ē bái . . .	She is ugly
i bē bái	She is not ugly.
i bô tōa-hàn	He is not big.
i ē sè-hàn . . .	He is small
i bē hñg	He is not far off.
i ū kīn	He is nearby.

An examination of this and other similar sentences eventually shows that some kinds of adjectives are used with *ū* or *bô* and others with *ē* or *bē*. Thus, *ū* and *bô* are normally associated with adjectives meaning near, cheap, strong, fragrant, or pretty, while *ē* and *bē* are associated with adjectives meaning far, expensive, weak, stinky, or ugly. Further, *ū* and *ē* indicate the presence of the quality in question, while *bô* and *bē* indicate its absence.

We can detect two components of meaning running through the four words. One is the component of absence or presence, and the other is the component of desirability, which has two values: desirable and undesirable.

	DESIRABILITY	
PRESENCE-ABSENCE	Desirable qualities	Undesirable qualities
Present	*ū*	*ē*
Absent	*bô*	*bē*

Once we have clarified these relations we are able to understand the difference between the following two sentences:

1   *i bô kín*   He is not fast.
2   *i bē kín*   He is not fast.

The speaker of sentence 1 considers that being fast is a desirable quality, which, unfortunately, the person he is talking about lacks. Speaker 1 is saying: "It is unfortunate, but he is not fast." The speaker of sentence 2, on the other hand, considers being fast to be an undesirable quality. Speaker 2 is saying: "Thank goodness, he is not fast." Speaker 1 may be discussing an Olympic runner, while speaker 2 may be discussing a loose pig he is trying to catch.

Most componential analysis is done on sets of words distinguished by more than two components, however, and often the components that are discovered have more than two values each. The words Zamenhof chose as kinship terms in Esperanto involve four components: lineality, generation, relationship through marriage, and sex. Of these, the first two can take any of several values, and the last (sex), either of two (male or female). Naturally, the picture is more complicated than it was with the Taiwanese verbs we just mentioned. Because the terms for females are formed regularly from the terms for males, we shall omit females from our calculation for the time being. We shall also temporarily ignore relationship through marriage. Let us begin with a conventional diagram of Esperanto kinship terms:

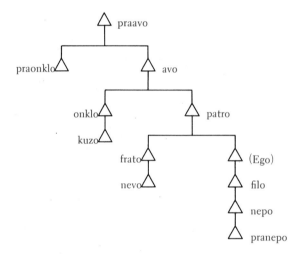

It is clear that one component of meaning underlying the differences between these terms is generation, ranging from the plus-three generation (*praavo*) to the minus-three generation (*pranepo*). It is also clear that generation alone will not explain the differences between all these terms, because in some generations there is more than one term. We therefore set up a component of "lineality." A plus-one generation term that is lineal is *patro*. The plus-one generation term *onklo* represents a kinsman who is not in Ego's direct line of descent, and we can call this collateral. In the zero generation, *kuzo* is a collateral term. *Frato*, also is in the zero generation, but, unlike *kuzo*, includes all of Ego's ancestors (though none of his descendants), a relationship we may call *collineal*. If we wish to diagram these words in terms of these two components of lineality and generation plus sex, we end up with a diagram like the following:

		Lineality					
		Lineal (ancestors and descendants of Ego)		Collateral (some but not all ancestors in common with Ego)		Collineal (all ancestors but no descendants in common with Ego)	
Sex		male	female	male	female	male	female
Generation	0	(Ego)	(Ego)	kuzo	kuzino	frato	fratino
	+1	patro	patrino	onklo	onklino		
	−1	filo	filino	nevo	nevino		
	+2	avo	avino	praonklo	praonklino		
	−2	nepo	nepino				
	+3	praavo	praavino				
	−3	pranepo	pranepino				

The component of sex could have been omitted here just as it was in our more traditional kinship diagram because all of the relations can be traced through any combination of male and female links, and the term used when the individual referred to is female differs from the male term in a completely regular way. Obviously such regularity exists by design; most natural systems are not so tidy.[11]

Analysis of a set of terms according to the components of meaning that underlie their contrasts is a very powerful tool for understanding some systems of terms. It has been conspicuously successful with kinship terminolgies in particular. It is less useful when the number of components is very great compared with the number of terms. Thus, the example of words for rice mentioned earlier would be clumsily handled by componential analysis because of the large number of components (hulling, cooking, transplanting, etc.) involved. Componential analysis also has difficulty dealing with polysemy, the father-kinsman and father-priest problem. Thus, different "components" are called into play in such pairs as "man" and "animal," "man" and "woman," "man" and "boy," "man" and "sissy," which are dependent upon the polysemy of the word "man." Similarly, relations of inclusion are difficult to handle componentially: in the United States the republic includes states, states include counties, counties include townships and cities, and cities include wards.

[11]Zamenhof also used another element, the prefix bo-, in his kinship terms to represent relations through marriage. Like the English phrase "-in-law," it is used to form names of Ego's spouse's kinsmen when used in the plus generations, to form names of Ego's kinsmen's spouses when used in the minus generations, and to form names both of spouse's kinsmen and of kinsmen's spouses when used in the zero generation. Modifying our diagram to include the meaning of components involved with forms in bo- would make it a far more complex affair. Even so, these forms are far simpler than comparable forms in many languages, and componential analysts normally omit in-law terms from their calculations.

Whether by componential analysis or in some other way, the advantage of including a body of related words in a single analysis is that it improves our sense of exactly what the word refers to by making clear where the boundaries are between it and some other word. It gives one a sense, as definitions of individual words seldom can, of the system of meaning that a given language is using in examining the world. By making this system explicit, it enables comparison with other systems in other languages.

Whorf and Linguistic Determinism of Thought

The fact that different languages seem to break up the world into categories differently has long been observed. The famous Italian proverb *Traddutore, traditore* (Translator, traitor) is a recognition of how different a translation is from an original. The interest of anthropologists focused on the problem of noncomparable categories in connection with their study of the aboriginal North American languages. B. Whorf in a series of famous studies of the Hopi language of the American Southwest tried to demonstrate that human thought is to a large extent a product of the categories of language.

> This fact [i.e., that different languages organize the world differently] is very significant for modern science, for it means that no individual is free to describe with absolute impartiality but is constrained to certain modes of interpretation even while he thinks himself almost free. The person most nearly free in such respects would be a linguist familiar with very many widely different linguistic systems. As yet no linguist is in any such position. We are thus introduced to a new principle of relativity, which holds that all observers are not led by the same physical evidence to the same picture of the universe, unless their linguistic backgrounds are similar, or can in some way be calibrated [Whorf 1940:214].

Important as such a finding might be, further research has not yet been able to substantiate Whorf's position in detail. It seems clear that our language requires that we note certain features of our surroundings because we need to do so in order to use the language to talk about them (as noting whether the rice has been cooked yet in Taiwanese), but it is not as clear that this precludes noting features of our surroundings that our language does not require us to use.

Some years back when I was driving down a crowded and icy street, the following conversation (or one very like it) occurred:

> My passenger: Watch out, she's pulling out.
> Myself (after hitting the brakes): You mean *he*; it's a *man*.

The sex of the driver of the other car was entirely irrelevant to the situation, yet my passenger was required to select the pronoun "he" or the pronoun "she." When he chose wrong, I corrected him before I even thought about it. The nature of English is such that sex (even when wrapped in winter coats and automobiles) *must* be correctly observed and reported. On the other hand, if we had been speaking Swahili, which does not require a choice comparable to the he/she choice in English in that sentence, it is perfectly possible that we might have noted anyway that the driver was male.

Some recent studies have shown that people seem to remember colors more accurately when the colors can be conveniently named in their language and less accurately when the colors are not distinctively named. This suggests that memory may involve linguistic coding of information and, therefore, that language can perhaps affect remembering more generally.

Language and Social Structure

Languages change over time. There are a number of reasons for this (most having to do with the fact that no two speakers of a language ever use it quite the same way), and a variety of patterns have been discovered in linguistic change. The reasons and patterns need not concern us here. What is important for present purposes is the fact that when a language is divided among several different speech communities, the version spoken in each of

**Development of Modern
European Languages.**

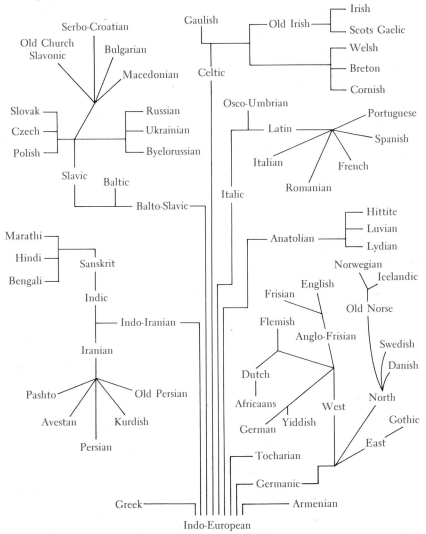

DIALECT *One of two (or several) mutually intelligible variants of a language, differing from other dialects in its body of speakers.*

SOCIAL DIALECT

A dialect that is distinguished from one or more other dialects of the same language; used by speakers not geographically distinguishable from speakers of another dialect. The contrasting term is "geographical dialect."

the communities tends to become distinctive to that community. Similarity from one community to another is maintained only by contact between them. The less the contact, the less the language of the two communities remains the same.

When the speech of two groups is not noticeably different and is mutually intelligible, the two groups are said to speak two different "dialects" of the same language. When the speech of two groups is mutually unintelligible, they are said to speak two different languages. If there is little communication between them, the speech of two speech communities originally speaking the "same" dialect gradually becomes different enough to constitute two dialects and ultimately may differentiate into two different languages. Historical linguists have documented this process for large families of languages. The accompanying diagram presents a schematization of the development of modern European languages from a (presumably unitary) Indo-European language hypothesized to have existed about 3000 B.C.[12]

Social dialects   Not all barriers to communication are barriers of distance and transportation, however, and not all dialect differences stem from geography. In recent years more and more anthropological attention has been focused on "social dialects," consistent differences in the speech of social groups that live adjacent to each other or interpenetrate geographically, but that differ in other respects, such as wealth, education, caste, ethnicity, or occupation. In the case of social dialects, unlike geographical dialects, it is more difficult to account for the differences by maintaining that there is little communication between them, although that is perhaps one factor. Instead, it has become clear that speaking a distinctive language, or a distinctive dialect, or even having a handful of distinctive words, phrases, or intonations can serve as a symbol of membership in a particular group or social category. Distinctive language is a symbol of one's status. Thus, the slang of a teenage gang serves as a symbol of each member's participation in the group. Similarly, the English teacher who says "It is I" instead of "It's me" signals by this grammatical (but rare) form that she is "educated" and an appropriate person to be teaching English. (The pupil who follows her example signals the same thing; in his case, it is patently false, and his speech is regarded as inappropriately formal; it increases the probability that he will be beaten up on the playground.)

Language difference is, of course, not merely a sign that a speaker occupies one status rather than another or is a member of group A rather than of group B. The reason that a person's language can be used by listeners to place him in a social status is that particular usages are expected from occupants of that social status. Like any other behavior, linguistic behavior is a focus of status expectations. And violations of linguistic expectations about a

---

[12]Because Indo-European is technically a hypothetical construct deduced from the relationships among modern languages, most linguists today avoid speaking of it as though it were a language actually spoken at some point in history. It is our nearest possible reconstruction of such a language. How close the reconstruction comes there is no way to tell.

status are potentially just as dangerous to the occupant's ability to keep occupying it as the violations of other kinds of expectations are. The English teacher shows that she is educated when she says "It is I," but she is also *expected* to say "It is I," and many people would maintain that she was not a very good English teacher if she did not. Similarly, in most college dormitories in the United States, the male student who does not use "four-letter, Anglo-Saxon words" fails to meet expectations about male college students (or possibly about maleness). This does not mean he will be discharged from the college or the dormitory, but it does mean that other students will relate to him differently, probably with some suspicion.[13]

In recent years, the work of William Labov on phonology in New York has provided some rich examples of differences in speech patterns of different social classes. Labov noted that New Yorkers vary in the frequency with which they pronounce their final "-r's," with which they change "-th-'s" into "-t-'s," and in several other features of their speech. He demonstrated that these differences were correlated with the social class of the speaker and with the formality of his speech: In our terms, it varied with his status and with the context of his speaking. The accompanying figures present Labov's findings for the "-th-/-t-" variation and dropping final "-r's."

Zamenhof's description of Warsaw in the late 1800s greatly emphasizes the fact that different social groups in the city were associated with different languages. The problem was not merely that they did not understand each other, but that the language difference was one of a variety of symbols of membership in one ethnic group as opposed to the others: "I was taught that all men were brothers, while at the same time in the street and in the court at every step everything made me feel that men as such did not exist: only Russians, Poles, Germans, Jews and the like existed." The problem would not have been solved if everyone learned Russian as the government proposed (or Esperanto as Zamenhof proposed), for the problem was not exclusively one of communication or lack of contact, but one of the use of language to symbolize membership in one or another group.

Even in the late twentieth century, there are many countries where the use of one language rather than another has important implications for

[13]An appropriate informant who happened to step into the room just now informs us that if someone does not use four-letter words in a college dormitory, "It is probably because he is in some religious group or something" or, if not that, then "You would think he was weird, peculiar, queer, maybe a homosexual, or something. There are things you wouldn't do with him, like go to bars or parties or things." The reaction illustrates the general force of the example.

Interestingly, there seems to be a tendency for the compulsory use of profanity to correspond with male statuses in which a man has relatively little control of his situation. Thus, men use four-letter words more than women, students use them more than businessmen, and the culture of the armed forces requires their use even more emphatically than that of students. This vocabulary of frustration and aggressive masculinity seems to function at least partially for the symbolic reassertion of control and dominance when actual control and dominance are absent.

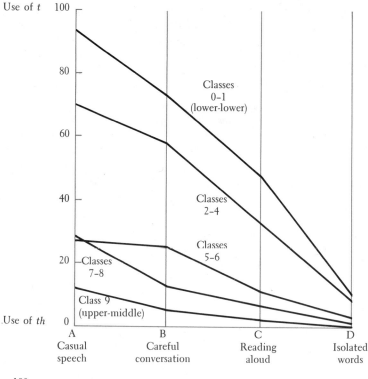

Use of *t*

Classes
0–1
(lower-lower)

Classes
2–4

Classes
5–6

Classes
7–8

Class 9
(upper-middle)

Use of *th*

A — Casual speech
B — Careful conversation
C — Reading aloud
D — Isolated words

Class Differences in New York in the Use of the *T* or *Th* Sounds in Words Beginning with *Th* ("Thanks," "Throw," Etc.). (Data from Labov 1968:243.)

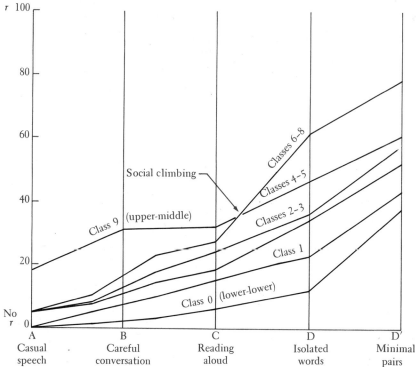

r

Social climbing

Classes 6–8

Classes 4–5

Classes 2–3

Class 9 (upper-middle)

Class 1

Class 0 (lower-lower)

No *r*

A — Casual speech
B — Careful conversation
C — Reading aloud
D — Isolated words
D' — Minimal pairs

Class Differences in New York in Leaving Out the *R* Sound in Words with *R* Following a Vowel ("Guard," "Beer," "Board," Etc.). (Data from Labov 1968:244.)

Welsh Language Riot.
About 300 Welsh nation-
alists demonstrated at
the university town of
Bangor in 1972, protesting
the excessive use of
English and (in their
opinion) inadequate use
of Welsh by the BBC.
Speaking Welsh is an
important symbol of
Welsh identity.

status. Thus, in Ireland the use of Irish has been promoted by those who would emphatically assert the independence of Ireland from the United Kingdom. Speaking Irish in modern Ireland signals either that one is a rustic who does not know English well (but an ethnically "pure" rustic) or that one is an anti-imperialist struggling for the maintenance of the Irish national culture. In Belgium the use of French or Flemish identifies the speaker with one or the other of these two competing groups struggling for their individual advantage. In the Philippines the use of Tagalog outside the Manila area is a symbol of solidarity with the government campaign for a unified national language and Philippine nationalism. It is also often interpreted as a betrayal of local interests.

Register and diglossia   As we noted earlier in our discussion of social struc-
ture, human beings do not occupy only one status each. Each of us occupies a great many statuses, often simultaneously. It is not surprising therefore to find that many individuals control more than one variant of a language (or more than one language) and that they switch back and forth among the variants depending on the situation in which they find themselves and the statuses that are activated at a given moment.

The particular form of a language that a particular individual uses in a particular status is called a "register." Many registers are shared by most or all speakers of a language, even if they themselves do not all have occasion to use all of the registers. Others are individual. One register in American English is that used by salespeople to customers. In this register (and almost nowhere else in the standard language) people are addressed as "sir" and "ma'am" or "madam." This register also includes the phrase "May I help you?" in a very special meaning and has certain intonations that are impor-

REGISTER   *One of two
(or several) variants of a
language shared by the
same speakers but used in
different circumstances.*

tant to it. Another register of American English is the peculiar jargon of the auctioneer. When we hear this register, we know both that an auction is in progress and who the auctioneer is. Another register is used for church sermons. Some families have peculiar words, often derived from the baby talk of one of their children, that are used only in a family context and become a distinctive part of the members' family register.

In Swahili a special register has developed as the language of city toughs. It is called *kibuhuni*, literally bachelor talk, or tough-guy talk. One of the most characteristic features is the replacement of standard Swahili *s* with *f* in a number of contexts. Thus, a word like *sehemu* (area) is pronounced *fehemu* in the *kibuhuni* register.

Even in Zamenhof's Esperanto some register variations have developed. Thus, faster speed of speaking, more intricate grammatical constructions, freer word order, and the use of certain neologisms are characteristic of speech among members of the Esperanto "youth movement." So is the use of a distinctive verb formation that sometimes replaces the occasional compound verbs of standard Esperanto (e.g., standard *estas parolinta*, meaning has spoken, sometimes becomes *parolintas* in the youth movement). There are also forms of Esperanto used entirely by speakers of the same nationality who share a language other than Esperanto. These forms involve cross-language puns and local references that are lacking in international usage. Both youth-movement Esperanto and national Esperanto are distinctive enough to be clearly recognizable, and speakers change from one to another form as occasion demands.

An Information Booth for the Esperanto Youth Movement. Even in Zamenhof's language, slightly different variants of the language are beginning to be associated with differences of social context; some forms are particularly characteristic of the youth movement.

Register differences in some languages are extreme and conventionalized into what is commonly known among anthropologists as "respect language." Japanese, Javanese, and Korean all exhibit the development of highly conventionalized differences in registers that are related to the sex of the speaker, the social status of the speaker in relation to the social status of the listener, the subject of conversation, and so forth. The complexity of this is shown by the accompanying Korean comic strip (from a Seoul newspaper).[14] In the first frame a bill collector approaches a man of vastly higher social status than he. The collector uses the "deferential" register of speech, while the executive responds with the "plain" form used to social inferiors. The cartoonist underlines the differences in status by having the collector bow very low and ask for a very large amount of back rent, presumably for a large and elegant building. Besides responding with the plain form, the executive sits back in his chair behind a desk with three telephones puffing a cigar. In the second frame the collector does not have to bow as low, and the rent is lower. The executive (with no cigar and only one telephone) still uses the plain form for social inferiors, but the collector has reduced his obsequiousness and used the "polite" form that is used among social equals who are not on particularly close terms. By the third frame the collector and the debtor (Ko Pa-u, the hero of the strip) are on more or less equal terms. The collector does not bow at all, but Ko Pa-u bows slightly. Both use polite forms. Throughout the sequence, the collector has become less formal. By the fourth and last frame, the bill collector is even standing back slightly, while the debtor grovels on the floor before him under the leaking roof of his miserable hovel. The collector still uses the polite form (the debtor is, after all, a customer of his company), but the drawing suggests that it is shouted, which changes its implications somewhat.

In Korean one or another of these registers must be selected for every conversation; the overriding determinant of selection is the comparative social class and intimacy of the parties to the conversation, just as the cartoon emphasizes.[15] The expectations associated with a particular social status include the expectation that in a given circumstance a person in that status will speak in the register that is conventional for that situation. The executive in the first picture of the cartoon strip would be acting unlike an executive if he were to use the deferential form back to the bill collector. And, indeed, he would be acting like a small executive rather than like a big executive if he were to use even the polite form, as the lesser executive in the second picture does. The bill collector would probably be thrown out of

꼬바우 영감

[14]We are indebted to C. Paul Dredge for bringing this example to our attention and providing interpretations of the Korean.

[15]The levels of formality in Korean are reflected in verb endings, among other things. The cartoon does not make use of all the levels of Korean respect language. One brief overview for beginning students of Korean, somewhat deceptively entitled *Korean in a Hurry* (Martin 1960:20–21), advises the beginner to familiarize himself with verb endings for styles called formal, plain, quotation, familiar, authoritative, intimate, and polite.

either of these offices if he were to use the plain forms rather than the polite or deferential ones. One does not speak to an executive in plain forms.[16]

The reader of the cartoon or the listener in a conversation in Korean can interpret the status differences from the speech. In Korean, as in all languages that have respect language, status is explicitly underlined in almost every speech act, and speakers must produce the speech differences correctly if they are to act according to the expectations of their statuses.

In some languages differences between some registers are so extreme that the language is effectively split into two different dialects or even two different languages. The term "diglossia" is used for such situations, first described by C. Fergusson (1959). Fergusson was able to note several features that are shared by many diglossic language situations. Typically, one finds diglossia in old, literate communities, where one form is associated with written language and the other with everyday conversational language. The written variant is typically more prestigious—Fergusson abbreviates it with the letter H for high—and the spoken form is less so (L for low). The L form is learned before the H form, which is typically studied in school. The H form is usually standardized (because it is normally the language of a body of written, sometimes sacred, literature). The H form is usually grammatically more complex than the L form, at least in overt ways such as the apparatus of word endings. There is normally a tremendous overlap in vocabulary, but enough words are different that practically any sentence can be assigned to the H or L category as soon as it occurs.

Most importantly, the two forms are normally in a stable relationship such that one is used in some contexts and the other in other contexts, with very little functional overlap (and hence very little competition between the forms).[17] Examples of languages that exhibit diglossia include Arabic, where the language of the Koran (H) contrasts with the numerous dialects of spoken Arabic (L) used in the Near East today; Haitian Creole, which is the L in diglossia with standard French as H; Chinese up to the early years of this century, where written classical Chinese was the H form, and the numerous spoken variants were the L. Similarly, Swiss German, modern Greek, medieval Latin, Norwegian, and Tamil are all involved in diglossic

DIGLOSSIA

A sociolinguistic situation in which two different dialects or languages are used in the same speech community but for different purposes.

Haitian Religious Rite. In Haiti, French is the written language, the official language, and the language of education and government. Creole is spoken at home, among friends, in markets, and in religious contexts, like the voodoo ritual shown here.

[16]Koreans actually do change their speech in this way, but what makes the cartoon funny to a Korean reader is presumably the emphasis upon the *extent* to which the bill collector's behavior—what he says, how he says it, and how he stands—depends upon the social importance of the debtor. The exaggeration of the social-class symbols in the cartoon points up the potential silliness of the custom when carried to extremes.

[17]Diglossia differs from bilingualism in that where there is diglossia, the two languages or forms of languages are functionally differentiated and not in competition, while where there is bilingualism, the two languages or forms of languages are used for the same purposes and are therefore in direct competition with each other. J. Fishman (1970) has argued that the purely bilingual situation tends to be self-liquidating as people come to use one language more of the time than the other. Fishman argues that purely diglossic or purely bilingual situations are in fact rare, most double-medium speech communities being actually a combination of the two.

language situations. In some parts of the world diglossia is appearing between the newly selected official languages of newly independent states and the spoken vernaculars of the people who make them up. Thus, Swahili seems to be stabilizing in rural Tanzania in a diglossic relationship (as H) to various other Bantu L languages.

SUMMARY

The analysis of language has involved two related ideas that have provided anthropologists with two of their most useful ways of looking at things: the emic-etic model; and the realization that what is random variation in one frame of reference can be patterned according to shared understandings at some other level. The emic-etic distinction has led to clearer thinking about the difference between how the anthropologist classifies the data he collects for purposes of comparison between one group and others, and how he studies the way the people he is investigating classify their own behavior in the context of the understandings, feelings, and institutions that make up their own, noncomparative context.

The analysis of native categories (emic analysis) has been applied to subjects ranging from myth to kinship and from disease to plant collection. The research that is most directly concerned with emic analysis is called "cognitive anthropology," and includes componential analysis and other techniques for collecting and analyzing information about how people understand their world. Much of the emphasis has been on the analysis of terms that people use to name events, physical objects, experiences, and social statuses. These techniques are only in the beginning stages of development, and most investigators have hopes of further developments in them that will make it possible to go beyond merely verbal categorizations.

The realization that what is random variation in one frame of reference is patterned in another has led anthropologists to the working assumption that virtually nothing is random, and that variation is worth investigating even when it seems to have no significance for the problem immediately at hand. In language an excellent example of this is the way in which speech can vary so much in the pronunciation of the same sentence (say) that it can be used to identify social dialects and registers. These entities are then used to identify and mark socially and psychologically significant entities (such as families, social classes, sermons, and auctions). Careful analysis can now be made of phenomena that were previously only "felt" to be important in much human interaction. But there is no reason to imagine that social dialects and registers occur only in language. Having observed these linguistic phenomena, anthropologists are now in a position to look for comparable cultural use of variation in other spheres (as our example of American academic gowns suggested).

One area in which the investigation did *not* prove very productive was in the search for regularities between the structure of a language, particularly the grammatical structure, and the world view of its speakers. These efforts, particularly associated with the name of Whorf, have been largely abandoned, at least for the time being.

Recent changes in the direction and emphasis of much research in technical linguistics have not yet been the basis for widely recognized approaches in general cultural studies. But a significant number of anthropological linguists are concerned with the applicability of new research in transformational linguistics to older anthropological problems. By studying the understandings that govern language, the anthropologist has a view of the understandings that govern and are governed by social structure and personality as well.

SUGGESTED READINGS

More on the case

Boulton, Marjorie   1960   Zamenhof: Creator of Esperanto. London: Routledge and Kegan Paul.

This book is a readable biography of Zamenhof by a prominent Esperanto writer. It includes a description of the creation of Esperanto and of the early days of the Esperanto movement.

Other readings

Fishman, Joshua A.   1970   Sociolinguistics: A Brief Introduction. Rowley, Mass.: Newbury House.

Fishman in this book (especially chap. 5) distinguishes bilingualism (the availability of two different linguistic codes in the same situation) from diglossia (the differentiation of linguistic codes such that the selection of one or the other is determined by context). This is an important contribution in its own right, but the point here is to suggest that people use (or can use) different forms of speech in different situations, depending on context.

Salus, Peter H.   1969   Linguistics. Indianapolis: Bobbs-Merrill.

A very brief introduction to linguistics for the reader without prior exposure.

Whorf, Benjamin Lee   1940   Science and Linguistics. Technology Review 42:229–231, 247–248. Reprinted in Language, Thought, and Reality: Selected Writings of Benjamin Lee Whorf, 1956. John B. Carroll, Ed. Cambridge, Mass.: Technology Press, and New York: Wiley, pp. 207–219.

Most of Whorf's speculations have been discredited over the years, but their influence was great and they are still seductive. Good example of Whorf's work.

10

Applied Anthropology

All progress is precarious, and the solution of one problem brings us face to face with another problem.

MARTIN LUTHER KING, JR.
STRENGTH TO LOVE, 1963

Indian tribesmen now living in the city of Khadi, taught weaving by social workers.

How is anthropological knowledge applied to everyday life?

What problems arise in problems of directed social and cultural change?

What sorts of understandings are affected by directed change?

Can people's culture make them refuse useful reforms?

Is it really ethical for anthropologists to participate in directed change?

**Nelida and the
Boiled Water:
A Case of Planned
Change in Peru**

The lower Ica Valley is a relatively flat plain area along the coast of Peru, about 170 miles southeast of Lima. A few years ago, a Peruvian government supported agency, the Ica Departmental Health Service, decided to promote the boiling of drinking water as a public health measure to reduce the incidence of typhoid and other water-borne diseases in this area.[1] To educate the local residents about the relationship between unboiled water and disease, and to convince them to boil water before using it, the Health Service hired twenty hygiene workers of both sexes. The workers were purposely chosen from the Ica Valley itself, and were given at least one year of training in hygiene, communicable diseases, sanitation, and domestic economy. The government's reasoning in choosing workers from the social group among which they would be working was that this would, it was hoped, make them more acceptable to the people they were trying to influence; it was thought that people would be more likely to accept changes from workers they recognized as being like themselves.

In addition to the hygiene workers, the Health Service sent physicians on lecture tours through the Valley, and these doctors explained scientific views of disease transmission and the importance of clean water in preventing illness.

One of the towns in the Ica Valley was called Los Molinos. Here a hygiene worker named Nelida worked for two years to bring the inhabitants to boil their water. Of the 200 families in the community, 15 were boiling water before she came. At the end of her two years of work, 11 more families were boiling their water. The decision to boil drinking water was made by village women; since women were in charge of most domestic tasks in this community, boiling water (or not) was strictly within their sphere of decision making, and Nelida worked closely with them and came to know many of them very well. Here are some of the women she dealt with:

Mrs. A was a woman in her early fifties who was a schoolteacher. Her husband drove the sole bus that traveled twice a day from Los Molinos to the town of Ica. In their house with them lived a son and an unmarried sister of Mrs. A's. The A's had more money than most families in the community because of the combined income resulting from Mr. A's bus driving and Mrs. A's teaching.

Mrs. A considered herself ill, and she told everyone that the doctors in Ica had diagnosed her as having sinusitis. The people of the village classed her as "a sick one." She was boiling water before Nelida came because, as she herself explained, boiled water is necessary for sick people.

The reason for this had nothing to do with microbes or water-borne disease, however. Instead the custom of boiling water for the sick was rooted in understandings about certain foods and drinks being "hot", and the relation of this "heat" to disease. For the people of the Ica Valley, as for many other people around the world, all foods and beverages can be divided into those that are "hot" and those that are "cold." This "hot" or "cold" quality of a food or drink is not related to its temperature, and is not a way of describing whether it is spicy. Being "hot" or being "cold" is rather a quality in the food similar to its color or texture. Thus, *pisco*, a local brandy, is very "cold" regardless of its temperature as measured by a thermometer, and pork is very "hot" regardless of its temperature or how it is flavored.

In the classification of substances used in the Ica Valley, boiled water is viewed as "hot," while unboiled water (or boiled water from the previous

[1] Our discussion of this project is based on Edward Wellin, "Water Boiling in a Peruvian Town" in *Health, Culture, and Community: Case Studies of Public Reactions to Health Programs*, Benjamin D. Paul, ed. with the collaboration of Walter B. Miller, New York, Russell Sage Foundation, pp. 71–103.

day) is considered "cold." It is thought harmful for sick people to eat or drink things that are either extremely "hot" or extremely "cold" in the local system of classification. "Cold" is especially dangerous for them. Water is boiled because this changes it from being a "cold" substance to a "hot" one. This is not a question of temperature (although boiling obviously raises that too, for a while), but of its "quality." Boiled water remains "hot" in "quality" even after it has cooled in temperature.

Because sick people must avoid "cold" substances, and because water is therefore boiled to remove it from the category of "cold" things before they drink it, boiled water is associated with sickness. It is sick people who are viewed as properly and correctly drinking boiled water, and this was precisely the reason Mrs. A boiled her water. She was, as she continually reminded people, sick. Mrs. A's boiling of water was accepted in Los Molinos as the natural and reasonable thing for her to do.

In fact, of the fifteen families that boiled water before Nelida came, eight had sick people in

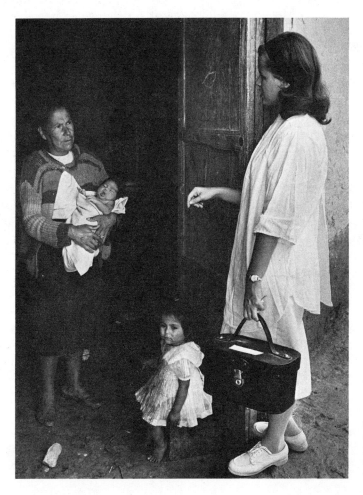

An American nurse and a new mother in the Bolivian Andes. A client's willingness to accept medical advice is partly dependent upon prior cultural understandings.

379

them. The remaining seven were all households in which the residents had some kind of association with the major cities of Peru and admired the ways of city people. One of these was the B household.

Mrs. B was a housewife in her middle fifties. She had been born and raised in Los Molinos, as had her husband, who owned a small plot of ground that he farmed and who also hired himself out from time to time as an agricultural worker on the local plantations. Both Mrs. B and her husband were *cholos*. *Cholos* are people of mixed European and Indian background.[2] They are the majority population in the Ica Valley, and about two thirds of the people in Los Molinos were *cholos*.

In the B house lived Mr. and Mrs. B, their grown son, two married daughters and their husbands, and three children belonging to the daughters: a total of ten people. Mrs. B prided herself on keeping her house extremely neat and clean, from the tile floor in the living room to the hard-packed dirt floor of the kitchen. In fact the B house was probably the neatest and cleanest one in the community. Mrs. B was not popular in Los Molinos. She was the subject of considerable gossip, and people criticized her, saying she "puts on airs and likes to pretend that she is better than she is." She herself claimed not to care what the people of Los Molinos thought of her, since they were, she maintained, dull, crude, and backbiting people, whose opinions did not matter. She had publicly commented that Los Molinos itself was a dreary place, and she made no attempt to hide the fact that she viewed herself as a person of high ideals and cleanliness living in the midst of people of low character and unclean habits.

A key fact about Mrs. B was that her brother had gone to the capital city of Lima many years before Nelida arrived in the community and had worked his way up to what was regarded in Los Molinos as a high position. He would visit Los Molinos for several days twice a year. During his visits, he spent a substantial part of his time expressing his pronounced views on politics, prices for agriculture commodities, home remedies for diseases, and many other topics.[3]

It is unclear exactly where Mrs. B got the idea that water should be boiled. Perhaps it came from her brother. In any case, she started boiling it for him when he came to visit, and ultimately she was boiling it for the whole household as a regular thing. Mrs. B was extremely friendly with Nelida, perhaps because she had few friends and because Nelida seemed more urbane than the local people did. Mrs. B attended several of the talks given by visiting doctors, including one about microbes in water, and she was apparently quite pleased with herself for having been a water boiler all along. After the talk she excitedly told Nelida: "Without even knowing, imagine doing such a good thing!" For her, microbes and dirt were the same thing, and she viewed having either one as a stain on her character and something any clean and decent person would avoid. That she had been "cleaning" her household of microbes when all about her had been ignoring them apparently confirmed her view of herself as cleaner and more decent than *some* people she could mention.

Unlike Mrs. A, Mrs. B was viewed as being "odd" about boiled water. After all, no one in her household was sick! Her water boiling was viewed locally as part of the same strangeness that could be seen in the "unnatural cleanliness" of her

---

[2] The term is used in this sense throughout most of South America other than Chile, where it is used to refer to Indians *without* an admixture of European background.

[3] The local children used to peer through the front door of the B house at him as he sat in the parlor delivering his opinions. They seemed especially impressed by his glittering gold front teeth.)

American Peace Corps Worker teaching Costa Rican farmer to find ear infections and ticks in cattle. A more productive way of teating cattle may be presented, but whether it is actually adopted depends much more on whether people consider ear infections and ticks a serious problem than upon simply learning how to treat them.

house and her tendency to "put on airs." She was what farmers of the American Middle West used to call "nasty clean," and that she boiled water without anybody being sick did not surprise anybody very much.

Mrs. A, like some others, boiled water because she was sick and needed to avoid "cold" foods. Mrs. B, also like some others, boiled water to be clean and (more importantly) "citified." But most of the residents of Los Molinos did not boil water when Nelida arrived. They were the people she came to "convert" to the Health Service's water boiling campaign.

Mrs. C was one of these. She was a Highlander from the Andes Mountains that loom above the Ica Valley. As a Highlander she was a member of an ethnic group considered lower than the *cholos*, the group to which Mrs. A and Mrs. B both belonged. Mrs. C wore her hair in the two long braids characteristic of Highland women, but she did not wear the colorful blouse and distinctive skirt that were (and are) typical Highland garb. Of course she spoke Spanish with the distinctive accent of the Highlands people. As we might have guessed from her keeping her Highland hairstyle, she made no secret of her background. On the contrary she was proud of it. Mr. C used to go back to the Highlands on regular visits in order to check on his small land-holdings and the cattle that he had there. The C's were people in the middle income group of Los Molinos society.

Highlanders in general viewed the coast as a good place to educate children, as a place having good fruit, and as being more prestigious than the high Andes. But they also thought of it as being ugly and oppressively hot, and they found the flat, brown terrain ugly. Furthermore, Highlanders viewed the coast as extremely unhealthy and ridden with disease. Finally, they were somewhat uneasy about living in the coastal area because they believed, with some justice, that Highlanders were treated badly there.

Nelida became quite friendly with Mrs. C. And although Nelida was a *cholo*, she did not make fun of Mrs. C's Highland accent as many *cholos* did. Mrs. C liked to talk to Nelida (and everyone else) about her native Highland village. She took up boiling water after many discussions with Nelida: it was clear that since, like other Highlanders, she viewed the area as unhealthy, she saw no reason not to follow the advice of her friend, Nelida. She did not consider herself a "real" member of the community and was not interested in the local view that only sick people boil water. She viewed the valley as unhealthy in any event, and if boiling water would reduce the health hazards living in Los Molinos, she was willing to boil water.

Mrs. D was 25 years old and a *cholo*. She and her husband had five children, and they had lived in Los Molinos all their lives. He was a plantation fieldhand, and the family was a poor one by local standards. Mrs. D was happy to have Nelida come into her house, and she listened with attention to what Nelida had to say about improving sanitation and limiting disease. She and her husband were considering building a privy as Nelida had suggested they should. On Nelida's advice Mrs. D went to the local health center for regular checkups during her last pregnancy. This was particularly striking because local women were extremely prudish concerning their bodies and disliked very much having anyone, male or female, see them undressed for any reason.

After Nelida's sixth visit to her, Mrs. D agreed that unboiled water caused disease, and she told Nelida that if she had had time, she would have been boiling hers, but that unfortunately she did not.

After Nelida's twelfth visit, a doctor came to town and gave a lecture which was attended by Mr. and Mrs. D and their five children. On Nelida's thirteenth visit to Mrs. D's house, Mrs. D frequently referred to the doctor's lecture and would point out memorable things he had told the audiences. She said that she had decided to begin boiling a kettle of water after breakfast every day, "just as the doctor said we should." Mrs. D did not widely advertise the fact that she had begun to boil water, but to those few friends to whom she did mention it she explained that she did it "because the doctor recommended it." Nelida was grateful that Mrs. D began boiling the water, but she was a bit annoyed that after all her patient explanations Mrs. D gave the doctor alone as the inspiration for her decision to begin boiling her water.

Mrs. D was not alone in this. Four of the eleven housewives who began boiling water did so immediately following a doctor's lecture, even though all of them had had considerable contact with Nelida first and had not been persuaded by her.

Mrs. E was a *cholo* who had lived in Los Molinos all her life. She had one daughter by a husband who had left her after a very brief marriage. In her household there were, in addition to herself and her daughter, her aged parents, her brother, and two teenage nephews, sons of a dead sister, who worked as fieldhands on a local plantation.

Mrs. E told Nelida that she agreed about boiled water and its usefulness in preventing disease, but she simply did not have time to prepare it. Unlike Mrs. D, it was clear that for Mrs. E finding time to boil water would in fact have been extremely difficult. Indeed Mrs. E's schedule was not much different from that of many other housewives in the community (except of course that women with unmarried adult daughters to help had a somewhat easier time, and women with smaller families had less work than those with larger ones).

Mrs. E arose at five o'clock each morning to make breakfast. After she had served breakfast to her nephews she would take breakfast to her old father, who would have been working in the fields since about five thirty. As she returned from that regular errand, she would collect faggots for the fire and fodder for the chickens and other animals. Upon her return home, she would wake up her daughter and supervise as the little girl splashed water on her face and pulled her cotton dress over the slip she slept in. Only then could Mrs. E sit down herself for a meager breakfast with her daughter. After breakfast she would send the daughter outside to play, help her old mother out of bed, and bring the old lady to the table to see that she ate some breakfast.

After this the "real work" began: she washed up the utensils and dishes used for breakfast; fed the chickens, pigs, and goats; and made two or more long trips to the well to bring back water (two five-gallon tins each trip). She also swept the floor of her house. All this time she had to keep an eye on her little daughter and somewhere during the course of things she would try to find an opportunity to use the privy in the front yard.

(Mrs. E's old mother disliked the privy very much because of its "evil odors" and possibly even "bad airs." Like "hot" and "cold," "bad airs" were a little different in the Ica Valley from what these words suggest in English. It was locally believed that illness could be caused by "airs," and part of the old lady's opposition to using an outhouse rather than the surrounding fields as had formerly been customary, was the fear of these "airs.")

By the time all the morning work was done and her mother taken care of, Mrs. E had to begin preparing lunch. This involved shelling corn or beans, grinding pepper on a flat stone, cutting up squash, kindling a fire in the stove, and putting together the soup which would be the main part of lunch. By now the heat of the day had started in earnest and would continue to increase until late afternoon.

After lunch had been served to everyone, Mrs. E could finally have an hour or so to relax and visit with friends and relatives. After this brief relaxation, Mrs. E returned to work to prepare the evening meal, which was served and completed before sundown, since there was little provision for artificial light. The day ended with her crawling into a pallet next to her daughter after she had washed up the evening dishes and perhaps talked with her old parents.

Nelida was especially pleased with Mrs. E because in their talks Mrs. E gained a working knowledge of disease transmission. She understood, for example, that flies were disease carriers, not agents of disease themselves. Mrs. E also understood, as Mrs. B, for example, did not, that hygiene was not a matter of being elegant but rather a matter of health, of keeping healthy by removing disease-causing conditions. She used her meager resources for health improvements like the privy she had built, rather than to show off. Despite all this, she still would not boil water for her family to drink.

Mrs. E's work schedule was clearly part of the reason she did not want to take on the project of boiling her drinking water. But another part of the picture was the equipment she used in her work. Her stove, like those of the other women in Los Molinos, was a waist-high, adobe-brick structure that burnt faggots. These were plentiful when the local vineyards were trimmed and when the old cotton plants were destroyed. But for about half the year this fuel material was scarce, and the women had to scour the fields and the banks of dry irrigation ditches in search of something to burn. Firewood was available from peddlers, but most people, and certainly Mrs. E, were forced to practice severe economy and could not possibly afford to pay for their wood. To conserve the little fuel that was found, the fire could be lit only to prepare the day's three meals.

This meant that water could be boiled only three times a day, when the fire was burning to cook the meals anyway. Here a further problem was encountered. The Peruvian adobe stoves were built so that they could take only two cooking vessels at a time, and some in the community were built to take only one. When the meal was cooking, it was very difficult, if not impossible, to find room on the stove to boil water too. Furthermore, Mrs. E's cooking equipment included only a frying pan, two metal pots, and some empty tin cans. This was typical of households of her economic level in the community. It meant that not only was there little space on the stove to boil water, but the cooking utensils were usually all being used to prepare the meals themselves and were not available for water boiling when the fire was going. Only after the meal was completed were utensils and stove space available so that water could be prepared. For poor families, that meant extra fuel consumption, which was not economically feasible.

But let us suppose the fuel problem could have been solved. At least during part of the year there was plenty of fuel, after all. The understandings about "hot" and "cold" food and drinks affected boiling too. If water was boiled and allowed to stand overnight, it became dangerously "cold." Traditionally, water boiled in the evening (for sick people) could not be drunk the next morning because it was now "cold." Given this belief, it would generally have been regarded as useless to boil water in the evening for use the next day: in local terms, day-old boiled water would just "come unboiled" again. For health workers it was hard enough to convince people that healthy people needed to boil their water at all, without taking on the problem of the "hot" and "cold" qualities and their relationship to the mysteries of the night. It simply had to be accepted that boiled water could not be kept to the following day.

People in Los Molinos drank most of their water, as would be expected, during the hottest part of the day. This meant that they needed drinking water from lunch onward. Furthermore they did not like to drink warm liquids when they were thirsty. Thus water boiled at lunch could not be used because it would not be cool enough (in temperature!) for people to drink. And we have seen that "yesterday's water" was not an alternative either. Only at breakfast time, then, could water be boiled in order to meet both the requirements of people's thirst and all the beliefs and scheduling constraints that surrounded water boiling.

But at the crucial period after breakfast, Mrs. E was busy. It was only after lunch that she had a brief period when she was not totally occupied in her work. Even if she had been willing to give up some of that rest period, it would not have been possible for her to boil the drinking water because it would not have been cool enough when they wanted to drink it, and it would have been thought to have "come unboiled" by the next day. So Mrs. E, while agreeing that boiled water was better than unboiled water,

New latrine installed by rural health center in Panama. In South America concern with illness caused by "bad airs" can affect rural people's willingness to use latrines.

continued to use water as it came. The logistics of water boiling were too overwhelming to do much else.

Mrs. F was a widow of about 60, and she lived in a household of twelve people. The family was black, and as a *cholo* Nelida had to take special care to avoid becoming entangled in the antagonisms that existed between *cholos* and blacks in the area. Nevertheless, that antagonism had its effects. "Racial" stereotypes existed on both sides. The blacks had derogatory names for *cholos* referring to their faded skin, the insipid foods they ate, their stolid pleasures, and their tendency to mimic their betters. And the *cholos* had derogatory terms for the blacks, referring to their relatively darker skins, their spicy foods, their alleged laziness, and their assumed fondness for engaging in sorcery.

Mrs. F was known in the community for her cooking, and from all over the village people came to ask her assistance at festival times. In many ways Mrs. F was a cultural conservative, and her famous cooking was of the traditional kind for this area. Her initial coolness to Nelida verged on hostility, partly because Nelida had come to the community to try to change it. There may well have been an element of ethnic hostility as well, since Nelida was a *cholo*. Mrs. F did not necessarily accept Nelida just because Nelida accepted her.

Mrs. F loved to try to trap Nelida into making definite statements that could be used to ridicule her. One day, when she heard Nelida saying something about child care, Mrs. F called loudly to her neighbor: "See how the young expert has come to tell us about raising our children." Similarly, one day Nelida made a comment about cooking, and Mrs. F called to all those within hearing: "Come and hear the expert teach me how to cook."

Mrs. F went to the doctor's lecture on microbes and believed some of what the doctor said. She did not, however, share with him the understanding of how disease worked. For example, local theory of disease held that there were certain illnesses that "stick to you." Syphilis and typhoid belonged in this category. Such diseases traveled from a sick person to a well one. Mrs. F believed that the microbes were the agency by which the disease traveled: they were like tiny birds or insects that flew across the space between people carrying the kinds of diseases that would "stick to them." They did not themselves *cause* disease; they were vehicles of disease.

Given this view of microbes, Mrs. F totally rejected many of the things that she heard about preventing disease. How, she wanted to know, could microbes fail to drown if they were put into *any* water? "Are they fish?" she would ask. And if not, why were they to be feared in water? Furthermore, she wanted someone to tell her how such small delicate things as microbes could harm anyone if they did not bring diseases along to help them. She did not believe they could be harmful in themselves.

Such microbes certainly did not strike Mrs. F as much of a threat, and certainly water-going microbes were quite outside her range of interests. Her view was that there were enough real threats in the world without worrying about tiny animals that might or might not inhabit water and might or might not bother to carry diseases about with them even if they were in the water. The twelve people in her household had to worry about "cold," about "airs," and about poverty and hunger. They had no time or energy to worry about tiny animals they could not even see, touch, hear, taste, or smell. To her boiling water was making a tempest in a teapot.

Analysis of the Case

What we have just seen is an example of an attempt to change people's practices and behavior. An outside agency, the Ica Departmental Health Service, was trying to change the way people acted by changing the understandings they had. Basically, they wanted only to bring people to boil water before drinking it in order that the incidence of water-borne disease might be lowered in the area. A well-trained health worker, Nelida, lived in the village for a prolonged period and came to know some of the women there very well. In addition, physicians made lecture tours of the Ica Valley villages, explaining the views of disease held by modern medicine and how boiling water could promote health.

Our six sketches of individual women do not represent the entire range of opinion about water boiling in Los Molinos. But they will serve to suggest something of the variety of opinions and situations that Nelida had to contend with. From examining them we can see some of the issues that must be faced in any sort of effort at planned change in human communities.

As we noted at the beginning, Nelida did not have very much success in her efforts. When she started work in the village of 200 households, 15 were boiling their water. When she left at the end of two years, only 11 more families had taken up the practice, an increase of only about 6 percent overall, or 3 percent per year. (And it was a matter of some frustration to her that her efforts were not even acknowledged by some of the "converts," who attributed their decision to the doctors' lectures.) Six percent can hardly be counted a very great success rate. We can imagine Health Service planners being both puzzled and discouraged. To understand the resistance to boiling water, we need to know how people made their decision to boil water or not. And to understand this, we must set boiled water and all of the things relating to the practice of boiling it into the wider framework of life as it is lived in Los Molinos.

We see immediately that boiling their drinking water was not merely meaningless to the people Nelida met in Los Molinos. Mrs. A boiled her water to make it suitable for a sick person, but she proceeded from a quite firmly held theory about why boiled water was better for sick people that was different from the theory Neldida may have held. (Actually, since Nelida was also from the Ica Valley, she may have held many of the same ideas she found in Los Molinos in addition to the new ideas about boiled water that she would have learned from her Health Service training.) With her concern for making metaphysically "cold" water into metaphysically "hot," Mrs. A was, in public health terms, boiling water for the "wrong" reasons. She did not share the Health Service's view of what it was about boiled water that made it desirable, and if she had got well, she probably would have given up the practice. And Mrs. B boiled water to show how sophisticated she was. Since she was imitating city people, who may have had the same view that the Health Service had, it might be possible to argue that she was ultimately boiling water for the "right" reasons, even if she did not know what they were, very much the way people in our own society avoid the "dangerous" practice of refreezing thawed meat without any understanding of why refreezing has any harmful effects. Both Mrs. A and Mrs. B were conforming to the "new" behavior of boiling their water, but neither was doing so for the reasons the Health Service had for advocating it. It would be a mistake to assume that because 15 of the 200 families already boiled water when Nelida arrived, the village was on its way to becoming a pure-water community. The lesson here is that people may do the same things for different reasons, and that the planner must be aware of why it is that conformists conform if they hope to gain wide acceptance for their plans.

We may be a little suspicious too of the women who began boiling water after the doctor addressed them or after Nelida had made several visits. They may have begun boiling water because they respected the authority and learning of the doctor or as a personal favor to Nelida, who may have been getting pretty desperate for water boilers as it became clear that the project was failing. Once again that would not mean that they were convinced, but merely that considerations of social structure, of statuses and the role relations among them, had brought pressure on them to perform a new behavior. As soon as the Health Service stopped sending people to Los Molinos, such people might very well revert to the use of the less troublesome natural water.

Introducing ox-drawn plows in Nyangombi, Zambia, 1977. The introduction of oxen as draft animals may seem backward when they are being replaced by tractors in other places, but successful development projects require assessment of local resources, understandings, and opportunities. Otherwise innovations are not widely adopted.

A planner must also take into account the very practical, entirely nonideological problems that people have with a new behavior. The Health Service apparently never considered the way it would fit into a farming wife's day to boil water: what was she supposed to do about the shortage of fuel, or about the demand for cold drinking water in the middle of the day, or about the limited space on the stove? These matters may seem trivial and unworthy of the attention of a highly educated central planner, but for the individuals who are to be convinced that a new scheme is worth trying (and worth continuing), they are crucially important. With behavior we are used to performing, we have all the details worked out. With new behaviors the details have yet to be worked out. Presumably, if very many Peruvian rural people took to boiling water, if it became "traditional," stove design would change in Peru as it has in some other parts of the world to include space on the stove for the water boiling equipment. But the Health Service had apparently not contemplated that problem. (We may hope that part of Nelida's job included recommendations to the Health Service.)

Actually, practical problems and beliefs are not really separable in this instance. The crisis of stove space came about only partly due to the shortage of fuel. Fuel was not in such short supply the whole year around. What made the stoves and available pans inadequate and required women to boil water at the time of the day when they were most busy were understandings: one understanding was that it was unpleasant to drink hot water at midday. Another was that the boiling would be undone if the water were allowed to stand overnight. Perhaps the reason that the Health Service had not anticipated the crisis of stove space and fuel was that the belief in water coming unboiled had not occurred to them; boiling had a different meaning in connection with microbes than it had in connection with theories about "hot" and "cold," and it may have taken an uneducated villager rather than an urban health officer to "confuse" these "two kinds of boiling" with each other!

In this chapter we shall discuss all of these problems in a little more detail and a little more abstractly, but still with specific reference to the problem of boiling water in Los Molinos. No two problems of planned change are ever the same, but problems *like* these seem to occur in virtually *all* planned-changes projects, and every experience of planning has lessons to teach the participants in every other.

Before we start we shall consider another matter: how anthropologists, as professional students of human society, can or should participate in planning efforts. Then we shall take up the problems of the cultural context for planned changes and the context in social structure.

The Ethics of Applied Anthropology

In the same sense in which any concern with human culture and society can be loosely called "anthropology," so, too, any application of knowledge about human culture and society to problems concerning human life and changes in

APPLIED
ANTHROPOLOGY *Any*
application of knowledge
about human culture and
society to problems
concerning human life and
changes in it.

it is called "applied anthropology." And even as people who are not anthropologists can be said to make "anthropological" observations or think "anthropological" thoughts, so planners who are not anthropologists can be thought of as doing "applied anthropology." However, just as the academic discipline of anthropology has developed distinctive concepts and methods for observing and explaining human behavior, so the application of these concepts and methods can be called "applied anthropology" in a more restricted sense. Anthropologists are rarely the only people involved in a project to introduce a change into the life of a community. Most often no anthropologists are involved at all. Many projects, however, do involve anthropological findings and concepts. And as anthropologists are in the business of analyzing human culture and society, we might expect that such projects will generally be more successful if they can draw upon the professional's knowledge and perspective about how human groups work.

In the case described here, anthropologists were not directly involved until after the project had been completed. Edward Wellin, the author of the report which was the basis for the case, arrived in 1953 after he had finished a couple of years of other work in the Ica Valley, and spent some months in Los Molinos studying the effects of the water boiling program and trying to discover the reasons for its successes and its failures. In some instances anthropologists are involved from the beginning. Anthropologists have played a direct role in such fields as birth control, uses of alternate sources of energy, implementation of modern agricultural programs, and acceptance of various health measures. There can be little doubt that applied anthropology is a growing field and that future anthropologists will be called on more and more to use the results of their discipline in promoting various kinds of changes in people's behavior by influencing the understandings that people share.

All this, of course, raises important ethical questions. At one extreme some anthropologists argue that the business of anthropology is to study people, not to change them. The use of anthropological knowledge in general, or of the knowledge of a particular community, in order to bring about a change in the community, is to betray it, it is argued. At the other extreme are anthropologists who argue that this is nonsense. As long as the changes made are for the good, it is argued, there is nothing at all the matter with making them, and if the anthropologist's knowledge can ease the transition from one moment in history to another, he not only ought to be allowed to use it that way but, like a doctor, even has a duty to do so.

Some people argue that because change is a continuing part of all human societies anyway, it is absurd to imagine that any end is served by refusng to participate in it. Others argue that anthropological knowledge, once published, will be used in planning programs whether or not it is professional anthropologists who use it, and anthropologists ought at least to show the responsibility to see that it is not used in a way that will accidentally cause pain and suffering rather than an improvement of the human condition.

In cases like inducing people to boil their drinking water, it is doubtful if

anyone but the most extreme purist of academic isolationism would maintain that an anthropologist was betraying the discipline to help. But many cases are not so clear. The recently contacted Tasaday of the southern Philippines are an example of a complex situation. It appears that the Tasaday were living in virtual isolation from other human societies when they were first contacted in 1971. They lived in caves, wore clothing made of leaves, lived by gathering wild foods, and used only stone and wooden tools, when newspapers around the world ran banner headlines about the discovery of a "Stone Age People" in the Philippines. Immediately they were visited by pouchers, tourists, officers of the Philippines commission on national minorities, the Philippine First Lady and her guests, and eventually even a couple of anthropologists assigned to get a study made while the Tasady were still pristine. The Tasaday may or may not have liked it, but they were isolated no longer. Overnight, they knew about helicopters, guns, cloth, steel, and all the rest. And indecision reigned about what Philippine "Tasaday policy" ought to be: should they be kept as they were? Presumably, they would not be dissatisfied simply to be left alone. Or was that even possible? With population growth as rapid as it is in the Philippines, how realistic was it to try to create a Tasaday reservation so big that they would never again have contact with outsiders? How desira-

Tasaday. Until 1971 the Tasaday lived in virtual isolation. With their discovery, an ethical question arose about what "Tasaday policy" ought to be.

Tasaday gathering
food.   Anthropologists
disagree about how deeply
they should be involved in
helping the Tasaday adjust
to their modern fate,
whatever it is to be.

ble was such a plan? Or should they be educated into the greater Philippine
society, so that they could cope with gun-toting surrounding peoples. The
classic debate about the "nobility" of the "noble savage" was the order of the
day. If the decision were to integrate the Tasaday into ordinary Philippine
life, could an anthropologist in good conscience offer his services in making
that transition as painless and rational as possible? Some would argue that
this was cultural genocide and that anthropologists should have no part of it.
Others would argue that to leave such a painful adjustment in Tasaday life in
the hands of administrators or others who were not anthropologists was
simply making it more painful and was yet more reprehensible. The stakes in
this are much higher than in the problem of boiling water in the Ica Valley,
and we can easily see how opinions would not only be divided, but would also
be firmly held.

But most situations are less momentous and there *are* some guidelines. More than thirty years ago the Society for Applied Anthropology formulated a code of ethics designed to protect the individuals and societies where programs of applied anthropology were being carried out, and to guide the anthropologist who wanted to participate in change projects without subjecting himself to criticism from less interventionist colleagues.

The basic tenet of this code of ethics is that the individual anthropologist has a prime responsibility to the people among whom he works, and not to the program or agency employing him. An anthropologist, in other words, whether a planner or a researcher, is not a spy, not the agent of an outside power, not the hand at the end of the law's proverbial long arm. The code specifically says that an anthropologist may not disclaim responsibility for a program in which he is involved by claiming that the goals of the program are decided by agencies and not by the anthropologist working in them. The anthropologist involved is still responsible for the effects of that program on the people with whom he works, whoever sets the goals, and this responsibility is specifically one that demands the anthropologist's allegiance to the welfare of the people in question. In general, anthropologists have construed this very conservatively, maintaining, for example, that the welfare of the subjects is not served by any program which they themselves believe is counter to their interest (even if the anthropologist believes or knows otherwise).

In the Los Molinos project that makes up our case, there can be little reasonable doubt that the goal of the program, the reduction in water-borne diseases, is a worthwhile one, and one which all the participants share; the ethical issues that face an anthropologist in a program such as this concern the

Water pump in Kenya. Few anthropologists would make ethical objections to development projects such as the water supply plant of which this pump is a part, completed in 1977 with aid from the Norwegian Agency for International Development.

way the project is carried out more than its goals. In fact, very few serious scholars would find the noncoercive techniques used in this project objectionable in the least.

Shared Understandings and Applied Anthropology

As noted earlier, a major issue in bringing about change in a community is the way in which the change is related to a broad range of understandings shared or partially shared by the people concerned. There is an old anthropological adage to the effect that everything is related to everything else, and in applied work just as much as in descriptive work the anthropologist is often and forcibly reminded how true this is. Perhaps the greatest source of failure in planning programs is the difficulty of foreseeing all of the connections between understandings that will eventually turn out to be relevant to whether or not the change is welcomed and adopted.

In the case at hand, the people of Los Molinos have at least four different sets of shared understandings that were relevant to their interest in drinking boiled water. First there were understandings about boiling itself. Then there were understandings about disease and how it was caused. Next there were understandings about the daily schedule and other physical routines. Finally there were understandings about different groups in the community. Let us look at these one by one.

The shared understandings the people of Los Molinos had regarding water and its boiling were part of an organized set of understandings they had regarding food and drink in general. We have seen that the people of this area classify all food and drink into "hot" and "cold," qualities understood to be inherent in the substances, and quite separate from temperature or spiciness. The fact that water was viewed as "hot" in a boiled state and "cold" when in its natural state (or leftover) was crucial in understanding the reaction of the village people to the attempt to get them to boil their water.

Equally important was the set of shared understandings concerning the sources of disease. The people of Los Molinos had their own shared understandings about what causes disease and these competed with the ones held by those who advocated water boiling. For the people of Los Molinos, disease could be contracted by exposure to "bad airs," by some diseases which traveled from a sick person and "stuck to" a well one, and by exposures to extremes of "hot" and, especially, "cold."

Another set of important understandings which are, however, indirectly rather than directly connected to water boiling in this case are all those that deal with work, eating, and drinking and that affect the daily schedule. We saw that the only time water could be boiled was after breakfast. This "practical matter" very much influenced the actual boiling of water, and its roots in local attitudes as well as in local equipment and available materials were crucial considerations in whether or not water would be boiled.

Finally there are the understandings which define the different groups in the community. These understandings tell individuals who is "like them" and who is different; they define the individuals whose opinions are most listened to and those whose opinions are less important; and they inform people as to what is proper behavior for the members of the various groupings. This last set of understandings is crucial to water boiling in several ways. One of these is that these understandings play an important part in the distribution of culture through the expectations (shared understandings regarding how different sorts of people should act in particular circumstances) that they partial out to the members of the community. In Los Molinos they included, for example, the relation that people saw between neatness and hygiene on the one hand and "putting on airs" or pretending to be higher than one really was on the other.

Culturally Constituted Environments

All human beings live in the same physical world, but their understandings about the world vary and their behavior is at least as much determined by those understandings as it is by the objects and people around them. This is because the *significance* or meaning of the objects and individuals that surround an actor are established not by those things themselves but by the understandings the actor has concerning them. How people treat others depends upon what they think those others are, what they believe those others can be depended on to do, and what ends the people themselves have. How they treat the objects they encounter is the direct expression of the understandings they have concerning these objects. The classification of food and drink into "hot" and "cold" held by the people of Los Molinos crucially determined their eating and drinking habits, including whether they were willing to boil water or not.

In short, in order for people's behavior to change, their understandings of the world around them must also change to some extent. In attempting to get the people of Los Molinos to change their behavior regarding water, it was vital that their understandings regarding both water and things indirectly connected with it also be changed. The job of applied anthropology, in fact, is to discover what shared understandings affect the objects and areas where change is desired and to indicate how changes in these understandings might be brought about.

The problem of apathy The difficulty of this task can be seen in Mrs. F's view of the world. When she says that for the "poor"—and by this she means people like herself in Los Molinos—there is enough to worry about in the world with poverty, "bad airs," "cold," and hunger without worrying about things "you cannot see, touch, smell, or feel," she is making the classical statement of a person resisting new understandings of his environment. To her, microbes may be real. The doctor says they are, so they probably are. But they certainly are not important given her understandings of the world. She sees them as simply "delicate little animals," and in her understanding of the world, there is no need to do anything about those animals, even granting that they do exist. The environment she "creates" by her understandings of the world simply provides no basis for boiling water as a means of avoiding sickness. Boiling water, or more exactly boiling water to kill disease-bearing microbes, is not a realistic idea for Mrs. F.

Nor is Mrs. F alone in viewing the world as one in which water boiling is, at best, an unnecessary activity for healthy people. The view of food and drink held by most of the people of Los Molinos is such that there is no reason for healthy people to drink boiled water, since in the understandings of disease shared in this area it is not the case that unboiled water causes disease. Extreme "cold" itself encourages disease and is especially to be avoided. It is for this reason that the water for sick people is to be boiled since boiling changes water from being "cold" to being "hot," which is why it is good for sick people. Boiled water in Los Molinos is rather like aspirin for many readers of this book. Aspirin is for people with a headache. If one's head does not ache, there is no need to take aspirin.

For the planner, having a reform regarded as unnecessary raises difficulties. Unnecessry reforms may be accepted for the time being, if for no other reason than for their novelty or to make the planner stop bothering people about them. It is worth a certain amount of expense or inconvenience, after all, just to make people stop urging one to do things. For example in most American cities the American Legion and other veterans' groups sponsor an annual "Poppy Day" just before Memorial Day, when volunteers walk the downtown streets "selling" paper and cloth "poppies" to collect money for various

Building Scandinavian-style agricultural machinery in Botswana. If people do not understand and believe the reason for a procedure, they are unlikely to follow it except in the presence of the developer. Belief depends partly upon the relationship between the new procedure and beliefs already established.

veterans' assistance programs. A pedestrian who displays a paper "poppy" on his clothing is not generally approached by a second volunteer, and many people buy a poppy early in the day less out of enthusiasm to support veterans' relief than to avoid being continually approached by eager volunteers. One volunteer in Chicago used to sell poppies with the call: "Poppies! Poppies! Buy your protection early!"

If people buy poppies for protection against other poppy vendors rather than to help veterans, they can hardly be thought of as very eager supporters of the veterans' programs; similarly people who adopt any behavior merely to satisfy the planner or get rid of him are unlikely to be very ardent enthusiasts. Conformity with a reform does not mean the planning program is successful because conformity without any enthusiasm often leads people to abandon the new behavior as soon as the planner's back is turned. As we suggested earlier, some of the water boiling women in Los Molinos might very well have given up the practice once Nelida was not around to care whether they did it or not.

The problem of negative associations Reforms perceived as objectionable present even greater difficulties than those merely thought unnecessary. The planner is unlikely to meet acceptance based only on the desire to please or be rid of him; instead he is liable to meet resistance and arguments that the proposed change is a bad thing, often for reasons he had never imagined.

There was no real harm in healthy people drinking boiled water, according to the understanding shared by most of the people in Los Molinos. It would not hurt them. But it was thought an unnecessary practice. The local opinion went beyond this, however. Not only was it unnecessary for healthy people to boil their drinking water, it was something of a crotchety luxury. The excessive weakness and ostentatious cleanliness implied by it led Los Molinos people to be suspicious. Everybody knew some people might boil water merely because they were "different" (like Nelida or Mrs. C, the Highlander, or like city people), but it was felt very probable that the reason "ordinary" people would boil water was more likely that they thought they were better than everybody else and wanted a way to show it. We saw that Mrs. B boiled water long before the workers from the Health Service came to the village. And we noted that she did it as part of her general demonstration of superiority to those around her. Her attitude was not lost on them, and any water boiler who was not sick opened the possibility that neighbors would view her as a person who was trying to "put on airs." If understandings about disease led people to think it unnecessary to boil water, understandings about putting on airs led people to *object* to boiling water. This provided a real obstacle to promoting the practice.

The Health Service did not expect people in Los Molinos to reject drinking water because of its being an effete custom, so far as we know, and yet the fact that healthy people who already boiled water did it to be fancy apparently made others unwilling to be associated with the practice. This reaction is not unfamiliar to any of us. Probably all of us take a dim view of practices that we associate with people whom we do not admire. Whether we

Rev. Sun Myung Moon. In order for an innovation to be adopted people need to see it as desirable or necessary. Negative associations hurt the chances of acceptance. Rev. Moon's efforts to change American life are probably weakened by stereotypes about revival meetings, "cults," the word "Moonies," or even the government of Korea.

think of some college students rejecting business suits and ties, or of American school boards outlawing the teaching of German during World War I, or of Old Money rejecting the flamboyant displays of the Nouveaux Riches, or of restaurant goers avoiding casseroles because they associate them with penny-pinching on the meat, we can easily recognize how people in Los Molinos might have felt about boiling water, given that the very people who boiled it were those who were unpopular for putting on airs.

Whatever the reasons in a particular case, a new behavior that has already been contaminated by such associations in people's minds must somehow be reinterpreted to them or it is probably doomed to failure. The popular association between drinking only boiled water and being hoity-toity was one of the most difficult problems that Nelida had to face in Los Molinos. She probably was not helped in this task by the fact that, with her superior education and urban contacts, she was, in a sense, a member of the very group that was admired and imitated by known water boilers. If Nelida and the doctor who lectured could have established that boiling water was not a citified attempt to show superiority, this would have facilitated water boiling even if the microbe theory of disease were not accepted. There were other obstacles to water boiling, but its association with attempts to make oneself superior was itself an important barrier to adoption of the practice. Judging from their rate of success, the health workers never solved the problem.

There are problems, then, when a reform is seen either as unnecessary or as objectionable. Without knowledge of the shared understandings that contribute to people taking these views, the planner is powerless to deal with them. Even with that knowledge the planner may have great difficulty making the plan seem like an improvement to the people he wants to have adopt it, however it may appear to the outside.

The problem of logistics A quite different sort of obstruction can be seen in considering Mrs. E's reaction to Nelida and the doctor's lecture. It will be remembered that Mrs. E agreed about the microbe theory of disease and agreed that boiling water was a desirable thing to do, but she explained that she simply "had no time" to boil the water. This was, in fact, true, given the daily schedule and kitchen equipment commonly found among the people of Los Molinos. Because of the shared understanding that water that "sleeps" becomes dangerously cold, it was impossible to boil water on the fire made to cook the evening meal. Because people wanted to drink most water at midday and were unwilling to drink warm water, it was not possible to boil on the fire made for the midday meal. Only the breakfast fire could serve for water boiling, and at that time of the day many women, like Mrs. E, were busy and could not possibly spare the time to put water on to boil. Even if they could do so the small number of cooking utensils they had and the construction of their stoves allowing only one or two vessels to be heated at once made this very difficult.

All the understandings that contribute to the work schedule, the allocation of resources so that few rather than many cooking utensils are acquired, and the desire to drink water only when it was cool, made it difficult for many people who had become convinced that water boiling was desirable to do anything about it. This obviously had important implications for the goal of bringing boiled water to Los Molinos. Even if the association with "putting on airs" could have overcome the obstacle presented by work schedules, stove construction, and cooking utensils would still have remained. In order to achieve a greater conversion to water boiling than was achieved by Nelida and the other workers from the Health Service, it would appear useful to encourage people to design their stoves to take more cooking vessels, to encourage them to acquire additional cooking utensils, and, perhaps, to advise a way for them to drink water boiled at the midday meal rather than at breakfast, since the established schedule seems to make the midday meal one where the cook is most likely to have a bit of time to use for boiling.

Social Structure and Its Influence on Boiling

In addition to the understanding we have already considered, those dividing the community into groups also affect the acceptance of water boiling. We saw in Mrs. C's case that a person who considers herself, and is considered, an outsider is in a different position regarding water boiling. Mrs. C was not particularly sensitive to the opinions of her *cholo* neighbors. She asserted her membership in the Highland group by wearing her hair in the Highland fashion, and she was not reluctant to call attention to her origin in the Highlands and her preference for that area. It is not clear whether or not the people of Los Molinos thought Mrs. C was "putting on airs" by boiling her water, but it is likely she would have been indifferent to any such gossip, since as a Highlander she believed the people of the lowlands, including Los Molinos, persecuted Highlanders anyway.

In addition the villagers were probably more likely to let Mrs. C behave in ways that they would not readily have accepted from people they considered "their own." They understood that Highlanders were different from themselves and did not expect their behavior to be the same as the behavior of people born in the village. Mrs. C occupied a status different from the status of locally born people, and people of Los Molinos were quite willing to overlook her "idiosyncrasy" in regard to water boiling.

It is an important aspect of the distribution of culture that the expectations applied to people considered to be like oneself are different from the expectations applied to people understood as different. These differences can be vital in the acceptance of such changes as water boiling. However it is probably also true that the fact that Mrs. C boiled water did nothing to promote water boiling among local people. Practices can come to be accepted when people view them as expected of individuals like themselves. So, for example, some people adopt clothing styles that they do not themselves necessarily find especially attractive because they believe that people in their position "ought to" wear such clothing. If enough people like oneself do something, one might well begin to do it too, even if one does not particularly like it, or even much understand it. So, if a large number of villagers in Los Molinos had begun to boil water, some of those who did not agree with, say, the microbe theory of disease, would nevertheless have begun to boil because they came to understand that boiling water was something people in their position should do. However, Mrs. C's boiling did nothing to help bring this about, since she was viewed as an outsider. Converting people like Mrs. C to water boiling was probably easier than converting people who were sensitive to the opinions of those around them, but the long-term effects of doing it may have been less helpful to the final goal of getting everyone to boil water.

Not all "outsiders" have the same status, of course. The doctor who came to lecture in the village was unquestionably an outsider, but he also had a special status as a consequence of his being a physician. Mrs. D accepted some

Group innoculation. Co-operation with a project such as this World Health Organization campaign against Yaws in Haiti is made easier by enthusiastic participation of people influential in forming local opinion. In rural Haiti, as in Los Molinos, the prestige of a doctor helps gain acceptance for the program.

of the changes proposed to her by Nelida, but she credited the doctor for her conversion to boiling water. And this happened despite the fact that Nelida had had more than ten visits to her house to discuss the matter. When Mrs. D finally did begin to boil water, she did not widely advertise her conversion, but when she did talk about it, she said she was doing it because "the doctor said to." It is obvious that as a member of the community with the status of "insider" she did not want to make too much of the fact that she was beginning a practice which might be considered "putting on airs." However some people were sure to know she was doing it, and she "covered herself" by explaining that it was the doctor who convinced her to do it. Again our information regarding the culture of the people of Los Molinos is incomplete and it is not entirely clear what expectations are attached to the status "doctor," but it appears that doctors are expected to advise people to do things for their health even when those things are not strictly in accordance with understandings shared by the villagers. By invoking the status of the doctor and its expectations, it appears that Mrs. D hoped to avoid the undesirable meanings that might be attached to her new practice.

Mrs. D's use of the doctor's status indicates an important means by which existing shared understandings that stand in the way of a desired behavior change can be overcome. If there is a status which is accepted as able to recommend things even if they are not completely in accord with local understandings, these things might be accepted by some local people because of the importance they attach to that status. Thus one researcher in a small Japanese village found that local people were quite open to educational changes advocated by the Ministry of Education and its local representatives even when they did not understand them. The attitude was that the Ministry knew about these things, and that whatever it recommended about education ought to be followed. Similarly one of the authors once heard a couple in a train disputing about the time it would arrive in Salt Lake City. In the absence of a schedule there was no way to resolve the dispute, but the wife attempted to win the argument by revealing that she had heard another passenger mention the time she was arguing for. Her husband claimed that he too had had his time confirmed by another passenger. The wife now clinched the argument by revealing that the passenger she had heard was "a professor." She hoped to imply that someone who specialized in knowing things could not possibly be mistaken about the arrival time in Salt Lake City. The status of professor attached to her advocacy was a good enough reason for her to feel quite sure of herself, and it seemed to her that with the prestige of The Academy behind her, her husband surely would have no choice but to come around to agree with her.

The snowball effect If there are enough people willing to follow a plan of action because it is backed by a person in a certain status, they can start a "snowball" process that is difficult to start with outsiders like Mrs. C. Sometimes not everyone in the community will follow the suggestions of the occupant of some particular status, but if it is somehow possible to get a considerable number to do so, it can begin the process of people coming to view whatever is suggested (such as boiling one's drinking water) as something reasonable people in the community are likely to do. Once that process is under way, a movement toward general conformity is begun. This did not happen in Los Molinos. It was the basic reason the Health Service sent doctors to lecture in the Ica Valley, although it is possible that they were not fully aware of precisely what it was they sought to do. An investigation of the expectations attaching to the doctor's status might have made it possible to maximize the effectiveness of his suggestions by identifying the areas in which these suggestions would most readily be accepted.

"One of us" Social structure refers to all the interlocked statuses in a group and not just those involving outsiders, of course. The people of Los Molinos were divided into three basic ethnic groups: *cholos*, Highlanders, and blacks. Nelida, the health worker, was herself a *cholo*, and her greatest success was among her fellow *cholos*. The community had only relatively few Highlanders, but a considerable minority were blacks. We saw in Mrs. F's case that there was considerable antagonism between blacks and *cholos*, and that Mrs. F was rather antagonistic to Nelida. It was a sound move on the part of the Health Service to train hygiene workers from the area where they were to work, but given the fact that the population was ethnically divided it was impossible for them to have a worker who could approach all parts of the group with equal ease. *Cholos* viewed Nelida as "one of us," and this had important advantages. It also, however, had disadvantages in that she became subject to the antagonisms that existed between the community's different groups. Her inability to convert Mrs. F to water boiling was probably as much due to Mrs. F's conservatism as to her being black, but it would be interesting to know if a black worker could have converted her. Perhaps a black worker could not have done so, but the relations between the black worker and Mrs. F would surely have been quite different, whether or not Mrs. F ultimately took up boiling her water.

Applied Anthropology and The Rapidly Changing World

Anthropologists have an important role in a world changing at a faster rate than it ever has before. In all parts of the world, people are in the midst of technological changes that uproot procedures followed by generations before them. Through a knowledge of the understandings shared by the members of groups undergoing such changes, the dislocation and difficulty associated with change can sometimes be minimized. Skilled anthropologists able to identify shared understandings that directly and indirectly affect reaction to change can have a powerful effect on the course of that change. In areas like Los Molinos, new health techniques are becoming available to people previously denied their benefits, and it is possible (indeed probably necessary) to use the concepts of an anthropologist's approach in order to succeed in encouraging the adoption of many of the procedures with the most promise to improve the general level of human health and well being.

Anthropology is still a young discipline, and its techniques are by no means

Komuna Paryska shipyard. This shipyard is in Poland, but it could as well be in Argentina or Taiwan. Industrialization now reaches all parts of the world. The question is how anthropology can help to ease the dislocations that go with the process.

as effective as anthropologists would like them to be, but it does have a great deal to contribute, and applied anthropology can have an important and constructive role in modern world society.

SUMMARY

Applied anthropology is the use of anthropological concepts and techniques in programs aimed at altering behavior of members of human groups usually through altering their understandings of the world around them. Clearly involved are the understandings people have that directly influence whatever behavior is the object of programs of change. But understandings less directly connected to the object can also have a powerful influence. In a program aimed at bringing about water boiling in order to lessen water-borne diseases, we saw that the people's understandings regarding the classification of food and drink also influenced their behavior, as did the understandings underlying their daily schedule, the construction of their stoves, and the number of cooking utensils they owned. The social structure of the community was seen to exert a number of powerful influences on the acceptance and rejection of the desired change. The expectations that attached to particular statuses in the community not only influenced whether their occupants accepted or rejected the proposed change, but also influenced the extent to which one individual's acceptance of the change encouraged others to accept it.

There are serious ethical problems involved in attempts to change people's behavior, and anthropologists are aware of these and have formulated a code to deal with them. A crucial fact to remember is that the knowledge derived from anthropology is likely to be used whether or not anthropologists agree to its use or participate actively. Anthropologists can often have a benevolent effect on governmental or private programs of social and cultural change.

The concepts and techniques of anthropology are still relatively simple and undeveloped, but an important role for applied anthropology already exists in the modern world with its very rapid change.

SUGGESTED READINGS

Foster, George M. 1973 Societies and Technological Change. New York and London: Harper and Row. (Second ed. First ed. Traditional Cultures and the Impact of Technological Change, 1962)

This new edition of the classic, introductory book in applied anthropology is aimed mainly at technicians concerned with planned change, but it is also an excellent introduction to applied anthropology for introductory students.

Colson, Elizabeth 1971 The Social Consequences of Resettlement: The Impact of the Kariba Resettlement upon the Gwenbe Tonga. Kariba Studies 4. Manchester: Manchester University Press.

This fascinating study of an African group that was forcibly moved from their home area so that the area could be flooded by a new dam begins with the sentence "Massive technological development hurts." The book shows dramatically what rapid, planned change can do and how people react to it.

GILLEN, JOHN 1949 Moche, A Peruvian Coastal Community. Smithsonian Institute of Social Anthropology, Publication no. 3, Washington, D.C.

An ethnographic account of a Peruvian community similar to Los Molinos in many respects.

BROKENSHA, DAVID 1969 Community development: an interpretation. Scranton, Pa.: Chandler Publishing Company.
Discusses successes and failures of applied anthropology, with a variety of case studies.

SECTION FOUR

Beyond Human Nature: The Anthropological Analysis of Life Among Nonhuman Primates

Anthropology, as the study of human beings and human society, is particularly concerned with culture and its variations. It is the conviction that all variations count as legitimately human that drives anthropologists to collect data on so many societies, whether large or small, and to continue considering theoretical generalizations in a relentlessly comparative framework. This same concern with culture that characterizes the physical anthropologist and leads him to consider human fossil ancestors with particular concern for their possible ability to participate in societies and maintain cultural understandings that might be considered recognizably "human" in type. Going back in history, the fine line between the human and the prehuman is difficult to draw. At what point in the long development of us moderns would we be willing to say that prehuman society and culture became human society and culture (even assuming we had all the evidence we wanted on the point)?

Many human capacities are not, after all, uniquely human. Our ability to walk, for example, is shared with most other animals, however crucial it is to the functioning of human society. On the other hand our ability to learn to make pizza is entirely limited to ourselves. No other animal has ever mastered this sort of skill. The family dog may be fond of pizza, but he is quite unable to master the skills involved in making it.

The student of human society and culture has a necesary concern both with the historical question of the gradual emergence of an animal with legitimately human abilities and potential, and with the larger question of the extent to which human skills are shared with other animals. People are not descended from apes any more than apes are descended from people. People are descended from protopeople, and apes are descended from protoapes, but if one goes far enough back there is ultimately a common ancestor (named Dryopithecus), a being that is at once a protoprotoperson and a protoprotoape, so that modern apes are therefore of particular comparative interest as the closest relatives to humans among all living animals.

Apes too have society, and apes too, we are beginning to realize, have shared understandings. From studying the abilities, the preferences, and the habitual behaviors of these related animals, anthropologists are gaining new insights into human abilities, human preferences, and habitual human behaviors.

We have seen how anthropology is able to

shed additional light on a culture of any particular human society by studying a wide variety of human societies and their lifeways. In a similar way it is possible to gain a better understanding of the capacities of humans in general through the study of non-human ways of life in comparison with human ones. By comparing different human societies, we learn more about each of them individually. And by comparing different primates (including humans), we learn more about them individually. The academic subdiscipline of anthropology that is particularly devoted to the comparative study of humans, apes, and monkeys is called "primatology."

Primatology is comparatively new as an integral part of cultural anthropology. Physical anthropologists have been concerned with the anatomy of nonhuman primates for decades, particularly as a help in interpreting the fossil evidence of ancient humans, prehumans, and nonhumans. But the emphasis on the comparative study of human and nonhuman primate behavior is comparatively recent, and yet to be entirely integrated into the general stream of cultural-anthropological research. In Chapter 11, we review some of this work, with particular reference to the topics raised about human beings in the earlier chapters of this book. There is no "case" to begin this chapter. Primate studies do not seem to us to lend themselves to using a case to start off the discussion the way the subject matter of the other chapters did, so the chapter begins directly with the general and theoretical discussion.

11

Learning from Monkeys and Apes

I confess to you, I could never look upon a monkey,
without very mortifying reflections.

WILLIAM CONGREVE
LETTER TO DENNIS, 1695

Lowland gorilla.

In what ways are we like the monkeys and apes?

Is their social structure similar to human social structure?

Do they have culture?

Is there such a thing as a moral ape?

How do these nonhuman primates communicate with each other?

Is our brain anything like the brains of these beasts?

Humans are mammals, and, like all mammals, many of their inherited traits are traits that contribute to greater effectiveness and greater complexity of behavior. Also like all mammals, and birds too, humans produce only a relatively small number of offspring and lavish a great deal of care and attention on those few they have. A substantial part of what is human can be attributed to the fact that humans are mammals. Even more of what is human, however, results from the fact that humans are primates. In a sense, primates are the mammals who carry mammalian characteristics the furthest. The long mammalian childhood reaches its zenith among the primates, and the highly developed and complex mammalian brain finds its most intense development and complexity in the primates. In mammals generally, the highly evolved brain and the long childhood combine to produce individuals with both the opportunity to learn a great deal in their prolonged association with their mothers and other adults and the neural equipment that gives this association its full impact and richness. In other words, much of what is distinctive about humans and their means of adapting themselves to the world and each other has its base in the heritage they have as mammals and, especially, as primates. In humanity's primate heritage are the foundations for human society, human culture, and human personality and, in fact, the beginnings of these human means of adaptation.

The Importance of Primate Child Care and Mother-Child Relations

It is impossible, of course, to know how primate young were cared for during the Miocene and earlier, but we can get an idea of the primate heritage in this area of behavior, as in many others, by examining what the different living primates do. We know that humans and the African apes are very close relatives, sharing common ancestors until only about 10 million years ago (see Chapter 6, "Human Beginnings"). Anything humans do that gorillas, chimps, and monkeys also do is almost certainly a part of the heritage humans derive from the ancestors they shared with these nonhuman primates and perhaps others whose lines of descent separated from the human line earlier. Of course, parallel evolution can give rise to similarities when quite different forms face similar problems under similar circumstances, but if all hominoids have the same trait, that trait is almost certainly a product of their common primate heritage. We study monkeys and apes, then, not only to find out what humans share with them, but also to gain insights into the behavior and adaptation of our early primate ancestors.

On the basis of molar wear we believe that dryopithecine apes and the first hominid, *Ramapithecus*, had the extended period of childhood dependence characteristic of contemporary primates, including humans. The presence of a long childhood in humanity's ancestors is certain. As Table 6 shows, the combined infancy and prepubescent ("juvenile") phases in the lives of primates are quite long in absolute terms, occupying roughly a

Table 6 Duration of Life Periods[a]

	FOETAL PHASE (days)	INFANTILE PHASE (years)	JUVENILE PHASE (years)	ADULT PHASE (years)	LIFE SPAN (years)
Lemur	126	$\frac{3}{4}$	$1\frac{3}{4}$	11+	14
Macaque	168	$1\frac{1}{2}$	6	20	27–28
Gibbon	210	?2	$6\frac{1}{2}$	20+	30+
Orangutan	233	$3\frac{1}{2}$	7	20+	30+
Chimpanzee	238	3	7	30	40
Gorilla	265	3+	7+	25	?35
Modern man	266	6	14	50+	70–75

[a]Table shows duration of life periods of primates derived from many sources. Foetal phase is equivalent to gestation period. Life span is the summation of the three postnatal phases. Uncertainty is indicated by ? or a + sign.

SOURCE: Napier and Napier, 1967, A Handbook of Living Primates, London, Academic Press, p. 40.

quarter of the total life span. Compared to those of other mammals, the length is even more impressive. The lowly lemur, for example, lives about as long as a domestic cat, but instead of that pet's roughly ten months of combined infancy and prepuberty, the lemur[1] has, perhaps, two years. The orang lives about as long as a horse, but instead of the horse's year or so of immaturity, the Indonesian ape has seven years. The mammalian trait of having a long childhood, then, is greatly extended in the primates, and this prolonged period of dependency is an important part of the primate heritage.

The main importance of the long childhood can be found in the relations between the child and its adult companions and peers. These relationships provide the basis for the complex primate social adjustment. During their early relationship with their mothers, most mammals learn to desire the company of others of their kind, and in primates this is intensified as so many mammalian traits are. Just how crucial the infant's experience is to adequate development can be seen by examining monkeys and apes whose infancies and childhoods have been disrupted. Numerous studies have shown that primates deprived of early contact with their mothers are unable to function as other animals of their group do even if their physical needs

[1]The late Professor Earnest Hooton of Harvard was a distinguished physical anthropologist and an irrepressible writer of amusing verse. His doggerel (1947:15) about the lemur expresses a view rather common among students.

The lemur is a lowly brute;
His primate status some dispute.
He has a damp and longish snout
With lower front teeth leaning out.
He parts his fur with this comb-jaw,
And scratches with a single claw
That still adorns a hinder digit
Wherever itching makes him fidget.
He is arboreal and omnivorous;
From more about him, Lord deliver us.

are met. The disruptive effect is intensified if they are also isolated from their peers.

Isolated primate infants A series of experiments in which baby rhesus monkeys were isolated from their mothers show how dramatically important the mother-child relationship is for the development of an adequately functioning adult (Harlow and Harlow 1962, 1965). Babies reared in cages by themselves grew up into desperately maladapted adults. Upon reaching physical maturity the monkeys reared in isolation cannot copulate as other monkeys can do. Female monkeys reared in isolation have been paired with normally reared males, some of which managed, with serious difficulty, to impregnate their partners. The mothers treated the babies born of these unions very differently from the way rhesus babies are normally treated. The mothers did not assist their infants in nursing as normal mothers do, and the infants that managed to find a nipple by themselves were ignored instead of being helped. Mothers reared in isolation physically assaulted their babies, striking them away, stepping on them, and grinding their faces on the cage floor. The babies had to be removed from their mothers' cages to prevent their destruction.

The isolated monkeys are also impaired in areas other than sex and mothering, and they do not interact with others of their kind in the usual ways. A good deal of their time in early life is spent in stereotyped behaviors such as rocking back and forth, hugging themselves, and sucking their thumbs or big toes. As these deprived animals get older, the stereotyped behaviors become less frequent, but they continue through their lives. Putting these monkeys together with normally reared monkeys after the early isolation diminishes the effect of that isolation, but the isolated monkeys never come to act as normal ones do. Monkeys reared in isolation showed either excessive excitement or, occasionally, apathy and fear when entering a novel setting, which had an obviously detrimental effect on their ability to learn new things.

Rather similar work with chimpanzees shows similar results (Turner, Davenport, and Rogers 1969). As with rhesus monkeys, chimps reared in isolation cannot perform the sexual act upon reaching maturity and do not interact with others of their kind in the usual ways. Like the monkeys, the chimps deprived of their mothers and other social contacts spend much of their time in early life behaving in ways characteristic of mentally deficient and severely disturbed human children, that is, rocking back and forth, hugging themselves, rolling their heads, and sucking their thumbs.

The effects of early deprivation are lessened when the isolated animals are put together with normally reared ones, and some evidence indicates that the chimps recover from early isolation more fully than rhesus monkeys do. The isolated chimps learn to perform sexually after a period of being reunited with others of their kind reared normally. The inability to deal with social situations as well as normally reared chimps can, however, persists through life, and excessive excitement in new settings interferes with the

Mothering Among Monkeys Raised in Isolation   Monkeys raised in isolation from their mothers and peers grow up into socially and sexually maladapted adults. When females of this type bear an offspring, they treat it very differently from the way normal monkey mothers would. The mother in (a) is grinding the baby into the floor of her cage. In (b) and (c), monkeys isolated in infancy engage in thumb-sucking and self-hugging, two common examples of the stereotyped behavior characteristic of monkeys deprived of early social contact. Socially isolated monkeys grow up to be either apathetic or, as in (d), excessively excited in contacts with other monkeys.

(a)

(b)

(c)

(d)

learning of new things even though general mental ability does not seem to be impaired.

As with the monkeys, being separated from the mother is very damaging to chimpanzees' ability to behave as other chimps do and to get along with others normally. Alison Jolly, looking at the results of maternal deprivation from a humane and human perspective, says: "The frightening part is that these differences [in learning ability between normal and isolated chimps] remain among adolescent chimpanzees who have been 'normally' caged with others for five or six years after their early isolation" (A. Jolly 1972:233).

The period from birth to some point well into childhood, then, is crucial for adjustment and development. This period of close attachment to the mother is an important part of the human primate heritage in a number of ways. It is during this period that the young individual develops social ties with the mother and others and, it seems, develops the motives and skills necessary for successful group life. Sexual skill, mothering, and at least some types of learning are all dependent upon satisfactory early-childhood relationships.

The incest inhibition   The mother is dominant with respect to the child, which is partly the basis for what can be called an "incest inhibition." This has been observed in operation in the relations between mother and son in at least four primate genera: Japanese macaques, rhesus monkeys, baboons, and chimpanzees. Mother-son copulation, in fact, has only rarely been observed in *any* of the free-living higher primates.

Observation of wild macaques over a period of several years revealed only one instance of mother-son copulation. This took place after the son had risen sharply in the group's social hierarchy, and it suggests that the incest inhibition, at least in part, can be understood as related to the mother's continued domination of her child even after he has outgrown physical dependency. Among chimpanzees living in their natural setting, the mother shows deference and respect for her grown son at the same time that he continues the deferential behavior toward her he showed when he was physically immature, and their relationship is one of mutual respect. Whether this plays a part in it or not, it appears that mother-son sexual relations are rare or nonexistent among chimpanzees. Goodall (1971) reports two instances of females in estrus who copulated with all the males present except their mature sons, who stood by and made no attempt to mount their mothers. This is despite the fact that during estrus females usually couple with all the males present. Among rhesus monkeys sons and mothers rarely mate, even if the sons are dominant over their mothers.

Goodall reports that wild chimpanzee brothers had sexual relations with a sister despite her screaming protest. There is a possibility that the incest inhibition among chimps is extended to siblings, but this remains to be established by more observations of free-living animals. Among primates living in multimale bands there is no way, either for the animals or the observer, to establish paternity, so there is no possibility of a father-daughter incest inhibition. Among single-male groups such as the hamadryas baboon, the father is known with reasonable probability, although the females in a group do sometimes mate out of the leader male's sight with "follower" males who stay near the group. Sexual relations between father and daughter are inhibited among hamadryas baboons by the fact that young males beginning their own harems "kidnap" immature females from their father's group before they are mature enough to interest the father, thus ensuring that daughters are out of the father's presence when they are sexually mature. This, however, is quite a different phenomenon from the active abstention from copulation characteristic of chimp mothers and sons.

The important fact is that for a number of genera of primates, there is an incest inhibition. More observation of free-living higher primates may reveal this inhibition to be present in additional genera, and more evidence of inhibition for siblings may be found. Even if it is not, a reasonable possibility exists that at least a mother-son sexual inhibition may have been present as part of the primate heritage as the early hominids began to evolve toward modern human status. This is important in a number of respects, but let us begin by examining its significance for the question of the presence or absence of culture among nonhuman primates.

Social Life: Learning and Protection

All modern primates, regardless of genus, live in social groups. Almost certainly, ancient ancestral primates did the same. Otherwise, how can we explain the universality of the practice among the diverse modern members of the order? A leading physical anthropologist and a psychiatrist who specializes in primate studies argue convincingly that social life among primates is derived from the opportunities this way of living provides for learning and the mutual protection it provides.

> Why does the [nonhuman primate] group exist? Why does the animal not live alone, if not all year at least for much of it? There are many reasons but the principal one is *learning* [emphasis in original]. The group is the locus of knowledge and experience far exceeding that of the individual member. It is in the group that experience is pooled and the generations linked. The adaptive function of prolonged biological youth is that it gives the animal time to learn. During this period, while the animal learns from other members of the group, it is protected by them. Slow development in isolation would simply mean disaster for the individual and extinction for the species. . . . Harlow's experiments have shown the importance of the mother-infant relationship and of the play group in the development of normal social behavior. Clearly, under natural conditions fundamental learnings take place inevitably. A monkey that did not learn to be social would be eliminated [Washburn and Hamburg 1965:364].

These points are important from the perspective of the evolutionary development of primate life. Judging from the facts that a long childhood is a very old primate characteristic and that modern primates have little but group living to protect the young and each other, it is very likely that the ancient primates with their long childhoods also relied on group life. We cannot know for certain what these early groups were like, but from examining the behavior of modern primates we can get some idea of how the groups offered protection and the sort of learning social life entailed.

Groups offer protection to their members in a number of different ways. Just being in a group does that to some extent as can be seen, for example, by observing African antelopes. These beasts graze together and flee together when they are attacked by a predator. Chasing a group is harder for the predator than chasing an individual, and sometimes at least the predator's charge is made fruitless by his going first after one antelope and then another, with the result that both get away. Some primates do more than that and either offer a defense against attack or distract the attacker. Some plains baboons are active defenders, and when they are threatened by a predator, the females and young come together and the adult males interpose themselves between them and the threat. Among pata monkeys there is only one adult male in each group, and in the face of an attacker he calls attention to himself while the others in the group flee in another direction. Chimpanzees do not seem to be subject to much attack by predators, but an observer put a stuffed leopard in the path of a group of free-living chimps. A large male picked up a stick and struck the leopard with blows sufficiently strong to have killed it had it been real and dim-witted enough to stay around and receive the blows.

Whatever the details of how different primates provide protection, social living is always involved in some way. Social living also provides oppor-

Baboons Treed by a Lioness. Group life offers protection at least to the extent that chasing a group is more difficult than chasing a single individual. Many times a predator will give up the chase when faced with five or six enormous adult male baboons.

tunities for learning that are particularly important for the young during their long dependency period when they most require protection. The two bases for social life are thus closely interrelated.

Groups, Evolution, and Learning

The idea that primate behavior is entirely instinctive, meaning that it is wholly determined by inherited mechanisms alone and that experience does not matter, is difficult to support, particularly in the face of what we have seen about the inability of monkeys and chimps to copulate when they have been isolated in their early years. If reproductive behavior does not appear "automatically" as a result of the creature's innate constitution and regardless of what experiences it has had, we must ask whether *any* complex behavior occurs without being influenced by social learning. The difficulties the isolated primates had in getting along with others of their kind and in caring for their young give some indication of how generally important social learning is.

Granting the crucial importance of social learning should not lead to the view that the biological basis for learning can be ignored. The fact is that some primates of the same species learn the same things even if their groups are separated by such great distances that there could be no contact between them. It is also true that primates fail to learn some things even though they are exposed to them for a long time.

David Hamburg, a psychiatrist, has an important idea that brings the biological basis for learning and learning itself together. It is called "ease of learning." The idea is both simple and useful.

Individuals seek and find gratifying those situations that have been highly advantageous in survival of the species [emphasis in original]. That is, tasks that must be done [for species survival] tend to be quite pleasurable; they are easy to learn and hard to extinguish. . . . Selection may operate on *differential readiness for learning responsiveness and attachment to others of the same species* [emphasis in original] [Hamburg 1968:254].

What "ease of learning" refers to is an evolutionary process whereby selection favors individuals who can and want to learn the things that the species requires for survival. Such selection produces individuals with the biological basis—in learning ability, perception, and motivation—for learning what needs to be learned for species survival. This process works on all mammals, but is particularly important among the primates with their very long periods of childhood and consequent opportunities to learn.

The individual must have the opportunity to learn, as isolated monkeys and chimpanzees do not, but he must also have the specific physical equipment with which to learn the particular thing. This equipment is provided for him by the evolutionary process that shaped him and all the other members of his group. For example, chimpanzees build nests for sleeping every night, and all chimps build in much the same way. Only chimps learn to build nests in this way, but *all* free-living chimps[2] learn it even if their groups are separated by great distances. Even so, the learning involved in building the nests cannot be dismissed. Baby chimps sleep with their mothers in the mothers' nests for the first four or five years of their lives, but during this time they observe their mothers making nests and play at nest building. Beginning as early as ten months, the baby chimp begins to bend twigs and grass into the semblance of an adult nest, and as it gets older it makes nests more and more proficiently. These early "play nests" are not used for sleeping. The infant or juvenile ape often makes them, bounces around in them a time or two, and then tears them apart to make a new one. Nest building is practiced and learned so that when the young is too old to sleep with its mother, it can make its own nest with no difficulty.

Similarly, chimpanzee adults shape grass stems to use in pulling termites from their mounds. An adult will select a longish stem and push it through the wall of the termite mound. When termites inside seize it with their jaws, they can be pulled out with the stem and eaten. Chimps have been observed to strip leaves and projections from twigs for use in their termite fishing, make a number of "fishing tools," take them to a mound, and put all but one aside until the twig or stem being used needs replacement. Young chimps learn this from observation, and Goodall has recorded a particular chimp child she called Merlin as it observed its mother termite fishing and learned how to "fish" itself over the course of two years (see Goodall 1971:227–228).

These behaviors are unquestionably learned, but at the same time they have a biological base. If they did not, how could we explain the undeniable fact that the behaviors are present in different chimpanzee groups separated by half the continent of Africa? The behaviors have a survival value for the species, and selection has gone on for many generations for individuals who are able and willing to learn them. The "ease of learning" of these behaviors for chimps is very high.

This does not mean that chimps *must* learn these behaviors or even that they *will* learn them, but only that they have the biological equipment to do so if the social situation presents them with the opportunity. If biology made no difference, we would not find the same nests in different chimpanzee groups on different sides of Africa. If social learning made no difference, how do we understand the monkeys and chimps that do not know how to copulate after they have been isolated in infancy? Social learning only takes place when the biological basis for it is present, but when that basis *is* present, behaviors can be transmitted by it from individual to individual. For example, young monkeys that have seen their mothers startled by seeing a snake in a laboratory box avoid that box although they themselves have not seen the snake that is in it.

---

[2]Chimps living in zoos do not learn to do it if conditions are not as in the wild.

One of the most impressive demonstrations of the place of social learning in primate behavior comes from the work of the staff of the Japan Monkey Center. Primatologists at the center studied a troop of free-living macaques (macaques are rather large terrestrial monkeys) on a small, isolated island. The island had a mountain and a forested area where the macaques did all their foraging and a beach area where they very rarely went and never foraged. None was observed to enter a stream flowing near the beach or to go into the ocean. In 1952 the primatologists began to leave sweet potatoes on the beach, and the monkeys came to the "new" area to select the ones most nearly free of sand and eat them. A year after the sweet-potato distribution began, a young female monkey was observed taking potatoes to the stream, holding them in the water with one hand, and brushing or washing the sand away with the other. This washing technique was taken up first by monkeys of the originator's age (around two) without regard to their sex. Within five years of the young female's first washing, more than three-quarters of all young animals were washing their potatoes. Adults, however, were much slower to learn, and within the same five years less than a fifth had taken up the practice. All the adult washers were female!

The explanation for this difference in learning is to be found more in the opportunity to observe others through feeding with them than in age and sex differences alone. The young fed together and thus had more opportunity to learn from the originator. Mothers feed with their young, and adult females have some chance to learn from their young. Male adults, however, feed away from the main body of females and young and thus had very little opportunity to observe the new practice. After a time the washing innovation was "taught" by macaque mothers to their young, and the behavior is now well established on the research island.[3] Lest it be thought that this whole phenomenon is divorced from the biologically based process called "ease of learning," it is important to note the comment on the macaques' potato washing by the primatologist Hans Kummer:

> These are the same movements baboons use when removing dirt or bristles from a fruit. Apparently these behavior patterns develop easily from the behavioral potential of ground-living primates, or in other terms, these species are genetically predisposed for brushing and rolling movements. In this case, potato-washing is new only insofar as the cleaning movements are performed in water [Kummer 1971:123].

Learning is a vital element, but so is the biological base established by generations and millennia of evolution of the species.

We could supply further examples of social learning by various sorts of primates, but the main point would still be this: Learning takes place in

---

[3]The description of the feeding experiment can be found in Kawai (1965). Kummer (1971:117–124) discusses the full implications of the washing behavior and another innovation learned by the troop from the same young female.

**Chimpanzee Investigates
Foot of Newborn Sibling.**
Primate learning takes
place in social settings and
involves a genetic predisposition to learn.

social settings, and it involves a genetic predisposition to learn. When that predisposition is present, the learning provides a means for transmitting information from individual to individual and generation to generation whether the information concerns nest building, potato washing, or any other complex behavior. Inasmuch as culture is primarily learning and the transmission of learning from generation to generation, the evidence from monkeys and apes requires that we consider the fundamental basis for culture as part of the primate heritage.

Although primates learn a great deal from their associations with others of their kind, it should be clear that there is no *teaching*. Knowledge is passed from generation to generation, but most or all of it comes from observation by the learner rather than from positive activity on the part of those that already have the knowledge. In the next section it will become clear that the moral force characteristic of culture is mostly or entirely absent from the knowledge shared by nonhuman primates, and because of this, these primates cannot be considered to have true "culture." We must also emphasize that the transmission of culture among humans involves active teaching, which is absent among primates. On this ground too, then, they cannot be said to have culture in its full sense. In the words of C. F. Hockett

(1959:36): "A behavior pattern is transmitted culturally if it is not only learned but *taught*, and if the teaching behavior, whatever it may be, is also learned. . . ."

Culture and Protoculture: Are the Apes Moral?

As we discussed in Chapter 2, culture is not simply a matter of learning. It is more than a series of understandings about what can be done or, even, what is a useful or effective way of doing things. *Culture has a moral element.* Its component shared understandings are prescriptive or proscriptive or both in stating what must or ought to be done and what must not or ought not be done. The importance of the moral force contained in the elements of culture is its role in influencing behavior by making understandings more likely to serve as actual guides for action rather than simply as information about how one might behave. The effect of moral force, in other words, is to increase the likelihood that shared understandings will actually serve as guides for behavior, which, in turn, makes it possible for the members of a group to predict (within limits) what their fellows are likely to do. Such prediction is essential to social life. For our present purposes the question is: Do the nonhuman primates have any trace of this moral force in the understandings that they have learned and that they share among themselves?

Predictability is essential to the social life of nonhuman primates in the same way it is for human social life. Among monkeys and apes, as among other nonhuman social mammals, predictability is promoted by the existence of a limited range of behaviors that *can* be learned by the members of each species. Investigation of the existence of variations in the behavior of nonhuman primates of the same species but living in different places and under different conditions has only recently been undertaken in a vigorous way, but it is clear that what these nonhuman primates *can* learn from each other in the wild is distinctly limited. In other words, the importance of moral restrictions is less for nonhuman primates than for humans because, as a simple matter of learning, the available alternatives are fewer. Even so, it is vital to our understanding of the primate heritage to try to find out if there is any sign of morality among monkeys and apes.

To do this, we must try to find a means of detecting the presence or absence of moral force in shared understandings. Such a measure would have to reveal in some way that the actor felt differently about behavior governed by an understanding with a prescriptive element than he did about behavior not governed by such an element. The feeling in question would have to be concerned with some idea of good and bad. If the actor has behaved in accord with what was called (in Chapter 2) a "prescriptive understanding," he would, if he really shared the understanding and its moral component, feel good. If he had not followed the prescriptive understanding, he would feel bad. With human actors it is possible to find out how they feel about what they do through conversations and interviews, a procedure hardly feasible with monkeys and apes. Any measure we might have for the non-human primates would have to derive from observations of behavior and inferences based on those observations. One sort of observation that can lead to the inference that understandings have moral force for nonhuman primates would be seeing a monkey or ape refraining from doing something pleasurable when there are no *practical* reasons for refraining.

This brings us back to the incest inhibitions we noted in the last section and why these are important to our consideration of the extent of the primate heritage in the area of culture. A particularly striking instance we cited was the two chimpanzee males that refrained from copulating with their mother when she was in estrus even though they were present when other males did so and even through an estrus female is normally mounted by every mature male chimp present. It might be that the males refrained from coupling with their mother because they were very severely punished for sexual advances when they were younger and learned a strong sexual avoidance of her. If that were so, we would want to know why there was such punishment, but the fact is that young chimpanzees are treated with extreme tolerance and are not severely punished by their mothers (or others, for that matter) for anything they do whether sexual or not.

The absence of mother-son copulation in certain primate genera might be due to the mother's dominance over the son in those genera. If it were, we would find that males of those genera do not in general copulate with females who are dominant to them, but this is not what we find. Instead, we find that older females of those genera who have held and helped younger males are serviced by those males quite as readily as by older males who were never in a subordinate position to them.[4] It may well be that the mother's dominance over her child continues into the child's adulthood and contributes to sexual inhibition, but if that were all there were to it, there would surely be evidence of similar avoidance in other formerly dominant-subordinate relations, and there is no such evidence.

Protomorality None of this proves that chimpanzees feel it is "bad" for mothers and sons to copulate. An abstract idea such as "bad" may be beyond even the impressive mental abilities of chimpanzees;[5] it does certainly appear, though, that there is something in the relationship between mother

---

[4]In fact, adult estrus females help juvenile males mount them by crouching down so the immature males can reach them (Goodall 1971:158–159).

[5]The chimpanzee "genius" Julia, raised by Rensch and Dahl in Germany, has solved problems such as the one in which a series of the correct six boxes out of twelve must be unlocked with "keys" to get the banana in the sixth box. Each of the boxes is unlocked with a key taken from the previous box, and the correct key can only be obtained by making the right choice among several boxes. The problem can only be solved "mentally," and this by looking at the final box and the shape of its "keyhole," finding the correct key in the choice boxes in the second-to-last series, and so on, backward to the beginning. This is what Julia did. See A. Jolly (1972:283–288).

and son which leads to an inhibition of the sort of sexual response that would occur between individuals not in that relationship. It has been suggested that the mother and the adult son continue to feel toward each other as they did when he was an infant. This feeling is sometimes taken to account for his refusal to copulate with his mother, and for her refusal to allow him to do so if he tries. It may well be involved in the sexual inhibition, but whether it is or not, the undeniable fact is that the inhibition is clearly *not* based on gaining pleasure or avoiding pain. Whether based in the male's retention of an infantile status regarding the mother or on something else, we can infer that whatever stops sexual behavior between the two is *something* different from what determines such behavior as eating, running away from a dangerous situation, or resting when tired.

It may well not be an understanding with moral force that governs the sexual relations between chimp mothers and sons, but the renunciation without external reasons of what is a pleasurable activity in all other relations makes this relation something special. Besides involving the guidance of behavior by considerations other than pleasure and practicality, full-fledged morality involves the existence of a hierarchy of values to which the individual can refer his conduct for evaluation. There is no evidence for such a thing in chimps or other nonhumans, but the incest inhibition seems to have at least one element of morality about it, behavior guided by something other than pleasure-pain avoidance and practical factors, so we can think of it as "protomorality."

"Proto-" is a Greek-based prefix that means first, earliest form of, or trace of. It is generally agreed that the higher primates have protoculture in the sense that socially transmitted and learned information plays an important part in their lives. It does not have the complexity of "culture" with no "proto" in front of it, of course, and though its contents are acquired by learning, there is little or none of the active teaching found in culture. "Protomorality" might be a reasonable term for what lies behind the incest inhibition, but it has to be recognized that there is no evidence for the presence of elaborate abstractions such as "good," "bad," "ought," and "ought not" in nonhuman primates. Such abstractions depend for their full development upon having complex language, and the apes and monkeys do not have it. Further, there is no evidence that anyone but the mother chimp and her son cares about the observance of the incest inhibition, so there is no community aspect to this protomorality.

There is also no convincing basis for believing chimpanzees or other nonhuman primates have the abstract mental ability needed to think of themselves as separate objects with continuity over time, which would enable them to apply a system of moral standards (if they were capable of one) to themselves in the way humans do. Thus, although it cannot be argued that moral force among nonhuman primates plays anything like the role it does in human culture, it is important to note that the primate heritage may well have contained bases for action—more accurately, refusals to carry out particular sorts of actions—that cannot be derived from seeking direct gratification or physical pleasure. In the incest inhibition of several genera of primates we see a renunciation of immediate gratifications without apparent external reasons for that renunciation, and this is what we mean by "protomorality."

Protoculture and Social Structure

The fact that all primates live in social groups is extremely important for understanding the primate heritage. Equally important are the sorts of social groups nonhuman primates have and the bases for statuses and roles in these groups. There can be no question about the importance of genetically imposed limitations on monkey and ape behavior in social relations as in other areas of activity. The similarity among the social groupings of primates of the same species even when there is no possibility of communication between them demonstrates the importance of their common biology. Their social relationships are not wholly determined by their genes, however. The interaction of the biologically given and the learned is complex, but in social relationships each plays a crucial role, as we saw in discussing ease of learning (see pp. 229–233). We shall focus our immediate attention on the part learning plays in social structure, but we should keep in mind the biologically based abilities for social life and the presence of biological determinants for learning different social structures in different species.

Primate protoculture includes such things as the learned ability to make termite-fishing tools among chimps, the newly discovered and socially transmitted interest in washing potatoes among Japanese macaques, and an incest inhibition among a number of genera of primates. Perhaps the most important aspect of protoculture to be considered is the basis provided by social learning, including learning from members of the previous generation, for the sort of social participation characteristic of the species. The isolated rhesus monkeys and chimpanzees could not carry out the social behaviors normally found among members of their species. This means that at least part of the basis for this behavior is protocultural in the sense that it is normally acquired through the social learning the isolated individuals missed. Actually, much of primate protoculture is concerned with social relations.

Nonhuman primates learn to recognize clearly defined social categories (e.g., "dominant male" and "dominant female"), and the members of these categories act and are treated in ways that would lead us to say there would be expectations associated with those categories if their occupants were humans. In the terms given in our discussion of social structure (Chapter 3), this means that there are statuses in primate groups. Further, inasmuch as the occupants of these statuses have different relations with occupants of other statuses according to what those other statuses are (for example, a dominant male behaves in one way toward a subordinate female and in another toward a male from another primate group of the same species), each status includes a variety of roles. As the discussion of ease of learning showed, we would expect a definite biologically determined limit to the extent of variation in the social structure of groups within a particular species,[6] but within those limits the statuses and roles are acquired through social learning, including transmission from generation to generation by that learning. Primate social structure depends upon protoculture in a way similar to the way human social structure depends on culture, although the possibility for variation in the latter is vastly greater than in the former.

All primate groups have a number of young living together with a number of adults, some of which are male and some female. This is the basic primate social pattern. In some cases the group is only a mating pair and its offspring (as among the gibbons), and in others it can include a number of adult males, adult females, and the offspring of the females. The larger groups of the last sort are organized in a number of different ways.

Hamadryas baboon social structure Among hamadryas baboons, the adult male has a number of females that mate with no other male. He keeps them near him by threatening or actually biting them when they wander away. A number of such "polygynous" groupings spend much of their time next to each other and unite against common enemies. This sort of mating group within a larger group is a basic pattern found in most human societies where there are a limited number of individuals with recognized sexual access to each other.

Another sort of multimale, multifemale grouping is found among chimpanzees. In this grouping, mothers and their offspring (often including grown offspring) wander around combining with other similar groups and with various groupings of adults on a temporary and amicable basis. Primatologists sometimes call this arrangement an "open community," and some believe it may have been the basis for very ancient hominid groupings. Others suggest that the polygynous, single-male groups within a troop made up of a number of such groups, as is found among hamadryas baboons, may have been the key part of our heritage. We will return to this issue when we examine the evolution of the australopithecines.

For the moment what is of most concern is the sort of protoculture that structures these primate groupings. All of them have a number of different statuses, none limited to such strictly biological categories as young and old, male and female. There is always at least one additional dimension of differentiation: dominance-subordinance. For hamadryas baboons the statuses of adult male and of adult female are quite clearly defined in the behaviors of animals occupying the statuses. We have already seen that an

[6]An idea of the limits on variation in primate social structure comes from Zuckerman's accounts (1932) of bringing hamadryas baboons to the London zoo. In the wild the hamadryas baboons live in social groupings that include a number of females for each male. Ignorantly, it is sad to say, the zoo brought more male baboons than females, which resulted in fighting over the females and many deaths. Each male tried to form a harem despite the impossibility of all the males doing this.

Male Hamadryas Baboon
Threatening. The status
of the adult male hama-
dryas involves his con-
trolling a number of
females. Making the
threatening gesture shown
is a common way of
compelling conformity
with his wishes.

adult male has a number of females that associate only with him. If any of
a male's harem is slow to follow him or moves away from him and his other
females, he threatens her with a stare, a tooth-displaying yawn, or a bite on
the back or neck, which brings her back to the harem. Other males will not
try to get the females away from the male who controls them even if they
are better fighters. In his status as "harem master" the male has a role
not only toward the females in his harem, but also toward other adult
males. This latter role involves the other males' recognizing his rights in
the females.

Kummer has carried out an experiment that illustrates the workings of
hamadryas social structure by showing the behaviors carried out in several
statuses and roles (1971:104–105). He trapped two male baboons from the
same troop and a female from an entirely different troop. He then put one
male and the female into an enclosure and the other male in a cage 10 yards
away where he could easily see the pair. The male in the enclosure immediately mounted the female (this gesture does not involve actual copulation), started grooming behavior with her, and got her to follow him in the
way adult males do with the females in their harem. After the other male
watched the pair for fifteen minutes, he was put into the enclosure with
them. He did not try to take over the female or fight with the first male.
He did not even look at them. He sat in the corner of the enclosure looking
up at the sky, fiddling on the ground with one hand, and intently studying
the distant landscape. He behaved, in fact, rather like an intruder on an
intimate scene in someone's home. The result was the same even with two
males purposely captured by Kummer because of their fighting ability and
even when the first male into the enclosure was clearly weaker than the

second. When two males were put in the enclosure without a female, there was no avoidance between them, and they interacted freely.

The statuses of the possessor male and the female include a clear role for each in their relations involving mounting, being mounted, following, punishing for not following, and mutual grooming. The male in his status as possessor has a role toward other males, and they a role toward him. This relation involves noninterference on the part of the outsider and what might be called confidence (as evidenced by not attacking) on the part of the possessor. That males have more than one status is illustrated by the fact that the males interact freely when females are not present. In their status of bachelor, the behaviors that would be called for if one of them were in the status possessor do not occur, but other, more affiliative, ones do. The tolerance males have for each other is probably related both to the fact that a number of male possessors and their groups of females can remain in the same area and be right next to each other without fighting and the fact that they are able to cooperate in the face of an external threat.

Although the hamadryas social structure has a definite biological basis, it can be unlearned by the females, and learned by female baboons of different but related species. It appears that the required behavior is within the behavioral potential of the whole genus or, at least, of a number of its component species. In as little as an hour after hamadryas females are transplanted to an anubis baboon troop where harems do not exist, they learn to associate with a number of males rather than only one and to stop the following behavior they show among their own kind. The anubis are a different species from the hamadryas, but do belong to the same genus and live in the same environment. Anubis females learn very quickly to manifest the behaviors appropriate to a hamadryas harem member. It must be noted, however, that an adult anubis male who lived in a hamadryas troop for several months did not learn to behave as a possessor and was totally without female companionship. The hamadryas males seem equally unable or unwilling to give up their possessor status if there are unattached females available.

Chimpanzee social structure   Chimpanzees' and gorillas' social structures do not entail the sort of exclusive relations between males and females characteristic of hamadryas baboons. Sexual relations for chimpanzees and gorillas are between all estrus females and all the males who encounter them during the period of "heat" save, for chimpanzees,[7] sons. Chimpanzees also have a distinctly casual social grouping in which only the mother and her offspring form a stable unit in an otherwise shifting series of relations. When there is a quantity of fruit in a small area, all the chimps within as much as 15 square miles may congregate there to eat it, but they break up into smaller groups again when the fruit is gone. A number of males will come together

---

[7]Not enough has been seen of wild gorilla sexual activity to know whether there is an incest inhibition in that animal. See Schaller (1963) for the only comprehensive report on the behavior of free-living gorillas.

Juvenile Chimpanzee
Interfering with Relations
between Adults.   Male
chimps are very tolerant
of juveniles and accept
juvenile interference, even
with copulation, with
better grace than adult
females do.

amicably to share the favors of an estrus female and then separate when her
receptivity is over.

The statuses of male and female chimpanzees are quite different in a
number of respects. In caring for the young, the females receive most of the
young infants' attention and spend a great deal more time with them than
males do. Males exhibit much more fighting and aggressiveness. Somewhat
surprisingly, however, the males are more tolerant of juvenile interferences
with their activities than females are. Their tolerance is most notable during
sexual intercourse when juveniles often jump on the male's back while he
is copulating and pull at him.[8] He generally responds to this by ignoring
them and continuing with his activity. Females are also tolerant and accept
a good deal of childishness from the young, but they are less easygoing with
young pests than the males are.

Chimp statuses and roles, however, are by no means limited to those
directly based in sex and the other universal (in all the primates including
humans) status differentiator, age. There are also statuses based on domination and on attractiveness. Males make fierce displays, hooting, banging on
things, and jumping into the air with their hair abristle, which are part of
individual males' movements up the hierarchy of their group. The higher
a chimp stands, the more others give way to him in beginning to feed on
scarce or especially desirable food, and the more he is followed by others

[8]Juvenile interference with copulation is very common among chimpanzees, and although
it is true that a mother's young leap on males who mount her during her estrus, this is not
limited to juveniles and their own mother. Young chimps pester males copulating with any
female, including females with no children of their own. Goodall says of this juvenile behavior:
"For the time being it must remain one of the many mysteries" (1971:159).

when he moves from one area to another. High-ranking individuals receive submissive behavior from those beneath them in the hierarchy more often than they show such behavior. This submission involves gestures of appeasement, crouching down and making soft panting grunts when the individual receiving these gestures acts in an assertive or aggressive way. Chimps are, however, complex animals, and an individual who occupies a dominant status in some situations may himself be submissive in others. There are no permanent chimpanzee leaders. An individual may greet a "subordinate" gleefully and receive the same sorts of greetings from him when there has been a separation; and individuals pat each other reassuringly on the hands or groin when one is frightened or frustrated without regard to their dominance or subordination. The same is true of kissing and hugging, which has the same significance as patting. Some of the preference dominant individuals receive is also given young infants and juveniles, at least by their mothers and siblings. The young infant and juvenile statuses are in no sense dominant, but they receive favored treatment in attention and grooming just as the dominant males do.

Goodall presents a useful summary of her findings regarding a social structure in chimpanzees.

> A chimpanzee community is an extremely complex social organization. Only when a large number of individuals began to visit the feeding area and I could make regular observations on their interactions one with another did I begin to appreciate just how complex it is. The members who compose the community move about in constantly changing associations, and yet, though the society seems to be organized in such a casual manner, each individual knows his place in the social structure . . . knows his status in relation to any other chimpanzee he may chance upon during the day. Small wonder there is such a wide range of greeting gestures, and that most chimpanzees do greet each other when they meet after a separation. Figan [an adolescent male], going up to an older male with a submissive pant-grunt, is probably affirming that he remembers quite well the little aggressive incident of two days before when he was thumped soundly on the back. "I know you are dominant. I admit it; I remember" is probably the sort of communication inherent in his submissive gesturing. "I acknowledge your respect; I shall not attack you now" is implicit in the gentle patting movement of Mike's hand as he greets a submissive female [1971:120–121].

Whether we are considering the casual but well-ordered intricacies of chimpanzee social structure or the more rigid and simple structure of hamadryas groups, there can be no question that nonhuman primates have elaborate systems of statuses and roles and that these go beyond simple distinctions based on sex and age.[9] The behavior appropriate to these statuses is probably the largest part of the protoculture of each group because although there are biological limits on the social structures of the nonhuman

---

[9]Careful and elegant studies of the nature and complexity of roles in monkey groups can be seen in Reynolds (1970) and Kummer (1967).

primates, individuals can perform the behaviors required of their statuses and roles only when they have learned to do so, with learning from members of the preceding generation (especially the mother) being particularly vital. We cannot consider the great variety of social structures found in different primate genera and species here, but all have well-developed ones involving numerous statuses and plural roles for those statuses. Our primate heritage and, more directly, that of our early hominid ancestors, includes a social structure with an important part of its basis in protoculture. That social structure may even have been similar to the two nonhuman primate structures we have just been considering, but we will return to this issue when we come to the evolution of the australopithecines in the next chapter.

Pongid and Human Structures

None of what has been said should obscure the fact that some highly important aspects of human social life are only vaguely suggested by pongid society or are altogether absent from it. Division of labor in pongid groups hardly extends beyond the fact that females have children and the breasts to feed them, while males do not and have not. It is true that males are almost always dominant over females. It is also true that in such activities as moving from one area to a distant one, leadership, and therefore dominance, is important. Further, different animals do quite different things. However, in the economic sphere there is no division except, again, that only females provide milk for the young. A partial exception exists with respect to the hunting that is done by chimpanzees and by baboons. This relatively infrequent activity was carried out only by males among Goodall's chimpanzees. Strum (1974) observed ninety-eight kills by a baboon troop in Kenya in a year, and some of the kills were made by females, although, she reports, only the males leave the troop to go on hunting "trips." These data on hunting suggest some slight division of labor in that activity, but there is no other suggestion of it in any other sphere of nonhuman primate life.

Another crucial aspect of human society, sharing, is almost nonexistent among pongids. In addition to the limited sharing of meat, chimpanzees do beg favored foods from one another and, occasionally, are given a bit, but even in the young, once they are weaned, each individual must find almost all his food for himself. The begging and occasional response to it, like the exclusively male participation in the hunt, may foreshadow important developments, but neither division of labor nor sharing can by any reasonable standard be said to play an important role in nonhuman primate society.

A final point concerning social structure among primates concerns the importance of sexual activity as the basis for social ties. On the basis of observing monkeys living in the London zoo, the famous primatologist of the first half of this century Sir Solly Zuckerman concluded that the primates, unlike other mammals, were sexually active most of the time because of

Baboon Eating an Antelope It Has Killed. Recent investigations show that, contrary to earlier beliefs, chimpanzees and baboons not only kill small animals, but also have a limited division of labor and share some of the food they hunt.

the almost constant receptivity of the females and the males' powerful sex drives. It has since been shown that this is not really true of monkeys (and apes) living in the wild who are much less sexually active than their caged (and very possibly bored) kinsmen. A. Jolly stresses the fact that most male-female bonding is not directly based on sex and estimates that "the females of most primates are unlikely to be in estrus for as much as twenty weeks of a twenty-year life span" (1972:201). Males and females are very closely bonded in many primate genera, and we have seen that sexually related activity such as the mounting of the female by the male among hamadryas baboons can be very important as a sign of possession, but that actual copulation need not be involved for the sign to be effective.

The role of sex in primate social groupings cannot be dismissed, of course, but to explain the life-long association of males and females in a group on the basis of sexual attraction alone is an error. Doing this ignores the crucial patterning by protoculture of other drives acquired during the long childhood and how adaptive this association is, given such requirements as infant and child care, mutual protection, and relations with others of the same species. There seems to be universal agreement among primate specialists that humans are the sexiest members of the order and that although sexuality plays a role in male-female bonds among nonhuman primates, it does not provide the sole basis for this bond in humanity's primate heritage.

Psychological Processes, Symbols, and the Primate Heritage

The definite and important resemblances between human and pongid psychological processes indicate that the primate heritage was rich in the material from which our own unique psychological abilities evolved. It is hardly surprising that there should be an extensive heritage in the psychological

Chimp Tool Use. Chimpanzees use such readily available objects as sticks for various purposes. The picture shows a small branch being used to retrieve a piece of food from a stream.

domain considering the many social and physical similarities among all the primates including man. As we will see in the next section, the higher primates resemble humans in many important anatomical and neurological features, and a combination of this with the long primate childhood and lifelong social existence could not fail to produce similar psychological processes. Among chimpanzees, and probably gorillas and other genera, mental processes are strikingly similar to human ones in many ways, but they differ in not involving fully developed symbolic ability. As Holloway says:

> Chimpanzees have been reported to fit together sticks and to use sticks to procure termites. These examples may represent simply ad hoc tool-use, but the borderline between tool-using and tool-making is probably very thin. These few instances, plus a wealth of examples of problem solving in chimpanzees, clearly indicate the presence of *thought* [emphasis in original] in these animals, even if the internal processes are not coded in extrinsic symbols. We are fairly certain that the chimpanzee is capable of conceiving invariant relations between his actions and the outside world. There is no way to know what the chimpanzee is thinking, but it does seem fairly clear that its thought processes differ from man's in the absence of arbitrary form [1972:400; references deleted from quotation].

The central place of what Holloway calls "extrinsic symbols" in human psychological processes is unquestionable. It is through their use that most of what is distinctively human occurs. A rather gloomy definition of humans is that they are the only animals with foreknowledge of their own death. They are also the only animals with knowledge of next week's party (and the ability to think of a "party" and plan it), next year's vacation at the seashore, and the delicious food eaten five years earlier at a little restaurant in Paris. Through their ability to manipulate symbols, in other words, humans can transcend time and space. The same ability also makes it possible for them to use and produce abstractions ("six," "sweet," "family," "evil," and so on). This ability has important but ill-understood roots in uniquely human evolutionary developments in the brain. Nevertheless, there is a primate heritage in the area of mental functioning and even in symbol use that needs to be considered for a full understanding of the emergence of humanity.[10]

The part of the primate heritage that is especially important is the extent to which ancestral primates may have provided a basis for the human use of symbols. For a long time in anthropology there has been a distinction between "symbols" and "signs." A picture of an apple is at one remove from the apple itself and that picture would be called a sign for an apple. The

[10]Holloway in the article quoted at the beginning of this section stresses the uniqueness of human thought and the inappropriateness of using nonhuman primate evidence to understand human psychological evolution. It is not clear from his article, however, that he views the use of primate behavior to illuminate the primate heritage as inappropriate; even if one wishes to emphasize human uniqueness—and who can deny it or wishes to?—it is not necessary to neglect sources in the primate past. Perhaps contemporary primate behavior is a poor window on the primate behavioral past; it is nevertheless the only window we have or ever will have other than the interpretation of physical remains.

word "a-p-p-l-e" is much further removed from the actual fruit and has, in fact, no intrinsic connection with it. Symbols or "extrinsic symbols" are representations that depend upon convention for their reference. Signs, also called "intrinsic symbols," operate through direct representation.

Mammals all respond to signs to some extent at least, as anyone knows who has been seen by a hungry dog carrying the dog's dish toward the dog-food cupboard. Symbols are more difficult for animals, but that some small symbolical ability, at least when humans involve themselves, exists is evidenced by the response of domestic animals to their names or other words. Mammals communicate with one another by such means as growls, hisses, displaying teeth, and so on. The extent to which these cues are extrinsic symbols rather than signs can be debated inasmuch as most or all of them involve behavior actually involved in what is being represented. Thus, a dog communicating displeasure or threat to another dog bares his teeth, which is, of course, a step in actually biting. Mammals do communicate with one another without human help, but this is done through the use of signs that are always connected to anger, fear, hunger, or some other emotional state.

Primates are much more sophisticated in their communication with one another, and their use of very complex signs, at least, cannot be doubted. Vervets, for example, have different danger calls referring to leopard danger, eagle danger, and snake danger. This rather impressive signaling, however, is limited to the here and now. The vervets cannot tell each other about dangerous animals that are not present but are likely to be found somewhere or about what they did the last time they encountered a predator of some kind.

It appears that when nonhuman primates are left to themselves, their ability to use symbols to refer to things across time and space is definitely limited. The reference of a primate communication is limited to what is now actually present in the animal's perception. Another limitation on communication among wild primates is that the elements which make up the communication—whether the communication be vocal or gestural—are emotionally based (grunts, hoots, bared teeth, and such) rather than arbitrary as are the sounds which make up human words.

In all languages, words are made up of discrete sounds that can be combined and recombined into a vast variety of symbols. The combination and recombination of the units is entirely arbitrary and is guided wholly by convention rather than by individual emotional states or anything else. The same conventional basis applies to the meanings of the words (or other symbols), but the conventions governing word meaning are separate from the conventions governing word formation. Linguists refer to this doubly conventional language feature as "duality of patterning,"[11] and it allows a very great amount of information to be transmitted with only a small num-

[11]Hockett (1973:98–121) has a very basic discussion of language, at once clear and informative. Actually, patterning is even more complex than we have indicated, and language is multiply patterned, not just dually, as will be explained in the chapter on language.

EXTRINSIC SYMBOL *A representation that depends on custom for its reference. It has no necessary relation to the thing symbolized.*

SIGN *A representation that depends on its resemblance to the thing symbolized for its reference; can also be called an "intrinsic symbol."*

Male Vervet Monkey. Vervets produce a variety of signals, including a threatening signal similar to the one produced by hamadryas males.

ber of discrete sounds. Without duality of patterning, complex communi-cation—including within the individual through thinking—is very much reduced.

A majority of authorities believe that only the human brain is able to create purely arbitrary symbols out of purely arbitrary units, although there is evidence that primates can be trained by humans to use impressively ab-stract symbols. In the wild, even complex signals such as vervet danger cries and the even more elaborate communication of wild chimpanzees are based in emotional outbursts rather than dependent for their meaning on shared understandings transmitted by learning, although the intensity of the signal and the status of the signaler do modify meanings.

Chimpanzee communication and learning Chimpanzees show the great-est communication skill of nonhuman primates, and studying them can help us form some idea of the sort of skills with complex signs our common ancestor bequeathed us. The age and sex of the animal communicating affect the message as does his prestige and the vigor he uses in making the sound or gesture.

Goodall reports a very wide variety of gestures used in communicating. Patting the hand or groin of another in reassurance and submission; grinning in fear and submission; embracing or holding hands with another for reas-surance; kissing and embracing on greeting another after separation or when faced with such a delightful thing as a pile of bananas; holding out the hand to beg for something another chimp has; and turning the back and bowing the head as a request for grooming—all are common gestures. There is also a rich repertoire of calls: one on finding good food; the "pant hoot" an-nouncing the presence of a particular individual; a danger call; and others. All these calls serve to communicate, and the pant hoot, for example, keeps the scattered chimpanzees aware of who is in the neighborhood just as the good-food call brings other chimps to the food. There are about thirty such calls, and they are sometimes combined to give more information.

A number of experiments have examined the symbolic capacity of apes. One of the most fascinating current studies involves teaching a female chim-panzee the sign language used by people who have been deaf from birth. Previous attempts to teach chimps to communicate have tried to use speech as the medium, but the difficulties an ape has in producing human sounds were a serious interference. The fact that the chimp who was raised as a human child learned only two words in several years may have been due to the lack of suitable sound-producing structures in chimpanzee anatomy rather than lack of symbolic ability. This is overcome in the sign-language experiment and the experimenters (Gardner and Gardner 1969, 1971) report that the young animal they have been working with is able to produce the signs for more than 100 words and has shown the ability to understand more than 300. In both producing "speech" and in comprehending it Washoe, the chimp in question, is able to deal with simple sentences as well as single words. An example of Washoe's sentences comes from an experience with one of her human friends, an assistant in the research project named Susan. This woman put her foot on a doll Washoe played with, and Washoe used her hands to make the signs saying: "Up Susan, Susan up, mine please up, gimme baby, more up, shoe up, baby up, [and] you up."

From the point of view of our interest in symbolic processes, perhaps even more fascinating than Washoe's impressive ability to reproduce symbols and to combine them in a meaningful, if very rudimentary, way is her ability to give symbolic recognition to her own separateness and individuality. We have emphasized throughout that the human social order is a moral order and that culture is effective because it has moral force. For this moral force to be effective, the individual must recognize himself as a separate being, continuing through time and the product, or at least sum, of what has happened to him. To have such an idea of self, the individual must be able to identify himself as the actor who yesterday did this or that and last year did something else. He also needs to be able to hold a moral code up to himself to evaluate his actions now, in the past, and, as projected, in the future. Washoe gives no indication of having the ability to conceive a moral code to which she can compare herself, but when asked what she saw in a mirror she signed back "Me, Washoe."

In humans the concept of the self has a vital role in psychological processes as the individual views himself at a psychological distance for planning and evaluating. There is no evidence that there is a concept of the self as a continuing thing among chimpanzees or, indeed, that such a thing is possible without language.[12]

More symbols and the primate heritage Another experiment with teaching a chimpanzee to communicate symbolically is being carried out by David Premack (1972) with a young female called Sarah. Sarah has been taught to use metal-backed pieces of plastic of different colors and shapes on a magnetic board to form sentences. She has learned concepts having to do with color, shape, and size, a connective form ("is" is a common one), negation, "if-then," and a few others. The experiment is less concerned with the chimp's total linguistic ability than it is with determining her ability to use symbols to represent reality. An instance of the work with her shows her startling ability to use the symbols she was taught:

> But she would go beyond merely applying a concept to exemplars not used in training; she could use the concept to generate new exemplars. In the case of "color of" this was seen in the introduction of the new color names, "brown" and "green." For instance, she was given the instruction, "brown color of chocolate." "Brown" was the only new word, both "color of" and "chocolate" having been established earlier. (In the same lesson, she was also given "green color of grape" as the second positive case, and "brown not color of grape" and "green

[12]The incest inhibition in chimps suggests the possibility of an ability to evaluate their own actions. This would imply a concept of the self, but more evidence will be needed to demonstrate that the inhibition is not due to some far simpler avoidance learning that has not yet been discovered.

**Chimpanzee Interpreting
Symbols.** The chimpan-
zee is handing her trainer
an apple as she has been
instructed to do by the
plastic symbols on the
magnetic board.

not color of chocolate" as the two negative cases.) She was then presented with
four wooden disks, only one of which was painted brown, and told "take brown."
She was consistently correct in her choice of the brown disk. Since the instruction "brown color of chocolate" was given her at a time when chocolate was
not present, and she was subsequently able to select the brown object, she must
have been able to generate an image of chocolate in the absence of the object
on the basis of the word alone [Premack 1972:54].

This impressive symbolic ability, like Washoe's, occurred with human
help and using symbols invented by humans. Still, the ability to use these
symbols had to come from the animals, which indicates that some basic
capacity for symbolic activity is present. Premack believes that some sort of
symbolic ability is part of all learning and that animals with less impressive
skills than chimpanzees do use symbols in a limited way. In his opinion symbols are used much more and in a vastly more complex way by humans
through language, but the difference between symbol use by humans and
by other animals is one of quantity or degree; it is not a difference in kind.
Whether or not this view is accepted, and his argument is an impressive one
(see Premack 1972:60–65), the existence of a strong primate heritage in the
area of symbol use seems strongly indicated by the evidence for symbolic
ability in nonhuman primates.

Another psychological dimension having a basis in the primate heritage
is personality. "Exposure to a group of adult chimpanzees gives one the
overwhelming conviction that one is dealing with an essentially human set

of attitudes and motives" (Hebb and Thompson 1954:543).

The primate heritage surely did include the biological bases for the drives that play a key part in human motives. Some of our most basic goals—including dominance in various forms, as well as food getting, sexual success, and other biologically based goals—are also present in the nonhuman primates and may well be a heritage we acquired from the primate ancestors that preceded even the men-apes. The enormous elaborations in motives, like the most intricate cognitive activities and their intricate organization, depend upon a uniquely human amount of symbolic activity. It may be that in many aspects of psychological functioning the differences between humans and other primates are differences in quantity rather than kind.

Recent evidence, in fact, suggests that in at least one band of wild chimps there is a greeting ritual absent in other bands and transmitted by learning (McGrew and Tutin 1978). This may suggest true culture, not just its bases, is part of our ancient primate heritage.

The Physical Heritage

The physical traits of the primates cannot be separated from their behavioral characteristics in any clear-cut way, of course. Nevertheless, it is useful to bring these traits into the center of attention so that we can see more clearly the part they play in the beginnings of humanity.

Natural selection proceeds through the ability of some individuals to have more offspring than others. This ability is based in physical structures, but it comes directly from the advantages bestowed by using these structures. Obvious though it may seem, it is important to remember that evolution proceeds according to performance or behavior, not on the basis of structures. Thus, it is likely that the first primates were small, early mammals which happened to have forepaws that allowed them to hold onto branches a bit better than their fellows and so to live arboreally. Being in the trees gave some advantage to those who lived there, and the descendants of these early branch graspers prospered and increased according to their ability to perform well in the trees.

The changes that took place in the bodies of the early primates were changes that came about through selection for performing well in the branches. The reduction of the olfactory center in the brain and the increase in the visual center are part of this same process because eyesight, especially three-dimensional eyesight, is extremely adaptive to feeding and moving in trees, whereas the ability to detect scents up where the breezes blow provides little advantage. The brain-eye-forepaw developments in early primates are part of the arboreal adaptation of these animals. The same complex of development gave these animals an increased ability to hold and manipulate food and other objects. For a fruit eater and insect catcher, the ability to grasp is not only useful with respect to tree branches. The early primate developments that led to a successful adaptation to life in the trees supplied the foundation for the emergence of a fully opposable thumb and for the brain development that provided a better memory, increasingly complex integration of information, and the basis for finer, individual control over the fingers. Total development in the higher primates is the result of a selection process that began many tens of millions of years ago with the ancient ancestors in the branches of the Mesozoic forest. Human manual skill and associated information-processing skill is a direct outgrowth of this long selection process.

Arms, shoulders, and gait   The hand-eye-brain changes that were involved in adapting to arboreal life are not, however, all there were in the primate heritage that set the stage for human manipulating skill. The forelimbs cannot play a constant role in locomotion if they are also to play a constant part in carrying or manipulating. Humans are the only fully bipedal primates, but the basis for freeing the forelimbs from locomotion is found in the earlier primates. Arm swinging, or "brachiation," the process of moving through the trees by means of the hands alone, is found only among the apes,[13] and it reaches its greatest development in gibbons and siamangs. Arm-swinging animals move with their bodies fully extended, and on the relatively rare occasions when gibbons and siamangs come to the ground they walk bipedally. A sophisticated recent study[14] suggests that the arm and shoulder arrangements characteristic of modern man evolved from an earlier primate arrangement involving arm swinging. Such appears to be the likeliest basis for the emergence of forelimbs specialized for manipulation, and it makes arm swinging a crucial part of the primate heritage of man. Further, apes are built so that they sit with their trunks erect, leaving their arms free for manipulating objects. Taken together with the structure of the arms and shoulder, the truncal erectness provides a basis for a fully bipedal gait. It does not by itself explain the evolution of the hominid shift in the spine, pelvis, foot, and leg that are also necessary to an upright posture, but the foundation for these traits lies in the ape.

Remembering that performance, not structure, is the basis for natural selection and, therefore, evolutionary change, the key question in human evolution is what favored a bipedal gait over arm swinging. We will consider this question in the next chapter when we consider the men-apes. For the moment, the important point is whatever the basis for freeing the forelimbs from locomotion, the earlier primates provided a physical heritage from which the human characteristics emerged.

[13]The New World spider monkey is a semibrachiator with a shoulder girdle similar to that of the apes. This is the result of parallel evolution rather than common ancestry.

[14]In two studies Oxnard (1969a, 1969b) examines nonhuman primate shoulder girdles from the point of view of which could be transformed into the human type with the least amount of change. He finds that shoulder girdles like those of orangutans require the least alteration to be made into the human type. His use of quantitative techniques to make the comparisons and alterations is interesting in itself.

(a)   (b)

Siamangs Brachiating (a) and Walking (b). A recent study suggests that modern arm and shoulder arrangements evolved from earlier primate forms associated with arm swinging. Ancient human ancestors, perhaps like these modern brachiators, may have had specialized forelimbs for swinging in the trees and used their hand limbs for walking on the ground.

Our nearest relatives, gorillas and chimpanzees, have the anatomy of arm swingers, with almost 180 degrees of possible arm rotation, but they spend a good deal of time on the ground (adult gorillas rarely or never go up a tree), where they move with a gait called "knuckle walking." Knuckle walking involves quadrupedal movement with the feet and the first two joints of the bent fingers touching the ground and a stance similar to that of a football lineman. The fact that an *Australopithecus* (a man-ape in the direct human line; see Chapter 8) that lived 1.8 million years ago had a hand half-way between a gorilla's and a human's strongly suggests that the heritage of knuckle walking is directly ancestral to a bipedal gait. It is important to bear in mind that the apes and chimpanzees move in a variety of ways, as does the (modern) human. Washburn's view of the emergence of the distinctly human means of locomotion emphasizes this variety and the gradual change in it as the way the primate heritage led to increasing bipedalism: "Chimpanzees knuckle-walk, climb, and brachiate [i.e., move by arm swinging]. From a similar pattern of behaviors, our ancestors may have decreased their climbing activity, added bipedal running, and retained slow knuckle-walking" (Washburn and McCown 1972:165).

A recent study of the biomechanics of the gait of the australopithecines (Lovejoy, Heipel, and Burstein 1973) convincingly argues that this direct ancestor had the same striding gait modern humans have. However, the possibility that it developed out of an earlier knuckle-walking gait of the sort indicated by Washburn definitely remains.

The primate heritage in gait is obviously important for human evolution, but so is diet. The relatively recent discovery of some hunting and meat eating among chimpanzees and baboons (Strum 1974) indicates an ancestral interest in hunting that may be as important in the ultimate development of humanity as any other single activity. We shall consider this more fully in the next chapter, but we need to note here that a taste for meat, together with the ability to hunt for it, is a very likely part of our primate heritage.

Chimpanzee Knuckle Walking. Humanity's closest relatives (gorillas and chimps) move across the ground with a gait called "knuckle walking." Some authorities stress the importance of this gait in the evolution of fully human bipedalism.

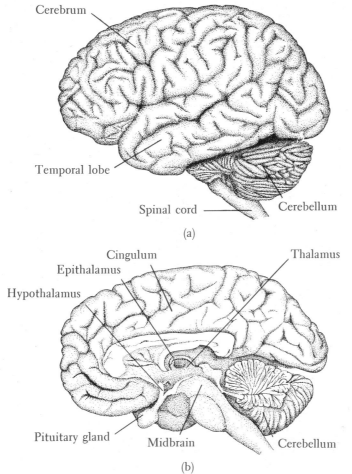

Cerebrum

Temporal lobe

Spinal cord — Cerebellum

(a)

Cingulum   Thalamus

Epithalamus

Hypothalamus

Pituitary gland   Midbrain   Cerebellum

(b)

Human Brain in Side View (a) and Lateral Section (b). Most of the enlargement of the primate brain has been in the cerebrum, which has gradually expanded until it covers the hypothalamus, midbrain, and other parts of the "white matter" identified in (b).

The primate brain   No part of the evolution of *Homo sapiens* is more distinctive than the evolution of his brain. In discussing the primate heritage in culture and in psychological processes we emphasized the need of a human brain to carry out the complex manipulation of symbols. Nevertheless, distinctively human brain evolution—like distinctively human evolution in posture and gait—did proceed out of a primate base, and some of our brain characteristics are shared with other primates.

The most striking of the general primate brain characteristics is the general enlargement of the brain. A few other mammals (such as whales and elephants) have very large brains, but as an order the primates must be viewed as the brainiest among the mammals, with the only close contenders being dolphins and whales. Most of the enlargement of the primate brain is in the cerebrum, the forepart of the brain, which deals with the integration of sensations and information. This brain part has two layers. The bottom, or inside, one is made up of white tissue, and the outer layer is composed of gray matter. The gray matter is called the "cerebral cortex," and it is in this part where most of the primate brain enlargement, relative to other mammals, has taken place. In primates the gray matter is wrinkled and folded, which provides more area in the space available than does the smooth cortex found in most other mammals. Having a large cortex is closely connected with the complexity of behavior found in primates because the cortex is the part of the brain that allows learning to be put to use in dealing with situations. In humans it is the cortex that is at the base of what we call consciousness, and something like consciousness is made possible for the other primates by this same area.

The whole issue of brain size has become controversial in the recent past. The assumption that humanity's unique mental processes are a direct result of the large size of the human brain is not as generally accepted as it once was. Size is important, but the view that brain organization is quite as important is receiving more and more emphasis. The organization of the human brain, that is, the relative size of the various parts of the brain, is unquestionably in the basic primate pattern with its emphasis on the cortex. In humans the frontal lobe of the cortex is expanded beyond that of any other primate, but the organizational emphasis is clearly the same one as in the other primates, where this lobe is also large. Similarly, the complexity of the convolutions (the wrinkles and folds) in the human cortex are greater than those in even the apes, but their brains have developed some complexity here so that the primate heritage in this type of organizational development cannot be doubted. As in so many areas we have considered, the *overall organization* of the human brain is a more elaborate development in a direction present as part of the primate heritage. As Holloway, a physical anthropologist, says:

> Basically, the human brain contains all the same structures as any mammal. On the other hand, the usual interpretation based on cranial capacity has assumed that the human brain is simply a four-fold multiplication of an ape brain, which then in turn is simply a four-fold increase over a macaque brain. Such a view is incorrect, since relationships between the "parts" have altered in the course of evolution and are specific to the particular species studied. . . . Quantitative shifts between components or substructures of the brain, as measured in terms of area or volume, have taken place under natural selection such that outputs of the system are different between the species [1966:106].

Holloway's main interest in the article just quoted centers on changes in the size and number of brain cells. He emphasizes that it is not brain *size* alone that makes ape behavior what it is and human behavior what it is, but that it is the relation among the brain's parts that is the vital determinant of what happens. As Holloway notes, the increase in brain volume in humans relative to apes and in apes relative to monkeys "is only the outward manifestation of internal changes." A crucial part of the internal changes in human, and to a lesser extent, ape, brains is an increase in the proportion of the brain mass devoted to the cortex. In humans, the parietal and frontal regions of the cortex, the areas at the center and top of the cortex, are particularly enlarged relative to other primates.

Much of the uniquely human brain organization is due to the key role of the newly expanded region of the cortex. The parietal area, sometimes called the association cortex, controls the bringing together of different information, as the cortex in general does, but this area has connections only with other nonsensory, nonemotional controlling zones. It is more purely connected than any other part of the brain with thinking and, especially, with abstractions. It is crucial to distinctively human mental processes, and it is little developed even in apes. David Pilbeam, a physical anthropologist, summarizes our current knowledge about this part of the brain and the general difference between human and nonhuman organization:

> The parietal lobe has expanded enormously [in humans]. It should not be thought, though, that human behavioral specificity lies in the parietal lobe, or indeed that it lies in any particular place. It is clear that the human brain has been reorganized internally, so that although it is still undoubtedly a primate brain its output is qualitatively different from that of other primate brains [1972:77].

In the organization of the human brain and in its output, then, we at last see a break with the primate past. In the next chapter we will see that the expansion and reorganization of the human brain involves the areas in the cortex and cerebellum that control manual manipulation as well as symbols and abstractions. We will see that the full flowering of this development did not come along until relatively late in hominid evolution.

SUMMARY

Humanity's primate heritage is very rich. Many of the most important human traits are shared with other contemporary primates, which shows that these traits have their roots in the common primate past. Human vision, forelimbs, hands, and even gait are closely related to those of various nonhuman primates. The social organization found in monkey and ape groups suggests some characteristics of human societies. Primate social life is differentiated beyond different statuses only according to sex and age, and there is every reason to look at nonhuman social structure from the perspective of individuals having a number of different statuses that, in turn, have different roles. The behavior called for in these statuses and roles is acquired through learning, without which the individual cannot perform adequately.

The primate's ability to participate in its group and to behave as members of its species ordinarily depends upon an infancy and juvenile period spent in close association with its mother and other members of its species.

During this period the group's ways of doing things are transmitted to the young through social learning. The biological foundation for what the members of each species learn comes from an evolutionary process that produced individuals who are able and motivated to learn what their group requires for survival. Under normal circumstances for the species individuals have the opportunity to do the necessary learning. This learning includes proper behavior in different statuses and roles and, in some species, something very much akin to toolmaking. Because social learning and the transmission of information from generation to generation is so important to primate adaptation, primates are said to depend upon protoculture for their way of life. It is called "protoculture," not because it has a biological foundation, (culture has that, too), but because its contents lack the fully moral quality found in human shared understandings. There is some suggestion of what might be called morality in the incest inhibition seen in a number of ape and monkey species.

In psychological areas the nonhuman primates, especially the apes, show cognitive skills similar in type to human skills. Some sort of limited symbolic ability seems to be present in chimpanzees, at least, although most nonhuman primate communication is with signs. Those who work closely with these animals see motives and attitudes in them they believe to be similar to those found in human personalities. Physically, the African apes show a high development of manipulative skill (as do a few sorts of monkeys), and this, together with the stereoscopic vision characteristic of all primates, makes quite elaborate manipulation possible. Human arm mobility and the arm-swinging ability of the apes seem to have a common basis in the ancestors of humans and apes before the evolutionary division 6 to 12 million years ago. The knuckle-walking gait of humanity's close relatives, the chimps and gorillas, is related by common descent to our own mode of locomotion. The primate brain is organized with an emphasis on the cerebral control of behavior, and this is much more true of primates than of any other mammals. Humans are distinctive in the extent of their ability to manipulate symbols, and this characteristic, unlike the others, may well be based in an important difference between the development of the human brain and the brains of the other primates.

SUGGESTED READINGS

HALLOWELL, A. I. 1956 The Structural and Functional Dimensions of Human Existence. Quarterly Review of Biology 31:88–108. Abridged and reprinted as Culture and the History of Man, *in* The Meaning of Culture, 1972. M. Freilich, Ed. Lexington, Mass.: Xerox College Publishing.

Although some of the data in this article are now outmoded, the questions about the evolutionary requirements for the emergence of human culture are well worth considering, as is the author's revealing perspective on the relationship between physical evolution and culture.

HARLOW, H., AND M. HARLOW   1962   Social Deprivation in Monkeys. Scientific American 207:137–146.

A description of the Harlows' classic experiments and the results. A key article for anyone interested in primate research and its implications for humans.

JOLLY, A.   1972   The Evolution of Primate Behavior. New York: Macmillan.

A thorough and easy-to-read overview of most of the recent work in nonhuman primate behavior.

KUMMER, H.   1971   Primate Societies. Chicago: Aldine.

A fascinating study of a single troop of wild baboons in Ethiopia with abundant material from the study of other primates and many general observations about the relevance of nonhuman primate studies to understanding humanity.

NAPIER, JOHN   1971   The Roots of Mankind. London: G. Allen.

A delightful and witty consideration of the main issues in understanding nonhuman primate behavior and its relations to human life.

REYNOLDS, V.   1970   Roles and Role Change in Monkey Society: A Consort Relationship of Rhesus Monkeys. Man 5:449–465.

This is a careful study of the nature and complexity of roles in monkey groups. Fascinating in itself and of theoretical value concerning the primate heritage.

Glossary

Affine A person related to Ego by virtue of a marriage between them or between two of their consanguines.

Agriculture The deliberate and methodical raising of plants for food. Some anthropologists distinguish "true agriculture," which makes use of a plow, from "horticulture," or gardening, which does not.

Animatism Belief in mana.

Animism The belief that all living beings and natural phenomena that appear to move or have life (sun, moon, rivers, etc.) have individual spirits (*animae*), some or all of which are appropriate objects of worship.

Anthropoids A classification of primates that includes apes, monkeys, and humans, but not prosimians.

Apical ancestor The person who is the common ancestor of all members of a descent group; on the basis of descent from the apical ancestor membership in the group is legitimately established.

Avunculocal residence The custom whereby a bride and groom take up residence with the groom's mother's brother.

Balanced reciprocity Reciprocal exchange in which values are calculated and equivalent items are exchanged, preferably simultaneously.

Baraza An East African dispute-settlement session in which a political official (headman or village chief) and fellow villagers try to find a solution for quarrels or disagreements.

Barter The exchange of one resource for another (sometimes with bargaining) without the exchange of money.

Basic understandings The parts of culture that fundamentally structure the experience of those who share them.

Bilateral descent Descent that is traced through parents of both sexes at each generation.

Bilocal residence The custom whereby a bride and groom take up residence either with the bride's parents or with the groom's parents.

Brachiation A mode of locomotion in which the individual is suspended by his hands and swings and leaps through the branches without using the feet or legs.

Caste Endogamous groups whose members have the same social standing and, sometimes, occupation.

Chattel art Works of art or decorated utilitarian objects that are small enough to be transported in the course of ordinary use.

Civilization A society that practices agriculture or herding or both and makes use of a written language; the state of culture that permits this.

Clan A lineagelike unilineal descent group (patri- or matri-) in which kinship links with the founding ancestor or ancestress are asserted but cannot be traced by the members. (In earlier usage, "clan" referred to a matrilineage.)

Classificatory system A system of kinterms that includes at least one term that refers to kinsmen in more than one genealogical relationship to Ego.

Coercion Support based on very definite and narrow expectations.

Compadre The term in many Spanish-speaking countries for the relationship between a child's godparent at baptism and his father or mother. The relationship between *compadres* is ideally and often actually one of mutual help and friendship.

Componential analysis A mode of analysis of sets of words or phrases that seeks to establish the minimum features that distinguish any one item in a set from any other.

Consanguine A kinsman related to Ego by virtue of their descent from a common ancestor.

Contagious magic Magical procedures based on the proposition that things once associated with each other continue to be mystically linked, so that what is done to one is also done to the other.

Corporate group A group whose members are responsible for each others' actions. There are property-owning corporate groups and others that do not jointly own property.

Cousin-marriage rule A rule to the effect that marriages should preferentially or prescriptively be made with a person in the status of cousin; typically this status refers to any same-generation kinsman of another lineage.

Cross-cousins The children of Ego's father's sisters and of Ego's mother's brothers.

Cultural relativism The view that the behavior of members of a group can be understood only according to the culture of that group. It is an intellectual tool and, quite separately, a moral and ethical point of view.

Culture The sum of the morally forceful understandings acquired by learning and shared with the members of the group to which the learner belongs.

Deme An endogamous, unilineal descent group.

Descent A person's claim to membership in a social category or group consisting of his ancestors and persons descended from them.

Descriptive system A system of kinterms that includes no term that refers to kinsmen in more than one genealogical relationship to Ego.

Descriptive understandings Shared understandings that state the way the world and its contents actually are when correctly understood; also called "cultural beliefs."

Dialect One of two (or several) mutually intelligible variants of a language, differing from other dialects in its body of speakers.

Diffusion The transmission of cultural traits from one society to another; sometimes called "cultural borrowing."

Diglossia A sociolinguistic situation in which two different dialects or languages are used in the same speech community but for different purposes.

Divination The activity of human beings in deciphering what are believed to be communications from supernatural beings or forces.

Duality of patterning The fact that the combinations of sounds that make up words in a language are governed by one set of conventions, while a separate set of conventions governs the combination of words into sentences. Two different patterning conventions for each language are thus provided.

Emic approach An approach to the analysis of a society or its culture that makes use of the categories of the people studied for organizing and interpreting data or that takes the discovery of these categories as an explicit research objective or both.

Endogamous Marriage only within a group.

Endogamy Marriage within one's own group.

Entailed understandings Understandings that are held partly as a consequence of accepting basic understandings.

Ethnocentrism Understanding and evaluating people, the way they act, what they believe, and what they value according to the culture of one's own group.

Ethnography The description of a society's way of life.

Ethnology The systematic comparison of different societies and cultures.

Etic approach An approach to the analysis of a society or its culture that makes use of preestablished categories for organizing and interpreting data.

Evolution A major biological process that includes the appearance of variety in a population and the operation of natural selection on that variety.

Exogamy Marriage outside one's own group.

Expectations Elements of culture associated with statuses that specify what behavior is appropriate in which situation and toward which people and the kind of response that behavior is likely to produce.

Extended family A family composed of a husband and wife (or a husband with more than one wife or a wife with more than one husband), plus at least one parent of one of them, plus at least one of their children. A typical extended family might consist of a man and his wife, his mother and father, and his children.

Extrinsic symbol A representation that depends on custom for its reference. It has no necessary relation to the thing symbolized.

Faction A political conflict group that is not corporate; it is recruited by a leader, and its members belong on the basis of different interests and desires.

Family A co-resident kinship unit that includes children and their mater and makes some provision for the rearing of the children. In *almost* all known instances, a family is a unit of economic production and includes adults of both sexes, at least two of whom maintain a socially approved sexual relationship.

Feudalism A system of economic, political, and social organization in which land is held by a tenant on condition that services are rendered to his overlord, who, in turn, may hold the land only on similar conditions from *his* overlord, in a hierarchy that reaches from a king at the top, who is the nominal holder of all the land, to serfs at the bottom, who actually farm the land.

Fission The breaking up of a group into its constituent parts; most often used when an inclusive group splits into the smaller groups that compose it.

Generalized reciprocity Reciprocal exchange in which individuals contribute goods or services as a matter of course without conscious calculation of return.

General-purpose money Money that serves as a general medium of exchange for all monetized spheres of economic exchange in a society.

Genetrix A biological mother.

Genitor A biological father.

Group A collection of people who are aware of their group membership and who carry out activities jointly or cooperatively. (See also *Inclusive group; Primary group; Secondary group; Corporate group; Society.*)

Homeopathic (imitative) magic Magical procedures based on the proposition that things which resemble each other are mystically linked, so that what is done to one is also done to the other.

Incest taboo The prohibition of marriage with particular categories of kinsmen.

Inclusive group A group all of whose members also belong to the same sort of smaller-scale group.

Jural rules Expectations that are culturally viewed as indispensable parts of a status. Violation of these expectations leads to the violator's being treated as a "bad" member of the status category or as having lost the right to be considered an occupant of the status.

Kinterms (kinship terms) The names that label kinship statuses in a society.

Kintype An abbreviation such as Br or DaHu or WiBrWiFa.

Legitimacy Support based on broad and general expectations.

Levirate The custom of a man marrying his brother's widow, usually to sire children for his deceased brother.

Lineage A localized, exogamous, unilineal descent group.

Linking understandings Shared understandings that make it possible for people to know what to expect from members of social groupings to which they do not belong.

Localized descent group A descent group in which the members of the group responsible for decision making are in the same locale as the resources belonging to the group.

Magic The belief in supernatural forces other than supernatural beings and procedures for the manipulation of those forces; the result of applying such procedures.

Mana Undifferentiated, impersonal, supernatural force.

Market exchange A mode of economic distribution in which resources are exchanged on the basis of prices established by supply and demand and expressed in generalized units of value.

Marriage An institutionalized way of providing that the offspring of a particular woman or of a particular woman by a particular man will be legitimate (i.e., will be the social kinsmen of some people rather than others and the social descendants of one set of ancestors rather than another).

Mater A social mother (as opposed to a biological mother).

Matrilineage A lineage in which descent is figured through a line of women.

Minimal pair A pair of words or phrases in a given language that differ from each other in meaning and in only one phoneme. A minimal pair is evidence that the two phonemes by which the two elements of the pair differ are separate phonemes. For example, "bit" and "pit" distinguish English /b/ from /p/.

Modal personality structure Common organization features in the personalities of the members of a group. These features concern which drives are more powerful than which others, which motives are most pervasive, and other relations among personality components.

Money A unit of value by which different items may be compared and in terms of which they may be exchanged; also a physical token of value that provides the means for making an exchange.

Monogamy A family system in which a given individual has only one spouse at any given time.

Morpheme A phoneme or fixed combination of phonemes having a meaning and not subdivisible into meaningful constituent parts.

Motivation A mental process composed of the serial operation of three other processes: drives, means, and goals.

Myth A story that embodies values of a culture and that has an aura of sanctity.

Natural selection A process resulting from the fact that some members of a population adapt to the environment better than others and have more offspring who inherit the traits that produced their parents' adaptive success.

Negative reciprocity Reciprocal exchange during which efforts are made to exploit the other party, as in bargaining and haggling.

Neolocal residence The custom whereby a bride and groom take up residence independently of either set of parents or other kinsmen.

Nomadism An adaptation that involves occasional movement of the group from one area to another for better resources. It does not include return to previous sites on a regular pattern.

Normative rules Understandings about what ought and ought not be done; based on cultural conceptions of what is good and ethical.

Nuclear family A family consisting of a husband and wife and their children.

Organization of culture The relationships among the understandings that make up the culture such as which understandings are more or less important, which are more or less general, and which go together with which others.

Organization of social relations The connections between social relations resulting from the ways the expectations in those relations influence each other; this can also be called "social organization."

Organizing understandings Shared understandings that dictate the relationships among other understandings.

Overdetermined behavior Behavior that is the result of more than one motive.

Parallel cousins The children of Ego's father's brothers and of Ego's mother's sisters.

Parietal art Works of art produced on walls and ceilings, especially cave paintings.

Pater A social father (as opposed to a biological father).

Patrilineage A lineage in which descent is figured through a line of men.

Personality The more or less organized collection of processes that goes on in each human mind.

Phoneme The range of sounds recognized by native speakers of a given language as one sound, such that the difference between one phoneme and another in a given utterance can potentially change or destroy the identity of the utterance. An English example is /t/.

Politics Activities concerned with establishing and achieving public goals, with what is "public" relative to the sort of group being studied.

Polyandry A family system in which a family is composed of one woman, two or more husbands, and the children of the woman.

Polygamy A family system in which a family is composed of one man, two or more wives, and the children of these women; or of one woman, two or more husbands, and the children of the woman. Polygyny and polyandry are types of polygamy.

Polygyny A family system in which a family is composed of one man, two or more wives, and the children of these women.

Polysemy The quality of having more than one meaning.

Power Control over other individuals and over resources.

Pragmatic rules Understandings concerning how to do things effectively without regard to whether the things are in accord with values or not.

Prayer A process in which human beings address words to supernatural beings; the words so addressed.

Priest A religious practitioner able to perform on behalf of the community or of individuals culturally sanctioned rituals that are directed toward supernatural beings, not all of which are concerned with producing specific results.

Primary group A group in which members have direct, face-to-face relations with each other, and every member has a relation with every other.

Procedural understandings Shared understandings concerning how things ranging from getting married or greeting someone to planting crops or programming a computer are properly done.

Race A population within a species that can be distinguished from other populations of the same species on the basis of genetically transmitted physical differences.

Rebellion Conflict over which individuals should hold offices or play particular roles in political processes rather than over the effectiveness or virtue of those offices or processes themselves.

Reciprocity A mode of economic distribution in which resources are presented by one person or group to another with the expectation on both sides that sooner or later the second will return something of about the same value to the first.

Redistribution A mode of economic distribution in which resources are presented to a central authority, which then allocates them for use to the members of the group.

Register One of two (or several) variants of a language shared by the same speakers but used in different circumstances.

Religion The belief in spiritual beings or forces.

Revolution Conflict over the virtue and effectiveness of existing political processes and offices.

Role The portion of all expectations associated with a status that is used in relations with occupants of some other status.

Secondary group A group in which members have direct relations with some other members, but everyone does not have a relation with everyone else.

Shaman A person routinely possessed by a supernatural being or beings for purposes of divination or healing.

Shared understandings Views of what is, what ought to be, and how to do things held in common by the members of a group.

Sib A union of two or more lineages related by a common, mythical ancestor. (In earlier usage, "sib" referred to a patrilineage.)

Sign A representation that depends on its resemblance to the thing symbolized for its reference; can also be called an "intrinsic symbol."

Social dialect A dialect that is distinguished from one or more other dialects of the same language; used by speakers not geographically distinguishable from speakers of another dialect. The contrasting term is "geographical dialect."

Social Organization See *Organization of social relations.*

Social relations The way people act toward one another in real situations.

Social structure The sets of interrelated statuses occupied by the members of a group.

Society The largest group people think of themselves as belonging to. It is almost always a secondary group.

Sorcerer A person who makes use of a series of procedures to bring about changes in the world on behalf of the community or individuals through the mediation of impersonal, supernatural power.

Sororate The custom whereby a man marries the sister of his deceased wife.

Special-purpose money Money that is restricted to one of two or more spheres of economic exchange in a society.

Status A social category and all the expectations assigned to the people in the category.

Sucking cure A typical element in a shamanistic performance wherein the shaman appears to suck a solid object from the body of a patient, to which the patient's illness or other disorder is attributed.

Superorganic Above or beyond the single individual.

Symbol See *Extrinsic symbol; Sign.*

Technical facts Unavoidable aspects of social and physical reality that are directly involved in shaping political activity by providing or excluding opportunities for particular sorts of actions.

True division of labor Division of labor following criteria other than sex or age.

Uniformitarianism The view that the geological processes now going on are not fundamentally different from ones that occurred in the ancient past. The doctrine is sometimes applied to the culture, society, and personality processes of ancient people.

Unilineal descent group An organized social group, membership in which is based on descent traced through a line of ancestors all of the same sex.

Unilineal evolutionism The view that all societies pass through the same stages of development in the course of their history; also called "parallel evolution."

Uxorilocal residence The custom whereby a bride and groom take up residence with (or very near) the bride's parents.

Values Shared understandings that state what is better and what is worse, what is beautiful and what is ugly.

Virilocal residence The custom whereby a bride and groom take up residence with the groom's parents.

Witch A person believed to bring about evil effects upon others through innate powers, and not through the use of ritual. (European "witches" are technically sorcerers, not witches.)

BIBLIOGRAPHY

ANASTASI, A. 1958 Differential Psychology. New York: Macmillan.

ARLOTTO, ANTHONY 1972 Introduction to Historical Linguistics. Boston: Houghton Mifflin.

BAILEY, F. G. 1969 Stratagems and Spoils. New York: Schocken Books.

———1973 Debate and Compromise. Oxford: Blackwell.

BARTH, F. 1959 Segmentary Opposition and Theory of Games: A Study of Pathan Organization. Journal of the Royal Anthropological Institute 89:5–21.

———1963 The Role of the Entrepreneur in Social Change in Northern Norway. Bergen: Norwegian University Press.

———1966 Anthropological Models and Social Reality. Proceedings of the Royal Anthropological Institute 165:20–35.

BARTH, F. 1966 Anthropological Models and Social Realty. Proceedings of the Royal Anthropological Institute 165:20–35.

BEAUCLAIR, INEZ DE 1969 Gold and Silver on Botel Tobago: The Silver Helmet of the Yami. Bulletin of the Institute of Ethnology. Academia Sinica 27:121–128.

BEIDELMAN, THOMAS O. 1961 Beer Drinking and Cattle Theft in Ukaguru: Intertribal Relations in a Tanganyika Chiefdom. American Anthropologist 63:534ff.

BENEDICT, R. 1932 Configurations of Culture in North America. American Anthropology 34:1–27.

———1934 Patterns of Culture. New York: Houghton Mifflin.

BERLIN, BRENT, AND PAUL KAY 1969 Basic Color Terms: Their Universality and Evolution. Berkeley: University of California Press.

BETEILLE, A. 1965 Caste, Class, and Power: Changing Patterns of Stratification in a Tanjore Village. Berkeley: University of California Press.

BOHANNAN, PAUL 1955 Some Principles of Exchange and Investment among the Tiv. American Anthropologist 57:60–70.

BOULTON, MARJORIE 1960 Zamenhof: Creator of Esperanto. London: Routledge.

BROKENSHA, DAVID 1969 Community development: an interpretation. Scranton, Pa.: Chandler Publishing Company.

BROWN, JUDITH K. 1970 A Note on the Division of Labor by Sex. American Anthropologist 70:1073–1078.

BURLING, ROBBINS 1970 Man's Many Voices: Language in Its Cultural Context. New York: Holt.

CAMPBELL, WILLIAM 1903 Formosa under the Dutch, Described from Contemporary Records, with Explanatory Notes and a Bibliography of the Island. London: Kegan Paul, Trench, Trubner.

CANNON, WALTER B. 1942 Voodoo Death. American Anthropologist 44:169–181.

CHIUSSI, ITALO, TRANS AND ED. 1969 La Nobla Korano. Copenhagen: T. K.

CLEMES, STANLEY 1964 Repression and Hypnotic Amnesia. Journal of Abnormal and Social Psychology 69:62–69.

COLSON, ELIZABETH 1971 The Social Consequences of Resettlement: The Impact of the Kariba Resettlement upon the Gwenbe Tonga. Kariba Studies 4. Manchester: Manchester University Press.

DALTON, GEORGE 1961 Economic Theory and Primitive Society. American Anthropologist 63:1–25.

D'ANDRADE, ROY G. 1966 Sex Differences and Cultural Institutions. *In* The Development of Sex Differences. Eleanor E. Maccoby, Ed. Stanford, Calif.: Stanford. pp. 173–204.

DAVENPORT, WILLIAM 1959 Nonunilinear Descent and Descent Groups. American Anthropologist 61:557–569.

DEVAMBEZ, PIERRE, ET AL. 1967 The Praeger Encyclopedia of Ancient Greek Civilization. New York: Praeger.

DEVORE, P., ED. 1965 The Origin of Man. New York: Wenner-Gren Foundation.

DIAMOND, NORMA 1969 K'un Shen: A Taiwan Village. New York: Holt.

DU BOIS, CORA 1960 The People of Alor. 2 vols. New York: Torchbooks. (First published in 1944.)

————1961 The People of Alor. Vol. II. New York: Academy Library.

DURKHEIM, ÉMILE 1960 Les Formes Élémentaires de la Vie Religieuse. Fourth edition. Paris: Presses Universitaires de France. (First published in 1912.)

EDGERTON, ROBERT B. 1965 "Cultural" vs. "Ecological" Factors in the Expression of Values, Attitudes, and Personality Characteristics. American Anthropologist 67:442–447.

————1971 The Individual in Cultural Adaptation: A Study of Four East African Peoples. Berkeley: University of California Press.

EISENSTADT, S. 1959 Primitive Political Systems: A Preliminary Comparative Analysis. American Anthropologist 61:200–222.

EKVALL, ROBERT B. 1968 Fields on the Hoof: Nexus of Tibetan Nomadic Pastoralism. New York: Holt.

ELIADE, MIRCEA 1964 Shamanism, Archaic Techniques of Ecstasy. Princeton, N.J.: Princeton.

EPSTEIN, SCARLETT 1959 A Sociological Analysis of Witch Beliefs in a Mysore Village. The Eastern Anthropologist 12:234–251.

ERIKSON, ERIK 1939 Observations on Sioux Education. Journal of Psychiatry 7:101–156.

————1945 Childhood and Tradition in Two American Indian Tribes. In Psychoanalytic Study of the Child. A. Freud et al., Eds. New York: International Universities Press. Vol. 1.

EVANS-PRITCHARD, E. E. 1937 Witchcraft, Oracles and Magic among the Azande. London: Oxford University Press. (Reprinted in 1963.)

————1940 The Nuer: A Description of the Modes of Livelihood and Political Institutions of a Nilotic People. Oxford: Clarendon Press.

————1951 Kinship and Marriage among the Nuer. London: Oxford University Press.

FERGUSON, CHARLES A. 1959 Diglossia. Word 15:325–340.

FESTINGER, LEON, ET AL. 1956 When Prophecy Fails. New York: Harper & Row.

FISHMAN, JOSHUA A. 1970 Sociolinguistics: A Brief Introduction. Rowley, Mass.: Newbury House.

FORDE, C. DARYLL 1963 Habitat, Economy and Society: A Geographical Introduction to Ethnology. New York: Dutton. (First published in 1934.)

FORTES, MEYER 1953 The Structure of Unilineal Descent Groups. American Anthropologist 55:25–39.

FOSTER, GEORGE M. 1973 Societies and Technological Change. New York and London: Harper and Row. (Second ed. First ed. Traditional Cultures and the Impact of Technological Change, 1962.)

FOX, ROBIN 1967 Kinship and Marriage: An Anthropological Perspective. Baltimore: Penguin.

————1968 The Evolution of Human Sexual Behavior. New York Times Magazine, March 24:32–35.

FREEDMAN, MAURICE 1970 Family and Kinship in Chinese Society. Stanford, Calif.: Stanford.

FRIEDRICH, P. 1968 The Legitimacy of a Cacique. In Local-level Politics. M. Swartz, Ed. Chicago: Aldine. pp. 243–269.

————1970 Agrarian Revolt in a Mexican Village. Englewood Cliffs, N.J.: Prentice-Hall.

GARDNER, R. A., AND B. GARDNER 1969 Teaching Sign Language to a Chimpanzee. Science 165:664–672.

————1971 Two Way Communication with a Chimpanzee. In Behavior of Nonhuman Primates: A Schrier and F. Stollnitz, Eds. New York: Academic. Vol. 4.

GARN, STANLEY M., AND WALTER D. BLOCK 1970 The Limited Nutritional Value of Cannibalism.

American Anthropologist 72:106.

GEERTZ, CLIFFORD 1966 Religion as a Cultural System. *In* Anthropological Approaches to the Study of Religion. Michael Banton, Ed. London: Tavistock. ASA #3, pp. 1-46.

GILLEN, JOHN 1949 Moche, A Peruvian Coastal Community. Smithsonian Institute of Social Anthropology, Publication no. 3, Washington, D.C.

GLUCKMAN, M. 1956 The Frailty in Authority. *In* Custom and Conflict in Africa. M. Gluckman, Ed. Oxford: Blackwell.

———1963a Custom and Conflict in Africa. Oxford: Blackwell.

———1963b Gossip and Scandal. Current Anthropology 4:307-316. Reprinted as Bobbs-Merrill Reprint A-299.

———1963c Rituals of Rebellion in South-East Africa. *In* Order and Rebellion in Tribal Africa. London: Cohen and West.

———1965 Politics, Law, and Ritual. Chicago: Aldine.

GODELIER, MAURICE 1971 "Salt Currency" and the Circulation of Commodities among the Baruya of New Guinea. *In* Studies in Economic Anthropology. George Dalton, Ed. Anthropological Studies Number 7. Washington, D.C.: American Anthropological Association. pp. 52-73.

GOLDSCHMIDT, WALTER 1965 Theory and Strategy in the Study of Cultural Adaptability. American Anthropologist 67:402-407.

GOODALL, J. 1971 In the Shadow of Man. Boston: Houghton Mifflin.

GORDON, CYRUS H. 1972 The Minoan Connection. Natural History 81:74-84.

GOUGH, E. KATHLEEN 1959 The Nayars and the Definition of Marriage. Journal of the Royal Anthropological Institute 89:23-34.

———1961a Nayar: Central Kerala. *In* Matrilineal Kinship. David M. Schneider and Kathleen Gough, Eds. Berkeley: University of California Press. pp. 298-384.

———1961b Nayar: North Kerala. *In* Matrilineal Kinship. David M. Schneider and Kathleen Gough, Eds. Berkeley: University of California Press. pp. 385-404.

GRAY, EDEN 1960 The Tarot Revealed: A Modern Guide to Reading the Tarot Cards. New York: Bell Books.

GRINNELL, G. B. 1923 The Cheyenne Indians: Their History and Ways of Life. New Haven: Yale.

HALLOWELL, A. I. 1950 Personality Structure and the Evolution of Man. American Anthropologist 52:139-173.

———1956 The Structural and Functional Dimensions of Human Existence. Quarterly Review of Biology 31:88-108. Abridged and reprinted as Culture and the History of Man. *In* The Meaning of Culture, 1972. M Freilich, Ed. Lexington, Mass: Xerox College Publishing. pp. 199-212.

HAMBURG, D. 1968 Emotions in the Perspective of Human Evolution. *In* Perspectives on Human Evolution. S. Washburn and P. Jay, Eds. New York: Holt. Vol. 1.

HARLOW, H., AND M. HARLOW 1962 Social Deprivation in Monkeys. Scientific American 207:137-146.

———1965 The Affectional Systems. *In* Behavior of Non-Human Primates. A. Schrier, H. Harlow, and F. Stollnitz, Eds. New York: Academic.

HARNER, MICHAEL J. 1972 The Jívaro: People of the Sacred Waterfalls. Garden City, N.Y.: Anchor Books.

HARRIS, M. 1968 The Rise of Anthropological Theory. New York: Thomas Y. Crowell.

HARRIS, M. 1968 The Rise of Anthropological Theory. New York: Thomas Y. Crowell.

———1971 Culture, Man and Nature: An Introduction to General Anthropology. New York: Thomas Y. Crowell.

HART, C, W. M., AND ARNOLD R. PILLING 1963 The Tiwi of North Australia. New York: Holt.

HAYS H. R. 1958 From Ape to Angel: An Informal History of Social Anthropology. New York: Capricorn Books.

HEBB, D., AND W. THOMPSON 1954 The Social Significance of Animal Studies. *In* The Handbook of Social Psychology. G . Lindzey, Ed. Cambridge, Mass.: Addison-Wesley. Vol. 1.

HERODUTUS 1955 The Histories. Translated and with an Introduction by Aubrey de Selincourt. Harmondsworth, Middlesex Great Britain: Penguin Books.

HOBBES, THOMAS 1881 Leviathan, Oxford: James Thorton.

HOCKETT, C. F. 1959 Animal "Languages" and Human Languages. *In* The Evolution of Man's Capacity for Culture. J. Spuhler, Ed. Detroit: Wayne State University Press.

———1973 Man's Place in Nature. New York: McGraw-Hill.

HODGEN, MARGARET T. 1964 Early Anthropology in the Sixteenth and Seventeenth Centuries. Philadelphia: University of Pennsylvania Press.

HOEBEL, E. A., AND KARL LLEWELLYN 1941 The Cheyenne Way: Conflict and Case Law In Primitive Jurisprudence. Norman: University of Oklahoma Press.

———1954 The Law of Primitive Man. Cambridge, Mass.: Harvard.

———1960 The Cheyennes: Indians of the Great Plains. New York: Holt.

HOLLOWAY, R. 1966 Cranial Capacity, Neural Reorganization, and Hominid Evolution: A Search for More Suitable Parameters. American Anthropologist 68:103-121.

———1972 Culture: A Human Domain: Current Anthropology. 10:395-412.

HOMANS, GEORGE C. 1941 Anxiety and Ritual: The Theories of Malinowski and Radcliffe-Brown. American Anthropologist 43:164-172.

HSU, FRANCIS L. K. 1961 Kinship and Ways of Life: An Exploration. *In* Psychological Anthropology: Approaches to Culture and Personality. Francis L. K. Hsu, Ed. Homewood, Ill.: Dorsey. pp. 400-456.

HULSE, F. 1971 The Human Species. New York: Random House.

JANSON, H. W. 1969 History of Art: A Survey of the Major Visual Arts from the Dawn of History to the Present Day. Revised edition. Englewood Cliffs, N.J.: Prentice-Hall, and New York: Abrams.

JENSEN, A. 1969 How Much Can We Boost IQ and Scholarly Achievement? Harvard Educational Review 39:1-123.

JENSEN, R. 1971 Can We Study Race Differences? *In* Race and Intelligence. C. L. Brace, G. GAMBLE, AND J. BOND, EDS. Anthropological Studies Number 8. Washington, D.C.: American Anthropological Association. pp. 10-31.

JOLLY, A. 1966a Lemur Social Behavior and Primate Intelligence. Science 153:501-506.

———1966b Lemur Behavior. Chicago: University of Chicago Press.

———1972 The Evolution of Primate Behavior. New York: Macmillan.

JOLLY, C. 1970a Letter. Man 5:518-519.

JORDAN, DAVID K. 1971 Two Forms of Spirit Marriage in Rural Taiwan. Bijdragen tot de Taal-, Land- en Volkenkunde 127:181-189.

———1972 Gods, Ghosts, and Ancestors: The Folk Religion of a Taiwanese Village. Berkeley: University of California Press.

KARDINER, A. 1945 The Psychological Frontiers of Society. New York: Columbia.

———1961 Conclusions to the Bibliographies. *In* The People of Alor. Cora Du Bois. New York: Academy Library. chap. 18.

KARDINER, A., AND E. PREBLE 1961 They Studied Man. Cleveland: World Publishing.

KAWAI, M. 1965 Newly Acquired Precultural Behavior of the Natural Troop of Japanese Monkeys on Koshima Islet. Primates 6:1-30.

KROEBER, A. L. 1948 Anthropology. New York: Harcourt, Brace.

———1953 (Ed.) Anthropology Today. Chicago: University of Chicago Press.

KROEBER, A. L., AND C. KLUCKHOHN 1963 Culture: A Critical Review of Concepts. New York: Vintage Books. (First published in 1952.)

KUMMER, H. 1967 Tripartite Relations in Hamadryas Baboons. *In* Social Communication among Primates. S. Altmann, Ed. Chicago: University of Chicago Press.

———1971 Primate Societies. Chicago: Aldine.

LABOV, WILLIAM 1968 The Reflection of Social Processes in Linguistic Structures. *In* Readings in the Sociology of Language. Joshua A. Fishman, Ed. The Hague: Mouton. pp. 240-251.

———1969 The Effect of Social Mobility on Linguistic Behavior. *In* Explorations in Sociolinguistics. Stanley Lieberson, Ed. Second edition. Bloomington: Indiana University Press. pp. 58–75.

LANCASTER, J. 1968 On the Evolution of Tool-using Behavior. American Anthropologist 70:56–66.

LE VINE, R. 1966 Dreams and Deeds: Achievement Motivation in Nigeria. Chicago: University of Chicago Press.

LÉVI-STRAUSS, CLAUDE 1955 The Structural Study of Myth. Journal of American Folklore 78(270):428–444. Reprinted in Claude Lévi-Strauss, Structural Anthropology, 1963. Garden City, N.Y.: Doubleday. pp. 202–228.

LEVY, JEAN-PHILIPPE 1964 The Economic Life of the Ancient World. J. G. Biram, Trans. Chicago: University of Chicago Press. (Reprinted in 1967.)

LEWIS, OSCAR 1959 Five Families: Mexican Case Studies in the Culture of Poverty. New York: New American Library.

————1964 Pedro Martínez: A Mexican Peasant and His Family. New York: Random House.

LI YIH-YUAN 1972 Aspects of Chinese Character as Viewed from Some Ritual Behaviours. In Symposium on the Character of the Chinese. Li Yih-yuan and Yang Kuo-shu, Eds. Taipei, Taiwan: Institute of Ethnology, Academia Sinica. (In Chinese.)

MARTIN, SAMUEL E. 1960 Korean in a Hurry: A Quick Approach to Spoken Korean. Revised edition. Rutland, Vt.: Tuttle Company.

MAUSS, MARCEL 1925 Essai sur le Don, Forme Archaïque de L'Échange. Année Sociologique: n.s. 1:33ff.

MEAD, MARGARET 1928 Coming of Age in Samoa. New York: L. W. Morrow.

————1935 Sex and Temperament in Three Primitive Societies. New York: Morrow.

————1949 Male and Female: A Study of the Sexes in a Changing World. New York: Morrow.

————1953 National Character. In Anthropology Today. A. Kroeber, Ed. Chicago: University of Chicago Press. pp. 642–667.

MALINOWSKI, B. 1921 The Primitive Economics of the Trobriand Islanders. The Economic Journal 31:1–16.

————1922 Argonauts of the Western Pacific. New York: Dutton.

————1925 Magic, Science and Religion. Reprinted in B. Malinowski, Magic, Science and Religion and Other Essays, 1948. Garden City, N.Y.: Anchor Books.

————1927 Sex and Repression in Savage Society. New York: International Library.

————1935 Coral Gardens and Their Magic. London: G. Allen.

————1939 The Group and the Individual in Functional Analysis. American Journal of Sociology 64:938–960. Reprinted as Bobbs-Merrill Reprint S-183.

————1944 A Scientific Theory of Culture and Other Essays. Chapel Hill: University of North Carolina Press.

MANDELBAUM, DAVID C. 1941 Social Trends and Personal Pressures. In Language, Culture, and Personality: Essays in Memory of Edward Sapir. Leslie Spier et al., Eds. Menasha, Wis.: Sapir Memorial Publication Fund.

MANN, A. 1972 Hominid and Cultural Origins. Man 7:379–386.

MERTON, R. 1940 Adult Roles and Personality. Social Forces 17:560–568.

MORTON-WILLIAMS, P. 1967 The Yorubu Kingdom of Oyo. In West African Kingdoms in the Nineteenth Century. D. Forde and P. Kaberry, Eds. Glasgow, Scotland: International African Institute, by Oxford University Press. pp. 36–39.

MURDOCK, G. P. 1949 Social Structure. New York: Macmillan.

————1959 Africa. New York: McGraw-Hill.

MURDOCK, G. P., AND CATERINA PROVOST 1973 Factors in the Division of Labor by Sex: A Cross-Cultural Analysis. Ethnology 12:203–225.

NAPIER, JOHN 1971 The Roots of Mankind. London: G. Allen.

NAPIER, JOHN, AND P. NAPIER 1967 A Handbook of Living Primates. London: Academic.

NASH, MANNING 1964 The Organization of Economic Life. In Horizons in Anthropology. S. Tax, Ed. Chicago: University of Chicago Press. pp. 171–180.

NICHOLAS, R. 1965 Factions: A Comparative Analysis. *In* Political Systems and the Distribution of Power. M. Banton, Ed. Association for Social Anthropology Monograph 2. New York: Praeger. pp. 21–62.

————1966 Segmentary Factional Political Systems. *In* Political Anthropology. M. Swartz, V. Turner, and A. Tuden, Eds. Chicago: Aldine. pp. 49–60.

————1968 Rules, Resources, and Political Activity. *In* Local-level Politics. M. Swartz, Ed. Chicago: Aldine. pp. 295–322.

PIDDOCK, STUART 1965 The Potlatch System of the Southern Kwakiutl: A New Perspective. Southwestern Journal of Anthropology 21:244–264.

————PITT-RIVERS, J. A. 1961 The People of the Sierra. Chicago: University of Chicago Press. pp. 145–159.

PREMACK, D. 1972 Two Problems in Cognition: Symbolization, and From Icon to Phoneme. *In* Communication and Affect: A Comparative Approach. T. Alloway, L. Krames, and P. Pliner, Eds. New York: Academic.

PRIVAT, EDMOND 1912 Historio de la Lingvo Esperanto: Deveno kaj Komenco 1887-1900. The Hague: Internacia Esperanto-Instituto.

POLANYI, KARL 1957 The Economy as Instituted Process. *In* Trade and Market in the Early Empires: Economics in History and Theory. Karl Polanyi, Conrad M. Arensberg, and Harry W. Pearson, Eds. New York: Free Press. pp. 243–270.

POWELL, H. A. 1960 Competitive Leadership in Trobriand Political Organization. Journal of the Royal Anthropological Institute 90:118–145.

QUEEN, STUARD A., AND ROBERT W. HABENSTEIN 1967 The Family in Various Cultures. Third edition. Philadelphia: Lippincott.

RADCLIFFE-BROWN, A. R. 1952 On the Concept of Function in Social Science. *In* Structure and Function in Primitive Society. A. R. Radcliffe-Brown, Ed. Glencoe, Ill.: Free Press. pp. 178–187. Reprinted from American Anthropologist 37:392–402 (1935).

RÄNK, GUSTAV 1967 Shamanism as a Research Subject: Some Methodological Viewpoints. *In* Studies in Shamanism. Carl-Martin Edsmann, Ed. Stockholm: Almqvist and Wiksell. pp. 15–22.

REMINICK, RONALD A. 1974 The Evil Eye Belief among the Amhara of Ethiopia. Ethnology 13:279–291.

REYNOLDS, V. 1968 Kinship and the Family in Monkeys, Apes, and Man. Man 3:209–223.

————1970 Roles and Role Change in Monkey Society: A Consort Relationship of Rhesus Monkeys. Man 5:449–465.

RIVERS, W. H. R. 1906 The Todas. London: Macmillan.

ROTH, CECIL, TRANS. AND ED. 1965 The Haggadah for Passover. Boston: Little, Brown.

SAHLINS, MARSHAL 1976 Culture and Practical Reason. Chicago: University of Chicago Press.

SAHLINS, M. 1959 The Social Life of Monkeys, Apes and Primitive Men. Human Biology 31:54–73.

————1961 The Segmentary Lineage: An Organization of Predatory Expansion. American Anthropologist 63:322–343.

————1963 Poor Man, Rich Man, Big-Man, Chief: Political Types in Melanesia and Polynesia. Comparative Studies in Society and History 5:285–303. Reprinted as Bobbs-Merrill Reprint A-339.

————1968 Tribesmen. Englewood Cliffs, N.J.: Prentice-Hall.

SALUS, PETER H. 1969 Linguistics. Indianapolis: Bobbs-Merrill.

SCHALLER, G. 1963 The Mountain Gorilla. Chicago: University of Chicago Press.

SCHEFFLER, H. 1964 The Social Consequences of Peace on Choiseul Island. Ethnology 3:308–402.

SCHWARTZ, THEODORE 1973 Cult and Context: The Paranoid Ethos in Melanesia. Ethos 1:153–174.

SEABROOK, W. B. 1940 Witchcraft: Its Power in the World Today. New York: Harcourt, Brace.

SEARS, R., AND G. WISE 1950 Relations of Cup Feeding to Thumb-Sucking and the Oral Drive. American Journal Orthopsychology 20:123–139.

SERVICE, ELMAN R. 1966 The Hunters. Englewood Cliffs, N.J.: Prentice-Hall.

SINGER, MILTON 1961 A Review of Studies in Culture and Personality. *In* Studying Personality Cross Culturally. B. Kaplan, Ed. Evanston, Ill.: Row, Peterson. pp. 9–92.

SLATER, MARIAM KREISELMAN 1959 Ecological Factors in the Origin of Incest. American Anthropologist 61:1042–1058.

SLOTKIN, JAMES 1965 Readings in Early Anthropology. Chicago: Aldine.

SPIRO, M. E. 1951 Culture and Personality: The Natural History of a False Dichotomy. Psychiatry 14:20–46.

———1954 Is the Family Universal? American Anthropologist 56:839–846.

———1956 Kibbutz: Venture in Utopia. Cambridge, Mass.: Harvard.

———1958 Children of the Kibbutz. Cambridge, Mass.: Harvard. (Paperback edition 1965.)

———1961a Social System, Personality, and Functional Analysis. *In* Studying Personality Cross-Culturally. B. Kaplan, Ed. Evanston, Ill.: Row, Peterson. pp. 93–128.

———1961b An Overview and Suggested Re-Orientation. *In* Psychological Anthropology. F. Hsu, Ed. Homewood, Ill.: Dorsey. pp. 459–492.

———1973 Social Change and Functional Analysis. Ethos 1(3):263–297.

SPIRO, M. E., AND ROY G. D'ANDRADE 1958 A Cross-Cultural Study of Some Supernatural Beliefs. American Anthropologist 60:456–466.

STEIN, HOWARD F. 1974 Envy and the Evil Eye among Slovak-Americans: An Essay in the Psychological Ontogeny of Belief and Ritual. Ethos 2:15–46.

STRUMS, S. 1974 Personal communication.

STUART, JAMES, AND D. M. MALCOLM, EDS. 1950 Fynn, H. F.: The Diary of Henry Francis Fynn. Pietermaritzburg, South Africa: n.p.

SUTTLES, WAYNE 1960 Affinal Ties, Subsistence, and Prestige among the Coast Salish. American Anthropologist 62:296–305.

SWANSON, GUY E. 1968 The Birth of the Gods: The Origin of Primitive Beliefs. Ann Arbor: University of Michigan Press.

SWARTZ, M. 1958 Sexuality and Aggression on Romonum, Truk. American Anthropologist 60:467–486.

———1968 Bases for Compliance in Bena Villages. *In* Local-level Politics. M. Swartz, Ed. Chicago: Aldine. pp. 227–242.

———1969 The Cultural Dynamics of Blows and Abuse among the Bena of Southern Tanzania. *In* Forms of Symbolic Action. Proceedings of the 1969 Annual spring Meeting of the American Ethnological Society. Seattle: University of Washington Press. pp. 126–133.

SWARTZ, M. 1969 The Cultural Dynamics of Blows and Abuse among the Bena of Southern Tanzania. *In* Forms of Symbolic Action. Proceedings of the 1969 Annual Spring Meeting of the American Ethnological Society. Seattle: University of Washington Press, pp. 126–133.

THAN TUN, A. 1973 Religion in Burma A.D. 1000–1300. Journal of the Burma Research Society 42:47–70. *Cited in* M. Spiro, 1973, Social Change and Functional Analysis Ethos 1(3): 263–269.

TOPLEY, MARJORIE 1955 Ghost Marriages among the Singapore Chinese Man. 55:29f.

———1956 Ghost Marriages among the Singapore Chinese: A Further Note. Man 56:71f.

TURNBULL, C. 1965 The Wayward Servants. Garden City, N.Y.: Natural History Press.

TURNER, C., R. DAVENPORT, AND C. ROGERS 1969 The Effects of Early Deprivation on the Social Behavior of Adolescent Chimpanzees. American Journal of Psychiatry 125:1531–1546.

TURNER, V. W. 1957 Schism and Continuity in an African Society: A Study of Ndembu Village Life. Manchester, England: Manchester University Press.

———1967 The Forest of Symbols. Ithaca, N.Y.: Cornell University Press.

TUTTLE, R. 1969 Knuckle-walking and the Problem of Human origins. Science 166:953–961.

TYLOR, EDWARD BURNETT 1871 Primitive Culture. London: J. Murray.

VOGET, F. 1975 A History of Ethnology. New York: Holt, Rinehart and Winston.

WALLACE, A. 1961 Culture and Personality. New York: Random House.

———1970 Culture and Personality. Second edition. New York: Random House.

WALTER, E, V. 1969 Terror and Resistance: A Study of Political Violence. New York: Oxford University Press, pp.. 109–219.

WASHBURN, S. L. 1960 Tools and Human Evolution. Scientific American 203:63–75.

———1973 Primate Studies and Human Evolution. *In* Non-Human Primates and Medical Research. New York: Academic.

WASHBURN, S. L., AND C. LANCASTER 1968 The Evolution of Hunting. *In* Man the Hunter. R. Lee and I. DeVore, Eds. Chicago: Aldine. pp. 293–303.

WASHBURN, S. L., AND D. A. HAMBURG 1965 The Implications of Primate Research. *In* Primate Primate Behavior. I. DeVore, Ed. New York: Holt.

WASHBURN, S. L., AND E. MCCOWN 1972 Evolution of Human Behavior. Social Biology 19: 163–170.

———1973a The New Science of Human Evolution. *In* 1974 Britannica Yearbook of Science and the Future. Chicago: Encyclopaedia Britannica. pp. 32–49.

WASHBURN, S. L., AND R. S. O. HARDING 1970 Evolution of Primate Behavior. *In* The Neurosciences. Second Study Program. F. Schmitt, Ed. New York: Rockefeller University Press. pps. 39–47.

WERNER, E. T. C. 1922 Myths and Legends of China. London: Harrap.

———1932 A Dictionary of Chinese Mythology. New York: Julian Press (Reprinted in 1961.)

WHITE, L. 1959 Man and Culture. *In* The Evolution of Culture: The Development of Civilization to the Fall of Rome. New York: McGraw-Hill. chap. 1.

WHITE, L. 1949a Energy and the Evolution of Culture. *In* The Science of Culture. L. White, Ed. New York: Grove Press, pp. 363–393.

———1949b The Expansion of the Scope of Science. *In* The Science of Culture. L. White, Ed. New York: Grove Press. pp. 55–117.

———1949c Culturological and Psychological Interpretations of Human Behavior. *In* The Science of Culture. L. White, Ed. New York: Grove Press. pp. 121–145.

———1959 Man and Culture. *In* The Evolution of Culture: The Development of Civilization to the Fall of Rome. New York: McGraw-Hill. chap. 1.

WHITING, J. 1954 The Cross-Cultural Method. *In* The Handbook of Social Psychology. G. Lindzey, Ed. Reading, Mass.: Addison-Wesley. pp. 523–531.

WHITING, J., AND I. CHILD 1953 Child Training and Personality. New Haven: Yale.

WHORF, BENJAMIN LEE 1940 Science and Linguistics. Technology Review 42:229–231, 247–248. Reprinted in Benjamin Lee Whorf, Language, Thought, and Reality: Selected Writings of Benjamin Lee Whorf, 1956. John B. Carroll, Ed. Cambridge, Mass.: Technology Press, and New York: Wiley. pp. 207–219.

WILHELM, RICHARD, TRANS. (FROM CHINESE TO GERMAN) AND ED. 1950 I Ching or Book of Changes. First edition. Carl F. Baynes, Trans. (from German). Bollinger Foundation Series Number 19, Princeton, N.J.: Princeton. (Third edition published in 1967.)

WILSON, BRYAN 1969 Society: A Sociological Comment. London: Watts.

WOLF, ARTHUR P. 1970 Child Association and Sexual Attraction: A Further Test of the Westermarck Hypothesis. American Anthropologist 72:503–515.

WOLF, MARGERY 1972 Women and the Family in Rural Taiwan. Stanford, Calif.: Stanford.

WU CH'ENG-EN 1958 Monkey. Arthur Waley, Abridg., Trans., and Ed. New York: Grove Press. (First published in 1943.)

YOUNG, FRANK W. 1965 Initiation Ceremonies: A Cross Cultural Study of Status Dramatization. Indianapolis: Bobbs-Merrill.

ZUCKERMAN, S. 1932 The Social Life of Monkeys and Apes. London: Kegan, Paul, Trench, Trubner.

Credits

Chapter 1 3 Photograph by Lola Romanucci Ross. 14 From Tengler, *Laienspiegel* (Mainz, 1508), reprinted in *Der Kelheimer Hexenhammer*, Munich, 1966. 7 Reprinted from Gisela M. A. Richter, *The Portraits of the Greeks*, vol. 1. © 1965 Phaidon Press Ltd., London SW 7. 19 Nationalmuseet, Copenhagen. 20 Culver Pictures. 21 (top) Lewis Henry Morgan Collection, The University of Rochester Library. 21 (bottom), 23 (top) Pitt Rivers Museum, University of Oxford. 22 Wide World Photos. 23 (bottom) Photograph by Esther Henderson. 28 The University Museum, University of Pennsylvania. 31 Blackstone Studios. 32 French Embassy Press & Information Division. 35 Drawing by Franz Krüger.

Chapter 2 43, 64 UNICEF photos by Horst Cerni. 45, 71 Photographs by Marc J. Swartz. 51 (top left) F.A.O. photo; (top right) Photograph by John Launois from Black Star; (bottom left) Photograph by S. Weiss, copyright Rapho Guillumette Pictures; (bottom right) Photograph by William Mares from Monkmeyer Press Photo Service. 59 From Thomas Gladwin and Seymour B. Sarason, *Truk: Man in Paradise* (copyright 1954 by Wenner-Gren Foundation for Anthropological Research, Inc., New York). 61 Pitt Rivers Museum, University of Oxford. 67 Photograph by Julia Sommer. 76 (left) South African Information Service; (right) Photograph by Myers from Afrique Photo. 78 Film Study Center, Peabody Museum, Harvard University.

Chapter 3 81 Stern/Scheler from Black Star. 86 Photograph by Arthur Soybel. 91 Photograph by Tobin Spirer. 93 F.A.O. photo. Photo from Bibliothèque national, Paris. 105 Film Study Center, Peabody Museum, Harvard University. 107 Courtesy of the American Museum of Natural History. 112 Photograph by Marilyn Silverstone from Magnum Photos, Inc. 115 Photograph by David K. Jordan. 120 Pitt Rivers Museum, University of Oxford.

Chapter 4 123, 153 National Film Board of Canada. 126, 127, 138 From Cora Du Bois, *The People of Alor*, University of Minnesota Press, Minneapolis. © 1944 by the University of Minnesota. 130 Wide World Photos. 133 Photograph by George Rodger from Magnum Photos, Inc. 136 Photograph by Ken Heyman. 143 Photograph by Ray Ellis, copyright Rapho Guillumette Pictures. 148 South African Information Service. 156 (top left), 157 (left) From *Yanoama, The Narrative of a White Girl Kidnapped by Amazonian Indians* as told to Ettore Biocca. Translation from the Italian by Dennis Rhodes, © 1969 by E. P. Dutton & Co., Inc., and George Allen & Unwin Ltd. Published in 1970 by E. P. Dutton; © 1965 Leonardo da Vinci Editore, Bari, Italy. Reprinted by permission of the publishers, E. P. Dutton & Co., Inc., and George Allen & Unwin Ltd. 156 (top right) (bottom), 157 (right) Photographs by Napoleon A. Chagnon.

Chapter 5 163 United Nations Photo. 164, 166, 192 Reprinted from *Schism and Continuity in an African Society* by Victor W. Turner by courtesy of Manchester University Press for the Rhodes-Livingstone Institute. 174 Irven DeVore/Anthro-Photo. 176 Photograph by Paul Hockings. 177 Photograph by Don Tuzin. 182 Reprinted from *East African Chiefs* by Audrey Richards, Faber and Faber, London. 183 Reprinted from *Our Primitive Contemporaries* by George P. Murdock. Copyright, 1934, by the Macmillan Company. 187 Photograph by Ken Heyman. 188 Photograph by David K. Jordan. 209 Wide World Photos.

Chapter 6 219 Irven DeVore/Anthro-Photo. 222 OAS Photo. 224 Rockefeller Foundation. 225 Embassy of Mexico. 226 Photograph by Betty and Arthur Reef. 230 F.A.O. Photo. 236 Unesco/P. Almasy. 237 Courtesy of the American Museum of Natural History. 239 National Museum of Canada, Ottawa, Canada. 242 Photographs by Robert M. Glasse. 246 Reprinted from *A World of Islands* by June Knox-Mawer (1968), Collins Publishers, London. 249 Photograph by David K. Jordan. 255 © F. Caracciolo-F. Banoun/Scala.

Chapter 7 259, 271 South African Information Service. 262 From *The Cheyenne Way: Conflict and Case Law in Prmitive Jurisprudence*, by K. N. Llewellyn and E. Adamson Hoebel. Copyright 1941 by the University of Oklahoma Press. 263 National Anthropological Archives. 264, 268 Photographs courtesy of Museum of the American Indian, Heye Foundation. 266 From *The Cheyennes: Indians of the Great Plains* by E. Adamson Hoebel. Copyright © 1960 by Holt, Rinehart and

Winston, Publishers. Reproduced by permission of Holt, Rinehart and Winston, Publishers. 273 Wide World Photos. 278 Office of Information, Papua New Guinea. 281 Photograph by Fievet from Afrique Photo. 287 Reprinted from *Purgatory and Utopia* by Alicja Iwanska, copyright 1971 by Schenkman Publishing Co., Cambridge, Mass. 293 National Anthropological Archives.

Chapter 8. 297 Photograph by Fujihira from Monkmeyer Press Photo Service. 300, 301, 303 Photographs by David K. Jordan. 306 Originally published by the University of California Press; reprinted by permission of The Regents of the University of California. 311 The Metropolitan Museum of Art, Rogers Fund, 1928. 313 Supplied by National Museum of History, Taipei, Republic of China. 316, 325 Courtesy of the American Museum of Natural History. 319 Photograph by Ken Heyman. 323 Photograph by Fievet from Afrique Photo. 328 Photograph by David Seymour from Magnum Photos, Inc. 330 The Metropolitan Museum of Art, Gift of Mrs. William H. Osborn, 1967, in memory of Johnston L. Redmond. 334 OAS Photo.

Chapter 9 343 Wide World Photos. 346, 611, 371, 372 Universala Esperanto-Asocio. 347 Belgian Esperanto Institute. 351 Universala Esperanto-Asocio, photograph by Fejer Zoltan. 361 Photograph by J. Nance from Magnum Photos, Inc. 374 Photograph by Eve Arnold from Magnum Photos, Inc.

Chapter 10 377 Embassy of India, Information Section. 379, 381 Courtesy Peace Corps. 385 Eric Schwab/WHO. 388, 393, 396 Norwegian Agency for International Development. 391, 392 Toby Bankett Pyle/Photo Researchers. 398 (top) Rhoda Galyn/Photo Researchers. 398 (bottom) Marc Rattner/Black Star. 401 United Nations. 404 Embassy of the Polish People's Republic.

Chapter 11 409, 428, 439 (right), 440 San Diego Zoo Photos. 413 Harry F. Harlow, University of Wisconsin Primate Laboratory. 416 Irven DeVore/Anthro-Photo. 420 San Diego Zoo Photo by F. D. Schmidt. 426 Joe Popp/Anthro-Photo. 430 Photograph by T. W. Ransom. 431 Photograph by London *Daily Express* from Pictorial Parade. 433 Zoological Society of London. 436 David Premack, University of California at Santa Barbara. 439 (left) San Diego Zoo Photo by Ron Garrison.

The homolosine equal-area projection used throughout this text is based on Goode Map No. 201HC World Homolosine, Goode Base Map Series. Copyright by The University of Chicago, Department of Geography.

Index

Linguistic models, 31
Linguists
   and componential analysis, 363–365
   and phonemes, 353–356
   and phonetic and phonemic analyses, 356–357
   and subphonemic variations, 357–358
Linking understandings, 55–56, 69
Linton, Ralph, 30
Llewellyn, Karl N., and E. Adamson Hoebel, 260–264
Los Molinos, 378, 379, 380, 382, 383, 384, 389, 390, 393, 394, 395, 396, 397, 399, 400, 401, 402, 403
Lovejoy, C., K. Heipel, and A. Burnstein, 440
Lowie, Robert, 23

Macaques, 411, 414, 419
Magic, 325, 327; *see also* Mana
Maine, Henry, 20
Malinowski, Bronislaw, 23, 24–25, 28, 242, 244, 277–278
   on magic and science, 325–326
Mana, 321–323
   Manipulation of 323–327
Mammals
   and care of young 410
   communication, 433
   see also Primates
Man-apes. *See* Hominids
Market exchange, 233, 248–250
   and money, 248, 250–255
Marriage, 185–187
   Alorese, 124–127
   and Australian moieties, 209–211
   Chinese, 179–181, 187, 188
   cousin, 204–209
   endogamy, 192
   exogamy, 191–192
   Ganda, 182
   ghost, 175
   and incest taboos, 189–191
   Nuer, 175, 187
   preferences and prescriptions, 191, 203, 204–211

Marriage (*continued*)
   prohibitions, 187, 191
   and residence rules, 197–203
   sister exchange, 191
   Tiwi, 185–186
   see also Descent groups; Family
Marriage wealth
   Alorese, 124–128
   Ganda, 182, 183
   Tiv, 254
Martinez family, 220–226, 246–247
Masai, 76, 77
Maternal deprivation, studies of, 412–414
   Alorese, 137–140
Maters, 175; *see also* Descent groups; Mothers
Matrilineage, 195, 205–207
Matrilineal societies, 199, 200
   avunculocal residence, 201–203
   Crow Indian, 214–215
   Ndembu, 168, 170–171, 174
   Trobrianders, 208
Matrilocal residence. *See* Uxorilocal residence
Mbuti Pygmies, 281–282
Mead, Margaret, 23, 29–30
Means, 131; *see also* Motivation
Melanesia, 242–243
Mexico
   subsistence village living in, 220–226
   and village factions, 287–288
Microbes, 386, 389, 395, 399
Milpa agriculture, 220
The Mind of Primitive Man, 23
Mind
   consistency of beliefs, 63, 67
   and culture change, 63
   as location of culture, 61, 79
Minimal pair phonemes, 355–356
Mixed-group organization, 116–117; *see also* Groups
Modal personality structures, 155–157; *see also* Culture; Personality

Mohammad, 300
Moieties, 209–211
Monetization, 251–255
Money, 248, 250–255
Mongols, 197
Monkeys
   communication of, 433
   and isolation studies, 412–413
   and social learning, 419
   see also Baboons
Monogamy, 178
Monotheism, 309–311
Montesquieu, Baron de, 21
Moral force,
   and shared understandings, 49, 70, 79
   social expression of (reward and punishment), 57
   and transmission of culture (learning), 63
   in Trukese understandings, 58–59
Morality
   and cultural conformity, 143–145, 152–153
   primate, 421–424
   and self, concept of the, 435
   see also Culture; Moral force
Morgan, Lewis Henry, 21, 22
Morphemes, 359–363
   and componential analysis, 359–361
Morton-Williams, P., 108
Mortuary rites
   Dani, 78
   Trukese, 59
Mothers
   Alorese, 137, 154–155
   chimpanzee, 427–428
   Chinese, 280
   and incest inhibition in primates, 414–415, 422–424
   and kinship statuses, 174–177
   mammalian, 411
   primate, 411
   and sexual division of labor, 230–231
   and status expectations, 93, 107–108, 111–112